Preaching the

Preaching the New Lectionary

Year C

Dianne Bergant, C.S.A.

with

Richard Fragomeni

A Liturgical Press Book

THE LITURGICAL PRESS
Collegeville, Minnesota

www.litpress.org

Cover design by David Manahan, O.S.B.

Year C: ISBN 0-8146-2474-X

1	2	3	4	5	6	7	8

Library of Congress Cataloging-in-Publication Data

Bergant, Dianne.
    Preaching the new lectionary / Dianne Bergant, with Richard Fragomeni.
        p.   cm.
    Includes bibliographical references and index.
    Contents: — [v. 2] Year B.
    ISBN 0-8146-2473-1 (alk. paper)
    1. Lectionary preaching—Catholic Church.   2. Catholic Church.
Lectionary for Mass (U.S.).   Sundays and feasts.   3. Bible-
-Homiletical use.   I. Fragomeni, Richard N.   II. Title.
BV4235.L43B47   1999
251'.6—dc21   99-16138
                                                           CIP

Contents

Ordinary Time (Part Two)

Ordinary Time (Part Three)

Ordinary Time (Part Four)

Solemnities of the Lord

Introduction

The Lectionary is a unique genre of ecclesial literature. It is part of the liturgical canon, a collection of books that also includes the Sacramentary, the Ritual Books for Sacraments, the Book of Blessings, the Pontifical, and the Liturgy of the Hours, to name a few. The Constitution on the Sacred Liturgy (no. 24) states that sacred Scripture is the source of the readings and prayers used in the liturgy. The Lectionary, while not identical to the Bible, is drawn from its contents, providing a kind of narrative infrastructure for celebration of the Liturgical Year. The Lectionary is drawn from sacred Scripture by selecting passages from the biblical material (decontextualizing) and then placing these readings within a new literary and liturgical context (recontextualizing), thus creating a new ecclesial genre.

This recontextualization of former biblical material calls for a new way of interpretation, one that takes into consideration the liturgical character and setting of the lectionary readings. The present commentary is an example of this type of interpretation. It will be fundamentally a literary reading of the texts, but it will also provide historical information whenever something in the text might appear foreign to the contemporary believer.

Features

This commentary is unique in several ways. First and foremost, it employs a literary-liturgical way of interpreting all four readings of each Sunday and major feast of the Liturgical Year. This includes the responsorial psalm, a reading that has seldom enjoyed the importance it deserves and has at times even been changed or eliminated. Second, it explicitly situates the interpretation of each day's readings within the theology of its respective liturgical season. This theology is drawn from the specific themes of the readings that make up that particular year rather than from general theological themes otherwise associated with the season. In this way the meaning of the entire season becomes the context for understanding its individual parts. Third, the lections of the season are read in sequential order, from the first Sunday of that season to the last (all of the first readings, all of the second readings, and so on). This kind of reading creates a kind of mini-reading and provides yet another way of understanding the riches of the readings (charts at the beginning of each season demonstrate this).

Limitations

The present commentary does have limitations. Unfortunately, it does not directly engage the other books of the liturgical canon, most importantly the Sacramentary. There are two reasons for this. First, various liturgical books are presently being revised. While the composition of the Lectionary has been determined, the form of the Sacramentary is still in transition. As important as this book is to full liturgical recontextualization, it did not seem appropriate to use the unrevised edition, nor was it deemed wise to delay the commentary until the revision of the Sacramentary appeared.

Second, inclusion of all of the relevant liturgical material would have made the commentary unmanageable. The method employed here is a relatively new one and is offered in a limited fashion. Those who find it helpful are encouraged to use it in other liturgical contexts.

Uses

The commentary is ordered in the following way. Each lectionary season is first presented by way of a chart showing readings for the entire season. This is followed by the **Initial Reading** of that season, which explains how the lections can be read sequentially across the season from the first Sunday to the last. This procedure is carried out with each of the four readings, so that the theological patterns that are unfolding within the weeks of the seasons can be seen. Because of its length, Ordinary Time has been divided into four sections: Sundays 1–10 (before Lent); Sundays 11–16; Sundays 17–21; Sundays 22–34 (the remainder of the year). Each of these sections has a particular thematic focus. After the theological themes of the season are uncovered, a literary reading of the lections of each respective Sunday is provided and the theological themes of that Sunday are brought into dialogue with each other.

Reading the Lectionary in the various ways provided here has great potential for many forms of liturgical ministry. It can quicken the religious imagination of homilists, thus providing fresh new possibilities for liturgical preaching. It can offer creative insights for those involved in the liturgical preparation for the celebration of feasts and seasons. It can also act as a valuable resource for liturgical catechesis. In so many ways the material in this commentary can contribute toward enhancing the liturgical lives of the faithful.

Development

It is important to acknowledge those upon whose groundbreaking work this approach is built. They are David N. Power, O.M.I., the inspiration of such an approach, and Bishop Blase Cupich, who wrote his doctoral dissertation under the direction of Professor Power on the topic of the Advent Lectionary.[1] In this work he laid the foundations for the literary-liturgical method employed here.

In the recent past three books have appeared that can act as companions to this commentary. Two of them suggest a way of understanding the Lectionary that corresponds to the one advanced here. In *Scripture and Memory*[2] Fritz West recounts the way lectionary patterns have been developed and are interpreted by various Christian denominations. He also explains the three-year cycle of readings, which originated within the Roman Catholic tradition but which then spread to the wider Church. In *The Sunday Lectionary*[3] Normand Bonneau provides an overview of the principles that determine the selection of lectionary readings and an outline of the patterns that shape the seasons of the Liturgical Year.

Very recently a third resource has appeared. In *Preaching Basics*[4] Edward Foley works from many of the same principles noted here as he provides a new way of thinking about preaching. Together these four studies offer a new way of understanding the Lectionary and of opening its riches.

Finally, a debt of gratitude belongs to Richard N. Fragomeni, who introduced me to this approach. He is the one who explained the textual mosaic that introduces each season, and his creative interpretations form the basis of the **Themes of the Day,** which completes the commentary of the Sunday or feast. His contribution to this project has been invaluable.

[1] Blase J. Cupich, "Advent in the Roman Tradition: An Examination and Comparison of the Lectionary Readings as Hermeneutical Units in Three Periods" (Ph.D. diss., The Catholic University of America, 1987).

[2] Fritz West, *Scripture and Memory: The Ecumenical Hermeneutic of the Three-Year Lectionaries* (Collegeville: The Liturgical Press [A Pueblo Book], 1997).

[3] Normand Bonneau, *The Sunday Lectionary: Ritual Word, Paschal Shape* (Collegeville: The Liturgical Press, 1998).

[4] Edward Foley, *Preaching Basics* (Chicago: Liturgy Training Publications, 1998).

Advent

First Sunday			
Jeremiah 33:14-16 I raise up David	Psalm 25:4-5, 8-9, 10, 14 I lift up my soul	1 Thessalonians 3:12–4:2 Strengthened at his coming	Luke 21:25-28, 34-36 Redemption is at hand
Second Sunday			
Baruch 5:1-9 Splendor of Jerusalem	Psalm 126:1-6 The LORD has done great things	Philippians 1:4-6, 8-11 Pure and blameless for Christ	Luke 3:1-6 All flesh see God's salvation
Third Sunday			
Zephaniah 3:14-18a Shout for joy, Jerusalem	Isaiah 12:2-6 Cry out for joy	Philippians 4:4-7 The Lord is near	Luke 3:10-18 Prepare for the Lord
Fourth Sunday			
Micah 5:1-4a He comes from Bethlehem	Psalm 80:2-3, 15-16, 18-19 Turn to the LORD	Hebrews 10:5-10 I come to do your will	Luke 1:39-45 Elizabeth recognizes the mystery

Advent

Initial Reading of the Advent Lectionary

Introduction

This section is an initial reading of the textual mosaic of the Advent Lectionary. It offers us a context for examining the individual lections of the season. It is based on the literary forms of the readings as well as on a preliminary interpretation of their content. In a sense, it presents the meaning of the entire season as the context for our understanding of the individual parts.

First Testament Readings

Reading the First Testament lections in sequential order from the first to the fourth, we discover an important theme. The mystery of God's saving action promised so long ago will be fulfilled within the ordinariness of human history. We see that the scandal of God's prodigious love unfolds in a particular place through a specific family. God comes into our world rather than calling us out of it into the realm of the divine.

In Jeremiah a new promise is made, assuring the anxious people that God's earlier promises will be fulfilled through a descendant of David. Although the people who first heard this prophetic announcement would have been thinking of the monarchy, today we know that the promise rested on the descendant and not on the political system identified with the original ancestor. The monarchy was not the promised Messiah, the Davidic individual was. As ambiguous as this promise may be, it does direct our attention to a particular family through whom God would work.

This promise of a brighter future is repeated in the readings from Baruch and Zephaniah. The city that was desolate for so long is now told to clothe itself in finery and rejoicing, for God has chosen it to reveal the mercy and splendor of God. Though Jerusalem is the name of a unique city with its own long and complicated history, it also refers metaphorically to the people of Israel, a particular people among all the nations of the ancient world. The choice made by God narrows further and further until the actual village where the promised one will be born is identified. Though only a stone's throw from the great city of Jerusalem, Bethlehem never really grew to be much. Its real importance was as the birthplace of David. Henceforth it would be know as the birthplace of the Messiah of God.

Psalms

While the first readings all look in anticipation to what God will do, the psalm responses begin with a plea to be led in the ways of God (First Sunday). This moves to a cry of exaltation for having been restored to peace and prosperity (Second and Third Sundays). The responses conclude with a final appeal for salvation (Fourth Sunday).

The responses also contain various images of God that together provide insight into God's extraordinary behavior toward weak, limited, even sinful humankind. In the first response God is good and upright, kind and constant, in covenant with others and cherishing their friendship. The second response states that God delivered captives and restored their fortunes. The response from Isaiah depicts a God to whom we can turn with confidence, a God who can alleviate our fears and concerns. In the last response God is characterized as a caring and protecting shepherd and as a meticulous vinedresser. Taken together, the responses create a collage of sketches of God as one who is intimately concerned with our well-being and who is able to effect change in the circumstances of our lives.

Epistles

Three of the readings from the epistles contain instruction for Christian living, either in anticipation of the definitive coming of Christ (First and Second Sundays) or for believers presently grounded in the reality of Christ's entry into the world to save us (Third and Fourth Sundays). Basic to all Christian living is love. It is this love that roots us in righteousness and makes us blameless in holiness before God. Christian virtue should be a witness to all, for that is how God is made manifest. The final reading describes the unselfish sacrifice of Christ. It was through this sacrifice that we have been consecrated and given the grace to live the kind of lives to which the other readings exhort us.

Gospels

The message of the first three gospel readings is anticipatory. Each reading directs our attention to some aspect of God's saving plan, a plan that will unfold in the future. The readings move from the expansive cosmic sphere, to the scope of the ministry of Jesus, to the events that took place just before the actual appearance of God in human flesh. They begin with an announcement of the final coming of the Son of Man. Though this momentous event will be preceded by signs of terror and destruction, we are assured that it will ultimately usher in the redemption of humankind. The second and third readings announce the inauguration of the public ministry of Jesus. The details of the accounts place this ministry squarely on the stage of history. While God's working may be depicted in descriptions that employ vibrant imagery, the events described were real events with historical significance.

The account reported in the final reading is descriptive of an event and also a kind of foretaste of future events. Elizabeth's unborn child recognized the child in Mary's womb. The one who would become the voice in the wilderness that pointed out the long-awaited one was first the child in the womb who alerted his mother to the identity of the child Mary was carrying. The one who was to come had already manifested himself, and even before his birth there were those who paid him homage.

Mosaic of Readings

This mosaic of readings shows that Advent is a time of great anticipation. It is a time for us to reflect on the wondrous fact that God in Christ has entered the events of human existence and from there has called us to live lives rooted in the same Christ. It is through this unique human reality that we come to know God, and it is to other human beings that we are sent to proclaim what we know. God came once in the flesh and became so much a part of our existence that never again will human life be bereft of the divine.

Readings

First Sunday of Advent
Jeremiah 33:14-16

The message in this passage enjoys prophetic authority. Spoken by the prophet, it contains the words of the LORD. It announces a future wherein the promise of God will be fulfilled. However, God made many promises to this favored people. To which promise does the oracle refer? The reference is clearly to a promise of redemption, and these few verses highlight several important theological themes that define this redemption.

First, although the oracle is directed to the chosen people, mention of both the northern kingdom of Israel and the southern kingdom of Judah indicates the inclusive nature of the promised redemption. There is no internal preference here. Though Jeremiah is a southern prophet, the redemption he announces is for all the people.

The second feature of this promise is its Davidic character. A shoot, a sign of new life springing from previous life, will be raised up for the Davidic house. While mention of this royal house has a southern connotation, it could actually be pointing either to the earliest phase of the monarchy, when all political groups were united under David, or to the time of Jeremiah himself, when there was but one nation under the jurisdiction of a descendant of David. The promised shoot probably comes *from* the royal line. However, the passage states it is raised up *for* the monarchy as well. This could suggest that while it will be an agent of God's redemption for the people, it will also provide the monarchy itself with another chance of being the means through which God will effect redemption. This will be accomplished because the shoot will practice justice and righteousness in the land, two characteristics associated with the anointed ruler (cf. Isa 9:6).

The oracle next turns its attention to Judah and Jerusalem. In the days of future salvation they will be safe and secure. This promise suggests they do not enjoy safety or security now. The oracle is a pledge of future redemption to a people in need of it at the present time. Mention of Judah and Jerusalem is significant. Judah represents the political identity of the people. However, the governmental seat of the nation, Jerusalem, is its religious center. The oracle promises that in the coming days of fulfillment a Davidic ruler will be raised up and the nation, which is really a religious entity, will be secure.

The last line holds profound importance. Jerusalem, the city whose name means "foundation of peace," is here given a new name, "the LORD our justice." From this, one could conclude that the real foundation of the city's peace is justice and that the basis of this justice is the quality of its commitment to the LORD. The message of this passage, then, includes an implied call for recommitment. The oracle itself sketches the character of the future covenantal relationship between God and the people. It begins with an announcement that God will deliver them to safety, and it ends with the people grounding their salvation in the righteousness of God.

Psalm 25:4-5, 8-9, 10, 14

The psalm response opens with a prayer for divine guidance. The word "way" has very close association with the Wisdom tradition and refers to a manner of living. Although the term often designates movement or direction on a road rather than the road itself, here it could refer to a style of life. This psalm limits its considerations to the way of righteousness. "Path" appears in parallel construction with "way" and also refers to a style of life. When this expression is used in reference to God, it can mean either God's own ways of acting or the ways God teaches humankind to go. The psalm seems to include both meanings.

If we understand the words from the perspective of God's way of acting we become attentive to the salvation accomplished by God (v. 5) and to God's own uprightness (v. 8). The psalm gives no indication as to the character of the salvation wrought by God. Was the psalmist in physical danger? Was the deliverance from personal misfortune? Whatever the case may have been, the psalmist asks for insight into God's saving ways, presumably in order to walk according to those ways, to sing God's praises, and to offer thanks for God's goodness.

The second stanza comments on the righteousness of God, which is attentive to both the sinners and the *anawim,* or humble (vv. 8-9). Both groups are taught the way of the LORD, the way God acts toward people's loyalty and infidelity. Presumably the sinners will be taught that wickedness will be punished, while the humble will be assured that their righteousness, which is in keeping with God's way, has not gone unnoticed.

The "way" the LORD shows probably refers to the manner of living God expects of humankind. In this psalm it is a reference to the law (v. 10), for it is there that the will of God is to be found. The psalmist is asking for guidance to discern God's will in order to live in accord with it. Such compliance is the only appropriate response of one who is in a relationship with God. The paths of the LORD, or the way of living that is pleasing to the LORD, promise the blessings of covenantal lovingkindness (*hesed,* vv. 10, 14) and truth or constancy (*'emet,* v. 10). These attitudes guarantee an intimacy of friendship or the kind of familiarity that results in trusting counsel *(sôd).* This is the kind of friendship that will be enjoyed by those who fear the LORD. Such fear is less an attitude of dread and trembling than one of awe in the presence of the majesty of God. The trepidation that may accompany fear stems more from reverence and wonder than from terror.

The Wisdom character of this psalm is apparent in these important themes: the way of the LORD, counsel or friendship with God, and fear of the LORD. The psalm clearly draws the connection between covenant and wisdom. An intimate relationship with God calls for a response from the covenant partners. The psalmist prays: Teach me your ways. Show me how you have acted; show me how I should respond. The psalm itself provides an answer to these questions: Walk in the way of the LORD!

1 Thessalonians 3:12–4:2

The passage consists of two quite different literary forms, each containing its own theological message. Placed together, however, a definite link can be discerned. The first (3:12-13) is a kind of wish-prayer, employing verbs in the optative (wish) verb form rather than the imperative (command) verb form. In it Paul expresses his desire for the spiritual growth of the Thessalonian believers. The second (4:1-2) is an exhortation that contains a tone of urgency, encouraging the believers to continue to live righteous lives.

It is Paul's wish-prayer that the Thessalonians increase (grow to produce an abundance) and abound (enjoy an excess) in love. He is asking for their spiritual growth and maturity. He does not ask that love increase but that the believers' capacity for growth be expanded so they can fill it with love. Furthermore, it is his wish-prayer that their love be both communal (for one another) and universal (for all). Such love breaks out of ethnocentric bounds and, like the love Paul himself possesses, resembles the inclusive love of God.

This kind of universal love pervades the entire being of the one loving because it flows from the heart, which is believed to be the seat of understanding and will and the place where the hidden motives of life and conduct take shape. When such a heart has been strengthened and expanded, love can overflow abundantly. Paul desires this kind of living for his converts so that when they must appear in the light of God's glory at the time of the coming of Christ, they will be found blameless in holiness.

In the eschatological thinking of Israel, which early Christianity inherited, believers maintained that at this end-time God, accompanied by angels, would come to render deliverance or judgment. In this passage Paul implies that the coming of the end-time should be an incentive to righteous living. This eschatological perspective is seen in Paul's view of the coming of Christ with his holy ones. Although for Paul "holy ones" usually refers to faithful Christians, his reference here is probably to heavenly beings (cf. 2 Thess 1:7). This first part ends with "Amen," a primitive Christian response that affirms the truth of what has been proclaimed.

The urgent exhortation that follows (4:1-2) encourages the Thessalonians to conduct themselves (the Greek verb is *peripateō*, or "walk") according to the ethical and moral standards of the Christian tradition. Behind the instruction Paul has handed down to them is the authority of the Lord Jesus. Paul is asking them to do nothing more than the teaching of Jesus requires of them. In the first part of this passage he expresses a wish that the Christians mature in their capacity to love. Here he urges them to advance along the paths of righteous living. He wishes and he exhorts so that these Christians will be blameless at the coming of the Lord Jesus.

Luke 21:25-28, 34-36

The coming events described by Jesus strike fear in the human heart. He speaks of cosmic disturbances and the distress on earth these disturbances will cause.

As startling as all of this may be, the upheavals are really signs that portend the advent of redemption. Cosmic turmoil calls to mind the primordial chaos out of which God brought order (cf. Gen 1:1-10) and the destruction at the time of Noah out of which God brought order anew (cf. Gen 7:12; 9:9-11). In the case described in this passage the disturbances are probably less predictions of actual historical events than metaphorical images portraying the end of one age and the birth of another. Apocalyptic imagery frequently is employed in describing the entrance of God onto the stage of world history (cf. Isa 13:9-10). While a theophany of this kind is generally associated with divine judgment (cf. Ezek 32:7-8), in this case it precedes the coming of the Son of Man and a time of redemption. In one of the long-standing messianic traditions, a mysterious figure who is "like a son of man" comes on the clouds to receive from God dominion, glory, and kingship (Dan 7:13-14). Early Christian theology appropriated this tradition in its characterization of the messianic role of Jesus. This is certainly how "Son of Man" should be understood in this gospel passage.

The upheaval described here, whether it is meant as cosmic, national, or spiritual, will cause such anguish that people will die of fright. Despite this, Jesus tells his listeners to stand erect and raise their heads when all of this happens rather than cower in fear. For those who have been faithfully awaiting the revelation of God, this will not be a time of punishment. Rather, it will be the advent of the new age of fulfillment. In order to ensure that this will indeed be the case Jesus next tells his listeners how they should prepare for that time (vv. 34-36).

The fundamental exhortation is: Beware! Take Heed! Be Alert! Don't be caught by surprise! Although there will be extraordinary signs announcing this upcoming event, the exact time of the revelation is unknown. That is why believers must avoid any kind of behavior that might jeopardize their watchfulness, whether it be carousing and drunkenness or simply preoccupation with the anxieties of daily life.

The "day" referred to is the ominous Day of the LORD, foretold by several Israelite prophets (cf. Amos 5:18-20; Isa 13:6; Jer 46:10). It will be a day of punishment for the wicked but a day of salvation for the faithful. It is ominous and threatening for all because no one knows exactly when it will dawn, and consequently everyone must be vigilant at all times and pray for strength to endure. This last admonishment acknowledges that all are subject to human weakness and even the faithful could fall away in the face of overwhelming afflictions. However, at the coming of the Son of Man (Jesus), faithful believers will be able to stand before him and receive the redemption he brings.

Themes of the Day

The readings of the First Sunday of Advent set the stages for our reflections on the entire season. The themes in these initial readings include the promises made by God; the coming of the Lord, the Son of Man; and the manner of living for those to whom the promises are made. Since these promises convey both specific historical and general eschatological significance, their fulfillment is not limited to the communities to which they were originally made but is intended for all who open themselves to them.

The Promises Made by God

The readings for this First Sunday contain a number of promises, all pointing to the same reality, namely, peace and fulfillment. Because there is here a promise of blessing, we can conclude that they were not yet a part of the people's lives. The pledge of a descendant of David assured the people that justice would eventually be established in the land and the people would then be able to live there in peace and security. The promise of the coming of the Son of Man was one of redemption rather than destruction. Clearly these are promises filled with hope.

The promises are made to needy people, people who are longing for peace and the fulfillment only God can give. Each of the readings depicts a dimension of suffering, suffering that has often been brought on by the people themselves. However, the promises are assurances that the end of their suffering was in sight. The promises actually tell us more about the God who makes them than about those to whom they are made. They reveal a loving and provident God, a merciful and forgiving God. This is a God who does not hold grudges but who gives second, third, even numberless chances. Furthermore, because it is God who promises we can be sure the promises will be fulfilled. These are promises full of hope.

The Coming of the Lord

In the readings for today the coming of the Lord is clearly envisioned as a time of expectation, not of fear and trembling. Although the earlier tradition about the Day of the LORD included the aspect of punishment of the wicked, the focus here is on redemption. This is true about each of the readings but especially the psalm response. In it we pray to be guided in the ways of God, who is our savior. The time of expectation may be preceded by apocalyptic occurrences—signs in the heavens and dismay on earth—but here the cosmic shift is expected to bring fulfillment, not destruction.

The suffering described in the gospel passage is the kind of distress that accompanies any major natural, social, or personal upheaval. At such times we may be shaken to our foundations; we are dismayed, frightened to death. Paul says the Lord will come with his holy ones; Luke says the Son of Man will come in glory and great power. This is the day when the love and providence, the mercy and forgiveness of God will be made manifest. As we enter into this season of expectation, we too are invited to stand before the Son of Man to receive the blessings promised by God.

The Advent Way of Life

What is expected of those who receive the promise? An Advent way of life exhorts us to "wait in joyful hope for the coming of our Savior Jesus Christ." However, it is not merely a life of passive anticipation. Rather, it is one of active discipline. Dependent on God, it is rooted in love and blameless in holiness. It is lived in the midst of a community within which God's promises have already been revealed. The Advent way of life not only anticipates the Day of the Lord's coming, but it incarnates that coming as well. As we live rooted in love and blameless in holiness, we make present in our lives that Lord who is to come. Thus we are summoned to live in the tension between the already and the not yet.

The Advent way of life is both simple and profound. It does not necessarily require unusual behavior on our part, but it calls us to live the usual unusually well. It affects the everyday events of life; it directs the way we interact with people; it informs the attitudes that color our judgments and motivations. It is as ordinary as the birth of a child; it is as extraordinary as the revelation of God.

Second Sunday of Advent
Baruch 5:1-9

Two movements appear in this dramatic depiction of reversal of fortune. In the first (vv. 1-4) the grieving city of Jerusalem is told to replace its mourning garb with garments that bespeak splendor and rejoicing. In the second (vv. 5-9) Jerusalem is directed to stand on the heights and watch the resplendent return of the previously captured citizens.

Jerusalem is first portrayed as a grieving mother. Her sorrow is not for herself but for those children who were carried off by enemies, scattered both east and west. Since this also meant the loss of any future for the family, one could say that Jerusalem was faced with extinction. Hence she is clothed in the traditional garments of a mourner.

Finding the city in such a state, the prophet directs her: "Take off your robe of mourning and misery!" Her attire is to be completely altered. In place of bereavement garb, she is told to clothe herself with the glory and justice that come from God and to wear on her head an imposing miter similar to the one worn by the high priest Aaron (cf. Exod 28:36-37; 39:30-31). This transformation is called for so the new splendor of the city will be seen by all the earth. Finally, the city whose name means "foundation of peace" is given a new name: "the peace of justice, the glory of God's worship." (*Theosébeia* [glory] might be better translated as piety or reverence for God. This explains the reference to worship.) The first part of the new name suggests that the peace Jerusalem represents is grounded in justice; the second part suggests that the city is garbed in divine splendor.

Transformed by the glory of God, Jerusalem is told to stand on the heights and witness a second reversal of fortune: those who had been taken from her as captives will return rejoicing; led away from her on foot, they will be carried back to her on royal thrones. The contour of the world will be transformed for the sake of the people of Israel. The route upon which they will travel will be made level to facilitate their crossing; the high places will be brought low and the depressions will be filled in (cf. Isa 40:4). Even the trees will shelter them as they return home. Just as those scattered will be gathered by the word of God, so it is God who will level their return route and bring them back to Jerusalem.

No explicit reason is given for God's remarkable magnanimity. It is simply extended to Jerusalem and to her children. The passage does state that the splendor God bestows upon Jerusalem will be revealed to all the earth, but it does not say that such witness is the reason the city is glorified. What is mentioned, along with God's justice, is God's mercy. It may very well be that God's mercy prompted the reversals, and the reversals witness to the world the mercy of God.

Psalm 126:1-2, 2-3, 4-5, 6

Believers trust that God will surely act on their behalf, because God has done so before. The great blessing of Israel's past was the return from exile. Zion, the mountain on which the Temple was built, became a symbol with many levels of meaning. It stood for the Temple itself, the city of Jerusalem, the southern kingdom, or the entire nation of Israel. Here it probably represents Jerusalem and the area surrounding it.

The response of the returnees was threefold: amazement, laughter, joy. Their release and return was so extraordinary it was almost beyond their comprehension. It was as if they were in a dream. This suggests that their situation could scarcely lead them to believe they could ever come back to the land from which they had been taken. Painting the situation in such bleak shades was a technique employed by the author to help the people see how helpless they were to improve, much less reverse, their predicament. In such circumstances only God would have the authority and power to change anything.

The graciousness of God, as seen in the deliverance of and blessings given to the Israelites, speaks volumes to the other nations. It throws into bold relief God's saving power. It also shows that this power is not bound by the limitations of geographic boundary or ethnic particularity. It was exercised over the Israelites, but it could be effective in a foreign country. This is a God who shows preference for those who are poor and marginalized in society, for the homeless and the foreigner, the displaced and the refugee. The portrait Israel's history paints of such a God has clarity, depth, and nuance. Seeing this history unfold before their very eyes, the nations will marvel at the greatness of a God who can accomplish such amazing feats, and they will acclaim the LORD.

The prayer for deliverance is straightforward: Restore us now as you restored us in the past. The image used as a comparison reflects the impossible character of the present situation. The restoration will be like a flood of water in the southern desert, which is not only infrequent but unlikely. The image itself contains a paradox. One element of it (torrents of water) is the complete reverse of the other (arid desert). This contradiction underscores the implausibility of what is being asked. However, the petitioner boldly offers the petition, because the grace requested had been granted in the past.

The reversal of fortune is further described in symbolic language: sowing in tears and reaping in joy; leaving with only the promise of harvest and returning with its abundant fruits. God will replace with good fortune the tragedy that now marks the circumstances of the people. This is their prayer; it is for this they hope. They are confident their prayer will be answered and their hope realized because God has been gracious to them in the past.

Philippians 1:4-6, 8-11

The affection Paul has for the Christians of the Philippian community is evident in this passage. His prayer for them, though it is one of petition, flows from his appreciation of their faithfulness to the righteousness God is effecting in them. The partnership or community *(koinōnía)* he enjoys with them is probably a sharing *in* the faith rather than a sharing *of* the faith in ministerial involvement. He commends them for having been partners with him in this faith since the first days of his founding of the church in Philippi. This is clearly a community dear to Paul's heart.

The affection Paul has for this community is more than merely human sentiment, as noble as that might be. The longing he has for them is identified with the affection Christ has toward them (v. 8). The Greek word refers to the deepest interior feelings, the bowels of the emotions *(splánchnon)*. It is a word that denotes compassion. Paul claims this is really the love of Christ expressing itself through him, and he calls on God to bear witness to this.

Although it was Paul who brought the good news of the gospel to these people, he acknowledges that it was God who made it take root in their hearts, and it is God who will oversee its maturation until it is brought to completion at the day of Christ Jesus. The spread and fruition of the word is God's doing. Paul is merely the instrument God has used to plant the seed.

The eschatological character of this passage becomes clear when Paul identifies the time of full flowering as the day of Christ Jesus. This reference probably springs from ancient Israel's notion of the Day of the LORD, that time when God will enter world history bringing salvation to the righteous and punishment to the wicked. From its very beginnings Christianity has interpreted the Day of the LORD (YHWH) as the Day of the Lord (Jesus) and has anticipated a second coming of Christ as judge. Paul's message here serves to assure the Philippians that this anticipated day will be one of rich harvest for them.

Paul's prayer for the Philippians is twofold: that their love for one another will increase, and that they will be pure and blameless for the coming day of Christ. The love of which Paul speaks *(agapē)* is selfless, like the sacrificial love of Christ. Here it has no explicit object. It is a disposition of openness to all. It both produces and thrives in the kind of moral insight that can discern (test by trial) what is of value. The purity and blamelessness for which he prays suggest the kind of Christian maturity that produces fruits of righteousness. If the believers are to be pure at the time of Christ's coming, they will have to have been living pure lives. This is the substance of Paul's prayer; he wants them to live out that for which he prays.

Paul concludes his prayer in the traditional style of both Jewish and Christian prayers of thanksgiving: "For the glory and praise of God."

Luke 3:1-6

The account of the ministry of John the Baptist is steeped in imagery that recalls both the Exodus from Egypt and the return from Babylonian Exile. However, lest it be seen in merely symbolic terms, the gospel writer places John's activity and the ensuing ministry of Jesus squarely in the midst of the broader world. The power structures in Palestine are identified, beginning with the Roman emperor himself (Tiberius Caesar) and moving through the list of regional authorities of occupation and the Jewish religious leadership. There is some discrepancy in the dating. However, the intent here is less an interest in chronological precision than in grounding the events of salvation in world history.

John the Baptist is a most fascinating figure. He comes from a priestly family (cf. Luke 1:5), yet he is found in the desert, a place that calls to mind the wandering of the people in the wilderness as they moved out of Egyptian bondage into the land promised by God. His activity occurred in the region of the Jordan, the gateway to the Promised Land. The river itself was crossed by the people before their entry into the land (cf. Jos 3:14-17). Thus crossing became a symbol of their entrance into a new life. All of this somehow marks John as an agent of momentous transformation.

This passage treats the kind of baptism John proclaims *(kērýssō);* it does not describe the actual rite. In the Jewish tradition baptism was a common practice that had a rich and varied significance. It was one of three requirements for becoming a Jew (along with circumcision and sacrifice). It was an ascetic act that at times signified turning away from evil and at other times represented cleansing from sin, which was the divine answer to repentance. In either case it carried an eschatological importance, marking the entrance into a new form of living. The baptism of John called for repentance *(metánoia),* a conversion, or change of heart. This conversion was for the forgiveness of sin. Clearly the eschatological significance of John's baptism was salvation, not judgment.

The messianic character of John's ministry becomes clear from the reference to the Isaian passage that follows (cf. Isa 40:3-5). In the earlier oracle the prophet applies the practice of preparing a fitting roadway, across which a conquering leader would travel home amidst great celebration, to the transformation that would precede the return of the people from exile. With a slight adjustment to the passage (in Isaiah, what was in the desert was the way of the LORD; here, it is the voice), the gospel text suggests that John is the herald of the coming of the Lord. Just as both the Exodus and the return from exile involved a desert crossing, so the eschatological renewal proclaimed by John begins in the desert.

Finally, as both of the earlier incidents were salvific, so will this new coming of the Lord be an event of salvation. However, it will not be limited to the people of Israel. As announced by Isaiah, this salvation will be universal.

Themes of the Day

The readings for the Second Sunday of Advent revisit the theme of promise and move it in a slightly different direction. First, they situate God's promise squarely within the context of world history. Then, they characterize the nature of God's promise as one of wondrous transformation. Finally, they provide examples of how this transformation takes place within the relationships that constitute the fabric of life.

The Sacredness of History

Ours is not an otherworldly religion that calls us to renounce the realities of human life. On the contrary, the advent of God's coming and the promise of fulfillment that accompanies it happen within world history. The first reading locates God's action of restoration in the city of Jerusalem. The gospel passage situates the ministry of John, the son of Zachariah, within a particular period of world history. It points us to historical experience as the place and the time of restoration, of incarnation, of redemption. It shows us that God works within everyday life, in conventional places, during regular time. In fact, from a human point of view the extraordinary events of salvation appear to have taken place within what was ordinary.

Our appreciation of the significance of history leads us to realize that Advent is not merely a time to remember something that happened two thousand years ago. Nor is it simply a time for anticipating some future event, whether that be the anniversary of Christ's birth or the mysterious time of his Second Coming. The adventing of God, the promise we are expecting, and the transformation it offers happen within the affairs of human life, of our life, of the here and now. Ours is the acceptable time! Ours is the day of salvation!

The Promise of Transformation

John proclaims repentance, the kind of transformation that results in a change of heart. The readings are filled with examples of reversals that characterize such transformation: the robe of mourning is replaced by the splendor of glory; tears are turned into rejoicing; those led away by enemies are brought back by God; valleys are filled, mountains are leveled, winding roads are made straight; even nature offers itself as shelter for the People of God. In a world that has been transformed those who are shamed and discarded are made glorious; those who suffer are comforted; the oppressed are freed; all life's obstacles are removed; the way to God is made straight; the natural world enjoys peace and harmony. This is the promise made to us in our time.

Advent is a time of yearning for such transformation. It is the time of preparing for its arrival. It is a time to open ourselves so that, as in the past, God can accomplish through ordinary human beings the necessary reversals that are part of this hoped-for transformation. It is the time of bringing the promises for the future, made in the past, to fruition in the present.

A Life of Repentance

The transformation, or repentance of heart, takes place within human life, within relationships of justice between people and with the earth, in right living, in genuine unselfish love. It produces the fruits of righteousness of which Paul speaks. The first reading suggests that the reversals are experienced by a people who grieve. The same transformation is particularly evident in our relationships with the people we offend or the people we discard, with the people of whom our own society takes advantage.

Advent living requires that we situate ourselves in our own lives, that we not try to escape our own history. It challenges us to see history as the very sacrament of God's advent. We do this with the eyes of faith opening us to the transformative future embedded in the present.

Third Sunday of Advent
Zephaniah 3:14-18a

The exaltation in this oracle of salvation is stated clearly at the outset: "Shout! . . . Sing! . . . Be glad and exult!" The people are told to cast aside all cautious reserve and to rejoice wholeheartedly. They are addressed in endearing terms associated with their election by God. Besides their customary designation as Israel, they are identified as cherished daughter. (Ancient cities or nations were characterized as female, and their inhabitants as children of the city/nation.) Though Zion and Jerusalem are usually associated with the monarchy, there is no royal reference here. The nation as a whole is being addressed.

The reason for this rejoicing is their deliverance from their enemies, a deliverance accomplished by God. The misfortune they endured was a punishment for their sins. Now God, as judge, has removed that judgment, and this is cause for great rejoicing. A further reason for rejoicing is the abiding presence of the LORD in their midst as King of Israel (v. 15) and as a mighty savior (v. 17). Both titles are associated with the early period of Israel's history, a time when God was the only king they knew and when, as a mighty warrior, God defended them from their enemies. Invoking these titles, the prophet is reminding them that their deliverance comes from no human savior but from the LORD.

"On that day" is an allusion to the Day of the LORD, a time in the future when the justice of God will be executed throughout the world. The people may have been unfaithful in the past, but because of the salvation won by God, that day will be a time of exultation for them. The words that announce a prophetic oracle of salvation will be spoken to Jerusalem/Zion: "Fear not!" (cf. Isa 10:24; 40:9). They are not to be discouraged (the literal translation is "let not your hands be slack," like one paralyzed, unable to move out of fear [cf. Isa 13:7]). God is in their midst as king and savior.

The concluding verses contain tender expressions of God's love. In the first phrase the rejoicing *(śimḥi)* of God is reminiscent of another prophetic reference. As a bridegroom rejoices over his bride, God will rejoice over the people (cf. Isa 62:5). Clearly, an intimate relationship is intended. In the second phrase the verb translated "renew" *(ḥāraš)* really means "to be quiet" in love.

In this context it suggests a disposition of love too deep to be expressed in words. Finally, God will rejoice *(gîl)* in singing *(rinnâ)*, the kind of exuberance characteristic of oriental weddings (cf. Ps 45:16).

Taken together, these phrases describe both the tenderness God has for this restored people and the joy their restoration elicits in God. The people are called to rejoice because God rejoices. This is further expressed in the reference to feasts. The joy and exultation to which they are called is the kind experienced during the time of festivals, those times of celebration when the people revel in their good fortune.

Isaiah 12:2-3, 4, 5-6

Although a passage from the prophetic material, this is really a hymn of thanksgiving that anticipates favors to be granted and enjoyed in the future. Because of its content it might also be considered a hymn of confidence. God is declared to be the source of salvation, and bolstered by this assurance, the writer claims to be unafraid and filled with courage. The prophet is also strengthened knowing that the source of salvation is the LORD rather than a mere human being. The theme of water appears here, not as threatening and chaotic as is so often the case but as transformative. In this passage it is the water of salvation. Those who draw this water as if from a well will be refreshed by God's salvific power.

The theme of universal witness reappears as prominent (vv. 4-5). The writer calls on the community to praise the glorious name of God, the name that represents the very character of God. They are to extol the marvels God has accomplished and to proclaim them to the nations. The most celebrated of these wondrous works is the transformation of the people themselves. Only God could have taken a people in need of salvation and transformed them into witnesses of God's power. In other words, the transformed lives of God's people will announce to the nations the marvels God has accomplished.

The third and final theme found in this response highlights the importance of Jerusalem. This city was both the royal capital of the Davidic dynasty and the site where the Temple was built. It is the second aspect that is the focus here. Although the Temple itself is not mentioned, its purpose as the earthly dwelling place of God is. The city is called upon to rejoice, and the reason for this exultation is the presence of God in its midst. Although the Temple was the concrete representation of God's own divine presence, it is this presence and not the temple building that is fundamental (cf. Jer 7:3-4). In this passage the theology has come full circle. The presence of God in the midst of the people is the source of the writer's confidence of future deliverance.

The title "Holy One of Israel" has cultic nuances. It comes from the Hebrew that means "set apart" or "consecrate" *(qādash)* and is opposed to what is secular or profane. God's holiness is usually manifested in some form of glory or majesty, and this frequently, though not always, occurs in the Temple, or "holy place." In the presence of such a God human beings recognize their own limitations and commit themselves to a way of life that separates them from the profane, consecrates them to God, and gives them access to what is holy. Chosen by God from among the other nations, Israel was set apart and consecrated to God. In this passage the psalmist calls the people to rejoice in this: the holy God is in their midst.

Philippians 4:4-7

Several elements in this short passage lead one to conclude that the community to which the letter was originally addressed was experiencing some form of adversity. First, the passage is introduced by Paul's emphatic double exhortation to rejoice, suggesting that joy is not a spontaneous response to the people's present situation. This exhortation is followed by another, perhaps more forceful, admonition: "Have no anxiety," which suggests that fear or dread are not far from them. Finally, Paul directs them to pray, indicating that they are indeed in need.

The joy Paul advocates is not merely the happiness that comes from enjoyment of life. It is a special kind of joy, joy in the Lord, the kind grounded in faith in Jesus Christ. Paul calls the believers to live lives of kindness, of gentle forbearance that does not insist on one's own rights, that is willing to forgo any form of retaliation, that is selfless in spite of the faults of others. Such genuine Christian behavior should be visible to all. In other words, all people should be the beneficiaries of this kind of Christian kindness. "The Lord is near" is an eschatological watchword acclaiming the future coming of the Lord to set all things right. If they have lived righteously, the Lord will come to them as a compassionate savior rather than as a severe judge.

The movement of the theology in this passage is clear. As stated above, if the Christians live righteously, God will come as a savior. Now they are told that abiding in the saving grace of God will eliminate all anxiety. In the face of this, the Philippians are advised to pray to God. Three different words are used in order to emphasize both how needy people are and how important it is for them to acknowledge their need. "Prayer" *(proseuchē)* refers to a very general prayerful attitude of mind; "petition" *(déēsis)* is a prayer of supplication expressing great need; "request" *(aitēma)* includes mention of those things for which they ask. This stress on prayer and the need that lies behind it underscore the reliance the Philippians have on God. Any virtue or righteousness on their part cannot be credited to their own resources. They are totally dependent on God, even for their piety.

The reward for such commitment to righteousness and to prayer is peace. This peace is extraordinary in at least three ways. First, it originates from God or it is somehow of God. Second, its value transcends anything that can be comprehended by mere human beings. Third, peace itself acts as a sentinel, keeping watch over human endeavors and withstanding any form of anxiety that might threaten human equanimity. This is certainly reason to rejoice.

Luke 3:10-18

The gospel reading recounts instructions given by John the Baptist to those who came out to see and hear him and to be baptized. It can be divided into two parts: answers by John to questions posed by people in the group, and John's acknowledgment of the superiority of Christ, who is to come.

Three times John is asked: What should we do? Although he himself lives an austere life removed from the ordinary pursuits of people, he does not ask his inquirers to dissociate themselves from their own lives or occupations. Rather, he challenges them to continue where they are but to carry out their daily responsibilities with concern for others, honesty, and integrity. The practical ethical instructions he gives are communal in character.

The first questioners are identified generally as "the crowds." John exhorts them to share their surplus with those who lack the necessities of life. The Greek word translated "cloak" (*chitōn*, v. 11) is the inner garment worn next to the skin, not the outer cloak often used as a covering at night. Not only clothing but also food should be shared. It is clear from John's teaching that not everyone is called to withdraw from the world as he did, but all are instructed to care for the needs of others.

Among the crowds are tax collectors and soldiers, two groups doubly despised because they worked for the occupying Roman force and frequently took advantage of the Jewish populace. Tax agents derived their livelihood from the money they collected. They frequently exacted more than the taxes required by the authorities, thus amassing their own fortunes at the expense of the people. They are not told by John to resign but to desist from exploitative practices. The soldiers referred to here were probably not members of Roman garrisons but may have been a form of police assigned to protect the tax collectors, for they too are admonished not to extort. The tax collectors call John "Teacher," the one who instructs in righteousness. His instructions are all relational in nature: share with the needy; do not exploit the vulnerable.

The expectation that filled the people was eschatological; they were looking for the Christ, the "anointed one." Lest they mistake him for this Christ, John contrasts himself with the one who was to come. He insists that he himself is not worthy to undo the sandals of that long-awaited one, a menial task even below the dignity of a Hebrew slave. His baptism with water was a ritual of repentance and cleansing. The Christ's baptism of the Spirit will purge and transform, and his coming will be a time of judgment, when the wicked will be separated like chaff from the wheat and be thrown into the fire. The harvest has already occurred; the time of judgment is now.

It seems that John's ministry precedes this eschatological crisis, and the urgency and stern demands of his instruction call for the kind of change of heart required of those who would be saved from its ravages.

Themes of the Day

We are at the midpoint of Advent. Today we celebrate Gaudete Sunday. The principal theme of the day is joy. The readings not only call us to rejoice; they also tell us why and how we should rejoice. The gospel confronts us with a very different though not unrelated theme. Employing John the Baptist as a model, it directs us to recognize our limits and not go beyond them.

Shout for Joy

Continuing our reflection on the Advent themes of promise and transformation, we can clearly see why joy is an appropriate attitude to adopt. Joy, which according to Paul is one of the fruits of the Spirit (cf. Gal 5:22), is the deep inner experience of satisfaction and exhilaration. The joy referred to here is a religious sentiment, not emotional happiness. Along with gratitude, it is the heart's response to God's goodness. Zion is told to shout for joy because it has been saved by God from its enemies. It is also assured that God is in the midst of the people. The psalm response proclaims the same message; the reading from Philippians announces that the Lord is near. This is cause for joy.

While we may not be inclined to "*shout* for joy," there is no reason for us to live lives devoid of it. The Lord is in our midst whether things are going the way we would like or not; whether we are prosperous or needy; whether we are vigorous or in ill health; whether we are enjoying life or struggling with death. The circumstances of life do not determine whether or not we should rejoice. The presence of the Lord in our midst calls us to it.

Advent Joy

Advent is a time for joy, not primarily because we are anticipating the anniversary of the birth of Christ but because God is already in our midst (Immanuel). The readings for this Sunday assure us that God is with us, not as a judge but as a savior (Zephaniah and psalm). We rejoice over the saving acts of God, which make us confident of God's care and unafraid of whatever may cross our paths. We rejoice in the peace of God that surpasses all understanding. Advent joy is like the delight that fills a woman who has just given birth, even if it occurred in the throes of birth pangs, in the midst of the fragility of life. Advent joy springs from the realization that the presence of God in our midst can so transform our lives that the promises of peace and security will be fulfilled. Advent joy is the way we live in the tension between already and not yet.

Be Who You Are

The marvelous things God has accomplished in our lives should not blind us to the reality of human limitations. John the Baptist is a model for us in this regard. He did not seek out public adulation even though it was probably within his grasp. He knew his limits, and he did not step beyond them. In the advice he gave to others he counseled them to know who they were and to recognize the extent of their occupational privileges. Collect just taxes but no more. Do not oppress those over whom you might exercise authority.

When we truly realize that God is in our midst, we have no need to deny our own limitations or the legitimate boundaries that define our lives. Realizing that our identities are rooted in being children of God, we will have no trouble admitting that there are others who are before us or beyond us. By the grace of God, we are who we are. Perhaps what we need most to be saved from is our fraudulent selves, selves that put on false airs in order to impress or fit in. Advent is a time to strip ourselves of such duplicity and to stand honestly and humbly before God, eager for redemption.

Fourth Sunday of Advent
Micah 5:1-4a

This oracle of salvation contains several important theological themes: salvation will come from an insignificant village rather than from the royal city; the power of the ruler comes from God; a time of trial will be followed by a time of security and peace. The message, as startling as it may be, can be trusted because it is the word of the LORD.

Since there were two Bethlehems, the prophet designated which one was meant. One was in Galilee in the land of Zebulun (cf. Jos 19:15). The Bethlehem referred to here was the one associated with Ephrathah, a clan related to Caleb and located in Judah. Because it was the place of David's origin, the reference is rich in early royal importance that is quite distinct from any association with Jerusalem, the dynastic capital of the reigning royal family. The ruler promised here is not to be understood as the successive Davidic king but as a new Davidic king, fresh and totally committed to God as the young

David had been. Bethlehem (meaning "house of bread") in Ephrathah (meaning "field of fruit") may not have been militarily significant, in contrast to Jerusalem; but it represented fruitfulness, and it produced the most prominent king Israel ever knew.

This new ruler will be called forth *for* God and strengthened *by* God to rule. The image used to depict his rule is that of a shepherd who leads, protects, and provides for those in his care. Although David had been a lowly shepherd, the shepherd image had royal connotations. Kings were frequently characterized as shepherds because of the responsibility they had for their people. This promised king will shepherd in the strength and majesty of God. The image also suggests a personal relationship, for shepherds knew their flock quite well and the sheep recognized the voice of their shepherd.

Elements in the oracle suggest that a time of tribulation will precede the birth of this ruler. First, the LORD will give up some people, presumably to suffering. This is followed by an assurance that kindred who have been separated will be returned. This could be a reference to some kind of exile or displacement, but in the future time, of which the prophet speaks, the people will be reunited. Finally, one of the ways of characterizing the arrival of the eschatological age of fulfillment was as a woman giving birth to new life. The suffering that is part of the birth process was considered the birth pangs of the Messiah. It reflected the struggle involved in letting go of one form of existence in order to emerge into a new one. Despite the agony, once the tribulation of birth is over, the joy of new life blots out the pain involved in delivery.

The promised ruler will be firm yet gentle, as a shepherd is. The people will be secure, no longer threatened with banishment ("they shall remain," v. 3). There will be a reign of peace *(shālôm)*, prosperity, safety, and good health. This prophecy is an affirmation of hope in the future, a hope grounded in the goodness of God rather than in human accomplishment.

Psalm 80:2-3, 15-16, 18-19

This communal lament contains several images of God: attentive shepherd and imperial ruler (v. 2), military captain and cultivator of vines (vv. 5-16). The shepherd was responsible for the care of the flock, leading it to verdant pastures and protecting it from danger. He had to be patient and solicitous, even when the sheep wandered off and placed themselves in peril. A good shepherd could recognize the unique bleating sound of his sheep, making him conscious of their whereabouts even when they were out of his sight. God was called the "Shepherd of Israel." Thus the psalmist cries "Harken!" and is confident God will hear and come to the aid of those in need.

The second image is of an imperial ruler, majestically enthroned. Cherubim, composite winged creatures with both human and animal characteristics, stood at the entrance of the Temple. Since many societies considered the monarchy divine, cherubim often guarded the royal throne. In Israel the monarchy was human, and cherubim guarded what belonged to God. They were in the garden of Eden (Gen 3:24), on the ark of the covenant (Exod 25:20), and around God's throne (v. 2).

The title "LORD of Hosts" is also associated with the ark of the covenant (cf. 1 Sam 4:4). "Hosts" is a military term meaning divisions of the army. "Hosts of heaven" refers to units of the heavenly defenders, those who fight cosmic battles and claim God as their military leader. Israel believed that God would marshal these forces of heaven and would fight for Israel (cf. Isa 40:26). This divine fighter was none other than the one who ruled from the heavenly throne, and so the psalmist cries out: "Look down from heaven and see!" The Ruler who sits in majesty is also the solicitous Shepherd of Israel, the one to whom the psalmist pleads "Rouse your power and come to save us!" The psalm may have originated in the north, since all the names mentioned are of northern tribes. However, here these few tribes represent all the people.

Finally, God is depicted as a keeper of vines. Cultivating a vineyard is demanding and tedious work, and it takes a long time to bring a vine to maturity. Vinedressers must be dedicated, patient people, not unlike shepherds. Both are dealing with living things that follow their own laws of growth, which the ones tending cannot really control. They must be willing to forgo their own comfort in the face of long hours and inclement weather. Picturing God in this way, the psalmist cries: "Take care of this vine!"

What apt images to characterize the relationship between God and the people! Though God is very powerful, like an imperial ruler or a military leader, the care God provides compares with that of an attentive shepherd or a patient vinedresser. The final plea for help mentions one who sits at God's right hand, traditionally considered the place of honor. This may have originally been a reference to the king, the one responsible for the safety and prosperity of the nation. Gradually it was applied to the longed-for royal Messiah.

Hebrews 10:5-10

This passage consists of a contrast between the sacrificial ritual that was formerly observed and the sacrifice of Christ. It is written in the form of a homiletic midrash, an interpretive approach in which a passage from Scripture is cited and then commented upon. Throughout the reading the author places various phrases in the mouth of Christ, thus giving christological authority to his own theology. He tells us that Christ proclaimed these statements upon his entrance into the world, suggesting that what is contained here is the precise reason for the incarnation. The statements themselves focus particularly on the excellence of Christ's physical body *(sōma)*.

Christ's words are a commentary on Ps 40:7-9. Four different sacrifices are mentioned: animal sacrifice *(thysía);* meal offering *(prosperá);* burnt offering *(holokaútoma);* sin offering *(perì hamartía).* Together they represent the entire sacrificial system. In the original psalm they are contrasted with an attitude of obedience toward God, demonstrating that interior obedience is preferred over mere external ritual. As it appears in this passage, the contrast is between those sacrifices and the body of the psalmist. Applied to Christ, his sacrifice is preferred over other sacrifices because of the preeminence of his human body as compared with the bodies of the sacrificial animals. Christ's compliance with the will of God is clearly stated, but here the specific focus is the offering of his body and not merely his obedience.

In his commentary on this christological reading of the psalm (vv. 8-10) the author of the letter makes explicit the contrast between adherence to the law and Christ's obedience to God's will. He claims that Christ annuls or takes away the first (external adherence) in order to establish the second (internal obedience). He then moves in his theological development from Christ's obedience to our own sanctification. By freely offering his body in sacrifice, Christ identifies his own will with the will of God. We are sanctified through this same sacrifice, not through any sacrifice required by law. For it was through his human body, a body like ours, that he demonstrated his obedience.

Finally, the preeminence of Christ's sacrifice of his body is stated again. He offered himself once for all (v. 10). The former sacrificial system required a variety of offerings to be repeated time and again. This multiplicity of sacrifices indicates the inadequacy of any single sacrifice. Because he was offering his own body, Christ offered himself only one time and in only one way, and it was enough. It is through this sacrifice that we are sanctified.

Luke 1:39-45

The report of Mary's encounter with Elizabeth can be divided into three parts: Mary's journey into the hill country in the south (vv. 39-40a); her greeting and its effects on Elizabeth and on her unborn child (vv. 40b-41); Elizabeth's jubilant response to all of this (vv. 42-45). The only geographic identification given in the account is the region within which Elizabeth and Zechariah live, the hill country of Judah. This reading does not identify the village or region from which Mary came. The major significance of the passage is the faith-filled avowal of Elizabeth.

The Greek verb used suggests that Mary's greeting to Elizabeth was a customary salutation *(aspázomai),* but its effect was profound. It caused the child in Elizabeth's womb to leap with joy *(skirtáō).* This is reminiscent of the joy that filled David as he leaped before the ark of the covenant, the symbol of God in the midst of the people (cf. 2 Sam 6:14-15). Elizabeth was filled with the Holy Spirit and proclaimed her faith in the child Mary was carrying. In the cases of both David and Elizabeth's unborn child, it was their realization of being in the presence of God that caused them to rejoice. It is as if Mary is the ark and the child within her is the glory of God.

In response to this wondrous experience, Elizabeth exalts first Mary and then her child (v. 42). The word translated "blessed" *(eulogéō)* means "to extol" or "to speak well of." Elizabeth does not pronounce a blessing over them. Instead, she recognizes the blessedness they possess and she praises it. This blessedness is derived from the dignity of the child, a dignity Elizabeth acknowledges by referring to him as her Lord *(kýrios)*. As David had wondered how the ark of God could come to him (cf. 2 Sam 6:9), so Elizabeth wonders how the mother of her Lord should come to her.

There is a sequence of recognition that begins and ends with Mary. At the sound of Mary's greeting the child in Elizabeth leaped for joy, thus signaling to her the presence of her Lord in the womb of Mary; at this, Elizabeth recognizes the blessedness of Mary's unborn child and, through him, Mary's blessedness.

The reading ends with a macarism, a literary form associated with the Wisdom tradition. It begins with "Blessed" or "Happy" and then celebrates the good fortune that will come to a person who has acted in a righteous manner. Mary is here called blessed *(makários)* for having believed what had been spoken to her by the Lord, a reference to the annunciation (cf. Luke 1:26-38). In this case it is faith, not some work of righteousness, that is extolled. She believed she would conceive and bear a son, and it had come to pass. It is this son that she carries in her womb that precipitated the events recorded in this passage. The way this good fortune will be manifested in Mary's life is not stated; she is merely called blessed.

Themes of the Day

In many ways the readings for the Fourth Sunday of Advent anticipate Christmas. They get us ready for the imminent future, giving us glimpses into the mysteries we will be celebrating. They do this by bringing together the major themes found in the first three Sundays: promise, repentance, transformation, joy. On this Sunday we are on the threshold of fulfillment, filled with anticipation of his coming, while we celebrate his presence in our midst.

The Threshold of Fulfillment

There is always excitement at this time of the year. It is as if everything is filled with promise. Animosities are set aside; estrangement dissolves into reconciliation; the whole world seems gentler; and we are filled with the spirit of generosity. In the days just before Christmas the possibility of newness is almost palpable. The spirit of the season seems to have caught hold of us even before the actual day has arrived. It is like the Hebrew verb form often used in prophetic pronouncements. The prophetic future form is really a present form, because the promises God makes begin to be fulfilled as soon as God makes them.

Today we stand on the threshold of fulfillment. The future God has prepared for us is open before us, even though we have not yet stepped out into it. We can see some of its contours, and it is very inviting. On this Sunday we are invited to pause at the threshold and gaze for a moment into this future. This invitation is extended to us so we can appreciate the gift being given to us.

His Coming

Both the reading from Micah and the one from Luke place us squarely in history. The child belongs to a particular people in a particular place at a particular time. The incarnation takes place in human history, thus affirming the fundamental goodness of human life and concerns and sanctifying them even further. The child comes from simple people, from a place that is relatively insignificant, thus underscoring God's preference for what is ordinary.

The reading from Hebrews tells us that in God's plan redemption is dependent upon incarnation. The body that was offered for our salvation, the body that consecrated us through having been offered up, was the body that grew in the womb of Mary. The extraordinary salvific deed of God was accomplished through his coming into the world as one of us. The obedience Christ played out through his body fulfilled for us the promises made by God.

The Celebration

Advent is the season when we stand on the threshold of fulfillment. However, it is the fulfillment of an event that has already taken place. We remember it, we ritually reenact it so we never take it for granted, so we never forget that it is in and through history that the marvelous deeds of God are accomplished. Each year we pause to celebrate these events, not because they have not yet occurred but because they *have* happened and are happening now before our eyes. The celebration of anticipation is also the celebration of fulfillment, fulfillment of the promises made, fulfillment of our redemption, fulfillment of our transformation. Blessed are we who believe that what was spoken to us by the Lord has been fulfilled!

The Nativity of the Lord (Christmas)

Mass at Midnight Isaiah 9:1-6 A son is given to us	Psalm 96:1-3, 11-13 Let the heavens be glad	Titus 2:11-14 The grace of God has appeared	Luke 2:1-14 Today a Savior has been born
Mass at Dawn Isaiah 62:11-12 Behold, your Savior comes	Psalm 97:1, 6, 11-12 A light will shine on us	Titus 3:4-7 Out of mercy, he saved us	Luke 2:15-20 The shepherds came
Mass During the Day Isaiah 52:7-10 Announce the good news	Psalm 98:1-6 All have seen God's salvation	Hebrews 1:1-6 God has spoken through the Son	John 1:1-18 The Word became flesh
The Holy Family of Jesus, Mary, and Joseph (1) Sirach 3:2-6, 12-14 Honor your parents	Psalm 128:1-5 Blessed are those who fear the LORD	Colossians 3:12-21 Over all these, put on love	Luke 2:41-52 Jesus in the Temple
The Holy Family of Jesus, Mary, and Joseph (2) 1 Samuel 1:20-22, 24-28 Samuel is dedicated	Psalm 84:2-3, 5-6, 9-10 Blessed are those who dwell with God	1 John 3:1-2, 21-24 Children of God	Luke 2:41-52 Jesus in the Temple

	Psalm		Gospel
January 1, Solemnity of the Blessed Virgin Mary, Mother of God Numbers 6:22-27 The LORD bless you and keep you	Psalm 67:2-3, 5, 6, 8 May God bless us	Galatians 4:4-7 God's Son was born of a woman	Luke 2:16-21 The shepherds came to Bethlehem
Second Sunday After Christmas Sirach 24:1-2, 8-12 Wisdom lives with God's people	Psalm 147:12-15, 19-20 God's Word became human	Ephesians 1:3-6, 15-18 We are children of God through Christ	John 1:1-18 The Word became flesh
January 6, The Epiphany of the Lord Isaiah 60:1-6 God's glory shines on us	Psalm 72:1-2, 7-8, 10-13 All nations will adore God	Ephesians 3:2-3a, 5-6 Gentiles are coheirs of the promise	Matthew 2:1-12 We saw his star
Sunday After January 6, The Baptism of the Lord (1) Isaiah 42:1-4, 6-7 Behold my servant	Psalm 29:1-4, 3, 9-10 The LORD will bless with peace	Acts 10:34-38 Anointed with the Spirit	Luke 3:15-16, 21-22 Jesus is baptized
The Baptism of the Lord (2) Isaiah 40:1-5, 9-11 God's glory revealed	Psalm 104:1b-4, 24-25, 27-30 Bless the LORD	Titus 2:11-14; 3:4-7 Bath of rebirth	Luke 3:15-16, 21-22 Jesus is baptized

The Nativity of the Lord (Christmas)

Initial Reading of the Christmas Lectionary

Introduction

Employing the same method of reading the Lectionary that was used in the Advent season, we interpret the constellation of readings the Christmas season offers. While the Advent season incorporates three cycles of the Lectionary, the Christmas readings, with the exception of the choices for the feast of the Holy Family and the Baptism of the Lord, do not vary. Each group of readings will be examined and interpreted. A presentation of the entire mosaic of readings will follow this exercise.

First Testament Readings

The Midnight Mass at Christmas begins the season. It is a word of emancipation. The people in darkness now see, for the child is born. The close of the season, the feast of the Baptism of the Lord, identifies the child as the servant, the one who brings about this liberation by the word of God that is proclaimed with power. The child-servant heralds a profound and wonderful reversal. Something cosmic has happened at Christmas. In the midst of the darkness the light that emanates from the child-servant reveals God's intentions to the ends of the earth.

The other First Testament readings in this season unpack the richness of the transformation this birth brings about. The people who were lost are no longer forsaken. The glad tidings of this good news will be sung by the servant, who proclaims liberty to captives and sight to the blind, who gives a name to the nameless and a voice of significance to women and children and those who are forsaken. The transformation touches the very heart of the domestic world of parents and children and calls for an ordering based in love and the promise of the world made new. In this order blessing is found, the blessing of peace, a blessing that is both a hope and a charge. It is a hope for God's peace among the people; at the same time it is a charge to live in such a way as to make the blessing of wisdom real in their lives and in their worlds.

At the end of the Christmas season we are told that God's glory goes forth from the city to the ends of the earth. All nations, races, peoples, tribes, and languages will proclaim the wisdom of God. The mystery of Christmas will gather all people into the promise of God. This is the work of the child-servant. It is a work that is caught up into the wonderful reversal of justice and compassion that still whispers in the night.

Psalms

The lectionary refrains for the Christmas season fall into three categories: declarations of the wonderful work of God among the people; the implications of these works in the lives of those who call upon the Lord; the universality of these works and the extension of God's glory.

Some of the refrains speak of the reality of the birth of a Savior. They declare that the birth takes place today; it is the present moment that knows the wonder of the Word made flesh. Other psalms are shouts of exultation and praise in face of this wonder. They express the unimaginable joy of those who receive God's gift and find in it their fulfillment.

Toward the end of the season the refrains move us into an understanding of the specific implications of the gift of the child born among us. They voice the happiness of those who know the Lord. The blessings of God abound, and this elicits the praises of all the people. The ultimate blessing given is peace.

Epistles

An examination of the epistles of the season shows they are an extended meditation on salvation. In these Christmas readings we are told that salvation has been given and now has appeared among us. It is offered to all people, and it brings with it the hope and promise of righteousness. Salvation is not our achievement; it is a gift that comes from God's Spirit.

The implications of this salvation are demonstrated in several epistle readings. Relationships change when salvation is received. First, we are called into forgiveness, patience, and the meekness that allows us to embrace each other in love and mercy. Second, the relationship with God is made intimate, and we are able to call God *Abba*. This new way of naming God allows us the inheritance of God, for we find ourselves to be children of God and sisters and brothers in Christ. All of these new relationships take place within the Church, which is not only the *place* of salvation but, more importantly, the *people* of salvation. The beauty of God and the wealth of the inheritance are ours in the community of faith.

Salvation is not confined; God's salvation is for all, Jew and Greek alike; and the wealth of it is to be shared among the nations. Peter preaches the universality of this gift in the name of Jesus, who was anointed by the Spirit. In the power of the same Spirit we are called to the same universality. In our day it takes the form of interreligious dialogue and recognition of the religious value present in other religions of the world.

The epistles offer an ever-widening understanding of salvation from the first appearance of the gift of Christmas to the preaching of the apostles to our own appreciation of it.

Gospels

The gospels for the Christmas season remain somewhat narrative, punctuated by passages from the Prologue of the Gospel of John, which reveals the theological significance of the Christmas story itself. There are two ways of viewing the gospels of the season. The first is a simple narrative reading that begins with the birth of Jesus and moves through the visit of the shepherds to a reading that provides a theological interpretation of the events recounted. The narrative continues with episodes from the life of the young Jesus, followed by a second theological interpretation. It concludes with two accounts of the manifestation of Jesus' true identity, the first to the Magi and the second at his baptism.

The gospels move from the birth to the baptism. They invite the religious imagination to accept the baby as the gift to the nations, the one whose ministry in the Spirit will make him a servant of God and humanity. The Christmas season ends with us poised for Jesus' mission and his entry into the place of testing, which will begin the lenten season.

The second way of reading recognizes a kind of chiastic structure:

a) birth

    b) shepherds

        c) theological interpretation

           d) visit to Temple

           d^1) visit to Temple

        c^1) theological interpretation

    b^1) Magi

a^1) baptism

The birth and the baptism are both forms of manifestation; the shepherds and the Magi represent all those to whom the revelation is given, both the poor and the prosperous, the Jews and the Gentiles; the theological interpretations can be matched, leaving the visits to the Temple as the focal point of the chiasm. In such a structure the accent of importance is placed on the texts at the center. In this case the religious observances in the Temple offer a key insight into the season.

Both accounts show that Jesus was grounded in the practices of his religious tradition. He is willing to be consecrated to God and to be incorporated into God's people. Both accounts also mention Mary's unique role in the drama of the incarnation. She realizes the uniqueness of her child when he is found in the Temple with the teachers and when the shepherds come prior to his circumcision. In both instances she stands in awe, not quite understanding. Jesus is the Lord who comes to his Temple; God has visited us in the form of a little child. Mary is the image of the Church; we rejoice in the birth of the child, but we do so not quite understanding the depth of this mystery. The child is born and redeemed, but only so we can be redeemed and reborn.

Mosaic of Readings

The Christmas cycle is a proclamation of the presence of God in human history. The Lectionary weaves narrative, prophecy, and exhortation together, producing a tapestry of breathtaking beauty. A threefold message is contained in this work of art: (1) Something definitive has happened in history, and it is the work of God; (2) this marvel is a gift that can be received by all people of goodwill, a universal gift extending to all the nations; (3) when received, this gift forms us into a community that lives by it and shows itself to be the place where God has pitched a tent among us. The Church is the community of grace and compassion for the life of the world. Christmas is the promise of Easter in the lives of those who receive the child-servant.

Readings

The Nativity of the Lord (Mass at Midnight)
Isaiah 9:1-6

The reading begins with the announcement of deliverance. Its message of hope and consolation is expressed through the contrast between light and darkness (v. 1). The darkness does not seem to be merely a temporary clouding of the light. Rather, the entire land is in darkness, and the people seem fixed in it. It is to them that a great light comes. This light ushers in a complete reversal of fortune, which the rest of the reading describes. The people did not bring this reversal on themselves; they are the recipients of God's good pleasure (v. 6).

After the initial announcement the prophet speaks directly to God, enumerating examples of God's acts of graciousness toward the people. First, the people embrace the entire experience of salvation with unbounded joy (v. 2). The rejoicing is of the kind that follows either an abundant harvest, when there is enough yield to satisfy the needs of all, or an assessment of the spoils of war after the battles have been won. In each instance there is a sense of relief that the hardships of the venture are over as well as great satisfaction with the respective fruits that have accrued from it.

The prophet next describes how God liberated the people from oppression (vv. 3-4). In the past they were shackled like oxen, forced to do arduous, ignoble tasks. They were subjected to physical abuse at the hands of another. But God intervened and destroyed the instruments of their servitude. The reference to Midian calls to mind the defeat of that nation under the leadership of Gideon (Judg 7:15-25). Not only was that defeat absolute, it was also miraculous, accomplished through divine power. Mention of this battle along with the military title "LORD of hosts" (cf. Advent 1, Psalm 80) may also explain the reference to spoils of war. The comparison is clear. God and only God has gained salvation for the people, and that salvation is absolute.

The final verses of the reading sketch a picture that is most astounding. The salvation reported is realized through the agency of a child (vv. 5-6). The responsibility for establishing the peace described here rests on his shoulders. The names ascribed to him signify the feats expected of him. Like every good leader, he will make wise decisions, and he will be able to guide others in their judgments. However, he will surpass all others in this regard; he will be a wonder! "God-Hero" comes from the Hebrew word *gibbor,* another term with military connotations. This child will be a divine warrior, capable of withstanding all the evil cosmic forces. He will be Father-Forever, unfailing in providing for those under his care. He is Prince of Peace, the one who both secures and safeguards it. This peace is more than the absence of war. It means wholeness, completion, harmony. It was a condition in which all things—human beings, animals, and plants—follow their God-given destinies undisturbed.

All these titles were in some way associated with the Davidic king. He was expected to be a wise ruler, mighty in battle, a father to his people, and the guarantor of peace. However, a more-than-human dimension has been added. This child may belong to the line of David, but he is an extraordinary descendant. The exercise of his dominion is the saving action of God.

Psalm 96:1-2, 2-3, 11-12, 13

The psalm calls upon the people to praise God for the wonderful acts of salvation God has performed (vv. 1-3). Three times the psalmist calls them to sing God's praises, each time highlighting a different aspect of the song. First, they are called to sing a new song. This is only appropriate, since their salvation has transformed them into a new people. No longer will laments be acceptable. The only kind of song worthy of the event of salvation that has unfolded before their very eyes is a hymn of praise.

Next, there is a note of universality to the singing. Not just Israel but all the earth is called upon to sing this song of praise. Finally, along with the call to sing is a summons to bless the name of the LORD. Since a name was thought to contain part of the very essence of the person, a call to bless God's name is really a summons to give praise to some aspect of God's character. The aspect to be praised is the salvation God has brought about for the sake of Israel. All the earth is called to announce the good news of this salvation and to announce it unceasingly, day after day.

God is here portrayed as enthroned as lord of the entire earth, accomplishing wondrous deeds that all the nations have been able to witness. The final verses (vv. 11-13) show that these deeds include the creation and governance of all the earth as well as the direction and judgment of all nations. Such universal power and dominion could only be wielded by a God who is above all other gods, one who reigns supreme in the heavens but who executes authority on earth as well. God not only performs these marvelous feats but does so with justice and faithfulness. This God is indeed powerful but also trustworthy. Such is the portrait of the God of Israel painted in this psalm.

The reasons for the praise for which the psalmist calls are specifically laid out. God is acclaimed as ruler of the heavens and the earth. It is quite understandable to claim dominion over the earth for God. Even minor gods were thought to exercise some power on earth. Since heavenly beings were frequently personified as deities in other ancient Near Eastern religions, it is a bit more difficult, though not impossible, to ascribe rule over them to God. It is clear from the early verses of this psalm that here the heavens were merely regarded as elements of natural creation. As such, they join in honoring the Creator. What is interesting in this chorus of praise is the inclusion of the sea and all the water courses over which it has control, since the sea was traditionally considered a mythological force of evil. That it is regarded as merely a creature of God is significant.

All the rejoicing is focused on an upcoming event, the advent of the LORD. The rejoicing itself does not overshadow the reason for the LORD's coming, which is judgment. God will judge the earth. As harsh as the notion of judgment may be, God judges with righteousness and truth (v. 13). Divine judgment is less a question of power than of harmony and right order. God's rule is one of right order. Salvation itself is really a return to this order. Therefore, the judgment of God is really the establishment of harmony, the establishment of peace.

Titus 2:11-14

This short excerpt from one of the Pastoral Epistles is a confession of faith in the saving grace of God. The verb "appeared" (v. 11) is testimony to divine revelation. The reading proclaims that God's grace is no longer something for which the people wait with longing. It has arrived; it is an accomplished fact. Furthermore, the universality of this salvation is clearly stated. It is not merely for an elect group, whether Jewish or Christian; it is for all humans *(ánthrōpois)*.

This grace, or good favor, takes the form of salvation, a theological concept with profound Jewish and Hellenistic connotations. In Jewish thought salvation was seen as rescue from the perils of life, and it was accomplished by God. Many narratives of the First Testament recount such salvation. In the Hellenistic mystery religions, which were so prominent at the time of the writing of this letter, the initiates shared in the mythical divine being's victory over death, and they were thereby assured a share in blissful life in the hereafter. In this particular passage the concept of salvation includes aspects of both views. It is because they have been saved from the perils of evil that the Christians have been empowered to live lives of moral integrity in this world. On the other hand, their salvation has come to them through the sacrifice of Christ Jesus, and they still await a future divine manifestation.

The reading also declares that God's saving grace imparts the kind of training necessary to combat the forces of a godless world and to live truly Christian lives (v. 12). The author of the epistle does not enumerate what these evil forces might be. (Discerning them may well be even more a challenge than opposing them.) What *is* confidently stated is the assurance that the power of divine grace will adequately prepare believers to live in moderation, righteousness, and piety, regardless of the opposition within themselves and from others that they may have to face. Such a courageous way of living is evidence that the age of fulfillment has indeed arrived. However, this indication of "realized eschatology" does not erase the expectation of a "future eschatology." Christians live an already-but-not-yet existence. Their moral lives are signs of and expectation of the final fulfillment.

Christ Jesus has achieved this great grace. His sacrifice of himself has redeemed and cleansed those who have accepted him. The moral character of this salvation is apparent in the final verse of the reading. The Christians are redeemed from lawlessness, and they are purified as a people who then perform good works. There is no doubt that this is God's saving grace, but it comes to the people through Christ Jesus. The Pastoral Epistles generally identify God as the savior of all. The Greek in this passage is awkward. It reads: "great God and savior of our Jesus Christ" (v. 13). It is only in translations that Jesus is identified as the Savior. Whatever version is chosen, the intimate relationship between God and Christ is obvious, and that is the point of the reading.

This passage does not call for hope. As a profession of faith it affirms a tenet of belief and holds it out as a truth that calls for commitment. Salvation has been won by Christ and offered to all. We decide how we will respond to it.

Luke 2:1-14

Luke's version of the birth of Jesus is one of the best-known stories of the Bible. It has inspired paintings and music down through the ages. Even small children know about the census, the swaddling clothes and manger, the shepherds and the angels' song. Our critical examination of the text should not so demythologize the imagery that we undermine popular religious imagination and overlook the power of its message.

The details of the story serve two important purposes: they situate Jesus in first-century history, and they link him with the house of David. The miraculous incidents that accompany this birth might lead some to conclude that the event recounted was too otherworldly to be genuinely historical. Such a position throws into question the very heart of the doctrine of the incarnation. Situating the birth within the world of real Roman rulers underscored its claim that God was indeed born at this time, in this place, among these people.

The details also identify Jesus as the Davidic Messiah. Since the gospel tradition maintains that Jesus was from Nazareth, it was important somehow to establish him in Bethlehem. The account of the census, regardless of how inaccurate its details may be, explains how his parents happened to be in Bethlehem at the time of his birth. The Davidic link is made again and again. Joseph was of the house of David, so he traveled to the town of David to be registered (vv. 4f.). The first to pay homage to the newborn were Bethlehemite shepherds, simple herders not unlike David himself. Mary and Joseph do not play the central roles here. Joseph is important because of his Davidic lineage, and Mary is identified as Joseph's pregnant wife. The entire focus of the story is on the child.

A second and related theme is God's choice of the most unlikely and frequently overlooked members of society to accomplish God's will. From the outset this child was treated like an unwelcome stranger, almost an outcast. He was deprived of the comforts that normally surrounded a birth, born away from the home of his parents, away from the warmth and love of an extended family. He was not visited by friendly neighbors but by shepherds, a class of people considered unclean because their occupation often required that they deal with both the birth and the death blood of their flocks. The stage is set to tell the story of God's predilection for the poor, the overlooked, and the forgotten. Like his ancestor David, the one who was destined for great things had a humble, even despised, beginning.

Despite the unconscionable affront by human beings, the birth of this extraordinary child was surrounded by celestial grandeur. An angel announced the wondrous event to the lowly shepherds and was then joined by countless other angelic beings who filled the night with their song of praise of God. The glory of God could not be contained, and it burst forth encompassing the shepherds with its brilliance. The disregard of the human community was outstripped by a display of heavenly exaltation.

This simple yet beloved Christmas story contains a complex christology. On the one hand, the author takes great pains to situate Jesus squarely within the human family of David. On the other hand, he identifies Jesus as Savior and Lord, and he paints a picture of heavenly celebration. Such is the mystery of Christmas.

Themes of the Day

The Church commemorates the birth of Christ with three celebrations of the Eucharist: at midnight; at dawn; and during the day of Christmas. These inaugural celebrations usher in the Christmas cycle with themes that will be revisited several times before the season ends. In the middle of the night the community gathers to meditate on three of these themes: the historical birth of Jesus, the liberating king, and the new age of fulfillment of God's promise inaugurated by this king.

The Birth of Jesus in History

The gospel clearly situates the birth of Jesus within a historical epoch, that of the Roman rule of Israel in the first century. The proclamation announced on this day places Jesus' birth within the affairs of human life with its struggles and cares. These historical and human details indicate this birth is not simply an otherworldly event, it happened at a specific time and in a specific place. The incarnation of God happened among us! God comes to us in our time, in our place, in our history.

Once the historical reality is established, the story reveals another dimension of this birth. The ordinary becomes transparent and reveals the extraordinary; the divine is known in the child. Angels appear in order to declare this is so. Night glows with the radiance of daytime, and the midnight hour is the breakthrough of everlasting light. Only those of humble heart come to know this wonder. The reality of the mystery is offered, but its significance is missed by many. In this case it is not the influential who recognize the gift but those society forgets. It is the shepherds, the poor and forsaken subjects of history, who happen upon this birth and believe. They behold it and they come to embrace it. In fact, it is the nature of this child, born in history, to reverse the orders of power.

The Liberating King

The readings contain strong images of the royalty of the Lord. God is portrayed as a valiant liberator worthy of praise and worship. It is God who champions the cause of justice and who brings a liberation that can reverse history and the ways of war, power, and oppression. The coming events will satisfy the needs of all. However, the reversal of the fate of history is made more shocking by the fact that the one who is the mighty warrior and conqueror of the nations is a child, one who rules with peace and integrity.

The child is Jesus. However, this child is the servant who can conquer the alienating forces of history, whose life is destined to change the fate of humanity. Furthermore, it is the child as the weak and voiceless one, the one who has neither power nor legal rights, who will shake the empire. God's reversal of the long-standing realities of this world is accomplished through the apparently insignificant through the gift of this child, who is given to us in the middle of the night.

The Age of Fulfillment Has Begun

With the birth of the child something new has happened: the age of God's fulfillment has arrived. This is an age of grace and fresh hope, made available to all people of goodwill. It is an era of redemptive presence, because now all people can walk in the newness of life and grace. This age has come about by the gift of Christ, poured out for us. We can see it, touch it, taste it. It is a time when justice and mercy appear, when nations seek the ways of peace, when reconciliation transforms us. And yet, while the age has begun, it is not yet fully realized.

We live in the traces of this hope, believing in its presence and awaiting its fulfillment. In a real sense, although we are celebrating Christmas, we are still an advent people who await the coming of the Lord in the abundance of mercy that is yet to erupt in history. We are a tensive people, not tense with the cares of this age but poised to receive the gift of the ever-deepening promise born among us and whose birth continues to astound us at every appearance of hope.

The Nativity of the Lord (Mass at Dawn)
Isaiah 62:11-12

The message of these two short verses is extraordinary in several ways. First, it has been prescribed by the LORD. Second, it concerns the redemption of Israel and is to be proclaimed to the whole world. Third, it deals less with the promise of a future salvation than with the announcement that salvation is already on its way. Fourth, it includes new names for the people and for the city of Jerusalem, names which show that both the people and the city have been radically transformed.

This prophetic notice repeats some of the content of an oracle that appears elsewhere in the book of the prophet Isaiah (40:10). In the earlier oracle it was the LORD God who was coming in might with reward and recompense. Here God is identified with salvation, and it is this salvation that comes with reward and recompense. Salvation has been accomplished. The new names for the people and the city make this clear.

In order to appreciate the significance of the title "the holy people," we must remember that ancient Israel was a nation whose political and social exile was interpreted by the people themselves as punishment for their sins. Now they have a new name, and that name implies they are not only forgiven but they enjoy a new identity as if newly born. The people are also called "the redeemed of the LORD," a title that marks a double relationship with God. The obvious meaning points to a bond between redeemer and redeemed. The former is someone who pays the debt of another and thereby provides deliverance from any kind of servitude; the latter is the one released from debt. The less obvious relationship implied in the title is kinship. Normally it was a close relative who paid the debt. These titles point to the intimate and remarkable attachment God has for this people.

Zion/Jerusalem is also given new names (cf. 62:2-4), indicating a new identity. The city that was overthrown, depopulated, and plundered will once again attract people to it. It will then be called "Frequented" or "Not Forsaken." The name declares that the desolation of the past is forgotten. Salvation has come to the city.

Psalm 97:1-6, 11-12

The psalm opens with the traditional enthronement declaration: "The LORD is king!" It is appropriately followed by the exclamation "Rejoice, and be glad!" The response suggests that the manner of God's rule calls for celebration, and this celebration extends beyond the confines of Israel to the entire world (v. 1).

A report of the manifestation of God's glory, composed of several commanding images, follows. It begins with a description of the divine king's throne, which is established on the firm foundation of justice (v. 2b). Unlike other regimes that are built merely on brute force or military victory, both of which might fail and result in dethronement, God's rule is constructed in the permanence of justice and right order. It is not only impregnable, it is immutable. It stands secure, enabling God to govern undisturbed by any threat and assuring reliable protection to all those under God's jurisdiction. The throne is surrounded by clouds and darkness (v. 2a), reminiscent of the theophany that took place on Mount Sinai (Exod 19:16-19) and the signs of the presence of God when the ark of the covenant was finally installed in the Temple in Jerusalem (1 Kgs 8:10-12). The cloud itself obscures the glory of God, leaving everything else in darkness.

Along with the image of a securely erected throne is a description of a royal procession (v. 3). A raging fire, symbolizing the purifying presence of God, is in the lead of this entourage, consuming the enemies of God in its path and purging the land as it proceeds. The verbs in this verse are in the Hebrew imperfect tense, suggesting that this refining manifestation is an event in the future.

The report of the dramatic features of the theophany continues (vv. 4-6). The verbs in this section are in the Hebrew perfect tense, implying that what is portrayed has already taken place or is presently unfolding before the eyes of those witnessing the spectacle. The event described resembles a forceful upheaval of nature, something like an earthquake that makes the whole world tremble. This disturbance is accompanied by an enormous display of lightning, enough to illumine the entire sky and all the earth below it. In many ancient Near Eastern religions, these spectacular demonstrations were frequently associated with a storm-god or variously credited to minor-gods, offspring of the principal deity. In this psalm they are nothing more than natural phenomena accompanying the theophany of the God who reigns as king of all creation.

The massiveness of mountains has led people to believe they are invulnerable. Such is not the case here. Instead, their durability is negligible, and they melt like wax before the intensity that attends the manifestation of God. The heavens, celestial beings that were considered divine in some religions but regarded in Israel as merely awesome creatures of God, join in praise of God's righteous rule. This colossal theophany is a phenomenon observed by all, and it challenges all to live righteously in accord with the righteousness of God that has been manifested (vv. 11-12). The psalm concludes with a glimpse into the lives of those who accept this challenge.

Titus 3:4-7

The appearance of the saving love of God is the theme of this passage, which was probably part of an early Christian baptismal hymn. The salvation achieved through Jesus Christ completely changed the lives of the newly baptized, drawing a striking contrast between the way they lived before their conversion and the way they live now. As in the reading for the Christmas Mass at Midnight, this passage announces what has already taken place. The love and kindness of God have appeared; it is not a future event for which believers ardently long. Furthermore, it has appeared in time, in history. The coming of Christ coincides with the ultimate manifestation of God's love.

It is clear this love is a free gift springing from the mercy of God and not simply compensation for righteous living. On the contrary, salvation is bestowed first so that, having received it, Christians might be able to live virtuously. It is this saving grace that justifies them, not any moral effort on their part. Everything is a free gift, bestowed out of divine largesse. This includes love, mercy, and justification in this life and the inheritance of eternal life. God's magnanimous giving is celebrated here.

A rudimentary trinitarian formula appears in the reference to baptism. The text explicitly states it is God's love that appears and it is God who saved us through the washing of baptism. It was God who poured out the Spirit through Jesus Christ. As with the passage from Titus read at the Mass at Midnight, there is no clear line drawn here between God as savior and Christ as Savior. It may be that such distinctions had not yet been sharply made. What is clear in this reading is that rebirth and renewal come through the Spirit and that divine titles (Savior) and activities (saving) are attributed to Christ.

Although the author uses commonplace Hellenistic religious language such as "rebirth" and imagery such as cleansing through water, the theology of justification is drawn from Jewish thought. There the righteous are those who, though unfaithful, have been acquitted by God. The initiative is always God's, and it is usually exercised in the face of human infidelity. From a human point of view the absurdity of such a situation is unmistakable. Still, accepting the opportunity of freely given justification is not an easy thing to do, and many people do not even believe it is possible. For those who believe it is both possible and desirable, reluctance to avail themselves of salvation is the real absurdity.

This baptismal hymn both proclaims tenets of faith and indirectly exhorts believers to embrace a life of virtue. Since they have been born anew, they can now act in a new way, walking blamelessly in this world in anticipation of the next. Christians are radically changed because God has entered their lives. The appearance of God's love has accomplished this.

Luke 2:15-20

It is because of the gospel reading that this Mass was formally referred to as the Shepherds' Mass. The passage itself is rich with theological themes: response to divine revelation, theological insight, evangelization, praise of God, contemplative reflection.

One of the reasons shepherds were considered irreligious by the self-righteous of the time was their failure to participate in regular ritual observance. Their occupation required them to be with the flocks, supervising their grazing and growth and protecting them from harm. This responsibility prevented them from being part of the worshiping community. That they would leave their flocks in the hills and go into Bethlehem in search of a newborn was extraordinary. Should anything happen to the sheep while they were gone, they would suffer a financial setback if the flock was theirs, or they would be liable to the owner if the flock belonged to another. The shepherds were most likely poor, and they would be well aware of the risk they were taking.

This did not deter them. They were responding to divine revelation and had received a heavenly directive. Rather than being irresolute they went in haste, leaving behind what gave them the little security they may have enjoyed. These humble shepherds were the first to respond to a divine invitation to leave all for the sake of this child. While it is true that they did return to their flocks, their willingness to initially leave them has religious significance.

When they saw Mary and Joseph and the baby, they understood what the angel had said. What was it that gave them insight? What enabled them to recognize their Messiah and Lord in this unlikely situation? What is it that enables any of us to see traces of the divine in the very ordinary of life? Might it be the openness to God and the willingness to accept the unexpected that provides eyes of faith that can see beyond appearances?

Themselves convinced of the arrival of the long-anticipated Messiah, they proclaimed this to all they met. Such behavior must have compounded the jeopardy into which they had placed themselves. They had not only abandoned their responsibilities and put their own futures at risk, they were now making incredible claims. The text does not say those who heard them were convinced by their words. It says they were astonished. Evangelization does not itself guarantee success.

The shepherds do not seem to have been influenced one way or another by the reactions of others. They return to their flocks praising God. Their lives may have resumed their normal pattern, but the shepherds themselves could not have been the same. They had had a profound religious experience; they had heard and understood a startling religious truth; they had placed this religious truth above their own personal needs and aspirations. These humble, probably uneducated, people had been transformed into believers, and their final response was praise.

The author inserts one sentence that has little to do with the shepherds. Mary reflected on all of this. She is the believer who has already experienced the power of God, and she stands silently before the mystery of what God has done. She treasures these things in respectful contemplation.

Themes of the Day

Traditionally, the Mass at Dawn is called the Shepherd's Mass, because the gospel text recounts the visit of the shepherds. The readings highlight four themes: God's initiative of universal transformation; the profound gratitude that ensues in face of this gift; the life of baptism that is receptive to God's initiative; and solidarity with outcasts as a sacrament of God's presence.

God's Initiative of Universal Transformation

God has taken the first step in our redemption, and the offer of grace is made to all people who can hear and who will embrace the gift. As a season, Christmas is really a time of universal goodwill. Widespread change seems to occur at Christmas; human hearts appear to soften, and we greet each other with good wishes and cheer. Because we remember the gift of God's love and receive it anew in our hearts, our interactions are transformed.

Left to our own designs, we tend to set limits and to remain caught in the status quo of our lives and our answers. God disrupts the order of life and by a divine undertaking of grace starts something that can impact the universe. The declaration of Christmas is bold: all of this possibility has already been realized; we can already live by the new name of God's compassion and justice. Transformative love comes alive in our midst, in the city where people dwell. The possibility of a new way of life happens now, and the future will usher it in among us. Receptivity is all that is asked of us.

A Matter of Great Gratitude

In response to God's gracious gift of transformation we are invited to rejoice with grateful hearts. The royal infant whose birth we celebrate is the one who was promised, the one who inaugurates the age of transforming grace. The child is, in fact, the long-awaited messianic king. He is the source of rejoicing in those who receive him with great gratitude. He is recognized by the angels and the shepherds but not by the power structures of the city. Only those who are open to God's gift can receive it with thanksgiving. When it is received, however, marvelous things happen. Our identities are changed, all the cosmos joins in the festivity, and righteousness blossoms in history.

The Life of Baptism

For Christian believers the life of baptismal fidelity is the grateful response to the gift of God's initiative. This baptismal life is rooted in the mystery of the triune

God, the God in whom believers are baptized. It is a life lived in the rebirth of the Spirit of God that animates us to live blamelessly, to live in a way that shows our appreciation of this gift, to live lives that are manifestations of holiness.

It is by living such lives that Christians are able to proclaim that God has truly appeared and to become the place of the ongoing appearance of God's gift of transformation. What becomes clear is that this is not our work; it is the work of God, who has come to dwell with us and in whom we find our cause for celebration. The baptismal life is a life of gratitude for the gift we have received, a gift whose fulfillment will be realized by God in the future.

Solidarity with the Poor

While Christmas morning may be a time for opening gifts and for family celebrations, it is also a time when people of means reach out to those who are less fortunate. Christmas celebrates generosity, first the generosity of God and then our generosity with one another, especially with the poor. Solidarity with the outcasts of society, with those who are barred from the power structures of society, is in keeping with the spirit of Christmas.

The birth of the baby is the source of joy for the poor and those who are scandalously forced to the fringes of Bethlehem. The despised shepherds become the privileged ones to whom the message is announced. God's gift finds a place among the outcasts and continues to dwell at home there. It is indeed a Christmas grace to be able to find God there, to rejoice in the gift, and to respond creatively to it. Thus we become the place where shepherds and kings meet in adoration and where the future of God's justice dawns.

The Nativity of the Lord (Mass During the Day)
Isaiah 52:7-10

The proclamation of good news is dramatically portrayed in this passage in several ways. It begins with a sketch of a messenger running swiftly over the mountains with the message of peace and salvation (v. 7). The focus is on the feet of the runner. This highlights his speed and determination. They are beautiful feet because of the message of deliverance they carry. There is an excitement in this scene; the message holds such promise. There is an urgency as well; the people to whom the messenger runs have been desolate for so long, waiting for a ray of hope. The content of the message is peace, good news, and salvation. The messenger announces to Zion that its God is king, the one who rules and controls the circumstances of its existence. By implication, this means that the city will be able to partake in the victory of its God.

The first ones to see the runner are the sentinels who stand watch on the walls of the city (v. 8; cf. 40:9). Since a messenger can bring either good news or bad news, from a distance these sentinels cannot be certain of the content of the message. However, their joyful reaction to the approach indicates that it signals not only a proclamation but the very actualization of the message to be proclaimed. In a way, the coming of the runner is itself the promise to be proclaimed. The people know what the coming of the messenger means, for what they have longed to see now unfolds before their eyes, and they shout for joy. As is so often the case with the prophetic word, its very proclamation effects the salvation it announces. Seeing the runner and hearing his words of peace and salvation are themselves the good news. With the announcement of peace and salvation, the LORD has indeed returned to the city.

First the sentinels cry out with joy. Then the very ruins of the city are exhorted to break forth in song (vv. 9-10). No longer need they lie destitute, unable to stand with dignity or protected with honor. God comforts and redeems the people dwelling within the ruins. The inhabitants are now a renewed people, and so the city itself is renewed. Peace is no longer a hoped-for dream, nor is salvation only a promise for the future. They are now accomplished facts for which to rejoice.

The prophet sketches yet another dynamic picture. In it we see the arm of God bared, revealing the source of the divine power that effected the deliverance the city now enjoys. This demonstration of strength serves to remind the people of the might of their protector. It also alerts the other nations to the seriousness with which God acts as protector of this people. It is not enough that Zion is rescued. The other nations of the world must see and acknowledge this power. They must recognize both the scope of God's power and the identity of the people who most benefit from it. Just as the messenger heralds peace and salvation to Zion, so the deliverance of the city heralds the mighty power of God to the ends of the earth.

Psalm 98:1, 2-3, 3-4, 5-6

The psalm belongs to the category of enthronement psalms, praising God as king over all (v. 6). It opens with a summons to sing a new song to God (cf. Psalm 96). The reason for this new song is the marvelous new things God has done. The psalmist follows this summons with an enumeration of some of the acts of God (vv. 1b-3).

God is first depicted as a triumphant warrior whose right hand and outstretched arm have brought victory. The victory sketched in these verses seems to have been historical, one that transpired on the stage of Israel's political experience. However, it is not too difficult for a god to defeat human forces. If God is to be acclaimed as king over all, there must be a more comprehensive victory, one that demonstrates preeminence on a cosmic scale. Behind the image of the triumphant warrior is just such an understanding. The divine warrior is the one who conquers the forces of chaos. This is a cosmic victory. These verses do include mention of a sweeping victory (v. 3). Thus it is correct to say that God's triumph is universal and undisputed.

The focus is on the particularity of Israel's salvation by God. Two aspects of this victory are mentioned. First, the victory, or demonstration of righteousness, is really vindication meted out in order to rectify a previous injustice. Second, the victory follows God's recall of the covenant promises made to the house of Israel. Lovingkindness *(ḥesed)* and faithfulness *('ĕmûnâ)* are closely associated with these promises (v. 3). It is important to remember that this particular psalm praises God as king precisely as a triumphant warrior. This implies that either the righteous character of God's rule or its universal scope had been challenged; therefore, any victory here is really a reestablishment of right order. In other words, it is vindication.

A second important feature of this reading is its statement about the relationship that exists between God's saving action and the promises God made. The psalmist claims that it was remembrance of the covenantal lovingkindness *(ḥesed)* that prompted God to save Israel. It was because of the promise made to the ancestors that the divine warrior stepped in and triumphed over Israel's enemies. That triumph, which was revealed to all the nations, is the reason for the psalmist's call to praise God in song.

The final verses elaborate on the musical element of the praise. The instrumental directions are specific. They could have originated in an actual enthronement ceremony. Two instruments are explicitly mentioned, the lyre and the trumpet. The first was frequently used as accompaniment for singing; the second might really be a reference to the ram's horn, which, like a clarion, announced days and seasons of ritual celebration. Here, as at the foot of Mount Sinai, it announces the coming of the LORD in glory (Exod 19:16).

Hebrews 1:1-6

This confessional hymn celebrates Christ as the agent of revelation, creation, and salvation. It begins with a comparison of the ways God communicates with humankind. In the past God spoke to the ancestors through the prophets; in the present God speaks a definitive word to the believers through God's own Son. Without disparaging the former way, it is clear that the author of this letter considers divine revelation through Christ far superior to the earlier method. The former method of revelation was fragmentary, incomplete. As a reflection of God's glory and an exact representation of God's being, Christ could be called the perfect revelation of God.

The Father-Son language found in most translations of this passage does not appear in the Greek, with the exception of the references included at the end of the reading (1:5-6). It is the sense of the overall passage that suggested the translations. Because of the Father-Son covenantal relationship, the Son of God enjoys a position of unrivaled privilege. The Son is the heir of all things and the agent through which the world was made and through which it continues to be sustained. In addition to preeminence, this assertion suggests preexistence.

The description of the relationship between the Son and God borrows elements from two very different yet related Jewish traditions: the monarchy and Wisdom. The first originated in the ancient Near Eastern world, where people believed their kings were either human manifestations of the deity or their actual physical offspring. "Son of God," a royal title usually conferred on the king at the time of his coronation, was understood literally. Such royal ideology was a serious religious threat to Israel, and many within the nation objected to the establishment of the monarchy (cf. 1 Sam 8:1-22). Political circumstances compelled the people to reconsider, and eventually Israel was able to reconcile having a monarchy within a monotheism (cf. 2 Sam 7:8-17). "Son of God" was demythologized, and the title was understood figuratively rather than literally.

Two of the references at the end of the reading (vv. 5-6) belong to this royal tradition. The first comes from an enthronement psalm (Ps 2:7), the second from the Davidic covenant passage (2 Sam 7:14). When this ideology is applied to Christ, an interesting reinterpretation takes place. The title "Son of God" is remythologized and understood literally once again. This is the meaning intended here.

The author also reinterprets the Wisdom tradition. There we find that it was through Wisdom that God created (Prov 8:22-31; Wis 9:9), and Wisdom is the pure emanation of the glory of God (Wis 7:25-26). In this tradition the line between Wisdom as creation of God and Wisdom an attribute of God cannot always be clearly detected. This very ambiguity lends itself to christological interpretation.

Since the Son is indeed the Son of God as well as the Wisdom of God, it stands to reason he would be superior even to the angels. As the agent of salvation he sits enthroned in the place of greatest honor, at the right hand of God. The author of this letter has used the royal theology of Israel to illustrate his christological faith. Jesus is indeed the Son of God, the Wisdom through whom all things came to be and remain.

John 1:1-18

The Gospel of John begins with one of the most profound statements about Jesus found in the entire Second Testament. Its lofty christology is comparable to that found in the reading from Hebrews. Both characterize Christ as preexistent; both depict Christ as an agent in the creation of the world. The reading itself falls easily into five parts: a description of the role the Word played in the creation of the world (vv. 1-5); a brief sketch of a witness named John (vv. 6-8); an account of the Word's entrance into the world (vv. 9-14); a second report about John (v. 15); an acknowledgment of our participation in Christ's glory (vv. 16-18).

The opening statement, "In the beginning," recalls a comparable statement in Genesis (1:1). This parallel may be the author's way of implying that the coming of the Word into the world is as momentous as was the first creation. The Word is then described in language reminiscent of the figure of Wisdom personified (Prov 8:30; Wis 7:25). Like Wisdom, the Word was actively involved in creation. Unlike Wisdom, the Word is explicitly identified as divine. In a free-flowing manner the author ascribes life-giving power to the Word, life that gives light. The mention of light enables the author to draw one of his many contrasts. This particular contrast is between light and darkness. At times the light is synonymous with life (v. 5a). At other times it represents truth (v. 5b). At still other times, the Word is the light (vv. 7-9).

The witness named John is not further identified. However, it is presumed it is the Baptist, since the words that appear here are later ascribed to him (v. 15; cf. 1:30). There seems to be a definite need to contrast the Word and John. While the Word is the true light that comes into the world, John is merely the witness who testifies to the authenticity (vv. 7-9) and superiority of this light (v. 15). Though designated by God as a witness to the Word (v. 6), John is neither a peer nor a rival of the Word.

Up to this point, only John is clearly a historical person. The Word resides in some primordial place. Now the Word enters into human history, and the next section describes both the incarnation and the rejection by human beings that the Word faced (vv. 9-14). In a third contrast the author distinguishes between those who were somehow intimately associated with the Word but did not accept him and those who did accept him and thereby became children of God. "His own" may be a reference to other members of the Jewish community. Here ancestry does not make one a child of God; only faith in the Word made flesh can accomplish this.

Several translations state that the Word "made his dwelling among us" (v. 14). A better reading of the Greek might be "tenting." It calls to mind the tabernacle in the wilderness, where God dwelt among the people (Exod 40:34), as well as the tradition about Wisdom establishing her tent in the midst of the people (Sir 24:8). The Word of God, who is also the holiness of God and the Wisdom of God, now dwells in the midst of humankind. Women and men have been greatly enriched by this divine presence, transformed by the love that first prompted God's revelation and Christ's incarnation.

Themes of the Day

With this set of readings the Christmas celebration gains a new depth of theological meaning. There is progression of insight from the midnight gathering to the assembly that takes place during the daytime hours. At midnight the birth in history was proclaimed. At dawn the initiative of God's gift was declared and the baptized community's joyful gratitude was announced. In this third celebration we meditate on the identity of Christ and on our own new way of life in the Word made flesh. Four themes can be identified: salvation takes place before our eyes; salvation is universal; the child is the reflection of God's glory; it is with eyes of faith that we recognize the Word of God made flesh.

Salvation in Our Midst

If our eyes are open and alert we can see marvelous things. We can see that God has won a victory for us. The victory is tangible; it is realized in our midst. What kind of victory is it? It is an overwhelming victory, one that conquers the enemy and conquers permanently. Strong military language accents this victory. The power of God brings about an unparalled sweeping triumph. What is conquered is evil itself, the disruptive powers of sin that choke off life and bring unbearable suffering to weak and strong alike. God has won victory for us, and blessed are those who have eyes to see the messenger and ears to hear the glad tidings of triumph. When the victory is experienced, salvation is ours. We can take it in and make it our own. By this victory God is glorified, the past is made right, and there is righteousness for all.

A Universal Salvation

God's victory has a profound impact on every place, every time, and every people. The birth of the infant, who is a king in David's line, promises salvation to all who long for it. This salvation is a new vision of wisdom, one that has been realized in Christ, who is God's agent of grace in the world. This means we humans have another chance at living lives of righteousness. We are now able to be forgiven and to forgive. We have been graced with the presence of one who can make a difference in our lives if only we are attentive to what is in front of us. It is a new world, one of inclusivity and righteous honor. It is a new age, ushered in by the child who is leading a victory procession.

The Glory of the Child King

Christ is the source and signal of God's universal salvation. The child king is the reflection of God's glory, and we are in awe of the wonder made known to us. What we need are eyes of faith to see this marvel of God's wisdom, this reflection of God's glory in the fragility of the child of Bethlehem. The clouds of heaven are opened for just a moment, but it is enough time for us to catch a glimpse of the divine character of this mysterious child. He is the exact representation of God; he sits at God's right hand; he is God's Word made flesh.

The Word of God Made Flesh

Ultimately the eyes of faith allow us to see the fullness of God's revelation. The glory of the infant king is the very presence of God made flesh. Jesus is the eternal incarnate Word, who has pitched his tent among us. Ours is not a distant God. Rather, the incarnate Wisdom of God is among us, and we are called to a change of heart that will allow us to see this wonder. But something more happens. In this turn of events, the participation in the mystery can be so complete that we can know a deep communion in the reality that is offered in Christ. The marvel is that the child who was born among us can be born again and again in those who believe. The divine Word continues to draw close to those who seek to live lives of sincerity and truth. We too can be children of light. Grace becomes incarnate in those who believe, for the salvation of God is made flesh in us. The tent of God is pitched wherever salvation is offered, and the ways of evil and death are overturned. All of this takes place right before our eyes.

The Holy Family of Jesus, Mary, and Joseph
Sirach 3:2-6, 12-14

The book of Sirach (or Ecclesiaticus) belongs to ancient Israel's Wisdom tradition. Unlike the prophets who either call the people back to the religious traditions from which they have strayed or console and encourage them to be faithful in the face of overwhelming suffering, the Wisdom tradition is a collection of insights gleaned from the successful living of life. It is instruction that provides a glimpse into a way of living that has brought happiness in the past, but it describes it in order to encourage similar behavior that will bring corresponding happiness in the present or future.

The reading for today is instruction about family life, identifying the kind of living that will result in family harmony. Although the teaching originated from a society that was patriarchal (the father is the head) and a perspective that was androcentric (male-centered), it continues to have value for societies that do not share these biased points of view. The focus is the respect and obedience children (both male and female) owe their parents (both mother and father). Finally, it is presumed that the children are adults, not young children. The final verses (vv. 12-14) make this clear.

In the face of the patriarchal nature of the original society, the admonition to honor one's mother (vv. 2-7) takes on added importance. The parallel construction within which each of these references to the mother is found suggests that respect and obedience are due both parents, not just the dominant father. We should not overlook the fact that the text states that the mother has authority over her sons and that this authority was confirmed by the LORD (v. 2). In the face of the androcentric bias found in the text, this point is significant.

True to the character of Wisdom instruction, Sirach lists the blessings that follow such a way of life. The dutiful child is promised life itself (vv. 1, 6), remission of sins (vv. 3, 14), riches (v. 4), the blessing of children (v. 5a), and the answer to prayer (vv. 5, 6).

The final verses exhort the adult son to care for his father in his declining years. The picture portrayed is moving. The weakness of the elder is contrasted with the strength of the son, who presumably is at the height of his own powers (v. 13b). This son is told not to use his strength against his frail, elderly father but rather for the older man's benefit. This should be the case, whether the father's infirmity is physical or mental. There is no mention of caring for his mother in the same way. This may be because in patriarchal societies it was presumed that women would be cared for by their fathers or brothers, then by their husbands, and finally by their sons. The head of the family was normally not so vulnerable as to be in need of care. At issue is not a question about which parent needs care but an admonition to give it where needed.

Finally, the entire teaching about respect for parents, from the commandment (cf. Exod 20:12; Deut 5:16) to this admonition in Sirach, takes on a completely different perspective when we remember it is addressed to an adult child, and the responsibilities of respect and obedience are those of offspring who are mature.

Psalm 128:1-2, 3, 4-5

This psalm is classified as a Wisdom psalm. It is clearly descriptive instruction that teaches rather than an address directed to God in praise or thanksgiving. The psalm contains themes and vocabulary associated with the Wisdom tradition, such as reward and punishment, happy or blessed, ways or path. It begins with a macarism (v. 1), which is a formal statement that designates a person or group as blessed (or happy). This statement includes mention of the characteristic that is the basis of the happiness and then describes the blessings that flow from that characteristic. In this psalm those called blessed are the ones who fear the LORD, who walk in God's ways (vv. 1, 4), and the blessing that flows from this attitude of mind and heart is a life of prosperity (vv. 2-3).

In the Wisdom tradition fear of the LORD is the distinguishing characteristic of the righteous person. It denotes profound awe and amazement before the tremendous marvels of God. While this may include some degree of terror, it is the kind of fear that accompanies wonder at something amazing rather than dread in the face of mistreatment. The one who fears the LORD is one who acknowledges God's sovereignty and power and lives in accord with the order established by God. If anyone is to be happy and enjoy the blessings of life, it is the one who fears the LORD.

The blessings promised are both material good fortune and a large and extended family. Large families, like vast fields, were signs of fertility and prosperity. They not only provided companionship through life and partnership in labor but also were assurances of protection in a hostile world. The promise of future generations (v. 6) guaranteed perpetuity for the family; its bloodline and its name would survive death and would endure into the next generation. Although the androcentric bias in the psalm is seen in its reference to the fruitful wife and numerous children (the Hebrew reads "sons"), the concern is really with the family as a cohesive and abiding unit.

The last verses of the psalm (vv. 12-14) redirect the focus from the good fortune of the individual to the blessing enjoyed by the nation. Mention of Zion, Jerusalem, and Israel indicates this (vv. 12-14). The reference to children's children holds both familial and civic importance. It bespeaks long life and the continuation of the family, but it also implies that the nation is prospering and that it will endure. The blessings come from God, but God resides at the heart of the nation in Jerusalem, the city of Zion (v. 5). The good fortune of the individual is a share in the good fortune of the nation.

The final statement of Psalm 128 (v. 6b) is less a prayer than an exclamation: "Peace be upon Israel!" "Peace," *shalom,* is fullness of messianic blessings. This includes personal contentment, harmony with others and the rest of creation, adequate material resources. All of this is the result of right relationship with God. The psalm begins and ends on the same note: "Happy are those who fear the LORD" and "Peace."

Colossians 3:12-21

An exhortation to virtuous living is introduced with the stated rationale for such a manner of life. Because the Christians are God's chosen, holy and beloved, they should act accordingly. This moving characterization is followed by a demanding program of behavior. The notion of clothing oneself with virtue does not suggest such behavior is superficial or merely outward show. It refers to the practice of wearing a uniform of some kind that readily identifies the role one plays in society. Christians are to be recognized on sight by their manner of living.

The virtues themselves (vv. 12-15) are relational. They are directed toward others, requiring unselfish sensitivity. They may demand great sacrifice. This is especially true about bearing with the annoying and even repugnant behavior of others and forgiving them when they have been offensive. The motivation for such self-sacrifice is the forgiveness the Christians have received from God. The list continues with an admonition to love, the highest of all virtues. The peace of Christ, which is placed before them, should not be confused with mere tolerance or control imposed by some outside force. It is an inner peace that comes from a right relationship with God and, therefore, true harmony with others.

The author seems to provide directives for some kind of communal practice. The Christians are urged to open themselves to the transforming power of the word of Christ, to instruct and advise one another, to join in praising God through psalms and other religious songs. These activities might take place during some kind of liturgical event or as part of everyday life. Whatever the case, the virtues fostered and the manner of living encouraged are all communal.

The final directives (vv. 18-21) reflect the household codes prevalent in the Greco-Roman world of the time (cf. Eph 5:22-29). This was a patriarchal world where the men who headed the families exercised total control over their wives, children, and slaves. There certainly must have been mutual concern within the families themselves, but it was not mandated by law. The heads of households held the lives of the members in their hands to do with them what they deemed fit. In such a social context the admonitions found in this passage are revolutionary.

While the author still insists that wives must be subject to their husbands, he instructs the husbands to act toward their wives with love and thoughtfulness. Children are still told to obey their parents, but fathers are advised to be moderate in the training of their children lest discipline become oppressive. The Christian virtues listed at the beginning of the reading, when practiced within the context of the family, appear to have transformed the patriarchal social customs of the day. What is emphasized in this Christian household code is not patriarchal privilege but male responsibility in the familial relationships. This means that in Christ the relationships between man and woman and child have been radically altered.

Luke 2:41-52

This is the only account in the gospel that gives us a glimpse of the years between the infancy of Jesus and the time of his ministry. Although the key element in the passage is the christological self-declaration of the young Jesus (v. 49), the context of the account depicts a very religious family unit and an equally submissive son.

Adult Israelite men were required to observe in Jerusalem the three pilgrim feasts of Passover, Pentecost, and Tabernacles. If, because of distance, they were unable to travel three times in the year, they were obligated to observe at least Passover in this way. The reading states that the parents of Jesus regularly met this obligation, participating in the week-long celebration. Jesus, identified as a child (*país*, v. 43), is twelve years old, the age when he is about to assume the religious responsibilities of an adult (cf. *Pirke Aboth* 5, 212). The story suggests that while Jesus considers himself ready for this transition, his parents may still perceive him as a child.

The sense of pleasant familiarity that accompanies travel with friends and family is abruptly replaced by anxiety when Jesus' parents discover he is missing. The mention of three days is probably not an allusion to the resurrection. The group had traveled for one day before his absence was discovered. It would take a second day to return to the city. His parents probably found him on the third day in the Temple, where, on feast days and Sabbaths, the Sanhedrin engaged in informal question-and-answer sessions rather than their normal judicial activities (cf. *Sanh* 88b). His parents were unprepared for this kind of behavior from Jesus; they were perplexed.

Those in the temple area who heard the boy were astounded at his understanding and his answers. The Greek word *(exitēmi)* is frequently used to describe human reaction to the manifestation of divine power associated with the age of fulfillment (cf. Luke 4:22). Although a popular tradition (found in some religious art as well) suggests Jesus was teaching in the Temple, the text does not state this. He was part of the exchange. This account has much in common with Greco-Roman tradition, which includes an episode recounting the exploits of a hero while still a child.

Mary questions her son, using a fixed formula of accusation: Why have you done this? (cf. Gen 12:18; Exod 14:11; Num 23:11; Judg 15:11). His response to her is less a counter accusation than a reply filled with surprise. Her reference to Joseph as "your father" is paralleled with Jesus' reference to God as "my Father," and herein lies the point of the narrative. There seems to be a conflict between Jesus' responsibilities of sonship in his relationship with Joseph and sonship in his union with God. However, in this account he is faithful to both. Approaching adulthood, he begins to assume a public role; having made a striking appearance in the Temple, he returns to a life of obedience to his parents. The implications of these events and Jesus' words are not lost on Mary. She may not understand them now, but she keeps them in her heart.

Themes of the Day

All the major themes found in today's readings highlight the relational character of family life. In Sirach some of the dynamics of family living and responsibility as exercised in the ancient world unfold before our eyes. The rewards of faithfully observing these family codes are showcased in the responsorial psalm. Paul directs our attention to the manner of relational living to which we are summoned as members of the family of God, a manner of living that flows from the bond of perfection that unites us. The gospel narrative provides us with a glimpse into the relational dynamics operative within the Holy Family.

Family Living

So much has been said recently about family values. But what exactly are they? The specifics of family customs and roles played within the family may be culture-bound, but the values out of which they emerge and which inform them are not. Sirach sketches a picture of ancient family customs, but it is easy to look beneath them and find enduring values that speak to us today. There we clearly discover the values of mutuality, respect, and service between wives and husbands, between parents and children, and between young and old. This does not mean there are no roles of dominance. However, these roles often disappear or, because of circumstances, revert to another family member. As Sirach demonstrates, the son who was once dependent on the father now becomes his caretaker. Despite the nature of the roles and the way they move from one person to another, mutual respect and care for those in need remains a constant.

These values challenge us today. Because of cultural differences we may not be inclined to live them in the same way, but mutuality, respect, and care for others should still be the backbone of our living together. The challenge before us is to devise ways for husbands and wives to live in mutual esteem, for parents to honor the dignity of their children at the same time children obey and show respect to their parents, for the elderly to protect the young even as the young watch over the elderly. Abuse occurs in far too many corners of the family, and no group seems to be spared its horror. The message from Sirach speaks to us today.

The Family of God

While this feast considers the family unit as such, it also celebrates the Church as the family of God. Thus the values of mutuality, respect, and service become characteristics of the Church, the ecclesial family. What binds the family of God together are virtues as relational as the ties that bind the members of the natural family together. While we use the metaphor of family and relate it to the Church, this does not mean that some within the community are mature and others are not. Within the family of God the virtues outlined by Paul are to be lived in a mature manner, not one that is infantile. The Church is a community of adults who are called in one body to live in a collaboration of love, mutuality, and service. They are joined in a bond of perfection, not in subservience or neurotic antagonism.

It may be more challenging to live out these values within the Church, for those who are called to put on Christ, bearing with one another in compassion, kindness, humility, gentleness, and patience, must relate in this way with people who may be strangers. The natural family bonds are absent. Within the family of God there is great diversity and significant differences. There it is neither blood nor marriage that binds but the word of Christ in the hearts of believers. It is no wonder that more than once in the reading for today Paul admonishes the Christians to forgive. The Church may be a different kind of family, but the values of mutuality, respect, and service are as essential here as anywhere.

The Holy Family

The model for both the natural family and the family of God is the Holy Family. There we find mutuality in the relationships; we find compassion, kindness, and humility; gentleness and patience; there we find obedience to parents along with respect for the uniqueness of children. In this portrait of the Holy Family people do not claim privilege. Jesus, who was the Son of God, submitted to his human mother and father. Mary and Joseph, who exercised authority over Jesus, also stood in wonder of him.

Together the members of the Holy Family observed the religious obligations of their faith, and when Jesus seemed to have moved out of his prescribed role as dependent, his parents may have questioned him, but they did not censor him. He, on his part, was sensitive to their anxiety. Though he would eventually assume a role that might be difficult for them to comprehend, for the present he would submit to their guardianship and adhere to their wishes. Mutual respect enabled the members of the Holy Family to resolve a difficult and painful situation without anyone being shamed or diminished in the process. This is a marvelous example of family values in operation.

A Celebration of Wisdom

It is not by accident that all the readings for today deal with the theme of wisdom, which can be understood as seeking and savoring those insights gained from the experience of life that enable us to live fully and with integrity. In each reading we see that we arrive at wisdom through the way we live out the relationships closest to us. In the family we discover that while children are taught and molded by parents, it is the children themselves that teach the adults what it means to be a real parent. In the family we discover that husbands and wives mold and shape each other into caring, loving, and forgiving partners. So it is in the family of God. There we discover it is only in trusting relationships that we can live lives of mutuality, respect, and service. Modeling ourselves after Jesus, we learn to be compassionate, kind, humble, gentle, and patient. In the family of God we take on the most basic family characteristic—we put on love.

Optional Readings for the Holy Family of Jesus, Mary, and Joseph
1 Samuel 1:20-22, 24-28

The story recounts the faithfulness with which Hannah and her husband, Elkanah, fulfill the vow Hannah made to God. At least two elements in this account make it an unusual story in a predominantly androcentric (male-centered) tradition. First, in this patriarchal society, the vows made by women are either assumed or annulled by the man under whose jurisdiction she lives, namely, her father, brother, husband, or son (cf. Num 30:14-15). Though obviously assumed by Elkanah, it is Hannah who fulfills the vow. Second, women are normally identified as the wives of their husbands. Here Elkanah is called the husband of Hannah. This suggests Hannah is more important than Elkanah.

There is a play on various forms of the Hebrew word for "ask" *(shā'al)* that is both interesting and confusing. Of interest is the connection between asking and the name of the child (v. 20). Some of this wordplay is lost in translation when forms of *shā'al* are rendered "give" and "dedicated" (vv. 27-28). The confusion is seen in the stated meaning of the name. Samuel *(sh⁽e⁾mū'ēl)* probably means "his name *[shēm]* is God *['ēl]*," not "asked of the Lord," which is a much better rendition of the name Saul *(šā'ūl)*. Scholars believe that since both Saul and Samuel were considered deliverers from Philistine oppression and since the names are so close in sound, the tradition about Saul could easily have been applied to Samuel.

The religious devotion of Hannah and Elkanah is clear. Faithful to his religious obligations, Elkanah goes to the shrine regularly, even when Hannah stays behind, presumably to care for the newborn child (v. 21). After the child had been weaned, Hannah fulfills her vow at Shiloh, the same place where she had originally made it (cf. 1 Sam 1:11). Children were often suckled until they were two or three years old (2 Macc 7:27), after which time a feast was held (Gen 21:8). The sacrifice described here probably corresponds to this occasion. A three-year-old bull is in its prime and therefore probably quite costly. An ephah of flour is equivalent to about a bushel. To this is added wine. The offerings described here comprise a substantial sacrifice.

As head of the family, Elkanah offers the sacrifice. When this has been accomplished, Hannah approaches the priest Eli and identifies herself as the one with whom he had conversed a few years earlier (cf. 1 Sam 1:12-18). Using an oath formula (v. 26), she reminds him of the earlier circumstances and assures him that she is there now to fulfill the vow she had made. Her discourse contains a play on the word for "ask" *(shā'al)*, perhaps influenced by the mention of Shiloh, another similar sounding word. Here the wordplay is with meanings rather than soundings. Hannah "asked" of the LORD, and now she is "lending" to the LORD so that the child will be "dedicated." All of these verbs are forms of the same *shā'al.*

Psalm 84:2-3, 5-6, 9-10

The psalm is usually classified as a Song of Zion, one that praises the marvels of the city of Jerusalem and the Temple, which is its crowning glory. It opens with an exclamation of praise of the sanctuary. The Hebrew for "lovely" *(yādîd)* can also be translated "well-loved," thus indicating the devotion the psalmist has for this place of national pride and worship. It is this devotion, rather than some external beauty, that causes the psalmist to yearn and to pine for the temple precincts and to cry out to the God who dwells there (v. 3).

God is addressed in several ways in the psalm, each reflecting some aspect of Israel's faith. First, YHWH (here translated "LORD"), the specific name of God, is an intimate name, so personal that not even Israel used it openly. It is associated with Moses' original revelation of God during his call to be the one to lead the people out of Egyptian bondage (cf. Exod 3:13-14). Even in that tradition the exact meaning and spelling of the name is circumvented out of reverence. The second name is the very popular title "LORD of hosts," or *Sabaoth* (vv. 2, 9). It originated in a military context, which explains the use of "hosts" (companies of warriors). After the period of occupation of the land it became a cultic name used to praise God's ongoing power to save and protect the people.

Third, the title "God of Jacob" recalls the patron God of the ancestor (Israel) who is considered the father of the twelve tribes. In the early ancestral tradition God is also referred to as "the Mighty One of Jacob" (cf. Gen 49:24), another indication of God's protective power. Finally, God is called "the living God," a God who both enjoys life and is able to ensure life for others. With the exception of the mysterious personal name of God, all these titles say something about God's gracious providential care of the people.

Two macarisms, declarations of happiness or blessedness, assert that both those who live in the Temple and those who visit the Temple as pilgrims are privileged and therefore are truly blessed or happy (vv. 5-6). Because of their proximity, those who dwell in the Temple are able to worship there regularly. Because of the strength God guarantees, the second group is able to embark on the arduous and oftentimes dangerous pilgrimage to the Temple, there to carry out their religious and cultic obligations.

The psalm response ends with a prayer for God's anointed one (vv. 9-10). Although both kings and priests were anointed, it was the king who was normally called the "anointed one." Furthermore, the poetic structure of the verse suggests that the reference is to the king. The parallelism is as follows:

behold   our shield

look upon   your anointed

Within this poetic construction, "our shield" refers to the same person as does "your anointed." Since the king was the protector or shield of the people, the allusion is clear.

1 John 3:1-2, 21-24

The first and more important point of this reading is the love God has for believers. A second theme is eschatological fulfillment. The second is dependent upon the first. In fact, it is a direct result of it. Believers are addressed as "Beloved" *(agapētoí),* a term of endearment that makes a connection between the love God has for them and the love they should have for one another.

The love *(agápē)* of which the author speaks is generative; it is transforming; it makes believers children of God. They are now a new reality; hence they are not accepted by the world, the old reality. Certain similarities between Jesus and the believers are drawn. The world, here meaning the entire inhabited world, which is subject to sin, recognizes only its own. It did not recognize the only begotten Son of God, and it does not recognize these new children of God. The implications of this are clear. Believers should not be surprised if they encounter the same kind of rejection, even persecution and death, that befell Jesus.

The already-but-not-yet of Christian eschatology is clearly stated. As a consequence of God's love believers have already been reborn as children of God. However, their transformation has not yet been completed, nor has it been fully made known to them. All this is dependent upon a future manifestation. It is not clear from the text whether this will be a manifestation of Christ or of God. However, any manifestation of the risen Christ is a manifestation of God, and in like manner the preeminent manifestation of God is found in the risen Christ.

As children of God, the believers are promised an even fuller identification with God. They will see God as God is, for they will be like God. The love God has for them far exceeds any guilt they may experience. They are called to believe this, thus making their faith one that is full of confidence, a confidence rooted in obedience to the commandments and manifested in the way they turn to God in prayer. Although only one commandment is placed before them, its focus is twofold. They are to believe in the name of God's Son, Jesus Christ, and to love one another. The mutual abiding character of the union that joins believers and God is clearly stated: faithful believers abide in God and God abides in them. This mutual indwelling is accomplished by the Spirit that was given to the believers by God.

The trinitarian theology is obvious. Viewing it from the perspective of the relationships in God, we see that Jesus is called the Son of God and the Spirit is identified as the gift of God that was bestowed upon the faithful. Viewing it from the perspective of trinitarian involvement in the lives of the faithful, we see that the ground of Christian confidence is the great love of God; the focus of Christian faith is commitment to the name (identity) of Jesus Christ, the Son of God; the assurance of divine indwelling is the gift of the Spirit.

Luke 2:41-52

This is the only account in the gospel that gives us a glimpse of the years between the infancy of Jesus and the time of his ministry. Although the key element in the passage is the christological self-declaration of the young Jesus (v. 49), the context depicts a very religious family unit and an equally submissive son.

Adult Israelite men were required to observe in Jerusalem the three pilgrim feasts of Passover, Pentecost, and Tabernacles. If, because of distance, they were unable to travel three times in the year, they were obligated to observe at least Passover in this way. The reading states that the parents of Jesus regularly met this obligation, participating in the week-long celebration. Jesus, identified as a child (*país,* v. 43), is twelve years old, the age when he is about to assume the religious responsibilities of an adult (cf. *Pirke Aboth* 5, 212). The story suggests that while Jesus considers himself ready for this transition, his parents may still perceive him as a child.

The sense of pleasant familiarity that accompanies travel with friends and family is abruptly replaced by anxiety when his parents discover Jesus is missing. The mention of three days is probably not an allusion to the resurrection. The group had traveled for one day before his absence was discovered. It would take a second day to return to the city. His parents probably found him on the third day in the Temple, where, on feast days and Sabbaths, the Sanhedrin engaged in informal question-and-answer sessions rather than their normal judicial activities (cf. *Sanh* 88b). His parents were unprepared for this kind of behavior from Jesus; they were astonished.

Those in the temple area who heard the boy were astounded at his understanding and his answers. The Greek word *(exitēmi)* is frequently used to describe human reaction to the manifestation of divine power associated with the age of fulfillment (cf. Luke 4:22). Although a popular tradition (found in some religious art as well) suggests that Jesus was teaching in the Temple, the text does not state this. He was part of the exchange. This account has much in common with Greco-Roman tradition, which includes an episode recounting the exploits of a hero while still a child.

Mary questions her son, using a fixed formula of accusation: Why have you done this? (cf. Gen 12:18; Exod 14:11; Num 23:11; Judg 15:11). His response to her is less a counter accusation than a reply filled with surprise. Her reference to Joseph as "your father" is paralleled with Jesus' reference to God as "my Father," and herein lies the point of the narrative. There seems to be a conflict between Jesus' responsibilities of sonship in his relationship with Joseph and sonship in his union with God. However, in this account he is faithful to both. Approaching adulthood, he begins to assume a public role; having made a striking appearance in the Temple, he returns to a life of obedience to his parents. The implications of these events and Jesus' words are not lost on Mary. She may not understand them now, but she keeps them in her heart.

Themes of the Day

The optional readings for the feast of the Holy Family provide us with an opportunity to reflect on "family values" in a slightly different way. The pivotal theme is the union we enjoy with God, a union of love that makes us children of God, members of the family of God. All other families find meaning and inspiration in this fundamental gathering. The stories of Hannah, Elkanah, and Samuel as well as Mary, Joseph, and Jesus are examples of how the plan of God unfolds within the everyday occurrences of family life.

Children of God

First and foremost, we are called to be children of God. It is out of love we are called; the initiative is God's. As children of God we are also joined to God's own Son, who has commanded us to love one another as God has loved all. If we are faithful to that commandment, Jesus Christ remains in us. The way we know we are united with him is that we keep the commandments. We are thus bound to Christ through the power of the Holy Spirit.

Human Families

The human family plays a significant role in the fashioning of the broader family of God. The larger family that God initiates is specified in unique historical families, as strange and as complex as those family relationships may be, with their joys and sorrows, their barrenness and fruitfulness. We see this in the family of Hannah and Elkanah. There is no way of separating this human family and the broader People of God. Hannah's barrenness became the occasion of prayer and dedication, which resulted in the enrichment of the entire People of God. The same was true with the Holy Family. When Jesus said he must be about the business of God, he was not pitting God's family against his human family. Rather, his human family was instrumental in accomplishing the business of God whether they knew it or not. The plan of God does not unfold in a vacuum but in the everyday family situations that include separation and misunderstanding as well as joy and celebration.

The broader family of God offers us opportunities to be enriched in ways our family of origin may have failed us. It allows us to find a dwelling place in the larger family relationships as found within the Church, within a religious community, within a prayer group, within any kind of gathering of believers committed to common goals or projects. If, like Jesus, we are about the business of God, we will not be hampered from accomplishing great things by the limitations of our families of origin.

The Home as a Temple

On this Sunday, with these readings, the Temple is used allegorically to refer to the home. Just as every individual is a temple of God, so every home should be like the house of God, a place where the members of the family can meet God and together offer praise and thanksgiving. We should not allow our structured concept of church or temple cloud our understanding of our own home as a dwelling place of God. Too often the sanctity of this place is violated by abuse or dysfunction. Today's feast is a time for us to look deeply into our homes, our family lives, and there to find or pray for the grace we need to be about the business of God, to dedicate ourselves and our families to God.

January 1, Solemnity of the Blessed Virgin Mary, Mother of God
Numbers 6:22-27

The blessing found in this reading may be one of the oldest pieces of poetry in the Bible. It is introduced by a statement that gives the content of the blessing both Mosaic and divine legitimation. Although it is the priests who ultimately bless the people, it is Moses who receives the blessing from God and delivers it to Aaron and his sons (vv. 22-23). These are examples of mediatorial roles, one played by Moses and another played by Aaron and the priests.

YHWH, the personal name of God, is repeated three times in the blessing (vv. 24-26). There is some question about the actual use of this blessing, since there is a tradition, standing to this day, that forbids the use of the personal name of God. People believed that a name possessed some of the very identity of the person named. To know someone's name was to possess intimate knowledge of and to enjoy some form of control over that person. To know and use God's name presumes this kind of intimacy and control. In order to guard against such presumption some other word or title was pronounced in place of God's name. According to the Mishnah, an ancient collection of Jewish law that dates back to about the third century of the common era, God's personal name was pronounced only when the blessing was used in the Temple. Whatever the case may be, the power of the personal name of God cannot be denied.

The blessing itself is crisp and direct. It is addressed to "you," a singular pronoun that can refer to an individual or to the entire nation understood as one. Each line invokes a personal action from God: to bless with good fortune and to keep from harm; to look favorably toward and to be gracious; to look upon and to grant peace. Actually, there is very little difference in the petitions. They all ask for the same reality, that is, the blessings that make life worth living. This could mean different things to different people at different times, but basically they are all asking for peace. Peace is the fundamental characteristic of Jewish blessing, the condition of absolute well-being.

The reading opened with God giving directions to Moses. It closes with a final word from God. The priests are told to invoke God's name on the Israelites. The Hebrew would be better read "put my name" on them. This evokes the image of placing one's name on property in order to certify ownership. The priests are instructed to put God's name on the Israelites, indicating that they belong to God and that God will certainly bless them.

Psalm 67:2-3, 5, 6, 8

The verb forms in this psalm make it difficult to be categorized. Some commentators believe the verbs are in past tense, and they classify the psalm as a prayer of thanksgiving for blessings already received. Others consider them a form of wish- or bidding-prayer, a moderate request for blessings that are not yet enjoyed. However the verbs are read, it is safe to consider the psalm as a prayer of blessing.

The psalm begins with a slight adaptation of the first words of the blessing used by Aaron and the priests who descended from him (v. 2; cf. Num 6:24-26). The use of this Aaronic blessing in a congregational prayer suggests the favors once promised to that particular priestly family are now sought for the entire people. The metaphor of God's shining face refers to the favorable disposition a smiling countenance reflects. The psalmist asks that God look favorably upon the people, that God be benevolent toward them.

God's goodness toward this people will redound to God's reputation among other nations. They will see the people's good fortune and will interpret it as the fruit of God's saving power on their behalf and God's continued rule over them. These other nations will conclude only a mighty and magnanimous God would be able to secure such good fortune. Here prosperity is not used as leverage against others. Quite the contrary, it benefits even those who may not be enjoying it. It does this because it is perceived as coming from God and not merely as the product of human exploits or ingenuity.

The psalm moves from an acknowledgment of divine rule over one people (v. 3) to an announcement of universal divine governance (v. 5). All nations will not only rejoice over God's goodness, they will also be guided by that same God and ultimately will praise that God (vv. 6, 8). In other words, the good fortune of one nation is testimony to salvific activity of God. This in turn becomes the occasion of salvation for all the earth. One nation is the source of blessing for all. This is the fulfillment of a promise made to Abraham (cf. Gen 12:2-3).

The psalm ends with a prayer for continued universal blessing. It is the past tense of the verb in this verse that had led some commentators to conclude that all of the blessings referred to earlier were also bestowed and enjoyed in the past. They maintain that the plea is that God continue to bless the people so that all nations will continue to revere God. Whether past or future, the psalmist believes all good fortune comes from God. Others see this and praise God, and in this way God is made known to all the earth.

Galatians 4:4-7

The mission of Christ to the world is the major focus of Paul's teaching in the verses that make up this reading. "The designated time" refers to that time in history when God brought the messianic expectations to fulfillment by sending his Son into the world. The word for "send" *(apostéllō)* carries the idea of authorization, as in the case of an envoy. The primary stress of this verb is less on the actual sending than on the commission, especially when it is God who sends. The passage, then, is concerned with the mission entrusted to Christ by God. Referring to Christ as God's Son establishes his divine nature; acknowledging that he was born of a woman establishes his human nature. The christology in this passage is rich and complex.

According to Paul, the goal of Christ's mission was to transform the Galatians from being slaves under the law to being adopted sons of God. Normally in patriarchal societies, only male offspring can inherit. Since legal status is the primary focus of this passage, its androcentric bias becomes obvious. In a more egalitarian society the fundamental message of change of status, while inclusive, would remain basically the same.

Paul is here setting up the contrast between servitude under the law and freedom in Christ. In order to do this he uses a social custom of his day. If an heir was too young to claim inheritance, a legal guardian was appointed until the heir came of age. Paul compares the believers to underage minors, who, until "the fullness of time had come," could not claim what might be rightfully theirs. The law acted as legal guardian. All of this changes with the coming of Christ. Christians are no longer minors bound to the tutelage of the law. They are legal heirs, adopted children because Christ is the only true Son. Does anyone need proof of this? The very fact that they are filled with the Spirit of Christ and dare to call God by the intimate term *Abba* should be evidence enough.

Paul's attitude toward the law is not as negative as it appears to be elsewhere (cf. Rom 7:7-24). Here it is a necessary guardian that carefully watches over minors until they are mature enough to take care of themselves. It is binding in order to teach; it restricts in order to instruct. Though it is inferior to the Spirit of Christ, it is faithful and trustworthy. However, once the Spirit takes hold of the believer dependence on the law ends, and freedom in the Spirit, the rightful inheritance of the children of God, begins.

The reading ends as it began, declaring that all this is God's doing according to God's plan. God sent the Son to make sons and daughters of the rest of us. This is accomplished by means of the indwelling of the Spirit, which empowers us to call God *Abba,* tender Father.

Luke 2:16-21

This reading for the feast of the Solemnity of Mary is essentially the same as that of the Christmas Mass at Dawn. However, these verses include mention of the circumcision and naming of Jesus. Although this is a slight difference, the addition shifts the focus of the passage away from the shepherds to the child and his parents. First, the sight of this lowly family opened the eyes of the shepherds so they could understand the meaning of the message announced by the angels. Then, Mary took all these mysterious events into her heart and there pondered their meaning. Finally, Mary and Joseph arranged for the child to be circumcised and named.

Circumcision was the ritual that initiated the males into the community of Israel. It was enjoined by God on Abraham and all his descendants, and from that time forward it was considered a sign of the covenant (Gen 17:9-11). As observant Jews, Mary and Joseph fulfilled all the prescriptions of the law, seeing that the child was circumcised as custom dictated.

In addition to being circumcised, the child was named. When the angel appeared to Mary and announced that she had been chosen to be the mother of the long-awaited one, the angel also told her the child would be named Jesus (1:31), which means "savior" (cf. Matt 1:21). Now almost everything the angel had announced has come to pass. Mary will have to wait to see how he will acquire the throne of his father David and rule the house of Jacob forever (cf. 1:32f.).

Themes of the Day

Liturgically, the Octave of Christmas commemorates several celebrations: the Solemnity of the Mother of God; the day designated for prayers for global peace; the beginning of the New Year. The Lectionary contains a variety of themes that resonate with these celebrations. The major themes are these: the person of Mary as the example of faith and of contemplation, and the blessing of peace for the New Year.

Mary

The gospel story, with the addition of the mention of the circumcision and naming of Jesus, is the same passage read for the celebration of the Christmas Mass During the Day. Placed within the context of the Solemnity of the Mother of God, however, the reading has a different emphasis. Here Mary is the focus, not the child. Although the shepherds are depicted as gaining insight into the presence of God by seeing this Holy Family, it is Mary who is described as holding all these things in her heart. She is the one who ponders the significance of these events.

By her willingness to hold all things in her heart, Mary becomes to Christians an inspiration of contemplation and reflection. She inspires us to consider deeply the significance of events rather than to go blandly through life without meaning or direction. She inspires us to constant reflection on the truths of the faith, which continue to be made real in life's experiences. She inspires us to fidelity to the practices of our faith, practices that are the disciplines of soul that lead the community to a clearer focus on God's presence in human affairs.

Blessings and Prayers for Peace in the New Year

The theme of peace appears on many levels; its meaning, "fullness of life," bursts forth in every reading for today. The ancient prayer/blessing of peace is an appropriate start for the New Year. In personal affairs, family concerns, in community and world organizations, peace is at a premium. We long for it; we pray for it. When God blesses us with peace, hearts are stilled and souls are at rest. This blessing of peace resonates well with the angels' wish for people of goodwill. The beginning of a new year is a good time to reach out to others and to pray for God's blessing of peace for each dimension of human encounter.

Peace is also our inheritance in Christ. As adopted children of God, we have been given the freedom to live in a godly manner, calling God our *Abba*. If we are resolved to live this new identity, we will be granted the freedom of heart that shows itself in works of peace and justice. Right relationships in the covenant activity of God are the pathways of peace. Our commitment to respond to God's initiatives in Christ and our willingness to be a new creation are solid New Year's resolutions for all who are interested in peace on earth.

Second Sunday After Christmas
Sirach 24:1-2, 8-12

In many ways this reading from Sirach resembles a poem found in the book of Proverbs (8:22-31). The characterization is interesting. First, Wisdom is personified as a woman. This is significant when we remember the high regard within which Wisdom was held. Second, she is not dependent on another to pay her homage. She sings her own praises, and she does this publicly, both before her own people and in the midst of the very court of God. From the outset it is clear this Woman Wisdom is no ordinary being. She is revered both on earth and in the heavens.

Wisdom's glory is really derived from the excellence of her creation by God. It is this she praises, and she does so among her people and within the divine court. It is unusual that a woman, even Woman Wisdom, should be granted admission to the court of God and be allowed to speak about anything, much less herself, before the high God and the hosts or courtiers of God. The origin and identity of this mysterious woman has challenged commentators from the beginning. The image has been interpreted in various ways. Some believe she was originally an ancient Israelite goddess. However, as Israel developed a monotheistic faith, she lost her divine prerogatives.

Other commentators consider Woman Wisdom a personification of a divine attribute. In this view she is not an independent deity but a characteristic of God. Although she is a creature of God, she enjoys extraordinary privileges. She exists before anything else has been created, and she does not seem to face death or destruction. The ambiguity of the text does not provide a definite explanation of this mysterious figure.

This reading from Sirach adds an element not found in earlier portraits of Woman Wisdom. It states that although she was free to roam throughout the universe, she was in search of a dwelling place for herself, a place where she would be able to rest. Her role in creation seems to have provided her some measure of universal influence, so she could have decided on almost any place. However, it was the Creator-God who determined where she would abide, and God decided it would be in Israel that she would dwell (vv. 8-12).

Deciding the proper place for Woman Wisdom to settle was not a divine afterthought. It was part of primordial creation itself. One can conclude from this that the establishment of cosmic Wisdom in the midst of Israel, decreed as it was at the primordial event, is here seen as part of the very structure of the created cosmos. Wisdom was there from the beginning, ministering to God but waiting to be revealed in a special way to the children of Israel. Once she was revealed to this people, she was exalted and admired, praised and blessed.

Psalm 147:12-13, 14-15, 19-20

This passage is from the final stanza of a hymn of praise of God. It highlights God's protection of and solicitude toward the people of Israel. Both Jerusalem, the capital of the nation, and Zion, the mount upon which the city was built, came to represent the people. They are called upon directly to praise God (v. 12). This summons is followed by a listing of some of the many wonderful works of God that elicit such praise. All of them point to the uniqueness of the bond that holds God and this people together.

God protects the people by fortifying the city. The ancient practice of building walls around cities provided them with a defense against possible attack and gave them a vantage point from which to observe the activity outside the walls (v. 13a). As strong as these walls might have been, the gates of the city put it in jeopardy, for they had to provide entrance for the normal traffic of the city, for travelers and traders, for those who farmed outside the walls. The city was somewhat vulnerable at its gates. The psalmist calls the people to praise God, who has strengthened them precisely at this their most vulnerable spot (v. 13).

Walls also act as borders. They define the limits of personal property, and they determine the sweep of the city. Protected as they are, the people of Jerusalem/Zion are truly blessed. They can go about their daily lives with a sense of security, for the fortification provided by God has assured them of peace (v. 14). Furthermore, this peace has enabled them to prosper, since they do not have to invest time or resources into defense measures.

Prosperity is symbolized by the wheat, which is abundant and of the finest quality. Both these characteristics represent the blessing bestowed by God. The abundance suggests either expansive fields that were never ravaged by wild animals or invading enemies, or else an extraordinary yield from a smaller plot of land. In either case the people would consider themselves singularly blessed by God. The exceptional quality of the wheat demonstrates the fertility of the land. Again, this is land that has been spared the despoiling that usually accompanies war. This is a land that has known peace.

The psalmist paints a dynamic picture of the powerful word of God. It is like an emissary who runs swiftly throughout the earth, both proclaiming and bringing about what has been proclaimed. God speaks, and it is accomplished. God promises to protect and provide for the people, and it is done.

This same powerful word is spoken to Israel, but with a different emphasis and with different consequences (vv. 19-20). It is God's special word, God's law, the law of life that will ensure God's continued protection and care. Just as Jerusalem/Zion (the people) is singled out for special consideration, here Jacob/Israel (the nation) is chosen for a unique relationship. No other nation has been so blessed. No other nation has been given God's law of life. This is the People of God. This privilege is the reason to praise God. Psalm 147 ends as it began, with praise of the LORD.

Ephesians 1:3-6, 15-18

The reading opens with a benediction (vv. 3-6), a common way to open letters as well as prayers (cf. 1 Kgs 5:7; 2 Cor 1:3-11). It also serves as a solemn, courtly form of congratulation (Ruth 4:14). This benediction blesses God, who has blessed us with "every spiritual blessing." As is always the case in Christian theology, the blessing of God comes to us through the agency of Christ. This agency is important enough to be mentioned in every verse of the benediction.

The blessings themselves are distinctively of a spiritual, even cosmic, nature. First is election in Christ. The theme of election has its origins in the Jewish tradition (Exod 19:5-6; Deut 14:2). What is unique here is the idea of primordial predestination. Predestination refers to that act whereby God's love, from all eternity, determines salvation in Christ. Although the author is writing to specific individuals, there is no sense that some are predestined for salvation and others are not. The point is that salvation in Christ is not an afterthought; it was in God's plan from the beginning.

The believers were not chosen *because* they were holy and blameless but *that they might be* holy and blameless. Once again it is clear that salvation is the cause and not the consequence of righteousness. The reading goes on to say that believers were chosen for adoption into the family of God. It is through Christ, the only real Son of God, that others can become God's adopted children. Although it is not explicitly stated here, the implicit baptismal theme is in the background of this passage. The benediction ends as it began, with a reference to praising God.

The second part of the reading is a twofold prayer: first, of thanksgiving that the baptismal grace referred to in the benediction has taken effect in the lives of the believers; and second, of petition that the believers will grow more and more into the kind of people they were predestined to become.

The author acknowledges the faith and love of the members of the community. Although there is warmth in the greeting, one does not get the sense that the author knew this community intimately. He has heard about them, commends them for their devotion by thanking God for it, and includes them in his own prayers.

The prayer itself is for wisdom, one of the primary baptismal gifts. The tradition of praying for wisdom can be traced as far back as Solomon (cf. 1 Kgs 3:5-9). Unlike this royal prayer, which asks for the ability to govern well, the goal of wisdom, for which the author prays, is spiritual: to know God; to understand the hope within the great call of election; to appreciate the excellence of the inheritance that comes with adoption as children of God.

John 1:1-18

The Gospel of John begins with one of the most profound statements about Jesus found in the entire Second Testament. Its lofty christology is comparable to that found in the reading from Hebrews. Both characterize Christ as preexistent; both depict Christ as an agent in the creation of the world. The reading itself falls easily into five parts: a description of the role the Word played in the creation of the world (vv. 1-5); a brief sketch of a witness named John (vv. 6-8); an account of the Word's entrance into the world (vv. 9-14); a second report about John (v. 15); an acknowledgment of our participation in Christ's glory (vv. 16-18).

The opening statement, "In the beginning," recalls a comparable statement in Genesis (1:1). This parallel may be the author's way of implying that the coming of the Word into the world is as momentous as was the first creation. The Word is then described in language reminiscent of the figure of Wisdom personified (Prov 8:30; Wis 7:25). Like Wisdom, the Word was actively involved in creation. Unlike Wisdom, the Word is explicitly identified as divine. In a free-flowing manner the author ascribes life-giving power to the Word, life that gives light. The mention of light enables the author to draw one of his many contrasts. This particular contrast is between light and darkness. At times the light is synonymous with life (v. 5a). At other times it represents truth (v. 5b). At still other times the Word is the light (vv. 7-9).

The witness named John is not further identified. However, it is presumed to be the Baptist, since the words that appear here are later ascribed to him (v. 15; cf. 1:30). There seems to be a definite need to contrast the Word and John. While the Word is the true light that comes into the world, John is merely the witness who testifies to the authenticity (vv. 7-9) and superiority of this light (v. 15). Though designated by God as a witness to the Word (v. 6), John is neither a peer nor a rival of the Word.

Up to this point only John is clearly a historical person. The Word resides in some primordial place. Now the Word enters into human history, and the next section describes both the incarnation and the rejection by human beings that the Word faced (vv. 9-14). In a third contrast the author distinguishes between those who were somehow intimately associated with the Word but did not accept him and those who did accept him and thereby became children of

God. "His own" may be a reference to other members of the Jewish community. Here ancestry does not make one a child of God; only faith in the Word made flesh can accomplish this.

Several translations state that the Word "made his dwelling among us" (v. 14). A better reading of the Greek might be "tenting." It calls to mind the tabernacle in the wilderness, where God dwelt among the people (Exod 40:34), as well as the tradition about Wisdom establishing her tent in the midst of the people (Sir 24:8). The Word of God, who is also the holiness of God and the Wisdom of God, now dwells in the midst of humankind. Women and men have been greatly enriched by this divine presence, transformed by the love that first prompted God's revelation and Christ's incarnation.

Themes of the Day

This Sunday could be called Wisdom Sunday. It celebrates Christ, God's incarnated gift, who comes to dwell in our midst. The divine Word, who has pitched a tent among us, is associated with the fulfillment of Wisdom and with our participation in her power. Several themes emerge from this association: Wisdom was present from the beginning of time as a cosmic force; Wisdom lives in the midst of the people; Christ is the fulfillment of Wisdom and the agent of our salvation.

Wisdom as Cosmic Force

Wisdom is part of creation from the beginning and holds sway over cosmic affairs. She inspires the praise of all creation. Told by God to live among the people, she is in their midst as a source of inspiration and encouragement. When joined with the Prologue of the Gospel of John, Wisdom is seen as incarnate in Jesus. In Jesus, Wisdom is the divine Word that dwells among us. In this Word all creation has come to be and is sustained in life and destiny.

Wisdom Lives Among the People

Wisdom dwells in Zion, in the Holy City of Jerusalem, in the midst of the city of God. When Wisdom dwells at the heart of the community, three changes occur. First, protection is offered to the people. There is no fear, no threat; all are secure in Wisdom's abiding presence. Second, with Wisdom comes a sense of God's sustaining mercy and love. Third, the protection and blessing Wisdom brings draw forth the praises of God. The people, all of the city, are inspired to give praise and thanks to God for Wisdom's wondrous gifts.

Christ, the Agent of Salvation

God is praised and blessed for the wonders of the divine gifts offered to us. Within this blessing there is the profound awareness that it is Christ who makes all good things possible. Christ is the agent of our salvation. In fact, the promise of salvation is proclaimed from the beginning of creation. Just as Wisdom was told by God to pitch her tent among the people, so the divine Word, bringing the gift of salvation, has pitched a tent amidst the people. This gracious act of God is an assurance that salvation is offered to all who are willing to receive it. Thus Christ, divine Wisdom and God among us, is the promise that all creation can be regenerated. This new life is the way of peace, the way of gratitude. It is the way of praise and thanks for the protection and blessing of God.

January 6, The Epiphany of the Lord

Isaiah 60:1-6

The reading opens with a twofold summons: Arise! Shine! The feminine form of the verbs suggests that the city of Jerusalem is being addressed. Although it had been downtrodden and enshrouded in darkness, it is now called out of this desperate state. The illumination into which it emerges is not merely the light of a new day, a new era of peace and prosperity. It is the very light of God; it is the glory of the LORD. This expression usually refers to some kind of theophany, some kind of manifestation of divine majesty. The oracle that follows the summons suggests the divine majesty that is revealed is the restoration of Zion/Jerusalem.

The assertion that Jerusalem enjoys the light of divine glory while everyone else is wrapped in a darkness that covers the entire earth (v. 2) is reminiscent of one of the plagues that befell Egypt when the pharaoh refused to release God's people from their confinement in that land (Exod 10:21-23). Certainly the allusion was not lost on those for whom this prophetic announcement was intended. The privilege Israel enjoyed in the first instance and the benefits this privilege afforded them serve here as incentive for relying on God's continued care of Israel.

This prophet states again and again that other nations will witness the glory of the LORD as it is revealed through the salvation of Israel (cf. 40:5; 52:10; 61:11; 62:11). Here the prophet makes the same claim (v. 3). The light Jerusalem provides for others is really the radiance of God's glory, and that glory is the manifestation of its deliverance. Thus Jerusalem's redemption enables others to behold and to walk in God's light. It is now the messenger of good news for others. This is why Jerusalem is summoned: "Rise up in splendor!"

Jerusalem is not only delivered from its misfortune by God, it is reestablished as a thriving city. Its dispersed inhabitants return; its destroyed reputation is restored; its despoiled prosperity is reconstituted (vv. 4-5). This is not a promise to be fulfilled in the future; Jerusalem's salvation is an accomplished fact. It is happening before its very eyes. The major centers of wealth and wisdom once again send their wares to Jerusalem. The wealth from land and sea pours into the city. Such good fortune is evidence of God's favor. This is another reason the city is summoned: "Rise up in splendor!"

Psalm 72:1-2, 7-8, 10-11, 12-13

In this royal hymn the psalmist is asking God to bless the king so the king in turn can bless the people. Ancient monarchs exercised incredible control over the lives of their subjects. Despite the scope and depth of this influence, the authority described here is not unregulated. Rather, it is under the jurisdiction of God.

The psalmist begins with a prayer, asking God that the king be given a share in God's own justice (vv. 1-2). This is the same justice with which God governs the world and all of the people in it. It is the justice that gives birth to harmony and to the peace (v. 7) that embodies complete well-being. This justice will enable the king to govern in a way that will provide the people with the peace and well-being God wills for them.

These people are explicitly identified as belonging to God, presumably the people of the covenant. Thus this is no ordinary king; he is one who has been placed over the covenanted people to rule them as God would, in justice and righteousness. The test of the character of the royal rule is the care given to the most vulnerable of the society, the poor. The psalmist asks God to grant righteousness to the king so he can protect the defenseless and guarantee for them a share in the prosperity of the nation.

The psalmist turns to the rule of the king itself (v. 7). He prays first for its steadfastness: may it last forever, until the moon is no more. It is not the reign itself that is the object of his prayer but the righteousness of the reign. Since it is really God's righteousness, he prays that it will take root and flourish throughout the rule of this particular king and that it will even outlast him, enduring along with peace until the end of time.

The psalmist next prays that this rule of justice be extended to include the entire world and all the nations within it (vv. 8, 10-11). Since the sea frequently symbolized chaos (cf. Ps 89:9-10), the expression "from sea to sea" (v. 8a) delineates the inhabitable land that lies securely and thrives peacefully within the boundaries of chaotic waters. "The River" (v. 8b) suggests a specific waterway that marks a land stretching to the end of the earth. Both of these sweeping images sketch a reign that encompasses all the world.

The kingdoms listed provide a specific profile of this universal rule (vv. 10-11). Tarshish is thought to have been a Phoenician commercial center in southern Spain; Sheba was in southern Arabia; Seba was a royal Ethiopian city in southern Egypt. If "the River" refers to the Euphrates, these sites trace the outline of the ancient Near Eastern world. The cities not only provide the borders of the reign of righteousness, they also signify its good fortune. They are all well established, flourishing, internationally respected centers of commerce and trade. If they are the outposts of this remarkable kingdom, how successful its center must be!

The reading ends with a picture of righteousness in action (vv. 12-13). If the test of justice is the solicitude shown the needy, the prayer of the psalmist has been answered. The kingdom is rooted in the righteousness of God, and the most vulnerable in the society have an advocate in the king.

Ephesians 3:2-3a, 5-6

The preaching of the gospel is the major focus of this reading. However, there are four significant themes connected with it and interwoven in the passage: ministry or commission; revelation; mystery; co-heir.

Oikonomía (ministry) comes from two Greek words: *oíkos,* meaning "house," and *nomós,* meaning "law." It means "law of the house." The word itself might be better translated "administration" or "management." This is because "ministry" has too often been understood as "works" rather than deputized responsibility for some aspect of the household, as is the meaning here. In this reading the *oikonomía* was assigned directly by God, thus making the writer of the letter both responsible for the believers and accountable to God.

The gospel message the author preached, specifically that in Christ the Gentiles are co-heirs, co-members, and co-partners with the Jews (v. 6), had been revealed to him by God. This is an important point, for within the early Church the gospel message was usually handed down from one member to another (cf. 1 Cor 11:23). It may be that new insights into God's plan were considered new revelations, and it might have been necessary to regard them in this way for them to be deemed genuine.

According to the author the status of the Gentiles had to be revealed because it had been secret until now (cf. Col 1:25-26). The apostles and prophets, to whom the Spirit revealed this message, constitute the foundation of the Church (cf. Eph 2:20). In other words, it is through this appointed messenger that the Spirit has revealed a new revelation to the established Church. The message of the new revelation is this: in Christ the Gentiles are co-heirs, co-members, and co-partners with the Jews.

Since what qualifies one as an heir is life in the Spirit of Christ and not natural generation into a particular national group, there is no obstacle in the path of Gentile incorporation. The body to which all belong is the body of Christ, not the bloodline of Abraham. The promise at the heart of gospel preaching is the promise of universal salvation through Christ, not of descendants and prosperity in a particular land. This is a radical insight for a church with Jewish roots and traditions.

The early Church may have cherished the hope and conviction of universality, but it had to rethink what this might mean. The message of this passage claims the Gentiles are co-heirs precisely as Gentiles and not as initiates who have come to Christ through the faith of Israel. This new revelation does not demean the importance of the Jewish faith for Jewish Christians. It respects it but does not insist upon it as a prerequisite for admission into the Church. The one thing necessary is to be "in Christ."

Matthew 2:1-12

As we near the end of the Christmas season we read another popular Christmas story: the three kings, or three wise men. Actually, they were astrologers, men who studied the heavenly bodies and there discovered the meaning of human life on earth. The account is a kind of *haggadah,* a Jewish story fashioned from diverse biblical material intended to make a theological point. This does not mean the story is not true. Rather, the truth of it is more in the total story and its meaning than in any or all of its details.

The story itself has developed a *haggadah* through which we now understand it. For example, the text says there were three gifts, not three men. It identifies the three gifts but does not relate gold with kingship, frankincense with divinity, or myrrh with suffering. It does not name them (Caspar, Balthasar, and Melchior), nor does it say that one was black. All of this is haggadic addition.

Modern astrologers tell us that there actually was an unusual astral phenomenon around this time. It is likely the author of this account provided a theological explanation of it. The story itself is dependent on elements from several earlier biblical traditions: the fourth oracle of Balaam the Moabite speaks of a star rising out of Jacob (Num 24:17); a reference to the kings of Tarshish, Sheba, and Seba, who render tribute and bring gifts (Ps 72:10-11); the promise that gold and frankincense will be brought on camels from Midian and Ephah and Sheba to Jerusalem (Isa 60:6).

Lest the astrological details lead us to believe this is a myth, the author situates the events squarely in time and place: the reign of Herod, Bethlehem and Jerusalem. Since they believed astral marvels frequently accompanied the birth of great kings, it is understandable the astrologers would go straight to the Judean king. The entire royal establishment (all Jerusalem) were frightened by news of this birth, for the child would be a potential rival. The learned of the court (chief priests and scribes) knew where to find the child. They relied on the prophetic message to tell them where to look, but they rejected its identification of the child as a legitimate ruler. Knowing the tradition is no guarantee of loyalty to it.

The report of the astrologers' veneration of the child is brief, yet stirring. The star actually led them to where he was. Finding him, they prostrated themselves before him and paid him homage. The text does not say they honored Herod in this way, so this should not be seen as tribute for a king. This is probably the kind of veneration they reserved for a god. The astrologers were adept at discerning truth. They read the astral signs, they recognized the true identity of the child, and they understood a message in a dream that told them to return home another way.

These anonymous men come out of obscurity and they return to obscurity. All we know is that they were not Israelite, and this is the whole point of the story. It illustrates that people of goodwill, regardless of their ethnic or religious background, are responsive to the revelation of God. Their openness brought the astrologers to the child, and they did not go away disappointed. This child draws Jew and Gentile alike.

Themes of the Day

The Christmas season reaches an apex on the Solemnity of the Epiphany. Traditionally known in many parts of the world as Little Christmas, it is a commemoration of the manifestation of God to all the nations. In some liturgical traditions this feast is the central celebration of Christmas. It commemorates not only the birth of Christ and the visit of the Magi but also his baptism in the Jordan and the manifestation of his glory at the wedding feast of Cana. In the Roman Catholic tradition the focus is on the first of these commemorations: the visit of the Magi and the implications of that visit for the glorious manifestation of God to all the peoples of the world. The readings for this solemnity develop the importance of this manifestation. Three themes dominate: Jerusalem is the source of light for the nations; Christ is the revelation of God to all the nations; new relationships are established in Christ between Jew and Gentile.

Jerusalem Is the Source of Light

There is a wonderful summons to alertness and presence of mind and heart, a call for all the nations to witness the marvelous works of God, which shine as light in the midst of the surrounding darkness. This is no ordinary light. It is a light that has God's Holy City Jerusalem as its source. The people of Israel have enjoyed the radiance of God's glory and are now set as a beacon for the nations. All the ends of the earth can witness the wonder of God's light in the midst of the city, its people, its rulers, and its way of life.

The light of God is known in the ways in which the most vulnerable in the city are cared for and acknowledged. In just action and righteousness the city becomes the beacon of God, and all the nations are attracted by this light. The quality of the light leads the way through the darkness and sustains the world in goodness and peace.

Christ as Light to the Nations

Led by a star, the astrologers come in search of the infant king. They have been attentive to the marvels of the universe, and there they have read signs in the heavens. They represent all who search for truth in the wonders of creation and in the wisdom of their own cultures of origin. Because they searched with eyes of faith they were able to recognize the gift of God when they found him, even though he did not conform to their initial perception of a royal heir.

They came from the far corners of the earth, Gentiles who followed the light and who found the new king whose reign would bring justice and righteousness into human affairs. They returned home, enlightened by their visit to God's place of revelation. Their encounter shows that in Christ the light of God is given to all people of goodwill, Jew and non-Jew alike.

The New Relationships Between Jew and Gentile

The manifestation of God among us changes the ways we perceive one another. Christ's birth provides us with the light by which we see a new criterion for relating. The Magi who come in faith to worship the child represent the multi-ethnic and cultural diversity in civic and parish situations, as well as the many religions of the world. To us who are related no longer merely by blood affiliation or national origin, Christ offers the Spirit of holiness as the ground for our relationships. This new universal belonging will be manifest in the community of believers who live no longer in darkness or exclusivity and sin but by a new dispensation of grace. All people, regardless of race or ethnic origin, can be co-heirs with Christ.

Sunday After January 6, The Baptism of the Lord
Isaiah 42:1-4, 6-7

This is the first of four passages (49:1-6; 50:4-9; 52:13–53:12) traditionally known as the Servant Songs. They constitute a unique set of poems that identify a mysterious figure who acts as a pious agent of God's compassionate care. Presumably it is God who speaks, and it is God who singles out this servant and gives him a special function to perform within the community. The uniqueness of this person can be seen in the title bestowed on him by God: "my servant." Very few people were so called by God: Abraham (Gen 26:24); Moses (Num 12:7); Caleb (Num 14:24); Job (Job 1:8). The one most frequently referred to in this way was David (2 Sam 3:8). The parallel construction in the first verse further identifies the servant as someone chosen by God and with whom God is pleased.

Most significant in this description of the servant is his having been endowed with God's own spirit. Earlier Israelite leaders were thought to have been seized by the spirit: judges (Judg 6:34; 11:29, 32; 14:19); kings (1 Sam 16:13); prophets (Mic 3:8; Ezek 11:5). Those who received the spirit were thus empowered to act within the community in some unique fashion. The particular needs of the community determined the character of this action. God's saving power was brought to the community through the agency of various individuals. The servant in this song has received the spirit of the LORD in order to bring forth justice to the nations.

The manner in which this justice is executed is extraordinary (vv. 2-4). It is not harsh and exacting, making a public pronouncement of God's judgment of Israel. Instead, it is gentle and understanding, willing to wait for the establishment of God's universal rule. This justice will not compound the distress of an already suffering people. Rather, it will be a source of consolation.

God speaks again, this time directly to the servant (vv. 6-7), indicating the role the servant is to play in the life of the community. The verbs all reveal the deliberateness of God's choice: "I called you; I grasped you; I formed you and set you." The mission of the servant is clearly determined by God, not by the servant himself. The parallelism between "covenant of the people" and "light for the nations" suggests that "covenant" is to be understood in a general sense, underscoring the universalism referred to elsewhere (vv. 1, 4), rather than in the exclusive sense usually associated with biblical covenant.

The responsibilities that flow from the servant's election are aspects of the commission to bring forth justice (vv. 1, 6). Although these tasks single out specific situations of human suffering, they probably stand for any form of darkness and confinement. Several themes converge here. The servant is called to bring forth justice to the nations and to be a light to the nations. This light will open the eyes of those relegated to the darkness of confinement. Most likely, the reference here is not to the release of Israelites but of those outside the believing community. The passage describes the deliverance of the whole world, not the rescue of Israel from its particular bondage. The universalism here cannot be denied.

Psalm 29:1-2, 3-4, 3, 9-10

This hymn of praise describes the LORD as sovereign over the heavens and the earth. It begins with a call to praise (vv. 1-2). Unlike most psalms of this kind, this call is addressed to heavenly, not human, beings. The scene is the celestial court with the divine council (the Hebrew reads "sons of God") assembled (cf. Job 1:6; 2:1). They are there in attendance, and they are called on to render honor to God. The imperative verb form indicates this is not an invitation; it is a command. These heavenly beings are charged to sing praise to God's glory and might.

The glory of God usually refers to some kind of divine manifestation. The psalmist declares that this glory is revealed in God's name. Traditional people believe there is power in a person's name, since the name embodies part of that person's very essence. How much more is this the case with the name of God! The great respect in which God's name was held explains why the people of Israel were forbidden to pronounce it. The psalm reports that this wondrous name was revered in heaven as well as on earth. The entire council is enjoined to pay homage to God, who is revealed as sovereign.

God's sovereignty is further manifested in the power God exercises over the forces of nature (vv. 3-4, 9-10). The voice of the LORD thunders over the waters (v. 3). This is a description of the mighty storm god, whose voice is the thunder itself, who in the beginning conquered the forces of chaos characterized as ruthless, destructive water. Although the characterization within the psalm suggests that God acts as a mighty warrior, the imagery paints a slightly different picture. According to this psalm God did not need a heavenly army to quell the chaotic waters. God's commanding voice was powerful enough. As in the first account of creation (Gen 1:1–2:4a), God's voice is itself creative power and divine splendor (v. 4).

God thunders. While this may appear to be a demonstration of the devastating power of God's voice, the context of the psalm reminds us that its focus is God's superiority over the forces of destruction. This verse is a reminder that the power of God's word can be felt both in heaven and on earth. In calling the heavenly beings to praise God, the psalmist is calling them to acknowledge all of these marvels.

The last scene brings us back to the divine council, to the heavenly temple and the throne of God. (vv. 9c-10). All who are present praise God with joyous acclamation: "Glory!" There God sits triumphant above the floodwaters. (The only other place in the Bible where the word "flood" is found is in the Genesis account [7:17]). The scene is majestic. God's thunderous voice has silenced the forces of chaos, and now God reigns supreme forever as king of heaven and earth.

Acts 10:34-38

The scene is the house of Cornelius, a newly converted Roman centurion. Normally an observant Jew like Peter would not enter the home of a Gentile. The first words of his discourse ("In truth, I see") indicate he was not always open to association with Gentiles as he is now. It was a newly gained insight about

God that changed his view of those who did not have Jewish ancestry. He realized that "God shows no partiality" (vv. 34-35; cf. Deut 10:17; 2 Chr 19:7) and therefore, neither should he. All are acceptable to God, Jew and Gentile alike.

According to Peter, God's message of peace was given initially to Israel, but this does not cancel that fact that it is meant for all. Inclusivity is the centerpiece of this reading. God shows no partiality, and Christ is Lord of all. Not even Peter, who knew the historical Jesus intimately and should have understood the implications of the message he preached and the example he gave, originally understood the radical nature of this gospel. But now he can testify that it is truly good news of peace.

Peter presumed that although they were Gentiles, they were living in Judea, so his audience would have heard something about the life and ministry of Jesus, if only in the form of gossip. As a Roman centurion stationed in this small country, Cornelius certainly must have known something, for his station would have required that he be informed of anything that might threaten the "Roman Peace." Mention of Jesus' baptism by John (v. 37) would have called to mind another disturber of the peace. Even though John was an irritant to the Jewish leadership, the unrest he caused would have been known to the Roman officials.

Although each of these incidents had a political side, this does not seem to have been Peter's motivation for referring to them. It seems, instead, that he was recalling incidents that manifested the power evident in the ministry of Jesus and the universal scope of that ministry.

The power of Jesus' ministry flowed from his having been anointed by God with the Holy Spirit. This reference to anointing is probably an allusion to his baptism, when the heavens opened and the Spirit descended upon him (Luke 3:21-22; 4:14, 18; cf. Isa 61:1). It was in and through this power that he had performed such miracles as releasing those who were in the grip of the devil. Peter makes a point of this last particular miracle, probably because those possessed by demons were considered the most unclean of the unclean. Despite this, Jesus did not relegate them to the margins of society as the self-righteous purists might have done. He touched them; he healed them. Like Jesus, Peter was now moving in circumstances (contact with Gentiles) that were considered by some as unclean. Like Jesus, he disregarded such a judgment, and he refused to conform to such a manner of estrangement. Peter was convinced that with God there is no partiality.

Luke 3:15-16, 21-22

The gospel reading consists of two distinct but related incidents. In the first John disavows that he is the Christ. The second is a report of extraordinary circumstances that followed Jesus' own baptism by John. The two incidents seem to be connected by the significance of the Spirit.

The expectation that filled the people was eschatological; they were looking for the Christ, the "anointed one." In a threefold manner John contrasts himself with the one who is to come, lest the people mistake him for this Christ. First he contrasts their respective baptisms. His baptism with water was a ritual of repentance and cleansing. The Christ's baptism of the Spirit and fire will transform and purge, thus making his coming a time of judgment, when the wicked will be separated like chaff from the wheat and thrown into the fire. It seems that the harvest has already occurred; the time of judgment is at hand.

John further admits that the one to come is mightier than he and far superior to himself. He insists that he himself is not worthy to undo the sandals of that long-awaited one. This menial task was even below the dignity of a Hebrew slave, although disciples were known to show their respect for their teachers in this way. There are no illusions in this austere man of the wilderness. Although he has caught the imagination of the hopeful people, he does not take advantage of this for self-aggrandizement.

It is clear that Jesus submitted himself to John's form of baptism, but there is no description of the actual event. Instead we have an account of what happened while Jesus was praying after the baptism had occurred. All of the verbs indicate the events happened *to* Jesus; they were not accomplished *by* him or *through* him. Jesus was the recipient of these extraordinary events.

First, the heavens were opened. This suggests some kind of apocalyptic phenomenon (cf. Ezek 1:1). Here it is the prelude for the descent of the Spirit. John had declared that the one to come would baptize with the Spirit. Before Jesus embarks on his ministry the Spirit descends upon him. This is not to suggest that in this way Jesus was filled with the Spirit, which does not seem to have been necessary. However, there is no question that Jesus is somehow intimately associated with the Holy Spirit. The dovelike form the Spirit takes is puzzling. Some commentators believe this gentle symbol is meant to counter the fierceness of the accompanying purifying fire, but there is nothing in the text to warrant this conjecture.

The trinitarian scene is completed with the voice from heaven, which identifies Jesus as "Son." The words spoken combine an allusion to the servant of the Lord (cf. Isa 42:10) and the enthronement of the king (cf. Ps 2:70), both passages rich with messianic significance. This episode has been considered by many as the divine commissioning of Jesus. As God's beloved Son he will baptize with the Spirit, thus bringing about the regeneration of the world.

Themes of the Day

This christological feast is the celebration of Jesus as the anointed servant of God. It brings to a close the Christmas season, which reveals who God is for us and who we are to be for others in Christ. The readings bring together various aspects of this mystery. Like a montage of snapshots, we are introduced to the image of the Isaian servant of God; we catch sight of Jesus, who fulfills the role of that servant; we see the fruits of Jesus' messiahship in the person of Cornelius; and we are brought to see the cosmic wonders of God's re-creative power revealed in this mystery.

The Baptism of Jesus

The baptism of Jesus inaugurates his ministry as the anointed one, or Messiah of God. The passage from Isaiah indicates the kind of Messiah God intends Jesus to be. He will not exercise harsh justice as a mighty judge would. Nor will he wield the sword of vengeance on the battlefield. The Messiah of God will be a servant, one who though mighty is gentle, one who is chosen by the high God yet committed to the needy and the marginal, one who is the proclaimed Son of God and who still attends to the least within the human community. The Messiah of God may have come from an insignificant village like Nazareth, but he was anointed with the Holy Spirit and with power. He taught those in the coastlands and healed those under the power of the devil. The Messiah of God does not conform to the expectations of a proud and self-absorbed society. Filled with the Spirit of God, the Messiah of God acts out of that gentle, compassionate Spirit.

For Whom Did He Come?

For whom did the Messiah of God come? For those whom the society discarded. He came for the people who were broken and suffering, for those who were blind, for those who were imprisoned. He came for people who are so easily pushed to the margins, beyond our view, where the circumstances of their lives will not trouble us—the homeless, the unemployed, the abandoned children, the helpless elderly, the mentally and chronically ill. He also came to people who, like Cornelius, do not belong to our inner circles, people who for any number of reasons threaten us, people we might actually despise. He came for the strangers among us, those who have different cultural customs, those who worship in different ways. He came for people we have pushed out as well as those we have refused to let in. The Messiah of God came for all people without distinction.

Cosmic Ramifications

While the psalm praises God the Creator, on this feast, joined with the other readings, it proclaims God's re-creative power. Through the servant in Isaiah,

God fashioned a new society, one of justice and compassion and healing and liberation. In Jesus the Messiah who came as a servant, the creative majesty of God is revealed in its premier form, and all creation is made new. Walls of enmity tumble, and all people are bound together in the peace of Christ. We who are baptized share in this new creation and in the messianic responsibility of declaring this good news to the coastlands. As disciples of Jesus the servant Messiah we continue the ministry he first took upon himself. Now it is through us that God re-creates society. Like Paul, we bring the good news of the gospel to all people. The Christmas season ends with us as participants in the servant messiahship of Jesus.

Optional Readings for the Baptism of the Lord
Isaiah 40:1-5, 9-11

The message of Deutero-Isaiah opens with the exclamation "Comfort my people" (40:1a). The plural form of the verb indicates that this imperative is addressed to more than one person, therefore the identity of the prophet is difficult to determine. The passage itself seems to be a kind of prophetic commissioning; God summons a group of people to speak God's own words of comfort. The phrases "my people" and "your God" are covenant language. They suggest that there still exists a covenant relationship between God and the people who have suffered.

The verbs "speak" and "proclaim" (v. 2) are also plural, most likely addressed to those called to comfort God's people. The Hebrew actually reads "speak to the heart." Since the heart was considered the organ of thought, the phrase means "convince Jerusalem" rather than "be tender toward her." But of what should Jerusalem be convinced? The first two verses suggest that the people of that suffering city had to be assured that they had indeed paid their debt and their suffering was now over. Perhaps they had to be convinced because there was no recognizable evidence to suggest—and so they did not readily believe—that their release was imminent.

The people are directed to act out their deliverance even before they see evidence of it. Some are told to prepare for the coming of their God by removing any obstacle that might prevent God's approach or obstruct the view of God's glory that onlookers might enjoy (vv. 3-5). The picture sketched here resembles the carefully repaired highway over which victorious kings or generals traveled in triumphant procession on their return home. The people who had suffered so long are told to prepare such a road, and upon its completion they will behold the glory of their triumphant God. There is an element of universalism here. Not only they but all humankind will see the glory of their

God. This wondrous display will be the first proof that they have finally been delivered from their suffering.

A second directive is given, this time to people within Jerusalem itself (vv. 9-11). The city, broken and depleted, is told to announce to the other vanquished cities of Judah the approach of this triumphal procession. The message they are to proclaim is not theirs; it is dictated to them. They are to be heralds of good news. They are to announce that the mighty, victorious God is coming. Though just, God comes with the solicitude of a shepherd. This is the good news of deliverance, and the people are urged to believe this message is true.

The builders of the highway are told to make God's approach possible; the citizens of Jerusalem are told to announce to others the good news of this approach. The highway builders are to complete their work before they see the glory of the LORD; the people in the city are to herald a procession they themselves have not yet witnessed. In both cases the people are directed to act out their release even before they have tangible evidence of it. What they have is the word of the prophet, whose message employs verb forms that suggest that future events are already accomplished in the present. The people's faith in this word is itself the strongest evidence of their deliverance.

Psalm 104:1b-2, 3-4, 24-25, 27-28, 29-30

The nature hymn, from which the psalm response is taken, is remarkable in its depiction of God as the creator and sustainer of all life. It is clear that the psalmist is overwhelmed by the splendor of the universe. God is described as robed in majesty and glory, wrapped around with radiant light the way the commanding gods of the ancient Near East were depicted. The psalmist does not claim that God is visible but that God's garments are discernible. In other words, the splendor the psalmist beholds is an indication of God's presence. God is perceived through the glories of creation. In fact, this awesome experience of creation is itself a revelation of God.

The allusions to ancient creation mythology abound. After the warrior-god had defeated the forces of evil, a palace was constructed for him over the conquered and now tamed chaotic waters. He would travel across the sky with the clouds as his chariot and the winds as his messengers. This is precisely the scene appropriated and depicted here (vv. 3-4). Not only is God declared sovereign over all the forces of nature, but the presence of God is discerned in the movement of clouds and winds.

The natural world is marvelous in its appearance, diverse in its manifestations (v. 24). The variety and complexity of its forms are astounding. Even the sea, once thought to be threatening, is now the habitat of various forms of life (v. 25). These natural marvels are attributed to the wisdom of the Creator. In the biblical tradition there is an intrinsic link between creation and wisdom (cf. Prov 8:22-31; Wis 9:9). Wisdom was understood as insight into, harmony with, or power over the orders of reality. These orders were established by God at the time of creation, and they are sustained by the same divine creative power.

God is extolled as the one who cares for all living things. All creatures look to God for sustenance. Creation is not a static act, completed once for all in the distant past. It is experienced as an ongoing event. The act of creation and power of the Creator are perceived in the constant renewal of life that unfolds before our eyes. In a very real sense creation is more than a primordial event, it is a personal experience.

The psalm insists that the life forces of the natural world do not operate in a manner independent of the divine will. None of this happens haphazardly, nor is there any struggle between God and the forces of nature. All of nature serves God's designs. God sustains life by providing food, but God can also bring on death by taking back the breath of life. When this happens the creature returns to the dust from which it was initially taken (cf. Gen 2:7; Job 12:10). God is both the original Creator and the one who continues to control the forces of nature.

Finally, God not only creates but re-creates as well. The word for "spirit" *(rûah)* is the same as that found in the story of creation, where a mighty wind swept over the waters (Gen 1:2). That was the first creation. The psalm claims that the spirit can also bring about a new creation.

Titus 2:11-14; 3:4-7

This reading from one of the Pastoral Epistles contains a confession of faith in the saving grace of God. The verb "appeared" is testimony to divine revelation. God's grace, in the form of salvation, is no longer something for which the people wait; it is an accomplished fact. Furthermore, salvation is not merely for an elect group, whether Jewish or Christian, it is for all humans (*ánthrōpois*, v. 11).

This grace, or good favor, takes the form of salvation, a theological concept with profound Jewish and Hellenistic connotations. In Jewish thought salvation was seen as rescue from the perils of life, and it was accomplished by God. In the Hellenistic mystery religions, which were so prominent at the time of the writing of this letter, the initiates shared in the mythical divine being's victory over death, and they were thereby assured a share in blissful life in the hereafter. In this particular passage the concept of salvation includes aspects of both views. It is because they have been saved from the perils of evil that the Christians have been empowered to live lives of moral integrity in this world. On the other hand, their salvation has come to them through the sacrifice of Christ Jesus, and they still await a future divine manifestation.

God's saving grace imparts the kind of training necessary to combat the forces of a godless world and to live truly Christian lives (v. 12). Virtuous living is evidence that the age of fulfillment has indeed arrived. However, this indication of realized eschatology does not erase the expectation of a future eschatology. Christians live an already-but-not-yet existence. Their moral lives are both signs of, and expectation of, the final fulfillment.

The grace of salvation has been achieved through the sacrifice of Christ Jesus. The Pastoral Epistles generally identify God as the savior of all. The Greek in this passage is awkward. It reads: "great God and savior of our Jesus Christ" (v. 13). It is only in translations that Jesus is identified as the Savior. Whatever version is chosen, the intimate relationship between God and Christ is obvious, and that is the point of the reading.

The second part of the reading is really a single sentence in Greek (3:4-7). It is a kind of creedal formulation of soteriology, God's saving grace given to us though Christ. This grace manifested itself through kindness *(chrēstos)* and generous love *(philanthrōpia),* the kind of love one has toward someone in need. Salvation is the central theme of the declaration. The rest of the sentence explores aspects of God's saving grace. Mercy, not righteous deeds, is the basis of this grace. Rebirth, renewal, and justification are its effects. Hope of eternal life is its goal.

The bath of rebirth or renewal *(palingenesía)* may be a reference to baptism. However, since it suggests that it is baptism that saves and not the mercy of God, the washing may here be merely a symbol of the removal of sin rather than the means of accomplishing its removal.

Luke 3:15-16, 21-22

The gospel reading consists of two distinct but related incidents. In the first John the Baptist disavows that he is the Christ. The second is a report of extraordinary circumstances that followed Jesus' own baptism by John. The two incidents seem to be connected by the significance of the Spirit.

The expectation that filled the people was eschatological; they were looking for the Christ, the "anointed one." In a threefold manner John contrasts himself with the one who is to come, lest the people mistake him for this Christ. First he contrasts their respective baptisms. His baptism with water is a ritual of repentance and cleansing. The Christ's baptism of the Spirit and fire will transform and purge, thus making his coming a time of judgment, when the wicked will be separated like chaff from the wheat and thrown into the fire. It seems that the harvest has already occurred; the time of judgment is at hand.

John further admits that the one to come is mightier than he and far superior to himself. He insists that he himself is not worthy to undo the sandals of that long-awaited one. This menial task was even below the dignity of a Hebrew slave, although disciples were known to show their respect for their teachers in this way. There are no illusions in this austere man of the wilderness.

Although he has caught the imagination of the hopeful people, he does not take advantage of this for self-aggrandizement.

It is clear that Jesus submitted himself to John's form of baptism, but there is no description of the actual event. Instead we have an account of what happened while Jesus was praying after the baptism had occurred. All the verbs indicate that the events happened *to* Jesus; they were not accomplished *by* him or *through* him. Jesus was the recipient of these extraordinary events.

First, the heavens were opened. This suggests some kind of apocalyptic phenomenon (cf. Ezek 1:1). Here it is the prelude for the descent of the Spirit. John had declared that the one to come would baptize with the Spirit. Before Jesus embarks on his ministry, the Spirit descends upon him. This is not to suggest that in this way Jesus was filled with the Spirit, which does not seem to have been necessary. However, there is no question that Jesus is somehow intimately associated with the Holy Spirit. The dovelike form the Spirit takes is puzzling. Some commentators believe this gentle symbol is meant to counter the fierceness of the accompanying purifying fire, but there is nothing in the text to warrant this conjecture.

The trinitarian scene is completed with the voice from heaven, which identifies Jesus as "Son." The words spoken combine an allusion to the "servant of the Lord" (cf. Isa 42:10) and the enthronement of the king (cf. Ps 2:70), both passages rich with messianic significance. This episode has been considered by many as the divine commissioning of Jesus. As God's beloved Son he will baptize with the Spirit, thus bringing about the regeneration of the world.

Themes of the Day

The Close of the Christmas Season

The optional readings for this feast recapitulate the themes of the entire Advent-Christmas season. Within the Christian tradition the voice that announces the future events is associated with John the Baptist. However, the reading itself proclaims the coming and manifestation of the LORD, clearly an Advent theme. The gospel reading from Luke moves us from anticipation of the coming of the Messiah to fulfillment of God's promise. This theme of fulfillment is at the heart of the Christmas message. In the baptism narrative we see that Jesus has come into our midst, not only as a helpless infant but as our anointed Messiah. There is a dimension of this same gospel reading that opens us to a future yet to be fully realized in our lives. The one upon whom the Spirit descends has come to baptize us in that same Spirit.

The reading from Titus is similar to the gospel in that it too both heralds the appearance of Jesus and promises a future fulfillment for us. Renewed by the Spirit, we will be justified and become heirs in hope of eternal life. The readings clearly announce that the LORD is coming; the Lord has come; the Lord will continue to come to and through us into the whole world.

Under all this rings the melody of God's creative power, as seen in the psalm response. Though a hymn that praises God's creative and sustaining power in nature, placed alongside the readings for this feast they take on another meaning. In view of the Isaian passage, God promises to create something new in the wilderness of chaos. There the glory of the LORD will be revealed. As the readings from Luke and Titus reveal, this glory has appeared not only in the marvels of the natural world but in an even greater marvel, the incarnation of God into this natural world. Finally, through baptism in the Spirit that was sent forth, we are saved in the bath of rebirth, and through us the face of the entire earth will be renewed.

(For further reflection, please refer to the themes for the primary set of readings for this feast.)

Lent

First Sunday Deuteronomy 26:4-10 Confession of faith	Psalm 91:1-2, 10-15 Be with me	Romans 10:8-13 Confession of faith	Luke 4:1-13 Led by the Spirit
Second Sunday Genesis 15:5-12, 17-18 A covenant with Abraham	Psalm 27:1, 7-9, 13-14 My light and salvation	Philippians 3:17–4:1 Changed into Christ	Luke 9:28b-36 Jesus is transfigured
Third Sunday Exodus 3:1-8a, 13-15 "I am who am"	Psalm 103:1-4, 6-8, 11 The LORD is kind	1 Corinthians 10:1-6, 10-12 The past is an example for us	Luke 13:1-9 Repent or perish
Fourth Sunday Joshua 5:9a, 10-12 The first Passover in the land	Psalm 34:2-7 Taste and see	2 Corinthians 5:17-21 Reconciled through Christ	Luke 15:1-3, 11-32 The prodigal son
Fifth Sunday Isaiah 43:16-21 A way through the wilderness	Psalm 126:1-6 The LORD has done great things	Philippians 3:8-14 All is loss but Christ	John 8:1-11 Neither do I condemn you
Palm Sunday of the Lord's Passion Isaiah 50:4-7 I gave my back for beating	Psalm 22:8-9, 17-20, 23-24 Why have you abandoned me?	Philippians 2:6-11 Christ humbled himself	Luke 22:14–23:56 Passion of the Lord

Lent

Initial Reading of the Lent Lectionary

Introduction

The comprehensive lenten Sundays' readings can be viewed as a theological matrix serving as a source for an interpretation of the readings of the individual Sundays and a key for an appreciation of the lenten season itself. The matrix presented is based on the patterns of meanings offered in the literary forms and the content of the readings themselves. Read in columns beginning with the First Sunday of Lent and concluding with Palm Sunday, the lections provide an overview of the meaning of the entire lenten season.

First Testament Readings

The first readings for the season of Lent provide us with a family photo album of important moments in the religious history of ancient Israel. The first picture is a composite. With very little detail it sketches Israel's origins in Aram (ancient Syria), its oppression in Egypt, its deliverance from bondage, and its entrance into the land of promise. The picture is framed with symbols of cultic celebration. The language is in the form of liturgical speech, and the picture itself is part of a harvest festival. It is an interactive picture; the one who reads it as a prayer is invited into the drama it captures.

The next two pictures reveal the depth of intimacy that exists between God and the people chosen by God. The first shows God calling one of our early ancestors, making very personal promises to him and forging a pact that sets him and all of his descendants apart. In the second picture God makes new promises to a later generation. In both instances it is God who takes the initiative. Extraordinary natural occurrences are included in both pictures. What is striking about these family pictures is the absence of women and children. Although they were obviously included in the marvelous deeds performed by God, the one who took the pictures seemed interested in only the men of the family.

Given all of the promises made by God, one would think this people would be spared devastating hardship. Such was not the case. There was intolerable servitude in Egypt and a period of exile in Babylon. Even though the people had to endure calamity, the loving care of God finally brought them out of each agonizing experience. The two snapshots are taken from these periods of deliverance and reestablishment. They both depict the joyful celebration of new beginnings; the first is more historical in character, the second is imagistic. All together, the album contains pictures of God's loving providence over a very needy people, creating for us the first composite lenten theme.

The final snapshot is jarring. It is the picture of a pious man who suffers at the hands of others. As with all the readings used on Palm Sunday, it prepares us for the sacred events we will celebrate in the ensuing days.

Psalms

The responsorial psalms furnish us with a second composite lenten theme. They move us from prayers of trust (First and Second Sundays), to thanksgiving (Third and Fourth Sundays), back to confidence (Fifth Sunday). Appropriately, the psalm used on Palm Sunday is a lament. The trust found in the first psalms is based both on God's power to defend and God's protecting presence. This trust is confirmed through an oracle of salvation in the first and praise of the goodness of God in the second. As we move to the Third Sunday we see that the trust was well founded, for the psalmist is filled with thanksgiving for the goodness of God shown to the people, specifically at the time of Moses, but more generally, at all times.

The lenten psalms (excluding the one for Palm Sunday) end on a note of confidence. In the midst of the calamitous experience of the destruction of the Temple, the end of cultic worship, and the devastation of the land of promise, there is the belief that God has not ultimately abandoned the people. The future will witness a reversal of fortune. We may regard Lent itself as a season of suffering and penance, but the repentance to which we commit ourselves will open us to a new life of promise. As with the other readings for Psalm Sunday, the psalm of the day—a lament—looks toward the passion of Jesus.

Epistles

The christological character of the epistles for Lent is prominent. In each one of them and in all of them together, Paul declares both the central role Christ plays in the salvation of the world and the total commitment this calls forth in Paul as well as in all others. This centrality is the principal theme of the First Sunday, and it sets the tone for all of the following Sundays. It is important to note that here centrality also incorporates the aspect of universality. This particular aspect is repeated on the Second Sunday, when we hear that all things will be made subject to Jesus Christ. Even events of the past occurred with an eye to Christ, as we read on the Third Sunday. We are exhorted to learn from those past events in order to be faithful to our commitment to Christ in the present and in the future.

Sin has separated us from God, but Christ has reversed this alienation, reconciling us to God. The old things have passed away; we are now a new creation (Fourth Sunday). The epistle for the Fifth Sunday brings all of these themes together. Because Christ is central to salvation, because salvation is universal, because God's action in the past provides us with examples for present commitment, and because Christ has reconciled us with God, we must commit ourselves wholeheartedly to Christ, being willing to turn our backs on all else if need be. The epistle for Palm Sunday places Christ before us as an example to follow. Taken together, these readings provide us with insights into the workings of salvation and with an explanation of why it operates the way it does and how we can enter into it.

Gospels

The gospel readings begin with a look at the paradoxical nature of Jesus' ministry. In the account of his temptations in the wilderness we get a glimpse of the struggles that may have accompanied him throughout his entire ministry. In contrast to this, the story of the transfiguration shows him radiant in glory. Although the shadow of death does raise its head at this time, the mystical experience assures the disciples, and us, that the drama of Jesus' life and death will end with resurrection.

The next three gospel accounts contain material intended for purposes of instruction. Jesus uses current events, events with which his audience would be familiar, to impress upon them the urgent need to be prepared at all times for death. He insists that if they do not heed this warning they risk the same shocking fate suffered by those who lost their lives (Third Sunday).

We are then treated to two stories of sinners who were snatched from terrible fates by the compassion and mercy of God. Both the prodigal son and the woman taken in adultery were guilty of sin; both stood humbly before the one who could inflict dire consequences upon them; both were treated instead with respect and kindness. It is this type of behavior that distinguished the kind of Messiah Jesus chose to be (First Sunday); it is this kind of behavior that revealed the glory that Jesus possessed (Second Sunday). Put simply, the lenten themes found in the gospel readings can be summarized as follows: suffering and glory; sin and reconciliation with God. The gospel for Palm Sunday is the passion of Jesus.

Mosaic of Readings

This mosaic of readings shows that Lent is a time to review the history of God's workings in human history. It begins with a composite of pictures showing God's loving providence. Reflecting on events such as these can only elicit sentiments of confidence and thanksgiving as found in the psalms. In the epistles we see the central role Jesus plays in the drama of salvation, and in the gospels we behold both suffering and glory, sin and reconciliation with God. The passion of Jesus, as terrifying as it was, reveals to us the depth of God's providence, the reason for our trust, and the efficacy of Jesus' sacrifice.

Readings

First Sunday of Lent

Deuteronomy 26:4-10

This passage contains one of the most important creedal statements found in the Pentateuch (cf. Deut 6:20-24; Josh 24:2b-13). The text indicates that this profession of faith was part of the Israelite celebration of First Fruits (vv. 4, 10; cf. Deut 14:22-29).The offering of the first fruits of the harvest acknowledged that the land itself was a gift from God. The cultic celebration described here consisted of both action (the offering of the basket containing the produce) and the recitation of the saving acts of God on behalf of the people. This passage describes Moses instructing the Israelites for the future observance of this festival. Since these directives come from Moses, the spokesperson of God, they have Mosaic and, therefore, divine legitimation.

Moses' exhortation (v. 5) contains a fixed pair of Hebrew verbs ("declare," *ʿānâ*; and "say," *ʾāmar*), which comprise a solemn declaration used in legal or cultic contexts. The creedal statement itself is an enumeration of the saving events that shaped Israel's faith. It includes an admission of its humble beginnings; a report of its oppression in Egypt; a testimony to its deliverance by God; an acknowledgment of God's gift of the land to them. This brief account covers three distinct periods in the history of the people: the age of the ancestors; the time of the deliverance from bondage; the period of the entrance into the land. The events sketch the story found in Genesis through Joshua. There is a noticeable change in language from third person (v. 5) to first person (vv. 6-9). This use of language and the fact that the various events were experienced by different people demonstrate how liturgical celebrations fuse the present community with the past.

The "wandering Aramean" is probably a reference to Jacob, who eventually becomes the father of the twelve tribes. The ethnic bias is clear in this designation. Not only was the ancestor not a Canaanite, but the tradition tells us that both Isaac and Jacob married Aramean women so the bloodline would be pure (cf. Gen 25:20; 28:1-2). The promise may have been handed down from father to son, but it was not the son of a Canaanite woman. The word for "wandering" *('ōbēd)* does not mean nomadic meandering but suggests being lost or being about to perish (cf. Jer 50:6; Job 4:11). It should be noted that it was when Jacob was most vulnerable in Egypt that he became a great nation. This is Israel's way of proclaiming that it was through the goodness of God that it survived and flourished.

Mention of the ancestor seems to be historical remembrance, but it is with the people who were in bondage that those reciting this creed most strongly identified themselves. They too suffered oppression; they too were delivered by God's strong hand and outstretched arm; they too were brought into the fertile land. Therefore, they too must observe the obligations of the festival of First Fruits. "Strong hand and outstretched arm" is an image that depicts military strength. It implies that the God of Israel conquered the forces of Egypt on Egyptian soil in order to deliver the people. This is an unmistakable statement about the indisputable sovereignty of God. Finally, the centrality of land is clear. It was given *(nātan)* by God (v. 9), and the offering of its first fruits is the way of showing gratitude for all the mighty acts of God.

Psalm 91:1-2, 10-11, 12-13, 14-15

Although we do not have Psalm 91 in its entirety, the verses that make up the responsorial psalm for today do yield what appears to be a kind of cultic liturgy: the worshiper is addressed (vv. 1-2); there is a message of assurance (vv. 10-13); the psalm concludes with an oracle of salvation (vv. 14-16).

The first two verses clearly fit together. The worshiper is first called upon and then is told how to turn to God in trust. The addressee is a devout person, one who lives near a shrine or perhaps even the Temple. In Hebrew parallel construction this sacred place is called the "shelter of the Most High." The reference to the "shadow of the Almighty" calls to mind the outstretched wings of the cherubim statues that were erected at the entrance of ancient temples. These creatures acted as honor guards or mythological protectors.

Four divine titles are found in these two verses. God is called "the Most High" *('elyôn)*, the name ascribed to the deity worshiped in Jerusalem even before David conquered that ancient city (cf. Gen 14:18-22). This particular title is used when God is described as Creator of heaven and earth who governs the entire universe rather than as a local deity who exercised circumscribed jurisdiction. "Almighty," or Shaddai *(shadday)*, is a name associated with the early ancestors (cf. Gen 17:1; 28:3; 35:11; 43:14; 48:3). The context for most of the appearances of this name is covenant commitment. "LORD," or YHWH, is the personal name of the God of Israel. The name is derived from some form of the verb "to be" (cf. Exod 3:14). However, its exact translation remains shrouded in mystery. Finally, the generic term "God" (*'el*) is used. Though each of these titles has a slightly different meaning, together they sketch a picture of a victorious Creator who has deigned to enter into covenant with human beings.

In the oracle of assurance (vv. 10-13) the protection God will provide is described with dramatic imagery. Messenger angels (*mal'āk*) become guarding angels (cf. Exod 23:20; Ps 34:8) who will step into the most perilous situations and protect the worshiper from certain harm. The promise made here is extraordinary. People who go barefooted risk injuries just walking. Not only will the worshiper be preserved from such common dangers as stubbed toes or injured feet, but God's protection will make this person immune to the dangers of snakebite and the threat of devouring animals. Rather than be vulnerable to such dangers, the worshiper will be able to trample them underfoot. In this psalm the protection of God is not circumscribed by the confines of the shrine. Instead, God protects wherever the worshiper needs God's protection.

In the oracle of salvation that concludes the psalm (vv. 14-16) God promises to deliver the one who devoutly clings to God and glorifies God's name. In other words, if the worshiper is faithful to the covenant, God will be faithful as well. The mutuality of the commitment here is obvious. So is the basis of trust. The worshiper is invited to move from seeking security in things or places to trusting in God.

Romans 10:8-13

In this reading Paul incorporates three important themes. First, he stresses the singular importance of faith as the basis of salvation. Second, he reinterprets Scripture from a christological perspective. Third, he proclaims the universal character of salvation through Christ.

The essence of Paul's preaching is twofold: the centrality of Christ in the drama of salvation, and the need to accept the gospel in order to open oneself to Christ's saving power. Paul emphasizes this both by the literary structure he employs and by the content of the statement he makes (vv. 9-10):

a) confess with your mouth

   b) believe in your heart

   b') believe with the heart

a') confess with the mouth

Since in a chiastic structure the theme at the center is the important one, it is clear that faith is literally the heart of this message. Furthermore, Paul states that justification comes not through works of obedience or devotion but through faith. While he does distinguish between believing and confessing, one follows and requires the other. Belief without some kind of public confession could be betrayal; confession without interior belief is hypocrisy.

Relying on his hearers' knowledge of Scripture, Paul alludes to two prophetic passages. In one (Isa 28:16) Isaiah speaks of a firm cornerstone God lays in Zion. Whoever puts faith in that stone will not be shaken. Including this reference (v. 11), Paul is claiming that Jesus is the cornerstone set by God and those who place their faith in Jesus will not be shaken. In the other (Joel 3:5 [Hebrew]), after Joel has described some of the terrors that will accompany the Day of the LORD, he announces that whoever calls on the name of the LORD will be saved. Here (v. 13) Paul identifies Jesus as this Lord.

This bold identification of Jesus as Lord is made earlier in the passage where Paul uses what most probably was an early Christian profession of faith (v. 9). In Diaspora Jewish circles *Kýrios* (the Greek for "Lord") was an equivalent for YHWH, the sacred name of God. To call Jesus "Lord" had ramifications in both Jewish and Hellenistic circles. Since Judaism is a monotheistic faith, it identifies Jesus with the one true God. In a Hellenistic culture that embraced many gods, it was a political claim as well. It stated that Jesus, and no other lord or master, was the one to whom wholehearted allegiance belonged.

All of this constituted a central part of the "word of faith" Paul preached. Joined with it was the proclamation that God has raised Jesus from the dead. Belief in the resurrection was the basis of salvation. According to Paul it was precisely by means of the resurrection from the dead that Jesus became the anointed *(Christós)* of God. Finally, the efficacy of these awesome realities was universal. There was no advantage in being a Jew, a member of the chosen race of yore, nor was there an advantage in being a Greek, probably a reference to the Gentiles who were not bound by the Law of Moses. It is faith in Jesus, a faith that can be professed by anyone, that justifies and saves.

Luke 4:1-13

The account of Jesus' temptations in the wilderness, though christological in its significance, contains many features that connect Jesus with ancient Israel. The wilderness was not a romantic place. It was replete with danger. Inhabited by wild animals, it was also the refuge of bandits and the discarded of society. It was believed to be the abode of demons. More significantly, it had been the place of Israel's testing (cf. Deut 8:2). This account shows that unlike that ancient people, Jesus did not fail his test. The length of Jesus' fasting also has ancient Israelite significance. The two men who represented Israel's law and prophets, Moses and Elijah, fasted forty days and forty nights. Moses fasted as he wrote the Ten Commandments on tablets of stone (cf. Exod 34:28). Elijah fasted the same length of time as he walked to Horeb (cf. 1 Kgs 19:8). It was in this same tradition that Jesus fasted.

The narrative states that Jesus was under the influence of the Holy Spirit. He was filled with the Spirit upon his return from the Jordan. Furthermore, it was the Spirit, not the devil, who led him into the wilderness. This event in the wilderness was no chance encounter. The temptations themselves occurred in three different places: the wilderness, on a high mountain, on the parapet of the Temple in Jerusalem. In each instance Jesus is challenged to prove he is the Son of God. In each instance he replies to the tempter with a reference to a passage from Deuteronomy. Jesus never directly addresses the question of his divine sonship, but he always shows himself to be faithful as Israel was not.

The temptation to produce bread recalls Israel's hunger in the wilderness and God's graciousness in supplying the people with manna. Here the devil insinuates that if he has divine power, Jesus should be able to produce the bread his body craves. To this Jesus responds that God's words (the Commandments) are as essential for life as bread (Deut 8:1-3). The second temptation occurs on a high place from which Jesus and the devil can view the entire inhabited world *(oikoumenēs)*. There seems to have been a tradition that evil forces exercised ruling authority over the world. This will be changed when the Messiah appears and takes back control of the world. It is out of this concept that the devil can offer to relinquish power in return for Jesus' homage. Jesus rejects this proposal with a quote from Scripture (Deut 6:13).

The third temptation takes place in Jerusalem, the city that is the center of divine activity, according to Luke's theology. The place referred to was probably the southernmost corner of the Temple, a spot from which one can look across the Kidron valley and view a vast expanse of land. This last test was an attempt to force God's hand. Quoting a passage from the Scriptures (Ps 91:11-12), the devil challenges God's promise of protection, suggesting that Jesus see whether God will in fact preserve him from harm. Jesus counters the devil's baiting with his own choice of scriptural passage: Do not put God to the test (Deut 6:16). Three times the devil tempts Jesus; three times Jesus proves his allegiance to God. Israel may have failed in the wilderness, but Jesus remains faithful. This episode of temptation was over, but the encounters between Jesus and the devil were not finished. The evil one departed only for a time.

Themes of the Day

Lent is God's time. We see this in the readings for today. It is a time when we are reminded that we are but dust of the earth and there is nothing we can do to win our salvation. It is a pure gift from God. Lent also warns us not to try to force God's hand. Like Jesus in the wilderness, we are to allow God's plan to unfold in and through us. Finally, Lent is a time for us to enter actively into the mysteries of the death and resurrection of Jesus and there to marvel at what God has done for us.

Salvation Cannot Be Earned

We begin the lenten season knowing that salvation is not something we can achieve on our own merits. There is no advantage to being a Jew or a Greek, simply being faithful to devotional practices or not. Lent is not a season for us to concentrate on what we are going to do to be saved. It is a time for us to reflect on what God has done for us by bringing us to salvation. What happens to us during this season comes out of the goodness of God. What happens to us in faith comes by way of the resurrection of Jesus, which is God's seal on the ministry of Jesus in the Holy Spirit. Lent is less a time for us to be doing religious "things" than for us to be open to the transformative "things" God wishes to do for us. For Paul this is the basis of our faith.

This same theme is picked up in the responsorial psalm, where the psalmist turns to God knowing that only through God's power can salvation be accomplished. It is God's intervening activity that saves, not our lenten practices, regardless of how sincere or difficult they may be.

Do Not Force God's Hand

The temptations of Jesus are the same temptations we face when we are inclined to think that somehow we are in control. While the goals of the temptations may be admirable—feed the hungry, bring the world under the control of good, trust in God's power to protect us—we often choose to accomplish them in ways that are less than admirable. We try to perform the extraordinary so what we do reflects favorably on us. We use brute force in order to achieve control. We put God to the test rather than live peacefully with God's plan as it unfolds within and around us. We seek to become the super-hero, the super-minister, the super-Christian, on our own.

In his responses to the tempter Jesus constantly defers to the power of God: it is not by bread alone . . . worship only God . . . do not put God to the test. In a real sense, these temptations are a reminder that the fundamental temptation is to deny our human limitations and to refuse to let God be God for us. Lent is a time for us to *remember* that we are dust and not merely to wear it on our foreheads.

Remember the Mysteries of Our Faith

Remembrance iş more than an intellectual activity. It is participation in the reality of what is being remembered. Lent, which is the season to allow God to free us so we might not succumb to the temptations that besiege us on every side, will be transformative only for a people who remember what God has done for them in their past. Just as ancient Israel remembered God's care for them from the time of the calling of their ancestors to the events in their own lives, so Lent is the time to remember the events of the paschal mystery. More specifically, it is a time to enter into them and identify ourselves with them. If we are honest with ourselves we will have to ask why this remembering of, this identifying with, the mysteries of God has not transformed us already. Perhaps that is why we have Lent each year, so that again and again God can offer us the salvation only God can give.

Second Sunday of Lent

Genesis 15:5-12, 17-18

The reading for this Sunday consists of three distinct though related parts. It opens with God promising Abram he will have a multitude of descendants. Abram puts his faith in this promise. This is followed by directions for a covenantal ceremony. The last part is a brief account of the actual ceremony and a further promise of land.

Two promises are made to Abram, namely, a multitude of descendants and a vast expanse of land to be given to those descendants. Abram's response is one of faith (*'āman,* the same word from which comes the affirmation *amen*). This response is credited as righteousness. The verb "credited" *(hāshab)* is the word used of priests approving an offering for sacrificial use (Lev 7:18; 17:4). Righteousness is a relational term. It denotes right relationship either with others or with God. It is normally through acts of obedience or the performance of ritual that one is declared righteous. Here the basis of righteousness is neither obedience nor ritual. It is Abram's faith. He accepted God at God's word.

The second section begins with a divine self-identification (v. 7) similar to the one that introduces the Decalogue (cf. Exod 20:2). This is followed by a promise of land. Abram's request for a sign of assurance is more an indication of uncertainty than of lack of faith. God replies with a directive that contains elements of a somewhat sophisticated ritual as well as an indication of mythological understanding. Abram is told to procure every type of sacrificial animal. However, though most of the animals are cut into pieces, they are neither burned on the altar nor eaten, as is usually the case with sacrifices. Instead, another ancient ritual known as "cutting the covenant" is performed. In it the covenant partners cross through the divided carcasses of the animals. This action is a dramatized curse. It means that if either partner transgresses the prescriptions of the covenant the other can inflict the fate of the animals on the violator (cf. Jer 34:18-20). The harshness of the penalty signals the seriousness of this covenant making.

The action described does not conform in every detail to this ritual. First, Abram does not seem to be conscious of the ritual performance. After he prepared the carcasses, he is cast into the same kind of trance *(tardēmā)* as befell Adam when God built Eve from one of his ribs (cf. Gen 2:21). It is almost as if what follows is too mysterious for human eyes to witness. Nor does Abram pass between the pieces as the partners would. Only flames, which presumably represent God, pass through them. Does this mean that only God is bound by the covenant? After all, it is God who made (the Hebrew has "cut," *kārat*) the covenant (v. 18).

It is probably the third and last section that answers these questions. The description of the ritual is introduced and followed by a promise of land. In fact, the cutting of the covenant is God's reply to Abram's request for a sign. It is as if God has magnanimously promised land and then ratifies this promise by cutting a covenant. Both the promise of descendants as numerous as the stars and the promise of land from Egypt to Mesopotamia are extravagant. Such is the generosity of God. It cannot be measured.

Psalm 27:1, 7-8, 8-9, 13-14

The psalm response is a prayer of profound confidence in God. Unlike most prayers of this type, which begin with a plea for help and follow immediately with expressions of confidence that God will indeed hear the cry for assistance or relief and will grant the petitioner's request, this prayer begins with the expression of confidence (v. 1) and only then moves to the pleas for help (vv. 7-9). The prayer of the psalmist ends with a final declaration of confidence (v. 13). The psalm itself concludes with an exhortation addressed to the psalmist (v. 14). The form of the pronouns serves to divide the psalm into these sections. The initial acclamation of confidence is third-person indirect descriptive language. The supplications and the final statement of confidence are addressed to God in second-person direct language. The final directive is third person.

God is initially characterized as using three distinct metaphors: light, salvation, and refuge. In a world where darkness was not only a danger to one's safety but also symbolized the forces of evil, light was seen as the force that dispels any kind of danger. Because it also regularly conquered cosmic darkness, light enjoyed mythological prominence as well. Salvation, or deliverance, was always granted out of the beneficence of another. One did not save oneself. The misfortune from which God might save could be personal or communal, physical or spiritual. In any case, God was the savior. Finally, a refuge is a place of safety to which one in danger could flee for protection. All three metaphors characterize God as holding unparalleled power and exercising this power on behalf of the psalmist, who was not only vulnerable but somehow besieged.

The supplications begin (v. 7) with the same invocation as Israel's foremost prayer, the *Sh*ᵉ*ma*ᶜ ("Hear, O Israel"). The verb itself carries the meaning "to hear and respond favorably." The idea of being heard is reiterated in the plea for pity, which follows immediately. The particular verb used there *(ḥānan)* denotes a heartfelt response by one who has something to give to another who is in need. God has been identified earlier in the psalm as light, salvation, and refuge. This might lead some to expect the psalmist is asking for some form of protection. Such is not the case. The psalmist is pleading for the presence of God. Since it was believed God was experienced at shrines or during some ritual enactment, many commentators believe there is a cultic dimension of this psalm. If that is the case, we might suppose the petitioner, filled with confidence in God's solicitude, has brought her or his concerns to the sanctuary (women too prayed at the sanctuaries [cf. Hannah, 1 Sam 1:9-19]), where the petitioner hopes for some reply.

The face (v. 9) identifies the person and reflects the attitudes and sentiments of that person. Thus it is used metaphorically as a substitute for the inner bearing of that person. To hide one's face means to show aversion or disgust; to turn away one's face means to reject. When anthropomorphically applied to God, the idiom takes on theological significance. God is further described as the psalmist's help (v. 9, ᶜ*ezrâ*, the same word Adam used to describe Eve, cf. Gen 2:18). Believing God is not only capable of loving solicitude but is eager to show such favor, the psalmist concludes with an expression of confidence. Burdened with some kind of misfortune that has diminished the joy of living, the psalmist is confident of being restored by God to full life.

The final verse (v. 14), though clearly an injunction, can also be seen as an answer to the psalmist's prayer. One does not encourage another unless there is some hope of being heard. To wait for the LORD *(qāwâ)* means "to look for with eager expectation." It involves the very essence of one's whole being. It is based on trust that all God has promised will eventually be realized. Every aspect of this psalm response proclaims trust in God.

Philippians 3:17–4:1

In his exhortation to the Philippians Paul compares the fate of the true believers with that of opponents of the gospel. He begins by admonishing his hearers to follow his own example and the example of those who have already imitated him in his commitment to Christian living. He does not speak out of personal arrogance but as a teacher of wisdom. According to that tradition there are only two possible ways of living: the way, or path, of righteousness and that of evil. Paul would have his hearers conduct themselves on the path of righteousness (v. 17; the Greek has *peripateō*, "walk") and not walk the path of wickedness (v. 18). The contrast he draws is striking:

enemies of the cross of Christ	faithful to the Lord Jesus Christ
their end is destruction	awaiting the coming of the Savior
their god is their stomach	their lowly body is transformed
their glory is their shame	share in Christ's glory
occupied with earthly matters	citizenship in heaven

It is not clear who these enemies were. Most scholars maintain they were Gnostic Christians, whose view of realized eschatology led them to believe they had already passed into a spiritualized form of existence and could live in this world unscathed by its allurements. They would see little or no value in embracing the cross of Christ, since they were already living resurrected lives. Believing theirs was a spiritual existence, they felt absolved from any kind of dietary restrictions and could occupy themselves with earthly matters without risk of infidelity. Little did they realize that for them the end-time would be destruction *(apōleia)*, an eschatological term for the final divine retribution. Whoever these people were, Paul had warned his hearers about them before, and he does so here with great emotion (tears). These tears may have been caused by the deep distress he felt in the face of the unfaithfulness of these misguided individuals.

True believers, on the other hand, were really aliens in this earthly place. Their citizenship was in heaven. Unlike the enemies of the cross, they knew they would have to embrace that cross, and then, with Christ's coming, they would be transformed into his glory. (The Greek for "body" is *sōma*, which refers to total earthly existence.) The fullness of their transformation was in the future, and it would be accomplished by Christ. While they were still in this life, they were to live as citizens of heaven, following the admonitions imparted to them by Paul.

The reading ends with Paul addressing his hearers and exhorting them to steadfastness (4:1). The introductory word "therefore" *(hōste)*, implies that what follows depends on what preceded. Having drawn the comparison between the two ways of life, he now admonishes them to be faithful. The tears with which Paul spoke earlier have been replaced by an expression of uncommon love *(agapē)*. Paul's attachment to and pride in this community are obvious. He not only takes joy in them, he compares them to the crown *(stéphanos)*, or laurel wreath, given to the winner of an athletic competition. Paul has indeed run the race and has been victorious. The Philippians are evidence of that. The exhortation is straightforward: Stand firm! Even here Paul situates their fidelity in God. The verb *(stēkō)* implies that in faith they will achieve a standing that is grounded in God.

Luke 9:28b-36

There are two segments to the report of the transfiguration of Jesus. The first is the actual transfiguration and the conversation between Jesus and the two men from heaven. This was a private experience of Jesus; the disciples were asleep during it. In the second section the disciples have awakened, and they become involved. The account is rich with symbolism, suggesting that its significance is less in its historicity than in its theological meaning.

Jesus goes up a mountain to pray. The identity of the mountain is not given. It is enough to know that mountains had theophanic importance. Both Moses and Elijah, the glorified men who join Jesus, had encounters with God on mountains. It was during his prayer that Jesus was transfigured both from the inside (his face was changed) and on the outside (his clothing dazzled). Moses and Elijah appear in glory, which probably originated from God rather than from themselves, as was the case with Jesus. These two men represent the law and the Prophets respectively, the sweep of God's unfolding plan as found in the Israelite religious tradition. It is in this glorified state that the men speak of Jesus' imminent exodus.

Commentators believe that Jesus' exodus, his "going out from," includes his death, resurrection, and ascension, all the important events in God's plan of salvation. These events took place in the city of Jerusalem, the city that, according to Luke's theology, was the center of divine activity. That the men were discussing these events indicates that Jesus' death was not a tragic mistake, something he was unable to avoid. Rather, it was known beforehand by those who represented the entire religious tradition of Israel.

When they initially went up the mountain, the men who accompanied Jesus were identified as Peter, John, and James—the privileged inner circle of disciples. When they awoke from their sleep and saw the glorified Jesus along with Moses and Elijah, they are referred to as Peter and his companions. This is probably because Peter takes an active, even though misguided, role in the rest of the narrative. Though glorified, Jesus is recognized by Peter. He calls him "Master" *(epistátēs)*. In Luke, with the exception of the ten lepers cured by Jesus (17:13), this title is employed only by Jesus' followers. Strangers call him "Teacher." Peter does not want the apparition to end. He offers to construct three tents, dwellings for the glorified men. (Do these tents have eschatological significance? Do they, like the huts set up during the feast of Tabernacles, suggest that the end-time of fulfillment has come?)

What was wrong with Peter's perception? Commentators believe it was in his having judged Jesus as an equal with Moses and Elijah. His misunderstanding is corrected by a theophanic experience that has profound christo-logical significance. They are all taken into a cloud, a symbol of the hidden presence of God, and a voice from that cloud proclaims Jesus' divine identity in words reminiscent of Isaiah (42:1) as well as those spoken at Jesus' baptism (Luke 3:22). Jesus is not at all like Moses and Elijah. The voice not only authenticates Jesus' person but also enjoins the disciples to listen to his words, regardless of how challenging or perplexing they might be.

The cloud and the glorified visitors vanish and only Jesus remains. The disciples reported this experience to no one at that time. It will take the actual unfolding of the events of Jesus' "exodus" for them to understand its meaning. But then they will proclaim the good news fearlessly.

Themes of the Day

The Second Sunday of Lent celebrates the epiphanies of God, the ways in which God's divine presence is revealed. If Lent is a time for us to be open to the ways through which God can bring us to salvation, we will have to be able to recognize these ways when we come upon them. Lent is a time for such recognition.

In the Covenant

The first divine epiphany is the manifestation of God as one who initiates a covenant, an intimate relationship with human beings. Not only does God initiate this agreement, but God also seals it with blood, making it official. This covenant is concrete, as the sacrifice illustrates. It is historical, made with a particular family in a particular place at a particular time. God continues to relate to people in this manner. We see this in the community of the Church, where, through our own rituals, God enters again and again into covenant with us. This is why incorporation into the community through baptism is both celebrated and renewed on Holy Saturday.

Although we ritualize our relationship with God in a religious setting, the call to enter into the covenant can come in the ordinary events of life. We could be gazing at the night sky or into the eyes of a loved one. We might be occupied with the things of God or with the affairs of state. The important thing to remember about this covenant is that God enters into our lives and initiates it. No life is too simple; no life is too busy. Human history in all its contours is the setting for the encounter with God.

In the Suffering Christ

The glory of God is revealed in the transfigured Jesus, the one who discussed his suffering and death with Moses and Elijah. Though, like the three apostles, we might want to share in his glory, we can only do so by sharing in his suffer-ing. Lent is a time for us to enter into this suffering, not merely though reflec-tion, prayer, and penance but concretely, by sharing in the suffering of the body of Christ. We see this suffering all around us—in the fear of children who have been deprived of the innocence of childhood, in the aimlessness of youth who do not appreciate their own worth, in the desperation of parents who must raise their children in the midst of violence, in the empty eyes of the aged who often forget and are themselves forgotten. The glory of God remains just beneath the surface of their lives.

It may be easier to see God's glory revealed through the suffering of others than through our own distress. It is much easier to preach to others, or to work to ease the pain of others, without even admitting that we ourselves carry a heavy burden. Lent is a time for us to step back from suffering in order to get a better look at it, to try to discern God in the midst of it.

In the Example of Others

God is revealed through women and men who live lives of Christian commit-ment: in those whose integrity strengthens us, in those whose religious senti-ments inspire us, in those whose endurance gives us confidence. God is revealed in those who get involved in bettering the lives of others. God's love is seen in the compassionate; God's understanding is seen in the patient; God's mercy is seen in the forgiving. There are many in our midst whose example we would do well to imitate. The plumber or carpenter who takes pride in doing a job well, the person who looks in on a neighbor who is ill, the grandparent who is willing to look after the children, the student who is appreciative of the commitment of the teacher. God is revealed in very ordinary ways if we but open our eyes to see.

Third Sunday of Lent
Exodus 3:1-8a, 13-15

This narrative can be divided into different parts: an account of the initial theophany (vv. 1-3); a self-identification by God (vv. 4-8a); the disclosure of God's personal name (vv. 13-15). Throughout the narrative the lowliness and neediness of people are contrasted with the mysteriousness and grandeur of God. All this emphasizes God's graciousness toward the people.

Moses is anything but a leader here. He is tending the flock of someone else. He may be in the wilderness with the Midianites, but he is identified as an Israelite ("the God of your fathers, the God of Abraham . . . Isaac . . . Jacob").

He too is a member of the people who are being oppressed by the Egyptians. Whether the text refers to the angel of the LORD (v. 2), the flaming fire (v. 2), the LORD (v. 4), or God (v. 4), the references are all to the God who speaks to Moses from the bush. "God" is the general term for divinity; fire is a traditional symbol of the divine; "angel of the LORD" is often a reverential way of referring to God; and, as this text reveals, "LORD" is the personal name of the God of the Israelites.

The mountain is Horeb, a Semitic name that probably means "desolate place." There God speaks to Moses from out of a bush (*sᵉneh* in Hebrew, most likely an allusion to Sinai). Not only are there two traditions identifying different mountains, but there is uncertainty regarding the location of either. This suggests that geography is not the issue here, theology is. This is a holy mountain ("Remove the sandals from your feet") because it is a place of divine revelation. What is revealed? First, that the God who speaks is the very God who was worshiped by the ancestors. It is important to note that this God is not limited by territorial boundaries. Not only is this God revealed in the land of the Midianites, but this same God will release the Israelites from Egyptian bondage in the very land of Egypt and will then lead the people into yet another land, the land of Canaan.

Moses asks for God's name, not because he doubts but because a new revelation of God requires a new name. If God is doing something new (delivering an enslaved people), old titles will be inadequate. Giving the people the new name of God will not only authenticate Moses' role as their leader, but it will also announce to them the mighty deeds God is about to perform on their behalf. God does reveal a name, a name that is both clearly grasped and difficult to understand. The name given is similar in sound and appearance to the first-person *qal* (Hebrew imperfect form of the verb "to be"). This form denotes continuing action, thus the name means "I AM always." The new name signals a new revelation; the verb form implies continuing active involvement; the promise of deliverance identifies the way God will be with the people: always present to deliver. This is the way God will be remembered through all generations.

Psalm 103:1-2, 3-4, 6-7, 8, 11

The responsorial psalm begins with a summons to bless the LORD. Although the word "bless" is often used as a benediction, a prayer for God's presence or grace for the future, in this case it is a call to praise or to thank God for blessings already received. The call to "bless the LORD" is normally addressed to someone other than the psalmist. Here it is a self-address (vv. 1-2). The Hebrew word translated "soul" *(nepesh)* comes from the word for "breath." It yields over twenty meanings, chief among them "life-breath" (or soul), "life," "living person." The reference here is probably to the center within a person from which all life forces flow. This is not merely a spiritual or immaterial reality; it is a dimension that encompasses every aspect of the person. This understanding is corroborated by the phrase "all my being."

In the biblical world a person's name was thought to be an expression of that person's unique identity. In many ways names held more significance for people then than they do today. One could exercise power over another simply by somehow controlling the other's name. There were times during Israel's history when, in their attempt to show great reverence for God, the people paid homage to God's name rather than directly to God (cf. Deut 12:11, 21; 14:23f.; 16:2, 6, 11). Even when they did this they were careful to avoid using the divine name itself. Still today we show the same respect when we merely use the consonants YHWH or the substitute "Lord" (small upper case letters) rather than use the divine name itself.

The reason for praising or thanking God, the benefits to which the psalmist refers, is God's willingness to secure and defend the rights of those in need. The entire history of Israel is a series of events that demonstrate this. When they were in bondage in Egypt, God intervened and delivered them. When they were vulnerable in the wilderness, God provided for them. All of these mighty deeds flowed from God's lovingkindness *(ḥesed)* and compassion (*raḥămîm*, vv. 3-4), two relational attributes of God closely associated with covenantal commitment.

Lovingkindness is a passionate commitment to another that demonstrates a depth of friendship or piety devoted to the preservation and promotion of the life of the other and even to intervening on behalf of the other. It pursues what is good for the other regardless of the cost. Compassion comes from the word for "womb" *(reḥem)*. Here it is much more intimate than empathy felt for those who suffer. It can best be described as womb-love. In other words, the love God has for Israel is like the love a mother has for the children of her womb. This explains God's commitment to the people, and it is certainly reason to bless the Lord. As is seen in the Exodus tradition, these characteristics are integral aspects of God's own name and identity (v. 8; cf. Exod 34:6). It is out of this kindness and compassion that God acts, not requiring the harsh punishment the sins of the people warrant.

The extent of God's lovingkindness is further sketched by comparing it to the vast expanse of the heavens. Human eyes can only envision a fraction of the stretch that lies between the horizons. What is perceived is infinitesimal; the scope of the heavens is beyond comprehension. So is the compassion of God. Out of covenant love God puts our transgression so far from us that the distance cannot even be imagined. This is reason to praise and bless the Lord.

1 Corinthians 10:1-6, 10-12

In this reading Paul engages in a very daring and complex method of interpretation in order to warn the Corinthians about overconfidence in their status as

Christians. He employs elements of typological exegesis as he draws connections between the fate of those Israelites who wandered in the wilderness during the time of Moses and the Corinthians of Paul's own day. However, he seems to be making an adaptation in the way this typology works. Rather than understanding Christian reality in terms of what preceded it, Paul interprets the past in terms of the present. The basis of Paul's method of interpretation is his belief that since Christ is the end (goal) of Israel's history, he is also there in its beginning.

The specific focus of Paul's instruction is the efficacy of sacramental life. Although baptism and Eucharist are means of union with God, they do not work automatically. Paul turns to the wilderness events to illustrate this. He uses baptismal and eucharistic allusions to describe the experience of the people. Immersed (baptized) in the waters of the sea, they were joined to Moses and to everything he represented. They were fed with bread from heaven and water from the rock, elements that had spiritual origin. However, these saving events were of no avail for most of the people of that generation.

Probably the most daring allusion Paul makes is to the rock that afforded the people the water they so desperately needed to survive. We can get an insight here into an aspect of Paul's method of interpretation. He alludes to the written accounts of the wilderness tradition (v. 11). The way he identifies Christ as the rock depends upon the narrative sequence of these accounts. Because they state that Moses got water from the rock both at the beginning of the wilderness sojourn (Exod 17:1-7) and at its end (Num 20:2-13), a tradition grew up claiming this miraculous rock must have followed them through the wilderness. Paul seems to have accepted this tradition. Furthermore, since God was frequently referred to as a rock (cf. Deut 32:4, 15, 18, 30, 31; especially Pss 18:3 [Heb.]; 19:15 [Heb.]) and Paul identifies Christ with the God who saves, he takes an interpretive step and claims it was really Christ who led the Israelites through the wilderness.

Next comes the principal point Paul wishes to make: "Yet God was not pleased." Despite all the wonders God had worked for them in the wilderness, the people grumbled, and so they were punished. These events in their totality, not necessarily each individual element of the typology, were types, or examples (*týpoi*, vv. 6, 11), of how God punishes infidelity, even if God had first miraculously provided for the people. Since the Israelites were ancestors in faith, their history was an example for the Corinthians. In it they were to see that God's wondrous gifts are no guarantee of God's continued favor. If the Corinthians followed the example of the murmuring generation of Israel, they too would lose God's favor. Their own Christian calling and their initiation into its mysteries was, in itself, no guarantee of salvation. They would have to demonstrate their fidelity again and again. Christian life required Christian living. Even though they lived in the "end of the ages" and their salvation was already accomplished by Christ, it was not yet complete in them.

Luke 13:1-9

The gospel reading consists of a narrative saying of Jesus (vv. 1-5) followed by a parable that illustrates a major theological point (vv. 6-9). Two violent incidents are referred to: the slaughter of some Galileans and the collapse on innocent people of a tower on the southeast corner of the wall of the Temple near the pool of Siloam. Although there is no biblical record of these events, there is no reason to doubt they happened. Actually, their historicity is not at issue here. It is the unexpectedness of their occurrence that is the focus of Jesus' instruction. Still, certain details of each event hold theological significance.

At the time of Jesus, Galilee was a hotbed of political agitation. For this reason the Romans did not trust these people. Even in the face of this kind of antagonism, to murder people while they are engaged in the very act of ritual sacrifice so their own blood mingles with the blood of the animals they are offering is an act of gross brutality. However, such brutality corresponds to the picture of a vengeful Pilate obtained both from the Gospels and from several extrabiblical sources. The second event mentioned is equally tragic, even if accidental. These two occurrences raised the question of culpability. Believing there is a direct corollary between the character of one's behavior and the circumstances of one's life, people would wonder what terrible things these individuals might have done to deserve such dire consequences. Jesus insists that the victims of these two incidents were no more guilty of sin than anyone else. Therefore, their misfortune cannot be blamed on their own moral state.

The point on which Jesus concentrates is the suddenness of these tragedies and the possible unpreparedness of their victims. When he exhorts his listeners to repent lest they suffer the same fate, it is not that they might be spared such calamity but that should something of the sort befall them, they not be unprepared. Instead, they should be reconciled with God before disaster strikes so that divine judgment does not accompany the misfortune.

Jesus tells a parable to demonstrate a point about the mercy of God. The owner of the fig tree had every right to expect his tree to bear fruit. It was not that his patience had been spent after waiting three years. Instead, he concluded the tree would never bear fruit and was only depleting the soil. It could be replaced by another, more promising tree. There was probably no theological significance to the number three. It merely indicated a sufficient period of time. However, the one who tended the tree requested another year of nurturing to see if it might still bear fruit. If it did produce, the tree would be saved; if it did not, it could then justifiably be cut down. With this parable Jesus is making the point that God is like both the owner and the diligent worker, willing to give us time to repent. During this time, every means for fostering our repentance is given. Still, we must avail ourselves of these means, for such opportunities are not endless. Final judgment is a real possibility.

The twofold lesson Jesus teaches is a sobering one. First, we never know what lies ahead for us, so we must be prepared for sudden death by being reconciled with God at all times. Second, while God may be patient with our procrastination, this patience requires that we participate with the opportunities God provides for our maturing in righteousness. We risk God's judgment if we disregard God's grace.

Themes of the Day

Reflecting on the readings for today, we see one major theme emerging, namely, the incomprehensibility of God. This characteristic of the deity becomes pronounced in the mysterious divine name, which distinguishes the God of Israel from all others and yet leaves us in the dark as to its meaning. In these readings we also find a God who deigns to communicate with us through inanimate objects and the people in our lives. Finally, we see that God both pardons iniquities and decides to root out unfruitful branches, and we are confused by such inconsistency. In all of this we wonder how the majestic Creator of the universe can act in such incomprehensible ways.

I Am Who I Am

The personal name of God tells us so much and yet so little. If what we have learned about names is true, that is, that they reveal something of the nature or character of the one named, then the nature of God is certainly shrouded in mystery, for the exact meaning of God's name eludes us. Nor do the various ways God acts in our lives give us a clue as to its meaning. At times God's behavior seems so paradoxical; at other times it appears contradictory. Is God capricious or just mysterious in relating to human beings?

Actually, the way we respond to God's initiative and ever-present grace seems to influence the way God will continue to interact with us. In the matter of salvation, though the initiative and the transforming power are God's and salvation itself is a gift of God, we are not merely passive puppets in the drama. God gives the invitation, but that invitation must be accepted if there is to be any saving activity. This means that the ways God is experienced, though clearly determined by and under the control of God, are influenced by our dispositions. When we are needy, God comes as provider; when we are frightened, God comes as comforter and strength; when we are recalcitrant, God comes as judge and disciplinarian. God is a burning bush that captures our attention and plunges us into mystery; God is a horticulturalist who cannot allow a fruitless fig tree to sap the life out of the soil that nourishes other plants. God comes to us in whatever ways we might need divine aid.

God Sent Me to You

One would think that a God as magnificent and powerful as ours would not need intermediaries. Or if they were used, they would be of greater value than bushes in a mountainous wilderness or hired hands in orchards. Yet that is just the way God seems to work. God uses whatever or whoever is at hand. This is true whether it is an element of the natural world that is normally indifferent toward human beings, or an uncomplicated person whose only concern is to do her or his job well, or an individual who has been thrust by circumstances into the limelight. In every life there are those who speak for or act in the place of God. Lent is a time given us to discern who these people or things are. Who communicates God to us? Who intercedes for us before the Holy One? On the other hand, in whose life do we act as emissary? How do we reveal to others the message of God we have received? How do we intercede on behalf of them? The challenge here is to listen to the messengers who bring us the name of God, even if it is not always clearly defined.

The Rock Is Christ

In the midst of this ambiguity we have one sure source of stability—Christ. It is Christ who reveals the nature and meaning of the divine name; it is Christ who intercedes for us before God. Christ, the one who set his face toward Jerusalem, there to suffer and die, is the great messenger through whom God is revealed. He is the one who reveals majesty through the simplicity of a bush; he is the one who judges with the patience of a gardener. However, the limits of the experience and mercy of God in our lives are defined by our own openness. Despite the blessings we receive in the wildernesses of our lives, it could happen that God is not pleased with us. We must not take God's goodness for granted.

These readings close on a note of caution. Take care! We are not told whether the fig tree ever did bear fruit. We might be able to rest secure in the knowledge of the love and mercy of God, but these readings tell us we should not dare to rest passively or complacently.

Fourth Sunday of Lent
Joshua 5:9a, 10-12

These few verses provide modest sketches of two significant transitions through which Israel passed. The first transition was social. No longer would the people have to endure the degradation that was their lot in Egypt. No longer were they a captive people. No longer did they need to perform menial tasks that did not benefit them. Instead, they had been transported into a land where they could worship their own God freely and openly. They could now feed off the produce of that land without being accountable to any other people. They would probably have to work hard there as well, but they would be the beneficiaries of their own labor. The reproach of Egypt had been removed.

The second transition was their passage from total dependence for their nourishment on bread from heaven (manna) to a dependence on bread from the earth. This change signaled the end of their desert experience. They were now able to settle in a fertile land; they could put down roots, both their own and roots that would eventually provide them with necessary sustenance. This was a new period in their history. The promise of a land flowing with milk and honey had been fulfilled.

There is a play on words and ideas in the name of the place (Gilgal, which means "circle of stones") and the mention of God "rolling back" (*gll,* "to roll away" rather than "to remove") the reproach of Egypt as if it were a stone. In addition, it was at Gilgal that the Israelites set up twelve memorial stones after having crossed the Jordan into the land of Canaan (Josh 4:20). Because of its name the city itself became a permanent reminder that God had "rolled back" the reproach of Egypt.

The passage records the first celebration of Passover in the land of promise. Discrepancies in the text lead us to believe this is more than a historical account. The story suggests that the people have just crossed the Jordan into the land. Yet they are said to have offered cakes and parched grain, products of the land into which they have just arrived. This implies that they had been settled long enough to have produced a harvest. Furthermore, the Passover celebration took place according to a strict calendrical dating. It is not likely that the people had mapped out their journey according to such a calendar. Rather, they structured their liturgical life around it. Finally, though the feast identified is Passover, there is no mention of the required lamb. Instead, there is a reference to unleavened cakes, suggesting the feast of Unleavened Bread. Israel did not combine the commemoration of these two feasts until much later in its history.

This account probably grew out of a liturgical celebration of Passover/Unleavened Bread, a celebration that included some form of historical recital. The importance of this tradition is found less in the historical accuracy of the account than in its theological meaning. It is clear that Passover, whenever it was celebrated, commemorated God's having rolled away the reproach of Egypt and having fulfilled the promise of land made to the ancestors.

Psalm 34:2-3, 4-5, 6-7

The psalm response is part of an acrostic, a poem whose structure follows the order of the alphabet. Although the content of such psalms may vary, the form (the entire alphabet) always signifies one point: completeness. This psalm is less a prayer than an instruction. Its teaching is the conventional understanding of retribution: the righteous will be blessed and the wicked will be punished. The psalmist thanks God for having been delivered from distress and invites others to join in praising God. The attitude of the psalmist gives witness to others within the community, and it develops into a pedagogical technique. By confessing the goodness of God, the psalmist is teaching others to act in the same way.

The psalm begins with an expression of praise of God and an acknowledgment of the appropriateness of blessing God. This praise probably takes place in some kind of liturgical setting, for it is heard by the lowly *('ănāwîm)*, those who live in trust and dependence on the LORD. All who hear the psalmist are invited to join in rejoicing and in praising God's name. Since the name is really a dimension of the very character of the individual, to praise God's name is to praise God.

Normally in psalms of thanksgiving the reasons for gratitude are recited. Such is the case here. Without going into detail the psalmist confesses having been in distress, having turned to the LORD, and having been rescued. This is the reason for gratitude and why the psalmist glorifies God and bids others to do the same.

The congregation is now given explicit directions. They are encouraged to look to the LORD so they too might rejoice in gratitude, their faces radiant rather than filled with shame. The face is the expression of one's dignity, of one's status in the community. To lose face is to lose honor or to be shamed. The companions of the psalmist are encouraged to attach themselves to God and, thereby, to enjoy the blessings this ensures. Faithful to God, they will have nothing to fear, and they will not risk being shamed. The good fortune of the psalmist is placed before them as incentive. They have the psalmist's witness. It is now time for them to experience God's goodness for themselves.

2 Corinthians 5:17-21

In this reading Paul develops an unusual argument to show how God goes about reconciling sinners to God's own self through the death of the innocent Christ. Paul begins his teaching by using one of his favorite phrases—"in Christ." While this phrase suggests some kind of mystical union with Christ, it is clear Paul is using it here in connection with an eschatological way of reckoning the ages. His primary focus in this passage is the contrast between this age, the age of sin and alienation from God, and the age to come, the age of fulfillment and union with God. Those who have been transformed in Christ are already living in this new age. To describe their transformation Paul uses imagery reminiscent of the prophets. He speaks of a new creation (cf. Isa 65:17, 66:22; Jer

31:31; Ezek 36:26), of former things giving way to new things (cf. Isa 43:18-19). According to Paul, those in Christ are living in the time of fulfillment.

Reconciliation is the heart of the message in this passage, a reconciliation that puts an end to any enmity with God. The new things of which Paul speaks are the reconciling action of God and the message of reconciliation that Paul is to preach. The second flows from the first. Paul's use of pronouns can be confusing: God reconciled *us* and gave *us* the ministry of reconciliation. Although he uses plural forms, he is clearly speaking of himself. Paul frequently offers himself as a prototype for other Christians. That is probably his intent here. However the pronouns are to be understood, Paul states very clearly that God and God alone is the one who accomplishes these marvels. Rather than hold former sins against the guilty, God reconciles them through Christ.

Paul uses the notion of substitutionary sacrifice in his explanation of how God's reconciliation is accomplished. This notion is reminiscent of the role played by the Suffering Servant found in the prophet Isaiah. That servant of God not only suffered at the hands of the wicked but for their sake as well. Though innocent, he carried the guilt of their transgressions, and thus he justified many (cf. Isa 53:5-11). So it is with Christ. Though he was innocent he became the sin-offering for the guilty. Joined to Christ, those very ones now share in the righteousness of Christ and, through Christ, in the righteousness of God.

Paul's ministry (*diakonía,* "service") of reconciliation is his proclamation of the message (*lógon,* "word") of reconciliation accomplished by God. Having himself been reconciled with God, Paul now becomes the agent through whom God works in the lives of others. There is a universal dimension of this reconciliation; it is offered to the whole world (the *kósmos*). Using imperial language, Paul describes himself as an ambassador, one who acts with the legitimate authority of the absent ruler. As he announces the reconciling action of God, he is also asserting his own apostolic authority. It is not something he claims for himself but a responsibility bestowed upon him by God. All of this God has graciously accomplished for sinners through the magnanimous sacrifice of Christ. This is the good news Paul preaches.

Luke 15:1-3, 11-31

The opening verses of the gospel reading set the stage for the parable Jesus tells. Two groups of people are singled out, tax collectors and sinners. Tax collectors were hated because they worked for the despised Roman occupiers. Their wages came out of the money they exacted from their compatriots. To this end, many of them extorted unreasonable sums, which added to the disdain in which the citizenry held them. People who followed occupations that prevented them from regular observance of the law were considered sinners. Such occupations included anything that made contact with death, contaminating blood, or unclean animals. To eat with such people was to somehow share life with them. These were the people who came to hear Jesus. On the other hand, the Pharisees and scribes, those who dealt with the law and the things of God, criticized Jesus for the company he was keeping. They maintained that Jesus' association with such unclean outcasts contaminated him. Jesus, on the contrary, saw this association as opening the reign of God to all.

We see from the beginning (v. 11) that the parable has a double focus. While it is clearly about the mercy God shows to repentant sinners, it also contrasts God's openness with the closed-mindedness of those who consider themselves faithful. The scene with the elder brother is not an afterthought. In fact, it returns us to the opening verses, which describe the disdain of the Pharisees and scribes. Within the parable itself the contours of each of the three characters are carefully drawn so the meaning of the story shines through clearly.

There is no question about the depraved behavior of the younger son. With his third of the father's estate (the elder son would get a double portion), he abandons his father's home and even his own country, and he embarks on a life of dissipation. Just as the separation with his past was decisive, so the straits within which he finds himself are extreme. He attaches himself to a Gentile (a disgrace for a Jew), and he is reduced to feeding swine (an occupation forbidden by the law). Added to this, he longs to eat what the pigs eat. His association with defilement is complete. However, his eventual repentance is as sweeping as was his disgrace. He is willing to acknowledge his sin and even relinquish any filial claims if he can only be treated as one of his father's hired workers.

The picture of the father is also straightforward. He initially put no obstacles in his son's path but gave him his share of the estate. He disregards convention and runs out to welcome this son home. He treats him as one brought back to life, lavishly clothing him, giving him sandals, which would distinguish him as a son rather than a barefooted servant, hosting a sumptuous feast in his honor. He is no less attentive to the elder son, going out to plead with him to join the celebration, assuring him the major portion of the estate. This picture shatters the traditional patriarchal image and offers us a radically different picture of fatherhood, a picture totally incomprehensible to both of the sons. The father is neither domineering nor disinterested. He respects the decisions of both his sons even when he disagrees with them. When it becomes clear they have been mistaken, he forgives them. This startling new picture becomes the metaphor for understanding God.

The elder son strikes an interesting pose. He resents his father's unrestrained joyous treatment of the errant one. Just as the younger son had formerly repudiated his family, so this son refuses to participate in a family affair, and he will not even refer to the younger son as his brother. Unlike that dissolute one, he has always obeyed orders; he has served his father like a slave (*douleúō*); and yet he has never even received a goat with which to feast.

Though the elder brother contrasts his loyalty with the infidelity of the younger one, Jesus is really contrasting the compassion of God with the mean-spiritedness of the Pharisees and scribes. Like the elder brother, they lack compassion, and they seem to resent the fact that God is merciful toward sinners who repent.

Themes of the Day

In the midst of Lent we are given a moment for rejoicing, Laetare Sunday. All of the readings provide us with reasons for this rejoicing. The overarching theme is the prodigal goodness of God. The sentiments found in the responsorial psalm set the context for the reflections. The other readings show how needy people were showered with divine favor. However, even in the midst of this rejoicing we find a challenge. We must undergo a change of heart if we are to rejoice in God.

The Bountiful Land

Our gracious God has given us a world that freely nourishes our every need. Never asking for payment, it quenches our thirst and satisfies our hunger. The banquet set before us is not only hearty but also abundant and varied. We can eat unleavened cakes and parched grain, or fruit muffins and nut bread. There is a profusion of seeds and roots and berries. By the goodness of God we all live in a land of milk and honey, and we live there as a people redeemed from bondage, from the bondage of sin but also from the bondage of one another. God has removed from each and all of us the reproach of servitude, fashioning us into a new people in a new land of promise fed by the yield of that land. For this we rejoice.

However, this picture of abundance is idyllic. We know that we fail even in the face of such blessing. We do not always live as freed people, and we do not always allow others to live freely. Sometimes we hoard the fruits of the land; at other times we ravage the land. We bring back upon ourselves the reproach that was lifted from us by God. This Sunday is a time for us to rejoice in the goodness of God and to recommit ourselves to fidelity to that goodness.

The Prodigal Father

The goodness of God is strikingly portrayed in the radically new image of father that enables us to understand God in remarkably new ways. This is a God who allows us to follow our own dreams, who is partial to no one, who faithfully and patiently waits for us to return, who gently corrects our misperceptions. God longs to be reconciled with us even more than we long to be reconciled with God, and it is God's desire that we be reconciled with one another as well. God's prodigality is incredible. No limit is set on the celebration for the one who was been brought to life, and the other one is told, "Everything I have is yours."

This parable reveals what is required of us if we are to rejoice. First, we must realize that the reason for rejoicing is the goodness of God. The wild son had to acknowledge his failure and humbly return to his father. It is only when we embrace such sentiments that we will be able to rejoice. The elder son would have to overcome his resentment of his brother's newly acquired good fortune and his disappointment in his father's willingness to forgive. It is only when we can embrace these sentiments as well that we will be able to rejoice. Rejoicing for God's reasons is not always easy. This Sunday is an opportunity for us to so do.

A New Creation

The challenges placed before us in the other readings set out some of the conditions required of us if we are to be a new creation. We are called to a profound and total reconciliation, first with God and then with one another. The actual reconciling act is God's, but as is always the case, we must freely respond to God's initiative. The extent to which God has gone to be reconciled with us is astounding. Christ was identified with sin so we might be identified with God's righteousness. Who would have ever imagined such a marvel? This is certainly reason for rejoicing. But once again, we must be open to God's graciousness in Christ; we must be willing to be reconciled.

Reconciliation requires that we be open to giving and receiving forgiveness. It requires that we both remember and forget. We must always remember the causes of alienation so we do not succumb to them again. However, we must forget the resentment we felt so we do not allow it to influence our lives.

The reconciliation that comes from God comes with a commission. Having ourselves been reconciled, we are given the ministry of reconciliation. We now become the instruments through whom the world is reconciled to God in Christ. We become ambassadors of salvation. The gospel story of the brothers is unfinished. Were they ever reunited? Perhaps their reconciliation is up to us.

Fifth Sunday of Lent

Isaiah 43:16-21

The reading is part of a proclamation of salvation. Speaking through the prophet, God describes the uniqueness of the regeneration that God's own saving power will effect. We find familiarity with the imagery employed, yet at the same time the passage contains a startling claim of newness.

Israel's faith was based on the liberating events of the past. Snatched from the bondage of Egypt, protected and sustained while in the wilderness, its self-identity was rooted in the memory of its history, and its liturgical celebrations reenacted aspects of this history. Israel was a people of memory. Therefore, to be told by God's spokesperson to "remember not . . . consider not" must have been unsettling. What could the prophet mean? This is especially true of Second-Isaiah, who, perhaps more than others, relied in his prophecies on the earlier traditions.

Most likely the prophet was calling the people away from inordinate dependence on the past, a dependence that prevented them from seeing the astonishing new thing God was accomplishing before their very eyes. Faithful reverence for tradition is one thing, but insistent absorption in it is quite another. When the former is the case, older traditions can serve to fashion the understanding of new events and insights. When the latter is the case, openness to the newness of God is very hard to achieve. God is doing something new here, and the people must put aside the past in order to receive God's new graciousness.

The new thing God desires to accomplish is a new creation, a new reality so overwhelming that the people of Israel could never have imagined it by themselves. In order to assure them that something extraordinary would indeed be brought forth, the prophet begins this oracle of salvation by reminding them just who it is that is promising a new creation. Although the description of God's former feats centers on the deliverance of the people through the sea, this imagery stems from the much earlier myth of creation. In it, the mighty warrior God defeats the forces of chaotic water, harnessing their power and taming their fury. Surely the God who was victorious in the primordial battle and who created the magnificently ordered universe out of its wreckage can create something new from a people who had recently been released from the control of their conquerors.

The water theme is evident throughout this passage. The waters were opened so the chosen people could pass through them to safety. These same waters became the grave of those who pursued God's people to force them back into servitude. In the myth behind this description, the Creator defeated the waters and then assigned them their place above the heavens and under the earth. Finally, God furnishes the people with life-giving water in the desert, the place of waterless death. The God who controls primordial water, the waters of the sea, and the refreshing waters of life can certainly fashion this defeated people into a new and vibrant race. This is the promise of salvation proclaimed by the prophet.

Psalm 126:1-2, 2-3, 4-5, 6

Believers trust that God will surely act on their behalf, because God has done so before. The great blessing of Israel's past was the return from exile. Zion, the mountain on which the Temple was built, became a symbol with many levels of meaning. It stood for the Temple itself, the city of Jerusalem, the southern kingdom, or the entire nation of Israel. Here it probably represents Jerusalem and the area surrounding it.

The response of the returnees was threefold: amazement, laughter, and joy. Their release and return was so extraordinary that it was almost beyond comprehension. It was as if they were in a dream. This suggests that their situation could scarcely have led them to believe they could ever come back to the land from which they had been taken. Painting the situation in such bleak shades is a technique employed by the author to help the people see how helpless they were to improve, much less reverse, their predicament. In such circumstances only God would have the authority and power to change anything.

The graciousness of God, as seen in the deliverance of and blessings given to the Israelites, speaks volumes to the other nations. It throws into bold relief God's saving power. It also shows that this power is not restricted by the limitations of geographic boundary or ethnic particularity. It was exercised over the Israelites, but it could be effective in a foreign country. This is a God who shows preference for those who are poor and marginalized in society, for the homeless and the foreigner, the displaced and the refugee. The portrait Israel's history paints of such a God has clarity, depth, and nuance. Seeing this history unfold before their very eyes, the nations will marvel at the greatness of a God who can accomplish such amazing feats, and they will acclaim the LORD.

The prayer for deliverance is straightforward: Restore us now as you restored us in the past. The image used as a comparison reflects the impossible character of the present situation. The restoration will be like a flood of water in the southern desert, which is not only infrequent but even unlikely. The image itself contains a paradox. One element of it (torrents of water) is the complete reverse of the other (arid desert). This contradiction underscores the implausibility of what is being asked. However, the petitioner boldly offers the petition because the grace requested had been granted in the past.

The reversal of fortune is further described in symbolic language: sowing in tears and reaping in joy; leaving with only the promise of harvest and returning with its abundant fruits. God will replace with good fortune the tragedy that now marks the circumstances of the people. This is their prayer; it is for this that they hope. They are confident their prayer will be answered and their hope realized because God has been gracious to them in the past.

Philippians 3:8-14

One way Paul extols the unparalleled excellence of his relationship with Christ is to contrast it with the life he led and the values he championed before his conversion. It is not that he denies the worth of such things, but he proclaims that knowing Christ is the supreme good and everything else is loss, and more than that, it is rubbish. Paul is quite emphatic here, using a vulgar Greek term *(skýbalon)* that might be better translated "dung." Why does he see no value in them? Because as noble as they might be, they cannot bring him to Christ.

The desire Paul expresses in this reading is twofold. He wants to be made righteous through union with Christ, and he wants to share in Christ's sufferings in order to attain resurrection from the dead. By the grace of God, Paul came to realize that it is union with Christ and not obedience to the law that makes one righteous. Laws set standards and determine whether these standards have been met; true righteousness depends upon Christ. In the Bible, righteousness is more a legal concept than a moral one. It is conferred on an individual; it is not earned. A judge pronounces someone righteous whether that person is innocent or not, though ideally the person is innocent. This is the sense in which Paul uses the word. The righteousness he previously sought by obeying the law now appears useless; righteousness comes only from God. Christ was faithful to God and, therefore, participates in God's righteousness. It is through union with Christ that Paul will participate in this righteousness as well.

The union Paul sought was participation in Christ's suffering, for he knew that it was only through identification with Christ's death that he would really know Christ and the power of his resurrection. Implied in this and referred to further in the reading is the acknowledgment that commitment to Christ does not of itself result in perfect Christian maturity. Profession of faith in Christ does not automatically transport one into a higher realm of being, as some Gnostics seem to have claimed. It is only by taking on the day-to-day struggle with the realities of life in a manner that conforms to the example set by Christ that this identification is possible. Such living is opposed to any over-confident assertion of perfection or any form of quietism that leads to disregard of eschatological hope.

Paul sees this struggle as ongoing: he has not yet taken hold of it; he has not attained it; he continues his pursuit; he strains forward. He is confident he will achieve his goal not because he has been faithful but because Christ has taken possession of him. Throughout this reading Paul rejects any thought of self-achievement. He admits that righteousness is conferred upon him and that Christ has taken possession of him. For his part, he can only be faithful to the course to which he has committed himself. He uses the image of the athletic games to describe the part he plays. Like a runner he strains forward, never looking back to what he has left behind. His eyes are riveted on the goal before him, the marks on the track that indicate the finish line. The prize for which he runs is the high calling in Christ Jesus, received from God.

John 8:1-11

The narrative of the woman caught in the very act of adultery is really a story of conflict between Jesus and some of the religious authorities of his time. It begins with the scribes and Pharisees testing Jesus about fulfilling an injunction of the law, and it ends with Jesus turning the tables on the ones who put him to the test. The woman herself seems to be of little importance to those who challenged Jesus. However, she is treated with compassion by him.

The outer court of the Temple was a public place. There students frequently gathered around their favorite scribes to be instructed in the observance of the law. This was a perfect setting for the large audience into which the adulterous woman was brought. The bias of her accusers is clear from the outset. If she was caught in the very act of adultery, why did they not bring in her partner as well? The law required that both of them be stoned (cf. Deut 22:22-24). It appears that the woman is only a pawn in the game they have chosen to play with Jesus. They see that he has set himself up in the Temple as a teacher (*didáskalos*), so they invite him to decide a point of law that is not only controversial within the community but the decision of which could place him in jeopardy with both the Jewish people and the Roman authorities.

There is no question about the woman's guilt, only about the suitable sentence to be carried out. If Jesus said she should be stoned as the law required, he would be appropriating to himself the right to pass a death sentence, a right that belonged to the Romans alone. He would also be acting against his own teachings on mercy and compassion, and he would probably alienate those in the community who already opposed this particular death sentence. If he forgave the guilty woman, he would be disregarding the legitimate Mosaic sentence, and he would probably alienate those who interpreted the law more literally. His opponents had carefully devised a complex problem that would trap him one way or another.

What Jesus might have written on the ground with his finger does not seem as important as his refusal to be caught in the web that had been spun to trap him. He spoke to his challengers only when they prevailed upon him. Without contesting the death sentence, he invited the one without sin to be the first to carry it out. A second time he ignored them; he would not play their game. Instead, he turned their test of his integrity into a test of their own. Realizing they had been thwarted, those who sought to trap him departed in shame, one by one. In a society governed by issues of honor and shame, they realized that Jesus has outwitted them. While he has grown in stature, they have been diminished.

It seems that the crowds dispersed as well, for the text says that Jesus is left alone with the woman. Only now does he act directly. He treats her with the respect and compassion he has always shown those who are open to him and his message of salvation. As he has done in so many other situations, he disregards proper protocol, and he speaks to this woman who is a stranger to him, a sinner, and he does this in a public place. He does not condemn her, but neither does he exonerate her. Acknowledging her obvious sinfulness, he exhorts her to sin no more. Compassion and mercy have won out.

Themes of the Day

Lent ends on a note of wonder. In the face of all the mighty works God has already performed for the sake of the people, God promises something even more magnificent, something beyond our imaginations to conceive. From the deepest recess of our souls we rejoice. We can only stand in awe and rejoice. There are no words to describe God's goodness; we can merely rejoice. In fact, it may be as difficult for us not to rejoice as it is for a child not to thrill with a delightful surprise. When we finally see the wonderful new things God has in store for us, we will realize that, by comparison, everything else is like rubbish.

I Am Doing Something New

Throughout this season we have reflected on the marvels God accomplished in the lives of the people—cutting a covenant with Abraham, leading the people out of bondage, revealing God's own personal name, bringing them into a land bursting with life. Now God says: You haven't seen anything yet. God has already been victorious over chaotic waters and has led the people into a new land. What could surpass that?

The first reading proclaims that something new is about to appear. In the gospel, this new thing unfolds before our eyes. Here we see Jesus neither rejecting the law nor changing it. Instead, he shows that the law, as good as it might be, serves something higher. The first reading does not condemn the things of the past. It merely says we should look beyond them to something new. Neither does Jesus condemn the things of the past. He simply shows that the mercy and compassion of God exceed the authority of the law. God has done something new; Jesus has turned the law on its head. If he accomplished this with the woman, who is to say what he can do in our lives, in our world?

Filled with Joy

Once again we see that the readings of Lent are less concerned with mortification and penance than with divine graciousness and our response of joy and thanksgiving. We rejoice in our deliverance by God; we rejoice in the abundant blessings bestowed upon us. We rejoice that we have been called into God's family; we rejoice that we have been forgiven our offenses. Though we knew weeping in the past, we have been given the opportunity of living in the present and entering the future with rejoicing. The cause of our joy cannot be emphasized enough. It has nothing to do with ourselves, with our strengths and our successes. The cause of our joy is our God who is so good! So generous! So forgiving! God has done great things for us; we are glad indeed!

All Else Is Rubbish

Paul seems to be the most exuberant. He is not satisfied with the blessings of the past. In fact, he considers them rubbish when compared with knowing and being united with Christ. The blessings of the past were as barren as a desert; life with Christ is like a desert transformed, like a way through the wilderness. Life with Christ transforms us from people who are caught in sin to women and men who have been forgiven. Life in Christ is the new thing God has fashioned for us. The suffering associated with Lent is the stripping away that must occur if we are to be made anew; it is the birth pangs that precede the new birth. Penance that does not flow from this is pointless self-denial, the rigor we take upon ourselves merely to pump up our own muscles. God is the one who creates something new; we are the ones who are re-created. This process of re-creation may be painful, but the new life that emerges causes us to rejoice. When it comes to the wonders God can accomplish, we haven't seen anything yet!

Palm Sunday of the Lord's Passion
At the Procession

Luke 19:28-40

The account of Jesus' entry into Jerusalem can be divided into two parts: a description of his directions to his disciples to procure the colt on which he will ride into the city (vv. 28-34), and his actual entry into the city (vv. 35-40). His actions in this account have symbolic meaning, since they reinterpret several royal messianic traditions. This is particularly true regarding the details surrounding the acquisition of the colt. Jesus does not enter the Holy City on foot as a pilgrim would. Instead, he rides in on a colt as a messianic king (cf. Zech 9:9). "Colt" could refer to the young of any number of animals. What is important is not the particular species but the fact that no one has yet ridden on this animal. In a sense, it has not yet been profaned.

Two other features of the account contain royal allusions. First, kings had the right to press privately owned animals into their service whenever the situation seemed to warrant such action. (Even today, in an emergency officials can similarly appropriate what they need.) This practice could explain both Jesus' directive and the subsequent compliance of those who initially questioned the disciples' behavior. Second, the explanation given, "The Master [kýrios] needs it!" suggests that some kind of prerogative on Jesus' part is in the background. Finally, Jesus is in complete control of this incident. He knows in advance what is available, what can be done, and what should be said. He gives his disciples directions to follow, and they find that in each instance he had foreknowledge and authority.

The narrative identifies both Bethany and Bethphage, two villages east of Jerusalem. Though Bethphage is closer to the Holy City, either village could have been the site of this episode. The point of the narrative is the dramatic scene of Jesus coming over the crest of the eastern hill at the Mount of Olives, a place long associated with the appearance of the Messiah (cf. Zech 14:4).

The people around spread their cloaks on the ground before Jesus as their ancestors had formerly done in deference to a king (2 Kgs 9:13), and they praise him with an acclamation taken from one of the psalms (Ps 118:25-26). The blessing became part of the liturgical greeting of those who met pilgrims as they entered the Temple. In this narrative the bystanders direct the acclamation to Jesus, thus making it a cry of homage and not merely one of greeting. In this portrayal the one who comes in the Lord's name is intimately related to the coming kingdom of David. We are drawn to conclude that this kingdom will be inaugurated by the one who comes in the Lord's name. These features point to Jesus as the fulfillment of the Davidic messianic expectations. This is reason to exult "in the highest!"

At the Mass

Isaiah 50:4-7

The dynamics of hearing and speaking focuses prominently in this passage. The claim is made that God has both appointed the speaker to a particular ministry and provided him with what is essential if the ministry is to be effective, namely ears to hear God's word and a well-trained tongue to speak that word to others. This word is alive and fresh each day, for God opens the speaker's ears morning after morning. This means he must be always attentive to hear the word that is given. Although the speaker is identified as a disciple (one who is well trained), the description is precisely that of a prophet, one who hears God's word and proclaims it.

The ability to speak and the words spoken come from God. They are given to the speaker, but they are for the sake of the weary. Although the text does not indicate who these weary might be or the character of the words themselves, it does seem to presume that these people are in some way downtrodden and that the words are words of comfort.

A heavy price is exacted of the speaker. He suffers both personal insult and physical attack. He is beaten; his beard is plucked; he is spit upon. Despite all of this he does not recoil from his call. More than this, he does not even seem to ward off the blows that come his way. He willingly accepts what appears to be the consequence of his prophetic ministry to the weary. No explanation is given as to why this activity should precipitate such a violent response from others or even who these persecutors might be. All we know is that the ministry generates such a response and that the speaker does not abandon it or take himself out of harm's way. The suffering endured is willingly accepted.

In the face of all the affliction, the speaker maintains that God is his strength. This is an unusual statement, for such maltreatment normally would have been interpreted as evidence that God was on the side of his persecutors. Although he has been assaulted, the speaker declares that he is not disgraced and he will not be put to shame. There are no grounds for the speaker to make these claims other than utter confidence in God, a certainty of the authenticity of his call, and a conviction of the truth of the words he communicates.

Much of the content of this passage resonates with that found in many of the laments. However, there is really no complaint here, just a description of the sufferings that accrue from faithfully carrying out the mission assigned by God. If anything, this passage resembles a declaration of confidence in God's sustaining presence.

Psalm 22:8-9, 17-18, 19-20, 23-24

The psalm is a combination of a lament (vv. 8-9, 17-20) and a thanksgiving song (vv. 23-24). The imagery is both vivid and forceful. In some places it is so realistic that one cannot distinguish with certainty factual description from poetic metaphor. While the psalm may have grown out of the struggle of one person, mention of the assembly *(qāhāl)* adds a communal liturgical dimension to its final form.

The opening verses describe the derision the psalmist must endure from onlookers. These spectators are not explicitly identified as enemies. They are merely people who look upon the affliction of the psalmist and revile him rather than comfort him. The actual taunt is graphically described. Those who mock him part their lips to sneer at him, perhaps to hiss. They wag their heads in ridicule. The most cutting derision may be the words they hurl at him. He is reviled not only because he suffers but primarily because in his suffering he clings to God in confidence. It appears that the onlookers are mocking what they consider to be the psalmist's misplaced trust. Their taunt throws into question whether there is any point to such trust. Does God really care what happens to this pitiful man?

The metaphors used to describe the bystanders are trenchant. They are characterized as encircling dogs or some other type of predatory pack ready to tear him limb from limb. They are bloodthirsty assailants assaulting his body. They are rapacious thieves stripping the very clothes off his back. Nothing is safe from their savagery, neither the psalmist's person nor his possessions. In the end he lies humiliated, stripped, wounded. His integrity has been challenged and his trust in God ridiculed.

Neither the mockery nor the brutality of these onlookers can undermine the devotion of the psalmist. In the face of all of this suffering he clings to hope. Turning to God, he prays for a sense of God's presence and for deliverance from his misery. He does not seek reprisals; he seeks relief. These verses do not tell us whether the psalmist perceives his suffering as punishment for some offense, but they do indicate that the psalmist does not believe his unfortunate predicament should keep him separated from God. Suffering and devotion are not incompatible.

The reading ends with an exclamation associated with thanksgiving. This implies either that the psalmist's entreaties have been heard and he has been granted relief from this suffering or that he is convinced it will happen and he rejoices in anticipation. Since one's name holds part of the essence of a person, to proclaim the name of God is to recognize and praise the greatness, in this case the graciousness, of God. The text suggests this acclamation will take place within a liturgical assembly. The psalmist will make a public declaration of gratitude and praise. Although the identification of the assembly as a gathering of brothers (v. 23) reveals a clear gender bias, the further mention of the descendants of Jacob (the Hebrew has "seed," v. 24) indicates the intended inclusivity. The psalmist will proclaim his praise and thanksgiving before all the people so that all the people can join him in praising God.

Philippians 2:6-11

This cristological reflection on the nature and mission of Jesus can be divided into two parts. In the first (vv. 6-8) Jesus is the subject of the action; in the second (vv. 9-11) God is. The first part describes Jesus' humiliation; the second recounts his exaltation by God.

The first verse sets the tone for the actions of Christ Jesus. He did not cling to the dignity that was rightfully his. Two phrases identify this dignity: he is in the form of God; he is equal to God. Since the form of something is its basic appearance from which its essential character can be known, if Christ is in the form of God he enjoys a godlike manner of being. The parallel phrase restates this in a slightly different way: he is equal to God. The verb reports that Christ did not cling to this prerogative; he did not use his exalted status for his own ends. Christ freely gave up the right to the homage that was his.

Once again the verb plays an important role in this recital. Not only did Christ relinquish his godlike state, he emptied himself of it. The contrasts drawn here are noteworthy. Though in the form of God, he chose the form of a servant or slave. Without losing his godlike being, he took on the likeness of human beings. This does not mean that he only resembled a human being but really was not one. Christ did take on human form, but the qualification suggested by "likeness" points to the fact that he was human like no one else was human. Although the word "Lord" (*kýrios*, a word also applied to God) is not found in these early verses, the contrast between Lord and servant stands conspicuously behind it.

Christ emptied himself and took on the human condition. The final verb states that he then humbled himself and became obedient. Having taken on the form of a slave, he made himself vulnerable to all the particulars of that station in life. For a slave obedience is the determining factor. The extent of Christ's obedience is striking. Compliance with God's will in a world alienated from God requires that one be open to the possibility of death. In a sense, Christ's crucifixion was inevitable. It was a common punishment for slaves, the nadir of human abasement. Such ignominy was a likely consequence of emptying himself and taking on human form.

The exaltation of Christ is as glorious as his humiliation was debasing. It is important to note that while Christ was the subject of his self-emptying, his superexaltation is attributed directly to God. Once again there is a play on words and ideas. Just as "form" and "appearance" denote being, so "name" contains part of the essence of the individual. In exalting Jesus, God accords his human name a dignity that raises it above every other name. It now elicits the same reverence the title "Lord" (*kýrios*) does. Every knee shall do him homage and every tongue shall proclaim his sovereignty.

The extent to which Christ is to be revered is total. The entire created universe is brought under his lordship. This includes the spiritual beings in heaven, all living beings on earth, and even the dead under the earth. Distinctions such as spiritual or physical, living or dead, are meaningless here. All will praise Christ, whose exaltation gives glory to God.

Luke 22:14–23:56

This passion narrative is really a series of discrete individual stories. However, together they weave a tapestry of vibrant color and riveting scenes. They include the institution of the Lord's Supper (22:14-20); Jesus' farewell instruction (vv. 21-38); the events on the Mount of Olives and Peter's denial (vv. 39-65); Jesus' trial, flogging, and sentencing (22:66–23:25); the way of the cross and crucifixion (23:26-43); and Jesus' death and burial (24:44-56).

The narrative of the institution of the Lord's Supper is a classic farewell scene. It consists of a meal followed by a discourse on future events and directions regarding the disciples' behavior. The connection with the Passover underscores the meal's eschatological significance; "covenant in my blood" points to its sacrificial character. Even this wondrous event is marred by the announcement of the betrayal by Judas (vv. 21-23); the dispute among those at table over which of them would be the greatest (vv. 24-30); and the prediction of Peter's betrayal (vv. 31-38). Just before the account of Jesus' ultimate sacrifice we are reminded of the human limitations of those for whom he suffered. Even the ones who were closest to him were undependable.

The events that took place on the Mount of Olives are the prelude to the rejection and the agony in store for Jesus. Faced with these terrors, he accepts them as the will of God for him. Although there is a moment of divine assistance, it is fleeting, and Jesus realizes he will have to endure his ordeal while experiencing utter abandonment. Here he is betrayed by a disciple and arrested. Later he is denied by one of his intimate companions. All this occurs under the cover of darkness, the symbol of evil and death.

The one who is judge over heaven and earth is then dragged from one judgment seat to another. The accusation lodged against him? He is a revolutionary; he forbids taxes to Caesar; he has claimed to be a king, the Christ, the Son of God. Through all of this Jesus never challenges the legitimate authority of the high priest, the Sanhedrin, or even Pilate. However, neither does he lose his composure before them. He conducts himself with great dignity despite the fact that, defenseless under the control of his captors, he is whipped and mocked. The earlier adulation of the crowds now turns to hatred and rejection as they cry out for the release of Barabbas and for Jesus' own death. Unable to save him, the cowardly Pilate hands Jesus over to be crucified.

The last lap of the road to redemption lies before Jesus. Acknowledged by many as innocent, he is nonetheless led off to his death. Throughout this passion narrative, Jesus is portrayed as the non-violent, innocent victim of the unwarranted hatred and bloodthirsty desires of major sections of both the Jewish and the Roman populations. These are the people for whom he will shortly lay down his life. Even though he is in such dire straits, Jesus continues to minister to others, first to the grieving women of Jerusalem, then to one of the men crucified along with him. In the end, his agony may have been prolonged, but in death he simply breathed his last. Because the Sabbath was about to begin he was hurriedly taken down from the cross and immediately buried. The execution is reported quite matter-of-factly. The culminating event of the redemption of the world has been accomplished with dispatch.

Themes of the Day

In this final Sunday, as we prepare to enter the sacred time of Holy Week, we look again at the significance of Christ in our lives. We recognize him as our Savior, but we look more closely in order to discover just what kind of Savior he is. We find that he has taken the form of a slave; he has been glorified with a name above all other names; he continues to suffer with us.

A Self-Emptying Savior

We have not been saved through military power but through the kenotic humility of Jesus. Though he was really in the form of God, Jesus came in the form of a slave. We have a Savior who was crushed for our iniquities, nailed to a cross as a convicted felon, and there endured a sense of abandonment. Why has God stooped so low? Why did Christ empty himself so completely? We could say that all of this happened because Jesus was obedient to God's will in his life, regardless of where it was to lead him. This may be true, but it does not answer the fundamental question: Why does God love us with such abandon?

A Highly Exalted Savior

We have a Savior who was lifted up and exalted precisely because he emptied himself of his divine prerogatives. He became one of us in order to show us how we are to live. Unlike conquerors who triumph by putting down their opponents, Jesus was raised up because he himself was first willing to be put down. The passion recounts the extent to which he willingly offered himself. Because of this he has been exalted above everyone and everything else. His glorification was won at a great price, but it is now his by victory and not by mere bestowal. His name commands the homage no other name can claim, and it does so because he first handed himself over for us.

An Example for Us

We have a Savior who first offered himself *for* us and then continues to offer himself *to* us as an example to follow. As he was willing to empty himself for our sake, so we are told to empty ourselves for the sake of others. The best way to enter Holy Week with him is in the company of those with whom he has identified himself: the poor and the broken; the humiliated and the marginalized; those who suffer the abuse of others; those who never use rank to force their will. If we are to be saved we must go where salvation takes place—in our streets and in our homes where violence rages; in the dark corners of life where despair seems to hold sway; wherever the innocent are abused or the needy are neglected; wherever there is misunderstanding or fear or jealousy. We must go wherever Christ empties himself for our salvation.

Triduum

Holy Thursday Exodus 12:1-8, 11-14 Passover meal	**Psalm 116:12-13, 15-16bc, 17-18** Our blessing cup is a communion	**1 Corinthians 11:23-26** Proclaim the death of the Lord	**John 13:1-15** He loved them to the end
Good Friday Isaiah 52:13–53:12 He was wounded for us	**Psalm 31:2, 6, 12-13, 15-17, 25** Into your hands	**Hebrews 4:14-16; 5:7-9** Jesus learned obedience	**John 18:1–19:42** Passion
Holy Saturday Vigil readings Romans 6:3-11 Christ will die no more	**Psalm 118:1-2, 16-17, 22-23** Give thanks to the LORD		**Luke 24:1-12** Why seek the living among the dead

Triduum

Initial Readings of the Triduum

Introduction

The readings for the Triduum offer us a very different kind of mosaic. This is because of the unique character of the readings of the Easter Vigil. While the epistle and gospel passages of all three days can be read in columns, the readings from the First Testament and the psalm responses for the vigil make up a unit in itself. Despite this slightly different configuration the patterns can be traced, and the meanings that emerge can provide a theological matrix for the Triduum.

First Testament Readings

The readings for Holy Thursday and Good Friday offer two examples of vicarious sacrifice. The Paschal Lamb was slain as a substitute for the lives of the people. The Suffering Servant was also sacrificed so that others might live. Both were innocent victims; both were led silently to slaughter. While these images might point implicitly to Jesus, the First Testament readings of the vigil service take us in another direction. They recapitulate the story of salvation, which leads us to the waters of baptism.

Our reflection begins in the darkness of chaos out of which God calls light. Human beings are created and history begins. A hint of the intensity of God's desire to provide a future that far exceeds anything we might imagine can be seen in the story of Abraham and Isaac. That God does not really want the children of promise to perish is clear from the account of their crossing through the sea into freedom. God's love has the passion of a spouse. Even if the covenant relationship is threatened, this love will remain steadfast. God will provide for these people in all their needs, quenching their thirst with waters of life. They have but to turn and walk in God's ways and they will find peace. Even if they turn away and are unfaithful, God will pour clean water over them and will give them new hearts.

Psalms

The psalm responses are variously songs of thanksgiving for the amazing care and protection we have received from God; hymns of praise of God's graciousness, which has saved us and led us into a place of peace and prosperity; cries for help when we face insurmountable challenges or adversities; promises of fidelity to God and the ways of God; and prayers that spring from hearts that long to rest in God. They are all brought to a conclusion with a psalm that rejoices in the victory of the one who was rejected but has been exalted at the right hand of God.

Epistles

The mini-epistle created when the three readings are placed end to end develops the theological meaning of the sacrifice of Jesus. It begins with the official Christian proclamation of the eucharistic meal as the reenactment of the death of the Lord. This is followed by a priestly interpretation of the meaning of his death. It concludes with an explanation of our participation through baptism in Jesus' death and resurrection. We begin with a report of events that transformed a festive meal, and we end with a reminder of how we are transformed by the saving action of God, which comes to us through these events.

Gospels

The gospel passages trace the theme of Jesus' selfless sacrifice of love, beginning with an account of his self-emptying service of others. Though he has the power of God at his disposal, he strips himself, gets on his knees before his disciples, and renders a service only the humblest servants perform. The passion narrative details the extent to which he was willing to humble himself. He endured rejection, ridicule, and abuse, and he did it with the dignity of a king—the beloved Son of God. Having been lifted up on the cross, he was also lifted up from the dead. The one who was cast down has now been raised up.

Mosaic of Readings

These three days have traditionally been set aside for our reflection on the most sacred mysteries of our faith: the suffering, death, and resurrection of Jesus. However, the readings offer us a slightly different picture to consider. Just as contemplation of his suffering and death always includes some mention of his resurrection, so the readings that report the events of his life all include mention of our participation in these mysteries. We do not sit on the sidelines as uninvolved spectators. This is our story and we are part of it, whether we accept the love that is offered us or not. We are the ones who are cared for and nourished by God; we are the ones God lifts out of darkness and leads through the struggles of life. Even in his resurrection Christ beckons us to join him.

Readings

Holy Thursday, Evening Mass of the Lord's Supper
Exodus 12:1-8, 11-14

The reading sets forth the ritual prescriptions for the annual celebration of the feast of Passover. The first verse states that the establishment of the memorial, the determination of its date, and the details of the rite itself were all decreed by God. Since the event of the Exodus marked Israel's beginning as a people, it is only fitting that the feast commemorating this beginning be positioned at the head of their year.

The very first words of the passage assert that the power of God is effective even in the land of Egypt. This is a profound theological claim for several reasons: (1) it means that rule of the God of Israel is not limited to the boundaries of the land of Israel itself; (2) it describes Israel's God as superior to the gods of Egypt, ruling where these other gods do not; (3) it implies that Israel's God exercises authority over the lives of the Egyptians themselves, striking down their firstborn.

The celebration takes the form of a meal, at the center of which is a lamb. Because of the significance of this ceremony the selection, slaughter, and consumption of this lamb are carefully determined by ritual ordinance. The lamb must be male because the people cannot afford to lose the reproductive potential of the females of the flock. It must be a year old so that it has enough maturity to embody the salvific significance that will be placed upon it, yet not so old as to have lost its fundamental vitality. Like everything set aside for consecration to God, it must be free of all blemish.

The Passover lambs must be slaughtered in the presence of the entire community and then eaten in the respective households. Presumably this is an evening meal, since the lambs are to be slaughtered at twilight. The entire household must join together for this feast, men and women, children and servants. The lambs must be eaten in their entirety; nothing of the sacrifice can be left over, lest it be thrown out like refuse. For this reason small households should join together to ensure total consumption of the animal. Even the manner of dress is prescribed. They must be clad like those in flight.

The ritual itself may have originated from an ancient nomadic ceremony. Herders frequently moved during the night from winter pasturage to places of spring grazing. Before their move, one of the choicest members of the flock was sacrificed in order to ensure the safety of the rest of the flock. Its blood was then somehow sprinkled around the camp. This was done because of blood's apotropaic value, that is, it could ward off any threatening evil.

Elements of this ritual can be seen in the Passover ceremony. The night travel, the slaughter, and the marking with blood have all now taken on historical meaning. What was initially a sacrifice for pacification of an evil deity is now a memorial of God's protection and deliverance. The blood of the lamb, which originally warded off night demons, was now a sign of salvation for all those whose doorposts were marked with it. The night journey in search of new pasturage became the flight for safety into the wilderness. This ritual was to be a perpetual memorial of the time when the LORD passed over the Israelites.

Psalm 116: 12-13, 15-16bc, 17-18

This psalm is an example of a temple service of thanksgiving. In it someone who made an appeal to God and promised to perform some act of devotion when the request was granted now comes to the Temple and, before God and the assembly of believers, gives thanks for the favor granted and fulfills the vow that was made. Most vows were promises to offer some form of sacrifice (cf. Ps 56:13): holocaust (cf. Ps 66:13; Lev 22:18-20); peace offerings (cf. Ps 50:14; Lev 7:16; 22:21-22); cereal offerings and libations (cf. Num 15:3, 8).

The psalm response opens with an acknowledgment that there is nothing the psalmist can do and no gift that can be offered that will even begin to compare with the favors received from God. Inadequate as it is, the psalmist still renders what can be offered, expressing devotion by offering a cup of salvation. It is not clear exactly what the cup of salvation is. It might be a libation that is offered in thanksgiving. Or it could be a festive drink, the wine that was shared at a sacred meal, a symbol of the joy God's graciousness has produced. Whatever its identify, it serves as a cup of joy for having been saved.

Along with the offering of this wine is the proclamation of the name of God. Since God's name holds part of the divine essence, to proclaim that name is to recognize and praise God's greatness, in this case the graciousness of God's saving action. The cup is taken up and God's name is proclaimed.

The psalmist insists that, contrary to any appearances, God is concerned with the fate of the righteous. The psalmist's own situation is an example of this. The psalmist may have suffered, but ultimately God did intervene. Mention of the righteous (*ḥāsîdîm*) indirectly identifies the psalmist as one of this group. The psalmist could be making another point here: virtue and misfortune are not incompatible; good people do in fact suffer. Still, the point of this psalm is not the sufferings the psalmist had to endure but the deliverance that came from God and the psalmist's response to divine graciousness.

The relationship between the psalmist and God is strikingly characterized in the metaphors "servant" and its parallel "son of your handmaid." Although the first image has taken on a profound theological connotation (servant of God), the second clearly identifies both images as classifications within a structured household. A slave born into a household had neither a justified claim to nor any guaranteed likelihood of emancipation. By using these legal metaphors to characterize his relationship with God, the psalmist is dramatizing his own situation. Like a slave that has no hope of release, he was bound to a life of great difficulty. However, God looked kindly upon him and loosed him from his servitude.

The last verses (vv. 17-18) clearly identify the ceremony that will take place as a public ritual. A sacrifice of thanksgiving will be offered (cf. Lev 7:11-18), the name of the LORD will be proclaimed, and vows will be paid in the presence of the People of God. The psalmist, who once faced the prospect of death, now stands in the midst of the assembly, humbled and grateful to God.

1 Corinthians 11:23-26

This account of the institution of the Lord's Supper draws on the "Jesus tradition." The language used is technical and formulaic; what Paul received he now hands down (cf. 1 Cor 15:3). This does not mean that he received this tradition in direct revelation from the Lord but that he received it by word of mouth, the usual way a religious heritage is transmitted. This manner of expression establishes the ecclesial authority of the teaching. It also demonstrates Paul's own conviction that the risen Christ transmits the tradition through the agency of the members of the body of Christ, the Church. Since such transmission of tradition was a custom in both the Greek schools and the Jewish synagogue, the audience would understand what Paul was doing regardless of their ethnic or religious background.

That the account comes specifically from the Jesus tradition and not from the early Christian tradition generally is evident in the recital of the words of Jesus. They actually give instruction for the continual celebration of the liturgical reenactment. The fact that they are the words of Jesus gives divine legitimation to the *anámnēsis* (ritual of remembering) that is enjoined upon the community of believers. The words themselves are found within a succinct account of Jesus' Last Supper, wherein he draws lines of continuity between the old and the new covenants and makes clear their differences.

Jesus' attention is on the bread and the wine. Faithful to Jewish table etiquette, as either the head of the household or the host, he gives thanks and breaks the bread (v. 24). He identifies the bread as his body about to be given vicariously on behalf of those present. The fact that Jesus was actually with them when he said this makes the meaning of his words enigmatic. Was this really his body? Or did it represent his body? Believers have interpreted this in various ways down through the centuries. One thing is clear; they were charged to repeat among themselves what he had just done.

When the supper was over Jesus took the cup and pronounced words over it as well (v. 25). This cup is identified with the new covenant (cf. Jer 31:31-34) and with the blood of the Lord, which, like sacrificial blood, ratifies the covenant. This statement shows how the Jesus tradition has taken the new covenant theme from Jeremiah and blood ratification from the Jewish sacrificial system, incorporated them, and reinterpreted them. This verse ends as did the previous verse, with a charge to repeat the memorial.

Jesus' sharing of the bread and the cup was a prophetic symbolic action that anticipated his death. The ritual reenactment of this supper would be a participation in his death and a sharing in the benefits that would accrue from it. In it the risen, exalted Lord continually gives what the dying Jesus gave once for all. In the memorial celebration the past, the present, and the future are brought together: the past is the commemoration of his death; the present is the ritual of remembrance itself; the future is his *parousía*, his coming again.

The reason for repeating Jesus' actions and words is that they signify his salvific death. Believers live an essentially eschatological existence, anticipating the future as they reenact the past.

John 13:1-15

The account of the washing of the feet is introduced by a few references. They include identification of the time of year as that of the feast of Passover; a note about Jesus' relationship with God and his foreknowledge of his own death; a statement about his love for those called "his own"; and a report about Judas' complicity with the devil. All of this information sets the context for the narrative that follows.

The actual washing of feet was unusual for several reasons. Although it was a common practice of Eastern hospitality, it should have been done upon arrival at the house and not when everyone had already reclined at table. It was normally done by people of negligible social station: by slaves in a class-conscious household or, in a patriarchal society, by women. Here it was done by the one who could boast divine origin and who was both Lord and Teacher of those at table. While foot washing was a common social practice, as a symbolic action it here had theological significance and was intended as an example to be followed by all those present.

What looks like self-abasement by Jesus is really an expression of his love. By washing their feet Jesus showed the extent of the love he had for his disciples. Because of his love he was willing to empty himself of all divine prerogatives and to assume the role of the menial household slave. Because of his love he was willing to empty himself of his very life in order to win salvation for all. The love he had for his disciples is the model of the love they were to have for one another. In other words, they were to be willing to empty themselves for the sake of one another.

This symbolic action of foot washing was misunderstood by Peter. He saw the humiliation in such behavior, but he did not perceive its real meaning. He would not allow Jesus, his Lord, to abase himself in this way. But Jesus would not allow Peter to refuse the gesture without dire consequences. To reject the symbolic action was to reject its profound theological significance. If Peter would not participate in Jesus' self-emptying, he could not enjoy the blessings it would guarantee.

In trying to explain the meaning of his action, Jesus played on the ideas of clean and unclean. Customary washing of feet could make the disciples physically clean, but this foot washing could make them clean in a spiritual way, that is, all of them but Judas. Jesus knew that Judas had turned traitor and so was not clean. On one level, Peter understood this explanation; on another level he did not. He seems to have thought the more he washed the more he would be spiritually cleansed. Since their being washed symbolized their participation in Jesus' self-emptying, limited washing was adequate. Jesus assured Peter he would understand later, presumably after Jesus' resurrection.

Never did Jesus deny the dignity that was his as God, but he did not use it to safeguard his own comfort or well-being. Instead, it became the measure of his own self-giving and the example of the extent of self-giving his disciples should be willing to offer others. During his Last Supper, Jesus gave himself completely to those present and charged them to give themselves completely as well.

Themes of the Day

This is the first day of the solemn Triduum, the most sacred moment of the Liturgical Year. On each of the three days we meditate on some aspect of the same question: What is the meaning of Passover? Holy Thursday opens this meditation by considering God's initiative in these wondrous events. Three themes are prominent: the Passover, which is the saving action of God; our response to God's Passover; the wonder of God's love.

God's Passover

At the beginning of our meditation on the Passover, we see that it is God who passes over, saving us, nourishing us, serving us. The initiative is God's; the magnanimity is God's; the self-emptying is God's. We have nothing to contribute to these amazing happenings. We have only to open ourselves to receive the wondrous gifts that have been won for us.

God passes over us as a protective angel, preserving us from harm, leading us out of bondage into freedom. All we have to do is accept the salvation offered to us through this spectacular act of love. God also passes through mere human companionship and becomes the covenantal meal that sustains us. Along with this heavenly bread comes the guarantee of eternal life. It is ours only if we will accept it. Finally, Jesus passes beyond being Lord and master and kneels before us as our humble servant. If we are to belong to him, we must allow him to wash our feet. In each instance, the saving action is God's. For no other reason but love God offers us salvation, nourishment, and service.

Our Response

"How shall I make a return to the LORD?" On this day of Eucharist our only response is thanksgiving. When we give thanks we are merely opening ourselves to the graciousness of God. We are giving God the opportunity of overwhelming us with blessings. We participate in God's many passovers by accepting God's magnanimity. Our sacrifice of thanksgiving is really our openness to receive the sacrifice of God—the sacrifice of the lamb, whose blood on the doorpost liberated our future; the sacrifice of Christ's body and blood, which became our food and drink; the sacrifice of Jesus' self-emptying service, which stands as a model for our own service of others.

The Wonder of It All

Who could have imagined that any of this would happen? A motley group of runaway laborers escapes from the clutches of their superpower overlords; bread and wine is changed into the body and blood of a man who is being hunted down; the Son who was sent by God into the world washes the feet of his disciples. This is all incredible; it is no wonder that Peter resisted. It is so difficult for self-possessed, self-directed human beings to relinquish control of their lives and to stand ready to receive the gift of God. We do not question whether God *can* do such marvels, but we stand in awe that God *would*. God's love for us is beyond comprehension.

Finally, on the first night of this holy Triduum, we are left with this directive: "As I have done, so you must do." The graciousness of God toward us prompts us to pass over from being served to serving others. Our thanksgiving is expressed in our own self-emptying service of others. Having received the gifts of God, we give them away; they flow from God through us to others.

Good Friday of the Lord's Passion
Isaiah 52:13–53:12

An account of the afflictions of a righteous man (53:1-11b) is here framed by two utterances of God (52:13-15; 53:11b-12). This portrait of innocent suffering challenges the traditionally held conviction that evil brings on its own penalty and, therefore, that misfortune is evidence of sinfulness. In place of this view of retribution is a picture of one who not only suffered at the hands of others but did so for the very people who had unjustly afflicted him. The framework of God's words serves to legitimize this unconventional theological position.

It is clear that God is speaking in the closing verses, because only God would be able to bless the servant in the manner described (53:12). Since the servant is similarly identified in both of the framing parts, it is safe to conclude it is God who speaks in the introduction as well. The overriding theme in both parts is the relationship between the humiliation of the servant and his exaltation.

The opening verses do not suggest that the servant's exaltation is reward for his humiliation. Rather, it is precisely *in* his humiliation that he is exalted. He is raised up even as the bystanders are aghast at his appearance (52:13-15). The closing words explain how this can be the case. The will of God is accomplished in his willingness to bear his afflictions at the hands of and for the sake of others (53:11b-12).

The actual account of the servant's suffering is narrated from the perspective of those who have been granted salvation through his tribulations. It begins with an exclamation of total amazement. Who would have ever thought that the power of God (the arm of the LORD) would be revealed in weakness and humiliation? The details of this humiliation are then sketched (53:2-9). Unlike many righteous individuals whose lives contain episodes of misfortune, this servant lived a life marked by tribulation from beginning to end. Added to his physical distress was rejection by a community that held him in no regard.

The account is interrupted by a confession of the narrator's personal guilt and an acknowledgment of the servant's innocence. The narrator first states the traditional way of understanding the servant's plight: "we thought of him . . . as one smitten by God" (v. 4). Then the new and astonishing insight is proclaimed: "he was pierced for our offenses" (v. 5). This startling insight contains two important points: innocent people do in fact suffer for reasons that have nothing to do with their own behavior; the suffering of one can be the source of redemption for another.

The account of the servant's sufferings continues (vv. 7-9). Here his nonviolent attitude is clearly defined. He did not retaliate; he did not even defend himself. In fact, he willingly handed himself over to those who afflicted him. The image of a lamb led to slaughter suggests the servant knew that he too would die at the hands of his persecutors. Still, he chose to be defenseless. Even in death he was shamed, buried with the wicked. There was nothing in this appalling life or death that served as a clue to the significance of this suffering, or its redemptive value, or the source of exaltation it would become. God's ways are astounding.

Psalm 31:2, 6, 12-13, 15-17, 25

The theme of trust permeates this psalm response (vv. 2, 15). Although it contains elements of complaint or lament and of petition, it opens with a testimony to the psalmist's conviction that there is refuge in God (v. 2). The image suggests that he (identified as a male servant, v. 17) is fleeing some kind of peril and turns to God as a sanctuary in this flight. Further in the psalm (v. 16) he pleads to be rescued from his enemies and persecutors. Thus, threatened by such dangers, the psalmist seeks protection in God, and he is certain he will find it there.

The covenant relationship between God and the psalmist is apparent in several places. First, he appeals to God's justice or righteousness, a characteristic of the covenant. This appeal also suggests the innocence of the psalmist. He would hardly call upon God's justice if he were in any way guilty. Evidence of the relationship can also be seen in the way the psalmist identifies both God and himself: You are my God (v. 15); I am your servant (v. 17). Finally, the psalmist appeals to God's lovingkindness *(ḥesed)*, a technical term describing covenant loyalty. It is clear that this relationship is the reason for his confidence; it is why he flees to God.

Complete confidence in God does not prevent the psalmist from pleading with God. His first concern is shame. This is not an inner attitude or state of mind. It is public disgrace. In many Eastern societies it is referred to even today as "losing face." It is the opposite of possessing honor, an attribute more important than riches. A man without honor is an outcast in society, and for many people death is preferred to such disgrace.

The psalm does not clearly explain the initial cause of the psalmist's loss of honor. In a society that believed suffering was the consequence of wickedness, it could have been almost any kind of misfortune. Whatever it was, the psalmist was regarded as someone who was not only dead but who was then forgotten (v. 13). Since in this culture at this time, the only way an individual could survive after death was in the memory of the living, to be forgotten was doubly deplorable. The psalmist was also treated like a broken dish, not only shattered but also discarded. Whatever the misfortune was, it was regarded as shameful.

The description of his shame is a collage of metaphors that characterize his disgrace. He is an object of reproach, a laughingstock, a dread. He is shamed before everyone—enemies, neighbors, even friends. He has already lost his honor. What will reinstate it is vindication, and only God can accomplish this. Only God can show that the psalmist was innocent in the first place.

The psalmist prays that God's face might shine upon him. Since the face identifies the person and reflects the attitudes and sentiments of that person, seeing the face of God would be a kind of divine manifestation. The psalmist is probably not asking for such a revelation but rather for the light that comes from God's face. In other words, he is asking for God's good pleasure. His last words are an exhortation to others to trust in God as he has. To the end, his confidence will not be swallowed up by any disgrace he might have to endure.

Hebrews 4:14-16; 5:7-9

The reading consists of two distinct yet related parts. The first (4:14-16) contains a double exhortation: Hold fast to faith; approach the throne of grace with confidence. It develops the theme of Jesus the high priest who intercedes for us. This is a high priest who was tempted in all things and, therefore, can sympathize with our struggle.

The basis of constancy in the confession of the community is the identity of Jesus. He is Son of God as well as the great high priest. Just as the high priest passed through the curtain into the presence of God in the holy of holies, there to sprinkle sacrificial blood on the mercy seat (Heb 9:7), so Christ, exalted after shedding his own blood, passed through the heavens into the presence of God. Being the Son of God, his sacrifice far exceeds anything the ritual performed by the high priest might have hoped to accomplish.

His exalted state has not distanced him from us. On the contrary, he knows our limitations. He was tried to the limit but did not succumb. Furthermore, it is precisely his exalted state that gives us access to the throne of God. Unlike former high priests, who approached the mercy seat alone and only on the Day of Atonement, Christ enables each one of us to approach God and to do so continually. This first section of the reading ends with the second exhortation. The confidence we have in our relationship with Christ should empower us to approach the throne of God boldly, there to receive the grace we need to be faithful. The second section (5:7-9) is confessional in character. Each of the three verses offers a slightly different view of biblical christology. The first refers to the depth of Jesus' suffering; the second to a major lesson he learned through suffering; the third to the mediatorial role he gained by that suffering.

"Days when Christ was in the flesh" is an allusion to Jesus' humanity. In the biblical sense of the term, flesh *(sárx)* is not evil, but it is fraught with limitations and weaknesses. Because it is subject to deterioration and death, it came to signify many things that were associated with human frailty, such as vulnerability and fear. For Jesus to have taken on flesh was to have taken on these limitations and weaknesses as well.

The reference to his anguished prayer calls to mind his agony in Gethsemane (Matt 26:36-46; Mark 14:32-42; Luke 22:40-46). The reference here is probably to a traditional Jewish image of the righteous person's impassioned prayer. Its sentiments are reminiscent of those found in the psalms that describe agony, terror, and depression (cf. Psalms 22, 31, 38). Jesus offered these prayers as a priest offers sacrifice, and he was heard because of his reverence, or godly fear.

Though Son of God, Jesus learned what every human has to learn: acceptance of God's will in the circumstances of life. The surest way to learn this lesson, though perhaps the hardest, is through suffering. This notion points once again to Jesus' willingness to assume every aspect of human nature. As mediator of salvation Jesus endured torment of body and anguish of soul. He knew agony, terror, and depression. He could fully understand human distress and the desire to escape it. He was truly one with the human condition.

John 18:1–19:42

This passion narrative can be divided into three parts: the arrest of Jesus and his examination by the high priest (18:1-27); the trial before Pilate (18:28–19:16a); the crucifixion, death, and burial (19:16b-42). Throughout this account Jesus is portrayed as serenely in control of the events that eventually culminate in his death. Again and again his kingship makes itself evident, until he is finally lifted up in exaltation on the cross. Unbelief is exposed as resistance to God, and those who condemned him by this fact condemn themselves. Blame is placed more on the Jewish authorities than on the Romans, not out of any deep-seated anti-Semitism but because the Christian community at the time of the writing of the gospel was in desperate need of Roman approval in order to survive.

The undisputed sovereignty of Jesus is seen from the very first to the last episode. A cohort of Roman soldiers, a group of about six hundred, along with representatives of the religious leaders of Israel, come to arrest Jesus. Not until he provides a display of his divine power does he allow them to take him. Later, he stands with authority before Annas the high priest insisting that he has been arrested without cause. He acknowledges his authority to Pilate, pointing out that his rule is not of this world. He further announces that while authority is his by right, Pilate's is merely by appointment. Finally, only when all things have been accomplished does he hand over his spirit. From beginning to end, Jesus is in complete control.

The divine identity of Jesus is the fundamental reason for both his authority and the calm he exhibits. This identity is established at the outset. In the garden, three times (18:5, 6, 8) he responds to those who have come out after him with a simple self-identification: *Egó eimi!* I AM [he]! This was not lost on his accusers, who argued with Pilate that to claim to be Son of God made Jesus liable to death. This claim struck fear in Pilate's heart, and instead of releasing Jesus, he handed him over to be crucified.

The title of king is an explicit point of much controversy. It is the center of the discussion with Pilate, who questioned Jesus about it and then retreated somewhat when Jesus openly admitted his royal status. Jesus' claim to kingship became the occasion for the mockery of the soldiers, the rejection by the religious leaders, and the crowd's choice of Caesar rather than Jesus. This possible conflict with imperial sovereignty influenced Pilate to capitulate to the people's angry demands and to hand Jesus over to be crucified, but not without asserting this kingship by means of the inscription on the cross. The kingship of Jesus plays a pivotal role in this drama.

There is no misunderstanding in the accusations made against Jesus or in the execution of the plan to put him to death. Those responsible know what they are doing. Judas, an intimate companion, betrays him; the same Roman soldiers who had been thrown back by his power arrest him; the religious authorities condemn him for the very messianic posture they should have recognized in him; Pilate hands him over to the Jewish authorities even though he finds no fault in him. In this account unbelief is exposed as resistance to God. Despite this, God's plan of salvation moves inexorably forward.

Themes of the Day

We continue our meditation on the meaning of Passover. On Good Friday we discover that Jesus is our Passover. Three different faces of Jesus our Passover are offered for our reflection: the prophetic Suffering Servant; the great high priest; the triumphant king. Today's meditation ends with reflection on the power of the cross.

The Prophetic Suffering Servant

Silent like the paschal lamb that was sacrificed on behalf of the people, the Suffering Servant of the LORD allowed himself to be handed over to the slaughter. Though innocent, he took upon himself the guilt of the very ones who were victimizing him. We marvel at the willingness of those who place themselves at risk in order to save anyone who is vulnerable or anyone whom they love. But to do so for one's torturers is beyond human comprehension. Yet that is what Christ our Passover has done. He is the true Suffering Servant; he is the one who has allowed himself to be taken, to be afflicted, to be offered as the sacrifice for others. It is his blood that spares us; it is his life that is offered. Through his suffering, this servant justifies many. He is our true Passover.

The Great High Priest

Jesus is not only the innocent victim, he is also the high priest who offers the Passover sacrifice. Because he is one of us, he carries many of our own weaknesses. But it is because he is without moral blemish that, in him, we all stand before God. On this solemn day we behold his battered body, but we also look beyond it to the dignity that is his as high priest. Garbed as he is in wounds that rival the ornate garments of liturgical celebration, he offers himself on the altar of the cross. He is our true Passover.

Triumphant King

"King of the Jews" was the crime for which he was tried and sentenced and executed. It was the title that was inscribed above his bloody throne. To those passing by he appeared to be a criminal, but he was indeed a king. His crucifixion was his enthronement. Lifted up on the cross, he was lifted up in triumph and exaltation. Furthermore, he was not a conquered king; he was a conquering king. He willingly faced death and stared it down. As he delivered over his spirit, death lay vanquished at the foot of the cross. Within a few days this would begin to become clear to others. He is our true Passover.

The Power of the Cross

On Good Friday the cross gathers together all three images of Christ. It is in the light of this cross that we see clearly how all three must be accepted at once, for we never contemplate one image without contemplating the others. In the midst of the passion, we see the victory; when we celebrate Easter, we do not forget the cross. As we venerate this cross, we gather together the memory of all the living and the dead. With our petitions we bring to the cross all the needs of the world. In this way, the cross becomes the true *axis mundi,* the center of the universe, and Christ is revealed as the true Passover.

Easter Vigil

Genesis 1:1–2:2 (First Reading)

This first creation account is remarkable in several ways. It is replete with measured literary patterns. Each act of creation begins with the phrase "And God said" and ends with the temporal designation "evening . . . morning . . . the first day . . . the second day. . . ." First the universe is fashioned, and then it is appointed with all the heavenly luminaries. Next the sea and the sky and the earth are prepared as resourceful habitats for various animals. The appearance of these living things is described with another pattern: "God said . . . God made . . . God blessed" (vv. 20-22, 24-28). The very structure of the narrative bespeaks order and rhythm, interdependence and care. Again and again an evaluation is pronounced: "God saw how good it was."

According to this account order is brought forth from chaos; light is summoned from the darkness. God's creative activity is effortless. It is all accomplished by divine word. God speaks and creation appears; the word is the deed. The universe moves according to unwritten yet well-known laws. One word from God sets it all in motion. The potential for life seems to be in the waters of the sea and in the earth itself. All it needs is a word from God and it will burst forth.

The most extraordinary creature is humankind. The woman and the man are the only creatures made after the image and likeness of God and given responsibility to manage (subdue and have dominion) the rest of creation as caretakers. Only when all was completed and deemed "very good" did God rest.

Psalm 104:1-2, 5-6, 10, 12, 13-14, 24, 35 (A)

The nature hymn from which the psalm response is taken recalls the Genesis story of creation and is certainly one of the most beautiful psalms in the Psalter. It begins with a self-summons to sing the praises of God. It is clear the psalmist is overwhelmed by the splendor of the universe and is brimming with praise for the Creator of such grandeur. In fact, this awesome experience of creation is itself a revelation of God. The brilliance of nature is God's glorious robe. To behold creation is to encounter God.

Of all the creation motifs present in the psalm, the most prominent is water. The earth itself was established amidst cosmic water and then covered with protective ocean water as with a garment. Hearty spring waters refresh the earth and the animals that find their home both on the land and in the sky. Water brings vegetation to life on the earth, making it a steady source of food. Although it was initially chaotic and threatening, through God's gracious act of creation water has become the indispensable source of life for all living creatures.

The creation narrative and this psalm response both underscore the fact of God's activity. None of this happens haphazardly, nor is there any struggle between God and the forces of nature. All of nature serves the designs of God. In fact, in the psalm it is God who acts through nature; God sends the springs and raises the grass. God has created these marvels and then works through them for the benefit of all. No wonder the psalmist is inspired by creation to sing the praises of the Creator.

Psalm 33:4-5, 6-7, 12-13, 20-22 (B)

The verses of this psalm response contain a collection of various themes. The passage opens with a statement that reflects the fundamental basis of ancient Israel's faith in God. This faith is rooted in the truth of God's word, in the faithfulness of God's works, in the justice of God's covenant, and in the steadfastness of God's love. Everything else flows from these convictions.

The psalm picks up the theme of God's word and carries us with it back to the creation account of Genesis, where this word establishes the heavens and separates the waters of the deep. The stability of natural creation is evidence of God's power and faithfulness. God's creation provides a welcoming and sustaining home for all living beings. Creation is so vast that the psalmist's gaze cannot even begin to encompass all the reasons for praising the great Creator-God.

The psalmist moves from creation in its universality to history in its particularity. One people has been chosen by this Creator-God to be a special people, to be God's own inheritance. The macarism, "Blessed [Happy] the nation," denotes election, returning us to the themes with which this response opened. The placement of these themes is significant. Creation imagery is bracketed by covenant language. This literary arrangement can make two startling theological statements. First, it implies that the covenant God made with this special people is as firm and reliable as is creation. Second, it suggests that from the very beginning creation serves the goals of the covenant.

Genesis 22:1-18 (Second Reading)

This passage is an account of the testing of Abram. However, here the son takes center stage. This is not some anonymous offspring; it is Isaac, Abram's only son, the one he loves. Abram may have had another son (Ishmael), but Isaac was the only son upon whom his dreams were pinned. He was the hope of the future not only of his father but of the entire people who would eventually trace their ancestry back to Abraham. Isaac was the child of destiny, both of his father and of the entire race.

Just as Abram appears to be willing to sacrifice his beloved son, so Isaac seems to be willing to allow this to happen. There is no mention of struggle on his part. Though he inquires about the sacrifice, the answer given him by his father seems to satisfy him. Isaac is the innocent victim, the one who carries the wood of the sacrifice on his back up to the mountain where his life will be offered.

The fact that in this story Isaac is spared does not mitigate the horror of the scene depicted, nor does it alter the portrait of a brutal deity. God requires the innocent blood of the beloved son, and the father is willing to comply. Abram relinquished his natural claim on the child of promise, and at the end of the account he is blessed with a promise of more children than he can count (cf. 12:2-3; 13:16; 15:5; 26:4, 24). We may not understand God's plan, but we cannot deny that though God may at first appear to demand the impossible of us, in the end God will not be outdone in generosity.

Psalm 16:5, 8, 9-10, 11

The psalm verses speak of covenant relationship with God and the confidence that abounds from it. Two images express this relationship. The allotted portion of land is the inheritance each tribe was given and which was handed down within the tribes generation after generation. This land provided the people identity and membership, sustenance and prosperity. Without land they had no future, and they would not last long in the present. Here the psalmist is claiming that God has replaced the land in the religious consciousness of the people; the blessings and promises customarily associated with land are now associated with the LORD.

The second image is the cup. This might be the communal cup passed around from which all drank. Such an action solidified the union of those who drank from the common cup. When this action took place at a cultic meal, those participating in the feast were joined not only to each other but to the deity as well. The psalmist declares that this unifying cup is really the LORD. In other words, the psalmist is joined so closely with God as almost to defy separation. God is there at the psalmist's right hand, standing as an advocate or a refuge.

Such protection is reason for profound rejoicing. Regardless of the terrifying, even life-threatening ordeals the psalmist must endure, God is steadfast. In the face of things, this kind of confidence in God may appear foolhardy, but the psalmist's trust is unshakable. Ultimately, the fullness of joys will abound in the presence of God.

Exodus 14:15–15:1 (Third Reading)

We have come to that point in the story of liberation where God takes complete control of the situation. This divine leadership was exercised under several forms: the words of God; the angel of the LORD; the pillar of cloud. First, God gives specific directions to Moses. Next, the angel leads the people to the sea and then moves behind them as they pass through the parted waters. Finally, the column of cloud, which originally led the people, moves to the rear of the company. There, along with the angel, it serves as a buffer between the fleeing Israelites and the pursuing Egyptians. The escape from Egypt has been accomplished through the power of God.

While this narrative may appear to be an account of the struggle between the people of Israel and the Egyptian pharaoh, it is really a battle between divine forces. The pharaoh, thought by his people to be a god, is in mortal combat with the God of Israel, and it is the God of Israel who emerges triumphant. Not only is the LORD able to protect the Israelites and secure their release, but this is accomplished in Pharaoh's own land and against his own armies. The religious establishment of Egypt is no match for the God of Israel.

The waters of the sea represent the waters of chaos. God parts them just as the great Creator parted the carcass of the monster of the deep at the time of creation. The jubilation that follows this defeat is not so much because of the death of the Egyptians as because of the victory of God over the forces of chaos, be they political or cosmic.

Exodus 15:1-2, 3-4, 5-6, 17-18

This is a hymn of thanksgiving for deliverance and guidance. It recounts the miracle at the sea, the event that demonstrated God's mighty power and put an end to Israel's bondage in Egypt, and it reports Israel's entrance into and establishment in the land of promise. Recalling these marvelous feats, the poet praises God's glorious triumph.

As comments on the preceding reading stated, this is less a description of violence and the destruction of enemies than of the deliverance of a favored people. The characterizations of God underscore this; they all represent some kind of relationship with the people. God is a savior; a patron God who guided and protected the ancestors; a warrior who conquered cosmic evil; a divine ruler who reigns forever and ever.

There is an explicit cultic dimension of this hymn. It contains a threefold mention of the sanctuary: the mountain of God's inheritance; the place of God's throne; the sanctuary itself (vv. 17-18). This sacred place was important because it was the spot where the people offered sacrifice to God. More than this, it was the privileged place on earth where God dwelt in the midst of the people. It was usually erected on that site believed to be the center of the universe, the place where heaven, earth, and the underworld met. The poet is here thanking God for deliverance, but also for God's perpetual presence among the people. This presence is important because it will ensure God's continued protection.

Isaiah 54:5-14 (Fourth Reading)

Metaphors taken from familial relationships in a patriarchal household are used to characterize the covenant bond that exists between God and the people. Both God's love and God's wrath are portrayed in terms of a marriage bond that was established, then violated, and finally reestablished. Although the reading does not say Israel has been unfaithful, the implication is there.

God is a loyal but dishonored husband, and Israel is an unfaithful wife. The male bias here is obvious.

Looking past these narrow and offensive gender stereotypes, we can still appreciate the underlying description of God's love. It is intimate, like a marriage bond (v. 5); it is forgiving and tender (vv. 7-9); it is everlasting (vv. 8, 10). Just as God originally created a covenant bond, so now God lovingly re-creates it. The reference to Noah and the new creation after the flood suggests this (v. 9), as does the description of the reestablishment of the people in a city decked out in precious jewels (vv. 11-12).

Covenant language is very strong in this psalm. The reconciliation promised is called a "covenant of peace" (v. 10). Lovingkindness, or "enduring love" (*hesed*, vv. 8, 10), denotes loyalty to covenant obligations. "Great tenderness" (vv. 7, 10), comes from the word *ráham* ("womb"), and might be translated "womb-love." It refers to a deep and loving attachment, usually between two people who share some kind of natural bond. It only appears as a characteristic of God's love after the human covenant-partner has sinned. Hence there is an aspect of forgiveness in the very use of the word.

Psalm 30:2, 4, 5-6, 11-12, 13

This is a psalm of thanksgiving for deliverance from the peril of death, the netherworld, the pit (v. 4). The reference to death can be to illness, to depression, or to any serious misfortune that can threaten life itself. Whatever it might have been, the danger is now past; God intervened and saved the petitioner. In addition to the actual calamity, the psalmist is also concerned with enemies who would take delight in the misfortune. The prayer asks to be preserved from this insult as well. Following the initial plea is an acknowledgment of deliverance. God has heard the petition and has granted the request.

The psalmist next turns to the congregation of believers and calls on them to praise God. As with the preceding reading, the psalm does not explicitly state that the suffering endured was the deserved penalty for some wrongdoing. However, since that was the customary explanation of misfortune, such a conclusion could be drawn. Still, retribution is not the point of the prayer. Rather, the psalm compares the vast difference between God's wrath and God's graciousness. The former is short-lived; the latter is everlasting.

The psalmist turns again in prayer to God, pleading for pity. There is no suggestion that God has turned a deaf ear to earlier cries. Quite the contrary. The psalmist announces that grief and mourning have been turned into relief and rejoicing. This is the reason for the thanksgiving in the first place. Regardless of the nature of or reason for the misfortune, God can be trusted to come to the aid of one who cries for help.

Isaiah 55:1-11 (Fifth Reading)

This powerful prophetic oracle contains some of the most moving sentiments placed in the mouth of God. First, God's invitation is extended both to those who are able to pay for food and drink (v. 2) and to those who are not (v. 1). All are invited to come to the LORD in order to be refreshed and nourished. The reference is probably to something more than ordinary food and drink, since those called are also told to listen. The word of God is itself a source of rejuvenation.

The real object of the invitation is God's announcement of the reestablishment of a covenant bond (v. 3). The reference is to the royal covenant, the one made with David and his house. Although it was instituted as an everlasting covenant, the people broke the bond by their sins. God is now eager to restore this bond. The oracle states that just as David's success proclaimed God's majesty to the nations, so the people called here will be a witness of God's mercy and love. Just as David was the source of blessing, peace, and fullness of life for his own nation, the people called here will be a comparable source of blessing for nations they do not even know.

After this bold promise is made, the people are told to turn to the LORD; sinners are exhorted to reform their lives and to seek forgiveness from God. These are not suggestions; they are imperatives. The people are summoned to repentance. Then God's plans will take effect just as the rain accomplishes what it is intended to accomplish. Unlike human beings who work for justice and reparation, God's way is compassion and re-creation, and this renewal will last forever.

Isaiah 12:2-3, 4, 5-6

This hymn of thanksgiving anticipates favors that will be granted and enjoyed in the future. Therefore, one might consider it a hymn of confidence as well. God is declared "savior," and it is because of this characterization that the writer is unafraid and takes courage. The theme of water appears here as it did in the preceding reading. Though the imagery is slightly different, in both cases the water is transformative. Earlier it represented new creation; here it is water of salvation.

The theme of witness reappears here as well (vv. 4-5). The writer calls on the community to praise the glorious name of God, the name that represents the very character of God. They are to extol the marvels God has accomplished and proclaim them to the nations. The most celebrated of these wondrous works is the transformation of the people themselves. In other words, the transformed lives of God's people will announce to the nations the marvels God has accomplished.

The third and final theme found in this response highlights the importance of Jerusalem. This city was both the royal capital of the Davidic dynasty and the site where the Temple was built. It is the second aspect that is the focus here. The city itself is called upon to rejoice. The reason for this exaltation is the presence of God in its midst. Although the Temple was the concrete representation of this divine presence, it is the presence of God and not the temple building that is fundamental (cf. Jer 7:3-4). The theology of the passage has come full circle. The presence of God in the midst of the people is the source of the writer's confidence in future deliverance.

Baruch 3:9-15, 32–4:4 (Sixth Reading)

This passage, taken from a book attributed to the secretary of Jeremiah (cf. Jer 36:4), is considered one of the Bible's hymns of praise of Wisdom (cf. Proverbs 8; 9; Sir 24:1-22; Wis 7:22–8:21). It begins with the characteristic summons "Hear, O Israel" (v. 9; cf. Deut 6:4) and continues with an explanation of the reasons for the nation's exile in the land of its foes. Basically it was because the people had turned from the law, the fountain of wisdom (vv. 10-13).

The mysterious female figure that appears in these verses is more than a wise woman; she is Wisdom itself. This representation of wisdom should not be considered a figure of speech. While many passages maintain that one of the chief characteristics of God is divine wisdom, the image found here suggests more. Wisdom Woman appears to enjoy an existence intimately associated with yet clearly distinct from God.

The description of Wisdom is reminiscent of images found elsewhere in the Wisdom literature. First, the question is posed: Where can Wisdom be found? (cf. Job 28:12, 20). In answer, the poet sketches an account of primordial creation. Wisdom was there with the Creator (vv. 32-35; cf. Prov 8:22-31; Wis 8:1), and only the Creator knows the way to her (v. 31).

Although she is inaccessible to all but God, she is given by God to Israel (3:36; cf. Sir 24:8-12). Because Wisdom is the way of God (3:13), she is also identified with the law (v. 4:1; cf. Sir 24:23). Ultimately, the way of Wisdom is conformity to the law; conformity to the law is the way to life; those who follow this way will be happy.

Psalm 19:8, 9, 10, 11

Six different synonyms are used to extol the glories of the law (*tôrâ*, meaning "instruction" or "teaching"). The psalm describes the blessings that acceptance of the law can impart, but it does so not merely to describe the law but also to persuade the people to embrace it as the will of God and to live in accord with it. What is described here is not just any religious law; it is uniquely Israel's, because in a very specific way it represents the will of the God of Israel.

In a very unique way, the law is that point where an encounter with God takes place. It consisted of directives for living a full and God-fearing life. The qualities associated with fulfillment of the law are some of the most highly prized attributes found in any religious tradition. The law is perfect or complete; it is trustworthy, upright, clean; it is pure and true. Fidelity to the law should lead one to the godliness enshrined within it.

The effects of the law are all relational, enhancing human life itself. The law imbues the soul with new vitality; it gives wisdom; it delights the heart; it enables the eyes to recognize truth; it generates awe; it is a path to righteousness; it is more valuable than gold; it is sweeter than honey. The law of the LORD is something greatly to be desired. This description of the law shows clearly that the psalmist found it life-giving and not restrictive, ennobling and not demeaning. Reverence for the law seems to promise the best things life has to offer.

Ezekiel 36:16-17a, 18-28 (Seventh Reading)

The prophet claims that the Israelites brought on their own downfall through lives of violence and idolatry. Their sinfulness polluted the land, and so they were expelled. What is more despicable, according to this prophet, is the fact that their shameful behavior and the punishment they had to endure because of it doubly dishonored the holy name of God. It was for this reason God relented and gave them another chance.

The renown among the nations of God's holy name is an important theme in this reading. The spectacular events of Israel's initial election and the prosperity with which the nation was subsequently blessed should have been a witness to the surrounding nations of the unbounded generosity of God. Because the people failed in this, God decided to re-create the nation and to do it in a way that the name of the God of Israel would be synonymous with mercy and compassion.

The regeneration of the nation is accomplished in several steps. The first is a ritual of cleansing. The people have polluted themselves, so God washes them with clean water. This symbolic action represents the inner cleansing that takes place. Next, God takes away their hard hearts and gives them tender hearts, and gives them a new spirit, which is God's own spirit. This new heart and new spirit will transform the inner being of the people, enabling them to live lives of integrity. Although the verbs are in a perfect or future form, it is a special prophetic perfect, implying that this future transformation has already been accomplished. God's regeneration of the people has already taken place.

Psalm 42:3, 5; 43:3, 4 (A: When baptism is celebrated)

These two psalms really constitute one song, so they are often linked together. The first is a lament expressing the longing for God the psalmist experiences. This is a profoundly spiritual thirst, probably a desire for some form of worship in the Temple. The liturgical imagery is obvious: procession to the house of God, keeping festival. It seems that the psalmist even exercised some form of leadership within the worshiping community, leading the procession. The context of the lament could be exile, making it a fitting response to the preceding reading. Despite the suffering that is evident, there is no despair there. The psalmist does seem to anticipate ultimately standing in God's presence, beholding God's face.

The lament of the first psalm is replaced in the second by the petitions addressed to God. Whatever the suffering may be, the psalmist experiences it as darkness and, consequently, pleads with God to send light that will lead the psalmist to God's presence (another reference to the Temple?). There is confidence here; God's fidelity is invoked. Where earlier the psalmist nostalgically remembered the house of God, here return to that house seems to be a future possibility.

The last verses of the psalm response resemble a prophetic announcement. It is cast in the future form, but it is less a hesitant hope than a confident expectation. The grief and lament of the opening verses have given way to gladness and rejoicing. God has heard and answered the prayer of the psalmist.

Isaiah 12:2-3, 4bcd, 5-6
(B: When baptism is not celebrated)

This hymn of thanksgiving anticipates favors that will be granted and enjoyed in the future. Therefore, one might consider it a hymn of confidence as well. God is declared "savior," and it is because of this characterization the writer is unafraid and takes courage. The theme of water appears here as it did in the preceding reading. Though the imagery is slightly different, in both cases the water is transformative. Earlier it represented new creation; here it is water of salvation.

The theme of witness reappears here as well (vv. 4-5). The writer calls on the community to praise the glorious name of God, the name that represents the very character of God. They are to extol the marvels God has accomplished and proclaim them to the nations. The most celebrated of these wondrous works is the transformation of the people themselves. In other words, the transformed lives of God's people will announce to the nations the marvels God has accomplished.

The third and final theme in this response highlights the importance of Jerusalem. This city was both the royal capital of the Davidic dynasty and the site where the Temple was built. It is the second aspect that is the focus here. The city itself is called upon to rejoice. The reason for this exaltation is the presence of God in its midst. Although the Temple was the concrete representation of this divine presence, it is the presence of God and not the temple building that is fundamental (cf. Jer 7:3-4). The theology of the passage has come full circle. The presence of God in the midst of the people is the source of the writer's confidence of future deliverance.

Psalm 51:12-13, 14-15, 18-19
(C: When baptism is not celebrated)

This may be the best known of the Penitential Psalms (cf. Psalms 6, 32, 38, 51, 102, 130, 143). Although it is considered a lament, it also contains elements of a confession of sin and a prayer for forgiveness. This passage opens with a plea for restoration. The clean heart and new spirit spoken of here correspond to the same themes in the prophetic reading for which this psalm is a response. Such a prayer could be considered a veiled confession of sin, for it is a request for inner transformation. This is reinforced by the plea that God not cast the psalmist out but rather grant again the joy of salvation.

The psalmist next promises to announce to other sinners the salvation of God. Gratitude for having been forgiven becomes active service to others. The new life that results from the clean heart and steadfast spirit becomes an outward proclamation of God's gracious mercy. Others will see it and will themselves be converted and return to God.

The interior nature of this transformation can also be seen in the character of worship that flows from it. External performance, regardless of how faithfully it is done, is not enough. The psalmist goes so far as to say that God is not even pleased with practices of worship. This may sound exaggerated, but it is in keeping with the theme of inner transformation so prominent in the prophetic reading and psalm response. Once again, heart and spirit are the focus of the psalmist's attention. The clean heart is now also a humble heart; the steadfast spirit is now also contrite. The inner renewal effected by God is now complete.

Romans 6:3-11

Paul here explains how baptism has enabled the Christians to participate in the death and resurrection of Jesus. As they were engulfed in the water, they were buried with him in death; as they emerged from the water, they rose with him into new life. Paul's real intent in drawing these lines of comparison between the death and resurrection of Jesus and the baptism and new life of the Christians is ethical exhortation. He seeks to encourage them to set aside their old manner of living and take on the new life of holiness.

While the descent into baptismal waters can symbolize Christ's descent into death, there is another dimension of the water imagery that strengthens Paul's argument. There is a long tradition that cosmic waters were chaotic, therefore death-dealing (cf. Gen 6-9; Job 22:11; Ps 73:13-14; Isa 27:1). To be engulfed by water is to be swallowed by chaos and death. Christ is plunged into the chaos of death; the Christians were plunged into the death of chaos. By the power of God Christ rose to a new life of glory; by the power of God the Christians are raised to the glory of a new life.

Paul characterizes their former lives as slavery to sin. This old enslaved self has to be crucified. Just as death had no power over the resurrected Christ, so sin would have no power over the baptized Christian. Crucifixion is a fitting image for Christian conversion not only because of the role it played in Christ's death but because the torment it entails exemplifies the suffering a change of life will exact of the Christians. However, the cross is the only way to new life.

Psalm 118:1-2, 16, 17, 22-23

The refrain, "His mercy endures forever," indicates that this thanksgiving psalm was intended for congregational singing. The psalm itself is a song in praise of God's power and victory. God is depicted as a mighty warrior whose strong hand prevails over forces that can threaten the life of the psalmist. God's goodness and mercy toward the house of Israel are seen in this victory. The communal character of these sentiments suggests that the threat from which the people have been saved is some kind of national enemy. Having been spared, the psalmist extols God's good favor, actually becoming a witness to the grandeur of the saving works of the LORD. The gift of salvation by God engenders witness to others of the graciousness of this saving God.

The final image is the metaphor of reversal of fortunes found so often in religious literature. The situation is always the same. A righteous person is rejected, sometimes even persecuted, by other members of the community. When the patron steps in to correct this unjust situation, the righteous one is not only vindicated but is also elevated to a position of great importance. Here, the stone that was rejected becomes the very foundation of the entire building. Applying this metaphor to the psalmist, one is led to conclude that the suffering endured was unwarranted. The stability of the entire community is dependent on the innocent one who was originally rejected. This individual was first a witness to salvation by God and is now the agent of salvation for others.

Luke 24:1-12

Many scholars believe the earliest resurrection accounts recalled the appearances of the risen Lord and only later did the tradition of the empty tomb arise. This is probably true because, given their understanding of the unity of human nature, the earliest Palestinian believers would not have conceived of a resurrection that did not include the physical body. Nonetheless, while appearances of the risen Lord in themselves are difficult to verify, an empty tomb really proves very little, for the body could have been stolen. Still, if the body had been taken away, how does one explain the presence of the burial clothes Peter saw when he bent down and looked into the empty tomb? The robbers would hardly have unwrapped the body as they took it away.

The incredulity of the followers of Jesus is undeniable. The women come to the tomb to complete the burial rites that were interrupted on the day of his death (cf. 23:54-56). They did not expect to find it empty. When they report what they have seen and heard, the eleven and those with them do not believe them. Was their response due to male bias against the credibility of women, or could it indicate their lack of faith? Most likely, it is both. Despite Jesus' own earlier predictions, they are not prepared to believe in his resurrection, and they certainly are not going to accept the fact of it on the word of women. Even Peter, who ran to the tomb upon hearing their story, goes home amazed (*thaumázo* can mean both "critical" and "curious"). His action may indicate that he was not as incredulous as the other men, but the text does not say he believed.

The women, who according to this narrative are the first witnesses to the resurrection, were devout followers of Jesus. Those who are named had accompanied him throughout his journeys, attending to his needs and the needs of his disciples (cf. 8:1-3). They continued to minister to him at his burial. Initially the empty tomb led to their confusion, not to any faith. Entering the tomb, they saw the two men in dazzling garments (cf. the transfiguration, Luke 9:29). It was to these woman the proclamation of Jesus' resurrection was first announced: He is raised; he is living!

It is the religious meaning of the suffering and death of Jesus that is the focus of the resurrection message, not its political implications. Jesus is identified as the Son of Man, that mysterious being from early Israelite tradition who many believed would come to inaugurate the reign of God (cf. Dan 7:13). Those into whose hands Jesus was delivered are not identified as Jews or Romans but as sinners. The men from heaven remind the women of Jesus' own predictions of his fate (cf. 9:22, 44; 18:32-33). Only then do the women remember and, presumably, believe. They go to announce this wondrous message to the eleven and the others with them. Now the women are not only the first witnesses to the resurrection but also the first heralds.

Themes of the Day

During the Easter Vigil on Holy Saturday evening, we complete our reflections of the meaning of Passover. On Holy Thursday we saw that God is the one who passes over; on Good Friday we recognized that Jesus is our Passover. Today we ourselves are drawn into the mystery as we contemplate our own passing over. Holy Saturday is a time of liminality. We are no longer in one place, but we have not yet arrived at the other. We are in the crossing. We are moving from darkness into light, and we do this by passing through water.

The Passage Through Water

The vigil readings recount our journey from darkness into light, from the chaotic waters of creation to the saving waters of baptism. We begin at the dawn of creation, when God separated the waters and called light out of the darkness, ordered the world and made it pulsing with life. The unfathomable nature of the trust exacted of us as we embark on and remain faithful to this journey is seen in the test to which Abraham is put. In order to embrace the new life God has planned for us, we must be willing to relinquish all we hold dear in this life. This includes all our hopes and dreams and even that upon which we have based our future. God must be our hope and our dream; God must be the foundation of our future.

In the dark of the night we must be willing to follow God into the unknown. If we can do this, if we can risk all and leave behind the life to which we have grown accustomed, we will be able to survive in this period of liminality. All we need to sustain us at this time is the confidence of knowing that God, who is our redeemer, loves us with indescribable passion. Secure in this love, we will be able to turn to God for all we need. Embraced by God's everlasting covenant, we believe we are being led to a land that is abundantly fertile and secure from all that might harm us. It is in this liminal stage that we can accept God's commandments of life and promise to live according to God's plan for us.

The vigil readings end with a promise of regeneration. The waters that at first threatened us now cleanse us. We are given new hearts, which will enable us to live the life of faith to which we will soon again commit ourselves. We now stand at the threshold of a new creation. The period of liminality is over. Our next step is into the waters of baptism, there to be re-created, to be born anew, to die and to rise in Christ. Then our passing over will be complete, and we will be embraced by Christ, our true Passover.

Easter

Easter Sunday Acts 10:34a, 37-43 We ate and drank with him	**Psalm 118:1-2, 16-17, 22-23** The day the LORD has made	**Colossians 3:1-4** Seek what is above (or) **1 Corinthians 5:6b-8** Clear out old yeast	**John 20:1-9** He is risen
Second Sunday Acts 5:12-16 Believers were added	**Psalm 118:2-4, 13-15, 22-24** Give thanks to the LORD	**Revelation 1:9-11a, 12-13, 17-19** Now I am alive	**John 20:19-31** Jesus stood in their midst
Third Sunday Acts 5:27-32, 40b-41 We are witnesses	**Psalm 30:2, 4-6, 11-13** You have rescued me	**Revelation 5:11-14** Worthy is the Lamb	**John 21:1-19** He fed them at the sea
Fourth Sunday Acts 13:14, 43-52 We turn to the Gentiles	**Psalm 100:1-3, 5** We are God's people	**Revelation 7:9, 14b-17** In the blood of the Lamb	**John 10:27-30** My sheep hear my voice
Fifth Sunday Acts 14:21-27 The Church grows	**Psalm 145:8-13** I will praise your name	**Revelation 21:1-5a** He will wipe away tears	**John 13:31-33a, 34-35** A new commandment

Sixth Sunday Acts 15:1-2, 22-29 Circumcision is not required	Psalm 67:2-3, 5, 6, 8 All nations praise God	Revelation 21:10-14, 22-23 The Holy City Jerusalem	John 14:23-29 The Spirit will teach you
Ascension Acts 1:1-11 Jesus was lifted up	Psalm 47:2-3, 6-9 All you people, clap your hands	Ephesians 1:17-23 (or) Hebrews 9:24-28; 10:19-23 Christ has entered heaven	Luke 24:46-53 Jesus is taken up
Seventh Sunday Acts 7:55-60 The stoning of Stephen	Psalm 97:1-2, 6-7, 9 The LORD is king	Revelation 22:12-14, 16-17, 20 Come, Lord Jesus	John 17:20-26 That they may be one
Pentecost Acts 2:1-11 Filled with the Holy Spirit	Psalm 104:1, 24, 29-31, 34 Send out your Spirit	1 Corinthians 12:3b-7, 12-13 Baptized in the Spirit (or) Romans 8:8-17 Children of God	John 20:19-23 Receive the Holy Spirit (or) John 14:15-16, 23b-26 The Spirit will teach you

Easter

Initial Reading of the Easter Lectionary

Introduction

The entire Easter season celebrates the membership of the newly initiated people. Within the context of the liturgy, the texts read during this time constitute a mystagogical catechesis, or formative instructions for neophytes. One of the distinctive features of this season is the inclusion of selections from the Acts of the Apostles rather than readings from the First Testament.

First Readings

The first readings for the season of Easter provide us with an abbreviated account of the early days of the Christian community. Peter preaches the good news to a Gentile household. From the very beginning God intended that the gospel be spread to all people. This meant certain features of the religious tradition would have to be reinterpreted. However, the enthusiasm of the preachers and the power of their message captured the minds and hearts of many, and believers were added to their number. Nonetheless, from the beginning the Church knew both tremendous success and fierce opposition. The missionaries seemed to be challenging the law. How necessary was its observance? This was the first major theological crisis facing the nascent Church. The issue was resolved in favor of the community moving with the Spirit.

The last three readings shift our attention from the life of the community to the mighty acts of God. Jesus ascends to the right hand of God, there to receive the exaltation that is his by reason of his triumph. Stephen, the first witness *(mártys)*, sees him there. Just as Jesus had promised, the Holy Spirit descends upon the community, filling them with the courage that enables them to move out of their places of safety into the whole world. The power of Easter has taken hold.

Psalms

The responsorial psalms all come from hymns of thanksgiving or praise. God's fidelity to the covenant is the focus of much of this gratitude. God made promises and has kept them. God promised to deliver the people out of the hands of their enemies, and they were rescued; God promised they would be victorious, and they triumphed; God promised to supply them with an abundance of good things, and they prospered. There was much for which the people had to be thankful, and the psalms show that they were. The last three psalms are slightly different. They praise God who is enthroned victorious above the heavens. By placing these psalms within a specific liturgical context, the praise and thanksgiving they extol is ascribed to the risen Lord, and a definite correlation is drawn between the themes they contain and the season and feasts being celebrated.

Epistles

The epistles for the season have a strong christological tone. Although liturgically the second reading is usually exhortative, in this collection they are usually descriptive. Together they create a brilliantly colored portrait of the risen Lord. First his resurrection is unequivocally announced. Then the eschatological dimension of his risen nature is featured. He is portrayed as the one like the Son of Man, and the Lamb that was slain. Because of him the Holy City, the new Jerusalem, is open to all who have washed their robes in his blood. His entrance into heaven is described in both priestly and eschatological imagery. The season ends with the listing of various gifts bestowed by the Spirit sent in Jesus' name.

Gospels

With the exception of the feast of the Ascension, all the gospel readings have been taken from the Gospel according to John. The first passage is a report of the empty tomb, but most of the other readings are resurrection narratives, relating some appearance of the risen Lord. In each case the risen Lord has a commission to impart to his disciples. He appoints them as judges regarding the forgiveness of sin; he commissions Peter to care for the People of God; he directs them to love as he has loved; he bestows his peace upon them. In all of the gospels Jesus seem to be preparing the disciples for the time when he will physically depart from their presence and they will have to carry on themselves the work he began. He commissions them and provides the instruction necessary for them to know what to do. Even then they will have to wait for their empowerment by the Spirit.

Mosaic of Readings

The Easter readings for this year clearly portray the unfolding of the power of the resurrection. Scene after scene in the epistles presents the glorious effects of Jesus' own eschatological transformation. Awed by these marvels, we can do nothing but praise and thank God through the psalms. The gospels provide us with another perspective of the risen Lord. He is not content to savor his victory alone. It is his wish that all will have a share in his triumph, so he prepares his followers to spread the word through all the world. Finally, the readings from Acts show us what can be accomplished by weak and struggling human beings when they commit themselves to the words of Jesus and follow the prompting of the Spirit. These narratives merely sketch the beginnings. The rest is up to us.

Readings

Easter Sunday

Acts 10:34a, 37-43

Peter's discourse is an announcement about the scope and the spread of the gospel. The story of Jesus from his baptism, through his ministry, to his death and resurrection, has been reported all over the land. The power of Jesus' ministry flowed from his having been anointed by God with the Holy Spirit. The reference to anointing is probably an allusion to his baptism, when the heavens opened and the Spirit descended upon him (Luke 3:21-22; 4:14, 18; cf. Isa 61:1). It was in and through this power that Jesus performed good works and healings. Peter lists himself as a witness to all of these wonders.

The text suggests Peter is speaking to a Gentile audience. Judea is referred to as the "country of the Jews," and the rejection Jesus experienced at the hands of his own people is mentioned. This indicates that "the Jews" were a group other than those being addressed. The allusion to the message of the prophets implies that the hearers would have known to whom Peter refers. However, this does not mean they were Jews, since there were many Gentiles in Judea at this time who were interested in Jewish tradition and practice and who would have been acquainted with the important prophetic teaching.

Although Jesus' ministry had a beginning, namely his baptism by John, it does not seem to have had an ending. It continues through those who were commissioned to preach the gospel and bear witness to it. This is precisely what Peter is doing in this reading, bearing witness to the resurrection of Jesus (v. 40) and proclaiming the universality of its effects (v. 42).

Peter's teaching regarding the resurrection includes several important components. First, it is clearly a work of God. Second, it is a genuine resurrection from the dead and not merely a resuscitation. That it occurred three days after Jesus' death is evidence of this. Third, Jesus was seen by some and then ate and drank with several of his followers, Peter among them. This demonstrates that the appearances of the risen Christ were genuine physical experiences and not some kind of hallucinations.

Finally, the fruits of the resurrection are both transformative and all-encompassing. Peter claims that Jesus, appointed by God, is the one who fulfills the role of eschatological arbiter, judging the living and the dead (v. 42; cf. Dan 7:1). He further asserts that this judgment scene was the wondrous event to which the prophets testified. Peter is here explaining the mystery of Jesus in terms of prophetic expectation and thus is at once both reinterpreting earlier prophetic tradition and developing new theological insight. With just a few words Peter has placed Jesus at the heart of both the prophetic and the apocalyptic traditions of Israel.

The judgment Jesus brings is one of forgiveness of sin. He judges not to condemn but to save and to transform. Furthermore, though born from the people of Israel and rooted within that tradition, he was raised up by God to bring forgiveness to all. The power of the resurrection is not circumscribed by ethnic or religious origin. It is open to all who believe in Jesus. This is truly good news to the Gentiles.

Psalm 118:1-2, 16-17, 22-23

The responsorial psalm is a song in praise of God's power and victory. The refrain, "His mercy endures forever," indicates that this thanksgiving psalm was intended for congregational singing. The communal character of these sentiments, seen in the reference to the house of Israel, suggests the threat from which the people have been saved is some kind of national enemy. God's goodness and mercy toward the house of Israel are made manifest in this victory. The Hebrew word for mercy *(ḥesed)* is a technical theological term denoting God's steadfast love for the partners in the covenant, the chosen people of the house of Israel. Having been spared, the psalmist extols God's good favor, actually becoming a witness to the grandeur of the saving works of the LORD.

God is depicted as a mighty warrior whose strong right hand prevails over forces that can threaten the security of the people and the very life of the psalmist. The bias for right-handedness is obvious. The right side of a person was considered the stronger side, the honorable side. Conversely, the left side was weak, untrustworthy, sinister. The image of God's right hand connotes strength and triumph. It suggests that God's victory was won in a righteous manner.

This divine achievement in itself made God deserving of praise and thanksgiving. However, there seems to be a personal element in this victory. In the wake of God's triumph the psalmist is preserved from death. As a result of this magnanimous deed the psalmist will publish abroad the mighty works of the LORD. Here again, the individual and the communal aspects of this thanksgiving psalm are intertwined.

The final image is the metaphor of reversal of fortunes found so often in religious literature. The situation is always the same. A righteous person is rejected, sometimes even persecuted, by other members of the community. When the divine patron of the sufferer steps in to correct the unjust situation, the righteous one is not only vindicated but is also elevated to a position of great importance. In this psalm the stone that was rejected becomes the very foundation of the entire building. The Hebrew identifies this stone as "the head of the corner." Although some interpret it as the capstone that completes the building, the reference is probably to the cornerstone, which links two walls at right angles, thus holding up a significant part of the building's weight.

It is not clear to whom the metaphor of the cornerstone refers. However, as the verses of this psalm are arranged for our liturgical use, it seems that the speaker who survived the threat of death is the referent. This salvation was brought about by God, and it is recognized as a marvel for which to give praise and thanks.

Colossians 3:1-4 (A)

The passage, short as it is, contains the fundamental teaching about the resurrection and the way the death and resurrection of Christ transform the lives of Christians. It is set against the backdrop of ancient cosmology. The verbs used are quite telling. Besides the imperatives, which both address the present and remain open to all future moments, there are also verbs in the perfect tense, denoting the finality of some actions.

Two realms are delineated: the world above and the world below. In a three-tiered cosmology this delineation has two possible meanings. On the one hand, it could refer to the earth and the netherworld; on the other, to the heavenly realm and the earth. Although early Christian theology spoke of Christ descending to the netherworld after his death, there to release the souls of the righteous awaiting resurrection, the reference in this passage to God's right hand indicates the second interpretation is the one intended. The earth is the world below and the heavenly realm is the world above.

Christ rose from the dead and is now in the realm of heaven. Two images characterize the relationship between the risen Christ and God. First, Christ is seated at God's right hand. This suggests a heavenly imperial throne room where God reigns supreme and Christ sits next to God in the place of honor. Enthroned at God's right hand, Christ both enjoys God's favor and, as God's "right hand," bestows blessings on others and administers God's righteousness. The second image states that Christ is "in God." This means that having died to human life, Christ has been raised to a new life. In a new and total way, Christ's being is rooted in God.

The admonition to the Christians flows out of belief in this reality. As believers, they are joined to Christ. Consequently, they have died with Christ and they have risen with Christ. Therefore, they should turn their attention away from the things of this world and commit themselves to the things of heaven. They are called to a life that reflects this new reality. The specifics of such a life are outlined elsewhere, but one can presume that being joined to Christ would result in behavior like that of Christ.

While the admonitions are explicit imperatives, the statements about dying with Christ and being raised with Christ are in the perfect tense. This is not a dimension of the Christians' future expectation but an accomplished fact. They are indeed joined with Christ, and so joined, they are already with Christ in God. They have not left this world, but they are summoned to be attentive to the things of another world. In fact, they live in two worlds, or to use eschatological language, they have already entered "the age to come."

The passage ends with mention of Christ's ultimate appearance and a promise that those joined with Christ will also appear in glory. Here is an example of a complex eschatological view: already, but not yet. Joined to Christ, Christians are living in the final age already, but this age of fulfillment is not yet complete.

1 Corinthians 5:6b-8 (B)

The reference in this reading to yeast calls to mind the Jewish feast of Unleavened Bread (cf. Exod 12:3-10; Deut 16:3-4), which marked the beginning of the barley harvest. Though originally an agricultural celebration, it was eventually joined to the herding feast of Passover, and together they became a commemoration of God's deliverance of the people from the bondage of Egypt. The reference to "Christ our Passover" marks this combining of festivals.

During the first seven days of the feast only bread made from the flour of the new grain was to be eaten. It was prepared without leaven, the dough left over from the previous baking. Because leaven ferments and also causes ingredients around it to break down, it was considered both corrupt in itself and an evil influence. Nothing from the old year, and certainly nothing corrupt, was to be brought into the fruits of the new harvest.

Paul uses this abstention from leaven, which marked the transition from one year to the next, as a metaphor for the Christians' conversion from life before Christ to life with Christ, from the old age to the age of fulfillment. He exhorts them to rid themselves of their former way of life, for even the slightest trace of corruption can undermine the good they might do. "A rotten apple spoils the whole barrel."

Continuing with imagery taken from these combined Jewish festivals, Paul emphatically states: "Christ our Passover has been sacrificed!" The allusion is to the death of Jesus, which, like the sacrifice of the Passover lamb, saved the people by vicariously assuming the guilt of the community. In order fittingly to celebrate this Passover, the Christians must now purge themselves of all leaven of the past. They must put aside works of corruption and wickedness and commit themselves to lives of sincerity and truth.

John 20:1-9

The resurrection stories begin with a report of Mary Magdalene's visit to the tomb. It is the first day of the week while it is still dark. Reference to darkness rather than the dawn of a new day, which would be traditional, may be the author's way of incorporating the light/darkness symbolism. In other words, lack of faith is a life in darkness. Identifying the day as the first of the week will take on significance in subsequent Christian theology. It will be likened to the dawning of a new creation, the eschatological time of fulfillment.

No explanation is given for Mary's visit. The text does not say she came to weep or to anoint the body. It simply says she came to the tomb. Seeing that the stone had been moved, she presumed that the body of Jesus had been taken away. She seems to have entertained no thought of his resurrection, only the removal of his body. She ran off to tell Peter and "the other disciple." The text is cryptic. For some reason Mary speaks in the plural: "We don't know . . . ," and the disciple who was with Peter is not named.

The reading contains a definite bias in favor of this other disciple. He is referred to as the one whom Jesus loved (an allusion to John?), and he is the only one in the account who is said to have believed. He is beloved, and he is faith-filled. The text also hints at Peter's privileged status within the community. He is the one to whom Mary runs, and when the two men hurry to the tomb, the other disciple waits until Peter enters before he himself goes in.

The details about the burial wrappings are significant. They are still in the tomb, though the body is not. If the body had been merely transported to another tomb, burial wrappings would still have been needed, and presumably they would have been taken along. However, if the body had been carried away in order to desecrate it, the cloths would probably have been discarded. No explanation is given for why the head cloth was rolled up separately. The interpretation of these details seems to have been left to the character in the narrative. We are not told what Peter thought about them, but the Beloved Disciple noted these things and believed. It is unusual that resurrection faith would spring forth from an experience of the empty tomb rather than from an appearance of the risen Lord, but it is the case here.

The reading ends on a curious note. The reason for the general lack of faith of the disciples is given: they did not understand the Scriptures concerning the resurrection of Jesus. Regardless of how Jesus might have instructed his followers while he was still with them, they were ill equipped to comprehend his suffering and death, to say nothing of his rising from the dead. They would need both a resurrection experience and the opening of their minds to the meaning of the Scriptures.

The choice of this reading for Easter Sunday highlights the incomprehensibility of the event. The fact that neither Mary, probably Jesus' closest female disciple, nor Peter, the leader of the Christian community, was prepared spontaneously to embrace the truth of the resurrection should caution us lest we too-glibly presume to grasp it. There is much in the reality of the resurrection that continues to challenge as well as sustain us.

Themes of the Day

Easter is the season of mystagogical catechesis, instruction that unpacks the hidden mystery experienced in the sacraments of initiation received or renewed on Easter. The readings of each Sunday concentrate on some aspect of this mystery. The central theme of this Sunday is newness of life in Christ. This newness is not without historical context. It burst forth first in the resurrection of Christ, and then through the preaching of the first Christians. History is broken open by this newness in unimaginable ways.

Newness in Christ

In the Northern Hemisphere the world is coming alive. You can see it in the trees; you can smell it in the air. There is a freshness about to burst forth. Newness seems to be standing on tiptoes eager to reveal itself, ready to be born. The life that was hidden in the darkness of winter is impatient to appear in all its glory. Nature itself seems poised to reenact the drama of death and resurrection.

On Easter Sunday the changes in nature all point to the transformation par excellence, the death and resurrection of Christ and the transformation that takes place in us as we participate in that resurrection presence. The readings testify that if we die with Christ we will appear with him in glory; if we cast out the old yeast we will be fresh dough. When this wondrous transformation takes place, everything is new; everything is fresh.

To what newness are we called? To what must we die in order to rise transformed? What old yeast of corruption must be cast out in order that we might be fresh dough? On Easter we renew our baptismal vows. What is it we really renounce? Ours is a world of violence, of prejudice, of indifference. Too often we harbor feelings of anger and resentment, of selfishness and disdain. Easter proclaims that Christ has died and has risen; with him we die to all the wickedness in our lives and in our world, and we set our hearts on higher things, on sincerity and on truth.

History Is Broken Open

Though we know well the Easter story, we never fully grasp its meaning. The stone has been rolled back and the tomb is empty; resurrected life cannot be contained. Like the first believers, we so often must continue to live even with our dashed hopes and our misunderstanding of God's mysterious power. Like the first believers, we come to the tomb and expect to find death, but instead we find signs of a new life we cannot even begin to comprehend. Like the first believers, we do not realize that history has been broken open and is now filled with the resurrected presence of Christ.

History no longer makes sense. The one who was maliciously singled out and shamefully hung on a tree was really the one set apart by God to judge the living and the dead. Who can comprehend such a paradox? But then, who goes to a tomb expecting to find life? History has been broken open, and now we really do not know what to expect!

This same resurrection power works in own lives today. "This is the day the Lord has made . . . it is wonderful in *our* eyes!" We too hear the Easter proclamation. By it, we too are brought into the power of the resurrection.

Second Sunday of Easter

Acts 5:12-16

This is one of the passages that form the basis of the idealization of the early Christian community (cf. Acts 4:32-35). Actually, it is less a coherent summary than a collection of motifs, even somewhat contradictory motifs. It offers us a collage rather than a picture of the community.

"Signs and wonders" is a way of describing the mighty works of God (cf. Exod 7:3; Ps 135:9; Acts 2:22, 43; 4:30). Here it refers to the miracles the apostles were able to accomplish through the divine power bestowed on them by Jesus (cf. Luke 9:1). Like their Master before them, they were able to effect cures simply through their touch. Furthermore, they performed these wonders openly in Solomon's portico, a colonnaded area on the eastern side of the Court of the Gentiles. People from all around brought their sick and disturbed friends and loved ones, hoping the apostles would cure them as Jesus had cured others (cf. Luke 4:40; 5:19; 6:18-19). The people at this time, unscientific as they were, believed the world was in the grips of evil spirits. In this way they explained both physical and emotional distress; the afflicted one was under the control of some evil or unclean spirit (cf. Luke 13:11). To cast out that spirit was to cure the person (cf. Mark 9:25). With the power of God, the apostles were about to accomplish such signs and wonders.

In this reading Peter is singled out. The sick are carried out into the streets, probably not because their illness might pollute the sacred precincts but because there was no room inside (cf. Luke 5:19). Some in the crowd do not think it necessary for Peter to touch the afflicted ones. The miraculous power of God could be transmitted through his shadow alone. This is striking, for even Jesus normally healed through touch. Two exceptions are the woman who was cured of her ailment by merely touching the fringe of Jesus' garment (Luke 8:44) and the cure from a distance of the Roman centurion's slave (Luke 7:1-7). The Greek word for "fall on" *(episkiázō)* is the same that appears in the accounts of the annunciation (Luke 1:35) and the transfiguration (Luke 9:34). In all these instances it is the mystery of God that overshadows and the power of God that effects wondrous things.

Evidence that this passage is a collection of motifs rather than a coherent summary is seen in the apparent contradiction between verses 13 and 14. The first states that others were afraid to join the community of believers; the second declares that great numbers were added to their ranks. Actually, both were probably true. The great accomplishments of the early Christians certainly struck fear in the hearts of some, while at the same time they attracted others. Fear and admiration can and do exist side by side, especially when the power of God is evident.

Psalm 118:2-4, 13-15, 22-24

The responsorial psalm consists of excerpts from a song of thanksgiving that seems to be part of a liturgical celebration. The psalm contains both individual and communal features: the language in the first and third sections (vv. 2-4, 22-24) is plural, while the speaker in the middle section (vv. 13-15) is clearly an individual. The refrain, "His mercy endures forever," establishes the psalm's congregational liturgical character.

The psalm itself begins with a call to give testimony to the goodness of God. This call is threefold in structure and inclusive in nature. The "house of Israel" designates the people of the covenant; the "house of Aaron" refers to the priesthood; "those who fear the LORD" is probably a reference to God-fearers, proselytes of non-Israelite origin (cf. Ps 115:9-11). The Hebrew word for "mercy" (*ḥesed*) is a technical theological term denoting God's steadfast love for those in covenant with God. Presumably the leader of the liturgical assembly calls out to the members of each respective group, and they in turn declare God's faithfulness.

The voice is singular in the second section of the responsorial psalm (vv. 13-15). It testifies to a time when the psalmist was under great duress, suffering at the hands of others and being overpowered. In the face of this oppression God stepped in and saved the psalmist from ultimate defeat. The acknowledgment of deliverance is followed by an individual song of praise (v. 14), which uses the language of one of Israel's oldest hymns of victory (Exod 15:2a). The song, long associated with God's deliverance of the people from Egyptian bondage, acclaims the faithfulness of God: "My strength and my courage is the LORD."

The rescue of the individual is linked to the salvation of the entire community. They are the righteous who live in tents (v. 15). This reference to tents could be another allusion to the Exodus experience and the sojourn in the wilderness, or to the feast of Tabernacles, when the people remembered and celebrated this emancipation and sojourn. Whichever the case may be, the shout of victory proclaims God's deliverance of the people.

In the third section (vv. 22-24) the congregation speaks again, announcing the reversal of fortune that has taken place. The one who had been rejected and hard pressed by enemies has now been saved and exalted by God. Throughout this account of suffering and salvation, it is very clear that deliverance and exaltation are the works of God and not the accomplishments of human beings. This saving act may have happened to an individual, but the entire congregation has witnessed it and marvels at it.

In genuine liturgical fashion, the responsorial psalm brings us to the present moment. Although the salvation described occurred in the past, the psalmist insists that *today* is the day the LORD has made, *today* is the day we rejoice in God's saving work. This liturgical perspective enables believers of any generation to identify their own time as the day of salvation and to rejoice in it.

Revelation 1:9-11a, 12-13, 17-19

The reading consists of a report of a commissioning vision that the speaker, who gives his name as John, received at an earlier time. Verb tenses make this clear. He is caught up by the Spirit and commissioned by God as were the prophets of old. The function of his vision was twofold: it clarified the nature of his task, and it conferred divine authority upon it. By referring to himself as a brother to the Christians to whom the letter is addressed, he identifies himself as a Christian as well. Furthermore, as a Christian he is a companion with the others in the suffering they endure for the sake of their faith. A dimension of this suffering is his apparent banishment to the penal colony on Patmos. This island off the western coast of Asia Minor was settled by political enemies of the Roman government. Since adherence to civil religion was considered the duty of every good citizen, preaching the gospel and testifying to faith in Jesus would have been considered a political breach that warranted severe punishment.

"The Lord's day" probably refers to the day of the week rather than to the eschatological Day of the LORD. The voice that spoke to John sounded and acted like a heralding trumpet. The experience was primarily visual; the loud voice merely directed him to write down what he saw.

The vision itself was of one like a son of man, who appeared in the midst of seven free standing golden lampstands. This individual recalls the figure from the book of Daniel who comes on the clouds (Dan 7:13). He is robed like a man of high rank, with a golden sash around his chest. Laborers wore the sash around their waist so they could tuck up their garments when work had to be done. The lampstands are reminiscent of the golden lampstand with seven lamps with their tubes from the vision of the prophet Zechariah (Zech 4:2). Though similar to these ancient images, the two details are significantly different in John's vision. In Daniel the one like a son of man is presented to the ancient one; here he is himself "the first and the last." In Zechariah it is a single lampstand set up before the LORD; here there are seven lampstands, and the Son of Man stands in their midst.

John was gripped with fear, literally frightened to death. The figure in the vision responded to this with the standard declaration of reassurance: "Do not be afraid!" (cf. Luke 1:13, 30; 2:10). He then identifies himself with the classic self-predication: I am *(égó eími)!* This is followed by three characterizations that find their origin in ancient Israelite tradition. The mysterious figure attributes to himself the epithet "the first and the last," originally claimed by the God of Israel (Isa 44:6). While this same God is also regarded as the living God (cf. Ps 42:1), the figure in the vision was once dead and is now alive. This is clearly a reference to Christ. Finally, having conquered death though his own death, Christ now holds the keys to death and the netherworld. The figure in the vision clearly appropriates to himself divine characteristics, while indirectly identifying himself as the crucified and now-risen Christ. In the new order, theophany (the revelation of God) is specifically christophany (the revelation of Christ).

The vision is not merely for the seer. Both at the beginning and at the end of the experience John is told to write down what he sees, both now and what will be revealed to him in the future. The vision is clearly for the churches, not for any individual.

John 20:19-31

Two resurrection appearances form a kind of diptych. The hinge that connects them is the person of Thomas. Absent for the first event, he is the central character in the second. His absence is curious, since on both occasions the doors of the room where the disciples were gathered were securely locked, "for fear of the Jews" (v. 19). Why had Thomas not gathered with the rest of the disciples? Was he not afraid? Or was he too afraid to be associated with them? The reason for his absence is never given. However, it does provide an occasion for another encounter with the risen Lord and the demonstration of faith that ensues.

The two resurrection appearances have several details in common: both occur on the first day of the week; despite the closed doors Jesus appears in their midst; he addresses them with a greeting of peace; he calls their attention to his wounds. Each of these details is laden with theological meaning.

The first day of the week is the actual day of the resurrection (v. 19) or the day that will eventually commemorate it (v. 26). The entire reckoning of time has been altered. Where previously the conclusion of the week had religious meaning, now the focus was on the beginning, on the future. The closed doors not only secured the disciples from those who would be hostile toward them, but they also underscore the mysterious character of Jesus' risen body, which is not impeded by material obstacles. The wish of peace, the common greeting of the day, was also a prayer for the eschatological blessings of health, prosperity, and all good things. Finally, by calling attention to the wounds in his hands and side, Jesus showed the disciples that he was really the crucified one now risen.

According to this account it is on the evening of the resurrection itself that the Holy Spirit is bestowed on the disciples. They are commissioned to go forth, to declare salvation and judgment. Though this charge comes from Jesus, it is a continuation of the commission he received from God. The trinitarian testimony is clear. The image of breathing life into another is reminiscent of the creation of Adam (cf. Gen 2:7) and the restoration of Israel (cf. Ezek 37:9). This very act by the risen Lord casts him in a creative/re-creative role.

Thomas represents the second generation of Christians, those who are called to believe on the testimony of others. The faith required of him is, in a way, more demanding than that required of those who actually encountered the risen Lord. Viewed in this way, his doubt is understandable. While we may judge him harshly for it, Jesus does not. Instead, he invites Thomas to touch him, an invitation not extended earlier to the other disciples. The story does not say Thomas actually touched the wounds, only that he cried out in faith, "My Lord and my God." The other disciples recognized that the one in their midst was their Lord. Thomas declared that the risen Lord was God, a profession of faith that outstrips the others.

According to Jesus, as profound as was Thomas' ultimate faith, it does not compare with the faith of those who do not enjoy the kind of experience of the Lord described here. Thomas should be remembered not because he was absent or because he doubted but because, like us, he was called to believe on the word of others. And like Thomas, we know how difficult that is.

Themes of the Day

The readings for the Sundays after Easter all provide mystagogical catechesis for the entire Church, with a special emphasis for the newly baptized. This instruction is meant to help us recognize the presence of the risen Lord in our midst. The overarching theme for the Second Sunday of Easter is the celebration of this presence in several manifestations. We believe in the resurrection, but we would like to have some concrete evidence of its power. Where is it in our lives? We want to touch it, to see it. We would like some kind of material presence.

While we might seek some obvious, tangible manifestation, each reading speaks of the presence of Christ in a way we would not expect Christ to be present. He is there in the very throes of sickness, in fear and doubt, in the celebration of the liturgy. These presences challenge us to go beneath appearances, beneath the mundane and banal of life, and there discover the risen Lord in personal mystical experience, in the ministry of the believing community, in the transformative possibilities of the liturgy.

Mystical Experience

The story of Thomas is the story of many Christians. Not content to take the word of others, they seek their own personal experience of the Lord. While in itself there is nothing wrong with such a desire, the disdaining of the word and witness of others can lead to arrogance and lost opportunities. However, the account shows both the patient understanding of Christ and the humble acknowledgment of error on the part of Thomas. It also shows that it was actually in the midst of the community, the place where Thomas least expected to meet the Lord, that the personal experience occurred. Finally, it was not at all what Thomas had expected. He demanded to touch the Lord, and when he was invited to do so, he instead expressed his faith in a gesture of adoration.

Mystical experiences are not reserved for extraordinarily holy people. Any one of us can be invited into a deep personal encounter when we least expect it, in the most unlikely places, with effects that overwhelm us. In fact, the risen Christ is always just around the next corner, eager to enter our lives with the transforming power of the resurrection.

Ministry of the Community

Unlike Thomas, who at first spurned the witness of others, the people who brought their sick to the apostles experienced the power of the risen Lord in the works of the community done in the name of that Lord. It was through the signs and wonders wrought by the disciples of Jesus that others were drawn to join the community of believers. So it is with us. There are people in our midst who serve the needs of others through visiting those who are sick and infirm, helping with the care of children, advocating for the protection of the vulnerable, repairing public roads and facilities, making sure our streets and neighborhoods are safe. There are those whose presence is a healing touch, whose smile warms our hearts, whose words of counsel illumine the darkness of our lives. There are people all around us who manifest the presence of the risen Lord if we but open ourselves to it.

We can be these people in the lives of others. We do not have to be professional ministers to witness to the presence of the risen Lord. We too have our Porticos of Solomon, our supermarkets, our gathering places, our offices and factories. We too can be the healing touch of the risen Christ in a world of suffering and violence. We can be the reason others come to the Lord.

Eschatological Liturgy

Being part of a community of believers in prayer can be one of the most profound religious experiences. It not only transforms the present, it also entrusts us with a vision of what is yet to be, an eschatological hope for a glorious future. This is the essence of the vision found in the reading from the book of Revelation, but it is also the possibility of every single Eucharist in which we participate. The wonder of the Eucharist is that it is present and future at the same time. It celebrates an encounter with the Christ who is with us now and who will be fully revealed in an eschatological future.

While it is important that everything connected with the liturgical celebration be done with the utmost care and reverence, the actual encounter with the Lord occurs beneath these exteriors. They can either aid us or act as obstacles, but they themselves are not the actual experience. They are gateways through which we pass into an encounter with the Lord. As we gather to celebrate we must remember that we are entering an eschatological moment in which we will encounter the presence of the risen Lord, glorified before the throne of God.

Third Sunday of Easter

Acts 5:27-32, 40b-41

The court scene depicted in the first reading for this Sunday describes apostles who are courageous witnesses to the resurrection of Jesus and heralds to the world of this wondrous event. Brought by the officers of the court, they stand fearlessly before the Sanhedrin, the supreme legislative council and highest religious and secular tribunal of the Jews. The high priest, the one who presides over this court, rebukes them for having disregarded a previous injunction to refrain from teaching in the name of Jesus. According to him, they have been quite successful in their preaching in Jerusalem, the city where Jesus had been tried and in the outskirts of which he was killed. In fact, they have been so successful that the high priest is concerned that the temper of the people may have changed and the ruling body might be assigned blame for Jesus' death.

Peter, acting as spokesperson for the rest of the apostles, replies in words similar to those spoken years earlier by Socrates when he was brought before the Athenian judges. Standing in opposition to tyranny, Socrates declares it would be better to obey the god(s) than some earthly court (cf. Plato's *Apology*, 29D). Peter then launches into a short sermon consisting of the fundamental apostolic proclamation. God has reversed the plans of those who put Jesus to death. They brought dishonor upon Jesus by crucifying him (cf. Deut 21:23: Cursed is the one who hangs on a tree), but God raised him from the dead and exalted him in a place of honor at God's own right hand.

Peter is intent on situating Jesus squarely within the tradition of Israel. He does this by identifying the God who exalts Jesus as the God of our (Peter's and the Sanhedrin's) ancestors. Furthermore, he claims this exalted Jesus is leader and savior, two roles traditionally played by Moses. Finally, Peter maintains that the opportunities for repentance, or change of heart *(metánoia)*, and forgiveness of sin, for which Israel awaits, will be granted through this once crucified now exalted Jesus. In a second way Peter points out the reversal accomplished by God. The one who will bring to fulfillment the eschatological hopes of Israel is the very one in whose name the apostles are forbidden to preach. Declaring that he and his companions are witnesses to the events that have occurred, he concludes by insisting that the truth of the apostolic message he proclaims is confirmed by the witness of the Holy Spirit.

Ordered once again to desist in their preaching, the apostles are set free. Their response is unusual. Rather than celebrating their dismissal, they rejoice in having suffered dishonor in Jesus' name. It is not that dishonor is something to be sought. Rather, in being witnesses to the marvelous deeds God accomplished in Jesus, and then being heralds of this good news, they now share in the dishonor Jesus suffered knowing they will eventually share in his exaltation as well.

Psalm 30:2, 4, 5-6, 11-12, 13

This is a psalm of thanksgiving for deliverance from the netherworld *(sheʾôl)*, the pit—the place of death (v. 4). This is the place of dismal darkness where the dead go. It is neither a place of reward nor of punishment. There is no differentiation of the dead, only a form of semi-life where there is no memory or praise of God. The allusion to death can also be an allusion to illness, to depression, or to any serious misfortune that can threaten life. In the ancient world people believed being stricken with illness was a sign one was actually in the grips of death itself. Therefore, to be brought up from the place of death is to be rescued from the threat of death. Whatever the actual danger might have been, it is now past; God intervened and saved the petitioner. In addition to the actual calamity, the psalmist is concerned with enemies who would take delight in the misfortune. The prayer asks that he be preserved from this insult as well. Following the initial plea is an acknowledgment of deliverance. God has heard the petition and has granted the request for rescue.

The psalmist next turns to the faithful ones *(hasīdīm)* and calls on them to give thanks for God's holiness, that quality that sets God apart from all that is profane. These are the ones who themselves have been faithfully obedient to the demands of the covenant. They are the ones who would be most familiar with and committed to God's holiness. The psalm does not explicitly state the suffering endured was the deserved penalty for some wrongdoing. However, since that was the customary explanation of misfortune, such a conclusion could easily be drawn, especially since there is no protestation of innocence. Still, retribution is not the point of the prayer; thanksgiving for deliverance is. In describing this deliverance, the psalmist compares the vast difference between God's wrath and God's graciousness. The former is short-lived; the latter is everlasting. The distress the psalmist endured is characterized as the darkness of night; the rescue the psalmist was granted, as the promise of dawn. The former occurred yesterday; the latter is experienced today.

The psalmist turns again in prayer to God, pleading once more for pity. There is no suggestion that God has turned a deaf ear to earlier cries. Quite the contrary. The psalmist proclaims that grief and mourning have been turned into relief and rejoicing, rejoicing taking the form of celebrative dancing. This reversal of fortune is the reason for the declaration of thanksgiving in the first place. Regardless of the nature of or reason for the psalmist's misfortune, God can be trusted to come to the aid of one who cries for help.

Revelation 5:11-14

The vision John describes reveals the heavenly throne room, where angels, living creatures, and elders surround the throne of God. There is no indication whether these angels were the cherubim, depicted as part human and part animal, who guarded the sanctuaries, or seraphim, the brilliant flaming fires that symbolized the purity and power of the heavenly court. Either of these or a combination of the two would have represented the magnificence of the scene. All we know is that there was a vast multitude of them.

We know much more about the living creatures. They were four in number, each with six wings and covered with eyes in front and back (cf. Rev 4:6-7). They had the same likenesses as did the four creatures in the vision of Ezekiel (cf. Ezek 1:4-13): a lion, an ox, a man, and a soaring eagle. Through the centuries many explanations of these figures have been advanced. They may be reminiscent of the complex-featured figures that stood guard at the entrance of temples. They may simply represent the excellence of all created beings: the most exalted of the wild (lion), the domesticated (ox), and the winged (eagle) animals, along with a human being. We see again how in this culture men, not women, stand for the entire race. The exact identity of these four creatures is not crucial for our appreciation of their importance. It is enough to know of a long Israelite tradition that stations them near God during extraordinary theophanies.

The elders number twenty-four. Several explanations of their number have been given, but none has proven satisfactory. Some think they stand for the sum of the twelve tribes and the twelve apostles. Others think they represent twenty-four priestly or Levitical orders. In the end they many simply represent a large number of Christians who have distinguished themselves by faithful service. Whoever they are, they join the four living creatures and the angels in praise.

The song is a doxology in the form of an acclamation. The seven prerogatives listed (v. 12) reflect a kind of royal investiture. They will be conferred upon the Lamb, because the Lamb has been found worthy of them. Each of these prerogatives belongs by right to God, but God bestows it on others (usually kings) to enable them to rule as God would rule. Since this investiture takes place in the heavens, and those around the throne witnessing the event represent all of creation, one can conclude that the rule conferred upon the Lamb is cosmic and universal. This is corroborated by the inclusiveness of the assembly, which cries out in praise. It consists of every creature in heaven and on earth, under the earth and in the sea. All four sectors of the universe are mentioned. There are no distinctions of gender or race or culture or even of species. All together, the living and the dead (those under the earth), acclaim the one who sits on the heavenly throne and the Lamb.

Although the focus is the investiture of the Lamb, the theology behind the vision is more specifically theological than christological. God is seated on the throne; the Lamb is not. Nor is the Lamb identified with God. Finally, any divine attribute the Lamb possesses has been given by God. Worship of and devotion to Christ must be understood in terms of his relationship with God. To this all cry out: "Amen!"

John 21:1-19

The gospel reading appears to be a composite of distinct episodes that have been brought together and now appear as one. It begins with an account of a miraculous catch of fish into which is woven a second report, that of a meal on the shore (vv. 1-14). This is followed by an exchange between Jesus and Peter (vv. 15-19).

The encounter of Jesus with the group of disciples begins and ends with the announcement that the risen Jesus revealed himself to his disciples (vv. 1, 14). This tells us that even those who had been his intimate companions did not recognize the Lord in his risen state (v. 4). Here recognition comes through Jesus' actions, not through his words. He called them "children" *(paidía),* a term that may be affectionate but that also carries the sense of undeveloped understanding. He directs them to cast the nets on the right side, the preferred side for right-handed people. Only after they pulled in the multitude of fish did the disciple whom Jesus loved identify the man on the shore: "it is the Lord." When they had come safely to shore, the others also recognized him, though there seems to have been a fundamental difference in his present state. They are tempted to ask who he is while at the same time somehow knowing his identity (v. 12).

Much has been made about the disciples having gone to Galilee and resuming their former occupations. Some interpret this as evidence of their lack of faith, even apostasy. This is not necessarily the case, since there was a tradition in the early Church that the risen Jesus told them he would meet them in Galilee (cf. Mark 14:28; 16:7). Besides, nowhere in this passage does Jesus reprimand them for their behavior. This group of seven included Simon Peter, Thomas, Nathanael, the two sons of Zebedee, and two unnamed disciples. The Beloved Disciple, though not clearly identified, was one of them. Most interpreters believe he was one of those not explicitly named. However, this could have included the sons of Zebedee, for they were not expressly named either. Though he was the one in the boat who recognized the Lord, he does not play an important role here. The primary focus is on Peter.

There are two major reasons for suggesting the report of the meal is a separate tradition. First, the episode of the miraculous catch is complete without it. Second, the net captures a multitude of fish (*ichthús,* vv. 6, 8, 11), but Jesus prepares other fish (*ópsárion,* vv. 9, 13). Verse 10 seems to link the two scenes. A meal prepared by Jesus, especially the risen Jesus, certainly has eucharistic or at least eschatological connotations. He feeds them, though he himself does not eat.

Finally, Jesus' exchange with Peter has many links with Peter's earlier denial of him. The charcoal fire (*ánthrakiàn,* v. 9) Jesus prepared is the same kind of fire near which Peter stood warming himself when he denied knowing Jesus (cf. 18:18). Having been sobered by this denial, Peter does not now declare that he is capable of being more faithful than the others (v. 15; cf. Mark 14:29-30; Matt 26:33-35). Three times Peter denied; three times he is called upon to declare his love. When he does, he is commissioned to assume the role of shepherd in the place of Jesus. He is now a shepherd who can show compassion to those who have failed.

The passage ends with a prediction of Peter's future death. It could well refer to the practice of binding the hands of the one to be crucified. Having been given the role of shepherd once held by Jesus, Peter is now told he will suffer a fate similar to that which Jesus suffered.

Themes of the Day

Continuing the theme of the manifestations of the risen Lord begun last week, today we concentrate on the different ways the witness of the community of faith manifests the Lord. We see it in the apostolic witness of service in leadership, in the witness of preaching and teaching, and in the witness of a life lived faithfully despite the high cost that such living might exact.

Service in Leadership

The apostolic witness of leadership and service accomplished by the various ministries within the Church is an example of the living presence of Christ. While today's gospel singles out Peter as a leader within the community, in no way does this mean that such providential care for the Church, the flock of God, is the sole responsibility of authorized leaders. Rather, it is the responsibility of all the baptized. The flock of the Lord is under the care of the shepherding community. All are called to feed and to tend the flock of God. However, some are given the added responsibility of overseeing this ministry. This is true of bishops, pastors, and all pastoral ministers.

In the world in which we live, a world of extensive dehumanizing poverty, of terrifying and continual violence, of the exploitation and criminal abuse of the defenseless, the Church is rightfully judged by the character and extent of the care it provides for the most vulnerable. Those called to this service, as Peter was called, should respond out of the same kind of humble love Peter did, for they should know it is only the saving power of God that enables them to persevere. Without it, they too might deny they even know Christ.

Preaching and Teaching

The apostles have crossed a threshold and through their preaching and teaching have led others across as well. They moved from one understanding of God's presence and activity in the midst of the people to another. This new understanding had the death and resurrection of Jesus at its core. The light of the resurrection had illumined their former religious convictions and aspirations, and they were undeterred in their commitment to spread this good news, this new word, this transforming light.

We are in a situation in the Church today that bears some resemblance to this earlier period. Our religious convictions and aspirations seem to be floundering, sometimes even languishing. The rapid pace of social change has caused many to relinquish any sense of religious purpose. The number of people not raised within a religious culture has increased sharply. There may be more need today for effective preaching and enlightened teaching than in the recent past. In a very real sense the risen Lord is made manifest in the preaching and teaching and catechizing of committed Christians, women and men who take seriously their baptismal responsibilities, as did the early Christians.

Witness—Mártys

A martyr is a witness. The Greek word suggests that a martyr is not so much one who dies for the faith as one who lives it so completely that that person is willing to suffer any consequence, even death, in order to be faithful. In the first reading the apostles are brought before the Sanhedrin because they refused to desist from proclaiming the good news. They rejoice that they have been found worthy of ill-treatment for the sake of the name of Jesus. In the second reading the Lamb who is exalted is the one who was slain. In fact, it is precisely in being slain that the Lamb is exalted. In the gospel Peter is told that, like his master, he will pay for his commitment with his life. Even the psalm alludes to the suffering that must be endured by those who have chosen to be faithful. This kind of steadfastness has always been a persuasive witness. The presence of the risen Lord is always loudly announced by the witness of those who persevere even unto death. The blood of the martyrs is the seed of the Church.

Our day has known its share of martyrs, brave women and men who have been silenced because they have cried out against injustice, against war, against poverty. There is the young priest who was murdered because he worked for land reform; the laywoman who was brutalized because she taught native women to cook and sew. There are people who have suffered the indignities of prison because they oppose war or nuclear weapons. We may not be called to this degree of martyrdom, but we must honestly ask ourselves, What price are we willing to pay for our convictions and aspirations? Will the risen Lord be made manifest in our witness?

Fourth Sunday of Easter
Acts 13:14, 43-52

This passage depicts the animosity that arose between the apostles and certain segments within the Jewish community, an animosity that precipitated the transition in Paul's ministry, addressing no longer the Jewish community but now the Gentiles. It is important to interpret the message of this passage carefully, lest we allow it to give birth to or nurture already present anti-Judaic sentiments that are more in the minds and hearts of the readers than in the biblical passage itself. The setting is Antioch in Pisidia, the administrative center of the Roman province of Galatia. Located in the southernmost part of the province, Paul and Barnabas, surnamed "Son of Encouragement" (cf. Acts 4:36), would have had to cross the Taurus mountains in order to reach it from Perga. The city boasted a military garrison with soldiers, who upon their conversion would be able to spread the gospel as they moved from assignment to assignment throughout the Roman territories.

There is an unusual paradox in this account of the ministry of Paul and Barnabas. They seem to fail in their preaching to the Jews of the Diaspora precisely because they have been too successful. It was the Jewish custom to invite visitors to speak in the synagogue on the Sabbath. This particular synagogue was made up of both Jews who had been born into the faith and proselytes who were in the process of converting. Unlike Gentile God-fearers who participated only minimally in Jewish religious practices, proselytes were allowed to worship. It was to this community that Paul and Barnabas came. They made such an impression that crowds returned to hear them on the following Sabbath.

This success engendered envy in the hearts of some, and in response to this they questioned the content of the apostles' preaching. It should be noted that the message of "good news" did not seem to bother them the first Sabbath but only as its popularity became obvious. While the text makes it sound as if all the Jews rejected the message and only the Greek proselytes were open to it, it was probably only the leaders of the synagogue who both contradicted Paul and blasphemed against Jesus. They were the ones who would have been offended by the success of other teachers, and they would be the ones who could influence prominent women worshipers and leading men of the city (v. 50). Their opposition could have stemmed from a theological sense that the requirements for salvation offered by Christianity were much too easy. On the other hand, they might have feared that their congregation would choose to follow Paul and that this might have financial repercussions.

The passage Paul cites comes from one of the Servant Songs of Isaiah (Isa 49:3). It declares that salvation will come to the Gentiles through the agency of the People of God. Paul reinterprets the passage to mean that he, Paul, will be God's light to the Gentiles. Since these Jews have rejected Paul's preaching, he will follow Jesus' injunction and will turn away from them (cf. Luke 9:5). With that, Paul and Barnabas leave for Iconium, in the region known as Lycaonia, the easternmost city of Phrygia, about one hundred miles to the east. As strong as this statement might be, it is clear that Paul does not totally reject the

Jews. As he moves from territory to territory he continues to go first to the synagogues to preach (cf. Acts 14:1; 16:13; 17:1, 10, 17; 18:4, 19; 19:8).

Despite the hardships the apostles are forced to face, the new converts (Jews or Gentiles?) were filled with the joy associated with the Holy Spirit, which they experienced in their newfound faith.

Psalm 100:1-2, 3, 5

The few verses in this responsorial psalm come from a hymn of praise that calls Israel to worship its God. There is also a universal dimension of this call; it is addressed to all the lands. It may be that the summons goes out to all, but the God to whom the praise is directed is clearly the LORD, the God of Israel. ("LORD" is a way of circumventing the use of YHWH, the personal name of God.)

In this response the call itself includes three imperatives: serve, come before, know. Each verb can be understood in its own distinct way. However, all three can also be different ways of saying basically the same thing. "Serve" can be understood in a general way as the function of a servant or a slave. In this sense it is appropriate to call people to serve God. On the other hand, it is also used in the context of worship, which is a particular kind of service. "Come before" implies entering the presence of God, clearly a reference to communal worship rather than individual devotion. The addressee is invited to enter the sacred precincts in order to give praise to God. In itself, "know" can mean simple recognition. However, when used of God, it carries a confessional connotation. We do not so much know God as we know the works of God, works of creation or salvation, both of which elicit praise from us. A summons to know God is a call to acknowledge the wonderful works of God. Since any summons to praise is itself a call to worship, all three imperatives convey the sense of worship.

The psalm uses two major characterizations of God, both of which reveal something of Israel's faith. God is described as Creator and shepherd (v. 3). The first image highlights the sovereignty of God, who as sole Creator conquered the primordial forces of chaos and continually holds these forces at bay. The second image portrays the tender provident care of God. In the ancient world shepherds devoted all their time and energy to the care and protection of their flocks. Because of the responsibility they had for the well-being of their people, kings were often characterized as shepherds. To refer to God as shepherd is to acknowledge divine providence but also to make a political statement. God, not some human ruler, is the one to whom allegiance is owed.

The response concludes with a description of God that consists of attributes associated with the covenant: goodness, lovingkindness, faithfulness. "Good" has a variety of meanings. It is normally used in the general sense of pleasant, favorable, or beneficial. Its precise meaning here will depend upon the meaning of the two words with which it is associated. "Lovingkindness" *(ḥesed)* describes God's loyalty to covenant obligations. It includes dimensions of providence, mercy, and deliverance. As a divine attribute it flows from God's fundamental goodness. The psalm declares that this lovingkindness endures forever (*'ôlām*), a word that can refer either to the remote past or the distant future, therefore, to perpetuity. "Faithfulness" (*'ĕmûnâ*) refers to God's total dependability, a dependability grounded in God's nature and underscored by God's covenant commitment. It is only right that we praise a God who is characterized as Creator and shepherd and described as good, kind, and faithful.

Revelation 7:9, 14b-17

Once again John, the seer, describes a portion of his vision. He sees an unnumbered multitude, one that cannot be counted. The scene calls to mind the promise made by God to Abraham that he would be the father of a multitude too numerous to count, like the stars of the sky and the sands of the seashore (cf. Gen 22:17). The multitude in John's vision is international in character, coming from every nation, race, people, and tongue. This fulfills another promise made to Abraham, that he would be the father of a host of nations (cf. Gen 17:4). This vast throng has inherited the blessings that may have been initially circumscribed by one people but now are opened to all.

The scene is one of extraordinary solemnity. The vast throng stands as a sign of respect and homage. This respect extends even to the reference to God: "the throne" is a circumlocution for the divine name. God's personal name is here given the highest respect by not being pronounced. Next to the throne stands the Lamb, the one whose blood enabled the throng to stand victorious and pure in the heavenly courts. Their victory and purity are expressed in several ways. First, white robes are a sign of both victory and of purity. The palms in their hands also signify victory. Finally, their robes are said to have been made white (pure) in the blood of the Lamb. It is clear that this multitude has been made worthy to participate in the heavenly worship.

John enters into the vision by carrying on a conversation with one of the elders who himself is part of the scene. Although this elder identifies the multitude, his explanation can be understood in different ways. It is not clear what is meant by the great distress. It usually refers to the tribulation believed to precede the time of eschatological fulfillment. For John that time had not yet come. However, his vision was a proleptic glimpse into the end-time, and those who constituted the multitude had already passed through their own period of distress (persecution and perhaps martyrdom).

To be washed in the blood of the Lamb can be a reference to Christ's redemptive sacrifice, the blood of which atoned for the sins of all. It can also be a reference to the baptism of the individuals gathered together, for it was though baptism that they were incorporated into Christ's death. Finally, it might mean that these people have paid the ultimate price for their commitment to Christ, shedding their blood as he shed his. The first two explanations are obviously assumed: all have been redeemed by Christ, and presumably all have been baptized. However, there is no certainty here about the question of their martyrdom.

It is because they have endured and have been made pure by Christ that they can stand before God and worship day and night without end. They are now protected from adversity. The description of their safekeeping is taken from the prophet Isaiah (cf. Isa 49:10), who looks forward to the day of return from worldly exile, the day that is fulfilled in John's sight. It is God who will wipe away tears (cf. Isa 25:8). This vast throng is sheltered by God and shepherded by the Lamb. They have endured, and now they can rejoice.

John 10:27-30

The characterization of Jesus as the Good Shepherd has many dimensions. The gospel reading for this Sunday reveals two of them: the relationship Jesus has with those who follow him and the relationship he has with God.

Jesus' sheep are those who hear his voice, recognize it, and follow him. This image originates in the world of herders. Sheep do in fact recognize the voice or sound of the one who cares for them, and they trustingly follow that voice, even into danger. Correspondingly, shepherds can recognize their sheep. This is because the shepherds and the sheep are together constantly and they become acquainted with the individual characteristics of each other. When applied to the relationship between Jesus and his followers, the image implies intimate knowledge on the part of both and unquestioning trust on the part of the followers.

Jesus makes two bold promises. He will give eternal life to those who are his sheep, and he will not allow anyone to take them away from him. He can promise eternal life because he has power over death. He can lay down his life and then take it up again (cf. 10:17). For this reason, if the sheep heed his voice, they will never perish. As with any flock, there seem always to be those who would snatch the sheep away from their rightful shepherds. Jesus claims this will never happen. If he has power over death, the ultimate peril, his hold over his sheep will certainly not be threatened by lesser evils. Furthermore, Jesus has the right to exercise this kind of authority over the sheep because they have been given to him by God.

The christological claims made in this passage are obvious. The very same words that describe the authority and control Jesus has over the sheep ("no one can take them," v. 28) are used in relation to God's control (v. 29). Furthermore, the passage ends with the declaration that Jesus and God are one. The Greek word used for "one" *(hen)* is neuter in form, suggesting the reference is to the identical manner in which Jesus and God care for the sheep. If the author wanted to say Jesus was identical with God, most likely a different form would have been used. Furthermore, Jesus consistently calls God "Father," the trinitarian designation that signifies distinction in divine union. Although the primary focus is on how Jesus cares for the sheep entrusted to him by God and in the same manner as God cares, it is clear that all Jesus says and does is the actual embodiment of God's will and not just behavior that is in conformity to it. Jesus and his Father are so closely associated that more than function is presupposed here. The shepherd who cares for the sheep is indeed one with God.

Themes of the Day

This Sunday is traditionally referred to as "Good Shepherd Sunday." However, the readings for today focus more on the flock than on the shepherd. The overarching theme appears to be unity in diversity. Placing this theme within the context of the Easter season, we might refocus it slightly and suggest that today we celebrate the presence of the risen Lord in communities of difference.

Trinitarian Unity

Unity in diversity is first found in the primordial divine union of the Trinity, the relationship between Jesus and the one he called "Father." United in the Godhead, they are still distinct. This is the foundational unity. All other models of unity flow from it. It is difficult to talk about this trinitarian unity. All we know about it are glimpses we can glean from the sayings of Jesus and the faith of the early believers. In the gospel Jesus describes the intimate relationship he has with his sheep, a oneness that cannot be undermined by another. No one will snatch the sheep out of his hand. The same is said about the Father. From this, one can conclude that Jesus and the Father exercise the same kind of oversight, thus making the relationship of the sheep with the Father similar to the union they enjoy with Jesus.

Communal Unity

Both the first and the second readings depict communities made up of people from every nation, race, people, and tongue, Jews and Gentile alike. This is precisely the makeup of most communities today. Parishes and religious groups born with a particular cultural identity have slowly, and sometimes not so slowly, changed in complexion and composition. Thriving young groups have given way to retirement communities; monocultural parishes are now bi- or tri-lingual. The melting-pot mentality, which frequently forced acculturation on newcomers, has been replaced by the image of the mosaic, where diversity is retained as a vital contribution to the entire design. Jesus' prayer that all might be one seems to have been heard.

Despite the obvious differences, all are children of the one God, all are joined in their common confession of faith, all share the same aspirations for final peace and fulfillment. Just as we must learn to look beneath the familiar to discover the presence of the risen Lord, so we must learn to look beneath the unfamiliar to find a sister or brother in Christ.

The Price of Diversity

Not everyone is happy with diversity. Some within the early community resented the success of Paul and Barnabas and tried to turn the people against them. These opponents may have resented their popularity, or they may have contested their teaching. Conflict could have arisen simply from what they perceived to be the threat of possible change. People generally like things the way they are and see no need to accommodate themselves to different people with different customs and ideas. Whatever the case may have been, some of the people instigated dissension among those listening in the synagogue, and they drove Paul and Barnabas out.

This sounds strangely familiar to us. Religious groups born out of struggle and hard work, lovingly nurtured as they grew strong, often resist what they perceive to be the invasion of foreigners. Rather than see this new group as a companion with gifts that can enrich them, they view them as usurpers, as people with little or no appreciation of the established form of life, manner of expression, or way of perceiving God. If these people could only take as their model the company of the blessed revealed in John's vision, they would see that those who have washed their robes in the blood of the Lamb, who are garbed in white robes of purity, and who carry palm branches of victory come from every nation and race and people and tongue. They would see that, in the end, unity in diversity will win out. In the end all will be united yet distinct, as are Jesus and the one he calls "Father."

Fifth Sunday of Easter

Acts 14:21-27

The missionary journey of Paul and Barnabas is resumed in this reading. From Derbe (v. 20) they retrace their steps through Lystra, Iconium, and Antioch of Pisidia. Continuing through Pisidia to Pamphylia, they preach in Perga and then set sail from Attalia, a seaport on the coast of Pamphylia, for their home base of Antioch on the Orontes. A map of the ancient world will show the ambitious scope of their daring apostolic venture. The success of their preaching is evident. They made a considerable number of disciples in Derbe (v. 21). The purpose of their return to cities visited earlier (v. 21) was to strengthen the converts they had already made. The report they gave on their return home indicates their missionary endeavor has been successful.

The apostolic activity of Paul and Barnabas had not been without difficulty (cf. vv. 1-19). In their exhortation to their Christian converts there is a subtle reference to the suffering they had to endure (v. 22). The statement does not mean that God requires suffering and then rewards it with citizenship in God's reign. It means, rather, that suffering is inescapable. Such a statement does not arise out of the concept of realized eschatology (Christians already live in the reign of God) but from the perspective of future eschatology (God's reign is not yet fully established). The Greek word for hardship *(thlipsis)* usually refers to the period of tribulation that precedes the ultimate appearance of God's reign. Such hardship is considered the "birth pangs" of the Messiah, the inevitable suffering that occurs when one passes from "this age" to the "age of fulfillment." This passage brings its own distress.

In the cities they are revisiting the apostles establish a kind of administrative structure not unlike that found in the synagogues. The need for organization is yet another evidence of the growth of the Church. The word for "appoint" *(cheirotoneō)* means "to stretch out one's hand" or "to lay hands on" in an official way. As was the case with the officials of the synagogue, these elders were probably entrusted with oversight of worship, discipline, instruction, and administration. This was not an innovative move on their part, for such structure seems to have been already established in the Church in Jerusalem (cf. Acts 11:30).

The apostles were not independent missionaries. They had been sent forth by the Church in Antioch, and it was to that same Church they returned and to which they reported what had been accomplished by God through them. It is important to note that the success of the mission is credited to God. The final verse contains a phrase intimately associated with the ministry of Paul. It was through him that the door of faith, an opportunity to believe in salvation through Jesus Christ, was opened for the Gentiles.

Psalm 145:8-9, 10-11, 12-13

The responsorial psalm for today is a hymn of praise of the greatness of God. In the first section the psalmist speaks about God, extolling divine mercy and compassion. In the second and third sections the psalmist speaks directly to God, praying that all God's works will give thanks and proclaiming the LORD's universal and everlasting reign.

The passage opens with an acclamation closely associated with the revelation of God and the acknowledgment of God's name, revealed at the time of the reestablishment of the covenant (cf. Exod 34:6). In these two verses covenant language abounds. God is described as gracious *(ḥannûn)* and compassionate *(raḥûm)* and filled with lovingkindness *(ḥesed)*. It should be noted that this divine goodness is not reserved for Israel alone but is extended to all God's works. This includes all peoples and nations as well as all natural creation. The covenant has been expanded to a universal embrace.

The works of the LORD include everything God has made as well as everything God has done, everything God has fashioned as well as everything God has accomplished. There is a comprehensiveness to this call for praise (vv. 10-11). The psalmist cries out to all the wonders of the created world, whose very existence testifies to the magnificence of the Creator. More than this, the God before whom the psalmist stands in awe is also a savior who has performed marvelous deeds on behalf of the people. God has delivered them from bondage, has provided for them in their need, has established them as a people, and has promised them a secure and prosperous future. As they unfold in the sight of all, these acts of graciousness themselves celebrate the LORD.

The faithful of the LORD are those who are holy *(ḥāsîd)*, those who are bound to God in covenant loyalty. Whether their holiness is the result of God's faithfulness to them or their faithfulness to God is not clear. It does not seem to matter to the psalmist, who is preoccupied with the praise of God and not with extolling others. These faithful are summoned to bless the LORD, to praise or honor God in reverence and awe. God is characterized as a monarch who rules over a kingdom. The word for "glory" *(kābôd)* means "heavy" or "weighty." Used here, it implies that God's kingdom is substantial, distinguished because of its magnitude, comprehensive in its splendor. The character and extent of God's rule demonstrates the essence and scope of God's power.

The final section of the psalm extols God's reign. The idea that gods ruled as kings was common in the ancient world, so to characterize the God of Israel in this way was not unusual. What is unique are the exclusive claims made about the reign of Israel's God. It is resplendent, as one would expect. But it is also universal, including all, and it is eternal. In this light, the covenanted faithful ones are called not only to praise God for the wonders God has accomplished in and for them but also to announce the glory of God's rule to the entire human race, to all the children of Adam. It is not enough that they enjoy the privilege of belonging to God's kingdom. Through them, God invites the entire universe to participate as well.

Revelation 21:1-5a

The vision reported in the gospel for this Sunday employs several images to characterize the new reality that will be brought forth in the age of fulfillment. First John sees the vision, and then he hears the voice from the throne explaining what it means. While the passage begins and ends with the theme of newness, its chiastic structure suggests it has a somewhat different theme as its focal point:

> a)new heaven and new earth (v. 1a)
>> b) former heaven and earth are gone (v. 1b)
>>> c) the sea is no more (v. 1b)
>>>> d) the city descends as a bride (v. 2)
>>>> d^1) God dwells with the people (vv. 3-4a)
>>> c^1) death is no more (v. 4b)
>> b^1) former things are gone (v. 4b)
> a^1) God makes everything new (v. 5a)

The pattern indicates that the middle elements (d and d^1) are the most important ones. In other words, this passage highlights the dwelling of God in the midst of the people. Every other theme serves this one.

The new heaven and new earth recall the prophecy of Isaiah (cf. Isa 65:17; 66:22), which promises a restored world for Israel after the Babylonian Exile. This has led some interpreters to believe the newness here is one of transformation or renewal. However, there is enough evidence to conclude the vision is describing something entirely new in nature. First, the Greek word used *(kainós)* denotes new in nature as distinct from new in time *(néos)*.

Second, the disappearance of the sea is significant. In ancient Near Eastern mythology, the sea was one of the most frequently employed symbols for chaos. It represented the primordial forces of evil that were defeated and restrained at the time of creation but never thoroughly destroyed. Even movements of genuine renewal were unable to completely eliminate the powers of evil. However, at the consummation of the world, when the final battle is won by the forces of good, the sea, the symbol of chaos, will be no more. Something completely new will then be established. This understanding of newness is substantiated by the statement that there will be no more death.

We must be careful, however, not to interpret the symbolic imagery literally. Just as a city will probably not descend from heaven, neither will a voice actually be heard coming from the heavenly throne, so the earth as we know it is not necessarily facing ultimate, total destruction. The imagery is describing something our faith tells us is real, but not precisely as depicted within the imagery itself.

The new Jerusalem fulfills for the people of the new age what the former Jerusalem meant for the people of the past. It was a sacred place, the place where God dwelt in their midst in a special way (cf. Isa 65:17-20). Beyond its importance as a place, the name "Jerusalem" also stood for the People of God, whether they lived within the city or not. In this vision Jerusalem probably represents the redeemed in whose midst God dwells. To characterize the city as a bride signifies not only its state of pristine innocence but also the intimate relationship of love that exists between God and the people (cf. Isa 61:10; 62:5). This intimacy is underscored by a version of the technical covenant formula (cf. v. 3, "I will be their God and they will be my people") (cf. Jer 31:33; Ezek 34:30; 36:28).

The old order has passed away, along with death and tears. In fulfillment of the prophetic promise (cf. Isa 25:8; 66:18f.) God will comfort the people who mourn, wiping away their tears. The reading ends in a summary note: All things are made new. While "new" is the eschatological catchword, the present tense of the verb is prophetic of God's new creative action.

John 13:31-33a, 34-35

The departure of Judas sets into motion the machinery of Jesus' arrest, trial, and execution. There is no going back now. The die is cast; the events of salvation are about to begin. The hour of eschatological fulfillment has come. While it looks like only suffering and death are on the horizon, this is in fact the moment of glorification. Lifted up in ignominy, Jesus will really be lifted up in glory, for surrender, death, resurrection, and exaltation are really all one event.

Having announced that this is the hour of his own glorification, Jesus explains how it is also the hour of the glorification of God. The Son of Man is glorified both in his own willingness to obey God even unto death and in the fact that God will glorify him by making his sacrifice effective for the salvation of all. Glorification does not cancel suffering. Rather, it is precisely at the moment of his being lifted up on the cross that Jesus will be lifted up in glory. Jesus' willingness to suffer also glorifies God, for it reveals the extent of Jesus' love for God and God's love for humankind. This mutual glorification flows from the intimate relationship that exists between God and the Son of Man.

Jesus addresses the remaining eleven apostles with the affectionate address of a teacher to students, "my children" (cf. Prov 1:8, 15; 2:1; etc.). It is followed by the commandment to love one another. A new situation is created by the sacrifice and glorification of Jesus. He will not remain with the apostles for long, and the love they show one another will be the earthly counterpart of the mutual glorification of God and the Son of Man. The command to love was given long ago: "Love your neighbor as yourself" (Lev 19:18). This is a new commandment, new *(kainós)* in nature as distinct from new *(néos)* in time. What makes it significantly different here is the measure of such love. They are to love one another with the same self-sacrificing love Jesus has shown them.

This kind of love will be the universal sign of discipleship of Jesus. It will establish a new kind of order. The disciples are to love one another as Jesus has loved them. His love is manifested in his willingness to sacrifice himself. His self-sacrifice is identical with his glorification. His glorification is also the glorification of God. In this way the love the followers of Jesus have for one another redounds to the glorification of God.

Themes of the Day

The several presences of the risen Lord we saw on the Second Sunday, the different ways of witnessing to this Lord that occupied our attention on the Third Sunday, and the various ways unity can exist in the midst of diversity that were plain to see on the Fourth Sunday, all point to the same reality: Everything is new! There is a new law of love, a new heaven and earth that is established in the Church, a new depth of communion there, and a new glory of God that shines forth from its members.

New Commandment

No society can survive without tolerance. No society can thrive without mutual respect. Yet none of this is enough for the new community Jesus has formed. It requires self-sacrificing love. Perhaps the greatest obstacle to this love is the diversity discussed on the Fourth Sunday. It is hard enough to love those who are like us; how can we possibly love those who are different? And how can we love those who do not love us? We have seen bumper stickers that read: Perform a random act of kindness. They have not yet made one that reads: Love those who hate you. If we love in this way how will we be able to fight wars? Or rob or cheat or destroy? Or punish with our power or undermine with our influence? How will we be able to ignore pleading eyes just because the face is a different color or the hair has a different texture? It is no wonder the commandment is called "new" *(kainós)*. This is something completely different.

New Heaven and New Earth

The new commandment is the law of the new heaven and the new earth established in the Church. Standards are entirely different there. The greater ones serve; the meek possess the earth; happy are the poor; woe to those who laugh. In the new heaven and the new earth children are cherished rather than ignored, those who are disabled are cared for rather than discarded, women and men are equally respected, all nations and tongues are welcomed. This is clearly a city that comes down from heaven, not one made by human hands. It is a city that embraces all who come to it. It is a city well beloved by God.

New Depth of Communion

God dwells in the midst of this city, in the heart of this people. God dwells with them and they dwell with God. Because of this special indwelling they are God's special people, and God is their special God, a God who is with them and for them. Previously they were considered children of God, born of the love that is God. In that new city they are joined to God as a bride is joined to her groom, in a love that reproduces itself, thus creating new life. Because of this love disciples go out to proclaim the good news, and other communities of love are established. Communities that so bind themselves in love become the living sacrament of God's presence.

New Manifestation of God's Glory

Through this new love, this new heaven and new earth, this new depth of communion, the glory of God is manifested in a new way. The eschatological future is anticipated in the present. The age of fulfillment has dawned. Because the glory of God is manifested in and through us in a startling new way, it is not necessary for the risen Lord to be tangibly present to us any more. From now on Christ will remain in the Church in an entirely new way— *through us* as much as *for us.*

Sixth Sunday of Easter

Acts 15:1-2, 22-29

The issue of conditions for membership was one of the most serious disputes that raged in the first years of the Church. As early as the first wave of Gentile conversions, it threatened to separate Christian from Christian, missionary from missionary. The reading for today gives us a glimpse into this matter and the way the leaders of the various churches resolved it.

Because the Jesus movement was originally seen as an internal Jewish renewal, the Jewish Christians continued to observe the religious practices of their former faith. There had always been Gentiles who were attracted to the fundamental integrity of the Jewish faith, such as the God-fearers (cf. Acts 13:16) and proselytes, or converts (Acts 13:43). Since there seemed to be no problem with their assuming the religious practices of Israel, most Jewish Christians expected Gentile converts to Christianity to do the same.

Two major factors brought this issue to a crisis point. Paul allowed his Gentile converts to refrain from Jewish observance. Probably not unrelated to the this was the fact that Gentile converts were multiplying rapidly, while the mission to Israel did not seem to be as successful. Some may have feared the movement might be taken over by pagans who knew very little if anything about the God that Jesus called "Father." It seems that some of the more reactionary Christians from Judea provoked dissension within the church in Antioch, insisting that circumcision was necessary for salvation. Not only were they challenging faith in Jesus as the sole means of salvation, but they were also trying to import the male bias that membership through circumcision reinforced.

The beginnings of church structure can be seen here. It is obvious that the church in Jerusalem enjoyed the place of prominence among the other churches. A matter that was probably more an issue in Antioch than it was in Jerusalem was, nonetheless, settled in the Jewish capital. Furthermore, delegates from Antioch were sent to represent the position of that church. Paul and Barnabas were chosen by the leaders of that church. Finally, the male bias of the churches is seen in the fact that positions of importance were held only by men (brothers).

An official letter containing the decision reached by the Jerusalem church was brought back by the original delegation, along with Judas Barsabbas (son of the Sabbath), a member of the Hebrew segment of the Jerusalem church, and Silas, a Hellenistic member of that church. Intended for the churches in the combined provinces of Syria-Cilicia, it opened with a rebuke of those Judaizers responsible for having instigated the dissension. The language that introduces the actual decision resembles the wording used in imperial and other official decrees. It shows that the leadership of the church in Jerusalem believed that it was the vehicle of the Spirit and that its decisions were one with the will of God.

While the Gentiles were not required to be circumcised, they were bound to four prescriptions: (1) abstention from eating meat that was first offered to idols and then sold in the market; (2) abstention from meat the blood of which had not been drained; (3) abstention from animals that had been strangled; (4) abstention from marriages within the degrees of blood relationship and affinity forbidden by the law (cf. Lev 18:6-18). Not only did this decree affirm the belief that salvation came only from Jesus and not even indirectly through the law, it also opened membership wide for women, who, under the regulation of circumcision, belonged to the Jewish community only through the membership of their closest male relative. In Christ, there is neither Jew nor Greek; there is neither male nor female.

Psalm 67:2-3, 5, 6, 8

The verb forms in this psalm make it difficult for it to be categorized. Some commentators believe the verbs are in past tense and classify the psalm as a prayer of thanksgiving for blessings already received. Others consider them a form of wish- or bidding-prayer, a moderate request for blessings not yet enjoyed. However the verbs are read, it is safe to consider the psalm as a prayer of blessing.

The psalm begins with a slight adaptation of the first words of the blessing used by Aaron and the priests descended from him (v. 2; cf. Num 6:24-26). This use of this Aaronic blessing in a congregational prayer suggests the favors once promised to that particular priestly family are now sought for the entire people. The metaphor of God's shining face refers to the favorable disposition a smiling countenance reflects. The psalmist asks that God look favorably upon the people, that God be benevolent toward them.

God's goodness toward this people will redound to God's reputation among other nations. They will see the people's good fortune and interpret it as the fruit of God's saving power on their behalf and God's continued rule over them. These other nations will conclude that only a mighty and magnanimous God would be able to secure such good fortune. Here prosperity is not used as leverage against others. Quite the contrary, it benefits even those who may not be enjoying it. It does this because it is perceived as coming from God and not merely as the product of human exploits or ingenuity.

The psalm moves from an acknowledgment of divine rule over one people (v. 3) to an announcement of universal divine governance (v. 5). All nations will not only rejoice over God's goodness, they will also be guided by that same God and ultimately will praise that God (vv. 6, 8). In other words, the good fortune of one nation is testimony to the salvific activity of God. This in turn becomes the occasion of salvation for all the earth. One nation is the source of blessing for all. This is the fulfillment of a promise made to Abraham (cf. Gen 12:2-3).

The psalm ends with a prayer for continued universal blessing. It is the past tense of the verb in this verse that had led some commentators to conclude that all of the blessings referred to earlier were also bestowed and enjoyed in the past. They maintain that the plea here is that God continue to bless the people so all nations will continue to revere God. Whether past or future, the psalmist believes all good fortune comes from God. Others see this and praise God, and in this way God is made known to all the earth.

Revelation 21:10-14, 22-23

The vision of the Holy City Jerusalem coming down out of heaven from God recalls several prophecies of ancient Israel, particularly from the book of the prophet Ezekiel (cf. Ezek 40:2; 48:30-35). While the Johannine description of the city is in many ways similar to the earlier tradition, there are significant differences. In the present account the author probably wanted to present the already constructed city as the fulfillment of what was envisioned in the earlier prophecy. However, as is so often the case with the things of God, the reality far exceeds the expectation. Though the city is on a high mountain, the traditional site of the dwelling place of God, it is coming down from heaven, a sign of divine condescension. Coming from God, the city is radiant with the splendor of God.

Two features of the city are given particular attention in this passage: the gates in its high walls and the foundation stones. Numbers often have symbolic meaning. This is true particularly in apocalyptic literature, such as the book of Revelation. Twelve suggests fullness, probably because of the number of months in the year and the number of astrological points in the zodiac. Therefore, the number twelve is grounded in the very structure of creation. The number four also has symbolic significance. Based on the four cardinal points of the compass and the four directions, it too signifies totality and is considered a fundamental feature of creation. It is no coincidence that both the tribes of Israel and the apostles of Jesus number twelve.

The meaning of the twelve tribes and twelve apostles has been variously interpreted. It is important to note that the latter do not replace the former. Each forms a very explicit part of the city. It is clear that the new Jerusalem is founded on the apostolic teaching, but the meaning of the role played by the tribes of Israel is not as evident. Perhaps they reflect an element of Jewish eschatology that expected the restoration of the twelve tribes at the end-time. If this is the case, it still does not explain the role these tribes play in the new Jerusalem. However, both groups retain their own identities and are incorporated as significant elements in the resplendent city.

The visionary seems surprised there is no temple in the city. This is understandable, since the rebuilding of the Temple was—and continues to be for some—the most concrete expression of hope for the future. However, Christian faith insists that the risen Christ is the place where God and human beings meet. Temple symbolism is thus fulfilled in God and the Lamb. Finally, the splendor of God gleamed through the city so completely there was no need for light from the sun or moon. This too was something that had been predicted earlier (cf. Isa 60:19f.). Even natural creation has been completely transformed in this wondrous eschatological event.

John 14:23-29

This gospel passage contains several major theological themes. It emphasizes the link between love and obedience, and it speaks of the presence of God with the one who loves. It provides us with a partial view of the internal relationships within the Trinity. It reports Jesus' farewell wish of peace.

Love is the fundamental message of Jesus. However, he calls for a demanding kind of love, one that is as self-sacrificing as was the love of Jesus himself. Only those who follow his example and obey his directives can be said to truly love, and those who love as Jesus did will in turn be loved by his Father. Such love is more than an emotional response. It is a state of being, a disposition within which one lives. The dwelling Jesus and his Father make with those who love like this is an abiding dwelling *(monē)* in contrast to a transitory state. Those who do not keep the word of Jesus will not be so blessed. Since the word of Jesus is really the word of the one who sent him, to reject that word is to reject both Jesus and his Father. They will not dwell with such a person.

While this passage cannot provide us with a complete trinitarian teaching, it does offer us some insight into the mystery of God. There is definitely an intimate relationship between Jesus and his Father. The very metaphor of father, which he uses to speak of God, is evidence of this. Furthermore, he and his Father together dwell with faithful believers. Despite this intimacy, they are distinct from each other. Jesus was sent by his Father, and it is to his Father that he will return. Jesus proclaims the word of his Father, and his Father sends the Holy Spirit in his name. Jesus even insists that his Father is greater than he is. This statement has led some to question Jesus' full divinity. However, it probably merely points to the Father as the fountainhead of the trinity.

Like Jesus, the Holy Spirit is sent by the Father, but the Spirit is sent in the name of Jesus, not in the name of the Father. The Spirit is not a substitute for Jesus but is an emissary, participating in the mission of Jesus by reminding the disciples the things Jesus taught them. To so remember is more than an intellectual act. It is a call to bear witness to the word of God. In this passage the coming of the Spirit appears to be distinct from the coming of Jesus and his Father to abide with the disciples. They come in order to abide in love; the Spirit comes to enlighten.

It is not clear how the departure and return of Jesus is to be understood. From a human point of view one can think either of his death and his return in resurrection or of his ascension and return at the end-time. In this gospel the death/resurrection/ascension are all one event of departure. However, Jesus does promise to dwell with believers even before his final return (v. 23). Here he is probably instructing them on how to live *with him* until he returns. The parousia, or final return, is anticipated during this in-between time.

Jesus' words end on a note of assurance. He bequeaths his peace. This is more than a wish, it is a blessing that includes all the benefits of the resurrection. His peace is utterly different from the peace of the world, the *Pax Romana*, which was won and preserved at the point of the sword. His peace is grounded in his relationship with his Father and his self-sacrificing love of the world. This peace is the legacy Jesus leaves with those who love him.

Themes of the Day

Our reflection for this Sunday both carries us back to the themes of last week and directs our attention to the ascension of Jesus, which lies ahead of us. We consider again the radical newness the resurrection brings, but we are also made aware of Jesus' departure. One might say that this week we examine Jesus' farewell gifts to us.

The New City

The new city of God is remarkable. It is built on the foundation of the apostles, but on its gates are inscribed the names of the tribes of Israel. There is no substitution here, one group of believers replacing another. There is only inclusion. Even if the names and numbers are symbolic, they represent openness to all nations, races, peoples, and tongues. Such inclusiveness will be radically new for people who are accustomed to privilege or discrimination based on gender or race or social class. In the city of God there are no foreigners, no undocumented immigrants. Whoever have washed their robes in the blood of the Lamb are welcome in the city of God.

In this city the indwelling of God will be so complete there will be no need for a temple, a special meeting place for God and the people. The glory of God will be so encompassing that all other sources of light will vanish in its brilliance. The resurrection of Jesus has radically transformed the way we live together and the way we live with God. It has assured us that regardless of outward appearances we have even here and now a foretaste of this heavenly city, if we but choose to live in the power of the resurrection.

A New Manner of Membership

What must we do to be saved? The question put to Jesus centuries ago is still asked today, and the answer is still the same. We must believe and we must love God and love one another. This sounds so simple, and yet it is so radical. We will be recognized as resurrection people by our active faith and our unselfish love, not by an exterior mark, regardless of how sacred. Ceremonial marks too often identify some as belonging while excluding others. They separate men from women, the young from the old, one race from another. What once may have been essential for membership has now lost its meaning. However, all obligations are not put aside. While we are still in this age of anticipation of the fullness of the end, we must live together with uncommon thoughtfulness. Along with strong religious conviction, we must be willing to make compromises for the sake of others. As Pope John XXIII has taught us, let there be unity in what is necessary, freedom in what is doubtful, and charity in everything.

This change in requirements for membership does not diminish the rigor of our religious obligations. Rather, it suggests that we may always have to reinterpret the law, for what is appropriate at one time and in one place may be inappropriate in another. Actually, the ability to discern God's will in new situations may be much more difficult than any consistent compliance to religious custom. With the early Christians, we will need the guidance of the Holy Spirit in this delicate process. This is why the departing Jesus assures us that the Spirit will come to us to teach us all things.

Christ's Peace

The final gift Jesus promises to give is his own peace. This cannot be a reference to safety from distress because the one who promises it is the one who faced humiliation and crucifixion. The peace Jesus bestows is a peace he has won by overcoming sin and death. While this peace probably does embrace human concord, it really encompasses salvation in the deepest sense. It issues from the union Jesus enjoys with God, a union we are now invited to share. It is a peace in which we can rest even while in the throes of life's struggles. Jesus bequeaths his peace to us just after he has assured us that God will send the Spirit to be with us in his absence. This is the greatest of his farewell gifts.

The Ascension of the Lord

Acts 1:1-11

The opening verses of the reading relate the book of the Acts of the Apostles to an earlier work, presumably the Gospel of Luke. Mention of the person of Theophilus (v. 1, cf. Luke 1:3) makes this clear. This man, whose name means "lover of God," may have been a patron of the author, perhaps responsible for the circulation of the writings. In this introduction, known as a proem, the author identifies the scope of the contents of the first book and then recounts the event of the ascension of Jesus, an event described at the end of the first book as well. The ascension thus becomes the transition from the earthly ministry of Jesus to the experiences of the early Church. The author further links these two moments in history with the activity of the Holy Spirit, through whom Jesus had previously instructed his apostles (v. 2) and in whose power they were to be witnesses to Jesus throughout the entire world (v. 8).

The author claims that the risen Jesus remained on earth forty days, appearing to his apostles and speaking about the reign of God. While this account suggests that only the apostles experienced the risen Lord (cf. vv. 2-3) and only they were present at his ascension (cf. "Men of Galilee," v. 11), other accounts describe a larger and more inclusive group of followers. The number forty is the same as the number of days during which Moses was instructed in the law (cf. Exod 34:28) and that Elijah journeyed toward the mountain of God (1 Kgs 19:8). This correspondence may be one of the details of the account wherein the author connects Jesus with the expectations of Israel. The importance of remaining in Jerusalem is another. The mission must go forth from that sacred city to the ends of the earth (v. 8; cf. Isa 2:3). Finally, Jesus' announcement of the apostles' baptism in the Holy Spirit recalls an earlier statement of John the Baptist (cf. Luke 3:16). These lines draw the continuity between Israel and the Church.

In most eschatological passages the Spirit is identified with the end-time. Here the activity of the Spirit is a characteristic of the new age, the time between the resurrection and the time of complete fulfillment. The author reports that the apostles confused these two moments as well as the nature of the new age that has dawned. Their misunderstanding presented an opportunity for the risen Jesus to instruct them one final time. They are to concern themselves with being Jesus' witnesses to the ends of the earth and not with the limited restoration of one nation. Furthermore, it is not for them to know God's timing. They will have the power of the Spirit to guide them for whatever length of time God desires.

When their responsibilities had been sufficiently explained, Jesus was taken from their sight. Several features underscore the supernatural nature of this experience. The cloud is a traditional symbol of the presence of God. The two men in white garments who interpreted the ascension are reminiscent of the two men in similar garb who were at the tomb and who announced the resurrection (cf. Luke 24:4-5). Though these men state that Jesus will return as he has left them, the symbolic nature of this description prevents us from knowing just what that might mean. With the apostles, we will have to depend upon the Spirit.

Psalm 47:2-3, 6-7, 8-9

A ritual of enthronement clearly unfolds in the verses of this psalm. It begins with a call to praise God with both a ringing cry and a clapping of hands. The cry *(rinnâ)* is a shout of jubilation connected with a divinely appointed sacrifice. Clapping hands is also a common ritual action. One of the derivatives of the Hebrew word for clap *(tāqaʿ)* is trumpet. Perhaps the liturgical clapping of hands is a substitute for the blowing of the trumpet. These two words clearly situate the psalm in a cultic setting.

The occasion for the liturgical celebration is the enthronement of God. Two very significant divine titles are used in this passage: Lord and Most High. Lord (YHWH) is the personal name of the God of Israel; Most High *(ʿelyôn)* is an ancient Semitic title that first appears in the Abraham-Melchizedek narrative (Gen 14:18-22). In that narrative it is the name of the god of Salem, a shortened form of Jerusalem. When the city became the center of Israelite worship, the title was applied to Israel's God. It now signifies the superiority of YHWH.

The enthronement itself appears to establish YHWH's sovereign reign. The Lord rules over all the earth (vv. 3, 8), over all nations (v. 9). In a world that believed each nation had its own divine patron, this was either a claim of the pre-eminence of YHWH over all other gods or an assertion of monotheistic faith. In either case, all people are called to acclaim the kingship of God (v. 8).

The notion of the kingship of the Lord has cosmic and mythological under-pinnings. The ancients believed that before creation the forces of good were in mortal combat with the forces of evil. A great cosmic battle ensued, from which good emerged triumphant. The divine leader of this victorious com-pany assumed the role of Creator and reordered the cosmos. When this was completed, a heavenly palace was constructed for this great god, who then as-cended the throne, there to rule over the entire universe, maintaining the order that had been established. In Babylon the enthronement of their god was repeated each year during the New Year festival.

While there is no explicit mention of cosmic victory in this psalm, there are reasons why such an understanding lies close to the surface of interpreta-tion. The most obvious is the title "Most High." In the earlier tradition, this was the name given to "the creator of heaven and earth" (Gen 14:19). When this title was applied to the God of Israel, all the attributes associated with that name were appropriated as well. Therefore, if and when the kingship of God was commemorated, even though the primary focus of attention was God's national or political significance this cosmic dimension would be in the con-sciousness of the people. In their minds their God was not only king over all the earth and the peoples that dwelt there but was also king over all the pow-ers of heaven.

Ephesians 1:17-23

This reading, though addressed to believers, is a series of intercessions. While the gifts for which the petitioner prays flow from faith in "our Lord Jesus Christ," the relevance of the Wisdom tradition is clear. The prayer is for a spirit of wisdom and revelation, gifts that are necessary for insight and understand-ing. Although this may sound a bit like Gnosticism, the belief that special God-given knowledge *(gnōsis)* set some people apart from the rest, it is clear that union with Christ is what sets Christians apart. The revelation referred to here is really the kind of enlightenment necessary for understanding the mys-teries that have already entered human history. The verb forms used in the passage indicate the action has been completed and the results of the action are effected in the present.

The prayer is for a threefold spiritual enlightenment, an enlightenment of the inner eyes. The petitioner asks that the believers may know (1) the hope of the calling they have received from God; (2) the riches of the glory of God's inheritance in the holy ones; and (3) the surpassing greatness of God's power to those who believe. These marvels have already taken place; it is for the be-lievers to acknowledge them in awe.

The power referred to throughout the reading belongs to God. It was God's power that raised Christ from the dead and seated Christ in the place of honor in heaven; it was God's power that made all things subject to Christ and exalted Christ as head of the Church. It is this same power that is now called upon.

The view of Christ contained in this passage is exalted. Having been raised from the dead, Christ now sits at God's right hand, high above all the other heavenly creatures. Most likely principality, authority, virtue, and dominion are references to celestial beings who were once thought to be divine but who are now considered classifications of angels. However they are understood, they were certainly considered superior to human creatures. The marvel is that here a human creature has been exalted above them. The mention of names being given in this age or in the age to come means that nothing is beyond Christ's rule (cf. Ps 110:1). His rule is universal in scope and duration.

The body metaphor characterizing the Church is introduced at the end of the reading. Exalted by God, Christ is made the head of the Church, which is the body of Christ. As members of this exalted body, believers share in Christ's fullness, in Christ's exaltation. Seated in the heavens above all other creatures, Christ's glory fills the universe. This reading is a prayer asking that the believers be granted the wisdom and insight to reverence these mysteries and to live lives informed by them.

Hebrews 9:24-28; 10:19-23

The unsurpassed excellence of the sacrifice of Christ is here contrasted with the previous sacrifices offered in the Temple. Normally temples were constructed over an opening that was believed to connect the three levels of reality, namely, heaven, earth, and the underworld. The opening, called the "navel of the earth," or *axis mundi,* made communication among these levels possible. By virtue of this communication the world was sanctified again and again. The Temple was believed to have been built according to the *imago mundi* pattern of the universe, the universe being considered the temple of the Creator-God. The Temple's structure reflected the four celestial horizons with their respective heavenly bodies, and its interior was decorated with elements of the natural environment within which it was built (cf. Exod 25:40). In this way the Temple itself demonstrated the connection between heaven and earth.

This reading plays on the differences between the true sanctuary and the one patterned after it. It claims that while the high priests performed their sacrificial duties in the earthly Temple, the exalted Jesus entered the true sanctuary. It further insists that the cultic system, which was established to enable the people to participate in certain cosmic events by reenacting them, was only able to actualize these events for a short period of time. This explains why the ritual of the Day of Atonement was reenacted year after year. In contrast to this, Jesus offered himself once for all. His sacrifice, like all cosmic acts, was unrepeatable. In the Jewish understanding of eschatology, at the end of time everything would be transformed. Holding to this idea, Christians believe the sacrifice of Christ bridged the gap between the time of human life on this earth and that time of final transformation, when Christ will return to bring irrevocable salvation to all who await him.

On the Day of Atonement the high priest would go behind the veil into the inner sanctuary and stand before the divine presence. There he would incense the mercy seat, believed to be the place on which God was enthroned and from which mercy was dispensed. He would then sprinkle the blood of the sacrificed bull on this mercy seat in an act of atonement. The author of this letter claims it is through his bloody sacrifice that Christ, the great high priest, enables us to enter boldly into the real inner sanctuary, the presence of the all-holy God. Furthermore, our hearts will be sprinkled with and made clean through the blood of Christ. The reference to cleansing the body with pure water is probably an allusion to baptism.

The reading ends with an exhortation to hold fast to the confession of faith *(homología).* This implies acceptance of, commitment to, and obedience to the gospel. If the people of an earlier time trusted that God would accept through the hands of their high priest the offering of the blood of a bull, how much more should the people of a new age trust that the blood of their great high priest would accomplish atonement for their sins.

Luke 24:46-53

In the gospel for today the author depicts Jesus as delivering one last instruction to his disciples before he ascends into heaven. In it, he states that his death and resurrection as well as the basic content of his preaching had been foretold. This is less an attempt to legitimize the authority of Jesus and his teaching than to place Jesus squarely at the heart of the tradition of ancient Israel. Since there is little if any explicit mention of these things in the early writings, this reference must flow from a certain type of biblical interpretation. Rather than regarding the earlier traditions as foreshadowing later events, the believers probably now understood those earlier traditions in the light of the later events. This would be particularly true with regard to the titles that were used of Jesus, namely Son of God, Son of Man, Savior, and especially Servant of God. Christological significance was read back into these Israelite traditions, thus reinforcing the promise-fulfillment motif already explicit there.

There is no question about the veracity of these events. The disciples were eyewitnesses *(aútóptai,* Luke 1:2) to them. Now Jesus tells them they must also be witnesses *(mártyres)* to them, testifying to the authenticity of their religious significance. They are to proclaim to all the nations that he did indeed die and rise, that he did preach repentance and forgiveness of sins. And they must present these realities as the fulfillment of God's plan of salvation. This last instruction was meant not only to bring the disciples themselves to resurrection faith but also to commission them to bring this faith to the world. The disciples finally understand what has happened, for they fall on their faces in homage to Jesus.

The actual account of the ascension is brief. Jesus leads the disciples to Bethany, he raises his hands in blessing in the manner of priestly benediction, and he is taken from their sight. There are no final words; there is no heavenly cloud; there are no angelic companions. It should be noted that there is neither grief nor fear on the part of the disciples. In fact, they return rejoicing and continue worshiping publicly in the Temple.

The importance that Jerusalem holds in this gospel can be seen in this final episode. Jesus ascends from Bethany, a village on the Mount of Olives just outside the city, and the disciples return to Jerusalem, participating in the religious practices of the city. He tells them to wait in Jerusalem until they have received the promise of God, which he is going to send them. There they were to wait until they had been strengthened with power from on high to proclaim the gospel to all nations, beginning with Jerusalem itself. Once again, this is the author's way of portraying the mission of Jesus as the continuation and fulfillment of the mission of Israel (cf. Isa 2:3).

Themes of the Day

The feast of the Ascension is a kind of liminal moment in the Easter season. It is a time between times; a moment when we have left one place in our journey but have not yet arrived at a second. While the narratives that describe the ascension fit well into the unfolding story of redemption, the feast celebrates one aspect of the resurrection itself, namely, the exaltation of Jesus. The readings help us through this paradox. They allow us to focus on this theological point while we commemorate a turning point in the life of the Church. We do this by considering the enthronement of Christ in the heavens and the new body of Christ on earth.

The Enthronement of Christ

Many of the Easter accounts have directed our attention to the appearances of Jesus, which were intended to strengthen the Christians' belief in his bodily resurrection. The emphasis was frequently on certain physical characteristics: he ate food, he invited Thomas to touch him. In many of these accounts Jesus seems to have been saying, "I am the same one who walked with you before. This is the body that you have always known." Today we stand awestruck, watching Jesus ascend into the clouds of heaven, there to be enthroned at the right hand of God. Today is a day to be overwhelmed by the reality of the divinity of the one we have known in his humanity.

Amidst shouts of joy and exaltation Christ is enthroned in heaven in both his divinity and his glorified humanity. Like the conquering creator-God, he has overcome his enemy (death) and now reigns over his new creation (the Church). For our part, we live between the time of his departure and the time of his return. Today we rejoice in one aspect of this mystery, his triumphant ascension; soon we will celebrate the second, the coming of his Spirit. Even though he has left us physically, we do not live without him as we wait. He is present with us in a new way, in a new body, in the Church.

The New Body of Christ

Christ, who ascended into heaven in his body, carries on what he began on earth through his new body, the community of believers. He teaches through its apostles and evangelists. He ministers through its prophets and pastors. In and through the Church, Jesus continues to heal and to comfort; to forgive and to include. We have not been left alone; we have his power, the same power with which he performed marvels when he walked the earth. We have not been left alone; we have each other. Together we make up the new body of Christ. Together we await the fullness of this body. It is this new body that stands in between the times—secure in what we have, confident regarding what we will be given.

Seventh Sunday of Easter

Acts 7:55-60

In many ways the death of Stephen parallels the death of Jesus. Like his master before him, Stephen made claims that, had they not been true, could well have been considered blasphemous. In this passage he insists that he sees the glory of God and Jesus in heaven with God, the same Jesus who had been found deserving of death by the religious leaders of the people. If the members of the Sanhedrin (cf. 6:12) had believed what Stephen was alleging, they would have had to conclude that Jesus' claims about himself were true and that they had wrongfully put him to death. Lest they begin to agree with Stephen and doubt themselves, they closed their hearts and covered their ears.

Like his master before him, the innocent Stephen was found guilty of the crime brought against him. For Stephen, it was blasphemy, and he suffered the punishment of that crime as prescribed by the law—stoning outside the camp (cf. Lev 24:14). Finally, like his master before him, Stephen prayed that the sin of his executioners not be held against them (cf. Luke 23:34) and that at death his own spirit would be welcomed in heaven (cf. Luke 23:46). The difference here is that while Jesus prayed to God, Stephen prayed to the risen Lord. This suggests that in the mind of the author, the risen Jesus was now identified with God. This account may have been an explicit example of what it meant for Christians to take up the cross and follow Jesus.

This is the only instance in the Christian Testament where the title "Son of Man" is found on the lips of someone other than Jesus. As reported in the Gospels, this is probably the title by which Jesus most frequently referred to himself (cf. Luke 5:24; 6:5; 9:22; 17:30; 21:27). The reference in this account is to the mysterious figure that appeared in Daniel's vision (cf. Dan 7:13). That heavenly being was closely associated with the Ancient One, an allusion to God. In a similar way, Stephen sees the Son of Man in heaven with God. He is at God's right hand, presumed to be the place of honor. Much has been written about him standing rather than sitting. This may reflect an element of Daniel's vision, in which the one like the son of man comes on a cloud and in an upright position. Or it could be a welcoming gesture; Stephen's prayer has been heard and the Son of Man is standing to welcome Stephen into the realms of heaven.

The stoning itself appears to conform to Israelite customs. It is done outside the walls of the city and was inflicted by those who had witnessed the offense (cf. Deut 17:5-7). The executioners would have removed their outer garments in order to give themselves freedom of movement. They placed them at the feet of young Saul (Paul, cf. Acts 13:9), as if for safekeeping. One cannot help but wonder why Saul was there. Was he a member of the synagogue of the Freedmen, the group before whom Stephen was speaking (cf. Acts 6:9)? Or was he merely a spectator? The reading tells us nothing more than that he was there and that he seemed to have been on the side of those who put Stephen to death. It is Stephen who is the hero here. He is the one who has successfully patterned his life and death after that of his Master.

Psalm 97:1-2, 6-7, 9

The psalm opens with the traditional enthronement declaration: "The LORD is king!" Behind this exclamation is the theme of divine kingship. The ancients believed that the gods were always vying with one another for power and status. The god who could be victorious over this chaotic situation, if only for a time, was enthroned as king over all. There are echoes of this theology in the responsorial psalm. The God who rules is the LORD, the God of Israel.

The exclamation is appropriately followed by an exhortation: "Let the earth rejoice!" God's victory and rule calls for a celebration that extends beyond the confines of Israel to many islands, an image that denotes the furthest parts of the world. God's throne is established on a firm foundation. Unlike other regimes that are built on brute force or military victory, both of which might fail and result in dethronement, God's rule is constructed in the permanence of justice *(ṣedeq)* and judgment *(mishpāt)*. It is not only impregnable, it is immutable. It stands secure, enabling God to govern undisturbed by any threat and assuring reliable protection to all those under God's jurisdiction.

With three phrases, the psalmist declares the sovereignty of the LORD. First, the reference to the heavens includes all the celestial beings once thought to be gods themselves but now merely luminaries or winds or forms of rain. No longer is there any vying among them. Instead, they are all intent on praising God's justice, the order that was set after the primordial battle had been won. Second, not only Israel but all people see God's glory *(kābôd)*, the splendor that shines from God's holiness and that is usually a characteristic of divine theophany or manifestation. Third, all other gods are prostrate before the LORD in an attitude of utter subservience. Actually, the verb *(bôsh)* means "to put to shame" or "to lose face." In a society where honor and shame play such important roles, this is a significant point. The universal kingship of the LORD is beyond question.

The passage from the psalm ends with a proclamation of praise addressed directly to the LORD. It captures the essence of the preceding verses. God is exalted above both heaven and earth. There is no threat of future upheaval or rebellion. God has no rivals. The divine king has been enthroned and the rule of this God will last forever.

Revelation 22:12-14, 16-17, 20

The eschatological character of this vision is clear from the outset. The risen Jesus announces that he is not only coming soon but that he is also coming as a judge. There are several other christological themes in this report. First, it is the risen Jesus himself, not an angelic messenger, who announces to John his imminent return. Furthermore, in two self-disclosive statements *(égō eimi,* I am) he lists five characterizations that describe him. The first three, Alpha-Omega, first-last, beginning-end (v. 13), mean basically the same thing. They are literary devices that name only the two poles of a certain dimension of reality but encompass everything that exists between those poles. Thus the alphabet includes every word that can be constructed from its individual elements; first and last include what in time sequence is between them; beginning and end implies the entire action. The risen Jesus here claims to be both origin and end of all things. By appropriating to himself attributes that belong to God he is claiming intimate unity with God.

The last two characterizations (v. 16) reflect messianic titles. Though "root" can mean "source" or "origin," it can also denote "branch" (cf. Isa 10:11). This latter meaning is probably the intent here. The light of Venus, the morning star, heralded the dawning of a new day and all the promise this might bring. This striking image became a reference to the Messiah (cf. Num 24:17). Because of their messianic implications, both "offspring of David" and "morning star" have been preserved in the Advent liturgy as two of the O Antiphons.

The risen Jesus announces that he will judge everyone not merely according to their faith but also according to their deeds. However, his attention is focused on those who have been faithful. He introduces them by means of a macarism: "Blessed are they!" He then describes them in three ways. They are the ones who have washed their robes. This is not necessarily a reference to baptism or martyrdom. Some kind of spiritual cleansing, symbolized by washing one's garments, was required for entrance into the presence of God (cf. Exod 19:10). The reference here may merely allude to this practice. These righteous ones are also given access to the tree of life, obviously a rescinding of the prohibition ordained in the Garden of Eden (cf. Gen 3:22). This would mean they would never have to face death. Finally, they are allowed to enter the city, the new Jerusalem, the renewed community, the place where God dwells eternally with the faithful. Moral or spiritual cleansing has taken place, all things have been fulfilled, the final consummation is at hand.

The righteous who are invited into the city are those who have thirsted for the gift of living water (cf. Isa 55:1). They are invited not only by the Spirit who calls but by the bride, the Holy City itself (cf. Rev 21:2). The words of the risen Jesus end as they began, with an announcement that he is coming soon. The Greek form of the verb "coming" is known as prophetic present, implying that the future is already in the present.

The reading itself ends with words that are both a prayer and a testimony to faith: "Come, Lord Jesus." It is probably a translation from the Aramaic *(marana tha)*. Although sometimes the eschatological overtones of the phrase were frightening (cf. 1 Cor 16:22), at other times it was prayed with confident anticipation (cf. *Didache* 10:16). The entire tone of this reading suggests that the Lord's coming is something to look forward to with joy.

John 17:20-26

This prayer of Jesus includes three major themes that together reveal something of the nature of God and something of the nature of the Church. These themes are creatively woven together into a kind of tapestry rather than logically developed into a theological thesis.

The first and perhaps the major theme is that of unity. It is the reason for Jesus' prayer. He prays for the unity of believers "that they may all be one" (vv. 21, 22, 23). He explicitly states that his prayer is not only for those who have heard and responded to his own preaching but also for those who believe in him because of the preaching of others. The mission of the apostles has been successful.

However, he does not want there to be even a hint of status. Eyewitnesses to the events of Jesus' life have no advantage over Christians of the twenty-first century.

The unity for which Jesus prays is anything but superficial. It is to resemble the unity that exists between Jesus and his Father. Here the image of father, as gender-biased as it may be, reveals the depth of the unity mentioned. Jesus proceeds from God as the image of God. We may be *made according to* the image of God, but the Son *is* that image. This notion of unity was reinforced as the historical Jesus conformed his will to the will of God. Thus the unity between Jesus and God flows from both the divine nature and the human obedience.

Jesus goes even further. The unity for which he prays does more than resemble divine unity, it participates in it. It is in faith that Christians are intimately united with Jesus. Therefore it will be through Jesus that they will be brought into the divine union, where the Father dwells in the Son and the Son in the Father.

The second thematic thread woven throughout this tapestry is glory (vv. 22, 24). Divine glory is the manifestation of God's character, or person. The glory of Jesus was believed to have been manifested through his death, his resurrection, and his exaltation by God. Joined to Jesus in faith, believers share in this glory because in a very real sense they share in his person. In this way they have entered into the very life of God and share in the union of Jesus and his Father.

Although it does not appear to be as prominent as the other threads, the world *(kósmos)* is important in this prayer. Presently, the world does not know God (v. 25). However, it is Jesus' prayer that this situation be changed. It will be accomplished through the witness given by the union that exists among and within the believers, Jesus, and his Father (vv. 21, 23). In other words, the world is the object of the ministry of the believers. To the world that does not yet know God, they are to manifest the divine union in which they participate. Through this manifestation the world will see not only that God sent Jesus but also that God loves believers with the same love with which Jesus is loved.

Jesus has made God's name known to believers. Now he asks that these believers might be with him. Since he has already spoken extensively about the union they enjoy with him, the reference here must be to something else—probably to the reunion at the end. This can be understood either as following the individual death of each Christian or the final consummation at the end of time.

The reading ends on the note of love. It is Jesus' prayer that the love with which God loves him may be in those who have believed in him. In this way Jesus himself will abide in them.

Themes of the Day

Over these past Sundays we have been considering the various ways the risen Lord is present in the community as well as the wondrous gifts he has bestowed upon it. Before we move into the mystery of Pentecost, we celebrate the risen Lord as exalted with God in heaven.

The Lord Exalted

We cannot even begin to fathom what the exaltation of Jesus means. On this Sunday, in our attempt to praise our risen Lord we compound image upon image, metaphor on metaphor. Jesus is the king who reigns in heaven; the victorious conqueror of primordial chaos; the one who governs both heaven and earth with justice rather than brute force; the one who elicits rejoicing rather than fear. He is the Son of Man seen by Stephen, standing in heaven in the place of honor at God's right hand; the one to whom were given dominion and glory and kingship. He is the consummation of all things; the Alpha and Omega, the first and last, the beginning and end. He is the long-awaited Messiah, who heralded the new day of promise.

Exalted by God

The exaltation of Jesus is a mighty act of God. The imagery from the psalm suggests it is akin to the marvel of creation itself. It is not something Jesus in his human nature could have accomplished on his own. This is an act of God. Jesus had been sent by God as he himself proclaimed, and he returned to God as Stephen testified. God's exaltation of Jesus is one more impenetrable mystery. Conscious of our own limitations, we might wonder how God can accomplish such things. An even more pressing question is, Why would God act in this way? Why raise to such heights one who shares our human limitations? Why exalt humanity with a share in divinity?

We have no answers to these questions. They are not intended to be answered. Rather, they must be asked again and again so that, in the absence of an answer, we can stand in astonishment and awe, realizing that all we can do is praise God and our exalted Lord.

Our Participation in the Exaltation

We have heard Jesus described with these images so many times they may have lost their power in our lives. If he is indeed all they imply, why is our faith so weak, and why are our lives so shallow? Stephen prayed to be received into the presence of this exalted Lord, and his prayer was answered. But he is not the only one invited to share in Christ's exaltation. All who wash their robes have been given a right to the tree of life and permission to enter the new city through its gates. Jesus prayed for *us*, not merely for his earliest followers. He wanted *us* to share in the intimate union that was his with God. It was his wish that *we* would be with him, that *we* would share the glory that had been his from the beginning and will be his forever in his exaltation. This Sunday we ponder these things as we await the power of the Spirit of God, which will soon take hold of us.

Pentecost Sunday

Acts 2:1-11

The Jewish feast of Pentecost was one of the three major pilgrim festivals of Israel. Originally an agricultural feast marking the end of the grain harvest, it was also called the feast of Weeks because it was celebrated seven weeks, or fifty days, after the feast of Unleavened Bread. As with the other two pilgrim festivals, it eventually took on historical importance, commemorating the giving of the law at Sinai. The fact that it was a pilgrim feast explains why devout Jews from every nation were in Jerusalem at this time. Although only devout men are mentioned (v. 5), we know that women and children also made the pilgrimage. This is an example of the author's gender bias.

The reading from Acts does not tell us precisely who were in the room when the Spirit descended. Was it the one hundred twenty that had gathered earlier (cf. Acts 1:15)? Was it only the twelve apostles (cf. 2:14)? Contrary to some translations the Greek does not use gender-specific language, so we cannot say it was a gathering made up exclusively of men. (The later reference to the Joel passage would suggest it was not; cf. 2:17-18.)

The external manifestations that accompanied the outpouring of the Spirit were all phenomena associated with a theophany, an experience of God. For example, thunder accompanied God's revelation at Sinai (cf. Exod 19:16); God spoke to Job from the whirlwind (Job 38:1) and to Moses from the burning bush (Exod 3:2). The text reports that these phenomena were audible and visible while the actual outpouring of the Spirit was not. However, as those in the room were filled with the Spirit, they began to speak in other languages, a feat that could only have some supernatural origin.

The same Greek word *(glōssa)* is used for the tongues of fire that appeared above each one and for the foreign tongues that were subsequently spoken. There is question whether the reference here is to communicative speech (foreign tongues) or ecstatic speech, called "glossolalia." Since the people who came to see what had happened did understand the bold proclamations of these Spirit-filled preachers, the meaning seems to be communicative rather than ecstatic speech (vv. 6-11).

The crowd that gathered because of the loud noise were confused, astonished, and amazed. They knew that those speaking were Galileans, presumably because of some feature of their speech. Yet the hearers were able to understand the message in their own dialects. Because the Galileans spoke in tongues and those in the crowd heard in their own speech, some commentators have suggested there was a miracle in hearing as well as in speaking.

The exact nature of this marvel is less significant than its meaning. It was clearly a manifestation of the universal presence and power of the Spirit. Some commentators believe it demonstrated the reversal of the fragmentation of peoples that occurred at Babel when languages were confused after the people attempted to construct the tower (cf. Gen 11:1-9). The outpouring of the Spirit and the preaching of the gospel to all nations are seen by some as the reuniting of the human race and the gathering of all into the reign of God.

Psalm 104:1, 24, 29-30, 31, 34

This hymn is remarkable in its depiction of God as the Creator and sustainer of all life. It begins, as do other hymns of its kind, with a summons to praise. The call to "bless the LORD" is normally addressed to someone other than the psalmist. Twice a self-address is used (v. 1, also v. 35). This forms a kind of *inclusio* that divides the responsorial psalm into two parts. The first treats God as the wondrous Creator; the second describes God's providential care.

The Hebrew word that is translated "soul" *(nepesh)* comes from the word for "breath." It yields over twenty meanings, chief among which are life-breath (or soul), life, living person. The reference here is probably to that center within the psalmist from which flow all life forces. This is not merely a spiritual or immaterial reality; it encompasses every aspect of the person. Every aspect of the psalmist's being is called upon to give praise to God.

God is described as robed in majesty and glory, wrapped around with radiant light. This is the way the commanding gods of the ancient Near East were depicted. The psalmist does not claim that God is visible but that God's garments are discernible. In other words, the splendor the psalmist beholds is an indication of God's presence. God is perceived through the glories of creation.

The natural world is not only marvelous in its appearance, it is diverse in its manifestations as well. The variety and complexity of its forms are astounding. This splendor is attributed to the wisdom of the Creator. In the biblical tradition there is an intrinsic link between creation and wisdom (cf. Prov 8:22-31; Wis 9:9). Wisdom was understood as insight into, harmony with, or power over the orders of reality. These orders were established by God at the time of creation, and they are sustained by the same creative power.

In the second part of the psalm God is extolled as the one who cares for all living things. All creatures look to God for sustenance. From a human point of view creation is not a static act, completed once for all in the distant past. We experience creation as an ongoing event. The act of creation and power of the Creator are perceived in the constant renewal of life that unfolds before our eyes. In a very real sense, creation is more than a primordial event; it is a personal experience.

The psalm then shows that the life forces of the natural world do not operate in a manner independent of the divine will. God sustains life by providing food, but God can also bring on death by taking back the breath of life. When this happens, the creature returns to the dust from which it was initially taken (cf. Gen 2:7; Job 12:10). God is both the original Creator and the one who continues to control the forces of nature.

Finally, God not only creates but re-creates. The ongoing forces of nature are re-creative. Life is sustained and perpetuated. The word for "spirit" *(rûaḥ)* is the same as that found in the story of creation, where a mighty wind swept over the waters (Gen 1:2). That was the first creation. The psalm claims that the spirit of the LORD can bring about a new creation. This is reason enough to bless the LORD.

1 Corinthians 12:3b-7, 12-13 (A)

This reading consists of three different yet related themes: an acclamation of the lordship of Jesus; a defense of diversity within the community; the body metaphor that characterizes that diversity.

The acclamation "Jesus is Lord" is rich in both Jewish and early Christian meaning. "Lord" *(kýrios)* was the official title of the Roman emperor. To proclaim Jesus as Lord was to set up a rivalry between the followers of Jesus and the ruling political authority. Since most if not all of the emperors claimed to be somehow divine, this rivalry was both political and religious. Furthermore, because the Roman government was involved in the death of Jesus, such a challenging claim would place those who made it at great risk for their lives.

The word "Lord" is also used in the Septuagint, the Greek version of the First Testament, as a substitute for God's personal name. To use this title for Jesus is to ascribe to him the attributes of God. This use may not have set up a political rivalry between Jesus and God, as was the case with the Roman emperor, but it certainly did make serious religious claims. It is important to note that the acclamation uses the name of the man Jesus, not his religious title, Christ. It is this man who is placed on the same level as the God of ancient Israel. No one would make such a claim were it not for the prompting of the Holy Spirit. This is a cry of faith, a testimony to the divine character of this man from Galilee.

Paul next launches into a discourse on the varieties of functions within the Christian community. In sketching this diversity he uses two triads: gifts, ministries, and works; Spirit, Lord, and God. Although the second triad suggests a trinitarian perspective that associates one set of functions with each of the divine Persons, it is clear from the text that all the activities are manifestations of the Spirit (v. 7).

"Gifts" *(chárisma)* refers to those operations of the Spirit, notably speaking in tongues and prophesying, that were usually operative during worship. Ministry *(diakonía)* was service within the community. It included duties that were often considered menial, like serving at table or collecting money. Paul may have included this reference in order to show that within the community of believers, no task is ignoble. "Works" *(enérgēma)* were feats of great energy or divine power. Since all these gifts or ministries or works were manifestations of the Spirit, no one was to be considered superior to another. Further, they were not given for the self-aggrandizement of the one who received them. All were given for the benefit of the entire community.

The diversity found within the community is compared to the complexity of the human body. Each part has its own unique function, but all parts work for the good of the whole. This metaphor characterizes several aspects of the community. First, it portrays unity in diversity, a unity that is far from uniformity. Second, it underscores the lack of competition among members, one activity elevating itself above the others. Lowly service is no less important than charismatic gifts. Third, it points up the interdependence that exists within the community.

In this community there are no more stratifications, whether religious (Jew or Greek) or social (slave or free).

Romans 8:8-17 (B)

Paul contrasts two ways of living: in the flesh and in the spirit. Although flesh and spirit can refer to two distinct aspects of human nature, they can also both connote the whole human being, but from a particular point of view or with a certain life-direction. When Paul refers to the flesh, he is not thinking of specific sexual behavior. He is speaking of human nature in all the limitations that sometimes incline one away from God. On the other hand, life in the spirit is attuned to God. It is that dimension of the human being that can be joined to the very Spirit of God.

Paul's denunciation of life in the flesh is unqualified. It cannot please God. Life in the spirit, on the other hand, is a form of union with God. He assures the Christians that they are in the spirit, if only the Spirit of God dwells within them. In true trinitarian fashion he likens the Spirit of God to the Spirit of Christ, and he maintains that it is through this Spirit that resurrection is promised. Paul speaks of life and death in two different ways. He states that those who live in the Spirit have Christ living in them. This is the same Christ who through his own death vanquished the powers of death. Though sin can still exact physical death, it cannot quench the spirit that lives because of righteousness. Just as Christ conquered death and lives anew, so those joined to Christ will share in his victory and will enjoy new life.

As far back as the traditions found in the book of Deuteronomy, Israelites believed they were children of God (cf. Deut 14:1). In that earlier tradition the idea of being children of God was associated with obedience to the precepts of the law. According to Paul, those who are children of God are so not because of obedience to the law but because they are led (compelled or constrained) by the Spirit. Paul uses "spirit" in various ways. The Spirit of God or Christ is a divine reality; the spirit of slavery is a disposition or mentality; the spirit of adoption is a relationship. He identifies children of God as those who are compelled by the Spirit. So compelled, we have been taken into the family of God and have the right to call God "Father."

We are also children of God through the sonship of Christ. First and foremost, Jesus is the Son of God. When we are joined to him we are led by the same Spirit that led him. Therefore we can say that it is with and through Christ that we become children of God. If Jesus can call God *Abba,* then we who are joined to him can as well. Here Paul's trinitarian theology springs from his conviction of our transformative union with Christ.

There has been a great deal of discussion about the Aramaic epithet *Abba,* "Father," which is a familial, colloquial term of intimacy. There is no reason to doubt that Jesus used it. What is remarkable is that he, who is son by nature, invites us, who are children by adoption, to address God in this way. Following Paul's argument, we are made children of God not by the Father but by the Spirit, or through the Son. It is the Spirit of Jesus in us that cries out.

Paul is making bold claims here. That could explain why he felt it necessary to call on witnesses to confirm the truth of his claims. According to law, two witnesses are required to corroborate a story. Paul's witnesses are the Spirit of God and our own spirit. Together they testify to the truth of what Paul says.

As children of God we are also heirs. But heirs to what? Although the text is not explicit, one could conclude that we are heirs to the very inheritance to which Jesus is heir—the glory of God in the coming reign of God. Whatever that inheritance may be, it is gained only through suffering. Once again, it is our union with Jesus that entitles us to privileges.

John 20:19-23

This appearance account treats the resurrection and the bestowal of the Spirit upon the disciples of Jesus as having occurred on the same day, for the event described took place "on the evening of that first day of the week" (v. 19). The account contains several salient details. First, the incident took place on the first day of the week. Second, it occurred despite the doors being closed. Third, Jesus appears in the midst of the disciples. Fourth, he addresses those present with a greeting of peace. Fifth, he calls their attention to his wounds. Sixth, he confers the Spirit on them and entrusts them with the power of binding or loosing. Each of these details is laden with theological meaning.

This first day of the week is the actual day of the resurrection (v. 19). It is clear that the entire reckoning of time has been altered by the event that occurred early in the morning. Where previously religious meaning was given to the Sabbath, the conclusion of the week, now the focus is on the beginning, on the future. The locked doors secured the disciples from those who had had some part in the arrest, trial, and crucifixion of Jesus. His followers had reason to fear that these people might be hostile toward them as well. The closed doors also underscore the mysterious character of Jesus' risen body. It is not impeded by material obstacles; it can move as it wishes and where it will.

The wish of peace, which was the common Jewish greeting of the day, was also a prayer for the eschatological blessings of health, prosperity, and all good things. When Jesus wishes peace for his disciples, he is proclaiming the arrival of this time of fulfillment. By calling attention to the wounds in his hands and side, Jesus shows the disciples he is not a figment of their imaginations or some kind of ghost from the netherworld. He is the same man who was crucified, but now he is risen. Apparently the disciples recognized the Lord, because they rejoiced at the sight of him.

The bestowal of the Holy Spirit is introduced by a second salutation of peace. The image of breathing life into another is reminiscent of the creation of Adam (cf. Gen 2:7) and restoration of Israel after the Exile (cf. Ezek 37:9). By breathing in this way, the risen Lord portrays himself as one who can create or re-create. One of the Hebrew words for "breath" *(rûaḥ)* is also translated "spirit," so there is long tradition of linking spirit and breath. The spirit of God is also the breath of God.

The disciples are commissioned to go forth, to declare salvation and judgment. The language describes the activity of a judge, who decides whether or not the defendant is bound to the consequences of the charges or loosed from them. Most likely, the authority here given to the disciples is much broader than this. The phrase "bind or loose" (retain or forgive) is similar to "flesh and blood," or "left and right." Each expression names the opposite poles, but together they are meant to include everything between them as well. These are ways of describing totality: "flesh and blood" refers to the whole body; "left and right" includes the entire horizon; "bind and loose" suggests complete authority. With the bestowal of the Spirit the disciples are authorized to continue the mission of Jesus.

John 14:15-16, 23b-26

This gospel passage contains several major theological themes. It emphasizes the link between love and obedience; it speaks of the presence of God with the one who loves; it provides us with a partial view of the internal relationships within the Trinity.

Love is the fundamental message of Jesus. However, he calls for a demanding love, one that is as self-sacrificing as was the love of Jesus himself. Only those who follow his example and obey his directives can be said to truly love, and those who love as Jesus did will in turn be loved by his Father. Obedience is not the requirement for love; it is the consequence of it. If the disciples truly love Jesus, they will keep his commandments. And if they keep his commandments, Jesus will ask his Father to send another advocate, the Holy Spirit, who will not leave them as Jesus is about to do, but who will remain with them forever.

Such love is more than an emotional response. It is a state of being, a disposition within which one lives. The dwelling Jesus and his Father make with those who love like this is an abiding dwelling *(monē)* in contrast to a transitory state. Those who do not keep the word of Jesus will not be so blessed. Since the word of Jesus is really the word of the one who sent him, to reject that word is to reject both Jesus and his Father. They will not dwell with such a person.

While this passage cannot provide us with a complete trinitarian teaching, it does offer us some insight into the mystery of God. There is definitely an intimate relationship between Jesus and his Father. The very metaphor of father, which he uses to speak of God, is evidence of this. Furthermore, he and his Father together dwell with faithful believers. Despite this intimacy, they are distinct from each other. Jesus was sent by his Father. Jesus proclaims the word of his Father, and his Father sends the Holy Spirit in his name.

Like Jesus, the Holy Spirit is sent by the Father, but the Spirit is sent in the name of Jesus, not in the name of the Father. The Spirit is not a substitute for Jesus but an emissary, participating in the mission of Jesus by reminding the disciples of the things Jesus taught them. To so remember is more than an intellectual act. It is a call to bear witness to the word of God. In this passage the coming of the Spirit appears to be distinct from the coming of Jesus and his Father to abide with the disciples. They come in order to abide in love; the Spirit comes to enlighten. The focus of the Spirit's enlightenment will be the words of Jesus. His words were not merely inspirational; they were the very words of God.

Themes of the Day

The community has been living in the in-between time since the ascension of the Lord. Today it celebrates the dramatic inbreaking of the time of fulfillment. The feast celebrates the fullness of the Spirit and the great gathering together of nations, and it also brings the Easter season to its conclusion. Like the finale of a majestic symphony, the readings for today recapitulate many of the themes that appeared throughout the Easter season: christology, trinitarian theology, reign of God, repentance, salvation, mission, universality. All are brought together as we are brought together into the body of Christ.

In the Fullness of the Spirit

At last the plan of salvation has been brought to conclusion. The risen Lord has been exalted to his rightful place next to God, and he has sent his Spirit to fill the earth with God's power. The world is charged with divine energy; it needs but a spark to ignite it with life and excitement. This vitality explodes into the extraordinary: tongues are loosed, and speech overflows its linguistic constraints; charismatic gifts flood the valleys of human habitation; barred doors are burst open, and frightened hearts are calmed. The Spirit of the Lord fills the whole world.

The Great Gathering

Once again we gather together for one reason, only to discover that God has gathered us for another. Strangers assemble to fulfill personal obligations, and they experience a phenomenon that bonds them together for life. Individual religious devotion is swept up into communal divine revelation. Through the Spirit of God we are reconciled to each other, and then together we spend ourselves for the common good. Through the Spirit of God the world is renewed, the community is revitalized, and we come to know the mysterious yet all-pervasive peace of Christ.

If this has all really happened, why does our world look the same? Why is there so much religious and ethnic rivalry? Why do we continue to make distinctions between Jew and Gentile, slave and free, woman and man, distinctions that favor one at the expense of the other? Why is there so little peace, or comfort, or solace? Why do we refuse to forgive or to be reconciled? Is Pentecost merely a feast we celebrate in red vestments? Has the face of the earth really been renewed?

The answer is yes! Resoundingly, yes! The Spirit has been poured forth and works wonders wherever human hearts are open to its promptings. The earth is renewed each time rivalries are resolved, distinctions are recognized as merely expressions of diversity, peace is restored, comfort and solace are offered, and forgiveness is granted. We are immersed in the vigor of the Spirit of God; all we have to do is open ourselves to it and the reign of God will be born in our midst.

Ordinary Time (Part One)

	First Reading	Psalm	Second Reading	Gospel
First Sunday (Baptism of the Lord)				
Second Sunday	Isaiah 62:1-5 The bridegroom rejoices in the bride	Psalm 96:1-3, 7-10 Proclaim God's marvelous deed	1 Corinthians 12:4-11 Different gifts, but the same Spirit	John 2:1-11 The sign at Cana
Third Sunday	Nehemiah 8:2-4a, 5-6, 8-10 The law was read	Psalm 19:8-10, 15 The law of the LORD is perfect	1 Corinthians 12:12-30 The body of Christ	Luke 1:1-4; 4:14-21 The Spirit is fulfilled
Fourth Sunday	Jeremiah 1:4-5, 17-19 A prophet to the nations	Psalm 71:1-6, 15, 17 I sing of your salvation	1 Corinthians 12:31–13:13 The greatest is love	Luke 4:21-30 Ministry to the Gentiles
Fifth Sunday	Isaiah 6:1-2a, 3-8 Here I am, send me	Psalm 138:1-5, 7-8 Sing the praise of the LORD	1 Corinthians 15:1-11 I hand down what I received	Luke 5:1-11 They left all and followed him
Sixth Sunday	Jeremiah 17:5-8 Trust the LORD	Psalm 1:1-4, 6 Blessed are the righteous	1 Corinthians 15:12, 16-20 Christ was raised, so we will be raised	Luke 6:17, 20-26 Blessed are the poor

Seventh Sunday 1 Samuel 26:2, 7-9, 12-13, 22-23 Spare the anointed of the LORD	**Psalm 103**:1-4, 8, 10, 12-13 The LORD is kind and merciful	**1 Corinthians 15**:45-49 The last Adam: a life-giving spirit	**Luke 6**:27-38 Be merciful as God is merciful
Eighth Sunday Sirach 27:4-7 Worth is revealed in speech	**Psalm 92**:2-3, 13-16 It is good to thank the LORD	**1 Corinthians 15**:54-58 Death is swallowed up	**Luke 6**:39-45 Speech reveals the heart
Ninth Sunday 1 Kings 8:41-43 Foreigners come to the Temple	**Psalm 117**:1, 2 Go out to all the world	**Galatians 1**:1-2, 6-10 An apostle from God	**Luke 7**:1-10 The faith of the centurion
Tenth Sunday 1 Kings 17:17-24 Your son is alive	**Psalm 30**:2, 4-6, 11-13 Rescued by the LORD	**Galatians 1**:11-19 Persecutor turned apostle	**Luke 7**:11-17 Young man, arise

Ordinary Time (Part One)

Initial Reading of the Ordinary Lectionary (Part One)

Introduction

This period of Ordinary Time is really an interlude between seasons. Christmas is behind us, and in a few weeks we will be entering the season of Lent. Although time and again we might catch a glimpse of the future, a hint of what lies ahead for Jesus and for those who are his disciples, during this interim period our readings invite us to reflect on various aspects of our discipleship.

The number of Sundays in this period prompts us to divide Ordinary Time into four sections. The absence of specific seasonal themes makes this division somewhat arbitrary. Since there is consecutive reading from the epistles, we could have allowed these readings to determine the divisions. However, we felt that since there is significant reading from some epistles and much less from others, such divisions would be quite uneven in size. Therefore, we simply divided the thirty-four Sundays by four and grouped the readings accordingly.

First Testament Readings

Although the first readings were probably chosen because in some way they reflect or support the theology found in the gospel selection for the day, when read according to the first column they offer a theological pattern with its own unique meaning. Read consecutively in this way, they yield four different themes. The Second and Third Sundays of the year pick up themes from the Christmas season, when we celebrated the inauguration of the reign of God on earth. These two readings provide us with pictures of re-created communities. In both instances the saving grace of God took people who had been unfaithful and reconstituted them as a new people, with a new name, and a new commitment to God. However, this reign has only been inaugurated. It must be proclaimed and spread, and for this we need ministers. The calls of Isaiah and Jeremiah orient us to this movement out of ourselves.

Once ministers of the word have been chosen and have accepted their election, the preached message begins to unfold. At the heart of the message is the call to trust in God. This is followed by the very challenging injunction to love one's enemies. Finally, we are shown that the gospel must take root at the very core of one's being, and the caliber of that commitment will be revealed in what we do and say. These first readings get us off to a good start in reexamining our call and our commitment to that call.

The first readings end with two narratives that demonstrate the universal character of the saving action of God. In the first Solomon invites non-Israelites to pray in the Temple; in the second the healing power of God cures the son of a woman of Sidon. Here we see that the power of God cannot be limited by ethnic, religious, or gender restrictions.

Psalms

Most of the psalm responses came from hymns of praise or thanksgiving, depending on the readings of the particular day. However, there is a Wisdom psalm that extolls the glories of the law (Third Sunday) and a lament that echoes the cry of those who suffer precisely because they are disciples (Fourth Sunday). It is appropriate that the examination of discipleship contained in the readings of this section of Ordinary Time elicit expressions of praise and thanksgiving.

Epistles

The Epistles from these first Sundays in Ordinary Time are taken from Paul's first letter to the Corinthians and his letter to the Galatians. Three themes can be gleaned. The first theme (Sundays 2–4) addresses aspects of the Christian community; the second (Sundays 5–8) focuses our gaze on the power that is exercised by the risen Christ; the third (Sundays 9–10) stems from Paul's own life as an apostle.

Paul's notion of community is remarkably vivid in its description. He uses images that underscore both the unity that is essential and the diversity that is unavoidable. He is not willing to relinquish one for the sake of the other. In his eyes, to do so would violate God's intent. Not only are we all members of the one body, but for the body to be healthy the members must be bound together by love. The hymn in praise of love reminds us of this.

The resurrection of Christ empowers us to rise as well. In this, death loses all jurisdiction that it might have exercised over us before our commitment to Christ. Before, we were simply earthly creatures; now we have been re-created in the image of the life-giving Christ. Total commitment to Christ alone can guarantee this. No religious practice, regardless of how cherished, can rival the saving power of Christ. This is the gospel Paul has preached ever since the day he encountered the risen Christ on the road to Damascus.

Gospels

The consecutive reading of the gospels reminds us of some of the same themes we found in the first readings. Here we see Jesus inaugurating his ministry (Sundays 2–4) and calling disciples to further the reign of God (Fifth Sunday). Instruction of the disciples follows (Sundays 6–8). The last episodes recount how the healing power of Jesus crosses ethnic, religious, and gender boundaries.

Jesus' ministry begins on an ambiguous note. On the one hand, he seems to be thrust into the public sphere before he is ready. Then, when he does reveal himself, his claims are met with mixed reaction. This is followed by an account of the call of the first disciples. The reception of Jesus' ministry should have alerted the disciples to the reception they themselves can expect. Their initial instruction includes a lesson on the paradoxes the reign of God will uncover, chief among which is love of one's enemies. Deeply rooted attitudes from which flow acts of righteousness are clearly preferred to mere external works that have no interior grounding.

The final gospel passages show Jesus disregarding the purity taboos and healing the servant of a foreigner, and bringing back to life a young man who was dead. It is clear from this that the reign of God has come for all people. Disciples come from various cultural backgrounds, all with their narrow viewpoints, and they will have to learn to be as inclusive as Jesus.

Mosaic of Readings

The major theological focus of this set of readings is discipleship. This discipleship is our participation in the ministry of Jesus. It calls people to live extraordinary lives and to accomplish wonderful deeds. Disciples are empowered to do this because they have risen with Christ to a new way of living. So empowered, they can accomplish the impossible. They can cast out the power of evil in others, and they can find it within themselves to love those who have been their enemies. Only God can accomplish this in frail human beings. Recognizing this, we sing out in praise and thanksgiving.

Readings

First Sunday in Ordinary Time
The Baptism of the Lord

Second Sunday in Ordinary Time
Isaiah 62:1-5

The reading consists of an oracle of salvation. The first verse is a prophetic promise of deliverance; the other four verses develop the theme through the use of marriage imagery. The prophet uses poetic parallelism to speak of God's inability to be silent in the face of Jerusalem's misfortune:

| for Zion's sake | I will not be silent |
| for Jerusalem's sake | I will not be quiet |

This poetic structure indicates that Zion and Jerusalem can be used interchangeably to denote the same reality. Furthermore, the rest of the imagery implies that the city really represents the entire nation. Therefore we can say that God promises not to rest until the nation is vindicated, until its righteousness *(ṣᵉdāqâ)* dawns and its salvation burns brightly. In other words, God will not rest until all behold the vindication of the nation. We are not told what precise crisis the nation has undergone that calls for such vindication. It could have been any kind of defeat or setback that would have caused it to lose face in the sight of the other nations.

There is a dramatic shift in the remaining verses of the reading. The message is now spoken directly to the nation itself, and God is referred to in the third person. The vindication in store for Jerusalem is more than a restoration. The city is promised a new name, spoken by the mouth of the LORD. A new name implies a new status. This is a kind of new creation. The marriage language and imagery make this clear, since marriage is itself the creation of a new reality. However, the language is first discouraging and only then encouraging. "Forsaken" can mean abandoned by one's husband; "desolate" can mean barren (cf. Isa 54:1). Previously the nation had been in such straits. But now the vindication and the new name indicate a total transformation. The people who were once forsaken are now the delight of the LORD; the land that once was barren is newly espoused.

As with all metaphors, the marriage imagery both adds a creative dimension to our understanding of the relationship between God and the nation and sets limits that can stereotype that understanding. Perhaps one of the best ways of portraying the passionate love God bears for us and the depths of the intimacy God desires is with marriage imagery. Within the context of such intimacy, what better way to describe the betrayal of love than the words "forsaken" or "barren"? How better depict the bliss of reconciliation than by taking delight in the beloved or in being espoused?

While the imagery is moving, it emerges from a patriarchal society where marriage is not a union of equals. Rather, the woman, not the man, is required to be faithful to the relationship; infertility was considered her burden, not his. The very language alerts us to this inequality. The Hebrew word for "espouse" *(bā'al)* also yields the nouns "husband," "lord," and "owner"; she is clearly under his rule. When the metaphor is applied to the divine-human relationship, the social inequality is reinforced, because God is indeed our LORD and ruler. However, rather than allow the image of God as ruler to reinforce patriarchal inequality, we must realize that the way God is characterized as husband undermines any domineering patriarchal stereotypes. God seems willing to do almost anything to reestablish the covenant bond the human partner has broken. Since that partner is represented as a woman, the metaphor can be taken to reinforce the stereotype that disadvantages women. However, patriarchy itself has been reinterpreted, and therefore, such a biased use of the metaphor would be inappropriate. (It would be interesting to depict the human partner as a cheating husband and see how God would then be depicted.) Whatever the characterization, God seeks reconciliation and will not rest until it is accomplished.

Psalm 96:1-2, 2-3, 7-8, 9-10

The psalm calls for praise of God for the wonderful acts of salvation God has performed (vv. 1-3). Three times the psalmist calls for this, each time highlighting a different aspect of the song. First, the song is to be a new one. This is only appropriate, since salvation has transformed the people—no longer will laments be acceptable. The only kind of song worthy of the event of salvation that has unfolded is a hymn of praise.

The song is directed to all the earth or all the lands (*'ereṣ,* vv. 1, 9). While the primary meaning of the word designates the earth in a cosmological sense, a second and equally significant sense denotes a particular territory. One can conclude that in this psalm both the natural world and human society within it are called to praise God. Finally, along with the call to sing is a summons to bless the name of the LORD. Since a name was thought to contain part of the very essence of the person, a call to bless God's name is really a summons to give praise to some aspect of God's character. The aspect to be praised is the salvation God has brought about for the sake of Israel. All the earth is called to announce the good news of this salvation and to announce it unceasingly, day after day.

All nations and peoples (v. 3) are to be told of the salvation God has brought to Israel. Though the passage does not explicitly mention Israel, we can presume Israel is the people referred to, because all the other nations are to be told of God's saving action. The glory *(kābôd)* of God refers to the visible manifestation of God's splendor. While it is usually revealed in the Temple (v. 9), here it is also associated with salvation (v. 2), with the historical events by means of which God delivered the people. In this, God has done a new thing, so it is only right that a new song of praise be sung.

Once the nations have seen the wonders God has accomplished on behalf of Israel, they too are summoned to praise the LORD. In fact all earth *('ereṣ)* is actually called to worship the LORD, who has been revealed in such a wondrous manner. The essence of their homage is the cultic cry: "The LORD is king!" This cry was frequently used during celebrations of the kingship of God. These either followed military victory or were celebrated at the new year, when God's primordial triumph over the forces of chaos was reenacted. During a cultic celebration the people at worship would proclaim the cry with joy; after the primordial victory both heaven and earth would acclaim God's dominion. In either case there is no question about the meaning of the psalm. The salvation God could accomplish for the people was evidence of God's victory over threatening forces and of God's continuing sovereign rule over all the earth.

This reign of God is acclaimed in three ways. First, the exercise of divine kingship is ascribed to the LORD. Second, the created world and all the societies within it are summoned to worship this God. Third, as king the LORD will govern or judge *(dîn)* the people in the manner they deserve. Thus sovereign, universal, and equitable rule are attributed to the God of Israel.

1 Corinthians 12:4-11

Paul launches into a discourse on the varieties of functions within the Christian community. In sketching this diversity he uses two triads: gifts, ministries, and works; Spirit, Lord, and God. Although the second triad suggests a trinitarian perspective that associates a specific set of functions with each of the divine Persons, it is clear from the text that all the activities are manifestations of the Spirit (v. 7).

"Gifts" *(charismáta)* refers to those operations of the Spirit, notably speaking in tongues and prophesying, that were usually operative during worship. "Ministry" *(diakonía)* was service within the community. It included duties often considered menial, like serving at table or collecting money. Paul may have included this reference in order to show that within the community of believers no task is ignoble. "Works" *(energēmata)* were feats of great energy or divine power. Since all these gifts or ministries or works were manifestations of the Spirit, no one was to be considered superior to another. Further, they were not given for the self-aggrandizement of the one who received them. All were given for the benefit of the entire community.

The list of manifestations of the Spirit is in no way exhaustive. It probably represents the reality of the community to which Paul is addressing his teaching. Many commentators believe they are enumerated in a descending order of value, as judged by Paul, with wisdom preeminent and speaking and interpretation of tongues less important. Probably the most significant aspect of this list is its diversity. There is a multiplicity of spiritual expressions, all of them manifestations of the Spirit, all of them given for the common good. Although they come from God, the needs of the community certainly influenced the nature of these manifestations.

The role of the Spirit in the life of the community is evident. It is through the agency of the Spirit that the community is blessed. In fact, these blessings do not merely come *from* the Spirit, they are produced *by* the Spirit and are manifestations *of* the Spirit. The challenge facing the community was the humble recognition of the manifestation of the Spirit wherever it is found and to whomever it is given. The various gifts, service, and workings were to be the cause of enrichment for the community, not dissension.

John 2:1-11

The author of the gospel ends the account of the wedding feast at Cana by referring to it as a sign *(sēmeíon),* a wondrous feat that points beyond itself to some deeper reality. While the specifics of the incident are important, their real significance lies in their relationship to this deeper reality. The event is the miraculous changing of water into wine. Every other aspect of the narrative must be understood in the light of this event. It includes the role played by the mother of Jesus, Jesus' hour, his glorification, and the belief of his disciples.

The personal name of Jesus' mother never appears in this gospel. It is important to know this when we wonder why he refers to her as "Woman." This address and Jesus' response to his mother's report about the lack of wine are ambiguous. For this reason we must be careful not to read more into them than the text warrants. "Woman" should not be seen as a sign of disrespect. Instead, it is akin to "Madam" or "Ma'am," expressions used by many people today. As for Jesus' response, the second comment in it is weightier than the first. Understanding the latter should give us insight into the meaning of the former.

Jesus' hour is the time of his glorification, the time when he will be manifested in all his glory. The culmination of this hour will take place when he is lifted up on the cross. However, throughout his ministry there will be times when some aspect of his identity will be manifested. Chief among these will be when he performs miraculous signs. The miracles of Jesus were never mere exhibitions of supernatural power. They were always revelations of the inbreaking of the reign of God, and the time when this inbreaking should begin was determined by God, not by Jesus and certainly not by his mother. Jesus was saying: We cannot preempt God's time. In response to this, Mary told the attendants to follow Jesus' directions. This can refer simply to the events of the wedding feast or it can have a much deeper theological meaning.

Evidently the hour of his glorification had arrived, for Jesus performed his first sign. Through it his glory was manifested to his disciples and they believed in him. The establishment of the reign of God had begun. Since the event was described as a sign and since a sign points to a reality deeper than what is obvious, their faith did not rest merely on Jesus' ability to perform miracles. They believed, or would eventually come to believe, the deeper meaning of the sign, a meaning somehow related to water and wine. The water was originally intended for ritual cleansing. According to Jewish custom it was to be available for rinsing the guests' hands and for washing the vessels used during the feast. On the other hand, a wedding feast with free-flowing wine was a standard image of the age of messianic fulfillment. In this first sign, Jesus transformed Jewish ceremonial into eschatological celebration, and his disciples believed in him.

Themes of the Day

The readings offered to us as we begin Ordinary Time carry over some of the themes we considered during the Christmas season. Then we celebrated the new era God inaugurated through the birth of Jesus. Now we look deeply into our minds and hearts to see just how open we are to the demands of that new year. Last Sunday we considered the manifestation of the Spirit at the time of the baptism of Jesus. This Sunday we contemplate the various manifestations of that same Spirit in our own lives. Finally, we are brought to realize that this variety of Spirit-filled ministries is intended to be a source of Christian unity and not of fragmentation or division.

Newness

One of the major themes gleaned from the readings for today is that of the call to newness. God summons us to something new, gives us a new name, provides us with new experiences, launches us into new ministries, and calls us to sing a new song of praise. All of this newness comes from God. As with the primordial creation, God creates out of chaos—God creates a new people out of one that was forsaken; creates a new land out of desolation; creates a new Spirit-filled community. Just as the first reading and the gospel show us that marriage is the creation of a new union, so is the salvation for which we praise God in the psalm.

Even Jesus experienced a call to newness. Through Mary, God called him out into ministry, a ministry that would bring the fruits of the eschatological age of fulfillment to the whole world. This transformation of the world will be the ultimate new creation of God. The new wine Jesus provides symbolizes the intoxicating nature of the newness he brings. Christmas was the season during which we beheld the inbreaking of God's newness. During Ordinary Time we see how the newness can transform the world.

Manifestations of the Spirit

We may be inclined to think of Pentecost as the one season of the Spirit, but in reality the newness of God always comes to us through the Spirit regardless of the season of the year. During Advent we saw that Mary was overshadowed by the Spirit; at the end of the Christmas season we saw that the Spirit was present at the baptism of Jesus; now we see that the new community brought to birth by God manifests the presence of the Spirit within it through various ministerial gifts. The Spirit of God is active wherever God is present to create something new.

Variety of Gifts

God always creates in extravagant variety. We see it in the world around us; we see it in the people who make up the world; we see it here in the gifts that are given to these people. All comes as gift from God, but not all comes in the same way. All must be given back to God in service, but not all will be given back in the same way. There are different kinds of gifts and different forms of service and different workings. In the world of the old age, diversity could be divisive; what one had could be a source of envy or jealousy in another. In the world of the new age, diversity should be unifying; one performs a service that is complemented by the service of another. It is in this way that the real glory of Jesus will be manifested. When this happens, the whole world will begin to believe in him.

Third Sunday in Ordinary Time
Nehemiah 8:2-4a, 5-6, 8-10

Ezra was the priest who acted as religious leader of the Jewish community recently returned from the Babylonian Exile. Nehemiah was the one who had led the people back and who then supervised the rebuilding of the walls of Jerusalem. Both of these men had been authorized by the Persian authorities.

The scene described in the first reading for today depicts an official religious assembly led by Ezra wherein the people commit themselves to the law.

The account contains a significant amount of ritual language and action, indicating its liturgical character. Ezra is acting in his capacity as priest, one who is responsible for interpreting the law. The assembly *(qāhāl)* is unusually inclusive, embracing not only the men but the women and children as well. The author of the account makes a point of the need for the children to understand the gravity of the occasion. This is not merely a communal gathering. Those who participate take upon themselves the serious obligation of observance of the law. As Ezra opens the scroll, the people stand in respect for the words they are about to hear. Ezra blesses the Lord, and the people raise their hands in a common expression of prayer, responding in affirmation: "Amen, amen!" They then prostrate themselves in reverence. All of this is in preparation for the reading. The ritual takes place in an open square in front of the northeastern part of the city wall known as the Water Gate. It was so named because it was opposite the Gihon Spring.

The reading itself takes about six or seven hours, from daybreak to midday. What was read is not specified, but the manner in which it was read is described. Interpretation was provided along with the reading because the community, made up of descendants of those who had been taken into exile, may not have understood the Hebrew in which the law was written. Perhaps the instructions had to offer a significant amount of translation or try to make relevant in new ways the requirements of a tradition that originated in the past. Such interpretation is always a challenge for a believing community. The law itself was probably not entirely new to them, but a contemporary way of living it would be. Ezra and those with him hand down the tradition they have received. Thus the people can accept it as their own and can identify with events and communities of the past.

Their response to this instructive reading is curious—they weep. The assembly itself was intended to be a joyful one, but the people weep. Perhaps they do so out of remorse for infidelity or because they are overcome by the grandeur of the sacred event. Whatever the reason, they are told to rejoice, to participate in a festive meal. The rich food and sweet drinks betray a community of means, one that has been settled in the land long enough to have been able to acquire such delicacies. It may be that the reading is more liturgical than historical, with some of the details of the narrative meant for future generations who will read the account as part of their own liturgical recommitment to the law.

Psalm 19:8, 9, 10, 15

Six different synonyms are used to extol the glories of the law. Although the general theme of the psalm is praise, its tone is didactic and exhortative. It describes the blessings that ensue from acceptance of the law. It does this not merely to describe the law but also to persuade the people to embrace it as the will of God and to live in accord with it. Each of the statements in this psalm identifies the law as belonging to the LORD. This is not just any religious law; it is uniquely Israel's, because in a very specific way it represents the will of the God of Israel.

When most people today talk about law, they normally mean legal enactments that have some degree of binding force. While this is certainly one dimension of the meaning of the Hebrew word, *tôrâ* might be better translated "instruction" or "teaching." As found in the Bible, the law consisted of directives for living a full and God-fearing life. Teaching the law was the special task of both the Wisdom school and the priesthood. The former group collected and safeguarded the insights gleaned from various life experiences. In a society that believed ultimate wisdom was revealed by the deity, the latter group functioned as mediators between God and the people.

If the law is understood as the will of God for human beings, then the qualities enshrined in that law could legitimately be considered reflections of divine attributes. If the law is thought to be the place an encounter with God takes place, then those shaped by the law will be godlike. The qualities associated with the law that are found in this psalm are some of the most highly prized attributes in any tradition. The law is perfect or complete; it is trustworthy, upright, and clean; it is pure and true. Fidelity to the law should lead one to the godliness enshrined within it.

The effects of the law enumerated here are all relational, enhancing human life itself. The psalmist maintains that the law imbues the soul with new vitality; it gives wisdom to those who would not ordinarily have it. It delights the heart; it enables the eyes to see dimensions of truth otherwise obscured. It establishes an enduring attitude of awe; it is a path to righteousness. This description of the law shows clearly that the psalmist found it life-giving and not restrictive, ennobling and not demeaning. Reverence for the law seems to promise the best life has to offer.

The last verse of the psalm ties the relational character of the law with the relational nature of the psalmist's association with God. Two metaphors are used to portray this. The LORD is addressed as rock and as redeemer. The first implies stability and security. God is strong. Furthermore, God employs this strength on behalf of the psalmist and is, therefore, trustworthy. The second metaphor provides us with an even more graphic image of God's providential care. A redeemer *(gōʾēl)* was a kinsperson who was obligated to redeem a relative from danger or debt. What is striking about this metaphor is not merely the lengths to which God seems willing to go in order to assist someone in need, as extraordinary as that may be. What is truly remarkable is that God should be characterized as a kinsperson, one who is as intimately related as are blood-kin. It is no wonder the psalmist prays with confidence!

1 Corinthians 12:12-30

Paul continues his instruction on the diversity found within the community by using the analogy of the body. This analogy was probably borrowed from Stoicism, but the way he uses it is reminiscent of the Jewish concept of corporate personality, where members of a family are somehow identified with the actions of the head of that family. In the body each part has its own unique function, but all parts work for the good of the whole. This figure of speech characterizes several aspects of the ideal Christian community. First, it portrays unity in diversity, a unity that is far from uniformity. Second, it underscores the absence of competition among members, since no one activity is elevated above the others. Lowly service is no less important than charismatic gifts. Third, it underscores the interdependence that exists within the community.

The unity within the community is based on common baptism. All were baptized in the Spirit, and all were baptized into the body of Christ. In this community there are no severely discriminating distinctions, whether based on religious background (Jew or Greek) or on social status (slave or free). Cultural and gender differences will remain, but they will not determine one's membership within the community. All drink of the same Spirit, so all live by the same life, the life of the Spirit. The metaphor of the body helps us see how important every member is. It is foolish to deny the diversity within this unity, and it is foolish to deny the unity within the diversity.

Paul insists that comparison for the sake of prioritizing abilities or functions is foolish. He ridicules first the attitude of inferiority ("I do not belong to the body") and then that of self-importance ("I do not need you"). By using exaggeration he makes clear the absurdity of such thinking. What would a body be like if it were only an eye or an ear or a head? Likewise, not all are apostles or prophets or teachers, and so on. However, just as all members are needed for the body to be whole, so all gifts and functions are needed within the Church if it is to fulfill its mission.

Commentators have long wondered about which parts of the body Paul considered weak or less honorable or less presentable. Since the head and the arms and the legs were almost always exposed, they conclude he was talking about some part of the torso. But which part? Each generation will probably interpret this according to its own set of standards. The point of the analogy, however, is Christian interdependence, not Paul's personal anthropological or physiological perspective. As we give extra attention to parts of the body that seem to be more vulnerable, so should Christians be particularly considerate of members of the community who are in need of care. God seems to care for the neediest, and so should the members of the Christian community. Finally, the solidarity that should flourish within the Church is poignantly characterized: If one part suffers, all suffer; If one part is honored, all are honored. There is no room for competition or resentment in this kind of community.

Luke 1:1-4; 4:14-21

The gospel reading begins with an address to Theophilus, whose name means "friend or lover of God." The respect the author accords this man suggests he is the patron who had assumed the responsibility of publishing this writing (cf. Acts 1:1). Here the author says some very interesting things about this gospel. It was one among several accounts of the events in the life of Jesus. It follows an orderly, presumably chronological, sequence. The events themselves are said to have fulfilled either the promises made by God or the expectations of the people that grew out of those promises. While the authenticity of the other accounts is based on the word of eyewitnesses who were also ministers of the word, this account is an interpretation of what was handed down by others. The author explicitly admits he is not an eyewitness by stating that this word was handed down "to us." "Handing down" *(parádosis)* is the technical word for passing on authoritative tradition. Theophilus is here assured of the authenticity of the instruction ("catechesis," from *katēchéō*) in the faith he has received. The eyewitnesses handed down the tradition to Luke, and now Luke hands it down to his patron.

The actual story begins with a summary statement. Jesus has taught in the synagogues of Galilee and has been praised by all. He now returns to his hometown and attends the synagogue service there. He is handed the Isaian scroll but seems to choose the passage (cf. Isa 61:1-2). There we find a prophet endowed with the Spirit, having been anointed by the LORD (v. 1). This anointing may be a figure of speech, but the duties that accompany it are very real and explicitly social. The principal function of the prophet is proclamation. He is called to announce liberty, release, healing, and the year of the LORD. It is clear most of the afflicted referred to in this passage are victims of a system. The good news proclaimed to them promises they will be the beneficiaries of the year of release.

The year of the LORD (v. 2) calls to mind the Jubilee year (Lev 25), the time when debts would be forgiven (cf. Deut 15), when land that had been forfeited would be returned to its original owners, when those imprisoned because of financial adversity would be set free. This was a time of great anticipation for the dispossessed and the impoverished. Conversely, it was a time of regret for those who would lose some of their wealth and power in the forthcoming economic redistribution. Whether or not such a year of release was ever actually observed, the idea became a powerful metaphor for general emancipation and economic restructuring as well as eschatological fulfillment. It symbolized the advent of a new era, a time of deliverance for the disadvantaged. This was a year that was instituted through the favor of the LORD, not the goodwill of others.

With the eyes of the synagogue fixed on him, Jesus makes a bold claim: "Today this Scripture passage is fulfilled in your hearing." He is the prophet who is filled with the Spirit; he is the one who inaugurates the year of deliverance; he is the one who has launched the era of eschatological fulfillment.

Themes of the Day

The primary theme that comes through the readings this Sunday is the word of God. Just as the Christmas season was the time to celebrate the incarnation of the Word of God in human form, so today we reflect on the proclamation of the word of God as found in the religious traditions that are handed down.

The Word Proclaimed

In both the first reading from Nehemiah and the gospel passage from Luke we see the dynamic power of the word of God as it is proclaimed. Paul's teaching originated as oral proclamation, and like the texts read by Ezra the priest and the one interpreted by Jesus himself, it was first proclaimed aloud. Only later were each of these proclamations regarded as the written word of God, handed down from one community to another, from one generation to the next. This word reminds the people of their identity as People of God. It situates them within the long and glorious stream of covenanted people. It calls them to the faithful living out of the implications of their identity.

There is something unique about hearing the word of God, realizing that it is fulfilled in our hearing. Part of this certainly stems from the oral character of our earliest ancestors. However, there is more to it. In a very real sense, the ear is the threshold through which the word of God penetrates the consciousness of the person. Thus the fundamental summons of the people of Israel was, Hear, O Israel! "Hear" means "take into yourself," allow it to penetrate the deepest resources of your being. Hear the word of God proclaimed and allow it to take root, like the seed that is sown by the sower.

The Word Is Fulfilled

The word of God elicits various responses from those who hear it. The first reading for today provides us with an example of openness to that word. The people who heard Ezra cried out in response: Amen, amen! So be it! We hear and we will obey! From the verses contained in today's gospel, we do not know how those who heard Jesus's interpretation reacted to it. We do know that both audiences listened intently to the sacred words of Scripture. Can we do less? The people at the time of Ezra were at a turning point in their history, and they knew it. The people in the synagogue of Nazareth were also at a turning point, but they probably were unaware of the importance of the moment within which they stood. We too are at a turning point, a new season of the Liturgical Year. The frantic excitement of Christmas is over; the ordinariness of life has taken hold. However, the word of God as proclaimed always insists we are on the threshold of the new age. And how will we respond?

Are we eager to obey? Do we view the law as a treasure, as life-giving? Have we learned to live with one another as members of one body, each member being important and contributing to the total health of the entire body? Have we moved into the new age of fulfillment eager to be transformed? Do we live differently in our families: Are we more patient, more understanding? Are we more generous in our local communities? In our churches? And what about our world? Is it more equitable? Less violent? Is there less desperation? Have we crossed into a new era with renewed commitment? Has hearing the word of God proclaimed made any kind of difference in our lives? Or do we have ears that are uncircumcised, closed to the power of the word of God?

Liturgical Assembly

Both Ezra and Jesus proclaimed the word of God within the context of a liturgical celebration, a setting similar to the ones wherein most people today hear God's word proclaimed. According to the teaching of Vatican II, the liturgy is described as the source and summit of our lives, and the Liturgy of the Word is an essential part of that celebration. With the people of Ezra we are invited to respond: Amen, amen! Thanks be to God!

It is also in the complex makeup of the liturgical assembly that we realize that though one body in Christ, we respond as different members of that body. Some identify with the hand, others with the foot. Some who hear the word proclaimed do so from situations of poverty, others from positions of power. Both women and men hear it, as do Asians and Hispanics and other indigenous people. In addition to this, Christians of various denominations hear the same word and respond in ways shaped by their respective religious tradition. All are open to the word, and it takes root in them as seed that is sown. It enjoys various yields because it takes root in different ground. This diversity need not separate us; actually, it can enrich us. We should be mindful of some of what we are accepting when we reply to the word of God being proclaimed: Thanks be to God!

Fourth Sunday in Ordinary Time
Jeremiah 1:4-5, 17-19

The first words of this call narrative are the same as those that generally introduce a prophetic oracle. With them, Jeremiah is declaring that his call from God was itself prophetic in nature. The divine words have come to us in the poetic structure of parallelism:

before I formed you	in the belly	I knew you
before you came forth	from the womb	I dedicated you
a prophet to the nations	I appointed you	

While the last phrase is not in strict parallelism, it does provide an interesting comparison. Several characteristics of Jeremiah's prophetic vocation emerge from this structure. The vocation itself was his destiny even before he was born; "belly," "womb," and the verb "know" *(yādaʿ)* all imply profound intimacy; "dedicate" signifies some kind of religious consecration; there was a universal character to the ministry ("to the nations"). Unlike many other prophets who were engaged in various occupations, the prophetic vocation was Jeremiah's entire identity. It took shape within him even as he was knit together in his mother's womb.

Having assured him of his prophetic call, God prepares Jeremiah for the fate that lies ahead of him. The expression "gird your loins" is a signal to prepare oneself for some kind of strenuous exercise. It resembles the modern phrase "roll up your sleeves." The free-flowing garment that men wore was girdled at the waist to allow free movement for running, physical work, or doing battle (cf. Job 38:3; 40:7). Jeremiah is told to get ready for some ordeal, and the ordeal is the proclamation of the word of the LORD. It is not going to be an easy task.

The LORD tells Jeremiah not to fear and then explains why there will be no need for fear. God will fortify the prophet as one would fortify a city. The imagery suggests a walled city with military fortifications. While the metaphor connotes extraordinary defense, it implies the possibility of massive assault. Jeremiah's assailants will be the very people to whom he is sent to prophesy. This includes both the Jerusalem establishment and the people of the land— probably those who owned land outside the city itself. They will not be merely unresponsive, they will vigorously fight Jeremiah. That is why he must prepare himself for battle.

The passage ends with words of encouragement. His adversaries will not prevail against the prophet, because the Lord will be with him. There is no promise here of deliverance *from* the onslaughts. The promise is that Jeremiah will not be crushed by them. With the strength that God will give him, he will be able to endure. If from the outset God knew the people would not be open to the message delivered by Jeremiah, why would God even send him? Why submit the prophet to such an ordeal? It may be in order that, looking back, the people would realize the importance of listening to the messengers of God. It may be more for the generations of people who follow than for those to whom the word was originally spoken. The last words are a kind of oracle of salvation intended for the prophet himself: "I am with you to deliver you!"

Psalm 71:1-2, 3-4, 5-6, 15, 17

The responsorial psalm for this Sunday contains several features of the traditional psalm of lament. It begins with a plea for deliverance from distress, even though that distress is not identified (vv. 1-4). This is followed by a prayer of confidence in God (vv. 5-6). It ends with the psalmist promising to make known the wonders God has wrought (vv. 15, 17).

The plea of the psalmist is expressed in four different ways: protect me; save me from shame; rescue me; hear me. Although the opening statement about taking refuge in God is often associated with seeking asylum at the shrine or in the Temple, there are no explicit cultic references in the passage. The imagery suggests the focus is on the safety God will afford the psalmist and not on the specific location where this will take place. The psalmist also asks to be spared from being put to shame. In a society where honor is a fundamental value, to be shamed or to lose one's reputation could actually be life-threatening. That the righteousness rather than the mercy of God is called upon suggests the petitioner is an innocent sufferer. This is confirmed when those threatening the psalmist are described as being wicked (v. 4). Finally, the psalmist prays to be heard by God. Being heard always means the petition is granted.

Different kinds of rock are used to characterize the trustworthiness of God. The first word denotes an immense rock, the massiveness of which makes it secure and dependable. It is the kind of rock upon which impenetrable and indestructible fortresses are built. The second kind of rock suggests a fissure or cliff. It is a rock formation upon which one can stand securely or under which one can be sheltered. These images demonstrate the way God is perceived and the confidence the psalmist has in God's willingness to aid those in need.

The trust the psalmist has placed in God is not a recent phenomenon, one that has merely arisen in the face of difficulty. Rather, it is a long-standing disposition, originating in the psalmist's youth. Earlier than that! The psalmist trusted even while in the womb. Trust in God has been an integral part of the psalmist's entire existence. This is a person who has been raised in the teaching of God (v. 17). The wondrous deeds of God are probably the saving acts God performed in the history of the people. One who has been raised within the religious tradition can frequently find in that very tradition reasons for trusting God. If God provided for the needs of the people in the past, surely there is reason to believe God will do the same in the present and in the future.

As the psalmist had called on the righteousness of God at the beginning of the prayer (v. 2), so that same righteousness is proclaimed at the end. It is the righteousness of God that will rectify the situation causing the distress. It is the righteousness of God that is the basis of the psalmist's confidence.

1 Corinthians 12:31–13:13

Paul's praise of love *(agápē)* is one of the best-known biblical passages. The first verse of this reading shows it is a continuation of a longer discourse. In the reading for last Sunday Paul insisted that all the gifts the Spirit bestowed upon individuals functioned for the upbuilding of the community. From the perspective of the community, one gift was not better than another. Each had her or his own gift to contribute to the common good. Today Paul concentrates his attention on love, the "more excellent way." This is not only the greatest of all spiritual gifts, but it is one all can possess.

In last Sunday's reading he spoke of the importance of several functions within the community. In this Sunday's reading he dismisses them as empty if they do not issue from love. He seems to order the gifts from the least important to the self-sacrificing service of others. As beneficial as tongues and prophecy and wisdom and knowledge and faith and generosity and even martyrdom may be, without love they are nothing. More than this, without them Paul himself is nothing. It is not that these gifts or functions are without value. It is, rather, that their value is transitory. They are useful now, while we are still in this world. However, at the end of this world their usefulness will come to an end, and they will cease to be. Love, on the other hand, will never cease to be.

Life in this world is further contrasted with life in the next. Despite all the gifts we receive from God, they are only partially realized here. The fragmentary nature of this life is compared to seeing a reflection, while the perfect nature of the next is like looking at someone face-to-face. Paul uses the analogy of human maturation to illustrate this transformation. As we move from this world to the next we leave behind the things of the former period, as an adult leaves behind the things of childhood.

Paul personifies rather than describes love, and he does it in both positive and negative fashion. Characterization follows characterization, until there are fifteen different ways love is represented. All of them reflect an aspect of open acceptance or unqualified respect. By stating what love is not, Paul is also suggesting what his hearers or readers really are: jealous, pompous, rude, quick-tempered. By indicating what love is, he is intimating that his hearers or readers could be patient, kind, and forbearing. While on the one hand, to love like this may appear an almost impossible task, on the other hand, we must remember that such love is a gift from God.

The last verse is difficult to understand. Paul says that faith, hope, and love all remain. Actually, faith and hope are necessary in this life. He has already said that in the next life we will see God face-to-face and then we will possess that for which we hoped. Only love will remain. One way to reconcile this discrepancy is to understand faith and hope as attitudes of total dependence on God, dependence that will last into the next world. With this understanding we can say that while they all last, love is the greatest of the three.

Luke 4:21-30

The Scripture to which Jesus refers in this reading is a passage from Isaiah read as part of last Sunday's gospel (cf. Isa 61:1-2). It announced the eschatological age of fulfillment. It provides a glimpse into the kind of Messiah Jesus will be, namely one who will refashion society for the sake of the oppressed. The response of those in the synagogue who heard Jesus is curious. At first they speak highly of him and are amazed at his words, but later in the episode they drive him out of the city to the brow of a hill to hurl him down. Their amazement stemmed from the fact that they presumed to know him. He was one of them, the son of Joseph, whom they also knew. How did one of their own get such wisdom? Might this amazement have contained the seeds of doubt? Might they have thought: He is one of us, how could he presume to be talking to us in this way? Some interpreters say their initial acceptance was superficial. Others believe they turned against him because of the proverb he quoted.

The connection between their amazement and Jesus' proverb is not clear. The people of Nazareth may have wanted Jesus to perform in their midst wonders like those they heard he had done elsewhere. The proverb would then mean: Perform miracles of healing at home. Jesus seems to have understood it this way, for he goes on to show that the people at home have no advantage over those who belong somewhere else. He introduces his examples with "Amen," the familiar exclamation of assurance, but Jesus uses it as an expression of self-affirmation. The woman in the Elijah story (cf. 1 Kgs 17:1-16) and the leper in the Elisha narrative (2 Kgs 5:1-14) were both Gentiles. Jesus has taken his examples of universalism to the extreme. The people of Nazareth may have envied other Jewish cities that had benefited from Jesus' power when they themselves had not, but Jesus suggests that God even goes beyond the confines of Israel into the territory of the Gentiles. Like the woman of Zarephath, Gentiles are open to the prophets of God; as with the Syrian leper, the healing power of God reaches out to them.

This is what filled the people in the synagogue with fury. To think that the prophetic promise of fulfillment or the saving power of God would be extended to the Gentiles was, in their estimation, pure blasphemy. In indignation they rose up against Jesus. Because it was unlawful to execute someone within the city, they drove him outside the city limits and sought to cast him down, perhaps in order to stone him (cf. Lev 24:14). This response gives us a second insight into the kind of Messiah Jesus will be. Not only will he fulfill the role of the prophet who announces the advent of the age of fulfillment, but he will also be rejected, as were the other prophets. Jesus is not accepted by his people because he preaches that he has come not merely for them but for any who will open themselves to his teaching. In fact, the point he makes in each of his examples is not that the Gentiles will join the Jews in their experience of

God's goodness but that this goodness comes to the Gentiles instead of the Jews. They are bypassed. This is a bitter message for a chosen people to hear, and they respond with fury.

Themes of the Day

This Sunday could be considered a continuation of our reflection on the major themes of last Sunday. Actually, we would have a rather distorted view of last Sunday's theology if we did not hold it up next to the theology of this Sunday. Last week's gospel stopped short with Jesus' interpretation of the prophetic passage read during the synagogue service. Looking only at the themes of last week, we considered the possibility of a positive reaction to the word of God proclaimed. This week we see the shocking reaction of those who heard Jesus' words, and we realize the complexity of any response.

Complexity in Our Response

In our moments of fervor we might wholeheartedly answer yes to the word of God, but in reality that yes is seldom uncomplicated. Even those who heard Jesus were first amazed at his words and then later sought to throw him off a cliff. They turned too quickly from their initial appreciation of him. Either their acceptance was shallow or they had not taken into account the ambivalence present in so much of human behavior. So many times we actually behave in ways we wish we would not, or what we want to do we fail to accomplish. In other situations we might stand in awe of others and yet turn against them because we are frightened of the power they exert, power we cannot understand, much less control.

A similarly complex situation existed in the life of Jeremiah. He was told of the great honor that was his as a prophet of God, called even before he was born. Yet he would have to fight against the people to whom he would be sent, the entire people of Judah—political rulers, priests, and people. The very people one would think should welcome his ministry are the ones who fight against him. Jeremiah is told that in the face of their resistance and their active opposition he will be preserved by God. God's ways are sometimes as complex as our responses to them.

Our motives and our reactions are generally quite complicated, even if our desires to be faithful are straightforward. Realizing this can cause us great frustration. Where can we turn for help? Who will be our support? The psalm response offers us a simple prayer, one that springs from true humility. In God we take refuge; in God is our trust.

Call to a Deeper Level

As important as are keen insight, total commitment, and courage under fire, the greatest response to the challenge presented us by the word of God is love. Despite the struggles that accompany its proclamation, despite the misunderstanding it might cause, the word of God cannot be silenced. Neither Jeremiah nor Jesus recoiled from the implications of their call, regardless of the resistance they experienced. Instead, they entered even more deeply into the call to love. Lest he brood over his injuries, Jeremiah is reassured of God's protection. And, without aggressively demonstrating his strength when he was threatened with harm, Jesus exhibited patience and kindness. Both men bore and endured their bitter misfortunes. This is the image placed before us as an example for us to follow.

The call to discipleship is a call to live in the eschatological age inaugurated by Jesus. In its own way it is to that reality Jeremiah was called; it is to that same reality we are all called; finally, it is this age of fulfillment that Jesus manifests in his power and glory. Returning again to the themes of last Sunday, we can say with certainty that God calls us to a new way of living. We may chafe under the suffering it could cause us, but we will not be left alone in our distress. As God was with Jeremiah, so we can depend upon God to be with us in our need. We must remember that however we do react, our response must be born out of love.

Fifth Sunday in Ordinary Time

Isaiah 6:1-2a, 3-8

The reading from the prophet Isaiah is an autobiographical report of a visionary experience he had during a liturgical celebration held in the Temple. The report consists of three movements: the theophany (vv. 1-2a, 3-4); the purification of the prophet (vv. 5-7); the prophet's offer to serve. The historical data situates the prophet's call to ministry in the actual history of Israel. King Uzziah ruled in Judah from 783 to 742 B.C.E. At his death the political circumstances of the nation changed radically. Isaiah's ministry is firmly rooted in this history.

The vision is one of uncommon majesty. The God of Israel is depicted as supreme among all other gods, since only the mightiest would be sitting on the throne of heaven. This is a bold idea for a nation in the throes of political unrest. The glory of God fills the entire earth and overflows into the Temple like the train of a royal robe. Seraphim, supernatural beings similar to the Sphinx, are stationed in homage. They were probably beings with animal bodies, wings, and human heads and hands. The very name is associated with burning flames. Hence it is fitting that one of their number should participate in the purification of the prophet.

The threefold acclamation of praise, Holy, Holy, Holy, is a way of expressing superlative. There is no god as holy as the God of Israel. This holiness is part of the very essence of God, the unapproachable divine mystery. God's glory, on the other hand, is the way God's holiness is manifested in history and in nature. They sing of God's holiness, but they experience God's glory. God is extolled as LORD of hosts, a reference to armies or military regiments. The heavenly hosts were those supernatural beings that first fought on the side of the deity and, once the battle was won, surrounded the divine throne as guards. The entire Temple shook with their thunderous acclamation, and it was filled with smoke. There may be a connection here between certain elements of the ritual celebration itself and details of the vision, for loud trumpet blasts and continual burning of incense were very much a part of Israel's cult.

The contrast between the holiness of God and Isaiah's own uncleanness causes him to cry out in despair. It is not by accident that it is his lips rather than his eyes or his hands that are cleansed. He will, after all, proclaim the word of the LORD. Now purified, he is ready to offer himself for that ministry.

The heavenly consultation (v. 8) suggests a form of divine council common in ancient Near Eastern theology. It usually consisted of lesser deities who owed allegiance to the more powerful god. Israel retained the concept but demoted the deities to the rank of angels. There is no way of knowing the references to the questions that were asked. They may in fact have been devices used to provide Isaiah an opportunity to volunteer for prophetic service. Whatever the case, the visionary experience of Isaiah both purified him and invited him into a life of service of God, an invitation he accepted with enthusiasm. This last verse shows that Isaiah was not merely a passive observer of the vision. In the end, he was an eager participant.

Psalm 138:1-2, 2-3, 4-5, 7-8

The responsorial psalm for this Sunday follows the general structure of the individual prayer of thanksgiving. Addressed directly to God, it begins with sentiments of thanksgiving along with a statement of the reason for being thankful (vv. 1-3). This is followed by a prayer that all, even those who do not belong to the immediate community of believers, might give thanks to the LORD (vv. 4-5). It ends with a statement of confidence in God's enduring faithfulness.

Evidently the psalmist had previously been in dire straits, had called upon the LORD for help, had been heard, and had been inwardly strengthened. This is the reason for the prayer of gratitude. The temple setting suggests that the psalmist has come there to worship and publicly to witness to the goodness of God. The angels (*ĕlōhîm*) suggest the court of heaven. In ancient Canaanite myths this court was made up of minor deities who stood in reverence around the throne of the principal god. As it developed its monotheistic understanding of God, Israel merely demoted these deities to angels, supernatural beings that were still under the dominion of the God of Israel. Thus the sovereignty of this God was not only emphasized by their subservience, but it was also enhanced by the homage they gave. Since the Temple was thought to be the earthly representation of the heavenly divine dwelling, it was not unusual to believe that these beings were somehow in the same kind of attendance in the Temple on earth. Therefore, standing in the Temple in the presence of God, the psalmist would also be in the presence of the attending angels.

The reason for the psalmist's gratitude is God's faithfulness to covenant commitment. This is clear from the employment of technical covenant language, lovingkindness *(hesed)*, and truth *('ĕmet)*. The promise referred to may be a pledge God made specifically with the psalmist, or it may be a reference to the general promise of protection and beneficence associated with the covenant made with the nation as a whole. In either case, God has been faithful, and the psalmist publicly witnesses to this faithfulness with gratitude.

The sovereignty of God in the heavens has already been proclaimed (v. 1). Next the psalmist turns to the peoples of the world (v. 4). The praise of God proclaimed by the psalmist is witnessed by the rulers of those nations, and they too will give thanks to the God of Israel. There is no coercion here, no suggestion of military defeat and forced subservience to the God of the conquerors. Rather, it is the devotion of the psalmist that will turn these kings to the God of the psalmist, and they too will cry out in a profession of faith: "Great is the glory of the LORD."

The right hand of the LORD is the hand of strength (a right-hand bias). This indicates that the reason for gratitude is the psalmist's rescue from some kind of adversity. We have already seen that God's goodness springs from covenant commitment. The psalmist concludes the prayer of thanksgiving on a note of confidence that this commitment *(hesed,* v. 8) will endure forever. God is not only faithful to past promises but will be faithful into the endless future.

1 Corinthians 15:1-11

This reading contains one of the earliest creedal statements. The authoritativeness of the gospel Paul preaches is seen in the technical language that he uses. He hands over *(paradídōmi)* to them what he has received *(paralambánō)* from others. The creedal statement itself is succinct: Christ died; he was buried; he was raised; he appeared. The first two components are facts that can be historically verified; the second two, while they did occur in history, are still statements of faith. This is the heart of the gospel. Everything else is interpretation or flows from these facts.

The proclamation that Christ died is itself a statement of faith, for it identifies the historical Jesus as the Messiah, the anointed of God. To this is added the declaration that his death was substitutional expiation; he died for our sins. Finally, his death was in fulfillment of the Scriptures. Thus the creed of the Christian community is rooted in the traditions of Israel. Most commentators believe the scriptural reference is to the tradition of the Suffering Servant (cf. Isa 53:5). Christ's burial was considered evidence of his actual death. It marked the finality of his death and prepared for the reality of his resurrection. If he was dead for the period of time that was considered proof of death, then only resurrection could explain his subsequent appearances as living.

The creedal statement maintains that Jesus was raised by the power of God, that he did not raise himself. This happened on the third day, in accordance with the Scriptures. This reference is even harder to verify (cf. Ps 16:10; Isa 53:11; Hos 6:2). No one saw him rise; they experienced him as risen. He appeared. The verb is strong and active. He was not merely seen by others. He manifested himself; the initiative was his. In a sense, it is the appearances that witness to the truth of the community's faith claims.

In Paul's account of the appearances we see both the conflation of various traditions and the selectivity that guided their development. Cephas is named first. That his Jewish name is used suggests the tradition's Jewish Christian origin. That he is mentioned first indicates his primacy. The number twelve cannot imply numerical accuracy, for Judas is no longer a member of the group, and his empty place has not yet been filled. It is probably a collective term the early Church used in referring to the original apostles. An appearance to five hundred is recorded nowhere else, so this may simply refer to a general appearance. The separate mention of James suggests he was not a member of the original twelve. His inclusion here may derive from the tradition of the Jerusalem church, of which he became the first leader. Nowhere is there mention of the strong gospel tradition that women were among the first to witness to the resurrection. According to John, Jesus appeared first to Mary (cf. John 20:11-18). Whether the bias is Paul's or that of the tradition he received, we do not know.

Paul adds his own name to the list. Jesus appeared to him. He likens himself to an aborted fetus, one that was rejected from a womb and was not ripe enough for a normal birth. This characterization may have come from his detractors, but he turns it into a profession of faith. Though once a persecutor, by the grace of God he now toils harder than all the others. His final statement is telling. It makes no difference who preaches the gospel so long as others hear it and believe.

Luke 5:1-11

Gennesaret is the fertile, heavily populated area at the northwestern corner of the lake known as the Sea of Galilee. In the gospel reading for this Sunday the name of this district is ascribed to the lake. The lake itself is seven hundred feet below sea level, thirteen miles long and seven miles wide and rich with an abundance of fish. As those who depend upon the yield of the sea know, night fishing produces the best yield. This is the setting for the gospel story for this Sunday.

The use of names and titles is revealing. The apostle Simon plays a very important role here. With one exception (v. 8) he is still known by his Jewish name, Simon (vv. 3, 4, 5, 10). When he recognizes Jesus' divine power in the miraculous catch of fish, he is referred to with a combination of his Jewish name and the name Jesus will later give him (cf. 6:14). For his part, Simon first calls Jesus "Master" (*epistátēs,* a word that is probably an equivalent to "rabbi" [v. 5]). Simon uses this title after Jesus has taught the crowds on the shore from Simon's own boat. Later, Simon, the experienced fisherman, follows Jesus' directive and is astounded by the yield of fish it brings. This causes him to prostrate himself before Jesus and to address him as "Lord" *(kýrios),* a title that combines the elements of power and authority.

Simon and those who are with him have a theophanic experience, a recognition of the divine power at work in and through Jesus. They are filled with astonishment or fear, to which Jesus responds in characteristic manner: "Do not be afraid" (cf. Luke 1:13, 30; 2:10). Usually when there is such an experience that fills the recipient with fear, the words of assurance are followed by some kind of commission. This suggests the commission is the point of importance. That is the case here. Jesus does not provide these fishermen a remarkable catch merely to cancel the frustration they experienced in an unsuccessful night of fishing. The miracle became an acted-out prophecy revealing both his own mysterious authority and the ministry to which they are being called. Jesus declares that a turning point in their lives has been reached. The commission states: "From now on . . . !"

Those who have made a living by catching fish are told that now they will cast a different net, one that will catch women and men. Jesus their Lord gathered crowds around him—men, women, and children who came to be captivated by his powerful words. From now on, if they will but follow the directives he gives them, regardless of how they might initially question them, they too will gather in hearers beyond number. The verb for "catching" *(zōgreō)* is in the continuous tense, indicating a habitual practice.

The astonishment of the fishermen turns to commitment. They leave everything—the incredible catch, their business (they were partners), the stability of their homes, families, and neighborhoods—and they followed him (*akolouthéō* suggests spiritual allegiance or discipleship).

Themes of the Day

The first Sundays of Ordinary Time dealt with the beginnings of the ministry of Jesus, the inauguration of the new age of fulfillment. The theme of this

Sunday shifts a bit, and we consider the call to continue the mission of Jesus by engaging in some form of ministry. The first and last readings for the day are call narratives; the epistle contains a statement of the faith that undergirds our response to our call; the psalm response celebrates the gracious goodness of God, which makes all of this possible.

Called to Serve

The call described today is more than a summons to faith; it is a call to ministry. Isaiah is called in order to be sent; the fishermen are called in order to gather others to Jesus. So it is with us. Our call is not merely to a life of personal holiness lived in union with God. As important as this might be, we are called by God to be sent out to the world. Our covenant with God is not a private affair; it is a communal reality. We belong to the People of God; we are members of the body of Christ. The faith has been handed to us, and we in turn hand it on to others. We have been prepared for this during the first few weeks of Ordinary Time. The moment has come for us to step forward and explicitly accept or refuse the call. We have seen how complex is the call and how complicated are our responses to that call. The examples of some of the prophets as well as of Jesus point the way to us. It is now the moment of decision.

Ordinariness of Life

As life transforming as this call may be, it comes to us in the ordinariness of life. It may come to us in our place of worship if we minister in the Temple as Isaiah did. It will usually come to us as we wash our nets or our dishes, as we teach or raise children, as we prepare a brief for trial or examine a patient; as we repair cars or work at the computer. The call of God comes to us in the ordinariness of life. This may sound scandalous precisely because of its ordinariness. However, God calls wherever the people are to be found, and if that means during the plowing, that is where the call of God will be heard. On the other hand, such a view sanctifies what might otherwise be deemed merely ordinary. The incarnation means that God took on human flesh and blood, human existence, human experience. The incarnation implies that God uses ordinary people, places, and things to reveal the extraordinariness of God. When we realize this we too will be able to cry out: "It is the Lord!"

Called to Witness

Our first and most fundamental service is to witness to the death and resurrection of Jesus. He died, he rose, and he lives on. This is the message that must be announced. This is the gist of Paul's instruction to the Corinthian community. It is the basis of all other ministries. We are called to proclaim the message of the resurrection by every means possible. Some, like Isaiah and the disciples of Jesus, will witness in open and dramatic ways. They will teach and preach; they will nurse the sick and care for the elderly. Others will witness in less conspicuous ways. They will insist on fair practices in their own workplaces; they will weed out expressions of prejudice and violence so that a new and just world can be fashioned for themselves and for their children. Called in the ordinariness of their lives, they will witness to the death and resurrection in that very ordinariness, thus transforming everything into extraordinariness.

Sixth Sunday in Ordinary Time
Jeremiah 17:5-8

The messenger formula, "Thus says the LORD," identifies the passage as a prophetic oracle. What is interesting about this section is the literary form used to express the message. It is a contrast statement that contains both a curse and a blessing, the kind generally associated with the Wisdom tradition. The insights contained within such statements are usually derived from human reflection on life experience. Here it is a statement that comes from God. Since neither the curse nor the blessing contains an introductory verb, it is not clear whether they are intended to be descriptive statements (cursed is . . . blessed is) or prophetic proclamations (cursed be . . . blessed be). Either interpretation is valid. What is important is that two individuals are contrasted, each representing a distinct attitude toward life. (Almost the identical contrast is found in the responsorial psalm.)

The Hebrew word translated as "one" is *geber,* a word that also yields the connotation "strong man." It is important to know this, because at issue in this passage is the source of a person's strength. The first one trusts in human beings and finds strength there. The second trusts in and lives by the power of God.

The contrast drawn between these two is striking. All the imagery used to characterize the one who turns away from the LORD describes barrenness and desolation. There is a play on the words for "barren bush" (*'ar'ār*) and "desert" (*'ărābâ*). The Arabah is a desert area that is part of the rift extending from the Jordan valley south to the Gulf of Aqaba. The wilderness referred to is burnt either from lava or from the unmerciful scorching by the sun. The earth is too salty to sustain life. Finally, this desolation is not a temporary situation that eventually will be remedied. There is no change of season here, no change of heart. On the other hand, the one who trusts in the LORD is firmly planted near water, the source of life. This one is not spared the hardship of heat, but because the source of life is so near and because its roots have forged their way underground to that source, the drought that often accompanies heat is not a serious threat. The one who trusts in the LORD is described as secure and productive.

As a description of these two contrasting life situations, the passage functions as an exhortation to the hearers to choose the way that guarantees security and productivity. As a prophetic proclamation it explains the reason for the fate of each so each can decide upon which path of life to take in the future.

Psalm 1:1-2, 3, 4, 6

The responsorial psalm is perhaps the best example of a Wisdom psalm. Not directed to God, it is less a prayer than an instruction for successful living. Its primary purpose is to provide direction as to a way of living that will result in happiness and prosperity. The teaching itself derives its authority from human experience rather than divine revelation. This should not be seen as humanism devoid of religious meaning. Rather, since Israel believed that the world and everything within it was created in an orderly fashion by a good God (cf. Gen 1:1-31), it also believed that all things within that world unfold according to the order God set in the beginning. Part of this order could be seen in the relationship between certain actions and their predetermined consequences. The challenge of life was to discover this order and live in accord with it. Israel further believed that its law and religious tradition offered insight into the order set by God. Therefore, to live faithful to the tradition would enable one to reap the fruits of this order.

This psalm contrasts two ways of living: the way of the wise or righteous and the way of the foolish or wicked. The former live in harmony with the order set by God. They delight in the law and follow it. The latter prefer to live against God's order. They choose the way of the wicked, the sinners, the insolent. Since the order within the world, established at the time of creation, somehow directs the outcome of one's behavior, a life that is faithful to this order will enjoy the fruits of order; a life that is unfaithful will reap the consequences of such behavior.

The psalmist draws on experience rather than religious tradition to illustrate the point of the instruction. The images used to demonstrate the differences in the two ways of life are vivid. The wise person is like a thriving tree that is well rooted near water, the source of life. Such a tree flourishes. In stark contrast, the foolish person is like useless chaff, rootless, with no source of life and no promise of productivity. The psalm ends with a religious statement: the God who created this order in the first place providently watches over it.

This psalm, like all Wisdom teaching, not only describes something from human experience but does so in order to exhort others to conform their lives to the insights already gained. In other words, this psalm describes the lot of both the wise and the foolish in order to encourage others to choose the way of life that promises prosperity rather than the one that results in meaninglessness. Proverbial teaching is always both descriptive and exhortative. The wise person is one who learns from life experience, either one's own or that of another.

1 Corinthians 15:12, 16-20

In the reading for last Sunday Paul proclaimed and interpreted the good news of Christ's resurrection. In today's reading he defends belief in the resurrection against those who do not believe in resurrection of the body. Such unbelief can be traced back to at least three groups of people. The first group is the Jewish Sadducees. They espoused a more conservative understanding of Judaism. Unlike the Pharisees, they held to a strict interpretation of the Scriptures, rejecting any development or modernization of the law. If something was not explicitly stated in the Scriptures, they did not accept it. Belief in reward and/or punishment after this life is one of the concepts they rejected. The second group is the Greek Gnostics. They highly valued the human soul, believing it to be immortal. They may have believed the souls of the dead would be somehow taken into glory, but they did not hold that this glorification would include some form of reanimation of the body.

Finally, there were those within the Christian community itself who labored under a misinterpretation of what has come to be known as realized eschatology. They seem to have believed that, through baptism, believers were joined to the risen Christ and were already living the resurrected life. In their eyes there was no need for any further resurrection after death. What they believed about the power of the resurrection may have been basically true, but the way they understood its effects in the lives of believers was seriously distorted.

Paul's argument about the fruits of the resurrection in the lives of others is based on his understanding of the union of Christ with believers. Because their resurrection results from their union with Christ, their failure to rise suggests that Christ never rose before them. The basis of their faith is his resurrection and not his miracles or his teaching a new way of living. Thus if he never rose, their faith is vain, empty, pointless. Worse than that, they are still in their sins. The argument goes as follows: If Christ did not rise, then he is still dead; if he is dead, then he has not conquered sin and death; if he has not conquered sin, then believers are unforgiven and still in their sins; if he has not conquered death, then those who have died in Christ have really perished. Rejection of the resurrection undoes both Paul's christology and his teaching on salvation. Paul insists that the hope believers have in Christ is not merely for this life. Rather, it is hope in a future life, a life when they will be able to enjoy fully the fruits of the resurrection.

Paul ends this instruction with a final declaration of faith, using an image from harvesting. As certain as the firstfruits are a promise of the quality of the coming harvest, so surely does the resurrection of Christ guarantee the resurrection of believers. As their resurrection is dependent on his, so their resurrection demonstrates the fruitfulness of his.

Luke 6:17, 20-26

The Sermon on the Plain is delivered to the disciples but in the presence of a much larger crowd. Three groups are identified: the Twelve, a reference to the apostles, who with Jesus have come down from the mountain; a group of disciples or followers of Jesus; and a large crowd of interested people who have come from as far south as Jerusalem and the area of Judea and from as far north as Tyre and Sidon in Syria. With all these people hanging on his every word, Jesus addresses his disciples with both macarisms and woes. The teaching is based on a practice associated with the Wisdom tradition. Certain behavior results in blessedness; misfortune is brought on by its opposite.

There is a perfect balance in the message of Jesus' sermon. He first singles out four situations in life that, he claims, make people blessed. He then identifies their opposites and declares them as being woeful. What is startling about Jesus' teaching is the reversal he proclaims. The blessed are those who are poor, who are hungry, who weep, who are persecuted, while the woeful ones are the rich, the satisfied, the joyful, the respected. Jesus has overturned the standards of this age and established new standards, those of the reign of God. While there is definitely a religious meaning to these beatitudes and woes, they should not be merely spiritualized. We must appreciate their literal meaning as well as their religious implications.

The poor (*ptōchoi*) were the economically impoverished and marginalized. They were frequently reduced to begging and were almost totally dependent upon the generosity of others for sustenance. While anyone can suffer an economic setback, the existence of a social class of poor is evidence the community as a whole had not taken seriously its covenant responsibility to care for the needy. When this happened, God sided with the poor and acted as their protector. This first beatitude announces that, unfairly deprived now, these poor will enjoy the reign of God. Conversely, the rich who did not address the needs of the poor will not enjoy the consolation of the reign of God. They have had their solace already. Those who are hungry now will be satisfied, and those who are satisfied now will be hungry. Those who weep now will laugh; those who laugh now will weep. The reign of God will turn standards upside down.

Perhaps the heart of this teaching is found in the last beatitude and the last woe. It is not just poverty or hunger or mourning that determines one's reward but the commitment to the Son of Man that may have caused the misfortune in the first place or that survived despite it. The followers of Jesus will be hated and marginalized and scorned because they are his followers. When this happens, they will be like the prophets, who, because of their call for repentance and renewal, were rejected by the ancestors. Conversely, the disciples of Jesus should be wary when they are accepted and esteemed in this world. This could mean that, like the false prophets of old, they enjoy approval because they deliver a message that unfaithful or disengaged people want to hear, a message that contains no call to conversion. The reign of God has turned the standards of the world upside down.

Themes of the Day

We who were called last week to witness to the death and resurrection of Jesus are instructed this week as to the meaning of that death and resurrection and the implications of this mystery in our lives. The death of Christ, which at first seemed like a curse, has been conquered in the resurrection of Christ. The curse has become the blessing.

A Transformed Life

Paul teaches us that united to Christ through faith and in baptism, we are united in his death and resurrection. With Christ we die to sin; with him we rise to a new life. Once again the ambiguities of human life may cloud our understanding of this mystery. We may be inclined to live our lives as if nothing transformative has occurred. It would be tragic if this were to happen. Our lives would be empty, our faith would be vain, and we would be people to be pitied. On the other hand, there is a way in which we can live ourselves into a new way of understanding. This can happen when actions performed in deep faith change the way we perceive the workings of God in our lives. If we live those lives as if we have really died to sin and have been raised to a new and transformed life, we may not only begin to believe we actually have died and been raised, but our lives will manifest the fact of this mystery. We cannot wait to see proof of our transformation before we change our actions. The proof is in the lives we live in faith. To deny that we have died and been raised is to deny the resurrection of Christ. Paul insists that they cannot be separated. The challenge is to live in and out of this faith.

Both Jeremiah and Jesus introduce us to such a way of living. It is a way of paradox, a way that moves us beyond the self-centered standards of the world. In the everyday give-and-take of living, the implications of faith work themselves out in blessing if we are faithful, in curse if we are not. The Wisdom form, which both men use, suggests that their teaching springs from the way life itself has been fashioned. In other words, the consequences of our behavior are not arbitrary; they flow directly from the behavior itself. However, dying with Christ and rising with him transport us into a new mode of being with consequences that are paradoxical. We are called to trust in God and the ways of God, which we cannot always see or understand, rather than in what is human, which we can grasp. Dying and rising turns the standards of living upside down.

A Paradoxical Life

In the world sketched in these readings the poor, the hungry, those who weep, and those who are persecuted are really the ones who are blessed. The victims of our social and economic systems, those who have been ravaged by war or have been made vulnerable by life itself are the ones who, if they place their trust in God, will be blessed in the end. They may appear to be the outcasts of this world, but if they are filled with faith, they will inherit heaven. The wealth of this world and its pleasures are not the blessings we might think they are. They can blind us to the real values of life and prevent us from dying to the world and living resurrected lives in Christ. It is neither poverty nor wealth that promises blessing or curse but commitment to Christ despite the poverty or wealth. Therein lies the paradox. The life of the tree is subject to the water that nourishes it; the life of the Christian feeds on faith in the death and resurrection of Christ.

Seventh Sunday in Ordinary Time
1 Samuel 26:2, 7-9, 12-13, 22-23

The story read today is filled with human intrigue and divine mystery. It contrasts the respect in which David held the anointed of the LORD with the murderous intent of Saul. Although David was the one hunted, Saul was the one caught. The king had an army of three thousand men, while David had one companion. It is clear that God had delivered Saul into David's hand. Still, David did not raise it against the king.

The king's spear was part of the royal regalia. It was more than a weapon. It was a sign of royal rank. When stuck in the ground, it marked the location of the royal tent. The ultimate disgrace would be to die by one's own spear. This is precisely what Abishai suggested. Abner had failed in his responsibility to protect the king. Furthermore, the very fact that David and Abishai were able to enter such a large camp without being detected could be credited only to God's intervention. Abishai offered to administer the blow so David would not have to live with the guilt of having killed the king. One might think David would be justified in killing the man who sought to kill him. However, by taking the symbol of royal rank he chose to shame his enemy rather than assassinate him.

Despite the fact that Saul was out to kill him, David refused to harm the king, for he was still the one chosen by God to lead the people. The fate of God's anointed one was in God's own hands. David explained this to Abishai while in the camp, and later, when he was at a safe distance, he announced it to those who were pursuing him. In this episode David is clearly favored by God, for the sleep that overcame Saul and his camp was not the normal sleep of fatigue. It was the same kind of deep slumber *(tardēmâ)* God had cast upon Adam when a rib was taken from him to fashion his companion (cf. 2:21), or when God cut a covenant with Abram (Gen 15:12), or when as punishment God withdrew prophetic guidance from the sinful people (Isa 29:10). Though clearly favored by God, David does not take advantage of this favor. Judgment is in God's hands, and God alone will reward or punish each one according to her or his righteousness *(ṣᵉdāqâ)* and faithfulness *(ʾēmet)*.

Psalm 103:1-2, 3-4, 8, 10, 12-13

The responsorial psalm begins with a summons to bless the Lord. Although the word "bless" is often used as a benediction, a prayer for God's presence or grace for the future, in this case it is a call to praise or thank God for blessings already received. The call to bless the Lord is normally addressed to someone other than the psalmist. Here it is a self-address (vv. 1-2). The Hebrew word translated "soul" *(nepesh)* comes from the word for "breath." It yields over twenty meanings, chief among which are "life-breath" (or "soul"), "life," and "living person." The reference here is probably to that center within the person from which all life forces flow. This is not merely a spiritual or immaterial reality; it encompasses every aspect of the person. This understanding is corroborated by the phrase "all my being."

In the biblical world a person's name was an expression of that person's unique identity. In many ways names held more significance for people then than they do today. One could exercise power over another simply by somehow controlling the name of that person. There were times during Israel's history when, in their attempt to show great reverence for God, the people paid homage to God's name rather than directly to God (cf. Deut 12:11, 21; 14:23f.; 16:2, 6, 11). Even when they did this, they were careful to avoid using the divine name itself. Still today, we show the same respect when we merely use the consonants YHWH or substitute "Lord" (small upper-case letters) rather than the divine name itself.

The reason for praising or thanking God, the benefits to which the psalmist refers, is God's willingness to pardon, to heal, and to redeem or save. These are all acts that flow from God's lovingkindness *(ḥesed)* and compassion *(raḥămîm,* vv. 3-4). These two attributes are not only closely associated with covenantal commitment but, as seen in Exodus tradition, are integral aspects of God's own name and identity (v. 8; cf. Exod 34:6). It is out of this mercy that God acts, not requiring the harsh punishment that the sins of the people would warrant.

The extent of God's mercy is further sketched by means of the figure of speech "east to west," which denotes immeasurable distance. Human eyes can only envision a fraction of the stretch that lies between the horizons. What is perceived is only infinitesimal; the reality is beyond comprehension. Using the figure of speech, the psalmist is claiming the same limitlessness for the compassion of God. Out of covenant love God puts our transgression so far from us that the distance cannot even be imagined. This is reason to praise and bless the LORD.

Finally the psalmist uses a familial image to characterize God's compassion. Although the reference is to the compassion of a father for his children, the word itself comes from the word for "womb" *(reḥem).* Here compassion is much more intimate than empathy felt for those who suffer. It is womb-love. In other words, the love God has for us is the love a mother has for the children of her womb. This explains God's commitment to us, and it is certainly reason to bless the LORD.

1 Corinthians 15:45-49

In this passage Paul continues the discussion on the resurrection that we have followed the last Sundays. Today he contrasts the ordinary human body with the resurrected body that believers will receive. He does this in several ways. First he draws a clear distinction between the first man, Adam, and the last Adam, Christ. As we read in the second creation narrative, when the breath of life was breathed into him, the first man became a living being *(nepeš ḥayyâ;* cf. Gen 2:7; the Greek "living soul," *psychē,* does not adequately capture the Hebrew meaning). In contrast, those possessing the spirit of the risen Christ have life through him, thus making him a life-giving spirit. Adam received life, while Christ gives it.

Some seem to have believed the man made in God's image in Gen 1:26f. was really an incorruptible heavenly being meant to serve as model for the rest of humanity, and that Adam, the man made from dust in Gen 2:7, was a material copy of that first man. If this were indeed the case, the man with the heavenly body would have already come, having preceded the man with the earthly body. This speculation would throw into question the authenticity of the human nature of Jesus, the last Adam, as well as the need for the resurrection. In the face of this possible misinterpretation of Christ, of resurrection, and of the creation accounts themselves, Paul insists that the natural preceded the spiritual. Thus it was necessary for Christ to die in order for him to be raised from the dead. Paul states this in another way: The first man (Adam) was out of the earth, made of its dust, while the second man, the Lord, by his resurrection was from heaven. Finally, those who come from the dust, as did the first man, will have natural bodies like that first man; those who are joined to the risen Lord will have resurrected bodies, as does the Lord.

The passage ends with Paul playing on the idea of being made in the image of another. Just as being made of dust we bear the image of the first man, who himself was made of dust, so sharing in the resurrection of the Lord we bear the image of the last man, the one who was raised from the dead.

Luke 6:27-38

Jesus' Sermon on the Plain, begun in the gospel for last Sunday, continues today. The primary focus of this instruction is love *(agápē)*, specifically, love of one's enemies. This injunction to love is stated in four different but parallel ways:

love	enemies
do good to	those who hate you
bless	those who curse you
pray for	those who mistreat you

In each case the disciples of Jesus are told to act toward their enemies in a way exactly opposite the way they themselves are treated. In other words, they are not to retaliate in kind. Furthermore, it is not enough that they refrain from retaliation; their love should not be mere passive acceptance. Rather, they are called to active love of those who do not love them.

Four examples of how this love is to be carried out are then given. All underscore the need to relinquish willingly what one may have a right to claim as one's own. There is question about whether striking the cheek is an act of violence or insult. The example seems less concerned about the nature of the blow than about the response of the one receiving it. Whether attacked or insulted by the blow to the cheek, one must be willing to be extravagant in one's resistance to retaliation. This same extravagance is illustrated in one's willingness to surrender even an undergarment when an outer cloak is taken. The disciples are told to give unquestioningly when asked and not to demand return of items taken. Such behavior may appear to be excessive, but it illustrates the extremes to which one must be willing to love enemies.

What has come to be known as the Golden Rule (v. 31) appears elsewhere in negative form: What is hateful to you, do not do to others (cf. Tob 4:15; *Didache* 1:2; *Sabbath* 31a). The negative form admonishes us to refrain from evil, while Jesus' positive, open-ended version is a call for active love. Three examples for living out this Golden Rule are given, each demonstrating that there is no credit (*cháris*) in simple reciprocity (vv. 32-34). The disciples must surpass others in loving, in doing good, and in lending. As children of God, they must model their love after the love God has for all, even for those who have turned away from God.

The disciples are called to be merciful (*oiktírmōn*) as God is merciful. The word is closely akin to the Hebrew word meaning "compassionate" (*raḥûm*), the attitude of loving attachment a mother has for the child of her womb. Here that loving attitude is attributed to God, who is referred to as "Father." Characterizing God in this way radically reinterprets the meaning of God's fatherhood. It is represented as lavishly loving and unselfishly attentive to others.

Finally, the way the disciples treat others will be the standard for the way they are treated by God. If they do not judge or condemn, they will not be judged or condemned. If they forgive and are generous, they will be forgiven and will receive generously. The extent of God's beneficence is illustrated through an image of measuring grain—good measure, pressed down, shaken together, running over from the fold in the outer garment that forms a kind of pocket. While we may be extravagant in our loving, the goodness of God far exceeds even the greatest human beneficence.

Themes of the Day

The schooling of the disciples continues. Here we see that such schooling is intent on changing the way we think as well as the way we act. Perhaps one of the most difficult lessons to learn in this area is forgiveness of those we consider our enemies, those who have wronged us. As challenging as this may be, the gospel calls us to an even higher standard: we must be merciful as God is merciful. If such perfection can become a reality in our lives, we will be able to forgive. Paul assures us that we can indeed attain such perfection, not by ourselves but through the power of the risen Lord, whose image we bear.

The Divine Image

Paul plays with the theology of creation. In the beginning we were made like the first Adam, earthly, limited, weak, concerned about the things of this world, and committed to our own well-being. Now we have been fashioned after the image of the second Adam, Christ, the risen Lord. Being like Christ, we become godlike, empowered with his saving power, transformed with him into new beings. It is now in our power, which is really the power of the resurrection, to be merciful as God is merciful. In the risen Lord we experience a mystical transformation. From now on all our actions can flow from this new reality.

Works of Love

Transformed by the power of the resurrection, we are capable of unprecedented good works. We can live without retaliation; we can render good for evil. We can be prodigal in our generosity toward others; we can relinquish any rights of proprietorship we might enjoy. We can live with others without unfairly judging them. We can be like God, boundless in our forgiveness. When we are transformed, God becomes the source of our spiritual power, the model after whom we pattern our lives, the incentive that spurs us on, and the ultimate goal of all our works. The works themselves are not mere external performances done out of obligation. They are visible manifestations of a deep inner reality, of the transformation that has taken place in our lives. Schooling for discipleship results in total transformation in Christ.

Eighth Sunday in Ordinary Time
Sirach 27:4-7

The first reading for today is a short collection of proverbs containing wisdom that has been gleaned from life experience. Though descriptive in form, the proverbs are intended to be directive in function. This is clear from the last verse, which is obviously an admonition. In its own way each proverb demonstrates how life itself is the test of the value of things. The specific aspect of life dealt with here is the revealing character of one's speech. A proverb frequently employs a nature metaphor to illustrate the point it is making. Here the sage uses metaphors from three different experiences of life: agriculture, the arts, and horticulture. The variety of situations considered helps us see that any situation can provide us with insight into life.

The first proverb insists that appearances are deceiving. When wheat is first cut, it contains the husk, some beard, and straw. Only with some kind of threshing does this refuse appear. So it is with people. First impressions are not always accurate. However, once someone starts talking the facade falls away, and the real person is revealed. The second proverb addresses the same issue, using an entirely different metaphor. It is impossible to fashion pots that will endure without firing them in a kiln. However, too much heat will crack the pots. The potter must know just how much heat the pottery can endure. So it is with people. Tribulation tests the mettle of the person, and that mettle is revealed in one's speech. Finally, the quality of the fruit reveals the degree of care given to the tree. So it is with people. By their fruits you shall know them. Their speech betrays their thinking. The final bit of advice provides the point of every one of the proverbs: Wait until you hear what people have to say before you praise them.

The theological value of the Wisdom tradition has often been challenged. How can we arrive at religious truth through purely human insight into mundane life experience? The ancient Israelites believed the reason life works the way it does is that God made it that way. Therefore, insight about life was really insight into the workings of God. From this we can see why they believed that through reflection on life they could discover God's plan, and knowing that plan and its origin in God they would be able to live according to it. This helps us appreciate the importance they gave to every aspect of life, and specifically on this Sunday the role speech plays.

Psalm 92:2-3, 13-14, 15-16

The psalm begins with a declaration of the appropriateness of thanking God. One's name was really an integral part of one's very being. Therefore, to praise the name of the Most High is to praise the LORD. Singing praises is a way of thanking God. Hymns of thanksgiving normally include reasons for gratitude. Although these verses do not mention specific examples of God's beneficence for which the psalmist is grateful, they contain an allusion to the goodness that God has shown and that should elicit thankfulness. Kindness (*ḥesed*) and faithfulness (*'ĕmûnâ*) are part of the vocabulary of covenant. Nothing is more worthy of our gratitude than the inestimable privilege of being in a covenant relationship with a kind and faithful God.

The cultic dimension of this prayer can be seen in the psalmist's declaration that it is good to praise God throughout the night, even until dawn. This suggests some kind of vigil, the kind that was normally part of the devotional life that unfolded at shrines. Individuals often held prayerful vigils in petition for some favor from God or in thanksgiving for a blessing received. As is frequently the case with religious people, thankfulness overflows and cannot be adequately voiced in a simple statement. Here the psalmist says that it is good to spend a night of prayer, giving thanks to God.

The rewards of righteousness are graphically sketched using imagery from the natural world of the Near East. The fertility of the familiar palm tree and the longevity of the neighboring cedar of Lebanon are apt metaphors for the blessings that will flow from fidelity to one's covenant responsibilities. The statement about the house of the LORD and the courts of God (v. 14) suggests the Temple and is a second allusion to worship. To be "planted in the house of the LORD" is probably a reference to temple devotion, which could be part of the life of any Israelite, rather than to temple service, which was reserved to just a few men. Just as trees were planted near water, their source of life, so the righteous are planted in the presence of God, their source of life.

The fruitfulness of the righteous is further described. It will endure even into old age, a time when living things normally cease to be productive. The vicissitudes of life that too frequently wear people down will not undermine the fruitfulness described here, because the righteous are planted in the presence of God, the source of all life. As long as they are faithful in their covenant commitment they will be able to draw on the strength and life-giving forces of this divine presence.

Finally, these remarkable lives will bear witness to the uprightness of God. Once again, the covenant relationship is the basis of this hymn of thanksgiving. The righteous are blessed because they have been faithful. However, the fruitfulness of their lives is a sign that God too has been faithful to the covenant promises.

1 Corinthians 15:54-58

We conclude our reflections on Paul's teaching on the resurrection by considering the vanquishing of death that Jesus accomplished. Again and again Paul has insisted that believers are joined to the risen Lord in faith and through baptism. Hence what is perishable and mortal because it was fashioned out of dust takes on the imperishability and immortality of resurrection. Although he uses the image of putting on garments, he is not suggesting this is merely a change in appearance. It is, instead, a radical transformation. This will happen, according to Paul, in fulfillment of the Scriptures.

Once again he has turned to the Scriptures in order to establish continuity between the cherished traditions of ancient Israel and the Christian faith. In order to make the point he wants, he reinterprets passages from two different prophets. The first is found in a description of a heavenly enthronement scene. It refers to that future day of fulfillment when the mighty God of Israel will vanquish the forces of evil once and for all, will be enthroned as conqueror on high, and in celebration will spread out a banquet for all the peoples of the earth to share. With this victory the LORD will swallow up death forever (Isa 25:8). Paul applies the meaning of this passage to Jesus, indicating that by his resurrection Jesus has accomplished this very feat. The second passage is part of a collection of judgment sayings. In it Israel stands before the ultimate sentence of death. In this context the words are a cry of triumph, and the triumph belongs to death (Hos 13:14). Paul reshapes the cry slightly and completely turns its meaning upside down, interpreting it as a defiant challenge.

Placing these two reshaped passages together, Paul has fashioned an entirely new poetic exclamation, which retains some of the original meaning of each yet creates an entirely new message. Death is now not only swallowed up, it is swallowed up in victory. Consequently, death itself knows no victory. Its sting (a reference to the sting of a deadly scorpion?) is no longer lethal. Paul then traces back to Christ the power that has conquered death. He begins his argument with the long-held conviction that death is the consequence of sin (cf. Rom 5:12). He moves then to the law which, regardless of its cherished value, not only directs people to righteous living but actually convicts people of sin (cf. Rom 5:13). However, God has given us victory over sin and death through the resurrection of our Lord Jesus Christ.

The instruction ends with an exhortation that is grounded in faith in the message just proclaimed: Therefore! Because of these things! The believers are told to be firm, to be steadfast. This suggests they are facing conditions that could cause them to waver in their faith. They are told to place their hope in the power of the resurrection and to live lives of dedication to the Lord. If they do this, they can trust that the risen Lord will bestow on them the blessings that flow from the victory that has been won.

Luke 6:39-45

The admonitions of Jesus set forth principles by which the followers of Jesus are to live. The first point deals with the kind of teachers one should follow and eventually become. The second addresses the relationship between the inner character of a person and the kind of behavior that flows from that character. Teaching from within the Wisdom tradition of Israel, Jesus uses metaphors taken from nature to illustrate the points he is making.

The teaching begins with two rhetorical questions, the answers to which are obvious. The first is No! The second is Yes! Many commentators believe this teaching is a veiled criticism of the scribes and Pharisees, the official teachers of Israel. This is not necessarily the case, since in the rest of the passage Jesus is exhorting his followers to be critical of their own behavior. One need not go outside the company of disciples to find attitudes and conduct that warrant censure. It seems that some of the disciples have not learned all the Master had to teach them. He accuses them of being too quick to find fault with others while at the same time remaining blind to their own shortcomings. Setting themselves up as judges in this way makes them blind people leading other blind people rather than faithful disciples of Jesus who are quick to forgive rather than judge.

The passage is riddled with male bias. The disciple and the teacher are men, as is the brother who is being corrected. All of this is evidence of a limited, male-centered society, perhaps the society of Jesus, certainly the society of the author of the gospel. Nonetheless, the message is intended as well for women.

A hypocrite is one whose outer way of living does not conform to an authentic inner disposition. The one who criticizes others without being self-critical is here accused of being a hypocrite. Jesus turns to the natural world to illustrate what he means. A tree brings forth the fruit it is disposed to bring forth: a good tree, good fruit; a rotten tree, rotten fruit; a fig tree, figs; a grape vine, grapes. Every good tree brings forth fruit "according to its kind" (cf. Genesis 1). Having made this point emphatically, Jesus applies the meaning of the metaphor to human beings. A good person brings forth good fruit; an evil person brings forth evil fruit. Actions flow out of the disposition of one's heart. This statement illustrates the conviction that character precedes action. While this is true, it is not the whole truth. It is possible to change one's inner disposition by first altering one's manner of living. However, the point Jesus is making is the importance of congruity between the inner and outer dimensions of a person. Where there is such congruity, there is integrity; where it is absent, there is hypocrisy.

Themes of the Day

The readings for this Sunday continue the schooling of the followers of Jesus as they are fashioned into true disciples. The overarching theme is similar to one found in the readings for last Sunday. It is the deceiving character of outward appearances. These readings insist there must be some kind of integrity between one's speech and one's actions. Both the reading from Sirach and the one from Luke, by employing Wisdom forms of instruction (proverb and parable), indicate the Wisdom character of the teaching. The settings are commonplace (agriculture and social interaction) demonstrating that the lessons of life are learned in everyday occurrences.

Integrity of Speech

It is unfortunate that we do not always value the integrity of speech as we might. We may even extol our ability to deceive others, to lead them on for our own advantage. We cannot take people at their word, not even those who hold positions of trust, such as politicians, newscasters, lawyers, ministers, even parents. We may not honor truthful speech as we should, but we still recognize the havoc dishonesty of any kind plays in a society. Some of us may want to get ahead any way we can, but no one of us wants to be a victim of dishonesty.

The Wisdom lesson for today addresses the question of integrity. We have learned from the experience of life itself that honesty is not merely the best policy, it is essential if a society is to survive and thrive. We recognize that there must be a measure of integrity between speech with which we communicate and the values and aspirations that motivate us. There must be a comparable measure of integrity between our speech and our deeds. It is not by accident that the Hebrew word *dābār* means both "word" and "deed." Words identify our deeds, and our deeds are expressions of the words that are formulated first in our minds and then on our lips.

Transformation: A Work of God

We must never forget that the transformation of life we seek is possible, not through our own efforts but through the death and resurrection of Christ. It was through his own death that death itself has been swallowed up; it was through his resurrection that human life has been changed for all time. He is the true Word spoken, the incarnate Word in the flesh. What he says and what he does are one. We are merely beneficiaries of the marvels he has wrought. It is because of him that we are able to persevere in the work of God, which we have taken upon ourselves. We can never forget that the good work we accomplish is accomplished in and through this Lord.

Orthodoxy

We have come to understand "orthodoxy" as meaning "correct teaching." However, the word itself comes from two Greek words meaning "right" *(orthós)* and "glory" *(dóxa)*. Orthodoxy, or right praise, is that which is both spoken and done at the same time. It identifies the integrity of which we have been speaking, an integrity measured by the right correspondence between speech and action. In form, the responsorial psalm is a hymn of praise. In a sense it is also an expression of this kind of orthodoxy. It describes the life of the righteous ones, whose integrity cannot be questioned. It declares that it is by a righteous life itself and not merely through prayers of praise that God is glorified. The glory of God is the human person fully alive (Irenaeus).

Ninth Sunday in Ordinary Time
1 Kings 8:41-43

This is an excerpt from Solomon's prayer in the Temple he built in Jerusalem. The foreigners for whom he prays are not the resident aliens *(gēr)* who had settled in the land and who were protected by law. Instead, they were strangers (*nokrî*) who had heard of God's great name (the name was the extension of the person) and had come from a distance to worship God in the Temple. They are evidence of the wide spread of God's fame. The text suggests these people have heard enough about God to come to the Temple, but it is there they will learn about the marvelous deeds wrought by God's mighty hand and outstretched arm. This phrase is identified with God's deliverance of the Israelites from Egyptian oppression (cf. Deut 26:8). Since recital of a creedal statement (cf. Deut 6:21b-23; 26:5b-9; Josh 24:2b-13) was an important component of Israelite worship, we may have here an allusion to this practice.

The concern for foreigners voiced in this prayer is extraordinary. While there are many passages that demonstrate Israel's universalistic perspective, they usually presume there will be conversion, that those who are outsiders will eventually become insiders. Such is not the case here. These strangers are not sojourners, people who have decided to live in Israel and, perhaps, even to become proselytes. Rather, these are people from another land who, while they do come to Jerusalem to worship, will most likely return to their land of origin. Solomon prays that God, who is in heaven, will hear their prayer. Thus as their prayers are answered, God's fame will spread even more across the world, and soon people from all the lands of the earth will know God's name, will stand in awe of God's power, and will recognize the Temple as the place to pray. This prayer says nothing about the value of other religions. It merely prays that all people will recognize the authenticity of Israel's.

Psalm 117:1, 2

The shortest psalm in the Psalter, this responsorial psalm is a classic example of a hymn of praise. The first verse is the imperative call to praise; the second is causative, giving the reason for such praise. There is no question about its liturgical character. However, there is not agreement as to whether the summons is merely a liturgical phrase or liturgical direction. The first verse contains an example of synonymous parallelism, in which the second of two lines of poetry parallel the first:

| praise | the LORD | all nations |
| glorify | him | all peoples |

This is a poetic way of reinforcing the meaning of the verse. It should be noted that it is not Israel but the nations who are called to sing the praises of Israel's special God (the LORD). They are called upon to give honor and glory to a God not their own. This speaks to the universality of the reign of God. Not only will God's dominion envelop all people, but all people will be embraced by God's care and protection.

The reason given for the praise of the nations is the goodness God has shown to Israel, not to the nations themselves. This further identifies the hymn as one of praise of the kingship of the LORD. Words associated with covenant are used—lovingkindness *(ḥesed)* and truth, or fidelity. The coupling of these words is closely associated with the revelation of God's name to Moses at the time of the remaking of the covenant (cf. Exod 34:6). God's lovingkindness is said to be steadfast, strong as a warrior *(gābar);* God's truth lasts forever *('ôlām).* Since this is the description of the God who enters into the covenant, it is a guarantee to Israel that the covenant itself will be strong and enduring. When the nations see and understand what God has done for Israel, they will surely sing God's praises.

Galatians 1:1-2, 6-10

In the beginning of this letter Paul identifies himself by means of his Roman surname. The origin of this name is unknown. Perhaps he chose it because of its similarity to Saul, his Jewish name (cf. Acts 13:9). He further identifies himself as an apostle. While the word itself designates one sent by another, it had a particular meaning in the Christian communities. It referred to those who had been especially chosen by Jesus and who, at the time of Paul, exercised authority from Jerusalem over the entire Church. Claiming to be an apostle appears to have been very important to Paul, for he follows it with a form of authentication. This suggests the legitimacy of his apostleship had been challenged. In the face of this, Paul insists he received his calling directly from Christ. He has not merely been authorized by one of the existing churches or by one of the leaders in Jerusalem. Regardless of what others may think of him, he is a genuine apostle.

Here we get a glimpse into Paul's christology and the current practice of missionary endeavor. He says he was called by Jesus Christ and God the Father, an expression with trinitarian nuances. Furthermore, he states that Jesus was raised from the dead by God. In other words, Paul believes that God was working in and through Jesus Christ. As an apostle Paul seems to write not only in his name but in the name of others. He refers to his companions as brothers. Either Paul did not travel with women missionaries, as did some of the other itinerant Christian preachers (cf. 1 Cor 9:5), or he is using "brother" for "brothers and sisters" in the stereotypically discriminating fashion of the day. Although they are not always given credit for their ministry, there is evidence that women were quite influential in the apostolic work of the early churches (cf. Rom 16:1-16; Phlm 2). Finally, the letter is written to all the churches in the province of Galatia, indicating that correspondence was passed around, probably by other itinerant apostles.

Paul writes out of astonished disappointment, even indignation. He rebukes the Galatians. Evidently they had fallen victim to preachers who perverted the essence of the gospel, and Paul writes to correct this. Initially they accepted the gospel Paul preached, but then, as if it never really took hold of them, they quickly subscribed to another teaching. This passage does not identify the error, but it certainly reveals Paul's passion in the face of it. Having initially emphasized his credentials as an apostle, he insists that anything that deviates from the message he has preached must be rejected. It must be rejected even if the message is received in what appears to be some form of heavenly communication. Paul's condemnation is searing. Let those who preach another message be cursed *(anáthema)!*

Paul ends as he began, with a defense of himself. He knows that such virulent condemnation will not endear him to some, yet he is not deterred in his reproach. His commitment is to Christ and to no other. This, and not acceptance by others, is what determined his ministry.

Luke 7:1-10

At the conclusion of the Sermon on the Plain Jesus went to Capernaum, a border town that could well have quartered Gentile soldiers. A centurion was a soldier with charge over one hundred men. This explains his comment about having soldiers subject to him (v. 8). As a man of importance, he would also have slaves. However, this particular centurion is unusual. He is particularly concerned about the well-being of his slave, who is sick unto death. He, a member of the occupying force of Rome, has endeared himself to the local Jews. He has shown his love for Israel by building, or contributing to the building of, their synagogue. The centurion is thought by some commentators to have been a God-fearer, a Gentile who believed in the teachings of Judaism and kept the moral law but did not become a proselyte. Whatever his status, he was considered a cherished patron of the community, for a delegation from the synagogue went to plead his cause before Jesus.

Besides being so good to the Jewish community, the man also believed Jesus had the power to cure his mortally ill slave. He had heard about Jesus. This is an example of faith that came not from direct experience but through the words of others, a point not to be lost on later generations of Christians. The faith of this Roman soldier is still more unusual. Understanding the operations of spheres of authority and power, he believes that Jesus would not even have to come to the sick man. If the centurion can issue an order from a distance and know it will be obeyed, certainly Jesus can as well. Finally, he refers to Jesus as "Lord" *(kýrios)*, a social title that shows respect but also a religious title that implies faith. If only the former meaning is intended, it is unusual that an occupying military commander would so address a simple itinerant teacher. If the title is to be understood in the second way, it is extraordinary indeed.

This extraordinary faith is accompanied by genuine humility. The centurion claims he is not worthy to have Jesus enter his home. Attentive to Jewish law, he would know that visiting a Gentile home would make Jesus unclean.

We see here an example of the social and religious distances that existed between Jews and Gentiles. Furthermore, the man does not seem to realize that Jesus frequently spurned such prohibitions in order to meet the needs of others. Whatever his reasons, he let Jesus know that he believed his slave could be healed from a distance by Jesus' word alone. The power of the word concerning Jesus brought him to faith; he believed the power of Jesus would bring his slave to life. Jesus marveled at this humble faith and contrasted it with the kind of faith he found among the Jews. Here was a man who had not been raised in the faith of Israel but who was better able to recognize the power of God working in Jesus than most Jews.

The story says the messengers sent to Jesus returned to the home of the centurion. It does not say Jesus accompanied them. We are led to believe that, as the centurion had said, Jesus has indeed cured the slave from a distance. Throughout the narrative there was no direct contact between Jesus and either the slave or the centurion. The power of God can operate across time and space. All it needs to be effective is faith.

Themes of the Day

An important lesson disciples have to learn is that the ways of God do not conform to human expectations. More often than not the reign of God operates according to different standards—the hierarchies of society are turned upside down; insiders are passed by in favor of outsiders. Disciples will not only have to understand this kind of paradox but will also have to recognize it when it is present.

Christian Freedom

Christian freedom is one of the realities that does not conform to our patterns of thought. How easy it is to misunderstand freedom itself and all it entails. This is at the heart of Paul's thought. It is not too difficult to understand observance of religious practices. Most people have been raised to appreciate the importance of such compliance. We also have a fairly good grasp of the meaning of freedom. Therefore, it may seem reasonable to presume that Christian freedom means non-compliance. If this is what Paul meant by freedom from the law, why did he so often insist on an ethical way of life? No, freedom in Christ means being free from the limits set by the law. It means that it is only of Christ that we can say: This alone! Everything else is negotiable!

Outsiders Come In and Insiders Go Out

In today's readings we see the saving power of God move beyond ethnic and religious barriers. Outsiders are brought in, and insiders follow the healing power of God as it moves beyond customary boundaries. The power of God moves unimpeded where it will, and those who are joined to Christ are impelled to follow its lead. While law is valuable in that it guides us along the path of God's will, it also makes distinctions that become divisions, that separate people from one another. That is the limitation of law, and it is a limitation to which the power of God is not bound. In Christ we are called to a freedom that takes us beyond those divisions and distinctions into universality of presence.

Solomon welcomed the foreigner into the Temple to pray. How welcoming are we? Are we eager to have others join us in the church? In the civic community? In the nation? Or do we keep them out lest they threaten the comfortable lives to which we have become accustomed? Are we willing to open our ranks to share power and influence with newcomers? With those of a different gender or cultural group? With the next generation? It is custom that has established rules of membership, and God transcends custom. Can we?

The healing power of Jesus reached out to the servant of a pagan centurion. In fact, it traveled to the sick man even without the immediate presence of Jesus. This is remarkable, because healing was a sign of the establishment of the reign of God, and this would mean the reign of God was open to outsiders. More than this, the reign of God went in search of the outsider. It is so typical of God to be untypical. Crossing boundaries before us, the power of God moves us out of ourselves and of our narrow worlds. We are compelled to break down the barriers that custom has erected so we might let people in, or out, as the case may be. The all-embracing power of God would have us go out to reach others wherever they are. It is in this way, not in mere compliance to regulations that set boundaries, that we fulfill the law.

Tenth Sunday in Ordinary Time

1 Kings 17:17-24

The miracle described in this account took place in the confines of Israel, to the north in Sidon. This is an important point, because it was performed in a land thought to be under the jurisdiction of another god. The LORD has such power in other lands; thus the God of Israel exercises universal power. From a slightly different perspective we can say that the God of Israel also lavishes blessings on those who are not Israelites. Both the power and the goodness of God disregard national boundaries.

The episode develops out of an act of hospitality. As was the custom of the day, the woman offers hospitality to one in need, but then she suffers misfortune. She links the illness of her son with the entrance of the prophet into their lives. Rather than consider him a source of blessing, she believes this man of

God has brought God's wrath to the household. Such an attitude reveals the woman's understanding of retribution—the belief that good is rewarded and evil is punished. Said another way, good fortune is a sign of righteousness and adversity is a sign of sinfulness. From the perspective of the woman the goodness of the prophet made evident her own grave but unrecognized sinfulness. It was this sinfulness that was then punished by means of the illness of her son.

The serious plight of the woman is described in very few words. She is a widow with only one son, and that son is either dead or next to death. She is facing a double tragedy. In a patriarchal society a woman could claim the major privileges of society only through the agency of the men in her life. From birth she was under jurisdiction of her father and, at his death, her brother. When she married, this jurisdiction was transferred to her husband and, at his death, her son. With no husband and now perhaps no son she did not easily fit into the kin structure. Furthermore, with the death of the only son, the family itself was at its end. There would be no descendants to inherit the estate, and the name of the father would not pass into the future and, therefore, would cease to exist.

Elijah performs what appears to be a form of homeopathic treatment, but what is really a kind of symbolic prophetic act. It is not the power from the body of the prophet that restores the boy but the power of God working through the prophet. The passage itself makes this clear; Elijah prays to the LORD, and the LORD hears his prayer. When her son is restored to her alive, the woman responds with an act of faith. Her living son is proof that God's power works through this man of God. Now she testifies that God's word comes from Elijah's mouth as well. God's life-giving power has been exercised in a foreign land for the benefit of one of the most disadvantaged of society, a widow.

Psalm 30:2, 4, 5-6, 11, 12, 13

This is a psalm of thanksgiving for deliverance from the netherworld *(she˒ôl)*, the pit—the place of death (v. 4). This is the place of dismal darkness where the dead go. It is neither a place of reward nor one of punishment. There is no differentiation of the dead, only a form of semi-life in which there is no memory or praise of God. The allusion to death can be extended to illness, to depression, or to any serious misfortune that can threaten life. The scope of meaning here is broad, because in the ancient world people believed being stricken with illness was a sign one was actually in the grips of death itself. Therefore, to be brought up from the place of death is to be rescued from the threat of death. Whatever the actual danger, it is now past; God has intervened and saved the petitioner.

In addition to the calamity itself, the psalmist is also concerned about enemies who might take delight in his former misfortune. He asks to be preserved from this insult as well. Following the initial plea is an acknowledgment of deliverance. God has heard his petition and has granted his request for rescue.

The psalmist next turns to the faithful ones *(ḥasīdīm)* and calls on them to give thanks for God's holiness, that quality that sets God apart from all that is profane. These are the ones who themselves have been faithfully obedient to the demands of the covenant. They are the ones who would be most familiar with and committed to God's holiness. The psalm does not explicitly state that the suffering endured was the deserved penalty for some wrongdoing. However, since that was the customary explanation of misfortune, such a conclusion could easily be drawn. This is especially true since there is no protestation of innocence. Still, retribution is not the point of the prayer; thanksgiving for deliverance is. In describing this deliverance, the psalmist compares the vast difference between God's wrath and God's graciousness. The former is short-lived; the latter is everlasting. The distress the psalmist endured is characterized as the darkness of night; the rescue the psalmist was granted, as the promise of dawn. The former occurred yesterday; the latter is experienced today.

The psalmist turns again in prayer to God, pleading once more for pity. There is no suggestion that God has turned a deaf ear to earlier cries. Quite the contrary. The psalmist proclaims that grief and mourning have been turned into relief and rejoicing, and the rejoicing takes the form of celebrative dancing. This reversal of fortune is in fact the reason for the declaration of thanksgiving in the first place. Regardless of the nature of or reason for the psalmist's misfortune, God can be trusted to come to the aid of one who cries for help.

Galatians 1:11-19

In this autobiographic sketch Paul reveals some of the details of his life as he defends the authenticity of his apostleship. Again this week we see him insisting on the legitimacy of the gospel he preaches. He knew there were valid reasons for others to distrust him. After all, he had persecuted the Church of God; he even ravaged it. Then, after acting with such vehemence, he made a complete reversal and began preaching the gospel without ever having been authorized to do so. He was doubly suspect. It is understandable that there would be some doubt about the sincerity of his conversion and that some would take exception to his claim to have received a personal revelation from God. Despite all appearances, this is a man whose robust self-confidence was rooted in God and whose total commitment cannot be questioned.

Both at the beginning of this reading and at its end we see Paul asserting his independence from other apostles, insisting that he is a disciple of no one but Jesus Christ. On this point some of the details are ambiguous and have caused confusion. For example, Paul insists that the gospel he preaches was not received from someone else, yet he admits that he went to Jerusalem to confer with Cephas. This apparent discrepancy can be resolved in the following way. Paul was an avid (zealous) adherent to the traditions of the ancestors.

The reference here is probably to the oral traditions the Pharisees had developed as they interpreted the Scriptures to meet the needs of the times. Whether Paul had ever met the historical Jesus (a possibility because he was in Jerusalem at the time of the stoning of Stephen; cf. Acts 7:58), he was certainly acquainted with the claims of Jesus' followers. They were the cause of his fury. In fact, the better he knew the traditions of the ancestors, the more he would realize the significance of the Christian teaching. It was, after all, claiming that the traditions to which he was so passionately committed had been fulfilled in the life, death, and resurrection of Jesus.

Paul was not ignorant of Christian teaching. Before his encounter with the risen Lord he probably knew about Jesus, but he did not believe. As a result of the encounter he believed and may have wanted to hear more about the life of Jesus as Cephas had known him. While others may have provided Paul with historical information, he insists that no one really instructed him in the faith. The truth of the resurrection of Jesus was revealed to him by God, not taught to him by another. While such insistence reveals a man of strong conviction, it seems to have been interpreted by some as arrogant self-confidence. Paul must have realized this, for he credited the grace of God for his change of heart.

Actually, Paul credits God for everything. He alleges that, like the prophet Jeremiah before him, he had been set apart by God even before his birth (cf. Jer 1:5). God called him; God revealed Christ to him; God gave him a commission to preach to the Gentiles. It is important to note that his call and commission were one and the same reality. He was not merely called to be a follower; he was called to preach to the Gentiles.

In a sense, Paul's resoluteness in the matter of his apostleship has implications for all those believers who were not eyewitnesses to the events of the life of Jesus. His experience of the risen Lord after the ascension was as significant as the appearances of the risen Lord that took place before the ascension.

Luke 7:11-17

The story in today's gospel is well known. Jesus and his disciples encounter a funeral procession leaving the city they are about to enter. It is the only son of a widowed woman. Jesus is overcome with emotion and, without having been asked, raises the young man to life. This apparently simple story is rich with christological meaning.

First, the popularity of Jesus is clear. He is already attracting crowds; therefore, this marvelous feat will not go unnoticed. Second, the miracle elicits the kind of response attributed to a manifestation of God; the people are struck with fear and they glorify God. Finally, they recognize the miracle for what it is, a demonstration of divine power. The bystanders proclaim this in two ways: they perceive Jesus as a prophet; they acknowledge that God has worked through him. Finally, the author of the gospel himself refers to Jesus with the post-resurrection title "Lord."

This is an unusual miracle, for Jesus seems to have performed it out of his own deep emotion *(splanchnízomai)* rather than in response to someone else's request or demonstration of faith. Jesus was deeply moved at the sight of the grieving mother. It was her only son, and she was a widow. The vulnerable position in society of this widow is the same as that of the widow of Zarephath of Sidon (first reading). Not only is she suffering the grief of loss, she now is also bereft of a legal advocate. This was truly a tragic event, and Jesus was moved to pity.

The body of the dead man was probably being carried on an open bier, as was the custom. Since dead bodies polluted the city, they were buried outside its limits. This explains why Jesus and his companions met the funeral procession where they did. Jesus himself disregarded the cultic prohibition against touching a corpse. Such an act would render him unclean. However, it was through this very act that the life-giving power of God was transmitted to the corpse. The same act that polluted Jesus raised the young man. He spoke, giving evidence that he was alive. Jesus gave him back to his mother, an act reminiscent of another prophetic raising (cf. 1 Kgs 17:23). Both Elijah (1 Kgs 17:17-24) and Elisha (2 Kgs 4:32-37) brought dead sons back to life. The people might have been referring to this when they declared that Jesus was a prophet from God.

There is no evidence in the text that the people were thinking of the passage in which Moses foretells the coming of another prophet, the messianic prophet (cf. Deut 18:15). However, if there were even the slightest reference here to that tradition, the episode would both illuminate and obscure the messianic character of Jesus. While he can clearly be seen as an agent of the miraculous power of God, the absence of any requirement of faith might suggest the Messiah is merely a wonder-worker, one who goes around doing good but who requires nothing of the people. It is clear from the gospel accounts that the miracles of Jesus are not the primary focal point of his ministry. The proclamation of the reign of God is. The miracles merely demonstrate the presence of that reign here and now in the lives of the people who believe.

Themes of the Day

Jesus' instruction of the disciples regarding the universal scope of God's loving care continues this Sunday. Once again we see concern for those who are pushed to the margins of society by certain laws or customs. Today the concern is not only for those who suffer because they come from a different ethnic background but also for women who are made vulnerable because of gender-biased laws. Jesus spent his time preaching and healing. In the readings for today we have examples of both these ministries. We also see today that there are no limits to the scope of these ministries. The love of God goes out to all.

Embracing All

There are no limits to the healing love of God. It embraces all regardless of race or gender. Neither the prophet nor Jesus withheld this power because of special social convention. No questions were asked; there was no hesitation. When it comes to the reign of God, all are invited. It is not a question of who is worthy; all are welcome.

However, the reign comes through other people, through those who have been sent to witness, to proclaim, to heal. God's love is all-embracing, but what about the disciples' love? Do we discriminate? In our service do we include some but exclude others? Do we allow biased social or religious customs to restrict our ministry, thereby withholding the healing love of God? Are we "faithful" to the law but unfaithful to the call of Christ? Who are the "least" in the community, who may in fact be Christ in disguise? Jesus risked becoming ritually contaminated in order to prevent a widow from being even further marginalized. What are we willing to risk for the sake of service to others?

Apostle to the Outsider

Just as the healing power of God moves out to those who have been excluded, so we, like Paul, have been commissioned to go out to those who have not been included—the poor and the dispossessed; the refugees and the displaced; those with unsightly disease or mental disability; those who are in prison or in exile; those who have in any way been made invisible by society. Paul's experience of call included his commission to proclaim the good news of Jesus Christ to the Gentiles. We receive a similar call through the sacraments of initiation. In a way, Paul takes us by the hand and leads us out into the world, a world that so desperately needs to hear good news, needs to feel a healing touch.

The point of such ministry is not to swell the ranks of church membership but to bring the message of salvation to all. The conversion of Paul demonstrates how the grace of God can break open our biases and transform us into agents of salvation for others. He progressed from being a man who persecuted those who did not believe as he believed to becoming one who disregarded all social and religious barriers, who invited all people into the loving embrace of God. The readings for today show us that the reign of God knows no boundaries. The lesson to be learned is that disciples of that reign must have the same kind of openness.

Ordinary Time (Part Two)

Eleventh Sunday **2 Samuel 12:7-10, 13** The sword shall not depart from your house	**Psalm 32:1-2, 5, 7, 11** Forgive my sin	**Galatians 2:16, 19-21** Christ lives in me	**Luke 7:36–8:3** Her sins are forgiven
Twelfth Sunday **Zechariah 12:10-11; 13:1** Look on him whom they pierced	**Psalm 63:2-6, 8-9** My soul is thirsting for you	**Galatians 3:26-29** We are all children of God	**Luke 9:18-24** You are the Christ
Thirteenth Sunday **1 Kings 19:16b, 19-21** Elisha followed Elijah	**Psalm 16:1-2, 5, 7-11** You are my inheritance	**Galatians 5:1, 13-18** Called for freedom	**Luke 9:51-62** I will follow you wherever you go
Fourteenth Sunday **Isaiah 66:10-14c** Rejoice with Jerusalem	**Psalm 66:1-7, 16, 20** Let all the earth cry out with joy	**Galatians 6:14-18** I bear the marks of Christ on my body	**Luke 10:1-12, 17-20** He appointed seventy-two
Fifteenth Sunday **Deuteronomy 30:10-14** The word is very near to you	**Psalm 69:14, 17, 30-31, 33-34, 36-37** Turn to the LORD or **Psalm 19:8-11** The law is perfect	**Colossians 1:15-20** Firstborn of creation	**Luke 10:25-37** Who is my neighbor

Sixteenth Sunday **Genesis 18:1-10a** Visitors to Abraham	**Psalm 15:2-5** Walk blamelessly	**Colossians 1:24-28** The mystery hidden	**Luke 10:38-42** Martha and Mary
Seventeenth Sunday **Genesis 18:20-32** Abraham intercedes	**Psalm 138:1-3, 6-8** You answered me	**Colossians 2:12-14** Raised with him through faith	**Luke 11:1-13** Ask and you will receive
Eighteenth Sunday **Ecclesiastes 1:2; 2:21-23** What profit comes from toil	**Psalm 90:3-6, 12-13** Harden not your heart	**Colossians 3:1-5, 9-11** Seek what is above	**Luke 12:13-21** Store up treasures in heaven

Ordinary Time (Part Two)

Initial Reading of the Ordinary Lectionary (Part Two)

Introduction

The initial readings for this segment of Ordinary Time continue the focus on discipleship. We may think the themes associated with this topic are not so engaging because they are often basic instructions. However, it is in this teaching that we discover what it means to be a follower of Jesus, and such instruction is always challenging. In these Sundays we will see what constitutes a disciple, what is expected of a disciple, and what might be exacted of a disciple.

First Testament Readings

The readings from the First Testament could be considered a random listing of "do's and don'ts" of a disciple. The first narrative would be subtitled: "Do not think that you are above the law." No one, not even the chosen King David, was exempt from obedience to it. When confronted with his sin, he did repent. We see on the Twelfth and the Fourteenth Sundays that the chastised house of David was promised eventual reestablishment, and that promise was fulfilled in the restoration of the city of Jerusalem. Those chosen by God have a serious responsibility to be faithful. Elisha shows disciples what to do: Commit yourself wholeheartedly. Whenever we may think this is too much to ask because we are not sure we can be faithful, Moses assures us that the law is really not as hard to follow as we are inclined to imagine.

The lessons of the last three Sundays are straightforward. As disciples, we are expected to be openhearted, to accept people as they come to us. As disciples, we will find ourselves called up to intercede for others, even presuming on our own relationship with God if need be. And finally, as disciples, we ourselves must realize the transitoriness of all earthly things. Our fundamental commitment must be to God.

Psalms

The psalm responses for this segment of Ordinary Time include most of the major categories of psalms. There are hymns of praise of God and gratitude that God has saved the psalmist from enemies and from the punishment of sin. There are prayers that express confidence that God will continue to protect the psalmist from danger. There is a Wisdom psalm that includes instruction for success in life, and there is an entrance liturgy that was probably used in Israel's cultic celebration. Finally, there is a lament that cries out for help in distress. These are all sentiments that spring spontaneously from the events of life. They are all sentiments that are part of the devotional response of disciples.

Epistles

The continuous reading, first from the letter to the Galatians and then from the letter to the Colossians, allows us carefully to trace the teachings of Paul to these two Christian communities. In Galatians Paul is intent on showing that faith in Christ is what justifies us, not faith plus observance of the law. Because his teaching about the law is so radically different from that of other Christians who insisted on its salvific power, Paul had to demonstrate the legitimacy of his discipleship. Today we may find ourselves in similar internal disputes. It is important that we have theological grounding for the positions that we hold.

In Colossians Paul situates discipleship squarely at the feet of his christology. In Colossians this is a "high christology." Christ is the firstborn of creation as well as the firstborn of the dead. Joined to him, we share in his exalted status. We are raised to new life with him in faith, and we live this new life with him in God.

Gospels

As the gospel readings recount the public ministry of Jesus, they also uncover the contours of discipleship. The disciple is one who is intent on serving the Lord regardless of the criticism, whether silent or spoken, from those who either do not understand or who do not approve. One's discipleship is shaped by the way one perceives Jesus. He clearly stated that he would suffer greatly, and those who would follow him should be prepared for the same fate. Their lives would be uncertain, and they might have to readjust their priorities. There would be no other way; commitment to follow him must be total.

Those who accept the challenge will participate in his ministry. Like him, they will know both success and failure. They will be called on to love with all their hearts and with all their beings. They will be called on to love people they don't particularly like or who don't particularly like them. They will be expected to serve unselfishly but in their service not to lose sight of their priorities. Disciples will find that they constantly turn to God in prayer for the needs of those they serve. And finally, like everyone else, they will have to learn that the value of committed life is in the authentic living of it, not in the goods we may have amassed, whatever these goods may be. The fundamental charge of the disciple is to proclaim by word and example that the only good in life that endures is commitment to God in Christ.

Mosaic of Readings

These readings create a mosaic of brilliant colors and muted hues. The boldest colors draw us to the divine nature of Christ. This is reflected in the picture of the historical Jesus that is sketched. In the shadow of the figure of the Lord we see the disciples, called to participate in the life of Christ and to further the establishment of the reign of God. As the disciples become more and more like their Lord, their ministry and life become more and more brilliant in color.

Readings

Eleventh Sunday in Ordinary Time

2 Samuel 12:7-10, 13

The major part of this reading is a prophetic oracle ("Thus says the LORD") delivered from God through the prophet Nathan to David the king. In the last verse David acknowledges his guilt and Nathan assures him he will not die for his sin. This is not to say there will be no punishment. Quite the contrary. In a very real sense, the punishment will fit the crime. Several themes are woven together to create a picture of the heinousness of David's sin. Most obvious are his lust and the murder he perpetrates. The indictment by Nathan clearly sketches the course of these events. However, there are also the issues of royal ascendancy and privilege. Perhaps most important is the question of the continuation of the bloodline.

David is reminded of the blessings God has bestowed upon him. It is clear the king's success was the work of God and not his own doing (vv. 7-8; cf. 2 Sam 7:8-9a). One practice listed among these blessings that is disturbing to contemporary readers is the transfer of the wives of Saul to David. Since inheritance of the land and property of a society or clan are essential for the survival of that group, it is important to guard vigilantly the inheritance rights. In patrilineal societies, as ancient Israel seems to have been, women of childbearing age were protected not for their own sake but in order to assure that the kinship line would be kept pure and there would be no question about lineage.

One way men established themselves as victorious over other men or over entire tribes of people was to violate the women of these people. In this way the inheritance rights of the offspring would be questioned and the estate might be alienated. Taking the wives of Saul may have been one way of showing that he, David, had not only captured the throne but had undermined the kinship structure of the previous king. He would then certainly be in charge.

When David took the wife of Uriah, he not only committed adultery with her, but he also cut off Uriah's line of descent. Uriah's murder merely brought this fact to completion. This meant that with no descendants Uriah's name would not endure into the next generation, his bloodline would dry up, and his property could be confiscated. With his adultery David destroyed an entire family. He abused his royal privilege with regard to both Uriah and his wife. He took the woman as one would take a possession, and he had Uriah cut down. The fact that the blessings of God are enumerated in the beginning suggests that the true sin against God is the king's desire to determine the future of the monarchy rather than allow God to direct it through him. Since descent was an important factor in David's sin, it will also play a major role in his punishment. As through intrigue and violence he cut off the bloodline of Uriah, so the history of his own bloodline will be one of intrigue and violence.

This episode reveals the precarious position women held in a society like the one depicted here. Their procreative potential made them both cherished and vulnerable. Some biblical accounts portray their strength in this area. This story highlights their vulnerability. The unimportance of the woman in question is demonstrated in the fact that she is not even named. Instead, she is identified as the wife of Uriah, evidence that male dominance and descent are a primary issue.

Finally, the punishment shows clearly that in Israel, unlike in most of the other nations of the ancient world, the king was not above the law. He may have been chosen by God and lavished with blessings, but he was still accountable to the law like every other Israelite.

Psalm 32:1-2, 5, 7, 11

The psalm response comes from one of the seven psalms known in Christian devotion as the Penitential Psalms. Though cast in the form of a thanksgiving, it might be more accurately considered a Wisdom psalm. It opens with a double macarism ("blessed" or "happy"), a literary form identified with the

Wisdom tradition. In a unique way this form highlights something of the value system of Israel (or of Christianity; cf. Matt 5:3-12; Luke 6:20-22). It states the *real* basis of happiness, as opposed to what might be conventionally considered desirable. More frequently than not, the macarisms are counter-cultural, challenging the merit of customary aspirations. The macarisms in this psalm response exemplify this.

The double statement of blessedness introduces a Wisdom teaching about the benefits of God's merciful pardon, something valued more highly than prosperity or reputation. In it the psalmist gives a triple description of sin and of the forgiveness God grants if there is repentance. "Fault" *(peshaᶜ)* is really rebellion, a rejection of God's authority. Through the mercy of God this rebellion has been "lifted up" *(nāśāʾ);* the burden has been taken from the shoulders of the sinner. "Sin" *(ḥăṭāʾâ)* means "failure" or "missing the mark." This failure to measure up is covered up *(kāsâ)* by God. "Guilt" *(ʿāwōn)* also means "iniquity" or "perversion." God does not pass judgment *(ḥāshab)* on whether or not the psalmist is sinful or perverse.

The psalmist declares that anyone so treated by God is truly blessed. God has protected the psalmist. However, this is not an example of "cheap grace." This blessing of forgiveness is not given indiscriminately. Rather, it is given to those who have honestly sought forgiveness, who have admitted their sinfulness and have repented of it. It is clear the psalmist is such a person (v. 5). Using some of the vocabulary found in the macarisms, the psalmist acknowledges sin, does not try to cover up guilt, and admits fault. Accordingly, God took away the guilt of the psalmist's sin. It appears that the objective description of the "blessed" is really a personal testimony of the psalmist's own experience of sin, repentance, and forgiveness.

The response ends with an exhortation to rejoice. Just as it had begun with the theme of happiness, so it closes with exultation. As with the discussion about divine mercy, so with this call to rejoice; it applies only to those who are righteous or upright in heart. However, if one is just, then rejoicing is not only encouraged, it may be a spontaneous response to God's magnanimous mercy.

Wisdom teaching consists of the insights into life gained by reflection on experience, insights that may have come from personal experience but that can be applicable for many. The teaching in this psalm response fits into this category. The psalmist's experience of personal contrition and divine clemency is offered as an example for others to follow.

Galatians 2:16, 19-21

This passage is a kind of summary statement of Paul's teaching about justification through faith in Jesus Christ. In it he contrasts the limitations of observance of the law with the power of the death and resurrection of Christ. His extensive discussion of the law suggests his hearers were Jewish Christians, women and men who, like him, knew the importance the Jewish tradition placed on observance of the law. However, with an allusion to a passage from a psalm, Paul reminds them that even that revered tradition questioned whether a person could be justified before God in any way at all (cf. Ps 143:2).

Israel believed that the law had been delivered to Moses by God. It was a teacher, a guide that pointed the way to the will of God. However, by itself it could not justify. Faith in Jesus, on the other hand, could justify, not because of the act of faith itself but because of the salvific act of Jesus. Obedient to the will of God, Jesus faithfully handed himself over to death. Paul insists that commitment to Jesus in faith is the way believers participate in his sacrifice and in his triumph. It is in this way that faith in Jesus Christ justifies.

Paul's argument may seem to be rather complicated. Everything depends upon faith in the power of Jesus to transcend the law. Jesus was faithful to the law during his lifetime. However, in death he moved out of the realm of the law, and by his resurrection he moved beyond it. Those who in faith join themselves to this risen Lord also move beyond the realm of the law. They no longer live in a world dominated by law but are now governed by faith. Crucified with Christ, they die to the law through the death of Jesus; joined to Jesus, they live for God through the resurrection of Jesus. According to Paul, his union with Christ is so intimate and so complete, that he, Paul, is really no longer living. It is the life and power of Christ that now lives in him, moves him, determines his actions, and shapes his attitudes.

Here Paul uses flesh *(sárx)* to refer to that aspect of human nature that is most susceptible to sin. Flesh is not evil in itself, but it is vulnerable to evil. Paul declares that while he is still living this vulnerable life, he lives it by faith in the Son of God. With this christological statement he traces the salvific power that has transformed his life, through Christ, back to God. It is the power of the Son of God that enables Paul to live a life for God. Arguing in this way, he insists that faith in Jesus in no way nullifies the grace of God. Either justification comes through the law, and then Christ died in vain; or justification comes through faith in Jesus Christ, and then life according to the law has been transcended.

Luke 7:36–8:3

There are two distinct parts to this reading. The first and more prominent one is an account of a specific episode in the life of Jesus (7:36, 50). The second is a summary statement of Jesus' ministry that names some of the women who accompanied him (8:1-3). The primary focus of the account is christological: Who is this who even forgives sins? In it, contrast is drawn between Simon, a respected Pharisee, and an unnamed woman who is publicly known as a sinner.

The social customs detailed within the story all serve the theological lesson Jesus teaches.

The dinner must have been either a banquet or a Sabbath meal, because those eating were reclining. This was the kind of table etiquette observed on special occasions. The woman had a reputation as a sinner, so Simon would not have invited her; yet she seems to have had free access to the dinner, suggesting it was not a strictly private affair. She was indeed a sinner, even Jesus admitted this, though her sin is not explicitly identified. Her demeanor suggests it was somehow sexual, for a respectable woman would not be unaccompanied, would not approach or touch a strange man, and would not loosen her hair in public. Jesus does not rebuff her, so Simon concludes that he does not know she is a sinner and, consequently, that he could not be a prophet. The parable Jesus teaches shows he not only knew she was a sinner, but he also knew Simon's thoughts. Furthermore, as a true prophet he does not reject the repentant sinner but assures her of salvation.

Jesus has Simon himself explain the meaning of the parable, and then he uses that meaning to contrast the attitudes toward him of both Simon and the woman. Though Simon had invited Jesus to the dinner, he had not provided a slave to wash the dust of the road from his feet; he had not given him a kiss of welcome; he had not anointed his head with olive oil. What Simon had omitted to do, although required according to the spirit of simple hospitality, this woman had extravagantly performed out of a spirit of repentance. She may have owed a great debt, but the parable implies that it had been forgiven, and her tears of remorse, kissing his feet, and anointing them with precious ointment demonstrate the degree of her gratitude.

When Jesus assured the woman her sins had been forgiven, those at table wondered about him. Their amazement stemmed from what they had heard. We do not know Simon's response, but he might have been doubly amazed, for he must have detected from the focus of the parable that Jesus had known his host's thoughts from the very beginning. Jesus' last words to the woman reveal the progression of her transformation: her faith was the basis of her love, which was demonstrated in her contrition.

There is a subtle but significant theological tension in this narrative between love and forgiveness. The point of the parable was that the one who had been forgiven much loved much in return. Love was the response to forgiveness. The woman, on the other hand, was forgiven because she loved much. Love seems to have been the reason for forgiveness. Lest we think forgiveness is earned, we must remember that the woman was present at Simon's house because she came to see Jesus. Her demeanor suggests she had already heard of his power to forgive. In her case, repentance precedes forgiveness.

This account is followed by a summary of Jesus' ministry and mention of the names of some who accompanied him. It is interesting that the only ones explicitly named are women. Some, not all, of these women followed Jesus after having been cured by him. We should not think of them stereotypically as women who merely take care of men. These were women of means who were his patrons, providing for Jesus and the others out of their own resources.

Themes of the Day

The themes of sin, repentance, forgiveness, and service dominate the readings for this Sunday. The narratives engage us because they are so boldly told but also because the truth they tell touches our own lives so deeply.

Naming Sin

Although the journey toward salvation is initiated by God and everything we need on that journey is supplied by God, salvation itself is never forced upon us. If we are to be saved, we must first acknowledge our need. If we are to be forgiven, we must first admit our sin. As strange as it may seem, such acknowledgment and such admission are difficult to acquire. Children seem able to acknowledge their need, but they too have difficulty admitting their error. But if we cannot admit our sin, we will not be able to acknowledge the magnanimous goodness of God in forgiving us. We will not be able to be grateful for the mercy shown us. Naming our sin before God is our first step toward reconciliation. In fact, we can only admit our sin and acknowledge God's mercy because that mercy has taken a step toward reconciliation even before we have taken ours. God's goodness toward us precedes any contrition on our part.

No sin once admitted is beyond the forgiveness of God. David violated the wife of Uriah, cut off his bloodline, and had him killed. Although he was punished, once he admitted his guilt there was no thought of his not being forgiven. The woman who came to Jesus demonstrated her contrition publicly, and Jesus publicly announced her forgiveness. We see the same dynamic in the psalm response. Although admission of sin may seem to the sinner an almost insurmountable obstacle, it is a very small thing compared to the overwhelming flood of mercy it will unleash. What is it that keeps us from opening the floodgates of this mercy?

Naming Grace

The corollary to admitting our sin is acknowledging the source of the grace of salvation. It is clear in both narratives that God is the one who assures the repentant sinner of forgiveness. Paul is insistent about this. We are not justified, we are not reconciled to God through our own works. We do not earn our salvation. It is granted to us through faith in Christ, which itself is a gift from God. Here the apparent tension seen in the gospel narrative takes the form of a question: Do we love because we are forgiven, or are we forgiven because we first love? Because of his struggle with those who claimed that observance of the law was essential for salvation, Paul was the one who most strenuously argued that forgiveness is never earned. We are not forgiven because we love. We are forgiven because we are loved. Repentance may precede forgiveness, but even repentance is a grace offered by God.

Gratitude Expressed Through Service

There is no way we can repay God for the magnanimous mercy shown to us. However, gratitude is often expressed through service of others. This is demonstrated in the gospel narrative. The repentant woman was possessed by a desire to serve, regardless of the fact that her actions were censured. Her service took the form of humble hospitality. The women who accompanied Jesus and his group also served. They provided for the group out of their means. How do we show our gratitude for having been forgiven? Do we realize that the reconciliation with God that we enjoy makes us ambassadors of reconciliation for others? Do we do what we can, give what we have, to further the ministry of reconciliation?

Twelfth Sunday in Ordinary Time
Zechariah 12:10-11; 13:1

This short reading is part of a prophetic oracle. Although the speaker is not identified in these few verses, it is clear that it is the LORD. The oracle itself contains elements of judgment and lament as well as of hope and salvation. The day to which the prophet refers is probably the Day of the LORD, that eschatological or future time of reckoning when the guilty will be punished for their sins and the righteous will be rewarded. It will be a time when all social and moral disorder will be corrected and the world will be under the salvific reign of God. This oracle seems to suggest that the people of Judah will experience this day first as a time of great mourning (v. 11) and then as a time of salvation (3:1). The Hebrew construction of this section is difficult to decipher. Some translate it to say the one who was pierced looks upon the speaker. Most commentators translate it to say those who did the piercing look upon the one pierced. The latter version is the one followed here.

The reason for the lamentation is the recognition of sin. By the grace of God both the Davidic monarchy and the general population of the city of Jerusalem are brought to see their culpability. They are responsible for the harm done to some man. Though not explicitly stated, the verb ("pierced") and the following description suggest the man died as a result of his wound. There is much conjecture as to the identity of this individual. He may have been an actual historical person, or the reference could be to an eschatological figure (cf. Isa 53:5). Whoever it may be, the focus of the reading is less on the victim than on the grief experienced by the perpetrators of the crime against him.

Realizing the gravity of their transgression, the offenders mourn with overwhelming grief, the kind of grief brought on by the death of a firstborn or an only son (cf. Gen 22:2; 2 Kgs 3:27). Such grief arises from more than profound emotional attachment to a child. This is the child on whom hang the hopes of the future of the patriarchal family. This is the one who will carry the bloodline into the next generation. This child *is* the next generation. To mourn such a child is to grieve the irretrievable loss of one's future.

This grief is further characterized in two other ways. First, it is compared with the kind of sorrow that comes when political hopes are dashed. This is seen in the reference to Megiddo. It was there in 609 B.C.E. that the young king Josiah was killed, and the hopes of a people died with him. His death plunged the nation into all-encompassing grief. Most commentators believe the second reference is cultic. Hadad and Rimmon were Syrian nature deities. Each year at the end of the growing season their demise was ceremonially mourned. Life had left the earth and the people were bereft, so within the context of the cult they allowed intense feelings of loss to overpower them. These images give us some idea of the degree of suffering and remorse felt by those responsible for the agony of the one pierced.

The oracle does not end on such a somber note. On the Day of the Lord the royal establishment and the inhabitants of Jerusalem will be blessed with water that will wash away their impurities. The fountain gives off moving or living water, not static or dead water. Those who were found guilty in the first part of the oracle are here cleansed. Judgment has turned into salvation.

Psalm 63:2, 3-4, 5-6, 8-9

Three religious sentiments are present in this psalm of confidence. It begins with expressions of longing, followed by a short hymn of praise, and concluding with words of confidence. "Flesh" *(bāśār)* and "soul" *(nepesh)* are two dimensions of a human being that constitute the totality of that person (cf. Gen 2:2). The metaphor used to portray the intensity of the psalmist's longing is arid land. This metaphor not only makes the longing concrete, it also suggests that the need for an experience of God is as natural and basic to a human being as water is essential for life itself. Without such an experience the person is devoid of the source of life, just as parched land is devoid of the source of its life.

Several elements of this passage suggest its setting is cultic or somehow liturgical. Most obvious is mention of the sanctuary. Added to this is a description of the psalmist praying with uplifted hands, a traditional stance of prayer. The prayer itself (calling upon God's name) could be offered anywhere, at any time, so it is not explicitly liturgical. However, given the other cultic features it certainly can be understood in this way. The verb for "seek" (v. 2) might be better translated "seek early," suggesting early morning prayer after keeping a night vigil. Finally, the psalmist actually does pray for some kind of theophany, a physical manifestation of God (v. 3) that would take the form of divine power (*'ōz*) and glory *(kābôd)*.

The psalmist contrasts the arid life without God with the sumptuous life with God. The satisfaction that comes with the experience of God is compared to marrow of bone and fatness of flesh, parts of an animal that are not only tasty but also contain life-giving properties. While in reality such a rich banquet satisfies the physical need, it is to be understood here figuratively as characterizing the satisfaction the soul experiences. Regardless of the importance of life and the joys one might receive when that life is lived in union with God, the psalmist insists that the covenant bond of lovingkindness *(hesed)* is more precious than life itself. Actually, the psalmist's trust in being heard by God is rooted in this covenantal bond.

The passage ends with several images that characterize the psalmist's trust in God. First, God is proclaimed the psalmist's help *('ēzer)*. This is not a hope for the future but rather a present experience. Next, the text depicts the psalmist under God's protective wings, a reference to the eagle that spreads its wings over its young. Finally, the psalmist clings to God and is upheld by God's right hand, a stereotype that signifies God's power. The psalmist has turned to God for life and security, and God has responded with the requested protection.

Galatians 3:26-29

With bold strokes Paul redefines the relationships that exist among all those who have been baptized into Christ. The context for understanding this is the Israelite concept of children of God. The Jews always took great pride in claiming that through Abraham they were indeed God's chosen children. They further believed their physical descent from this ancestor would entitle them to the promises God made to him long ago. Paul neither denigrates this ancestry nor regards as revoked the promise associated with it. Rather, he argues that physical descent from Abraham no longer determines lineage or guarantees the right of inheritance. Faith in Christ does.

Paul insists that through baptism the Galatians have entered into a new form of life, a life in Christ. During the baptismal ceremony they symbolized this by removing the clothing of their old existence and donning the white baptismal robes. A reference to this ritual is probably behind Paul's statement about putting on Christ as one would put on a garment. The garment was an external sign of a profound internal transformation. In this new life former social distinctions are reinterpreted, and so the racial, class, and gender discriminations of the past have been erased. There are still distinctions, but they do not benefit some to the disadvantage of others.

Whether or not being children of God gave the Jews status in the broader society, in their minds it was the distinguishing trait that set them apart from the other nations. This distinctive lineage was handed down from generation to generation through the patrilineal bloodline. However, with faith in Christ any privilege that came with physical descent vanished. Once they had been delivered by their God from Egyptian bondage, the Israelites clung tenaciously to the idea of being free. While they themselves occasionally held slaves, it would be unthinkable that an Israelite would be so bound, since slaves of any origin were degraded. However, with faith in Christ, any sense of superiority associated with freedom vanished. In androcentric societies what is male is the norm and what is female is considered either secondary or totally insignificant. Whatever right or privilege a woman enjoyed, she did so because of her connection with an adult man, either her father and at his death her brother, or her husband and at his death her son. With faith in Christ, the privilege that came with gender vanished.

All those baptized into Christ were one with Christ and thereby one with each other. In fact, they were as if one body. Paul is not naive about the genuine differences that are present in any group. Not only are individuals unique, they contribute to the group in various ways. However, these differences do not constitute exclusive classes within the community. All are true children of God; all are genuine descendants of Abraham; all are heirs to the promises made by God. The Christian community is an inclusive group, embracing even those people the broader society has relegated to its margins.

Luke 9:18-24

The passage consists of the confession of Peter and a prediction by Jesus of his passion, death, and resurrection. The christological focus is obvious. Jesus first asks who the crowds think he is and then who the disciples think he is. Only after hearing the misconceptions of others does he reveal something about his true identity.

By the time of Jesus there were several prominent messianic traditions. Chief among them were royal (son of David), priestly, and apocalyptic (Son of Man). The crowds seem to have thought he was a prophetic figure. The structure of the Greek, "But who do you say?" suggests the disciples should think otherwise. Acting as spokesperson of the group, Peter shows that they do: You are the Christ of God! "Christ" *(christós)* means "anointed one, Messiah." Peter's confession declares Jesus to be the long-awaited one. He further identifies him as the Christ of God, the one who is anointed by, or of, or for, God. Jesus is the one promised by God and now sent by God. In response to Peter's testimony, Jesus charges the disciples to reveal his true identity to no one. This is probably because if the people have so misunderstood his identity, they would no doubt have significant misconceptions about the role of the Messiah. They were, after all, an occupied people, and they might expect that the anointed of God would be a political leader who would free them from the subjugation of the Romans.

Messianic misunderstanding could well be the reason Jesus first associated himself with the Son of Man tradition rather than that of the royal Davidic king, and then went even further in his self-revelation, predicting his own suffering, death, and resurrection. This prediction shows that the rejection and crucifixion Jesus would endure were not mistakes but, as difficult as it was to fathom, were part of the very plan of God.

Mention of the elders, chief priests, and scribes is significant. They were three groups that constituted the Sanhedrin, the highest court of the Jewish nation, which, with permission from Rome, was allowed to exercise religious authority. We must be careful how we interpret this passage. Too often the opposition of these people to Jesus has led to anti-Judaism rather than being seen as a way of showing that Jesus was rejected for religious as well as political reasons. The unrest he caused may well have been a political threat to Rome, and the bold claims he made greatly troubled the religious leaders.

The passage ends with instruction for discipleship. Those who follow Jesus must, like him, deny themselves of self-interest and self-fulfillment. Those who take up the cross do so realizing their fate is sealed, since one never puts the cross down again. There is a play on the words "save" and "lose." Those who selfishly save themselves really lose themselves; while those who unselfishly lose themselves really save themselves. This is what following Jesus means.

Themes of the Day

As disciples we often wonder who we are. We look at ourselves in order to discover our identities, when actually we should look first to Christ in order to discover who it is we are serving. This will influence the kind of disciples we will be.

Who Do You Say I Am?

This was a determining question for the disciples, and it is a determining question for us as well. Though he was a descendant of David, though he sprang from the root of Jesse, he refused to be seen as a political Messiah. He was put to death by those in power, but he himself was not part of the power structure; he was not identified with any political party or faction. He came to establish the reign of God, which could exist within any or every political system but which was identified with none of them.

There was something very prophetic about Jesus. He called people to reform and he promised salvation, just as the prophets had. However, they proclaimed the word of God while he spoke from his own authority. He was more than a spokesperson. His message was not conditioned by the times in which he lived, as were the prophecies of the others. While it did address the present moment, it was the norm for all other times and determined all other teaching.

Jesus identified himself as a suffering Messiah. Though he referred to himself as the Son of Man, he aligned himself with the figure of the Suffering Servant found in Isaiah. He attracted people from every walk of life and from every political and social sector of the population. This is the christological image that will determine the character of our discipleship.

Who Are We as Disciples?

Since Jesus was not a political Messiah, his followers would always have to struggle with the vagaries and ambiguities of political power. Since he was more than a prophet, his followers would always have to struggle with the radical challenges and incomprehensible mysteries of and inevitable resistances to his teaching. However, he himself alerts them to the fact of their future suffering. He was rejected because he did not conform to political expectations and because of the radical nature of his teaching. Those who follow him can expect nothing less.

Jesus invited all people to follow him. Paul develops this notion more explicitly when he says that identification with Christ in discipleship breaks down the barriers set up in society by the differences between Jew and Greek, slave and free person, male and female. The privilege often associated with political classification is canceled. Not even disciples can claim privilege. This is the kind of Messiah Jesus was. This is the kind of discipleship to which we are called.

Thirteenth Sunday in Ordinary Time
1 Kings 19:16b, 19-21

This fast-moving story is an illustration of prophetic succession in ancient Israel. The spoken word was not the only way prophecy was handed on; certain symbolic action also carried prophetic meaning. The symbolic act by Elijah of throwing his cloak over Elisha is one such example. It can be interpreted in more than one way. It indicates that Elisha has been invested with the power and authority of Elijah. It also suggests that the kind of activity in which Elijah was engaged has come to an end and a new generation of prophets is on the horizon. Elijah, then, is a kind of precursor, a sign of what is to come.

The names of the men are telling. They reflect the ministries they performed. Elijah, whose name means "my God *[El]* is the LORD *[jah],*" fought syncretism, insisting that the LORD and the LORD alone is God. The focus of the ministry of Elisha, whose name means "my God *[Eli]* saves *[sha],*" is the salvation God effects for the people. These ministries do not conflict each other. They actually complement each other, even though one chronologically succeeds the other.

Elisha is called while he is plowing a field, not unlike Saul, Israel's first king (cf. 1 Sam 11:5). He is either quite well-to-do, having twelve yoke of oxen, or he is part of a communal effort at agriculture, the oxen of individuals having been brought together for plowing. In either case, the story says that Elisha immediately left his plowing and eagerly ran after the prophet. He had no second thoughts about following his call. He only asked leave to say farewell to his parents. Kinship ties are very important in traditional societies like that of ancient Israel. To say good-bye has less to do with emotional attachment than to kinship responsibilities. It is important to note that both father and mother are mentioned. This might reflect the kind of lineality operative within the group.

This account describes the conflict that exists between two fundamental responsibilities: fidelity to the call from God and fidelity to one's primary family obligations. Elijah does not grant Elisha permission to leave, but he does respond. His response may sound harsh, but it is no harsher than that of Jesus, as we read in today's gospel. In fact, it is not even as harsh. However, the implications are demanding. Elisha has been commissioned by God to be a prophet, and it is up to him to decide whether or not he can make the radical break from the past that this commission requires. His response is wholehearted. His slaughter of the oxen and his destruction of the plowing equipment were symbolic acts of severing his ties with his past. He was now totally committed to the ministry of the people. He demonstrates this by feeding them. The narrative ends with Elisha in a subservient position. Though he had been commissioned as Elijah's successor, he would first minister to him as attendant. It would seem that his time of independent prophetic activity had not yet come.

Psalm 16:1-2, 5, 7-8, 9-10, 11

This psalm of confidence opens with a declaration of trust that God will protect the psalmist from danger (v. 1) and ultimately from death (v. 10). A confession of faith follows: The LORD is the only God for the psalmist. The psalm speaks of a covenant relationship with God and the confidence that redounds from it.

Two images express this relationship. The allotted portion of land is the inheritance each tribe was given and which was handed down within the tribes generation after generation. This land provided the people identity and membership, sustenance and prosperity. Without land they had no future, and they would not last long in the present. Here the psalmist is claiming that God has replaced the land in the religious consciousness of the people; the blessings and promises customarily associated with land are now associated with the LORD. Furthermore, this portion of the inheritance is safe, for it is the LORD who holds it fast.

The second image is the cup. This may refer to the cup passed around from which all drank. Such an action solidified the union of those who drank from the common cup. When this action took place at a cultic meal, those participating in the feast were joined not only to one another but to the deity as well. The psalmist declares that the unifying cup of which he speaks is really the LORD. In other words, the psalmist is joined so closely with God as almost to defy separation.

Three strong features suggest that the context of this psalm is the cult. The psalmist is counseled by the LORD. This could refer to the practice of a worshiper approaching a priest in order to receive counsel in a particular matter. A second feature is mention of prayer at night. This is probably an allusion to night vigil, the devotional ritual of spending the entire night at the sanctuary or in the Temple praying for a favor from God. Finally, the psalmist mentions the joy that is experienced in the presence of the LORD, what might be considered another allusion to the sanctuary. The psalmist clearly respects the importance of the cultic practices of the people.

The psalmist's entire being is filled with confidence and gladness. Two major dimensions of the human person are joined in order to demonstrate the comprehensiveness of the psalmist. They are the heart, which, understood figuratively, refers to the inner or spiritual dimension of the person, and the flesh, the physical or exterior dimension of the person. The reason for this rejoicing is the rescue from death that God granted the psalmist. Regardless of the fact that Christians consider these as strong proleptic references to resurrection, the psalmist was probably merely thinking of being rescued *from* death, rather than *after* death.

The protection represented in these verses is reason for profound rejoicing. Regardless of the terrifying, even life-threatening ordeals that must be endured, the psalmist proclaims that God is steadfast. In such difficult circumstances this kind of confidence in God may appear to be foolhardy, but the psalmist's trust is unshakable. Ultimately the fullness of joys will abound in the presence of God.

Galatians 5:1, 13-18

This reading is a discourse on the nature of Christian freedom. Paul introduces it with a statement containing both an assertion and a command based
on that assertion. It is an indicative followed by an imperative: because you are
. . . therefore be! The indicative assertion does not merely proclaim Christian
freedom, it also states that Christians have been freed for the sake of freedom
itself. In other words, Christ did not free them from one form of bondage only
to have them submit themselves to another. This is clearly stated in the imperative. They are told to stand fast in their freedom and not to allow themselves to
be bound again. This passage does not explicitly identify the slavery to which
Paul refers. However, mention of the law and the description of styles of living
indicate he is talking about ethical behavior.

The form of indicative followed by imperative has eschatological implications. The Christians are already free, but they are not yet totally free. It is not
merely that they could lose their freedom, though this is clearly a possibility.
Rather, the reason they might lose it is that, though freed by Christ, they are
not yet completely free within themselves. Habits of mind and heart, addictions of all kinds, retain their hold even after they are renounced. Freedom itself is a frightening thing because it requires the willing renunciation of
whatever compensations people have cultivated in order to cope with those
habits that enslave them. Paul realized this, so he exhorts the Galatians to
stand fast in their freedom.

Having warned the Galatians against reverting to some form of slavery
after being set free by Christ, Paul next addresses the opposite inclination. He
insists that the freedom to which the Galatians have been called is not an invitation to license. It is not an opportunity for throwing off all moral restraint
and indulging in some form of libertinism. Though no longer under the
bondage of the law, they are not free to live lawless lives. In fact, they are expected to "love your neighbor as yourself" (cf. Lev 19:18). Though not slaves
of the law, they should be servants of one another in love. In this way, though
they may not accomplish all that the law requires, they will have fulfilled all
that the law intends.

Paul contrasts life lived in the Spirit with life lived in the flesh. Elsewhere
he uses "flesh" in several different ways, but here he is referring to that aspect
of human nature considered susceptible to evil. While not itself sinful, because
of its vulnerability it is inclined toward sin. The flesh is often contrasted with
the spirit, that aspect of human nature associated with the spiritual realm, the
realm of God. It is this spiritual dimension of the human being that is joined
with the Spirit of God. In this passage it is not always clear whether Paul is
speaking of the spirit of the person or the Spirit of God. What is clear is his assertion that if the Galatians are guided by the Spirit of God, they will not be
enslaved by the law.

Jewish anthropology of the day maintained that the inclination toward good, which resided in the spirit, and the inclination toward evil, which resided in the flesh, were in constant contention within the human being. It is this inner struggle Paul has in mind. He insists that if, through a false sense of freedom, the Galatians give in to the inclinations of the flesh, they will eventually destroy one another. However, if they serve one another in love, they will live lives of genuine freedom guided by the Spirit of God.

Luke 9:51-62

Jesus' journey through the territory of the Samaritans contains several subtle allusions to the prophet Elijah. The account begins with a reference to Jesus being taken up just as the ancient prophet was (cf. 2 Kgs 2:11). While this may not have the exact meaning in each case, the phrase in Luke's Gospel would recall the similar phrase in the book of Kings. When the Samaritans refused to welcome Jesus and his company, James and John suggested that Jesus call down fire from heaven, just as Elijah had done when the enemies of Israel approached the prophet (cf. 2 Kgs 1:10). Finally, long before someone asked to say farewell to parents before following Jesus, the same request was made of Elijah by Elisha, his disciple (1 Kgs 19:20). Perhaps the author of this gospel is trying to show that Jesus transcends the expectations associated with the great prophet of ancient Israel.

The antagonism the Samaritans felt toward the Jews can be traced all the way back to the return of the Jews from the exile in Babylon (ca. 536 B.C.E.). Because some of the people in the district of Samaria had remained in the land during the period of exile and had intermarried with foreigners who lived in the vicinity, the returning Jews considered them social and religious half-breeds and, consequently, culticly unclean. For this reason they were kept from helping with the rebuilding of the Temple in Jerusalem. In reaction to this, the Samaritans built their own temple. Although the Jews later destroyed it, the Samaritans continued to worship God on Mount Gerizim, an action the Jews considered illegitimate. This explains why the Samaritans refused to show hospitality to Jews who traveled through Samaria on their way to worship in Jerusalem.

A second and unrelated episode follows this account. In it we see someone step forward and offer to follow Jesus, and later two others are called by Jesus to be disciples. The attitude of these three toward discipleship and Jesus' response to them is revealing. The first enthusiastically offers commitment, the other two wish to postpone joining Jesus until they have put their immediate affairs in order. In each instance Jesus emphasizes the demands that discipleship will exact. With the first, Jesus points to the price commitment will require. A follower of Jesus must be willing to relinquish all. The example given to illustrate the degree of surrender required is the willingness to forgo the sense of belonging somewhere. Jesus underscores the same demand when responding to the other two individuals. To one he insists that even religious ceremonial customs must be set aside if need be when commitment to Jesus is at stake. With the other he maintains that not even family ties can take precedence over discipleship.

The advice to the first person seems to be contradicted by the advice given the other two. However, this contradiction is only apparent. Discipleship does require wholehearted commitment to Jesus, but this commitment must be embraced realistically. While followers should be enthusiastic in their dedication, they should also be prepared to pay the price of wholehearted commitment.

Themes of the Day

Last Sunday we considered the cost of discipleship. Today we look more intently at some of the personal difficulties we might have to face as disciples. As members of societies and groups we have responsibilities toward the people who make up these groups. Jesus said we must "hate" them if we are to follow him. Surely he did not intend that we take this injunction literally. What happens to the responsibilities that are already ours when we follow the call to discipleship?

Wholehearted Commitment

There is no part-time discipleship. Our commitment must be wholehearted and complete. We must have a willing attitude that frees us interiorly from all other concerns so we might be able to follow Christ regardless of our state in life or our occupation. This attitude of commitment comes not merely from our own generosity of heart but also from our having been transformed into Christ through faith and baptism. With the psalmist we cling to God, who is our allotted portion and our cup. Such wholehearted commitment is an interior reality, not an exterior demonstration. It is not for the few; it is required of all.

The Cost of Discipleship

The readings for this Sunday invite us to meditate on the conflicts that face us when our various allegiances seem to clash. We may have family responsibilities. There are children to raise, elderly parents or infirm relatives to care for. What does discipleship require of us? We must earn a living. Are we expected to leave our employment to follow Jesus? And if so, what then will we do? All disciples must face the interior struggle caused by the conflict of legitimate responsibilities. The gospel draws the lines of such conflict with bold, even harsh, strokes. The commitment must be radical. But what does this imply?

Love Your Neighbor

The interior dilemma described above is resolved in the exhortation to love. The freedom of which Paul speaks is neither license nor halfhearted commitment. It is the freedom that comes with genuine love. If out of love we can negotiate successfully these conflicts caused by competing responsibilities without compromising our total commitment to Christ, we will find a new kind of freedom. This is the freedom that enables us to be faithful to both sets of responsibilities according to the proper priority. We will see that commitment to Christ is primary and the circumstances of our lives with the accompanying responsibilities set the parameters within which we live out our commitment. It is not in opposition with these responsibilities or despite them but by means of or through them that we live out our discipleship.

Fourteenth Sunday in Ordinary Time
Isaiah 66:10-14c

The first reading for today is an oracle of salvation ("Thus says the LORD"). The reason for the rejoicing is the future restoration of Jerusalem (v. 12). The ones called to rejoice are those who had previously mourned for the city (v. 10). The author adroitly employs the metaphor of motherhood to characterize the relationship that will exist between the city and its inhabitants as well as the loving care this relationship will provide. Like a nursing mother, Jerusalem will give of herself, feeding her inhabitants from the fullness of her own body. The Hebrew word for "comfort" or "consolation" *(tanḥûm)* comes from the root for "repent," "regret," "be sorry." It would seem that the people will be sorry and repent, and the city will then hold them to her bosom and comfort them. The very city for which they had previously mourned will comfort them! This is truly reason for rejoicing.

This touching maternal scene is interrupted for a moment, as God promises anew to lavish abundant blessing on Jerusalem. Using poetic parallelism and a second metaphor, the author once again depicts the city's life-giving properties. Water is essential for life in any part of the world, but especially in arid sectors. Since the land of Israel was bounded on several sides by deserts or barren wildernesses, the people would be keenly aware of their need for water. Flowing water, or water that was constantly being renewed by its source, was considered living water and came to be a symbol for life itself. The generous contributions of rivers or water torrents cannot be exaggerated. As they flow in their paths, they yield riches beyond imagination. They bring to the surface food of all kinds, and like a devoted mother they ask for nothing in return.

The author returns to the motherhood metaphor to illustrate the tenderness the city has for those who are her children. She carries them; she fondles them; she comforts them. We must remember that this is the same city for which the people mourned not so long ago. The contrast highlights the scope of the restoration accomplished by God. Jerusalem has gone from devastation to abundance. This is certainly reason for rejoicing.

After using the motherhood metaphor to represent the city's solicitude toward its inhabitants, the prophet next uses it to characterize the tenderness God will show to those who are in Jerusalem. Some today, who are so accustomed to think of God in exclusively male terms, might find this characterization bold, even shocking. The ancients seem to have been less restricted in their use of metaphors. What better way to describe the self-giving nature of God than as a nursing mother who protects and soothes and plays with her child? What is startling is not that the author would feature God in this way, but that God could be thought to possess such features.

The poet returns to the eschatological oracle. On the day Jerusalem is so transformed, the people will rejoice with their entire being, with their hearts and their bones *('esem)*. This will be a wonderful day. The power of God will shine forth from the restored city, and the People of God will rejoice.

Psalm 66:1-3, 4-5, 6-7, 16, 20

Today's responsorial psalm consists of two major parts. It begins with a three-fold summons to praise God followed by reasons for giving such praise (vv. 1, 7), and it ends with individual expressions of thanksgiving. Although the summons is directed to all the earth, it is clear from the content of the psalm that the intended audience was the people who dwelt in the lands. Each part of the summons adds a slightly different dimension to the praise that is sought. First, it is universal in scope; all the earth is called to praise the God of Israel. Second, the object of the praise is the name of God, which name identified the very essence of God. Third, the praise given to God is glorious, weighty, not to be dismissed casually. The psalmist then gives the reason for glorifying God in the first place. It is because of the wondrous feats God has accomplished.

The works of the God to whom the psalmist refers are the wonders God has accomplished in the history of Israel. Although the text leads one to believe the deeds were done for all women and men, the deeds mentioned are specific to Israel. It may be the psalmist believes that what was done explicitly for Israel would redound to the benefit of all. Using a literary form known as "merism" (the first in a list of several consecutive items represents all of the others), the author recalls Israel's history from its release from Egyptian bondage to its entrance into the land.

Since subduing chaotic waters was at the basis of all creation activity in the ancient Near Eastern creation tradition, historical water crossings always contained a dimension of creation. This bears out in the stories under consideration. It was in the wilderness that the motley group of slaves was fashioned into a nation. The water passages that frame this chapter in their history act as the boundaries in a rite of passage. At both ends of the chapter they moved from one stage of existence to another. Thus while the reference itself describes the historical event, it can serve to characterize any event of passage. This is certainly cause for praise. Furthermore, in the creation story, after the forces of evil have been vanquished, the victorious warrior is acclaimed king over all creation. Traces of this royal acclamation are found here (v. 7; cf. Exod 15:1-8).

The communal dimension of the first section of the responsorial psalm gives way to an individual focus. Perhaps it means that the psalmist benefits from the blessings bestowed on the nations. Or it may be that the psalmist has been a recipient of some particular individual blessing. In either case others are invited to join the psalmist in grateful praise of God.

Galatians 6:14-18

At first glance the reading appears to be a string of discrete sayings that have little or nothing to do with each other. A closer look will show this is not the case. Paul begins and ends with reference to suffering, first to the death of Jesus and then to the evidence on his own body of the sufferings he endured as a result of his commitment to Christ. We may not realize how shocking Paul's boast is unless we remember the ignominy of crucifixion. It was a degrading death reserved for slaves, violent criminals, and political rebels. It was not only an excruciating death, it was also a sign of ultimate defeat. Jesus died as a convicted felon, and it is in the sign of this death that Paul boasts. Paul evidently suffered greatly because of his commitment, and his body carried the marks of that suffering. Having boasted in the suffering of Christ, he then used his participation in that suffering as reason for forestalling opposition from others.

Paul moves step by step through his argument. First, he speaks about his relationship with the world. Although he uses "world" in several ways, here he means that aspect of human experience that is opposed to God. It is the old age of sin and rejection opposed to the new age of grace and fulfillment. A world where the cross is central is a world that has been turned upside down. Having been joined to the death and resurrection of Jesus, Paul has struck a death blow to the world and its system of values, and that world is now dead to him.

Next he treats the question of circumcision. This was the ritual act that symbolized membership in the People of God. It separated Jew from Gentile and men from women. Here Paul insists it really makes no difference whether one is circumcised or not. The age of fulfillment has come and brought with it a new creation. Faith in the power of the cross of Jesus is the sign of membership in the People of God. Thus women and men from every race and ethnic origin are welcome in this community. Paul pleads for peace and mercy for all who accept this rule or principle. Commentators disagree about the meaning of the conjunction "and" and therefore about the identity of the Israel of God (v. 18). Is it an appositive of those who accept this teaching (enlightened Christians?)? Does it mean the Jewish community? Mention of a new creation suggest it is a reference to the eschatological community.

The passage concludes with a traditional prayer of benediction, which is also a profound christological statement. It is a blessing of salvation that comes from Jesus Christ (the anointed one) who is the Lord. The blessing ends with the prayerful affirmation: Amen! So be it!

Luke 10:1-12, 17-20

The mission of the seventy-two disciples is symbolic of the ultimate mission to all the nations of the world (cf. Genesis 10). Although this reading alludes to the universality of the salvation Jesus brought, it is particularly concerned with the manner of life lived by the missionaries while on mission and the character of the success they experienced.

Jesus uses two metaphors to represent the mission: harvest, and lambs among wolves. Harvest connotes the readiness of the world for the ministry of the missionaries. This is a positive image suggesting that planting and growing have been accomplished. It only remains for the seventy-two to gather up the fruits of the work of others. Someone else had planted and watered. They were now there to harvest the yield. The second metaphor adds a sobering tone to the picture. Although the harvest is ready, harvesting itself is a dangerous occupation. The field of ministry is threatening, and the missionaries themselves are vulnerable. The directives Jesus gives accentuate this. The disciples are told to go into the world with only the bare essentials. No purse, no traveling bag, no extra sandals. They are to trust in God and depend on the hospitality of those to whom they go. Since their housing was intended merely as a support of their ministry, they were not to haggle for better accommodations, nor were they to decide the menu of the place even if there was some question about dietary purity. Finally, since two witnesses were necessary to verify any legal claim, they were to go in pairs.

Besides using the metaphor of harvest to characterize the urgency of the mission, the disciples were also told to refrain from engaging in the kind of prolonged greeting that was commonplace in the ancient Near East at that time. There was no time for social niceties. Peace! would be an adequate greeting. While Peace! was a typical Jewish greeting, it was more than that. It had become a synonym for messianic salvation. On the lips of a Christian it announced the presence of the age of eschatological fulfillment. Acceptance of such peace became the condition that determined the future of those to whom the disciples were sent. This peace rested on some but not on others. Those who were open to the message were blessed, but those who refused the missionaries determined their own sorry fate. The missionaries were told to shake the dust of that town from their feet. This also reflects the urgency of the time. The missionaries did not have the leisure to cajole those who were not open to the message. In a situation such as this the rejection was now mutual.

At the end of the mission the seventy-two joyfully returned with stories of success. They had cured the sick and announced the advent of the reign of God. In this they had witnessed the power of God triumphant over the powers of evil, symbolized by serpents and scorpions. Jesus confirmed their appraisal of their accomplishments. Satan had indeed been cast down. This entire experience was then put into context by Jesus. As important as were the wondrous deeds they had been able to perform, more wondrous still was the fact that their names had been inscribed in the heavenly book (cf. Exod 32:32f.).

Themes of the Day

Once again we look to the image of Jesus in order to understand something about the nature of discipleship. Here we see the cross of the Lord Jesus Christ. It is in this sign that we have been called; it is in this sign that we have been sent; it is in this sign that we understand our mission.

The Cross of Jesus Christ

The cross of Jesus Christ creates all things new. It reorders our priorities; it refashions our identities; it puts us in opposition to the standards of the world. No longer do we judge success or failure as before. No longer do we separate people by gender or race or religious tradition. A new reality has been formed, with peace and mercy as its identifying characteristics. The cross is the standard of everything. It is the cross that marks the disciple.

A Life of Discipleship

Although the gospel story is a report of ministerial commissioning, it contains elements of discipleship in general. Most obvious is the disciples' dependence on Jesus. They are not independent missionaries. They are called by him; they are sent by him; it is to him they return and report. To be a disciple is to be a follower. A second point that should be noted is the communal dimension of discipleship. While there is certainly a personal relationship between Jesus and each disciple, discipleship itself is not a singular privilege that one hugs to oneself to the exclusion of others.

Disciples minister to the needs of others, whatever those needs may be and with whatever abilities the disciple may possess. There are various kinds of healing. A friendly smile, a word of gratitude, a soothing touch, can go a long way in a world where pain and suffering seem to reign. We can teach the lessons of life in classrooms, in playrooms, in kitchens, in boardrooms. There are many ways we can cast out the demons that hold our world by the throat, demons of poverty and oppression, demons of addiction and slavery, demons of disdain and neglect, demons of hatred and violence. If they are not cast out by us, then by whom?

The Sign of the Cross

A life of discipleship is not an unmixed blessing. Because disciples are marked by the sign of the cross, they must expect suffering. The gospel speaks of rejection. Not everyone will welcome the message of the cross. Not everyone will appreciate the new creation it brings. Because they do not live according to the standards of the world, disciples will be judged as fools. Some of them will be subjected to even greater suffering. It makes one wonder who would even want to take on such a life. It seems like one is constantly going against the tide. And yet, if we are honest, we will have to admit that much of what the world promotes really goes against the grain of what is truly human. In the face of this, the disciple proclaims that true fulfillment is only found in God! In reality it is the world that is upside down, not the life of discipleship. And it is the cross that sets things right.

Both the first reading and the psalm response give us a glimpse of what can happen when things are set right, when the words or life of the disciple are taken seriously. The city is renewed; the world is rejuvenated; the prosperity of God is enjoyed by all; those who suffer are comforted; the kindness of God fills the whole world.

Fifteenth Sunday in Ordinary Time
Deuteronomy 30:10-14

Almost from its beginning Christianity seems to have pitted faith in Jesus against observance of the law. This has often led to a misunderstanding of the true nature of Christian freedom, and it has frequently reinforced anti-Judaic sentiments. This is unfortunate, because neither Jesus nor his disciples ever sought to abolish the law. Rather, they insisted that a proper understanding of the law is essential. Law, as found in the Mosaic tradition, continues to play an important role in both Jewish and Christian life today.

In the first reading for this Sunday Moses instructs the people about the law's importance and its accessibility. There are indications that the setting of the narrative is a covenant renewal ceremony. An important component of such a ceremony was the reading and acceptance of the law (v. 11). Mention of the people's return (v. 10) suggests they had turned from the LORD in disloyalty, had returned to the LORD in repentance, and were now entering into a renewed covenant relationship. "Book of the law" (v. 10) is a technical reference to Israel's earliest traditions, some of which were written in legal form and others in narrative. It refers to material that today is found in the Pentateuchal Torah, the first five books of the Bible. Finally, "all your heart and all your soul" is a technical phrase that denotes all of one's being. It is associated with love of God, the first and greatest commandment within which all other statutes and ordinances find their completion (cf. Deut 6:5).

To those who may say the law is too difficult to understand or so lofty it is almost impossible to observe, Moses replies: No! It is neither mysterious nor remote. It does not belong to the secrets hidden in heaven awaiting the end-time to be revealed. Because of human weakness it may be a challenge to follow, but it is relatively simple to understand. Nor is it located across some impossible divide, unattainable for most of us. Even a cursory examination of the law will show that while it is indeed the word of God, it arises from the experience of women and men: worship one God; do not steal; do not lie; and so on. The law of God is as close to us as our own human life. This is a bold claim, not because it minimizes the value of the word of God because it does not. It is a bold claim because it identifies human experience as the place where the word of God is to be found. It is in our mouths and in our hearts. This is less a statement about what we call "natural law" than a reference to the will of God that we have learned and interiorized. Moses insists that his audience knows God's will. What they must do is carry it out.

Psalm 69:14, 17, 30-31, 33-34, 36, 37 (1)

Elements of a psalm of lament can be detected here. There is the cry of lament itself (vv. 14, 17), the reasons for the lament (v. 30a), expressions of confidence that God will heed the psalmist's plea (vv. 33-34, 36, 37), and thanksgiving for having been heard (v. 31). Unfortunately, we are not accustomed to cry out to God in lament. Perhaps some think it unseemly to complain to God. However, a lament is a statement of profound faith. It acknowledges that God has power over the circumstances of life, and it is an expression of humble faith that God will come to the aid of those who cry out.

The cry of lament (vv. 14, 17) contains several words closely associated with the theme of covenant. The technical covenant term lovingkindness *(ḥesed)* appears in both verses. In addition we find truth *(ʾĕmet)* of salvation *(yēshaʿ,* translated "constant help," v. 14) and passionate love *(raḥămîm),* love like that of a woman for the child of her womb (v. 17). By arguing in this way the psalmist is bringing the strength and the personal dimension of the covenant to the plea for deliverance. The petitioner is not merely someone who has fallen on hard times. This is a member of the covenanted community. Surely God will turn an understanding ear to this plea.

This passage has a very brief statement of the reasons for the lament. The psalmist claims to be afflicted or lowly *(ʿānî)* and suffering. The lowly ones or the poor are the very ones who are called on to experience the goodness of God, and the psalmist is somehow identified with these people. This raises the question of what has come to be known today as "God's preferential option for the poor." The biblical tradition certainly seems to suggest that God is particularly inclined to hear their cry. But why should they be so privileged? The answer is found in covenant theology. Implied in this sacred agreement are two major issues: a promise by God to care for the needy and the responsibility of humans to care for one another. Israel believed that when someone within the covenant community was disadvantaged and not cared for by others, God would step in and redress the imbalance. The psalmist seems to be counting on a display of such divine justice here.

Confidence in God's being faithful to covenant promises and hearing the plea for deliverance is evidence of the psalmist's faith. Even before there are clear signs of deliverance, the psalmist trusts. God is extolled with songs of thanksgiving, rounding off this powerful hymn of lamentation and profound faith. The psalm ends with a final expression of confidence. The specifics mentioned in these verses are telling. The salvation of Zion and the rebuilding of the cities of the southern kingdom of Judah call to mind the time after the Babylonian Exile. While the details are rooted in historical events, they are often interpreted metaphorically, referring to other situations wherein God is called upon to save.

Psalm 19:8, 9, 10, 11 (2)

Six synonyms are used to extol the glories of the law. Although the general theme of the psalm is praise, its tone is didactic and exhortative. It describes the blessings that acceptance of the law can impart. It does this not merely to describe the law but also to persuade the people to embrace it as the will of God and to live in accord with it. Each of the statements in this psalm identifies the law as belonging to the LORD. This is not just any religious law; it is uniquely Israel's, because in a very specific way it represents the will of the God of Israel.

When most people today talk about law, they normally mean legal enactments that have some degree of binding force. While this is certainly one dimension of the meaning of the Hebrew word *tôrâ*, it might be better translated "instruction" or "teaching" than "law." As found in the Bible, the law consisted of directives for living a full and God-fearing life. Teaching the law was the special task of both the Wisdom school and the priesthood. The former group collected and safeguarded the insights gleaned from various life experiences. In a society that believed ultimate wisdom was revealed by the deity, the latter group functioned as mediators between God and the people.

If the law is understood as the will of God for human beings, then the qualities enshrined in that law could legitimately be considered reflections of divine attributes. If the law is thought to be that point where an encounter with God takes place, then those who are shaped by the law will be godlike. The qualities associated with the law found in this psalm are some of the most highly prized attributes in any tradition. The law is perfect or complete; it is trustworthy, upright, and clean; it is pure and true. Fidelity to the law should lead one to the godliness enshrined within it.

The effects of the law enumerated here are all relational, enhancing human life itself. The psalmist maintains that the law imbues the soul with new vitality; it gives wisdom to those who would not ordinarily have it. It delights the heart; it enables the eyes to see dimensions of truth otherwise obscured. It establishes an enduring attitude of awe; it is a path to righteousness. This description of the law shows clearly that the psalmist found it life-giving and not restrictive, ennobling and not demeaning. Reverence for the law seems to promise the best that life has to offer.

The law is said to be more valuable than gold and sweeter than honey. Gold is precious not only for its own sake but also for the use to which it can be put. In like manner, as the word of God, the law has its own intrinsic value. However, as the psalm demonstrates, its worth is also found in its ability to accomplish the effects listed here. In its purest state the sweetness of honey delights the palate. As a sweetening agent it can completely change the taste of food. In like manner, as the word of God, the law is to be savored for its own sake, but it also provides a particular flavor to everything within its influence. The law of the LORD is something greatly to be desired.

Colossians 1:15-20

The christology in this hymn praising Christ is referred to as high christology. It extols the divine character and activity of Christ rather than his human nature and the physical life he lived on earth. Paul uses several striking terms to characterize Christ: image of God; firstborn; the beginning; head of the church. Each one adds a significant dimension to our understanding of Christ. An image can either represent something or it can be a visible expression or manifestation of it. It is precisely because images function in this way that the ancient Hebrews forbade fashioning images of God. Once God was so represented, God could always be represented in such a limited way. It is clear from the passage that Christ is here considered more than a symbol. Rather, he is a visible manifestation of the invisible God. To say that Christ is the image of God is not meant to limit our understanding of God. Rather, it extols the person of Christ. "Firstborn" can also be understood in two ways. It can refer to priority in time or to primacy in importance. Since this hymn is extolling the divine nature of Christ, the reference is probably not to Christ as the first created being but to the sovereignty of the power he exercises.

Christ occupies the place of preeminence over all the rest of creation, a preeminence that makes creation dependent upon him. He is the agent through whom all was created, and he is also the goal of all creation. This characterization is reminiscent of the feminine figure of Wisdom, who, though still a creation of God, was present at and somehow participated in primordial creation (cf. Prov 8:22-31). Christ's rule extends over the angelic realm as well (dominions, principalities, powers). He is said to be before all things. While this can suggest preexistence, it also means priority of distinction. The latter idea is certainly present in what follows: Christ holds all things together.

Paul ties creation together with redemption. Using the metaphor of body, he depicts both the union that exists between Christ and the Church and the preeminence that is Christ's as head of that body. However, the theme of church is not developed here, since this section follows one that addresses cosmic reality. Thus this reference may reflect the Greek idea of creation as a cosmic body, with Wisdom or the Logos as its head. Redemption is accomplished through Christ's resurrection. Priority of time and preeminence are both present in the reference of firstborn from the dead, for Christ is both the first one raised and the one through whom all others will be raised.

Finally, as image or manifestation of the invisible God, the fullness of God dwells within Christ. In this capacity Christ is the agent of reconciliation. This reconciliation has a universal scope. It includes all created things in heaven and on earth, things visible and invisible. Though we are accustomed to thinking of reconciliation purely in human or social terms, the text is clear. All things are reconciled. We are only beginning to explore the ecological implications of this. The means of this reconciliation that Christ brings is the blood of the cross. Thus the sacrificial death of the human Jesus becomes the means through which the cosmic Christ reconciles all creation with God.

Luke 10:25-37

In this well-known conflict story one skilled in the law challenges Jesus' knowledge of that law, probably in an attempt to publicly shame him. Certain verbs betray his motives. He puts Jesus to a test (v. 25), and when Jesus answers his challenge correctly, the lawyer attempts to save face by justifying himself (v. 29). Jesus not only shows himself as one who knows and conforms to the law, but he turns the lawyer's challenge back on him by asking him to answer his own questions. The lawyer asks about inheriting eternal life, not about earning salvation. Inheriting means receiving blessings bestowed by another. Eternal life is an allusion to the reign of God. In a very real sense the lawyer is asking the right question, but his reason for asking is wrong: to catch Jesus in some error.

In answer to his own first question, the lawyer quotes the two passages from Scripture that encompass all of one's responsibilities. We must love God with all the powers of our beings (cf. Deut 6:5), and we must love our neighbor (originally interpreted as another Jew) as we love ourselves (cf. Lev 19:18; at times resident aliens were included in this injunction, Lev 19:34). Jesus recasts the lawyer's second question, "Who is my neighbor?" and tells a story to demonstrate what it means to be a neighbor. When Jesus asks the recast question, the lawyer is caught in his own snare. He is shamed, while Jesus emerges from this confrontation with even greater honor.

The story itself draws obvious lines of contrast. Priests and Levites were temple personnel, jealous of their ritual purity. In this account they are caught in a dilemma. Even if they wanted to help the man on the road, he may have been dead, and they would incur ceremonial defilement by touching him. Should they fulfill their social obligations to another human being, or should they protect their cultic purity so they might fulfill their ritual obligations? They chose the latter. On the other hand, the Samaritan had no ritual obligations. He was one of the despised half-breeds (cf. Thirteenth Sunday) and was already considered unclean by the Jews. However, the text clearly states that he did not attend to the man because he had nothing to lose. Rather, he was moved with compassion *(splanchnizomai)*, the same emotion that overwhelmed Jesus when he saw the grief of the widow of Nain (cf. Luke 7:13) and the father when he saw his prodigal son returning (cf. Luke 15:20). The Samaritan responded out of love, a love that encompassed all the powers of his being.

The lawyer had asked about works and was told to love. The Samaritan loves and demonstrates it through works. He goes out of his way to meet the needs of this stranger. He cleans the wounds with the alcohol composition of the wine; he soothes them with oil; he puts the man on his own animal and walks beside him to the nearest inn; he himself cares for the man; and he pays for the care provided by another.

In this episode Jesus is not interested in merely telling the lawyer who it is that deserves his love and attention. Rather, he reveals what it means to be a loving person. The focus shifts from the other to oneself. The admonition is striking: Go and do likewise! Put aside all racial or religious prejudices in order to meet the needs of others! Put aside all other responsibilities in order to love the other! In this parable Jesus is not the good Samaritan; the lawyer must be.

Themes of the Day

It was not enough to want to follow Jesus and to be committed to him. Discipleship also demanded a certain ability to make the necessary shifts in understanding in order to recognize what following Jesus required. He did not merely repeat the religious tradition in which he had been formed; he reinterpreted it. Today's disciples face a similar challenge. We too are called to understand the religious meaning of the words and deeds of Jesus, but we must also know how these words and deeds themselves called for adjustments of understanding on the part of those who first heard and witnessed them. This will help us appreciate the need for today's disciples to make comparable shifts of understanding in order to bring the message of Jesus into conversation with the contemporary world.

Open to the Unexpected

Perhaps one of the most exciting and at the same time unnerving aspects of our religious tradition is its nonconforming nature. We think we finally understand the way God is working in our lives, and then something happens that seems to turn our understanding inside out. We extol Christ as the exalted image of the invisible God, as the firstborn of all creation, the one in whom all else was created, and then we stand at the foot of the cross seeing the blood flow from his crucified body. The exalted one is humiliated, and it is precisely through his humiliation that he is exalted.

We are told to love our neighbor, and when we ask who that might be we are told a story that turns the question around. "Who is my neighbor?" or "Whom should I love?" becomes "Who acts as a neighbor?" or "Who shows love?" Attention shifts from the object of our love to the character of our loving, from deciding who deserves our love to loving without deciding who is deserving. The respectable person asks about righteous living, and the genuinely righteous person turns out to be the one who was not respected. The ways of God are indeed paradoxical.

Love of the Law

The same Sunday that we reflect on the paradoxical nature of the ways of God, we are told that the law of God, which appears to be so lofty, is really very close to us, in our mouths and in our hearts. This too is an unusual claim. Yet if we understand ourselves to be part of the body of Christ, as depicted in the epistle, and if we love the Lord our God as totally as the gospel exhorts us to love, we will allow the law to take hold of us in such a way that we will esteem it, as the psalm response suggests. This is not to promote a kind of legalism. Rather, it is a way of living inspired and informed by love, love of God and love of others, even, and perhaps especially, those whom we are not inclined to love.

Sixteenth Sunday in Ordinary Time

Genesis 18:1-10a

The reading from the book of Genesis follows a classic story form that was well known in the ancient Near East. In it, heavenly beings come in disguise to a humble home, receive hospitality from those living there, and reward that family with the announcement of the future birth of a child. Israel made use of this form in telling the story of the promise of a child to Abraham, whose name means "father of a multitude of nations" (cf. Gen 17:5). There appears to be some discrepancy regarding the number of men who visited Abraham. The narrative itself states there were three, with one of them at times acting as spokesperson. However, the passage opens by saying it was the LORD (singular) who appeared to Abraham. Furthermore, if these men were strangers, as the text states, how did they know Sarah's name? While their sudden appearance and the fact that they know what will transpire in the future suggest they are heavenly beings, it is probably best to allow the ambiguities and discrepancies to stand and simply concentrate on the movement of the story and its meaning.

The context and theme of the account is nomadic hospitality. There is a certain protocol that was to be followed. Since all strangers who came out from the desert were potential enemies, it was important to treat them as honored guests. In this way, a relationship of cordiality would be established at the outset. Furthermore, if the host took the initiative here, the host would always have the upper hand. Therefore, when Abraham sees the men, he goes out to them and compels them to accept his hospitality. It would be a breach of etiquette if he did not act in this way, just as it would be a breach of etiquette if they refused his overtures. Refusal by either side could be properly interpreted as a threat to the safety of the other. Upon receiving guests, the host was bound to refresh them and to offer them food and drink, the quality of which indicated the degree of importance the host accorded the guest. Abraham is portrayed here as the perfect host.

In the final section of the story both the visitors and Abraham disregard protocol. In a patriarchal situation such as this it would be presumed that the desert sheik's wife along with the servants would be out of sight but responsible for the meal. Still the visitors ask about her. Such a query violates the conventions of hospitality. Guests have no right to personal family information, particularly information about the women. This could be understood as a challenge to the authority of the male head of the family. Abraham responds without hesitation, a second unconventional move. This breach of etiquette is probably a narrative device that alerts those hearing or reading the story to the remarkable event about to take place. One of the visitors, presumably a perfect stranger, foretells the birth of Sarah's son. Sarah's significance is clear. First, she is named rather than merely identified as Abraham's wife. Second, the child is identified as her son rather than Abraham's. Obviously this woman will play an important role in the life of her son. All of this points to the extraordinary nature of the yet unborn child. His birth is mysteriously foretold by strangers who appeared from out of the desert and who not only know his mother's name but identify him with her.

Psalm 15:2-3, 3-4, 5

The psalm addresses the question of religious fitness. Although the presence of the LORD is generally a liturgical reference, it has a broader meaning as well. We have come to realize that God is present among us in various ways. However, the requirements for standing in the divine presence are the same regardless of how the phrase is understood. The answers given in this responsorial psalm describe moral fitness. Furthermore, the requirements are communal in nature. In other words, those who are worthy to stand before God are those who live virtuously with others.

The first list of requirements (v. 1) sets the context for the rest. "Walk" denotes a way of life rather than individual actions. The foundation of this way of life is righteousness or justice, a characteristic of God. It refers to the divinely established norm against which everything else is measured. Whatever conforms to God's norm is considered righteous. In the human sphere it takes on the meaning of justice. In this psalm it refers to those who act in ways that are faithful to God's will. Such faithfulness is not merely external conformity; it originates in their innermost being. Their thoughts are aligned with the truth of God's righteousness, and their tongues speak accordingly.

What follows (vv. 3, 5) are examples of concrete behavior in everyday life. "Friend" or "companion," rather than "fellow" (v. 3), is a better translation of the Hebrew word (*qārôb*). It includes the idea of personal closeness, and it is not gender specific. Frequently the quality of one's virtue is tested in the intimacy of close relationships. Walking on the path of righteousness calls to mind the Wisdom theme of choosing one of two ways. This theme appears again. The righteous person disdains the reprobate who has rejected God but honors those who fear the LORD. If one is to live in the presence of God, one must choose the way of God.

Human beings are dependent in all ways on the natural world. Economic systems are established to ensure that needs are met and prosperity is possible. In many societies lending money is done as a service to others, not as a way of increasing one's own capital. In such situations demanding interest is unacceptable, even unjust. (Without feeling we must adopt the economic practices of ancient Israel, we can still be motivated by some of the principles of fairness and attention to the needs of others upon which they are based.)

Those who stand in the presence of God do not take economic advantage of others. The psalm verse singles out two forms of economic vulnerability. One example is the need to borrow money in the first place. It is hard enough to suffer want; having to pay interest is an additional burden. The second example is victimization through bribery. This practice is doubly heinous when it abuses the innocent. The psalm ends with a promise of blessing for those who live with others in this righteous manner. They will know peace and security.

Colossians 1:24-28

This reading contains two important themes: the sufferings Paul endures, and his ministry to the Gentiles. Paul's teaching about his own sufferings is an issue that has generated much discussion. That he rejoices in these sufferings should not surprise us, for he believes they will benefit the Colossian Christians. The question arises when he claims that the sufferings *(páthēma)* of his own flesh *(sárx)* fill up what is lacking in the afflictions *(thlípsis)* of Christ's body *(sōma)*. The vocabulary itself indicates that the body of Christ is clearly something other than his physical being. It is the Church. The Greek title, "the Christ," includes a definite article, suggesting that this is not an alternate name for Jesus the Lord but a reference to the long-awaited Messiah. Furthermore, *thlípsis* is never a reference to the sufferings of the historical Jesus. It refers to the tribulations that, according to Jewish eschatological thinking, will precede the coming of the Messiah. Therefore, Paul is saying that his own physical sufferings contribute to what have come to be known as the "woes," or "birth-pangs of the Messiah."

Paul would never say that the sufferings of Jesus were in any way lacking in their atoning efficacy. Rather, he believed that, joined to Jesus, his own sufferings had merit and could be seen as part of the sufferings that would inaugurate the messianic age (a future coming according to Jewish tradition; a present as well as future reality in Christian faith). This is why Paul can claim to rejoice, regardless of the agony he might be enduring. They are hastening the time of ultimate eschatological fulfillment. These sufferings are substitutionary: "on behalf of." Paul is a minister, a servant *(diákonos)* with the responsibility of stewardship *(oikonomía)*. Since the term "stewardship" is derived from "household" *(oíkos)* and "rule" *(nómos)*, we can say that Paul understands his ministry as the service of management of the goods of the household of God.

Paul's stewardship consists in preaching the word of God, specifically the doctrine of salvation to the Gentiles. He considers this a mystery hidden for ages. He ascribes no blame to those Jews or Christians who reject the idea that Gentiles can be saved without having first to convert to Judaism. The Gentiles are included along with the other holy ones, for according to Paul, all those who have been baptized have been transformed in Christ; they are the saints. Having tasted the glory of Christ at the time of their baptism, they await in hope the fullness of that glory.

Ultimately the real message that Paul proclaims is Christ the risen Lord. To borrow from the great Jewish rabbi Hillel: Everything else is commentary! However, commentary is necessary for us to understand the specific impact of the message in every time and place. As steward of the household, it is Paul's responsibility to make sure that in the domain of his ministry everything is perfect.

Luke 10:38-42

Over the years this vignette about the sisters Martha and Mary has been interpreted in various ways. In many instances the ambiguities within the text have led interpreters to read their own biases into the story. While such interpretation might be able to bring the story into the experience of the readers, they risk missing some important points in the narrative itself.

The first point to be considered is the question of gender. In several ways the scene depicted is extraordinary. It is Martha who welcomes Jesus into her house. Though the explanation for her ownership is not given here, in many patriarchal societies ownership by a woman is unusual though not impossible. Jesus is portrayed as interacting alone with women who are not members of his family, thus challenging that restrictive taboo. Mary's depiction is important. She is seated at Jesus' feet, the customary place of a disciple, and she is listening to his words, a technical phrase that connotes either the fundamental proclamation of the good news or the instruction that flows from it. Here the faithful disciple is a woman.

For her part Martha is not only overwhelmed with the traditional household duties of a woman, she is also fulfilling the customary responsibilities of hospitality. She is distracted from attending to Jesus' words by her service *(diakonía)*, a word that came to have specific ministerial connotations. Just as in last Sunday's gospel Jesus chose the figure of a despised outsider as an example of unselfish neighborliness, so today we have women as examples of two different forms of ministerial activity.

In their own ways both sisters are faithful disciples of Jesus, one listening to his word and the other performing service. It is this very difference that seems to be the source of the tension in the story. The text does not say Martha wants to sit at the feet of Jesus; it states that she wants her sister to share in the responsibilities of service. Martha rebukes Jesus for his apparent indifference and then gives him directions for remedying the situation. Jesus is being asked to do more than intervene in a domestic squabble. He is being called on to decide which responsibility of the disciple takes precedence over the other. Jesus' response, though clearly stated, is somewhat ambiguous. What exactly is the better part that Mary chose? Is it reflection over action? Is it a choice for the things of God over basic human needs?

The context of the story might give us a clue to the meaning of Jesus' response. It opens with a statement about hospitality. Martha welcomes Jesus into her house. Might the answer be as simple as this: is true hospitality found in giving personal attention to the guest rather than in being distracted from that person by the duties associated with hospitality? Last Sunday we saw that attention to the person in need is to be preferred over the fulfillment of one's responsibilities, regardless of how noble those responsibilities might be. We also saw that when one's priorities are in order, one need not choose one obligation to the exclusion of the other. The story of Martha and Mary seems to be another example of this principle. The better part is to be attentive to the person. This attentiveness will eventually express itself in appropriate service.

Themes of the Day

The readings for this Sunday might all be reflected upon under the heading of openness. Abraham was open to receive the heavenly visitors; Martha opened her home to Jesus; Paul was open to the sufferings he endured for the sake of the Church. While each instance is different in itself, this Sunday we will consider openness in the form of hospitality.

Hospitality

When we think of discipleship and hospitality we normally focus on how disciples are accepted by others. Back on the Fourteenth Sunday we watched the seventy-two disciples being sent out to preach and to heal. We heard Jesus tell them to accept the hospitality offered to them and, when it was not forthcoming, to shake the dust of that town off of their feet. In today's readings the circumstances are reversed. Here we see the People of God offering the hospitality rather than receiving it, first Abraham and then Martha. What lessons of discipleship can be learned from these readings?

First and foremost we see how important openness is, for in each case those to whom the hospitality was offered were divine visitors in human form. Martha may have known that it was the Lord she was entertaining, but initially Abraham did not recognize the true nature of his visitors. We can never be sure under what guise God will come to us. It could be the person on the street who asks for directions, or the one who comes to our place of work to engage the service we provide. It may be the friend who comes to dinner or the co-worker who acts in a way we did not expect. God comes into our lives in unexpected ways, and we must have an open attitude of hospitality if we are to receive the blessings that might come with such visits.

Tasks Versus People

If our hospitality is genuine, we will share the best we have to offer. We will give of our time, and we will do what we can to meet the needs of those who come to us. Perhaps one of the greatest challenges disciples face today is finding the right balance between the tasks we have to accomplish and the needs of the people we serve. The tension between Martha and Mary illustrates how difficult this is. Martha was busy with the legitimate responsibilities of hospitality, but her complaint showed she was more concerned about her duties than her guest. With all the responsibilities we carry today, it is so easy to lose sight of the people involved. Parents can be so overwhelmed with the demands of making a living that they have little time for those for whom they are making the living. Doctors can be so intent on curing the illness that they are insensitive to the fears of the one who is ill. Pastors can be so overworked with administrative duties that they have little time for pastoring. All these duties are important, but not as important as the people for whom we do them. How hospitable are we to the people who come to us?

Fill Up the Sufferings

Throughout these Sundays of Ordinary Time we have considered many of the challenges that face disciples. This Sunday is no exception. We know we cannot lay aside the various responsibilities of our lives in order to sit with Mary at the feet of Jesus. However, we cannot allow ourselves to be held captive by these responsibilities, regardless of how legitimate they may be. And so we continue to struggle; to carry our burdens for the sake of the people we serve; to serve the people in our care realizing we will probably not be able to accomplish all our tasks, or at least not as well as we would like. This is the struggle that faces disciples today. It is in this way that the reign of God struggles to be born.

Seventeenth Sunday in Ordinary Time
Genesis 18:20-32

The account of the dialogue between Abraham and God over the fate of Sodom and Gomorrah is too complicated to be classified simply as an example of Near Eastern haggling. Nor is this a story about divine mercy. It is really a theological inquiry into the nature of divine justice. There is no question about the sinfulness of the cities. The outcry is for help in time of distress; it is a cry against oppression. At issue here is the extent to which the righteousness of some can off-balance the sinfulness of most.

The setting of the story is interesting. God has heard the cry and wishes to investigate the situation before deciding on a course of action. Abraham's visitors go ahead to the cities, while the LORD remains behind with Abraham. The underlying question that drives the exchange between Abraham and God is one of justice. The question as stated is: Should not the judge of all the world act with justice (v. 25)? The answer is obvious. Of course! However, the question as intended is: What is justice in a situation like this? The answer to this question is not so obvious. There is a tension here between communal guilt and innocence and individual guilt and innocence. If the city is guilty it should be punished. But what if there are innocent individuals in that city? Is it fair that they should suffer along with the guilty ones?

The question can be looked at another way. In traditional societies, identity and significance are more communal than personal. More emphasis is given to the group than to the individual member. Furthermore, the consequences of the actions of the head of the group are felt by the members (for example, the effects of the first sin). This thinking explains why individuals in the biblical stories often appear to us to be sacrificed for the sake of the group. Within the context of this theory known as "corporate personality," one can ask: If the guilt of some can result in the suffering of all, cannot the innocence of some hold back the hand that inflicts the suffering?

Abraham demonstrates extraordinary deference toward the LORD. In customary Near Eastern style he prefaces each of his inquiries with adulation. However, it is still he who boldly initiates the exchange that probes the nature of divine justice. Six times he questions God about the parameters of divine justice, and six times God appears to adjust them. Actually, we never really know the exact measure of these parameters. We know only the lengths to which Abraham inquires about them. He moves progressively from fifty to ten people whose innocence is strong enough to withstand the punishing arm of God, which is raised against the city. The account demonstrates the power of the righteous. Only a few can be salvific for many.

Psalm 138:1-2, 2-3, 6-7, 7-8

The responsorial psalm for this Sunday follows the general structure of the individual prayer of thanksgiving. Addressed directly to God, it begins with sentiments of thanksgiving, followed by a statement of the reason for being thankful (vv. 1, 3). It ends with a declaration of confidence in God's enduring faithfulness.

Evidently the psalmist had previously been in dire straits, had called upon the LORD for help, had been heard, and had been inwardly strengthened. This is the reason for the prayer of gratitude. The temple setting suggests that the psalmist has come there to worship and publicly to witness to the goodness of God. The angels (*'ĕlōhîm*) suggest the court of heaven. In ancient Canaanite myths this court was made up of minor deities who stood in reverence around the throne of the principal god. As it developed its monotheistic understanding of God, Israel merely demoted these deities to angels, supernatural beings who were still under the dominion of the God of Israel. Thus the sovereignty of this God was not only emphasized by their subservience, but it was also enhanced by the homage they gave. Since the Temple was thought to be the earthly representation of the heavenly divine dwelling, it was not unusual to believe that these beings were somehow in the same kind of attendance in the Temple on earth. Therefore, standing in the Temple in the presence of God, the psalmist would also be in the presence of the attending angels. The reason for the psalmist's gratitude is God's faithfulness to covenant commitment. This is clear from the presence of technical covenant language, lovingkindness (*ḥesed*) and truth (*'ĕmet*). The promise referred to could be a pledge God made specifically with the psalmist, or it might be a reference to the general promise of protection and beneficence associated with the covenant and made with the nation as a whole. Regardless of the case, God has been faithful and the psalmist publicly witnesses to this faithfulness with gratitude.

The psalmist acknowledges that the LORD is exalted, lifted high in glory, yet attentive to those who are humble or of mean estate. The right hand of the LORD is the hand of strength (a right-hand bias). This indicates that the reason for gratitude is that the psalmist has been rescued from some kind of adversity. We have already seen that God's goodness springs from covenant commitment. The psalmist concludes the prayer of thanksgiving on a note of confidence that this commitment will endure forever. God is not only faithful to past promises but will be faithful into the endless future.

Colossians 2:12-14

In what appears to be baptismal instruction Paul describes the effects of the triumph of the power of God in the lives of believers as manifested in the resurrection of Christ. He does this by relating Christ's burial in the grave of the earth with the Christian's burial in the waters of baptism. The death of Christ was historical; the death of the Christians is death by identification. It is clear in this passage that it is not the ritual of baptism itself that saves but rather the faith in Christ present in the Christian who submits to the ritual. Joined to Christ in faith, through baptism they enter the grave, the realm of the dead, only to rise with Christ to a new life.

Paul moves from the concept of actual physical death to that of spiritual death. This is the condition of those who, because of sin, are separated from God, the source of life. It is important to note that it was precisely while they were sinners that they were saved. In the past the Colossians were dead not only because of sin but also because they had not undergone the ritual of circumcision, the ceremony the Jews maintained initiated the men into the company of the saved. Paul, himself one of the circumcised, shifts from speaking exclusively about the Gentile Colossians (brought you) to speaking inclusively about all who were guilty of sin (forgiven us). In this way, without rejecting the rite itself Paul acknowledges circumcision's inability to forgive sin. Only interior faith in Christ manifested in the external expression of baptism can accomplish that.

The baptized Christians have gone down into death with Christ and have been raised with him to new life. The new life into which they have been raised brings with it a new standard of living, a new ethical code. Since they have died and are living a new life, the legal claims of the past are no longer binding, claims that appear to have been more a burden than a guide. Furthermore, the debt owed because of the transgressions of the past is canceled. The image Paul employs suggests this debt was originally set to writing but has now been expunged. Just as indictments of death were nailed to the cross of the criminal, so this notice of cancellation of debt is also nailed. Just as the cross was the instrument for carrying out the death sentence, so it is now the source of life.

Luke 11:1-13

This discourse on prayer can be divided into three separate but related segments: the Lord's Prayer (vv. 1, 4); an example of persistence prayer (vv. 5-8); the assurance of being heard (vv. 9-13). It was Jesus at his own prayer that prompted his disciples to ask for direction in their prayer, just as the disciples of other religious leaders had been taught to pray by them. There is some question about whether this should be seen as an actual prayer or as a pattern to follow in praying. Most commentators believe it is the latter or both. The plural pronouns in the prayer denote its communal character. The prayer consists of an invocation, appeals for the glorification of God, and the petitions of the supplicants.

The invocation "Father" suggests a relationship that is intimate and child-like. Furthermore, it came from Jesus, so it is evidence the prayer is intended for those who enjoy this relationship because of Jesus, for it was Jesus who called God "Father" and who here invites his disciples to do the same. Since the name of a person comprises the character of that person, to pray that God's name be made holy is to pray that God be given appropriate honor. The prayer for the coming of the reign of God is a prayer for eschatological fulfillment. These two pleas are found in the same order and almost the same words in the Qaddish prayer that ends the synagogue service. Though this prayer is later than the passage from Luke, it does suggest that the prayer of Jesus has much in common with traditional Jewish prayer.

There is a question about the meaning of the rare word that modifies "bread" *(epioúsion)*. Most commentators agree that "daily" best captures its intent. The verb form used in this petition denotes continuous giving. These features point to constant dependence on God rather than some form of eschatological satisfaction. The next plea includes an acknowledgment that forgiveness by God assumes the petition's forgiveness of others. The final petition prays that one not be overwhelmed by temptation. These petitions all point to the continuing need for God in the present struggles of life.

The persistence with which one should pray is characterized by the story of the man who woke his sleeping friend. That friend was not upset because he was awakened, nor was he unwilling to share his bread with his friend. He was upset because he did not want to disturb his family. However, he finally gave in, because his insistent friend would not. What was not achieved because of friendship was accomplished because of persistence.

The lessons to be learned about prayer are finally explicitly articulated. Like the man who was awakened from sleep, God is willing to give, but one must ask; God is willing to reveal, but one must seek; God is willing to open the door, but one must knock on it. God is willing to answer prayers, but one must pray. God's willingness to grant petitions is described through the use of a Jewish form of argument: "from the lesser to the greater." If a human father gives good things rather than harmful things to his children, how much more will the Father in heaven give good things to those who ask for them, the greatest good being the Holy Spirit? This entire discourse encourages the disciples to persevere in prayer.

Themes of the Day

The readings for this Sunday offer us an opportunity to reflect on the prayer of the disciple. They suggest some of the predispositions for praying; they reveal some of the content of Christian prayer; they offer us an idea of what can happen to us when we pray. Finally, Jesus himself gives us the Our Father, a prayer that contains within itself all of the characteristics of prayer that we will consider.

Predispositions for Prayer

As children we learned there are different kinds of prayer: praise, contrition, thanksgiving, and petition. All these different prayers recognize two fundamental realities: we are a dependent, needy people; our needs can really only be adequately met by our sovereign God. In the gospel Jesus instructs us to ask for what we need, to seek what we desire, to knock on the door behind which we hope to find our fulfillment. He assures us we will receive what we request, we will find what we seek, and the door will be opened to us. In other words, God is more than willing to give us what we need. However, for this to happen we must turn to God and humbly acknowledge our need.

Characteristics of Prayer

Our prayer is always directed toward God, as we see in the Our Father. Even if we pray to Mary or to one of the saints, we are still praying to God because these others only act as intermediaries for us before God. Therefore the first characteristic of prayer is that it is directed toward God. Regardless of whether it is an explicit prayer of praise or contrition or thanksgiving or petition, as prayer it acknowledges the majesty of God and is, therefore, a prayer of praise. In the Our Father, we praise God's name.

While many of the psalms, and the Our Father as well, include mention of the petitioner's own needs, the two narratives read this Sunday describe prayer offered for someone else. Abraham asks for mercy for the people of Sodom and Gomorrah, and the man in the gospel asks for bread for his friend. Generosity of heart is a second characteristic of prayer.

The most obvious characteristic depicted in the readings for this Sunday is persistence. Neither Abraham nor the man in the gospel was deterred by any obstacle. They show it is not so much that we persist in prayer in order to change God's mind as it is that we persist in order to discover what God's mind might be. How would Abraham have known the number of righteous required to save a city if he had not gradually reduced the number? How would the man have known he was willing to risk his friendship with another in order to fulfill his obligation of hospitality? Persistence in prayer reveals to us the lengths to which we are willing to go for another.

The Effectiveness of Prayer

The salutariness of prayer is often found in the change it effects in us, not in God. While it is true our prayer may not change the situations for which we pray, it is also true that frequently we change in the praying. By persevering in genuine prayer we may come to acknowledge that all things are in God's hands and that we can rest content to leave them there, trusting the situation will be cared for as God sees fit. It seems trite to say God hears all prayer and sometime the answer is No! It is better to say God respects the freedom of people and will seldom intervene to change the way events unfold. Still, prayer can change the one who prays and also the one for whom the prayer is offered if only human need is recognized and divine solicitude is acknowledged.

Eighteenth Sunday in Ordinary Time
Ecclesiastes 1:2; 2:21-23

The first verse of this short reading sets a tone that may appear to some to be an exaggeration. The word "vanity" appears five times. In Hebrew this is even more pronounced, since in that language the verse consists of only eight words. The construction "vanity of vanities" is the way the superlative is expressed in Hebrew. The word itself means breath or vapor. It denotes transitoriness or the lack of substance. It is from this that we get the idea of meaninglessness. We should not conclude that the author is suggesting that something is necessarily meaningless in itself, since breath is certainly very important. It is the transitoriness that is of concern here. Therefore, just as some have translated the phrase as "Meaninglessness of meaninglessness. . . . Everything is meaningless," one might also read it as "Transitoriness of transitoriness. . . . Everything is transitory."

Qoheleth is less a name than an occupational title. It is a feminine participle of the Hebrew verb meaning assemble *(qāhāl)*. The construction itself is curious, because it is quite clear that Qoheleth is a man. His occupation is generally understood to be that of teacher or preacher. This is not an insignificant point, given the position of importance accorded the teacher in ancient Israel. The designation prevents us from too readily dismissing the lessons taught by this teacher, regardless of its bleak tone. Still, Qoheleth could not be more emphatic in his pronouncement. He not only employs the superlative form, he repeats it and then restates his appraisal: All is vanity!

Qoheleth provides an anecdote to illustrate the point he is making. According to conventional Wisdom teaching, one should be able to enjoy the fruits of one's labor, provided it was done in a fitting manner. Good work should be rewarded. The man described here "labored with wisdom and knowledge and skill." There is no question about his right to take pleasure in the fruits of that labor. However, here the transitoriness is found in life itself. It seems the man does not live long enough to enjoy his goods. Furthermore, these goods will go to one who did not earn them, so there is a double inequity.

From this example Qoheleth frames his conclusion in the form of a rhetorical question, a technique that draws the reader into the argument. He comments on the effort the man put into his work, effort that included both labor itself and anxiety day and night. He then asks: And what did it get him? The manner in which Qoheleth sketches the man's experience and the fate that was his suggests that satisfaction is to be found at the completion of the task, in the ultimate fruits of the labor. There is a kind of continuum that presumes successful passage through each stage. When for any reason this passage is not completed, frustration sets in and the entire enterprise is considered pointless, meaningless, futile.

If we remember that "vanity" also means "transitoriness," we will be able to see the point Qoheleth is making in a slightly different way. Rather than presume that he is passing judgment on the entire enterprise, we might see it is really the anticipation of future satisfaction that is futile. Our own transitoriness places the future in jeopardy, so it is vain to locate our satisfaction there. This does not necessarily mean we should refrain from commitment and hard work. It does suggest the real fruits of our labor are found in the laboring itself rather than in what we might be able to enjoy of them in the future.

Psalm 90:3-4, 5-6, 12-13

The responsorial psalm has features of the lament, but its primary theme comes from the Wisdom tradition. The issue that seems to consume the psalmist is the transitoriness of human existence. Unlike God, for whom a thousand years are but a blink of the eye, humans have a very brief life span. When the time they do have is spent in suffering and misfortune, their agony can be intensified, and life can seem futile. The images in the psalm response depict this: dust, grass that wilts and fades. The psalmist prays for wisdom of heart, the kind of interior insight that will enable the people to live the few days they have committed to the things of God.

This prayer comes from a community in great distress. Apparently it has been suffering for some time, for it cries out to God in prayer: "How long?" They feel deserted by God, unable to free themselves from their plight: "Have pity!" Israel's way of understanding suffering was complex. They seldom questioned why their enemies were burdened with misfortune. The reason for this was obvious to them: enemies of God's people were enemies of God, so they deserved to suffer hardship. The misfortune that befell Israel was seen as quite another matter. If it was a punishment for ungodly behavior, it was seen as necessary recompense meant to restore the harmony that had been disturbed by the sin. However, even this kind of distress was thought to be only temporary. The people expected that the guilty ones would recognize their error and reform their ways, and then good fortune would return. The pleading found in this psalm arises from a situation from which relief has been long in coming, perhaps too long.

Daybreak usually brings thoughts of hope. The gradual appearance of light dispels the darkness of despair and speaks of promise and well-being. However, when it appears that relief is not on the horizon, which is slowly taking shape, discouragement turns to desperation, and hope evaporates like early-morning dew in the light of day. In such a situation each new day is an added burden rather than a herald of hope. The psalmist has known both kinds of day. Here the prayer is for days of gladness rather than days of affliction. The psalmist is pleading for a reversal of fortune. The confidence in God's willingness to relent from chastising the community and to grace it with kindness is based in the covenant relationship of lovingkindness (*ḥesed*) that it shares with God. God has made a promise, and even in the face of the people's infidelity God will honor that promise.

The psalm ends with petitions: Fill us with your lovingkindness! Grant us your gracious care! Prosper the work of our hands! Despite the hardships the people must have been enduring, their prayers are filled with hope. The God with whom they are in covenant will surely hear their cry and come to their aid. These are the sentiments behind the petitions.

Colossians 3:1-5, 9-11

Once again Paul begins his discourse with the indicative/imperative form: You have been raised with Christ, so act as risen people. He contrasts heavenly reality with earthly existence. This is the side of power for right-handed people, and because power is ascribed to that side, anyone who is stationed there is close to the seat of power and participates in that power. The spatial reference should be understood figuratively. The things above are the things of God, things that are essential for salvation, things with ultimate meaning. They belong to the realm of the redeemed. Paul encourages the Colossians to seek the higher things not in order merely to discover them but in order to live by them.

Paul also exhorts the Colossians to set their minds with intent and determination on the things of heaven. He gives three reasons for doing this. First, they are now joined to the risen Christ. Second, Christ's life is the new source for their own lives. Third, joined to the risen Christ, they will share in his ultimate manifestation in glory. This manifestation is a future event. Until then, they live hidden in Christ. This does not mean that their Christian way of life will go unnoticed. Quite the opposite. It will be seen by all, but it will not be esteemed by the world because the Christians will not be living according to the values of the world. They will have to wait until Christ is manifested in glory before the value of their lives is acclaimed. Until then they will have to accept misunderstanding, vilification, even persecution. However, when Christ appears, they will be vindicated.

Paul goes even further in his censure of the things of the earth, identifying them with moral depravity. He lists some of the vices to which believers are inclined despite their new existence in Christ. This is another instance of Paul's already-but-not-yet eschatological perspective. The exhortation directs the Christians to die to a sinful way of living. Of the vices listed, four are of a sexual nature, the fifth is more general, and the last is contrary to truth and love, the basis of life in common. All are regarded as earthly desires because they are deviations of concerns of this world—sexual behavior, the use of material goods, and the truth about the foundation upon which society is based. If the Colossians set their minds on the things above, they will engage in earthly affairs in the proper manner.

The transformation the Colossians have undergone is characterized as putting off the old self and putting on the new, as one would change clothing. This may well be yet another allusion to the change of garments that was part of the ritual of baptism. Paul combines this metaphor with the notion of renewal of the self that was originally made in the image of God (cf. Gen 1:27). Sin distorts the way one manifests the image of God; transformation in Christ renews it. The present passive verb form indicates this renewal is both continuous (always present) and the work of God (passive with regard to the person).

Finally, Paul insists that in this new way of living there are no distinctions that feed bias or discrimination, whether that bias be based on race, religious origin, gender, culture, or social status. In Christ it makes no difference whether one is a Greek or a Jew, circumcised or uncircumcised (this is also a gender bias), barbarian or civilized, slave or free. While the actual distinction does not fade, the bias that accompanies it has dissolved. There are no longer such separations. Christ is the exclusive and determining force in all.

Luke 12:13-21

Jesus is approached by a man who wants him to act as arbiter between himself and his brother. The dispute is over inheritance, but what follows shows the real issue is greed. Jesus uses this encounter as an occasion to teach a lesson about the futility of a life spent in amassing material possessions. Two important features of this teaching event highlight its Wisdom character. The teaching method itself is a parable, a form associated with the Wisdom tradition. It draws on what is commonplace in order to teach something deeper about life. The man in the parable is judged by God to be a fool, someone who has not learned the important lessons life has to teach. Though "foolish" (from the Wisdom tradition) and "wicked" (from the moral tradition) are often used interchangeably, this is a classification based on the standards of wisdom, not those of strict morality.

The rich man is not censured because of his wealth. Nor is he criticized for not attending to the needs of those less fortunate than he. His foolishness is much deeper; it is the attitude of greed that underlies his actions. Such an attitude determines how he values his wealth and what he will do with it. His life consists in amassing more and more. His folly is evident in the fact that he stores his grain without safeguarding it from decay. This point is important for the parable. It is an example of how goods that are not used will not last. The only way he makes use of his wealth is to indulge in a life of hedonistic excess (cf. Isa 22:13; 1 Cor 15:32).

The man's death is not a punishment for his greed. It is simply the end of his life of excess. It points out the futility of that life. He spent it collecting what does not last and what is thereby ultimately valueless. Before he told the parable Jesus already alerted the crowd as to its meaning: One's life does not consist in possessions. Possessions do not last. At death they are passed on to another, and there is no way of knowing whether that other person will use them well or not (cf. Eccl 2:19). Jesus draws out the moral of his story. It is foolish to devote one's life to amassing goods and to be bereft in what matters to God. Jesus is not specific here about what matters to God, but it is clear it is not material possessions.

Themes of the Day

The readings for this Sunday pose a fundamental question that can be stated in several ways: To what do we commit ourselves? Where are our hearts? What is most important in life? The Wisdom character of these questions cannot be denied. As we have seen so often, this tradition occupies itself with the basic questions of life: What is the meaning of life? Where do we find our fulfillment? These are questions all women and men of every time and place and culture ponder. The disciples of Christ are no exception to this questioning. However, they will be identified as disciples in the way they answer.

The Transitoriness of Life

Both the first reading and the psalm response speak about the transitoriness of life. It is all we have, and it is so fragile, so fleeting. It seems we just learn what living is all about and then our lives begin to diminish. We don't have the time to enjoy what it is we have discovered. This does not appear to be the case with children. They seem to live the present moment with abandon, with little thought to the future. They seem not to doubt they will have a future. Somewhere between the naiveté of children and the disillusionment of many adults is the realization that this is the life we have and it has been given to us to live fully with God and with one another.

What frequently keeps us from living life fully is the thought that we can only do so if we have accomplished particular feats, gained a certain reputation, and secured desired goods. While there is nothing wrong with any of these goals, there is no guarantee they will deliver the fulfillment we expect of them. And if we have denied ourselves and others the joy of real living in our attempts to obtain them, we have been wasting the life given to us.

The time we have in this life is not only transitory, it is also fleeting. It flies by. When we realize this, we may fear that in the end we will have nothing to show for our lives. How sad to think such thoughts! They show we have not learned the most basic lesson of life, which is: Life is to be lived!

The Vanity of Goods

Living creatures live off the fruits of the earth. This is certainly true of human beings. We need food and water to survive; we need material for clothing and shelter. We are artists, and so we use the elements of the earth to reproduce it in new and creative ways. We are toolmakers, and so we use the stuff of the earth to make life more comfortable. The goods of the earth are not only good, they are essential for our survival and advancement. However, they do not satisfy the deepest longings of the human spirit. They do provide us with pleasure and challenge, but they cannot shield us from the transitoriness of life itself. In the face of such impermanence they are ultimately worthless. When the fruits of the earth are not used to enhance the life of the earth, they lose their value; they spoil and even decompose. Life itself is the far greater good; goods only enhance life.

Life Hidden with Christ in God

Recognizing the transitoriness of life and the vanity of goods, we come to see that the only reality worthy of our total commitment, the only reality not transitory or vain, is our relationship with God in Christ. Though made of dust and thus subject to perishability, we are joined with Christ and promised imperishability. Having died to the vanities of this world, having taken off our old selves with their evil desires, we can now live in this world with a new self, in generosity rather than greed, with openness to others rather than religious or gender or social biases. In our commitment to Christ we will discover that we can transform what is transitory in life by giving it away in love. If we can live in this way, life is anything but vanity!

Ordinary Time (Part Three)

Nineteenth Sunday Wisdom 18:6-9 You saved your people	Psalm 33:1, 12, 18-22 Exult, you just	Hebrews 11:1-2, 8-19 Abraham lived by faith	Luke 12:32-48 Be prepared
Twentieth Sunday Jeremiah 38:4-6, 8-10 A man of contention	Psalm 40:2-4, 18 LORD, come to my aid	Hebrews 12:1-4 Keep your eyes on Christ	Luke 12:49-53 I bring division, not peace
Twenty-First Sunday Isaiah 66:18-21 They come from all nations	Psalm 117:1-2 Praise the LORD	Hebrews 12:5-7, 11-13 The discipline of the LORD	Luke 13:22-30 They come from east and west
Twenty-Second Sunday Sirach 3:17-18, 20, 28-29 Humble yourself	Psalm 68:4-7, 10-11 God makes a home for the poor	Hebrews 12:18-19, 22-24a The city of God	Luke 14:1, 7-14 The humble will be exalted
Twenty-Third Sunday Wisdom 9:13-18b Who knows God's counsel	Psalm 90:3-6, 12-17 You are my refuge	Philemon 9-10, 12-17 A brother, not a slave	Luke 14:25-33 Renounce your possessions

Twenty-Fourth Sunday Exodus 32:7-11, 13-14 A stiff-necked people	Psalm 51:3-4, 12-13, 17, 19 Have mercy on me	1 Timothy 1:12-17 Christ came for sinners	Luke 15:1-32 Joy in heaven over those who repent
Twenty-Fifth Sunday Amos 8:4-7 Woe to those who oppress the poor	Psalm 113:1-2, 4-8 Praise the LORD	1 Timothy 2:1-8 Offer prayers for all	Luke 16:1-13 You cannot serve God and mammon
Twenty-Sixth Sunday Amos 6:1a, 4-7 Woe to Zion	Psalm 146:7-10 Praise the LORD	1 Timothy 6:11-16 Keep the commandments	Luke 16:19-31 Lazarus was carried to Abraham

Ordinary Time (Part Three)

Initial Reading of Ordinary Time (Part Three)

Introduction

During this period of Ordinary Time the lectionary readings address many of the issues and concerns of ordinary life. At times the themes appear to follow one another logically; at other times they seem to be chosen in a random fashion. But that is the way life is. Ordinary Time is for the ordinary life of ordinary people. The lessons to be learned are lessons about discipleship and the kind of community this discipleship creates.

First Testament Readings

With the exception of a passage from Exodus, the First Testament readings for this section of Ordinary Time come from the Wisdom tradition and the Prophets. They offer a kind of kaleidoscope of images and themes that call to mind aspects of our religious tradition, and they challenge us to shape our lives in accord with the theology found there. They begin with a reminder that God provided protective care for our ancestors during their deliverance from Egyptian bondage. This theme sets the context for the rest of the readings of this section.

We read that Jeremiah was rejected by the very people to whom he ministered and that the king who should have protected him did nothing in his defense. It was God who, through a foreigner, came to his rescue and drew him out of the pit. God's care is also seen in the gathering of all nations in Jerusalem at the holy mountain of the LORD. Two Wisdom readings emphasize our need for humility in our dealing with others and our relationship with God.

The readings for the last three Sundays of this section are sobering. They lay bare our human weakness and our propensity for sin. Like the Israelites, we are often stiff-necked people, people who take advantage of the less fortunate and who are complacent in our good fortune. However, as the opening theme reminds us, despite our failures God is there to bring us out of our bondage to sin.

Psalms

The psalm responses provide us with one fundamental image of God, that of the divine provider. Most of the responses are songs of confidence in the goodness of God or hymns praising God for blessings already received. One of them, Psalm 51 (Twenty-fourth Sunday), comes from a lament. Even such a prayer demonstrates the confidence the psalmist has in God's goodness, for it would not be prayed if the psalmist did not think God would answer. The psalms reveal a trust in God's tenderness, in God's concern for the poor, and in God's fidelity to the covenant. Only the lament is a cry for mercy and forgiveness.

Epistles

The selections for the epistle readings provide us with continuous readings from the letter to the Hebrews and the first letter to Timothy. One reading from the letter to Philemon separates them. The letter to the Hebrews underscores the need for faith and the wonderful effects it will have in our lives. It encourages us to persevere in our struggles and to accept the hardships of life as opportunities to be strengthened by God. It calls us to participate in the incomparable covenant established by Jesus through the shedding of his blood.

The reading from Philemon shows a tender side of Paul. Respecting Philemon's rights, he pleads on behalf of the runaway slave. The basis of his entreaty is his insistence that the converted slave should now be treated as a brother in Christ.

Paul's attitude toward Timothy is no less solicitous. He both encourages him in his timidity and confirms him in his responsibilities. He begins by admitting his own former failings. He advises that prayers be offered for all, and he concludes by exhorting Timothy to stand fast in his faith. Paul is very attentive to the needs of those under his supervision.

Gospels

Every one of the gospel readings depicts Jesus engaged in teaching. Sometimes he is addressing his disciples; at other times he speaks to a broader audience. He begins with a message of encouragement, acknowledging that the reign of God makes great demands on those who would enter. Disciples should not lose heart. They must be vigilant so they are ready for the return of the Master.

Through these readings he teaches about the reign of God. He describes who will gain entrance and the price that will have to be paid.

The reign of God will consist of people from every corner of the world. It will include those frequently overlooked by society. Those who would enter must put Jesus above all their possessions. They may even be called upon to sacrifice family loyalties. Sinners will not be excluded, as long as they repent. The reign of God is open to all who are open to it. The section closes with a startling picture that challenges us to be attentive to the needs of the people around us. We may not hear their cries for help, but God does.

Mosaic of Readings

The readings for this time of year move easily from one area of life to another. Sometimes they open us to new challenges, but most of the time they are like reruns, lessons we may already have learned but must always learn anew. These readings do not contain trivial themes. On the contrary, they address many of the realities of everyday life, those frequently overlooked because of their ordinariness. Ordinary does not mean banal. It is the warp and woof of life; it is the normal place we encounter God. Even if we take a vacation from the responsibilities we carry throughout the year, the readings for the first Sunday of this section remind us there is no vacation from our responsibilities of Christian living. Furthermore, we must always be vigilant, for we do not know when we will be asked to be accountable.

Readings

Nineteenth Sunday in Ordinary Time
Wisdom 18:6-9

This reading from the book of Wisdom is an interpretation of the account of the deliverance of the chosen people at the time of their bondage in Egypt, specifically of the events of the night of their Passover. While the passage suggests the speaker is addressing God, the author employs a Greek literary form known as the syncrisis, a kind of comparison that points out the contrast between the plight of the Israelites and that of the Egyptians. This form is astutely used to show that God reversed the very means the Egyptians had employed in hopes of afflicting the Israelites. Thus the Egyptians themselves were smitten, while the Israelites escaped unscathed. The focus in this account is on the providence of God in sparing the people of Israel.

Many of the details of the original account (cf. Exodus 7-12) are presumed in this interpretation, though it does say the Israelites had been alerted in advance and so were ready. They took a great risk in deciding to flee the place of their oppression, but they put their trust in the promises of God. This is a very strong biblical theme. Past favors of God are remembered in order to instill trust that God will be no less provident in the present or future. In this hope the people waited, not knowing for what they were waiting but knowing in whom they had put their trust. The text suggests they knew they were to be saved while their enemies would be destroyed. Whether this was actually the case, it is a clear example of the syncrisis method of exposition.

The author boldly moves beyond the simple comparison of the syncrisis and claims that God reversed the fates of the two peoples and that the very means with which God punished the Egyptians in turn glorified the Israelites. At the very time when the angel of God was moving through Egypt killing the firstborn of every household, the Israelites were offering a lamb in substitutionary sacrifice. The blood of this lamb became their protection against the bloodletting suffered by the Egyptians.

The text says this liberating action on the part of God brought glory to the Israelites. This is a curious statement, because throughout its religious tradition Israel always insisted the glory belonged to God. Even when God performed wondrous feats, they were ultimately accomplished for the glory of God's name, never for the glory of Israel itself. This verse probably means their deliverance would show the Israelites to be the chosen People of God. This was a point of pride for them, but the glory always reverted to God, who delivered them.

Psalm 33:1, 12, 18-19, 20-22

The responsorial psalm opens with an invocation to praise. Everything in this response speaks of covenant relationship with God. First, only the just and the upright, those who have remained faithful to their pact with God, are called upon to praise the LORD. Second, only one nation was chosen by God to be a special people, to be God's own inheritance. That was the covenanted nation of Israel. The macarism ("Blessed" or "Happy") is spoken of Israel, the nation chosen as God's inheritance. Finally, the technical covenant term lovingkindness (*ḥesed*) is repeated (vv. 18, 22). The response clearly focuses on the theme of covenant.

The psalm employs the idea of inheritance in an interesting way. Inheritance normally refers to land handed down within a family from generation to generation. This social custom soon came to be used as a metaphor. The land of Israel was thought to belong to the various tribes only as an inheritance from God, who was the real proprietor. This led to an ever more extensive use of the metaphor, as found in this psalm. Inheritance indicates that Israel itself is not an independent entity; it belongs by right to God. This notion does not so much limit the freedom of Israel as underscore the passion with which God clings to the people.

The psalmist moves from consideration of covenant commitment to that of divine providence. For whom does God care? For all those who fear the LORD. "Fear" means standing in awe and wonder of someone or something, trembling in the presence of a great power or majesty. The psalm states that the LORD looks upon the people, presumably with eyes of compassion and love. God is characterized as a savior, one who will deliver them, one who will preserve them in the face of great need.

God is described as our help (*'ēzer;* the same word that describes Eve in Gen 2:18, 20) and our shield *(māgēn).* Together, the two words suggest some kind of military protection. There is no indication in these verses that the People of God are under any siege, but it may be because God, who has chosen to be in covenant with them, is always attentive to their safety and is with them as protector. The last verse is addressed directly to God. It is a prayer for the covenant bond of lovingkindness. It is for just such a relationship that the people hope.

Hebrews 11:1-2, 8-19

The first verse of this reading is one of the best-known passages from Scripture. It demonstrates the author's position that faith is more an openness of mind and heart than a set of theological propositions. The author uses the tradition about the faith of Abraham to illustrate what he means. The narrative is interrupted by theological interpretation intended for the author's own audience.

The story of Abraham's faith begins with his call from God to leave the home of his father and go to a land God would show him, a land he would receive as one receives an inheritance. The original story (Genesis 12) says nothing about faith or obedience, while this version is riveted on these two themes and declares it was because of his faith that Abraham obeyed. He left the familiarity of one land for the uncertainty of another, and all because of his faith in God. The sojourn of Abraham is seen as more than a search for a place to settle. The author of this letter, in a manner that today we would call anachronistic, credits Abraham with the desire he (the author) is trying to instill in the early Christians, a desire for a heavenly home. He is probably alluding to the heavenly Jerusalem, which is the true goal of all sojourners. In this way he links the religious journey of his Christian audience with the sojourn of their ancestor in faith.

At the time of the conception of Isaac, Abraham's faith became apparent again. Both he and Sarah were beyond their childbearing years, yet he believed the impossible was possible with God. Abraham was told he would have not only one heir but heirs beyond counting (cf. Gen 15:5; 22:17). God promised that this man, whose generative powers were as good as dead, would produce numerous descendants. Abraham's faith was rooted not so much in God's power as in the promise God had made, and because of this faith he received generative powers.

Once again the author interrupts the story for the sake of theological interpretation (vv. 13-17). He begins by stating that because they all died, the ancestors did not see the fulfillment of all the promises made to them. Still they believed. He returns almost immediately to the earlier point he made about a true and lasting homeland, stating that the ancestors were strangers not merely in the land that had been given to them. Like the Christians for whom this letter was intended, they were strangers on the earth itself.

Finally, Abraham's faith was manifested in his willingness to respond to God's further testing of his utter trust by sacrificing his only son, Isaac. The foreseeable consequences of his conformity to this testing are shattering. Isaac is the child through whom descendants will continue. To sacrifice him is to nullify God's initial promise and to forfeit his (Abraham's) future and the future of his household. Just as his faith led him to leave the blessings of his past (v. 8), so his faith leads him to relinquish the possibilities of his future.

Even though Isaac was not actually sacrificed, the text says that Abraham did indeed offer up his son. Once again, his faith is based on God's ability to bring life where there is no life. Could not God, who brought life through a man who was as good as dead, raise someone who was really dead? Believing that God could bring about the first marvel enabled Abraham to believe that God could also accomplish the second. The author states that Abraham's receiving Isaac back is a symbol. But a symbol of what? Does this refer to the eventual resurrection of all? This may well be the reference, but the text is not clear.

Luke 12:32-48

The gospel reading is a discourse intended for the disciples. It can be divided into three parts: a teaching on possessions (vv. 32-34); a story that demonstrates the importance of watchfulness (vv. 35-40); and instruction about responsible leadership (vv. 41-48). The first part is quite discrete, but the other two address the manner in which disciples should await the return of the Son of Man.

Jesus' address to his disciples reveals the tender nature of their relationship. The metaphor of a flock suggests both intimate knowledge and wholehearted commitment on the part of the shepherd. With this term of endearment Jesus assures the disciples that his teaching, regardless of how demanding it may seem, has their best interests at heart. He first announces that the reign of God is theirs; he then exhorts them to live lives that demonstrate their citizenship in that realm. With one admonition he exemplifies the kind of total commitment required of citizens of the reign of God. The admonition itself sounds radical. It was probably not intended to be taken literally, for total divestment would have turned the disciples into paupers, making them dependent on others for survival and sustenance.

Jesus does not denounce material possessions as such but only the amassing of such goods: he tells the disciples not to have money bags for carrying their surplus. He knows that trust in riches can stand in the way of trust in God, so he tells his disciples to get rid of what they do not immediately need and to concentrate their energies on the things of God.

Jesus introduces his teaching about watchfulness with a twofold admonition. He tells the men to tuck their flowing robes under their belts and to prepare for strenuous activity and then to light their lamps, suggesting they will have to be watchful even into the night. He is not explicit about the reason for this; he merely instructs them to be prepared, like servants awaiting the return of the householder. The reference to guarding a house against thieves is a second though unconnected example of the need for constant vigilance. There are eschatological nuances in the parable. First, the householder was away at a wedding, a favorite image for the celebration of the end-time. Second, the reward for watchfulness is a banquet served by the master himself, an allusion to the messianic banquet. Finally, Jesus links the return of the householder with the coming of the Son of Man. Since there is no telling when he will arrive, loyal servants must be prepared at all times.

In response to Peter's query, Jesus tells a second story that describes not only the watchfulness required of disciples but also the way leaders or managers of the household *(oikonōmos)* are to carry out their responsibilities while the master is away. The first manager is conscientious in the care of others, while the second is not only remiss in carrying out the duties of stewardship but actually abusive and self-indulgent. Other servants are chastised not because of what they did but because of what they failed to do. Preparedness does not mean simply waiting. One must be responsible during that wait.

The entire teaching ends with an explanatory saying. Everyone will be held accountable. Those to whom much has been given will be accountable for much; those to whom more has been given will be accountable for more. There is no thought here of having been given little.

Themes of the Day

In the middle of Ordinary Time we are confronted with a theme normally associated with the end of the Liturgical Year and the season of Advent. It is the theme of vigilance in anticipation of the return of the Master. This vigilance demands that we live lives of faith.

Vigilance

We might think this call to be vigilant is a proleptic view of the future, a kind of long-range preparation for Advent. However, the theme is probably placed before us today to remind us that we must be vigilant always, not simply at the beginning and the end of the Liturgical Year. We must always stand ready for the return of the Lord, for we really do not know when he is coming. This is true about waiting for the end of time as well as for the end of our specific time. However, it is also true about other times, for we do not know when God will open the door or window of our existence and call us into a deeper realization of the sacred dimension of life itself. Vigilance is a characteristic of a Christian at all times, for all times.

We must be ever vigilant so we can recognize the Lord in the people with whom we live and work. We must be ever vigilant so we can recognize the advent of the Lord in the world events of which we are a part. We must be always ready to respond to the call of discipleship, to serve where there is need, to carry out our life responsibilities in a fair and equitable fashion. We cannot be sure of the hour of our calling, because in a sense, every hour is the hour of our calling. Therefore, we must be ever vigilant.

We Live by Faith

While we live in the expectation of the full and ultimate coming of God in the future, we also live now in the presence of God. This means that God is present with us now as a companion in our lives. It also means that it is within God's presence that we live; in fact, God's presence is the context within which our lives unfold. However, until all things are brought to fulfillment we live in this presence by faith. At the time of the Passover the people put their faith in the promises God had made to them, and they were saved by means of that faith. Throughout his life Abraham lived by faith, clinging tenaciously to it despite what appeared to be impossible odds. Faith is the way we live when we do not see what we think we must see in order to go on.

It is through faith that we cling to the essence of our dreams when they seem to be dashed before our eyes. It is through faith that we launch out into new vistas when we are invited into the lives of others. It is through faith that we courageously endure the heartbreaks of life and the diminishments we all must face. It is faith that is the inner light that enables us to carry on in the dark.

Faith and hope are intimately joined. As believers we are called to trust in the promises of God, even when what is promised seems impossible. Faith is the way we live our lives before these promises unfold. We are promised a life of peace and harmony. As people of faith we are called to live in this world of hatred and violence as if that promise had already been fulfilled, for it is through our living in that faith that it is indeed brought to birth.

Faith Is Its Own Reward

A life lived in faith is its own revenue, its own reward. We are assured that we will be blessed, but we can never be sure of the exact nature of the blessing. The Israelites were freed from bondage only to find themselves in the wilderness facing yet another test of faith. Abraham offered his son, not knowing the ultimate sacrifice would not be required. Had he been assured that Isaac would be saved, it would not have been a question of faith. A life of faith can guarantee only one thing, that we will be able to live by faith. In faith, we put our trust in God and then carry out our responsibilities. In faith we wait for the Lord, who is our help and our shield, not really knowing under what guise he will come to us. Faith is both the cost of living as a disciple and the reward.

Twentieth Sunday in Ordinary Time
Jeremiah 38:4-6, 8-10

The reading for this Sunday is a drama of national crisis, prophetic involvement, and political power plays. The fate of the prophet Jeremiah seems to be in the hands of a vacillating king who is influenced first by the power establishment of Judah (v. 5) and then by a lone court official from the land of Cush (Ethiopia; v. 10). Zedekiah, whose name is derived from the word for "righteous" (*ṣaddîq*), was the last of the kings of Judah before the Babylonian Exile. He was no match for the political intrigues of his day, as can be seen in the reading for this Sunday.

The city in question is Jerusalem. It is under siege and seems to be losing the battle, as evidenced in the fact that there is no more food (v. 9). The princes are enraged because of the message Jeremiah had been preaching. We are not told what it was, but its effect on the soldiers was devastating. They are demoralized. The Hebrew says: He weakened the hands of the men of war. At a time of national crisis, as was facing the nation, such behavior was an act of treason punishable by death. The princes prevail upon the king. It sounds like King Zedekiah would have preferred to follow another avenue. Perhaps he was open to the message of the prophet. However, he was powerless against the princes, and thus he handed Jeremiah over to them. Here is an instance in which the word of God spoken by the prophet and the policies of the nation are in deadly conflict. In such a situation the one who speaks in God's name is likely to pay the price, exactly as happened in this case.

The princes chose a death without bloodshed. Their reasons are not given. Perhaps they were reluctant to have the blood of a prophet on their hands. The man who saved Jeremiah was a foreigner whose name means "servant [*ʿebed*] of the king [*melek*]." His reasons for saving Jeremiah are also not given. However, his explanation to the king regarding the inevitable death of the prophet seems somewhat strange, since that is precisely why Jeremiah had been put in the cistern in the first place. Furthermore, the king was well aware of it and had given his approval. However, at the urging of Ebed-melech he gave permission for Jeremiah's rescue.

The unrest in the kingdom is almost tangible. Not only do the people have to contend with a nation mightier than themselves, but there is no stability in their own government, and they are divided over the matter of prophetic proclamation. In this passage Jeremiah appears to be the center of contention.

Psalm 40:2, 3, 4, 18

This is a prayer of thanksgiving for past deliverance. In view of this deliverance, the psalmist pleads for further help from God (v. 18). To wait for the LORD is to stand patiently until God comes to one's assistance. Here the assistance of God is characterized as reaching down into death in order to draw up the afflicted one. The danger into which God reaches in order to rescue the psalmist is the pit or the swamp, both metaphors for death. The reference may not have been to death itself, yet anything that diminished life, whether sickness or misfortune, was often characterized as death. The imagery is reminiscent of the ancient seasonal myths in which one of the gods descends into the abode of the dead only to rise again to new life. The metaphor gradually came to be used to speak of the descent of human beings in general. This psalm includes the hope of rising from misfortune.

The psalmist is rescued from what might swallow up her or him. This is followed by the establishment of the psalmist on reliable rock. The contrast is obvious. The psalmist had been at risk of falling further and further into the pit, of slipping deeper and deeper into the mud of the swamp. Having been drawn up out of danger, the psalmist is placed on a secure rock, a place of sound footing. The rescue is celebrated with a new song, probably one that extols the exploits of the LORD in this event of deliverance. It could also refer to the move from the cry of lament in the face of suffering to a song of praise and gratitude for deliverance. The proclamation itself is not only a hymn of praise of God, it also serves as a witness to others of God's goodness to the petitioner and to the might that God showed on behalf of the psalmist.

Two stereotypical words are used to describe the psalmist: "afflicted" *('ānî)*, and "poor" *('ebyôn)*. These words eventually became synonymous with the righteous ones who, though deprived of protection by the power structures of the world, were favored by God and supported precisely because of their vulnerability. Once again God is referred to as help *('ēzer)*, this time coupled with deliverance *(pᵉlêt)*. Past favors are the basis of present cries for help. God delivered the psalmist in the past, surely God will repeat the act of deliverance in the present and even in the future.

Hebrews 12:1-4

In this exhortation to endurance the author of the letter to the Hebrews skillfully employs the metaphor of a race. Since the games were one of the major events of the Greco-Roman world, this metaphor was a marvelous way of encouraging the people to persevere in Christian living.

Just as the games were often held in a large stadium or amphitheater that could hold the crowds that came to watch, so Christians are surrounded by a great crowd of witnesses *(mártys)*. There is no way of knowing whether the author was thinking of those who had given their lives in witness to their faith or simply of faithful Christians who themselves gave witness. It really does not matter, for the point of the image is the encouragement these people would give to those running the race. Just as athletes are spurred on by the cheers of the people in the stands, so too Christians are encouraged by those who have preceded them.

Runners must strip themselves of anything that might encumber them. They must carry nothing that is not necessary for the race, and they must wear the kind of clothing that will allow free movement. This is true with regard to Christians as well. They should not be impeded by unnecessary weight, the heaviest burden being sin itself. Although the word for "sin" *(hamartía)* really means "missing the mark," as sometimes happens when one throws an object, it also denotes "guilt" or "rebellion." To carry such a burden would deprive the runner of the freedom necessary to move swiftly or would make running so difficult the runner would tire very quickly.

Success in any athletic venture requires that one have a goal and that this goal be kept uppermost in the athlete's mind. The author insists that Jesus should be the goal continually held before the eyes of the runner. Like the witnesses in the stands, Jesus would urge the runner to strain further and further. He would do this because he has already run the race and won it. He faithfully endured both the cross and the opposition of others. Having been put to death, he now is seated triumphant in the place of honor in heaven next to

God. He has run the race; now he enjoys the crown that is the reward for his success. As the runners begin to tire, they can look to him. This last point suggests that, like a marathon runner rather than a sprinter, the Christian runner is in for the long haul.

A very different image is used in the last verse of this passage. The author speaks about struggling and shedding blood, two characteristics of boxing or wrestling rather than running. Whatever the case, the message is still one of encouragement. Despite the hardships involved, Christians are not alone in their struggle. They have Jesus as their model, and they have the encouragement of the other witnesses.

Luke 12:49-53

The picture Jesus paints of himself in this gospel passage is troubling if we think of him merely as a gentle Messiah who came to spread peace throughout the world. Here he insists that his coming is comparable to a dramatic prophetic visitation. He says that he has come to cast fire on the earth, to be baptized, and to cause division at the very heart of human society. It is not that Jesus is eager for these disturbing events in themselves to unfold. Rather, he himself burns with zeal for the accomplishment of his earthly mission, which, in calling for radical change, will inevitably include such consequences.

The reference to casting fire on the earth probably denotes severe judgment, as did a similar action of the prophet Elijah (cf. 2 Kgs 1:10-14). Some commentators hold this to be a reference to the Spirit, who will come in fire. However, the negative tone of this passage suggests otherwise. It is more likely an allusion to the refiner's fire of which the prophet Malachi spoke (Mal 3:2). Along with this fire, which will purify the earth, Jesus speaks of the baptism he will have to undergo. It is clear he is talking about the suffering and death he will endure. While he dreads it he also embraces it, for he knows it will be the avenue through which he will accomplish his mission.

The linchpin that holds all the elements of this discourse together is the complex issue of division. While Jesus himself may have been a man of peace, the message he proclaimed was clearly divisive. Many of the claims he made cut to the core of the dominant social and religious custom and understanding of the time. He made demands on people that challenged them to the very heart of their being. He insisted that commitment to him and to his message must take precedence over any political and even kinship loyalties. This was the cause of the division described in the passage. Those who were originally bonded to each other by the closest human ties were often torn apart by loyalty to him. Some who were able to accept him and his teaching were even ostracized by those who did not. The animosity Jesus generated was also the cause of his own rejection and ultimate suffering and death.

This teaching is presented from Jesus' perspective. However, from the perspective of the one hearing his teaching, it unfolds in the following manner. Jesus' teaching and his demands bring on the division and antagonism that in turn resulted in his death. His death was the baptism into which he was destined to be baptized. The fire of judgment that he cast was the inevitable consequence of the choice that was made in his regard. Its purifying flames separated those who accepted him from those who did not. There is no consoling conclusion to this discourse. Here Jesus has described the effects his teaching will have on others. It is for those who hear this message to decide which course of action they will choose.

Themes of the Day

The readings for this Sunday provide us with an opportunity to continue to meditate on various aspects of the theme of discipleship begun last week. This week we look again at the cost of discipleship. This leads us to the realization that only if we have some kind of assistance can we pay the price. Finally, we realize that discipleship is lived out within the context of community.

The Cost of Discipleship

We might wonder why anyone would want to be a disciple, because so much is demanded. As disciples we commit ourselves to values and principles that are not cherished by everyone. We can be misunderstood for our beliefs, even ridiculed. In fact, our lives may actually be a reproach to those who do not share our aspirations. There may be times when we must stand in opposition to others. All of this tends to alienate us. It could even place us at enmity with those we love.

Yet, if we are genuinely committed, we realize there is also a price to pay if we are *not* faithful. It is very difficult to live with ourselves when we disregard our deepest convictions and ignore the promptings of God we experience within ourselves. As difficult as a life of faith may be, we know that such a life is the only way to live in this world. We realize that we do not control life. Rather, we are carried by it, and so we must make friends with its mystery and ambiguity. Fidelity may exact a dear price, but it is the only way open to us if we are to be true to ourselves and to God.

Divine Assistance

Faced with the cost of discipleship, we are brought to the realization that by ourselves we do not have the resources to pay it. We need assistance. The readings today remind us that we have the assistance we need. Both the reading from Jeremiah and the psalm assure us that God will stoop down and draw us out of the pit within which we find ourselves. We might find, as did the prophet, that this aid will come from places we have never expected. Strangers can help us; children can open our eyes to reality; the elderly can provide us with insight. We may discover that those closest to us are not supportive, but there are others who appreciate the stands we take, the directions we set for ourselves. We may discover that while we lose some brothers and sisters, we gain others.

The real support and assistance we get is from Jesus, who came to set the world and our hearts on fire. He endured the cross and gave us an example to follow. Actually, as disciples we do not have to do heroic deeds. We only have to live our normal lives in heroic ways. But people do that all the time. Parents sacrifice themselves for their children; police and firefighters put themselves at risk for perfect strangers. Daily we hear of ordinary people acting heroically. The grace of God is mediated to us through these people. Whether stranger or friend, they belong to the throng that surrounds us. Through them the grace of God can accomplish extraordinary feats.

The Communion of Saints

Paul assures us that there is a vast throng cheering us on as we run the race of discipleship. They are not merely spectators; they are those who have already run or are still running their own race. We are not alone in our commitment, in our struggle. There are many witnesses, many examples for us to follow. Some of these people may have already died, but their lives remain as testimony to the value of commitment. We may have known these people. They could be relatives who were examples of unselfish commitment to others. They could be strangers whose courage in the face of death has caused us to stand in awe. They could be people in the neighborhood or the workplace whose friendliness brightened our day. This is the great crowd of witnesses that cheer us on. There are also many saints who are still alive, who continue to act in these ways. It is through them that God draws us out of the pit; it is through them that God comes to our aid.

Twenty-First Sunday in Ordinary Time
Isaiah 66:18-21

The scene in the first reading for this Sunday depicts a great ingathering. It is an unusual scene, for the people brought together come from every nation.

These are not Israelites returning home from the Diaspora; they are pagans (*gôyim*), probably people from surrounding lands. They are not captives of war who have been forced into the land by victorious Israelites, there to serve as slaves. Rather, they are brought in by God and to them will be revealed the glory of God.

The prophet next announces that these foreign people are called together by God and will become a sign to other foreigners of the glory they themselves have seen. Some of their number will be sent out to distant places, such as Tarshish, a Phoenician colony in southern Spain; Put and Lud, most likely nations in Africa; Mosoch and Tubal, nations southeast of the Black Sea; and Javan, a Greek colony. These are nations known for their exploits in war and trading (cf. Ezek 27:10, 13; 30:5) but who had never heard of the God of Israel.

This prophetic vision is surprising, for Israel was not a nation that engaged in much missionary activity. Most of its Scripture shows it to be quite ethnocentric, concerned with its own needs and development. Such isolationism is understandable for a relatively small nation that for most of its existence had to struggle for survival amidst larger and more powerful peoples. While at times it did believe that all the nations of the world would eventually come to Jerusalem, Israel did not seem to believe these nations would be brought in, especially by other nations.

Furthermore, Israel had an all-consuming concern for ritual purity. In its desire to worship God in as perfect a manner possible, it developed stringent laws that separated what was considered clean from what was judged unclean. This included foreign people as well. Here, foreigners are brought together by God to behold divine glory. They are also sent out to announce God's fame abroad and to bring their new converts to worship the God of Israel in the Temple in Jerusalem.

Both the universal nature and the cultic character of the vision become clear. Those who come from foreign lands are joined with the Israelites at the Temple in Jerusalem. There both groups offer sacrifice to the LORD. The kind of sacrifice mentioned is the *minḥâ* (v. 20), a generic name for cereal offerings. While the Israelites seem to bring an actual cereal offering, the others bring new recruits as a symbolic offering. The prophet paints an extraordinary picture. People stream to Jerusalem from all four directions. Warriors come on horses; the wealthy come in chariots; women are carried on litters; the poor come on mules; merchants come on dromedaries. They all come to worship on God's holy mountain.

What may be the most amazing feature of this vision is found in the final verse. It is from these foreign people that God will call forth priests and Levites. Formerly only men from priestly or Levitical families were accorded this honor. Those who were chosen for this service were then responsible for the observance of all of the cultic regulations pertaining to purity. Here it appears that both ethnic privilege and cultic regulations are set aside, and this all happens through the action of God.

Psalm 117:1-2

The entire psalm consists of these two verses. It is a hymn with a universal point of view. All nations *(gôyim)* and all peoples *('ûmmîm)* are called on to give praise and glory to the God of Israel. The reason for this praise is the wonderful deeds God has accomplished on behalf of Israel. Two technical covenant words are used to describe God's beneficence: lovingkindness *(ḥesed)*, and truth, or "fidelity" *('ĕmet)*. Most likely the reference here is to the deliverance God granted the people of Israel and the subsequent covenant commitment God entered into with them.

It may seem strange that other nations are called upon to praise God for the blessings bestowed upon Israel. It is certain that many of these blessings would have redounded negatively on some of these nations, particularly the ones who stand as enemies of Israel. Because of Israel's insignificance on the world scene, its victory and the corresponding defeat of other nations and peoples would be considered by them as an act of God's goodness.

This brief psalm points out an important dimension of the election of Israel. The blessings granted Israel were not intended for that nation alone. Israel was to be the instrument of God's universal goodness. Others were to look on Israel and see not a great nation but a lowly one, a nation that became great through the mercy of God. This was the message Israel was chosen to proclaim, this was the good news of universal salvation.

Hebrews 12:5-7, 11-13

It seems the community to whom the letter to the Hebrews was addressed was undergoing some form of misfortune and was unable to arrive at an explanation for it. The traditional reason given maintains that suffering is the inevitable consequence of imprudent or sinful behavior. However, in situations where no fault can be found this explanation is seriously wanting. A second and perhaps less satisfying reason given suggests that suffering is really a form of discipline intended to make one strong. This second explanation does not so much address the cause of the misfortune as it suggests an attitude that will enable the one suffering to make the most of a difficult situation. It is the second explanation that is being advanced here.

The author of the letter first rebukes the community for not having remembered the teaching found within its own religious tradition. He then appeals to a well-known proverb that provides the explanation he is suggesting (cf. Prov 3:11-12). Since the Wisdom tradition was primarily anthropocentric (human-centered) in its concerns and in the formulation of its teaching, we should not be surprised that an androcentric (male-centered) society would view universal human concerns from an exclusively male point of view. This bias is very clear in the passage for today. However, in most cases this does not prevent us from reinterpreting the teaching more inclusively.

Both the original proverb and the author of Hebrews attempt to soften the view that suffering is discipline from God by appealing to the relationship of parent to child. One can say it is out of love and concern that parents discipline their children. Furthermore, it is important to remember that the Greek word for discipline *(paideía)* does not mean punishment but instruction, or training for life. This is what the community seems to have forgotten, and this is what the author is exhorting them to remember. Suffering is the rigorous training God puts us through so we might be strengthened for life itself.

The author next develops the Wisdom theme in a very creative way. Having argued that suffering is not always the consequence of foolish or sinful living, he now maintains that the endurance of suffering, which is surely an act of virtue, will earn a reward for those who suffer. There may be pain now, but there will be joy later for those who are trained *(gymnázō)* in it. This verb introduces the theme of physical exercise. Drooping hands and weak knees, symptoms of exhaustion, further develop the theme of athletic performance. According to the Wisdom tradition an individual must choose one of two paths, the way of the wise or the way of the foolish. The path referred to here is the way of the athlete, and the advice given admonishes the runner to make sure the path is straight so there will be no mishap.

Suffering, then, can be compared to the training a concerned parent provides for a beloved child or to the discipline an athlete undergoes in order to be prepared to run the race.

Luke 13:22-30

The gospel account contains both soteriological and christological teaching. Its literary form can be divided into an initial question that introduces the issue of salvation (v. 23), an illustrative allegory (vv. 24-27), a judgment scene (vv. 28-29), and a concluding saying (v. 30).

The questioner is not identified. While there seems to have been a difference of opinion in Jewish thinking of the time regarding the number of those saved (cf. *Sanhedrin* 10:1), there is no reason to think the questioning was an attempt to trap Jesus into answering in a way that could cause controversy. However, Jesus gives no direct answer to the question but turns the focus from curiosity about the salvation of others to concern about one's own future, not unlike the shift he made when the lawyer asked him to identify his neighbor (cf. Luke 10:25-37; Fifteenth Sunday).

Jesus introduces his story with an exhortation: "Strive" *(agōnízomai)*, a word used when describing the energy put forward during athletic competitions. With this exhortation he is telling his hearers to struggle for the prize, to commit themselves wholeheartedly, for the task before them is not an easy one. He then tells a story to illustrate how difficult it will be for some to be saved. This does not suggest that salvation is open to only a few. Rather, it shows that some do not make the necessary effort to get into the banquet hall. They either do not respond to the invitation in a timely fashion and then come too late to be admitted, or they presume that casual association with rather than genuine commitment to the master of the house (presumably Jesus) is adequate. In both cases those outside who expect to be admitted are turned away. To add to their dismay, they are told that some whom they look down on as outsiders will be brought in to the festivities while they will remain outside, weeping in disappointment and gnashing their teeth in envy. The people who will come from the four corners are probably the righteous Gentiles who will be invited to dine with the heroes of Israelite history.

This gospel shows some of the surprising reversals the reign of God will bring forth. Salvation is not promised exclusively to one group and not to another; the contrasts drawn are not all-inclusive. Still, the surprise will be in seeing who is saved and who is not. Insiders will be kept outside, and outsiders will be brought in; Jews will be barred from the messianic banquet, while Gentiles will feast at it; outcasts will be welcome, but religious elites will not. While this is true only of some members of each group, the reversals themselves will startle many.

Themes of the Day

The theme of community, which we considered last week, is found again in the readings for this week but with a slightly different focus. Here we are offered a threefold meditation on salvation and the role discipleship plays in it. We see the universal scope of God's salvific grace sketched again and again. It is a grace that draws people into the community and sends disciples out from that community to proclaim the good news of salvation.

Universal Salvation

The vision of a disciple must be the vision of God. It cannot be myopic or parochial. Disciples must see with wide-angle lenses, which enable them to recognize that God offers the grace of salvation to all. The passages from both Isaiah and Luke are astounding in their inclusivity. They show that God's saving grace is unbounded. It reaches out to those whom the People of God may not only distrust but sometimes even despise. From their, or our, point of view only those who have been faithful deserve salvation. Only those who belong to the right religious groups, who believe the correct religious doctrines, and who follow an approved way of life should be gathered into the company of the saved.

There is something dangerous about being smugly convinced of one's own salvation. Usually when this is the case, it is because we ourselves have followed the rules, important rules to be sure, but nonetheless rules. When we are so sure of ourselves, we can easily fall into the error of being as sure of the moral failure of others as well. The gospel warns us against such judgment. Our claim of knowing the Lord is not adequate for entrance into the banquet hall. The first reading clearly shows that salvation comes from God and not from anything we might have done. Our entrance into the banquet is a free gift from God, and anyone who will receive it as freely given will be welcomed.

The Gathering

Women and men are gathered into the community of the saved, primarily because others have been sent out to get them. The psalm refrain is the command to go out to the whole world. The first reading describes God sending fugitives back home to get their relatives. People come from all over because someone is sent to get them.

Today the command is directed to us. We are the ones who are being sent out to bring others to God. Every eucharistic liturgy ends with this commission, to which we may unthinkingly respond: "Thanks be to God!" The readings for this Sunday shake us awake to this responsibility. We are all sent back to the people and circumstances of our lives, there to be ambassadors of the saving grace of God. Others will hear of the fame and see the glory of God only through us. We are sent to be the light shining on the hill for all to see; we are sent to be the yeast that enables the dough to rise. We proclaim the God we worship and serve in the way we transact our business in our offices, in the supermarkets, in the classrooms, in the neighborhood, or in family gatherings. The way we live proclaims to the world in which we live that salvation is for all, and we are evidence of this.

The Need for Discipline

Unfortunately there are many people who do not believe they are fit to be evangelizers. They do not feel that they have the necessary theological training or that they are assertive enough to go out and bring others to God. They may think the work they do or the lives they live do not lend themselves to the task of spreading the good news of the gospel. They do not realize that all Christians are called and sent. This is not an option; it is a responsibility. They may not be professional ministers, but they are ministers nonetheless. They proclaim the message of salvation in everything they do and in the way they do it.

The reading from the letter to the Hebrews shows us that the key requirement for evangelization is discipline in the way we live our lives and carry out our responsibilities. All of us Christians are baptized into the life of Christ; we all are called to witness to Christlikeness in every facet of our existence. We must be disciplined enough to be willing in every circumstance of life to manifest Christlikeness to the world. We must encourage one another in our common efforts to be faithful; we cannot be at odds with one another. The Christlike life of Christians is the fundamental proclamation of the gospel. This is what draws others to the community of believers. As Christians, we are called to this and given what is necessary to carry it out.

Twenty-Second Sunday in Ordinary Time
Sirach 3:17-18, 20, 28-29

These few verses provide us with a short discourse on humility. What appears to be a title of endearment ("My child") may simply indicate the relationship between a teacher and a student. It sounds at first as if the motive for humility is purely utilitarian: so that you might be loved more than those who give gifts (v. 17). This is a criticism frequently lodged against the Wisdom tradition generally. However, this discourse is not lacking in religious motivation, for humility is said to find favor in God. It is clear from the text that the advice given here is not meant for those who lack standing in the community (v. 18). It insists, instead, that one's humility should increase as one's status does.

The author admonishes the student to be content with things within the realm of possibility. Don't reach for what exceeds your grasp; don't try to do what is beyond your strength. Since this is a discourse on humility, the implication is that one might attempt to do this in order to promote one's reputation in the eyes of others. Still, the value of this advice, as with all Wisdom teaching, depends upon the circumstances. In some situations it would be foolhardy to do otherwise. In others this advice might curtail creativity. It is important to remember that the only way we discover whether we are attempting the impossible is to try. Failure to achieve our goals will help us recognize our limitations. Even this does not adequately address the question, because one failure does not necessarily mean we should not try again. It is precisely in situations of ambiguity such as this that we exercise our wisdom and gain more.

A proverb is a concise poetic form that succinctly describes an aspect of reality. It is like a snapshot that captures one moment in all its splendor. But also like a snapshot, it removes that moment from its broader context. Proverbs are descriptive in form; they state how things are. However, they are intended to be exhortative in function: this is the way things are, so live in conformity with it. A good proverb is a distinctive work of art. It requires astute attention and creative composition. It is no wonder the wise appreciate proverbs (v. 28).

The reading ends somewhat abruptly with a poetic phrase that introduces a distinctly new theme. It is a kind of proverbial comparison. Though it does not explicitly state it, the saying implies that as water quenches fire, so alms atone for sin. Both the water and the alms wipe out what is detrimental. As stated above, descriptive proverbs are meant to function as exhortation. It is clear this particular proverbial saying promotes the giving of alms. Taken together, the advice contained in this passage directs the student to develop a attitude of humility regardless of status within the community and to meet the needs of the less fortunate. It is good counsel for all, regardless of one's social standing.

Psalm 68:4-5, 6-7, 10-11

The verses that make up today's responsorial psalm sketch two very different images of God. The first is a picture of the protector of the vulnerable; the second depicts God as the source of life for the earth. Together they illustrate the power of God in history and the created world.

The response itself begins with a statement describing the praise God receives from the righteous. Several words for rejoicing are used, emphasizing the extent of the delight they take in God. The phrase "before God" (in the face of God) is frequently associated with being in the presence of God during some cultic celebration. Later, mention of God's holy dwelling (v. 6) confirms this meaning. The actual call to praise speaks of God's holy name. Since one's name was synonymous with one's identity, this is clearly a call to praise God.

The LORD is depicted as father of orphans and defender of widows, two categories of people who, in a patriarchal society, had no legal protection. For this reason God steps in and becomes the paternal protector. Though not explicitly stated here, the imagery leaves no doubt in our minds that it is because of a previous covenantal commitment that God fulfills these roles in this way. The people are referred to as the inheritance of God (v. 10) and as the flock of God (v. 11), both references to their special election. Other imagery seems to allude to the release of the People of God from Egyptian bondage and to the ultimate settlement of those people in a land of their own (v. 7). Such historical recital was a part of many of Israel's liturgical celebrations. They were meant to recall God's goodness and to act as incentive for the praise to which the people were summoned. God is here praised as the savior of the people.

In the second portrayal, God is cast in the guise of the storm god from whom comes the fertility of the land. In ancient Canaan, this distinction belonged to Baal. One of the first major feats the religion of Israel was able to accomplish was the repudiation of that Canaanite storm deity and the appropriation of Baal's prerogatives and powers to the God of Israel. Now it is the God of Israel who rains down life-giving water so the land that has been given to Israel will flourish and the people who settle there will be prosperous. God is here praised as the Creator.

As Israel brought together these two images of God, that of Creator and redeemer, it was making a very bold statement. It was not unusual to believe that one's God was a protector of the vulnerable of society. However, to claim God was Creator was to make God sovereign above all the other powers of heaven. This was because in ancient Near Eastern mythology the creator was the one who had conquered the forces of evil and then reigned supreme above all. Israel is here saying that its God, who cares for widows and orphans with the care of the father of a patriarchal family, is the very God who brought order into the universe at the beginning of time and who continues to provide the earth with the necessary waters of life.

Hebrews 12:18-19, 22-24a

The reading contains a comparison between ancient Israel's experience of God on Mount Sinai and the eschatological experience of God on the transformed Mount Zion. Wherever there is a contrast between the old and the new, the former and the present, we must be careful how we interpret it lest we find ourselves guilty of anti-Judaic sentiments. While the text speaks of approaching the mountains, the verb that is translated "approach" *(prosér-chomai)* is the same word from which "proselyte" is derived. Thus the approach has more than spatial significance; one comes to the mountain in order to commit oneself. Finally, both scenes are cultic in character. However, they engender very different religious responses.

Although the first mountain is not named, the description of the activity that transpires on and around it clearly points to Mount Sinai, the place where God established a covenant with Israel. The darkness, the fire, and the storm are all universal characteristics of a theophany, and they attended the experience of God as described in Israel's earliest traditions (cf. Exod 19:16-19; Deut 4:11-12). The trumpet was probably the summons that called people first to the experience of God and later to its liturgical reenactment. These sensory perceptions created an atmosphere of dread for the people. This was coupled with a certain amount of distress generated by the message delivered during the theophany. Finally, the people were forbidden to advance too closely. As basic as was the covenant established at this time, the author claims that all these elements discouraged access to the divine.

On the other hand, the encounter with God on Mount Zion described here is unique. We must remember that the mount in question is not merely the hill associated with the kingdom of David and upon which Solomon constructed the Temple. While this rich tradition is certainly in the background, the present scene is eschatological in nature, not political. Zion, along with the city of Jerusalem within which it stood, was considered the special dwelling place of God on earth. For this reason it became the symbol of the eternal dwelling place of God, the mount upon which, in the age of fulfillment, all people would eventually gather to worship. This is the scene described in the text.

Unlike the experience on Sinai, this theophany on Zion is surrounded with festive celebration. Here we find angels, the assembly *(ekklēsía)* of the firstborn of heaven (probably those who preceded the author's audience into the presence of God), and the spirits of the just (a reference broad enough to include the ancient Israelites). God is here as judge and Jesus is here as mediator of the new covenant. It should be noted that the efficacy of the blood of the innocent Christ is compared to the blood of the innocent Abel and not that of the Passover sacrifice. This suggests the scene is not so much a repudiation of the first covenant as it is a description of the eschatological fulfillment accomplished by means of the second.

Luke 14:1, 7-14

The events depicted in the gospel reading for this Sunday take place on the Sabbath during dinner at the home of one of the leading Pharisees. All these details are important for the lessons Jesus will teach. Sabbath dinners were occasions for inviting guests who were not family members. This explains why Jesus was present. Furthermore, such gatherings were times for theological discussion and, in the case of Jesus, an opportunity for the religious leaders present to put his orthodoxy to the test. Finally, the saying with which the episode closes would have been of great interest to Pharisees, who believed in resurrection.

The text says Jesus was watched by the other guests at the dinner. However, he is the one who found fault, and he is the one who delivered two ethical directives, one intended for the guests and the other for the host. He first told a parabolic story that addressed proper placement at banquets. This was an important issue for a society preoccupied, as was Israel of the day, with questions of honor and shame. One's place at table was indicative of the degree of honor with which the host regarded the guest. The story shows the folly in presuming importance at a public banquet. It may be that another guest will arrive and be given a higher place of honor, and then one will be shamed into taking a less significant seat.

Jesus does not criticize this practice. Instead, he finds fault with the arrogant attitude of those who think they are more important than they really are. He actually seems to uphold the practice, admonishing the guests to take lower seats so they can glory in the public acclaim that will be theirs as they move to places of greater honor. This is the society of which he is a member, and he uses its social practices to make his points. This first part of his instruction ends with an admonition that seems to turn priorities upside down. Societies that are driven by questions of status seldom advocate humbling oneself. In fact, the contrary is usually true; they humble others in order to exalt themselves. What Jesus advocates is just the opposite. He would have people humble themselves and refrain from self-exaltation so they can be exalted by God rather than by others.

Turning to the host, Jesus criticizes the practice of inviting to a banquet only those who are able to reciprocate in kind. There is no generosity in giving to those who can repay. Rather, give to the poor and to those in need, the very people who could in no way advance one's sense of honor but who might in fact undermine one's reputation. Inviting the needy will show that one's generosity comes from the kind of open attitude toward others that Jesus preached. The Pharisees may not have agreed with this particular admonition of Jesus, but they would have understood his statement about reward to come at the time of resurrection. Unlike the Sadducees, who only accepted what was written in sacred Scripture, Pharisees did believe in the resurrection. The reference to resurrection of the righteous does not suggest there will be no resurrection for the wicked. The statement may have been formulated in this way because the behavior described will warrant reward, not punishment.

Both parts of Jesus' teaching in this account challenge the prevailing principles of honor and shame. Jesus first redefines what is honorable behavior, and then he redefines who are honored guests. Insisting that the kind of behavior he is advocating will be rewarded at the resurrection implies that one's status is determined by God, not by some biased social convention. The people at table have come to observe him carefully. The reading does not tell us how they responded to his teaching.

Themes of the Day

The overarching theme for this Sunday is generosity in giving. The particular focus is the invitation to share in a meal that celebrates community. The readings describe the attitudes we should have when we give and when we receive. They emphasize the undesirability of merely a sense of reciprocity and the desirability of humble and unconditional openness.

God's Bounteous Generosity

The exquisite nature of God is seen in the extravagant generosity with which God gives gifts. This is described in the psalm through imagery that captures both its boundlessness and its universal scope. Like the rain that falls on the entire landscape, the blessings of God are showered on all. The chief recipients are those who are not only needy but who have no way of repaying the blessings bestowed. In other words, these blessings are true gifts. They have not been earned, nor can they be repaid. Such is the nature of God's giving.

God's openness to include all is also seen in the reading from the letter to the Hebrews and in the gospel. All are invited to approach the heavenly city; the heavenly banquet will be open to the poor and to those who have no way of repaying. Neither status nor worldly possessions nor accomplishments is an adequate coin of recompense. The only recompense acceptable is a heart open to receive.

Only God can give gifts in this way, because only God has an infinite supply of blessings to give and no need to receive in return. Yet we are admonished to be generous in this way. In the gospel we are told to open our tables and our hearts to those who are unable to respond in kind. There are to be no restrictions on our openness to others, on the generosity with which we give of ourselves and our possessions. We must be as prodigal in our generosity as God has been toward us.

A Humble Heart

Only those who are humble can receive the gifts of God. Only those who can acknowledge that they are needy possess the openness necessary to realize that God's blessings are gifts freely given, not compensation for a job well done. Humility is the prerequisite for receiving gifts. Without a humble spirit we are unable to receive gifts as gifts. This is because we are either too proud or we do not know how to receive with the open hearts of children, who never think they must return in kind. This is the kind of humility recommended by Sirach. This is the kind of humility possessed by the disadvantaged pictured in the gospel.

It is very difficult for most people to be humble receivers of gifts. We have such a need to return the favor. These readings do not encourage a kind of selfishness that only wants to get without giving. Rather, they are calling our attention to a fundamental characteristic of human nature, a characteristic very difficult to admit. That is, because of our finite natures we need more than we can give. Despite the magnificent accomplishments we have achieved, we are really dependent on the goodness of others. While the exchange of gifts may be a common and, indeed, noble practice, in those areas of life that are most important we must be humble receivers. We receive life, we receive love, we receive forgiveness, all because the other is generous, not because we deserve it.

We Give as We Have Received

As we have received from the bounty of God, so we are called to give to others. Only those who have received with a humble spirit can give with the generosity of God, for they know they do not deserve God's goodness, so they do not require anything from those to whom they give. There is no quid pro quo, no "this for that." Everything is freely given and humbly received. The blessings of God are given to us so we in turn can give them to another. It is like love that is not really love until it is given to another. We live within this paradox of receiving and giving, and we are transformed as the process unfolds.

Twenty-Third Sunday in Ordinary Time

Wisdom 9:13-18b

The poem from the book of Wisdom declares in various ways the limitations of human wisdom. Although the book was written in Greek, the form of argument used is frequently found in Hebrew literature, that is, arguing from the more important to the less important, or vice versa (for example, "If these things are done when the wood is green what will happen when it is dry?" [Luke 23:31]). Because it is a poetic form and because the method of argumentation may be foreign to contemporary readers, it might be helpful to lay out the points of the argument in a logical manner before we examine the passage verse by verse.

It begins with rhetorical questions in parallel construction:

| who (*ánthrōpos*) | can know | the counsel | of God |
| who | can conceive | the intentions | of the Lord |

The intended answer to both questions is, of course, "no one." No one can fathom the mind of God; no one can know God's will. Yet we are required to live according to it. Therefore, somehow the will of God will have to be revealed to us.

The Wisdom tradition of Israel is a treasury of insights and perceptions gained through the conscientious reflection on the experience of life. Grounded in authentic experience, it is generally not speculative. It contains the kind of truth that, though specific, cannot be questioned because it reports the way life works. However valuable this information may be, no one bit of wisdom is universally applicable, nor can all of the wisdom together answer the most fundamental and pressing questions of human existence. This is not merely because of the ambiguity of life but primarily because of the mysterious character of the human person.

This tradition acknowledges that we are creatures of the earth limited by the elements of our own constitution. It admits that we discover new things about our world and our lives, frequently before we have an understanding of what it is we have discovered. As the text says: "The deliberations of mortals are timid, and unsure are our plans" (v. 14). In most cases certainty does not precede our actions but follows them. The very method that produces the wisdom that is valued so highly is the trial-and-error approach. Such is the thinking behind this passage.

The tradition also acknowledges that dimension of human beings that seeks a wisdom beyond that achieved by reflection on experience alone. We seek to know the things of God, the mysteries of heaven. Recognizing this, an ancient sage declared that God has put the timeless into our hearts without our ever discovering what it means (cf. Eccl 3:11). And if this were not enough, there are the struggles that results from the fact of human mortality (v. 15). Here we see the Greek notion of the superiority of the immaterial soul, or mind, over the corruptible body. All of this points to the inability of human beings to discern the will of God. The Hebrew form of argument states it clearly: We can scarcely discover the meaning of the things of the earth; how can we expect to search out the things of heaven? (v. 16).

It is the realization of human limitation that prompted the author to exclaim that we will attain the wisdom we so sorely seek only if God bestows it upon us. The holy spirit of which the author speaks should not be understood as the Third Person of the Trinity. The sense of the spirit found here eventually may have been incorporated into Christianity's trinitarian theology, but here it probably only refers to the immateriality of the things of God.

Psalm 90:3-4, 5-6, 12-13, 14-17

The responsorial psalm has features of the lament, but its primary theme comes from the Wisdom tradition. The issue that seems to consume the psalmist is the transitoriness of human existence. Unlike God, for whom a thousand years are but a blink of the eye, humans have a very brief life span. When the time they do have is spent in suffering and misfortune, their agony can be intensified and life can seem futile. The images in the psalm response depict this: dust, grass that wilts and fades. The psalmist prays for wisdom of heart, the kind of interior insight that will enable the people to live the few days they have committed to the things of God.

This prayer comes from a community in great distress. Apparently it has been suffering for some time, for it cries out to God in prayer, "How long?" They feel deserted by God, unable to free themselves from their plight: "Have pity!" Israel's way of understanding suffering was quite complex. They seldom questioned why their enemies were burdened with misfortune. The reason for this was obvious to them: enemies of God's people were enemies of God, so they deserved to suffer hardship. The misfortune that befell Israel was seen as quite another matter. If it was a punishment for ungodly behavior, it was seen as necessary recompense meant to restore the harmony that had been disturbed by the sin. However, even this kind of distress was thought to be only temporary. The people expected that the guilty ones would recognize their error and reform their ways, and then good fortune would return. The pleading found in this psalm arises from a situation from which relief has been long in coming, perhaps too long.

Daybreak usually brings thoughts of hope. The gradual appearance of light dispels the darkness of despair and speaks of promise and well-being. However, when it appears that relief is not on the horizon, which is slowly taking shape, discouragement turns to desperation, and hope evaporates like early morning dew in the light of day. In such a situation each new day is an added burden rather than a herald of hope. The psalmist has known both kinds of day. Here the prayer is for days of gladness rather than days of affliction. The psalmist is pleading for a reversal of fortune. The confidence in God's willingness to relent from chastising the community and to grace it with kindness is based in the covenant relationship of lovingkindness (*ḥesed*) it shares with God. God has made a promise, and even in the face of the people's infidelity, God will honor that promise.

The psalm ends with petitions: Fill us with your lovingkindness! Grant us your gracious care! Prosper the work of our hands! Despite the hardships the people must have been enduring, their prayers are filled with hope. The God with whom they are in covenant will surely hear their cry and will come to their aid. These are the sentiments behind the petitions.

Philemon 9-10, 12-17

Paul's letter to Philemon is a personal appeal to accept back with no recriminations a slave who had escaped Philemon's household and his control. While there is no direct teaching, Paul uses a pedagogical technique as he tries to persuade Philemon to acquiesce to his wishes in regard to this runaway slave. Commentators do not agree on the meaning of *presbutēs*. Some translate it "ambassador," while others render it "elder" or "old man." Since Paul makes a point of not using his authority in this matter, ambassador does not seem to fit here. If Paul is referring to himself as an old man or an elder, he might still be trading on the fact of his having labored for many years for the sake of the gospel. There is probably no way Paul's prominence in the Christian community can be ignored. Even if he does not insist on it, he must know it will be considered. Besides, he couples this with a reminder that he is even now suffering for the sake of Christ. All of this adds a certain amount of authority to his wishes.

The first item to address is the issue of slavery. Paul has been criticized by many for not condemning the practice. To expect him to do so would be anachronistic. However, he does suggest a mode of action that will eventually undermine the philosophy that undergirds slavery. It was a legal custom, and Paul recognized Philemon's rights within it. Nor would he use conversion to Christianity as a refuge from the difficulties of human existence. Although Paul would have liked to keep the man with him because of the service he could offer him, he still sent Onesimus back to Philemon. However, he now relies on Philemon's own understanding of mutual brotherhood and sisterhood in Christ to transform his attitude toward his slave. Paul had taught that in Christ there were no longer slaves or free persons but that all were children of God (cf. Gal 3:28; Col 3:11). Now he challenges Philemon to witness to his own belief in this teaching. He relies on his insistence that partnership in the Lord has broken down all barriers. He asks Philemon to treat Onesimus like the Christian brother he has now become rather than the slave he once was.

There is a very personal dimension to Paul's request. He claims to be Onesimus' spiritual father, and he looks upon him as his child. He even considers him his very heart. There is no way of knowing the grounds for such a claim. Had Paul converted the man? Baptized him while he was in prison? Or was the bond forged because Onesimus attended to Paul in his time of need? This personal relationship probably placed even more pressure on Philemon to receive the slave warmly upon his return.

Paul's belief that God can work wonders in any circumstances can be seen in the way he reinterprets Onesimus' escape, seeing it as the occasion of significant changes. Though a criminal act in itself from the perspective of Onesimus, it transformed a pagan into a follower of Jesus Christ. From the perspective of Philemon, it turned a slave into a brother in Christ.

Paul ends his request with a final plea: "Welcome him as you would me." We do not know whether Paul means that he is a Christian brother as I am, or that he is a part of my very heart. Perhaps it makes no difference. Paul appeals both to Philemon's Christian conscience and to his indebtedness to Paul. The man in prison can do little else.

Luke 14:25-33

The cost of discipleship is the basis of the teaching of Jesus in this gospel passage. It is important to note that despite what appear to be extreme demands, the instruction is addressed to the crowds and not simply to those who have already committed themselves to basic discipleship and who are now being called to even deeper commitment and intimacy. Three conditions for discipleship are given here: subordination of everything to commitment to Jesus, acceptance of the cross, and relinquishment of all possessions.

Jesus' admonition to "hate" one's closest family members has been the subject of extensive concern and interpretation. Surely Jesus could not have meant this injunction to be taken literally, since the entire basis of his teaching is love. There is no thought there that one cannot love both God and neighbor. In fact, one is commanded to love both. The expression probably springs from a Semitic idiom that refers to first loyalty, which implies that in choosing one thing one thereby excludes everything else. We see this expressed in Jacob's sentiments toward his two wives, Rachel and Leah (cf. Gen 29:30-31). Thus "hate" means "love less." Jesus insists that nothing, neither the closest family ties nor love of one's own life, can be placed in conflict with commitment to him. Whoever cannot make this sacrifice cannot be his disciple.

The second condition for discipleship is willingness to carry one's cross. Jesus' total commitment to his mission resulted in his own suffering and death. The commitment of those who would follow him can be no less. The demands this will exact will differ from person to person, but the requirement is the same—wholehearted commitment. Realizing that initial enthusiasm can cloak a superficial attempt at dedication, Jesus insists that potential disciples first take stock of their resources before they commit themselves to him. They should not rush into discipleship without examining what is involved. On the one hand, they must be aware of the cost that may be exacted of them; on the other, they should have some sense of their own ability to meet that cost. To say it another way, they have to reckon whether or not they can afford to follow him as well as whether or not they can really afford to refuse his demands. They should not step forward unless they are willing and able to expend all they have to carry through with their decision. Whoever cannot make such a wholehearted commitment cannot be his disciple.

Finally, would-be disciples must be willing to relinquish all their possessions in order to possess and to be possessed by Christ. This is not a new or different requirement. In a sense it contains within itself the other two. Total commitment to Jesus requires the willingness to give up the comfort and security of a stable family life as well as the willingness to spend all one has on that venture. Whoever cannot make such a wholehearted commitment cannot be his disciple.

Themes of the Day

On this Sunday we are once again confronted with the need to make choices. The Wisdom tradition, from which the first reading is taken, is rooted in the fact that life is a series of choices. The epistle and the gospel reading provide us with examples of the way Christians should choose. Finally, the psalm's description of the fleeting nature of life sets the context and tone for our decision making.

Priorities

We live in a world that seems to offer limitless choices. Opportunities for work and living, for education and recreation, for entertainment and relaxation abound. We are even free to choose the values we would espouse to support our choices. There is so much from which to choose, and all of it is presented as acceptable by the world. Discipleship demands that in the face of all this we keep our priorities straight. We must seek the counsel of wisdom so we choose the right path. True wisdom is knowing where to put our energies, how to focus our attention, with whom to commit ourselves. In the gospel Jesus insists that we must be single-minded. We must cling to the one thing necessary, and that one thing is authentic discipleship.

Throughout these days of Ordinary Time we have been looking at what discipleship requires. It may be demanding, but it is not impossible, for we are given the grace of God to sustain us and the community of other disciples as a support. All of the readings promise that if we make the right choices our lives will unfold in ways that will enrich us. The challenge is knowing which choices are right, and then having the courage to make them. In order to do this, we need the wisdom that comes from God, the wisdom sketched in the gospel reading. We must be willing to put our lives on the line for the choices we make.

Choices

In choosing Jesus, we choose other things as well. We choose new relationships with the very people to whom we have already been committed. Those who were slaves, or lower class, or employees, or providers of service, are now regarded as sisters and brothers in Christ. They may continue performing the same service as before, but we now perceive them in a new way, and we now treat them as equals. Those who are related to us through blood are now considered also bound to us by the grace of God. Our former ties are not severed, they are augmented.

In choosing Jesus, we also choose the cross. We choose to live in a way that calls us to travel the high road: to forgive offenses committed against us; to live simply so others can simply live; to take responsibility for the moral character of society. This way of living is very demanding, yet not very rewarding in the rewards of this world. We might even lose the little we have. In choosing Jesus we willingly relinquish our hold on the people and the goods we cherish lest they rival our commitment to him.

The Fleeting Character of Life

The fleeting nature of life as characterized in the psalm forces us to look at the meaning of life. When the day dawns for us to return to dust, what will we have gained from life? From our possessions? From the towers we construct? From the battles we have won? They will seem like the grass that wilts and fades, like the corruptible body we have been born with. What will it have been worth? The realization of our finiteness and the transitory nature of life should help us set our priorities right and should give us the courage to remain faithful to them. Throughout the Wisdom tradition the sages all place the meaning of life within the context of its brevity and the suddenness of its ending. In the face of this, it becomes clear that living in right relationships, following the straight path, choosing the wisdom of a covenant with God, is the only way to spend the brief time we have here on earth. Nothing else is really worth it.

Twenty-Fourth Sunday in Ordinary Time

Exodus 32:7-11, 13-14

This reading reports a dramatic exchange between God and Moses. The Israelites are guilty of having violated the first two commandments: You shall have no other gods; you shall not carve idols. They have made themselves a molten calf. In the ancient Near East it was common practice to construct pedestals upon which the images of gods were placed. Since Baal, the major fertility god of Canaan, was represented as a young and vigorous bull, it is possible that the Israelites had fashioned a pedestal in the form of a bull, intending to worship their own God. However, as the text says, the pedestal itself became for them an idol. They wrongly perceived it as the god who brought them out of Egypt. In response to their infidelity, God seems to disown them, insisting that they are Moses' people, whom he, Moses, brought out of Egypt. For his part, Moses will not allow this shift in association to take place. He insists that these are God's own people whom God, and no other, brought out of Egypt (v. 11).

God accuses the people of being stiff-necked. The description is of an ox or mule that will not respond to the tug of the rope around its neck. It resists by stiffening its neck. This is a colorful way of describing stubbornness. However, the association of the metaphor with plow animals also debases the person so described. Judging the people to be an impossible lot, God considers destroying them and beginning anew with a people that springs from Moses. God makes the same promise to Moses as was made to Abraham (Gen 12:2): "I will make of you a great nation."

It is probably here more than anywhere else that the greatness of Moses is seen. Rather than accept this amazing offer, Moses pleads for the preservation of the people of whom he is a member. His appeal is twofold. He first insists that the Israelites are God's very own special people. They are the people God brought out of Egypt with a strong hand and an outstretched arm, amid signs and wonders. It would be a shame to destroy them now. Moses then appeals to the promises God made to the ancestors of the Israelites. God promised to make their descendants, not Moses' descendants, a great and numerous people and to bring them into a land that was to be theirs forever. How could God possibly renege on those promises?

As the story is told, Moses has been successful in his defense of the sinful people. God relents of the severe punishment intended. This is an example of anthropopathism, ascribing human emotions to God. It is a way of showing God's passionate involvement in the lives of the people. Depicting God in human ways has both advantages and disadvantages. On the one hand, it brings God very close to our own reality. On the other, it saddles God with our limitations. In order to portray Moses as an unselfish mediator between God and the people, God is depicted in a less than flattering manner. Still, God does listen to the entreaty of Moses; God does relent; God does give the people another chance. How else but through anthropomorphism can we depict the passion God has for us?

Psalm 51:3-4, 12-13, 17, 19

This is one of the best-known of the Penitential Psalms. The response for today consists of a plea for mercy (vv. 3-4), a prayer for transformation (vv. 12-13), and a request for the opportunity to praise God (vv. 17, 19). In the initial plea the psalmist appeals to God's covenant dispositions: goodness *(ḥesed)* and compassion, or womb-love, the kind of attachment a mother has for the child she has carried in her womb *(raḥămîm)*. The first refers to the steadfast love that characterizes the relationship between covenant partners; the second is the attitude that only appears in narratives that recount God's disposition after the people have violated the covenant bond (cf. Exod 34:6-7). God's womb-love is for sinners, not those who have never failed. The psalmist probably appeals to these dispositions of divine graciousness in order to set the context of the prayer for transformation. If God has already been so gracious, surely a prayer for transformation will be heard.

Realizing that the seriousness of the offenses acknowledged requires a thorough transformation, a total change of heart *(metanoia)*, the psalmist prays for a clean heart and a right or true spirit (cf. Ezek 11:19). The technical verb for "create" *(bārā')* is used, indicating the psalmist is asking for a transformation that possesses a kind of pristine quality, a transformation that is really a re-creation. The same prayer is then made but in a manner that might be called a mirror projection. In negative terms the psalmist pleads for a continued relationship with God: "Cast me not from your presence, and your holy spirit [here used as a synonym for 'presence'] take not from me." The psalmist is here praying for the reestablishment of the covenant relationship that was shattered by the psalmist's own sins.

The response ends with a prayer that the psalmist might be empowered or permitted by God to sing a song of praise. Such a request could spring from the psalmist's sense of guilt, of realizing that sin alienates us from God and relegates us to a place distant from God where praise is inappropriate. Though now reconciled with God, the psalmist does not presume intimacy with God but asks permission to be counted again among those who do praise God. Coming before God to worship, the psalmist brings a most worthy gift, a spirit that was once proud but has been broken and humbled and is now contrite. The psalmist knows God cannot resist such a spirit, for God is truly compassionate. Finally, having been reconciled with God, the psalmist knows that all these things—the covenant relationship itself, forgiveness of sin, transformation of heart, and the ability to praise God—are gifts of grace from God.

1 Timothy 1:12-17

This short reading is a bold statement about the mercy of God toward sinners. Paul begins it with an expression of gratitude for God's goodness toward him, and from this he moves into a personal testimony that demonstrates the extent of God's goodness. Paul states that he is grateful Christ strengthened him and found him worthy to proclaim the gospel. In itself this could be an audacious claim. However, lest it sound like he is bragging he quickly admits to the character of his former life. Previously he had denied everything he had heard about Christ; he hunted down those who were his followers, and he stood in judgment over them. He is a perfect example of one who deserves punishment at the hands of God. However, the opposite occurred. He was treated mercifully. His admission that he acted in ignorance should not be taken as an attempt to excuse himself. Rather, it suggests that only the grace of God could help him see the truth.

In another bold statement he claims that just as his offense was great and his need for mercy was great, so the effects of God's grace in his life have been abundant. Regardless of what Paul says about himself and the success of his ministry, he always clearly insists that the grace of God was given him before he was able to accomplish anything he might have done. With grace as the prior disposition, Paul can say almost anything about himself.

His instruction on God's mercy continues with a pronouncement of the trustworthiness of the statement he is about to make, in which he maintains that redemption was the reason for the incarnation. In other words, the merciful love of God toward sinners prompted the coming of Christ Jesus into the world. For Paul salvation is an eschatological reality. It is concerned with ultimate human destiny. However, it is not something that occurs only at the end of life or at the end-time. Rather, salvation has begun in the work of Christ, and the unfolding of that work occurs as sinners are saved from their present sinfulness.

Once again Paul turns his attention to his own culpability. He considers himself the foremost sinner because of his previous opposition to God's grace in Jesus Christ. This is not false humility. He stresses his sinfulness so that he can emphasize God's mercy. The greater his own failure, the more remarkable is God's success in him. In fact, according to Paul that is the very reason God took the prominent persecutor and transformed him into an apostle. His own change of heart reveals the breadth of Christ's patience.

Paul ends his instruction with a doxology composed of several divine epithets, all of which originated in the Jewish tradition. The title "king of ages" was probably taken from synagogue worship; "incorruptible" is a term found in the literature of Hellenistic Judaism; "invisible" is an attribute retrieved from the earliest Israelite traditions. Finally, the basis of Israelite monotheism is the claim that there is only one God, and the God to whom all these characteristics belong deserves honor and glory forever.

Luke 15:1-32

The opening verses of the gospel reading set the stage for the parables Jesus tells. In them, lines are drawn between scribes and Pharisees, who were considered righteous religious leaders, and tax collectors and sinners, who were social outcasts. To share a meal with the latter group was to share life with them. These were the people who came to hear Jesus. The Pharisees and scribes criticized Jesus for keeping company with them. They maintained that Jesus' association with such unclean outcasts contaminated him. In contrast, Jesus saw this association as an opportunity for opening the reign of God to all. He illustrated God's care for the outcasts by means of three parables.

The first two are parallel stories. In them Jesus depicts the extravagant solicitude of the shepherd and the woman in order to demonstrate the extent to which God will go to rescue even one lost individual. It should be noted that divine solicitude is characterized by a woman's concern as well as a man's. The joy that both the shepherd and the woman experience in finding what was lost cannot be contained. They invite their friends and neighbors to share in their celebration. It is not that the shepherd cares less for the ninety-nine who were not lost, but both parables state that repentance generates more joy in heaven and among the angels than does faithfulness. This is more clearly stated at the end of the third parable: The one who was dead has come back to life again!

The third parable has a double focus. While it is clearly about the mercy God shows to repentant sinners, it also contrasts God's openness with the closed-mindedness of those who consider themselves faithful. The scene with the elder brother is not an afterthought. In fact, it returns us to the opening verses that describe the disdain of the Pharisees and scribes. Within the parable itself the contours of each of the three main characters are carefully drawn so that the meaning of the story shines through clearly.

There is no question about the depraved behavior of the younger son. With his third of the father's estate (the elder son would get a double portion) he abandons his father's home and even his own country, and he embarks on a life of dissipation. Just as the separation with his past was decisive, so the straits within which he finds himself are extreme. He attaches himself to a Gentile (a disgrace for a Jew), and he is reduced to feeding swine (an occupation forbidden by the law). Added to this, he longs to eat what the pigs eat. His association with defilement is complete. However, his eventual repentance is as sweeping as was his disgrace. He is willing to acknowledge his sin and even relinquish any filial claims if only he can be treated as one of his father's hired workers.

The picture of the father is also straightforward. He initially put no obstacles in his son's path but gave him his share of the estate. He disregards convention and runs out to welcome this son home. He treats him as one brought back to life, lavishly clothing him, giving him sandals, which would distinguish him as a son rather than a barefooted servant, hosting a sumptuous feast in his honor. He is no less attentive to the elder son, going out to plead with him to join the celebration, assuring him the major portion of the estate. This picture shatters the traditional patriarchal image and offers us a radically different picture of fatherhood, a picture that was totally incomprehensible to both of the sons. The father is neither domineering nor disinterested. He respects the decisions of both his sons even when he disagrees with them. When it becomes clear they have been mistaken, he forgives them. This startling new picture becomes the metaphor for understanding God.

The elder son strikes an interesting pose. He resents his father's unrestrained joyous treatment of the errant one. Just as the younger son had formerly repudiated his family, so this son refuses to participate in a family affair, and he will not even refer to the younger one as his own brother. Unlike the dissolute one, he has always obeyed orders; he has served his father like a slave (*douleúō*); yet he never even received a goat with which to feast.

Though the elder brother contrasts his loyalty with the infidelity of the younger one, Jesus is really contrasting the compassion of God with the mean-spiritedness of the Pharisees and scribes. Like the elder brother, they lack compassion, and they seem to resent the fact that God is merciful toward sinners who repent.

Themes of the Day

This Sunday we divert our attention for a moment from our consideration of discipleship and community in order to meditate on the character of God and the nature of Christ.

The Search

So often we say we are searching for God. In a sense such a search is futile because we are really not sure what we are looking for. And if we are sure, then it probably is not God for whom we are searching. Besides, we do not really "find" God. Rather, God is revealed to us. What is so shocking about this is that the God who is ultimately revealed is a God we would never have thought of seeking. The God who spoke to Moses is pained by the depravity of the people yet moved to show them mercy. Who could ever have imagined such a God? The God depicted in the gospel actually searches for what is lost. He seems to abandon the safe ones for the sake of the one who has strayed. She goes to great lengths to find one coin. As a spurned yet loving father, God patiently waits until we have come to our senses. Who could ever have conceived of such a God?

It is not enough that God chooses to enter into covenant with us. Our God is foolishly consumed with an insatiable desire to reestablish a relationship with us after we have turned our backs on God, have chosen to commit our loyalties elsewhere, have thoughtlessly wandered off into danger that threatens our well-being, not God's. What is it about us that makes us so desirable? The answer, of course, is that it has less to do with us than with the magnanimous character of God. It is almost as if unconditional love is not simply a characteristic of God but God's very essence, and no human frailty or depravity can change this.

God's Celebration

In the gospel reading the jubilant father graced his son with fine clothing and all the trappings of a sumptuous banquet. Once our covenant relationship has been reestablished, what blessings does God bestow upon us? The first is mercy, the intimate womb-love only a parent can know. It is almost as if God cannot reject us, because it would be like rejecting a part of God's very self. This mercy compels God to forgive us as totally as God forgave the perfidious Israelites and as the loving father forgave the chastened and repentant son. God's mercy and forgiveness take the form of freedom from slavery, and if not slavery from Egypt, certainly slavery from evil impulses, from addictions and habits that can destroy us. The younger son left his dissolute life behind him. The elder brother could have been freed from envy and resentment had he opened his heart to the loving concern of his father.

The celebration that follows the return of the lost nation, the lost sheep, the lost coin, the lost son, is open to all who will attend. And who will they be? Only those who admit they are sinners and who repent of their sin will recognize the need to celebrate. Those who have no sin to repent have no reason to rejoice. Only those who share the joy of God in the repentance of others will recognize the need to celebrate. Those who envy the celebration or who harbor resentment because of God's mercy will have no reason to rejoice.

Through Christ

Paul insists it is through Christ that all of this is accomplished. It is through the sacrifice of Christ that the depraved are forgiven, that sinners are saved, that the lost are found. It is through Christ that we are sought by God, and Christ is the very gift of mercy, the forgiveness of our sins, the celebration of our return. Paul is overwhelmed by God's goodness to him through the agency of Christ Jesus. He is the classic example of the forgiven sinner. In his repentance he is a model for us to imitate. He is certainly one over whom the angels of heaven rejoice. And what of us? Will we join the celebration?

Twenty-Fifth Sunday in Ordinary Time
Amos 8:4-7

This prophetic oracle is one of condemnation. Here the prophet denounces unscrupulous merchants for their false piety, their avarice, their dishonest business practices, and their exploitation of the poor and defenseless.

The text shows that Israel observed a lunar calendar, celebrating the new moon at the beginning of each lunar month. Special celebrations, which included sumptuous feasts and specific sacrifices, were prescribed for these days (cf. Num 28:11-15). As was the case with the observance of the Sabbaths, all business was suspended. While the merchants appear to have observed these religious obligations, they did so hypocritically, for in the midst of the celebration they were eager to resume their dishonest business.

The poor referred to here are the landless, those who do not harvest their own crop but must purchase grain and wheat for their food. Thus they are dependent on the honesty of the merchants, who not only measure out the produce on their own scales but who are in a position to determine the prices to be paid for the staples of life. These are the people who are frequently brought to such extremes of poverty they are forced to sell themselves into slavery in order to survive. These are the very people who are victimized by the unscrupulous merchants to whom this oracle is addressed.

The merchants describe their own dishonesty. There are three different ways by which they cheat their customers. When gauging the amount of grain, they do not measure out an entire ephah (a dry measure that corresponds to a bushel) but give the buyer less than the amount for which they pay. A second way of defrauding was to use shekels as measures. Since there was no way to ensure that each shekel weighed the same amount, it was easy to use only light-weighing shekels when measuring. The grain was then paid for with the amount of silver coins that corresponded to the number of shekels used as weights. More light-weighing shekels brought more silver coins. Finally, the scales themselves were fixed so the merchant always got more than was deserved.

The last verse reports the judgment of God, which is passed in the form of an irrevocable oath. Amos prophesied to the northern kingdom, often referred to as Jacob. The reference here to the pride of Jacob is probably an allusion to the arrogant self-indulgence of those tribes. As this oracle shows, the people of privilege frequently took advantage of the vulnerable poor. God swears an oath by this pride showing that the evil perpetrated as a result of it will not be forgotten. This is truly an oracle of judgment.

Psalm 113:1-2, 4-6, 7-8

The responsorial psalm is a hymn of praise of the LORD (*Hallelujah* in Hebrew). Such hymns have a definite pattern. The summons itself *(hallelu)* appears in a plural verb form, suggesting a communal setting, and it contains an abbreviation of the divine name *(jah)*. In this psalm the word is used as a refrain, a response to a series of statements that offer examples of God's indescribable graciousness. The psalm itself is a classic example of a hymn of praise. It begins with the imperative summons to praise God (vv. 1-2), followed by the reasons for praising (vv. 4-8). The call is to praise the name of the LORD, an expression found frequently in the psalms and referring to the very essence of God. The servants of the LORD who are called to praise could be the priests or Levites, making this a psalm for cultic use. However, it is not necessary to limit the reference to specific religious leaders. The term could be understood more generally and would then refer to all who owed any allegiance to God.

God is depicted as enthroned high above the heavens. This is the privileged place of honor that by right of conquest belongs to the victorious Creator of the world. After having vanquished the forces of chaos, this God reordered the universe and was then installed high above everything else, there to rule unchallenged by any power of heaven or earth. In a question that really seeks no answer, the psalmist inquires: Is there any one equal to this God? Could there possibly be a god to match—much less rival—the LORD, our God, the God of Israel? It is important to emphasize the magnificence of this deity in order to appreciate the significance of God's eagerness to attend to the needs of the lowly.

In synonymous parallel construction the psalmist traces the extent to which the solicitude of God will reach:

| raises up | lowly | from dust |
| lifts up | poor | from dunghill |

The lowly *(dal)* and the poor *(ʾebyôn)* refer to the lower economic class. Because humans were thought to have been made from dust and it was clear that after death they deteriorated into dust, dust itself *(ʿāpār)* became a symbol of human mortality, human finitude, and human insignificance. The dunghill or ash heap *(ʿēper)* was the place where worthless things were thrown or the refuse that remained after rubbish had been burned. The metaphors indicate that the very people society had discarded were the ones the exalted ruler of heaven stooped to lift up. Furthermore, they were then seated in places of honor among the royal rulers of the people.

The reversals are obvious. The God who reigned from the highest heaven reached into the reputedly lowest regions of human existence. Those who were lowly and poor were seated with the high and mighty. This condescension on God's part is reason for the praise to which the servants of God are summoned.

1 Timothy 2:1-8

Paul instructs Timothy to see that prayers are offered for the salvation of all. He is not speaking here of private prayer. Rather, in addressing the leader of a Christian community, he is giving him directions regarding prayer during times of public worship. The first three types of prayer mentioned are various forms of petition, and the subtle differences among them need not concern us here. The fourth kind, thanksgiving *(eucharistía)*, adds gratitude to the reasons for praying.

The major point of this instruction seems to be the all-inclusive scope of Christian prayer. Twice Paul states that prayers should be offered for all people (vv. 1, 4). Special attention is given to civic leaders. This indicates that Christianity was not fundamentally inimical toward those who wielded worldly power. Besides, if all power comes from God, as Christians believed, then rightful leaders govern by God's authority, and this authority should be respected. We must also remember that the early Christians lived under Roman rule. Therefore, their leaders were probably pagan and had little interest in winning the approval of an insignificant colonized people. This means that the Christians were admonished to pray for those who did not necessarily look kindly upon them.

Two reasons for such prayer are given. The first appears to be pragmatic: Pray for them so that you can experience peace in their midst. However, a closer examination shows that the goal of their prayer is really not simply peace but, rather, the salvation of others. Paul is urging prayer for the conversion of the leaders. If they are converted, then they will recognize and accept the teachings of the gospel, and all will be able to live tranquil lives. Devotion refers to one's religious attitude in the deepest sense; it is true reverence for God. Dignity is the moral earnestness that is manifested in one's outward demeanor. If the Church enjoys a congenial relationship with civic authorities, its members will be able publicly to live out the values they espouse.

The second listed reason for praying for these officials is the primary reason: It is God's will to do so. It is God's will that all come to know the one God and Christ Jesus, the only mediator between God and humankind (*ánthrōpos*). Belief in the universality of salvation through Christ should spur the Christians on to this kind of prayer. Not only through preaching will all women and men be converted to the gospel but through prayer as well.

The phrase "testimony at the proper time" is difficult to understand. Most commentators believe it refers to the ransom Christ paid for all. His death ushered in the time of universal salvation. It was to this universal ministry that Paul himself was called as herald and as apostle to the nations. Therefore, it is only right that the Church pray for the conversion of the Gentiles. The reading concludes with a final injunction to pray in every place with hands uplifted, a common posture for prayer.

Luke 16:1-13

This is the story of the steward or household manager (*oikonómos*) who rewrote the debts of his employer in order to ensure a financial future for himself after he is dismissed. It has often raised more questions than it has answered, because it seems as though Jesus is commending him for his unscrupulous behavior.

The man is being released because his did not fulfill his charge in a responsible manner. The text does not say he swindled his master; it says he squandered the property. Therefore, the dishonesty of which he is later accused is not traced to his initial mismanagement. The reason for the master's judgment appears only later. The man's inner quandary gives us a glimpse of his circumstances. He does not have the physical strength for arduous manual labor, and because of the social status he presently enjoys, lowering himself to the level of begging would be too humiliating. He decides to alter the accounts of his master's debtors. This gives us a new insight into the character of the man. He was not careful enough when managing the household resources for his master's benefit, but he is more than industrious when his own future is at stake.

Various explanations for the debt reductions have been given. Some believe the man only subtracted the commission he would have received. Others think he forgave the interest the master may have been illegally charging. There is no way of knowing which circumstances Jesus may have had in mind. The prominent status of the steward is implied in the fact that he would assume authority as he did. Even a trusted slave would never have been able to act in this way. This was a man who was able to make legitimate decisions in the name of his master, decisions the master would have to honor.

The judgment passed on the steward rests on the meaning of the Greek word *ádikías* (v. 8). While the word does mean "unrighteous," it usually refers to a violation of a law, to what is against custom rather than what is impious. It is clear the steward has violated customary law. It was his duty to advance his employer's position by enhancing his financial holdings. Instead, he reduced them for his own benefit. Despite this, the master of the household, not Jesus, commends him for acting shrewdly (from *phrónēsis*, the word for "practical wisdom"). Jesus seems to step back from this particular incident and use it to draw a religious conclusion: children of this age (or children of the world) have more practical wisdom than do children of light.

In his admonition Jesus interprets several elements from this story in order to point out how children of light should act. He first instructs his disciples to act with the same kind of practical wisdom but to use it to ensure places in an eternal dwelling. He then comments on the character of one's stewardship. The way one handles small matters will determine the way one handles weightier responsibilities. If one cannot exercise practical wisdom when dealing with the mammon or wealth of unrighteousness *(ádikías)*, how can that one be trusted with the real thing *(to alēthinon)*? If one cannot be relied upon as overseer of the possessions of another, how can that one be deemed adequate to be an independent proprietor?

The real point of the story is found in the last verse. Though shrewd in the ways of the world, the steward chose to serve his own financial needs rather than the economic interests of his employer. This made him an unreliable or dishonest servant. One cannot serve both the master of the household (God) and one's own personal interests (mammon). One must choose.

Themes of the Day

We have reflected on questions about discipleship and community. The readings for today focus our attention on a slightly different matter. It is a complex and sometimes divisive theme, that is, the proper use of money and the goods of this world.

Children of This World

We are creatures of this world. We are made of it, and we are totally dependent upon it for our very existence. We require its air, its water, its food, its heat. We need it for covering and for shelter; we need it to stimulate our minds and our spirits. Therefore, our use of its phenomenal resources cannot in itself be immoral. What is questionable is the character of our use. How much do we really need? How much do we have a right to use? What constitutes exploitation? When are we hoarding?

It is not uncommon for high-minded people to be concerned about economic equity. They have always struggled to ensure just distribution of the riches of the earth. However, until recently the question of the balance of the resources themselves has seldom been an issue. Today we are beginning to realize the folly in devising methods of distribution or redistribution without first taking stock of the measure of the resources we are considering. We do not have an unlimited supply, and exploitation is already resulting in certain ecological imbalances.

The Right to Life

The right to life includes more than questions about reproduction or war or capital punishment. It means we have a right to eat, to be clothed, to be sheltered, to be nourished by the beauty of the world of which we are a part. But how much and what quality of food do we have a right to when others who have the right to eat do not have enough to live on? How many changes of clothing do we have a right to when others who have the right to be clothed go naked? How elaborate a home do we have a right to when others who have a right to shelter are homeless? How much beauty do we have a right to when other gentle spirits live in squalor?

There are many circumstances that contribute to the complexity of these questions, making them very difficult to answer. Surely the merchant in the passage from Amos had a right to his business. He should not be faulted because he was prosperous while others were poor. Nor should the householder or the steward in the gospel be criticized for not being needy. We cannot be censured for putting resources aside for future use, for the education of children, for possible medical needs, for retirement, even for vacation. But how much do we really need? How much do we have a right to? Our consumer society might tell us we have a right to everything we can earn. But do we? In a world of limited resources how much do we have a right to? What does the balance of the natural world tell us? What do the legitimate needs of others tell us? What does our religious tradition tell us?

Children of Light

There are no easy answers to these questions. We live our lives on the horns of a dilemma. We have the right to use and to enjoy the marvels of our world, but we cannot do this free of responsibility to one another and to the world itself. The men in today's readings are not condemned because of their economic privilege but because they used it only to their own advantage. As Christians we are not merely children of this world; we are also children of light. Paul's admonition to pray for our civic leaders reminds us that we do indeed live in the real world, but we are called to live there according to standards worthy of our calling. We are more than insatiable consumers. Our value is not found in the measure of our possessions. It is in the quality of our relationships, in particular with our relationships with our deprived sisters and brothers.

We are not called to disown the world. It is impossible for us to do that because of our total dependence on it. But we are called to live in it gently, using what we need and sharing what we can. We may never be sure we have made the right decisions in this regard, but we must be ever conscious of our need to grapple with these issues. We are not the only ones involved in our economic decisions, and so we cannot make them lightly. We cannot afford to squander the resources of our world. We must make decisions as trustworthy stewards of the household of God, not like the man in the gospel who was only concerned with his own well-being. We must serve God, not mammon.

Twenty-Sixth Sunday in Ordinary Time

Amos 6:1a, 4-7

The prophet Amos appears to be condemning the enjoyment of extravagant wealth, an occupation frequently embarked upon by social reformers. However, the very first verse of this reading shows this is not the case. His denunciation is not of wealth itself but of the complacency that often accompanies it. He is distressed because the affluent entertain themselves with wantonness while the social structure of the northern kingdom of Israel disintegrates. The prophet's condemnation could not be more severe. He pronounces "Woe!" upon the people. Only funeral dirges begin in this way. The use of such denunciation here denotes the degree of the prophet's disdain. He believes the degenerate nature of the wealthy indicates that real life has died in them, and so a dirge is appropriate.

The particular aspect of their lives that he censures is their habit of self-indulgence at feasts. First, they lounge on elegant couches luxuriously appointed with costly inlaid ivory. Their posture on couches offers a good deal of comfort and is an invitation to spend a long time dining. The opulence of their surroundings is matched by their menu. A diet of meat was a rarity in ancient Israel. Animals constituted the livelihood of most of the people, not their food. They were important as a means of transportation or as work animals.

They produced the wool and the milk so necessary for life. Only on rare occasions was their flesh part of a meal. Because of the sacred importance of the life-blood of any living thing, the slaughter of animals was considered a religious act. Here the rich dine on the meat of lambs and calves, the very animals used for sacrifice. Young animals were offered in sacrifice in acknowledgment of God's sovereignty over the life of the flock or the herd. At these lavish banquets they are eaten by the rich because their meat is tender. The fastidious tastes of the wealthy expose their arrogance.

Nothing is said about the attire of the people who are dining, but mention is made of the costly oils with which they anoint themselves. Such perfuming was both a cosmetic practice and a sexual stimulation. Perhaps the most excessive example of dissolute dining is their manner of drinking wine. Not content to sip from goblets, they guzzle from wide-mouthed bowls. One can only imagine the result of such drinking.

The prophet has gone to great lengths to paint a picture of the dissolute character of the wealthy. In contrast to this, with one simple but piercing phrase he describes the condition of the nation as "the collapse of Joseph." The profligacy of the wealthy in the face of social breakdown is evidence of their self-indulgence and complacency. However, their affluent lifestyle will be cut short, and in an ironic turn of events those who always thought of themselves first will be the first to be deported into exile.

Psalm 146:7, 8-9, 9-10

As was the case with the psalm response for last Sunday, the responsorial psalm for this week is a hymn of praise of the Lord (*Hallelujah* in Hebrew). The pattern includes the summons itself *(hallelu)*, which appears in a plural verb form, suggesting a communal setting. It also contains an abbreviation of the divine name *(jah)*. In this particular psalm the word is used as a refrain, a response to a series of statements that offer examples of God's indescribable graciousness.

There is an allusion here (v. 7) to God's deliverance of the people from the bondage of Egypt and to God's providential care of them during their sojourn in the wilderness. God has been faithful. This is reason enough to praise the Lord. God's graciousness to the vulnerable is next extolled (vv. 8-9). There are many situations in life that can force one to be bowed down—a physical disability, a mental or emotional affliction, an economic or social disadvantage. Whatever the situation, God raises up the needy, enables them to stand with pride, reestablishes them in security. Strangers or aliens lack certain legal rights, and since it is not their own nation they may not be familiar with the rights they do have. Insensitive or unscrupulous people can easily take advantage of them. These vulnerable strangers are precisely the kinds of people the God of Israel chooses. Israel itself is the prime example of this. It was when they were aliens in Egypt that God took them and made them God's own people. This is certainly reason to praise God.

In patriarchal societies only adult free men enjoy certain privileges. As part of the household, women and children are under the jurisdiction and care of such men. Women belong to the households either of their fathers, their brothers, their husbands, or their sons. Here widows probably refer to women who cannot return to their home of origin because they have married but whose husbands are now dead and they have no adult son to care for them. Such women are marginal in society and need some patron to care for them. Likewise, it is presumed that the orphans referred to here have no extended family within whose jurisdiction they might take refuge. These are the ones for whom God cares.

The final verse praises God as sovereign and eternal ruler in Jerusalem. All the other verses of the psalm testify to the glory of this God who reigns forever from the very hill that is at the center of the lives of the people. This is not a God who is distant or remote. This God has entered into their history and into the social fabric of their existence. Such a God deserves praise.

1 Timothy 6:11-16

Paul addresses a personal message to Timothy. In it he delivers a fourfold charge: pursue the virtues; fight for the faith; grasp eternal life; keep the commandments. He calls Timothy to responsibilities any Christian would have assumed upon initiation into the Church. However, he expects that Timothy will fulfill them in ways that reflect his pastoral office. The reading begins with the emphatic "But you," implying that the life to which Paul summons Timothy is in sharp contrast to the lives lived by some unidentified others. This suggests there is a tension, either within the Christian community or within society in general.

The righteousness Timothy is called to pursue is right conduct in human affairs; the devotion is openness to the will of God. Faith is an attitude of trust in God; love is benevolence and goodwill toward others. Patience, or endurance, is staying-power, and gentleness is the kind of meekness that will inherit the earth. Though addressed to one who has been especially commissioned for ministry, these fundamentally Christian virtues will take forms that differ according to the life circumstances of those who practice them.

Paul employs an image from athletic competition in order to illustrate the struggle that being faithful often entails. It is not clear whether he was thinking of running, boxing, or wrestling. In any case, he exhorts Timothy to perform energetically in order to grasp the prize that is given to the winner. The prize Paul has in mind is eternal life. This is not to suggest Paul thought one could earn eternal life. Rather, he is working here with a metaphor that, in this particular case, cannot adequately represent both the incomparable desirability and the transcendent character of eternal life. What is clear is that Timothy, like all other Christians, was called to eternal life at his baptism. And now, again like all other Christians, he must fight for the faith so that he can attain it.

Paul underscores the seriousness of his admonitions. He charges Timothy, before God and before Christ, to obey the commandments in anticipation of Christ's glorious manifestation *(epiphάneia)*, a word that denotes divine self-disclosure. Here it is probably a reference to the Second Coming. When this great event will transpire is known only by God. As was the case in the reading for the Twenty-Fourth Sunday, the epithets applied to God all come from Jewish tradition. "Blessed and only ruler," "King of kings," and "Lord of lords" all extol the universal and singular authority of God. Invisibility and unapproachability are long-standing attributes, and the notion of immortality comes from Hellenistic Jewish thought. This is the God who will ultimately determine the time of Christ's return. This is the God whom Paul extols in the final doxology.

Luke 16:19-31

The gospel reading for this Sunday is a narrative that painstakingly paints a picture of radical reversals. The man who during life was treated as a castoff enjoys the bliss of heaven, while the one who savored the pleasures life has to give ends up in great torment in the netherworld. The story has two parts. The first describes the situations and fates of the two men (vv. 19-26). The second describes the man's concern for his brothers (vv. 27-31).

Jesus goes to great lengths to contrast the lives of these two men. The wealth of the first man is seen in his manner of dress, in the style of his home, and in the quality of the table he spreads for himself. He dressed like the wealthy people of his day, who used a very costly substance obtained from the shellfish murex to dye their outer clothing purple, while they wore undergarments of fine linen. He lived in luxury everyday, enjoying sumptuous meals and a home that boasted a large gate or portico. By contrast, the poor man, Lazarus, whose name is the Greek form of Eliezer (my God helps), was destitute. He lay begging at the gate of the home of the rich man, hoping for crumbs from his table. His condition was so debased that the scavenging dogs licked his sores. He was not a leper, for had that been the case he would not have been able to enter the city.

Neither description comments on the moral rectitude of the man. However, the unclean state of Lazarus is obvious, and it is reinforced with the licking of the impure dogs. Then why is Lazarus rewarded while the rich man suffers? Is there merely a bias in favor of poverty here? The answer is found in the understanding of covenant responsibility. Both men are somehow associated with Abraham and therefore belong to the people of Israel. Abraham tells the rich man that his brothers have Moses and the prophets, a reference to the religious traditions of the people. From this we can conclude that though the social conditions of the two protagonists were diametrically opposed, these men were bound together by the covenant. This means they had responsibilities toward each other, particularly the rich man toward the poor man. The story shows that he ignored these responsibilities.

The rich man was indifferent to the needs of the covenant brother who lay at the gate of his home. The fact that he named the poor man when he asked Abraham to send him refreshing water indicates he was not ignorant of him. When he asked that Lazarus be sent to warn his brothers to change their way of life *(metánoia),* he was told that they had the same religious tradition he had, a tradition that clearly charges the wealthy to meet the needs of the poor. If they were not attentive to that tradition, they would not heed a resurrected Lazarus. When he was alive and in a position to help Lazarus, he disregarded him. Now that he is in need, he asks that Lazarus first comfort him and then warn his brothers. Even in death the man is self-serving.

The male bias of the rich man is obvious. He asks that Lazarus go to his father's house, a clear indication of patriarchal organization, but he is only concerned with the men of his family. One could rightly counter that he may have had no sisters. However, extended families, such as were prominent at the time, certainly included some women. The entire character of the man shows he is concerned only with himself and with those who are like him. This is why he suffers. He has not been faithful to his covenant responsibilities, and his life witnessed no *metánoia.*

Themes of the Day

On this Sunday we take up again the question of our responsible management of money and the social relationships that influence it. The significance of covenant is clearly sketched, as is the harsh reality of judgment. It is Paul who offers us an alternative way of living that will stave off the punishment that results from disregard of our commitments.

Covenant Responsibility

Both the reading from the prophet Amos and the gospel narrative pointedly condemn the lifestyles of the rich. Again, it is not wealth itself but the complacency and disregard for others that it too frequently generates that is denounced. When we are relatively secure and satisfied with the circumstances of our lives, it is easy for us to take these blessings for granted, to think we have a right to all our good fortune. This is particularly the case in societies that foster a sense of individual opportunity and advancement in contrast to those that are more communal in their perspective. There we find the sense that "I earned this and so I have a right to enjoy it as I see fit."

On the other hand, biblical covenant is a communal concept. It emerges from a society that insists on mutual responsibility. With the exception of the Davidic covenant established between God and one family (cf. 2 Sam 7:8-17), all biblical covenants presume that God entered into a solemn pact with the entire people. While individuals do have rights and obligations, they carry them as members of the group, not merely as individuals. Furthermore, these rights and obligations flow from the relationships with one another as well as the relationship with God. It is for this reason that social justice was such a fundamental concern of the prophets in ancient Israel.

These readings are held up before us so we can compare our sense of covenant with that of the people portrayed within them. To what extent have we even been aware of our covenant bond with others? And conscious of it, how faithfully have we carried out our responsibilities? Unlike the people depicted in last Sunday's readings, those appearing here are not accused of dishonest behavior. They are not guilty of sins of commission, infractions of the law. They are guilty of sins of omission, sins that flow from a casualness toward covenant commitment. How do we measure up in this regard?

Judgment

There is a theme in these readings we do not like to face. Although the fundamental image of God is one of mercy and compassion, we cannot disregard the fact of judgment. Amos pronounces a woe against his own people; Abraham declares there is an unbridgeable chasm between the saved and the condemned. These are harsh condemnations, but they cannot be softened. Their very harshness lays bare the gravity of indifference to the sorry plight of others. As we move closer and closer to the end of the Liturgical Year, we will be reminded of this judgment. Even Paul speaks here of the appearance of the Lord Jesus Christ. Though he does not say that Christ will bring judgment when he comes, the nuances of this idea are present. Judgment will be determined not primarily in terms of our obedience to law but in view of our fidelity to covenant commitment.

Pursue Righteousness

Righteousness is a covenant term. It is a quality of God that is shared with us by means of our covenant bond. Paul admonishes Timothy, and us, to pursue this righteousness, along with devotion, faith, love, patience, and gentleness. Some of these virtues focus on our relationship with God, but most are directed toward our relationship with others. Those who are less fortunate are our sisters and brothers. If we take lightly our covenant obligations and allow them to languish at our gates, we will have only ourselves to blame when we find ourselves facing the harsh judgment of God.

Ordinary Time (Part Four)

Twenty-Seventh Sunday Habakkuk 1:2-3; 2:2-4 The just live by faith	Psalm 95:1-2, 6-9 Harden not your heart	2 Timothy 1:6-8, 13-14 Do not be ashamed	Luke 17:5-10 Have faith
Twenty-Eighth Sunday 2 Kings 5:14-17 There is no God but the LORD	Psalm 98:1-4 The nations see God's salvation	2 Timothy 2:8-13 If we persevere, we shall reign	Luke 17:11-19 The foreigner gives thanks
Twenty-Ninth Sunday Exodus 17:8-13 Moses' hands raised in prayer	Psalm 121:1-8 Our help is from the LORD	2 Timothy 3:14-4:2 Scripture is inspired by God	Luke 18:1-8 Persistent prayers are heard
Thirtieth Sunday Sirach 35:12-14, 16-18 Prayers of the lowly are heard	Psalm 34:2-3, 17-19, 23 The LORD hears the cry of the poor	2 Timothy 4:6-8, 16-18 The crown of righteousness awaits	Luke 18:9-14 The tax collector is justified
Thirty-First Sunday Wisdom 11:22–12:2 All things are God's	Psalm 145:1-2, 8-11, 13, 14 I will praise your name	2 Thessalonians 1:11–2:2 Christ's name is glorified	Luke 19:1-10 The Son of Man saves what was lost

Thirty-Second Sunday **2 Maccabees 7:1-2, 9-14** God will raise us up	**Psalm 17:1, 5-6, 8, 15** Attend to my outcry	**2 Thessalonians 2:16–3:5** May the Lord encourage you	**Luke 20:27-38** The God of the living
Thirty-Third Sunday **Malachi 3:19-20a** The sun of justice will shine	**Psalm 98:5-9** The LORD comes to rule	**2 Thessalonians 3:7-12** Those who don't work, don't eat	**Luke 21:5-19** Your perseverance will secure your lives
Thirty-Fourth Sunday **(Christ the King)** **2 Samuel 5:1-3** David is king of Israel	**Psalm 122:1-5** Let us go rejoicing to the LORD	**Colossians 1:12-20** All things were created in him	**Luke 23:35-43** Jesus, remember me

Ordinary Time (Part Four)

Initial Reading of the Ordinary Lectionary (Part Four)

Introduction

This last section of readings for Ordinary Time begins with a continuation of our reflection on discipleship and community. Then about half way through the weeks we encounter an abrupt change. We turn our gaze to God, not so much to grasp the meaning of divinity as to stand in awe of what divinity has planned for humanity. All of this is brought to conclusion with the readings of the last weeks. There we see that the mysterious workings of God, which we have considered throughout the year, find their culmination in the establishment of the reign of God and our invitation to enter into that reign. Even the readings that describe the end-time really point to the time that follows the end. This helps us realize that the end is not destruction but the threshold of the new age. The final words of the year are telling: "Today you will be with me in paradise."

First Testament Readings

The first readings for this last part of Ordinary Time were probably selected because they contain a theme found in the gospel readings of each Sunday. During these weeks of Ordinary Time we have been meditating on various aspects of discipleship. Several readings from the First Testament continue that theme, while others refocus our lens so we can concentrate on the marvels God accomplishes on our behalf. We are told at the outset that faith is the foundation stone of our lives, but then the reading moves away from what is expected of us to the unexpected that God accomplishes, and we see the foreigner Naaman profess his faith in the God of Israel.

The role of prayer is next considered. Not only was Moses' supplication required for victory, but the assistance of others was necessary for Moses to persevere in his prayer. This speaks eloquently to the interrelationship between religious leader and those who benefit from that leadership. The final passage that highlights the life of the disciple reminds us of the attitudes that should be ours when we come before God in prayer. We must identify ourselves with the lowly and the needy and humbly bring our petitions before God, confident God will hear our prayers.

The greatness of God is evident in the teachings on creation, on the resurrection, and on the coming of God at the end-time. The last three Sundays open us to the possibilities of living in this age as if we have been transported into the age of fulfillment, for indeed we have been. The focus on God reminds us we cannot hope to live such transformed lives without the strength that comes from God.

Psalms

The psalm responses create an assortment of prayerful responses to God. There is a hymn of praise (Psalm 145) and a prayer identified as prophetic proclamation (Psalm 95). There is a lament (Psalm 17), a prayer of confidence (Psalm 121), and one of thanksgiving (Psalm 34). While these three types may have once been consecutive parts of one long prayerful movement, they are now separate psalms. Each stands on its own and can be viewed as responding to some theme found in the first reading rather than to the religious sentiments of the other two psalms. In addition to these more personal prayers there are two parts of a hymn that praises God, who is the king of the universe (Psalm 98), and a final psalm that acclaims the great city wherein God's presence has been established in a very special way (Psalm 122). The diversity demonstrates the wide variety of prayers found in the Psalter and the various ways they can be incorporated as responses to lectionary readings.

Epistles

With the exception of the reading for the feast of Christ the King, a reading chosen specifically for the feast, the epistle passages are continuous readings from the second letter to Timothy and the second letter to the Thessalonians. Timothy's timorous spirit is behind much of what Paul says. He reminds Timothy about some of the fundamental tenets of the Christian faith, not because Timothy does not know them or hold them as true but because Paul seems afraid that the hardships of ministry and Christian witness will overwhelm his disciple. Paul seems intent on emphasizing the power of God's saving grace so Timothy will rely on it and not on himself.

Paul also prays that the Thessalonians will be strengthened in their faith so they will be able to spread the good news of the gospel to others as Paul has brought it to them. Without an ounce of pride, he offers himself as an example of commitment and steadfastness in the face of misfortune.

The passage from Colossians celebrates the many marvelous facets of Christ, who rules over us all as king of the universe.

Gospels

The gospel readings for this last section of Ordinary Time are a collection of the teachings of Jesus. The one account of the healing of the ten lepers ends with an instructive saying, and the report of Jesus' visit with Zacchaeus is a lesson in action. The teaching itself focuses on four major themes: the question of faith, aspects of prayer, the universality of salvation, and the aspects of the end-time.

It is only appropriate that our reflections on discipleship should end with considerations of faith as the basis of discipleship, and prayer as the fundamental practice of it. Jesus first explains the extraordinary potential of faith and then, with a healing narrative, illustrates its power. His teaching on prayer is also made immediately applicable through the parables he uses. This teaching device enables all of us to see ourselves in the characters of the stories.

There is a definite shift in perspective with the story of Zacchaeus. From this point to the end of the Liturgical Year the focus is less on the responsibilities of discipleship than on the marvels God accomplishes in our midst. The great work of God, whether we think of it as salvation or transformation, is ultimately the establishment of the new age of the reign of God. The advent of this new age is preceded by the collapse of the present age. This collapse is the subject of much of our reflection during these final days of the Liturgical Year.

Mosaic of Readings

We live in the time between. The reign of God had been established already, but its full flowering is not yet accomplished. All the readings address some aspect of this in-between time. We find instruction and clarification, encouragement and warning. We are given models to follow and examples to avoid. We are reminded of God's goodness and compassion as well as God's justice. But above all we are reminded that we have indeed died with Christ and we have risen with him, and so we have nothing to fear. All we have to do is open ourselves to the wonders prepared for us.

Readings

Twenty-Seventh Sunday in Ordinary Time
Habakkuk 1:2-3; 2:2-4

This reading from the prophet Habakkuk consists of two parts. The first (1:2-3) is a direct address spoken to God by the prophet. In the second (2:2-4) the prophet reports the response he received from God. The opening words of the reading are forceful and disturbing. The prophet cries out to God with the words of a psalm of lament: "How long?" "Why?" Although these are accusatory questions, it is not uncommon that those in torment should cry out in this way. In fact, complaint to God is an expression of profound religious sentiment. It is an acknowledgment of both human limitation and divine power. One would not turn to God if one did not believe God could remedy the situation. Lament is also an expression of hope. One would not turn to God if one did not trust that God *would* intervene. The case of Habakkuk is unusual. He begins by lamenting what appears to be God's indifference. It seems that God has turned a deaf ear to his anguish. It is not enough that he is engulfed by misfortune; he must also endure God's impassivity. And so he cries out.

The circumstances within which he finds himself are overwhelming—violence, ruin, misery, and destruction. He faces strife and discord. It seems to be more than he can handle, so he cries out: Why? Why do I have to be a witness to all of this, especially since you do not seem to be open to my call for help? The prophet is not using figurative language to describe his own inner turmoil. He is lamenting the social conditions of the people. The text does not contain any clues that might reveal the specifics of the situation. That is not the point of his complaint. What he grieves is the absence of God's tender solicitude for the covenant people in their need.

Finally, God does respond, not with an answer but with a vision. Though we are not told the content of the vision, Habakkuk is instructed to write it on tablets so the message conveyed can be announced even before the events described come to pass. Writing the vision on tablets accomplishes at least three things. It is a means of publicizing the message. It keeps this message before the eyes of those who might need to seek comfort in it before it transpires. Finally, when the contents of the vision do come to pass, the tablets stand as an affidavit, a concrete witness to the reliability of the prophetic word.

The vision, the fulfillment of which is in the future, does have its appointed time of disclosure. However, the exact time of this disclosure is known only to God, and contrary to what appearances might suggest, God is indeed in charge of the events of life. Habakkuk, and everyone else with him, will just have to wait patiently until the appointed time arrives.

Two possible contrasting responses to the waiting are given. Here we find what is probably the principal theme of the entire speech. The one who is rash or puffed up *('upp^elâ)* does not have an upright soul. In contrast, the one who is just *(ṣaddîq)* lives by faith *('ĕmûnâ)*. Faith is a disposition closely associated with the covenant. It means fidelity, trustworthiness, or steadfastness. This word from God clearly though indirectly addresses Habakkuk's initial accusatory questions. Without telling him why he has had to carry the burden of suffering or how long he will have to wait, God instructs him in the manner of his waiting. The righteous wait in faith.

Psalm 95:1-2, 6-7, 8-9

The responsorial psalm combines an invitation to praise, a plea for openness, and a word from God. The invitation is given three times: "Come, let us sing joyfully" (v. 1); "Let us come into his presence" (v. 2); "Come, let us bow down" (v. 6). Together they seem to be a reenactment of a liturgical movement. There is the initial summons to praise followed by an invitation to enter the presence of God (presumably the Temple), there to bow before God in worship. God then addresses the reverent community.

The relationship that exists between God and the people is characterized by means of several metaphors. God is the Rock of their salvation (v. 1). A rock is solid and secure. It affords grounding for whatever relies on it. Natural formations of rock also provide refuge and shelter from inclement weather and from various dangers. It is an apt image to refer to God as the protector of the people. God is also clearly identified as Creator (v. 6). This can be a reference to God as the Creator of the universe and everything within it, or it can be a more personal reference to the fashioning of a disparate group of individuals into a coherent community. The image that follows suggests the latter interpretation.

The psalmist identifies the community as the flock and God as the shepherd (v. 6). In a pastoral community such a relationship was quite intimate. Shepherds took total responsibility for their sheep, caring for them and protecting them even at the risk of their own lives. For reasons such as this, "shepherd" became a fitting metaphor to describe the monarch, who was expected to act in this same way on behalf of the people of the realm. In this psalm the images of rock and shepherd illustrate the people's perception of God as protector.

Having depicted God as a caring and devoted protector, the psalmist turns again to the people and issues a serious plea to be open to the voice of God. This plea suggests that "today" the people who have been gathered together will hear God's voice. Since this gathering is clearly liturgical in character (v. 6), it is safe to conclude that the word from God will be a part of the actual liturgical celebration. The people have come to worship God and to receive some word from God that will comfort them or set a direction for their lives.

The word that follows is an appeal by God to respond positively to God, not in the spirit of rebellion that governed their ancestors while they were in the wilderness (cf. Exod 17:1-7; Deut 6:16). During that earlier time the people had demanded signs that would prove the presence and power of God acting on their behalf, despite the fact they had witnessed God's gracious deliverance of them from Egyptian bondage. God desires hearts that are open, not hearts that have been hardened by selfishness or lack of faith. "Today" the descendants of those rebellious wanderers are called upon to respond with open faith and willing obedience.

2 Timothy 1:6-8, 13-14

Paul here appeals to Timothy, one who was his own disciple and on whom Paul had laid hands, a ritual that commissioned individuals for ministry. It is an appeal to courage in the face of hardship. In these few verses Paul admonishes Timothy to renew his zeal, to be unashamed of the gospel, to bear his share of suffering, to adhere to Paul's teaching and to safeguard it.

Timothy was quite a bit less forceful than his colleague Paul. While there is no question about the steadfastness of his faith, it appears that he struggled with a certain degree of cowardice, the kind of terror that grips the timid in the face of extreme difficulty. The zeal that previously blazed within him seems to have waned, and Paul challenges him to fan it back into flame. He received a particular charism on the occasion of his commission for ministry. It is this gift he must rekindle. Timothy needs the power, the love, and the self-discipline that will enable him to stand up courageously and witness to his faith.

Paul is aware of the risk one takes in publicly professing faith in Jesus Christ. There is a stigma attached to such testimony. After all, Jesus was a political threat to the Roman Peace, and he died the death of a convicted felon. All those who stand with him and proclaim what he preached place themselves in jeopardy. Paul himself is a political prisoner for this very reason. In the face of such possible peril Paul exhorts Timothy to witness to the Lord without shame, adding that he should not be ashamed of Paul either. Others may think Paul is a prisoner of the state and may thereby hold him in contempt. He insists he is really a prisoner of Christ, a distinction of which he boasts and which should make Timothy proud as well.

Furthermore, just as Paul is, Timothy should be willing to accept and embrace the suffering that will inevitably befall him as a minister of the gospel. He must be ready for misunderstanding, resentment, and hostility. He must face the possibility of imprisonment just as did Jesus, and Paul after him. Though Paul does not mention it here, it is conceivable he may even be called upon to offer the ultimate sacrifice of his life for the sake of the gospel. Such a likelihood would cast fear in the hearts of even the most stalwart. Still, Paul insists that nothing should undermine Timothy's confidence, for he can be strong with the strength that comes from God.

Having addressed Timothy's personal conflict, Paul turned to the substance of his preaching. Paul had handed on to Timothy the essence of the gospel. It was now Timothy's turn to carry it to others. He was not merely to repeat Paul's words. They were to be the norm, the standard against which all other teaching would be measured. Just as Paul did in his own ministry, so Timothy would have to refashion for new situations the teaching he received. The ministerial approach Paul advocates is what we today refer to as recontextualization. Then and now it requires that the minister be both faithful to the tradition and creative in articulating it in a new way. Timothy must guard the trust that is his but allow the Spirit to move where it will.

Luke 17:5-10

There are two independent sayings in the gospel reading for this Sunday. The first treats the power of prayer; the second addresses the responsibilities of disciples. Arranged next to each other as they are, they share the explanatory phrase, "The Lord replied." Thus they should both be read as instruction for the apostles.

As is so often the case, Jesus' response to a request includes a shift in perspective. The apostles ask for an increase of faith and Jesus speaks about its nature. They are interested in quantity and he is concerned about quality. He employs an image that suggests size in order to describe effective authority. The mustard seed was considered one of the smallest seeds. The mulberry tree had a very deep and extensive root system that was thought to remain for a long period of time. For this reason it was difficult to uproot the tree. Jesus uses the image of the seed metaphorically to illustrate how very little faith is needed to accomplish extraordinary feats. Thus it is not necessary to procure more faith. Rather, one should be concerned to secure even a small amount of genuine faith. Such faith will be able to realize even what is impossible.

Frequently Jesus first exemplifies the point he is trying to make and then at the end of his instruction explicitly draws the conclusion he intends. The second saying is an example of this pedagogical technique. Jesus begins his saying with a question that, at the outset, forces his audience to agree with what is described. It appears that the staff of the household under consideration is relatively small, for the servant is expected to perform several tasks—plowing, tending sheep, preparing food, serving at table. We may think the householder is unreasonable in the demands that are being made. We may not believe the servant should be invited to sit at table with the householder, but we might expect a bit of consideration toward one who had already been involved in strenuous service. However, the story is not about being considerate but about social convention. Jesus is teaching about the obligations of the one in service, not about the responsibilities of the one being served.

Disciples of Jesus should expect a similar lot. They have been called to labor, and when they fulfill their duties faithfully, they have only done what is required of them. The saying challenges any form of self-adulation based on accomplishments. The servants are unprofitable not because they do not do good work but perhaps because they are regarded as replaceable. When they can no longer fulfill their responsibilities, there will be someone to take their place. As harsh as this may sound, it is true. The rewards of discipleship must be sought in something other than a bonus.

Themes of the Day

The readings for both this Sunday and the next call us to faith. Today we reflect on the sense of the absence of God as the crucible within which this faith is forged and refined. We also acknowledge that faith is a gift from God, not a personal disposition of soul or a prize we have won. Finally, while faith may come to us from God, it is mediated through the community.

The Absence of God

In our struggles to be faithful disciples we frequently must endure periods of time, some quite short and others unbearably long, when we feel abandoned by God. Such experiences are difficult under any circumstances. When we have been intent on serving God with genuine devotion, such times are particularly trying, for one would expect that God would not withdraw consolations. However, even the righteous sometimes feel abandoned by God. When this happens, the broken heart and the strained spirit cry out to God in complaint: How long? Why?

Times of near despair know no restrictions on age or gender or class. Teenagers often search frantically for meaning and identity; people in midlife crises may desperately question their life choices; the elderly can feel that everything they have held dear is either taken from them or is slipping away. People fall victim to natural disasters wherein they lose everything that gave their lives meaning. Husbands and wives are betrayed by their partners, and their entire lives crumble before their very eyes. Illness strikes indiscriminately, and death's shadow looms over all. Finally, we have all known the tedium of life. We have all been worn down by it, tempted to give up, too weary to go on. These are all moments when we stand before the doors to faith and to despair, trying to decide through which one we will pass.

The Gift of Faith

Faith in God is a gift for which we pray. It enables us to accomplish marvelous feats; with it we can move mountains. As unprofitable servants we do not earn it; we have no right to claim it as our own. If we are honest, we will have to admit that there are many people we know who are more generous than we are, who are more patient and loving, who live lives of greater integrity—yet who do not have the faith we do. If we are honest, we have to ask ourselves: Why are we, and not they, so disposed toward God? And there is no answer to this question, except to realize that the faith we have is a gift from God. In God's goodness, these others will be cared for, but we are the ones to whom faith has been given. And therefore we are the ones from whom faithful service will be expected. We will be sent to plow the fields and tend the sheep. We will be called to serve at table.

Faith Comes Through Hearing

The faith that is ours has been mediated to us through the community. We have heard about God and about Jesus from others—from our parents and families, from our teachers and those who preach, from those with whom we work and play. Faith comes from God, but through the mediation of the community. Timothy received faith from his mother and grandmother. It was strengthened in him through the imposition of Paul's hands and through his preaching of the word of God. Furthermore, what Paul taught had first been handed down to him from those who preceded him. God grants us the gift of faith, but it comes to us through others. Perhaps those whom we know to be better people than we are have not yet met someone through whom this gift can be mediated. The challenge could be ours.

Twenty-Eighth Sunday in Ordinary Time
2 Kings 5:14-17

The first reading for today is a narrative about healing, gratitude, conversion, and worship. It recounts an episode from the collection of stories about the prophet Elisha. The primary character in the story is Naaman, a foreigner who was cured of leprosy and converted to the God of Israel.

This is a most unusual healing story. Although Elisha gave instructions concerning the ritual Naaman should perform, the prophet himself had nothing to do with the cure. In fact, he was not even present when it happened. There is a hint of primitive ritual, almost magic, in the sevenfold immersion, the reason for which is not given. The term "leprosy" covers a variety of skin diseases, least of which is Hansen's disease, which we today know as leprosy. Because of leprosy's skin eruptions, the one suffering was rendered unclean and was forced into isolation. Israel had many regulations governing leprosy (cf. Leviticus 13–14). Washing was part of the rite of reincorporation into the community, but it was not itself a remedy for the illness, as is the case here. Miraculously the waters of the Jordan transformed Naaman's flesh into that of a child.

Naaman was a man of means. He traveled with a retinue, an entourage that probably included attendants of various kinds. Suffering from leprosy must have been a terrible physical affliction and an unbearable social stigma as well. When he realized he had been cured, his indebtedness prompted him to return to Elisha and offer him a gift. This should not be construed as payment for services but rather as an expression of gratitude.

Naaman's cure was miraculous. All he had to do was submit himself to the prescribed ritual. "To go down" *(yārad)* might have a double meaning here. It describes Naaman's descent into the waters of the Jordan, and it can also demonstrate the humility of this man who, though he had people under his command, obeyed the directions of a lowly prophet from a nation not his own. Having experienced the power of Elisha's God, he proclaims there is no other God but the LORD. Evidence of the sincerity of his conversion is seen in his desire to worship the God of Israel even when he is back in his own land. Since it was believed that one could only worship a god in the land of that god (for example, Gen 4:16; 1 Sam 26:19), Naaman asks permission to take some earth back home with him so he will then be able to worship the God of Israel even outside of the land.

The story of Naaman champions monotheism and universalism. It is not surprising that an Israelite would claim there is no God but the LORD. When a non-Israelite does, it is truly remarkable. Naaman may have needed a miracle to recognize this truth, but recognize it he did! Something else makes this story exceptional. When there were many people suffering from leprosy in Israel, God chose to heal a foreigner. This demonstrates God's love and concern for all, Israelite and non-Israelite alike. One feature of this story betrays the uneven development of Naaman's monotheistic faith. While he does declare that the LORD and only the LORD is God, he has not yet realized that this means God's power extends over the entire world. Naaman does not need the land of Israel to ensure the presence of the God of Israel.

Psalm 98:1, 2-3, 3-4

This psalm belongs to the category of enthronement psalms, praising God as king over all (v. 6). It opens with a summons to sing a new song to God (cf. Psalm 96). The reason for this new song is the marvelous new things God has done on Israel's behalf. The psalmist follows this summons with an enumeration of wondrous acts of God (vv. 1b-3). Some of them are historical, other are cosmic in scope.

God is first depicted as a triumphant warrior whose right hand and outstretched arm have brought victory. The victory sketched in these verses seems to have been historical, one that transpired on the stage of Israel's own political experience. Actually, it is not too difficult for a god to defeat mere human forces. If God is to be acclaimed as king over all, there must be a more comprehensive victory, one that demonstrates preeminence on a cosmic scale. Behind this image of the triumphant warrior is just such an understanding. The divine warrior is the one who conquers the primordial forces of chaos. The victory referred to here is a cosmic victory. These verses include mention of a sweeping victory that is seen by all the nations (v. 3). This justifies the psalmist's claim that God's triumph is universal and undisputed.

The focus in this psalm is on the particularity of Israel's salvation by God. Two aspects of this victory are mentioned. First, the victory, or demonstration of righteousness, is really vindication meted out in order to rectify a previous injustice. Second, the victory follows God's recall of the covenant promises made to the house of Israel. Here we find covenant vocabulary. Lovingkindness (*ḥesed*) and faithfulness (*'ĕmûnâ*) are closely associated with these promises (v. 3). It is important to remember that this psalm praises God as king precisely as a triumphant warrior. There is an implication that either the righteous character of God's rule or its universal scope was challenged. That means any victory of God is really a reestablishment of right order. In other words, it is vindication.

A second important feature of this psalm is its statement about the relationship that exists between God's saving action and the promises that God made. The psalmist claims it was remembrance of the covenantal lovingkindness (*ḥesed*) that prompted God to save Israel. It was because of the promise made to the ancestors that the divine warrior stepped in and triumphed over Israel's enemies. That triumph, which was revealed to all the nations, is the reason for the psalmist's call to praise God in song.

2 Timothy 2:8-13

This Sunday we continue Paul's appeal to Timothy begun in last Sunday's epistle reading. The fact that Paul writes from prison makes his appeal even more poignant. It begins with what appears to be a form of creedal statement, and it ends with what Paul himself identifies as a trustworthy saying.

Paul exhorts Timothy to remember what is at the heart of the gospel Paul has preached. He is speaking here of a manner of remembering that is far more than merely calling to mind. It is a way of witnessing to the authenticity of what is remembered. In this case it is a truth that is twofold: Jesus Christ is raised from the dead and he is a descendant of David. The first component of the testimony is the very basis of Christian faith. The title "Christ" means "anointed one," the long-awaited one who would inaugurate the reign of God and bring it to fulfillment. This was accomplished through his death and resurrection. The fact that he came from the line of David shows that he fulfilled all the expectations and promises associated with that royal family. This is the gospel to which Paul committed himself and for which he was now suffering imprisonment.

Paul's attitude toward his confinement is complex. While he considered it a privilege to suffer the same fate as did his Lord, it was still a great affliction for him. It prevented him from engaging in the ministry in which he took such pride. It kept him from the people whose lives he had touched and who had touched his life. More than this, Paul was a freeborn Roman citizen. It must have been a great humiliation for him to have been treated like a common malefactor, a slave, or a conquered captive. He calls himself a criminal, a term generally used to designate burglars, murderers, traitors, or other serious offenders. Still, the greater his humiliation and torment, the more he rejoices in participating in the sufferings of Christ.

The agony and indignity Paul bears are seen by him as a share in the birth-pangs of the Messiah, that necessary suffering that would precede the birth of the reign of God. The idea that there was a predetermined amount of suffering that had to be endured before this glorious reign could come seems to lie behind Paul's thinking here. He believed that the more suffering he would contribute the less the rest of the Church would have to undergo and the sooner the reign would appear. He seems to have been assured of his own salvation, and in this way he sought to assure the salvation of others as well—not that he could earn it but that he could actively participate in its dawning.

The structure of Paul's trustworthy saying suggests a liturgical hymn. It consists of four conditional clauses with protases (if) that describe an action of the believer, and apodoses that state a corresponding action of Christ. The first two are positive; the second two are negative. The first saying reflects the fundamental belief in the fruits of the resurrection in the lives of believers. Joined to Christ in his death, we will be joined to him in his resurrection. This is baptismal language. The second attests to the need to remain faithful in order to share in Christ's reign. This particular saying may have been the primary reason for Paul's instruction of Timothy. The third describes the alternative to fidelity. The fourth saying addresses again the question of faithfulness, but it does not follow the pattern of the previous three. This is probably because there was no thought that God could be faithless. In fact, the opposite is true. That is the paradox of divine love. Human faithlessness only highlights divine faithfulness.

Luke 17:11-19

The gospel narrative echoes the story recounted in the first reading. It is the story of a foreigner who suffered the pain and indignities of leprosy. He was cured by the power of God and returned to give thanks. While similar lessons are taught in both narratives, each contains its own meaning. The gospel reveals the power of God working through Jesus and the power of faith to save.

The geographic data is confusing. If Jesus was traveling to Jerusalem, as the opening verse states, he would travel first through Galilee and then pass through Samaria. Galilee is to the north, Jerusalem to the south, and Samaria lies between them. While the order of the geography may not be important, mention is made of Samaria because one of those who came to Jesus was a Samaritan.

The abhorrent nature of leprosy can be seen in the fact that the ethnic and religious rivalry that existed between the Jews and the Samaritans was superseded by the disease. In a sense, the disease took complete control of them. They had no other identity but the disease of leprosy. They could claim no ethnic or political privileges, and they were barred from religious practice. According to the law they were to be isolated outside the cities and villages, segregated from all the normal activities of life (cf. Lev 13:46; Num 5:2-3), crying out "Unclean" should anyone approach them (cf. Lev 13:45). This law was binding on both women and men who suffered from the disease. However, only men *(leproì andres)* are involved in this story.

These outcasts recognized Jesus, for standing at a distance, they cried out to him by name. They also addressed him as Master *(epistátēs)*, a term only the disciples used for Jesus. They did not ask for alms, as was customary for destitute people who sat outside the villages begging for food or money. They asked for mercy, for compassion. Knowing who Jesus was, this probably meant they were seeking a cure. Jesus neither touched them nor spoke words of healing over them. He merely sent them away with directions. He put their faith to the test by having them go to the priests presuming they would be healed. They were sent to the priests who, as cultic functionaries, were responsible for protecting purity and guarding against impurity (cf. Lev 14:2). They did as Jesus directed them, and on the way, they were healed.

Only one man returned to thank Jesus. He is described with bold strokes: he glorifies God; he prostrates himself before Jesus; he is a Samaritan. He is not surprised that Jesus healed him. He, along with his companions, had recognized Jesus earlier and had hoped for a cure. Nor is he the only one who had faith. They all believed Jesus had the power to heal them, and they all went off to show themselves to the priests. What makes this man unique is his gratitude. Furthermore, it is a Samaritan, one who is despised by the Jews, who shows gratitude to the Jewish wonder-worker—a point Jesus clearly makes.

Jesus commends the man for his faith. Once again the last (a Samaritan) will be first (held up as an example).

Themes of the Day

The readings for today suggest a journey. They trace the stages of Christian conversion from sin through healing to gratitude and finally to the privilege of living fulfilled lives in the eschatological age.

Sin: Separation from God

The journey begins with the stories of Naaman and the ten men who had leprosy. Their leprosy, which was the principal alienating disease of that day, serves as a metaphor for our sinfulness, the condition that makes us unfit for the presence of God and despicable in the eyes of others. Separated from God and alienated from society, we are truly in a deplorable state, a state out of which we are unable to extricate ourselves.

Salvation: Healing

Into these seemingly hopeless conditions step the prophet Elisha and Jesus. Each in his own way brings the healing power of God, the saving grace of God. Paul is such a mediator as well. He brings the gospel to those who are in need of salvation. When people are open to his preaching, they are transformed and made ready to receive eternal glory. It is interesting to note that in both narratives the agent of God's healing did not belong to the social group of the one healed. In other words, God's grace does not move along ethnic or racial or gender or class or generational lines. God's healing grace is sometimes available to us through unfamiliar means. Had Naaman not crossed ethnic boundaries, he would not have been healed by waters that were foreign to him. Had the Samaritan man not been in the company of the other leprous men or had he not approached the Jewish Jesus, he would not have been healed. God's grace comes to us from unexpected quarters and in unexpected ways.

Thanks and Praise

The next step in our journey of conversion is the response of gratitude and praise. Both Naaman and the lone Samaritan are so filled with gratitude they return to the one responsible for their healing. They are not so preoccupied with their good fortune as to forget that it came to them as a gift. They must have known unbelievable joy in their cure, but the narratives depict them as overwhelmed with gratitude. Their response is the kind of thanks and praise proclaimed in the psalm and also celebrated at each Sunday Eucharist. We have been saved from our alienation from God and one another. Let us give thanks to the Lord.

New Life

Those who know they have been healed, who realize this was a gift freely given to them, and who return to give thanks have, by these acts of devotion, stepped over a threshold into a new way of living. Their thanks and praise usher them into the new age of eschatological promise: if we have died with him, we will live with him. This new life is completely dependent upon faith. For Naaman it was faith in the words of the prophet; for the leprous man, it was faith in the words of Jesus; for the people to whom Paul wrote, it was faith in the words of his teaching. We see this Sunday what we have seen on earlier Sundays, that is, the importance of faith and the role played by the community in bringing the promises of God to fulfillment.

Twenty-Ninth Sunday in Ordinary Time
Exodus 17:8-13

The account of the battle with Amalek demonstrates conclusively the favored status of the people of Israel. The Amalekites were a nomadic confederacy of tribes that roamed the region of Sinai and the neighboring wilderness. The Bible records a long history of enmity between these two nations. The particular battle reported here may have been over watering holes or pasturage for animals, both precious commodities in the desert and the reason for constant warfare. Four prominent Israelite heroes play pivotal roles in this drama. Moses, the central figure, and his brother Aaron were the ones who confronted Pharaoh and led the Israelites through the sea into the wilderness. Joshua was a military figure subject to Moses. Hur was the son of Caleb, who along with Joshua would be one of the few who left Egypt and actually entered the land of promise. These men form a kind of bridge between Israel's experience of deliverance and its eventual occupation of the land.

Many people have been troubled by the militant character of these Israelites and the thought that God not only endorsed their aggressive behavior but actually directed it. Wars were generally fought over land or resources, essential if a people is to survive. Maintaining that their God was committed to them in a particular way, the Israelites believed their God would want them to do whatever was necessary for their survival. They also believed that because they were God's special people, their enemies were God's enemies. Therefore, in fighting their own battles they would be fighting God's battles. Furthermore, they believed God was with them in their conflict fighting for their cause. This is not meant to justify their militancy but to explain their perspective.

It is clear the Israelites were no match for the Amalekites, for the only thing that prevented their defeat was the intervention of Moses. The staff of God may have been the same staff Moses used to perform wonders before Pharaoh (Exod 4:2-4) and with which he parted and then gathered back the water of the sea (Exod 14:16, 26-27). Some manuscripts say that Moses held up his hand; others say hands. Whichever version is used, the point is the same. When Moses' hands were held up, the Israelites prevailed; when Moses let them down, the Amalekites advanced. There is a hint of magic in this. The uplifted hands of Moses resemble a ritual that must be performed with great precision if the desired effects are to be achieved. It is almost as if Moses was a conduit of divine power. There is no question about it being the power of the God of Israel, but the text does not say that Moses raised his hands to heaven or that he prayed to God for help. In fact, God is not even mentioned here. This might be a remnant of a more primitive understanding of divine involvement in war.

The support Moses gets from Aaron and Hur is probably symbolic. While these men certainly played important roles in the history of Israel, stories such as this serve to legitimize the power they exercised within the community. Furthermore, although Joshua and the men he had chosen to fight with him ultimately put the Amalekites to the sword, it was really the conduct of Moses that won the battle. However, his involvement in the victory established Joshua as a trustworthy leader for the future.

Psalm 121:1-2, 3-4, 5-6, 7-8

This psalm of confidence is also a psalm of ascent, a song that contains sentiments associated with a pilgrimage to Jerusalem. Although this particular identification is not explicitly made in the psalm, there are several features of it that point to such a designation. Chief among them is the reference to God as the Creator of heaven and earth. This was an epithet of the Canaanite god who was worshiped at Salem long before David seized the city (cf. Gen 14:18-20). It is believed that when David took over the city, the religious leaders he brought with him appropriated as much of the religious tradition of the place as they were able to incorporate into the worship of the God of Israel. Thus the divine epithet remained in the city, but it now identified the LORD. A second point that suggests a temple context is found in the final verse of the psalm. Coming in and going out was a common way of describing a visit to the Temple.

Mountains were considered sacred sites. Their majesty inspired confidence, and they came to be considered places of refuge and safety. Because they seemed to reach high into the heavens, they were thought to be places where the gods dwelt, or at least from which the will of the gods was made known. Israel was no stranger to this kind of thinking. Not only did momentous events of its history occur on mountains (cf. Exodus 19), but Solomon had the Temple constructed on one (cf. 1 Kgs 8:1). That the psalmist should look to the mountains for help is very much in keeping with traditional Israelite piety. In the first verse the psalmist seems to ask a general question: From where does my help come? In the second, a very specific answer is given: My help comes from the LORD, who dwells in Jerusalem.

If the context of this psalm is the Temple, it is possible that the one who now speaks to the worshiper is a priest, for it was the practice in the Temple to inquire of a priest who would then pronounce a word of the LORD. Whether or not this is the case here, the message delivered to the psalmist is one of promise or blessing. God is described as a solicitous protector, one who watches day and night, attentive to the needs of the entire people ("guardian of Israel") as well as to those of the individual worshiper ("your guardian").

God is said to be at the right hand of the psalmist. Since in times of assault most people will grasp whatever is at their right, God is here described as the support that is ever there, waiting to be called upon. The sun and the moon were polar realities considered to be quite dangerous. Many people believed that fever and leprosy were caused by lunar disturbances and that those who were moonstruck were possessed by demons. The psalmist is promised that besides holding back such evils, God will act as a shade, protecting against sunstroke and the ailments that often accompany it. Every aspect of the psalmist's life will be in the safekeeping of this provident and sheltering God.

2 Timothy 3:14–4:2

As he continues to instruct Timothy, Paul expounds on the excellence of the sacred Scriptures (holy writings) and their usefulness in the lives of Christians (3:14-17). The reading for today ends with an exhortation to proclaim this magnificent word. Both Paul and Timothy were sons of Israel. This means that from a very early age they were well schooled in its religious traditions. In the first century a rabbi wrote that by the age of five a child should be studying the Scriptures (cf. *Pirke Aboth* 5:21). The holy writings to which Paul refers are what we today call the First or Old Testament. All of the praise he directs to the Scriptures is directed to this tradition. It is important that we recognize this, since there have been Christians down through the centuries who have erroneously believed the Second or New Testament made the message of these writings obsolete. This passage argues against such a position. It also demonstrates beyond a shadow of a doubt that, though Paul insisted that only faith in Christ Jesus saves, he did not harbor anti-Judaic tendencies.

Timothy is reminded of those teachers from whom he learned the message of the Scriptures. In his infancy and youth it would have been his mother, Eunice, and his grandmother, Lois (cf. 2 Tim 1:5). More recently it would have been Paul himself. Loyalty to his teachers is given as one reason for his faithfulness to the teaching of the Scriptures. The witness of the writings is further cause for fidelity, for it is within this tradition that the wisdom for salvation is found. Paul does not mean that salvation is found in the Scriptures themselves. Rather, they prepare for and point to the one who brings salvation, Christ Jesus. Paul does not repudiate the basic teachings in which both he and Timothy were raised. On the contrary, he maintains that they continue to reveal God's saving purpose, but they do so now through faith in Christ.

Paul believed that all Scripture was inspired by God and that it plays a very important role in the lives of believers. In it are found the history of salvation from the beginning of time up to their own day, the law that God gave through Moses, the message of the prophets, and instruction for wise living. Its teaching can be used to refute false doctrines; its laws and its counsels can direct those who are openhearted; the discipline it promotes can lead to righteous living. Training in the Scriptures, interpreted through faith in Christ, can help believers fulfill their religious duties.

Having expounded on the glories of the sacred Scriptures, Paul solemnly charges Timothy to remain faithful to his ministerial responsibilities. The seriousness of Paul's charge is seen in its strong eschatological tenor. He calls Timothy into the presence of God and of Christ, to whom he attributes lofty characteristics. He insists that Christ's sovereignty is seen in his role as universal judge and king of all. Paul believed that Christ would return and bring his reign to fulfillment. Until that day dawns, Timothy is charged to proclaim the word, to be resolute at all times, to correct those in error, to rebuke those who have gone astray, and to encourage all. He has the power of Christ Jesus to accomplish this, so he should not be fainthearted.

Luke 18:1-8

On the Twenty-Fifth Sunday of Ordinary Time we read the story of the unjust steward. In today's gospel Jesus tells the parable of the unjust *(adikía)* judge. He draws sharp lines of contrast between this man and a widow who comes to him for justice. The earlier story compared the practical wisdom of the unjust steward with that of the children of light and found the latter lacking. Here it is the vindication of God that is compared to the judge's execution of justice. The point of the parable is the need for persistence in prayer.

The judge is described as fearing neither God nor human beings. The fear of God is the quintessential characteristic of the pious person. By his own admission the judge is devoid of such devotion. This is a way of saying he did not hold in regard the pivotal commandments of love of God and love of neighbor. He was unjust not because he was an active adversary against another but because he failed to ensure that justice was served in the lives of all. This is an extraordinarily serious charge against a judge, whose very function is to secure justice for all, especially the most vulnerable of society. Sins of omission can be as devastating as sins of commission.

The woman, on the other hand, is a widow, a member of one of the most oppressed classes in Israelite society. It would seem she is not only widowed but also alone in the world, for it would be customary for a male member of her family to appear before the judge to plead her cause. The text does not identify the specifics of her complaint, but it would be safe to conclude that it has something to do with property or possessions. In other words, she is at risk of becoming even more defenseless. Though vulnerable, this woman is bold. She is already the victim of injustice, but she appears here before the judge, pressing him for a hearing. As indifferent as the judge seems to be toward her case, so is she persistent in her demands of him. He will not give in; she will not give up.

We are not told how long this standoff continued, but it was long enough to wear down the judge. He finally relents, and with a bit of exaggerated humor, he states that he will render her justice before she gives him a black eye. Today he might say, "She's in my face!" At this point in his instruction, Jesus introduces an *a fortiori* argument: If the judge who is unjust will finally vindicate those who have been mistreated, how much more will God vindicate those who are the chosen ones, who pray continually, crying out to God day and night? The persistence of the woman becomes the model of resoluteness for God's chosen ones. Like the woman in the parable, they cannot be certain regarding when God will respond, so they must persist.

Jesus' disciples are admonished to persevere in prayer day and night, regardless of how closed God might seem to be to their pleas. This parable shows them that in God's regard, it is not a question of disinterest but of timing. God will answer in God's time. This eschatological note leads into the final saying. Using the title with which he generally identifies himself and the character of his messiahship, Jesus implies that he is the one who will ultimately come to execute justice. The question he poses is sobering: "Will he find faith on the earth?" Following the parable as it does, this could mean: Will there be people who persevere in prayer? He leaves the question unanswered so the disciples can ponder it.

Themes of the Day

The theme of faith we have been considering these last two weeks takes a slightly different turn this Sunday. Today we consider the spiritual disciplines that exercise us in that faith and that deepen our faith as they do so. The over-arching discipline is prayer. The readings today offer various aspects of this prayer for our consideration. There is the spiritual discipline of prayer itself, which is essential to the life of the disciple; there is the communal dimension of prayer; and there is the ministerial commitment that is born of prayer.

Ceaseless Prayer

Our personal prayer must be persistent. Like Moses and the woman in the gospel reading, we must be ceaseless in our prayer, not discouraged by difficulties we might have to face. The woman's persistence finally opened the door of the judge. This story only captures one facet of prayer, namely, God's openness to us. In reality, prayer develops a mutual openness: God is open to our desire for God and we are open to God's desire for us. In the gospel account it is the woman who was persistent; in reality, it is God who prevails upon us to open ourselves. The gospel only hints at this particular aspect of prayer. It states that the Son of Man will come seeking faith.

Communal Assistance

Regardless of how strange the first reading may appear to be, it very strongly emphasizes the communal dimension of prayer. The Israelites would not have been able to prevail against the Amalekites without the prayerful action of Moses, but Moses would not have been able to persevere in his action of entreaty had not Aaron and Hur supported him. The stress in today's world on the importance of the individual, as important as this may be, has obscured the reality of our social nature and our inability to thrive or even survive without others.

What is true about life is true about prayer. We were saved as a people. Salvation may unfold in each life in a particular way, but it is not simply an individual quest or a personal blessing. Christ saved all of humankind. To develop a communal sense may be one of the most challenging aspects of discipleship for many of us today, but develop it we must.

Ministerial Fulfillment

As minister of the word, Timothy is admonished to keep preaching the gospel, to keep spreading the good news, to allow the Scriptures to continue to be a source of wisdom for himself and, through him, for all of the people who hear him. To have this kind of facility with Scripture requires that one enter into the deep meaning of the Scriptures and make them the basis of one's prayer. One must engage in what the monks call *lectio divina*, prayerful reflective reading of the Scriptures. This practice, or spiritual discipline, gives us access to God, and it also gives God access to us. It moves us out of our penchant toward isolated devotion into ministerial commitment. It gives us the courage and the gentleness to teach, to refute, to correct. When our ministerial activity flows from prayer, it also flows from and strengthens right relationships with God, with the religious tradition, and with the community. When this becomes a reality, the Son of Man will indeed find faith on earth.

Thirtieth Sunday in Ordinary Time
Sirach 35:12-14, 16-18

The reading from the Book of Sirach is a discourse on both the impartiality of God and the prayer of those in need. Although these are very different themes, in this reading one flows from the other.

Sirach is part of the Wisdom tradition of ancient Israel. This means that its teaching addresses some of the most fundamental questions of life. However, its limitations must be acknowledged. Along with several of the other Wisdom writings, it has been accused of favoring the worldview of those who are in power or who are in some way privileged. Its insistence that upright living will be rewarded and sinfulness punished presumes there are no obstacles in the way, obstacles such as often hold captive the lives of the less privileged. The Wisdom tradition seems to presume that all people really do have equal opportunity to pursue their dreams and to find fulfillment, a conviction the disadvantaged know to be false. For this reason the Wisdom tradition has been accused of class bias.

So much of the Bible, especially the prophetic material, seems to espouse what has come to be known as the "preferential option for the poor." This position claims that God favors those who are less fortunate. At first glance it might appear the Wisdom tradition, with its upper-class bias, is in conflict with the prophetic tradition, with its preference for the poor. A close look at this reading will show that such is not the case.

Sirach states that the justice of God is an established fact. In this he stands within a long tradition in Israel that professes this belief (cf. Deut 32:4; Ps 145:17; Isa 45:24; Jer 23:6; etc.). He also states that God knows no favorites, neither the privileged nor the dispossessed. He is not hereby challenging the prophets' obvious bias in favor of the poor. Rather, by making this statement he is indirectly showing that if there is any partiality, it is ours and not God's. He insists that God is concerned with justice, not favoritism; when God takes the side of the poor, it is for the sake of justice, not poverty. According to covenant theology, we are all responsible for one another. The well-off are obliged to address the needs of those who suffer misfortune. This is a matter of justice, not charity. With this view we can see that there is no intrinsic conflict between the Wisdom and prophetic traditions. The one presumes right order, the other condemns its violation.

Sirach contends that God hears the cry of the oppressed, those who are the victims of wrongdoing *(adikéō)*. Actually, the verb suggests that God does more than hear; God obeys *(eisakoúō)*. The oppressed cry out, the orphan wails, the widow complains, and God yields to their requests. These are all people for whom there seems to be little redress. It is almost as if God is bound to respond positively to them. As a covenant partner God is accountable to them, especially when other covenant partners disregard their own responsibilities. Sirach assures these forlorn people that their entreaties will not go unheeded. Like the persistent widow in last Sunday's gospel reading, they will not cease praying until they accomplish their goal, until justice is reestablished.

Psalm 34:2-3, 17-18, 19, 23

The responsorial psalm is less a prayer than an instruction. Its content teaches that the righteous will be blessed and the wicked will be punished. The verses that make up this response do not explicitly state the psalmist has suffered in some way. However, that is the implication. It seems the psalmist endured some misfortune, was rescued by God, and now sings the praises of this gracious God. The restoration of the psalmist can now serve as a lesson for others that demonstrates the benefits that can be derived from remaining faithful to God even in the face of hardship.

The contrast between the just and the wicked is clearly drawn. Besides being identified as servants of the LORD, the righteous are also referred to as the lowly *('ănāwîm)*, the brokenhearted, and the crushed in spirit, all indications of great suffering. The psalmist proclaims that God looks favorably toward these righteous ones. Their cries for help will be heard and God will provide them with what they need. The fortunes of the wicked will be just the reverse. The face of the LORD will be set against them, and they will experience God's hostility in the worst possible way. Remembrance of them will be wiped out. In a society that does not have a clear teaching about life after this life, such a fate means that no trace of the person will survive, and it will be as if that person had never existed.

The psalmist is not naive about the vicissitudes of life, even the life of the upright. In many instances the theory of retribution advanced here is more a statement of faith in God's justice than an accurate description of the circumstances of life. Not only do good people suffer, but sometimes it seems they suffer precisely because they are good, perhaps because they are more sensitive to right and wrong, or because they are the victims of the sinfulness of others. Whatever the reason, the lives of the righteous are often fraught with trouble, while at times the wicked seem to prosper.

The psalmist claims that if the righteous turn to God in their pain and misery, God will hear their cry and draw them out of their afflictions. However, whether they are rescued from their affliction or not, the just stand under the promise of God's loving presence. Because suffering is often perceived as the result of alienation from God, assurance of God's nearness, as is expressed in this psalm, can alleviate the distress such a misperception might cause.

2 Timothy 4:6-8, 16-18

The epistle reading for this Sunday reveals that Paul is aware that his days are numbered, that his death is imminent. He does not resent it, but neither does he run toward it eagerly. He faces it with the calm resignation that springs from deep faith. He uses moving imagery to characterize his death. The first metaphor is taken from the context of the cult. There we find the rite of pouring out wine as a kind of drink offering (cf. Num 15:5, 7, 10). This practice may have been introduced into the ritual as a substitute for blood libation. Paul states that he is being poured out like this sacrificial blood. Not only is every drop of life being exacted of him, but his offering of it is viewed as a sacrificial act.

A second metaphor is no less poignant. Paul views his death as a departure, a kind of leave-taking (*análýō*, a compound derived from *lýō*, meaning "to loose") associated with sailors weighing anchor or soldiers breaking camp. Like them, Paul has completed a demanding tour of service and is now preparing to return home. The references suggest eager anticipation. In none of these metaphors is Paul in control. The cultic image suggests that he is poured out by another. Although the sailor and the soldier perform important roles in their leave-taking, they certainly did not make the decision to leave on their own. They were merely carrying out the decisions make by another.

Finally, he uses imagery derived from athletic competition to evaluate the course of his ministerial commitment. He has competed well; he has finished the race. To this he adds that he has kept the faith, an idiomatic expression that means remaining loyal to one's oath. He has done what he could. Now he has only to wait for the conferral of the crown promised by God. The reference is to Christ's eschatological manifestation. For a moment Paul moves away from focusing solely on his fate in order to join with all the others who will be awarded the victorious crown. He claims no special privilege. This man, who is facing death at the hands of others, is looking forward to a time of communal fulfillment.

Paul compares the trustworthiness of God with the unreliability of human companions. It seems that everyone deserted him during one of his trials. Perhaps it was because they would have been putting themselves in jeopardy had they stood with him. Whatever the case, Paul is not resentful, for God was there to strengthen him when all others fled. Throughout this discourse he extols the marvelous deeds God has done on his behalf. He even maintains that the gospel benefited from his adversity. His imprisonment and trial provided an opportunity for him to proclaim the good news to the people involved. Because of it he was able to spread the word even more broadly, despite the difficult circumstances in which he found himself.

Paul is confident that just as God had previously rescued him from peril, so God would rescue him again. He is not speaking of being freed from prison but of being preserved from anything that might threaten his spiritual well-being and prevent him from being led safely into the kingdom of heaven.

Luke 18:9-14

The story of the Pharisee and the tax collector is so well known to us that we risk missing the full force of it. It is an example of divine reversal that surprises the hearers and obliges them to examine anew the values and standards by which they live. In it two men are contrasted not only by their exterior behavior but by the way each understands and describes himself. The judgment that is passed is based on self-assessment, not on the evaluation of another.

Pharisees were religious leaders who, though they were relatively liberal in their interpretation of the Bible, were quite rigorous in their compliance to religious practice (cf. Acts 26:5; Gal 1:14). The man in this story is a model of Pharisaic observance. Everything about his demeanor bespeaks propriety. He stands, according to the customary posture for prayer, and his conduct has been exemplary. He is innocent of greed, dishonesty, and adultery. His practices of piety exceed the requirements of the law. He fasts twice a week, when fasting is only mandated for the Day of Atonement; he tithes on all of his possessions, not merely on his earnings, as the law states. It would appear the man is beyond reproach. His description of himself is probably accurate, and his negative estimation of the tax collector may be accurate as well.

Tax collectors were despised because they were part of the economic system put in place by the occupying Romans. They were not paid by their employers, so they added fees to the taxes collected. There was no standard scale governing this added charge, and tax collectors often exacted exorbitant amounts. They could easily fall under the Pharisees' category of the greedy and the dishonest. The tax collector in this narrative does not deny his involvement in such offensive practices. In fact, his prayer for mercy seems to be an admission of his guilt. His demeanor is radically different from that of the Pharisee. He stands at a distance, suggesting that the other man either stood in the front or in the midst of those in the Temple. He does not raise his eyes to heaven, suggesting that the Pharisee did. He beats his breast while the Pharisee's arms were conspicuously raised high. His repentant manner marks him as a sinner.

There is no question about which of these men has lived a righteous life and which has not. The men have described themselves correctly. However,

Jesus' evaluation turns the story upside down. The Pharisee's self-estimation is really a self-eulogy. While he may be living an upright life, he takes credit for his virtue, and he claims superiority over others who may not be as compliant as he is. The tax collector, on the other hand, acknowledges that justification comes from God. The word translated "mercy" *(hiláskomai)* really means "cover over." From it comes the word *hilastērion,* the gold plate on top of the ark of the covenant believed to be the place from which God dispensed mercy. The tax collector prayed that his sins be expiated, and his prayer was answered. The Pharisee asked for nothing and received nothing. The saying at the end is the final judgment. The men's lives may have been the reverse of each other, but the judgment of Jesus exposes the real reversal.

Themes of the Day

Our reflection last Sunday examined various aspects of the prayer of the disciple. Today we reflect on the attitudes one brings to prayer rather than on the prayer itself. They illustrate basically two opposing attitudes: self-righteousness and humility.

Thank God I'm Better Than Others

It is very easy for religious people to fall into a kind of self-righteousness. Their very enthusiasm and generosity can plant the seeds of religious arrogance. They discover what commitment demands of them; they experience relative success in their endeavors to be faithful; they distance themselves from what they think might threaten their resolve; and then they pass judgment on those who do not share their values or experience their success. The growth of this kind of arrogance is often imperceptible, because there is enough truth in every step along the way that it is difficult to recognize when one is veering off the track.

The fact is that some religious people are better than the rest of us. At issue is the reason *why* they might be better. The arrogant Pharisee clearly believed he was better because of what *he* had done. He had been observant, and he was proud of it. The tax collector, on the other hand, was ashamed of what he had done. More to the point, he knew what God was able to do in the face of his sinfulness, and so he asked for mercy. Justification comes from God; it is not an equitable return for a job well done. The tax collector knew this; the Pharisee did not. The tax collector asked God for mercy, and he was granted his request. The Pharisee asked for nothing of God, and so he received nothing.

There are various ways in which we show we are self-righteous, but basically they all show we have forgotten that God is God and we are not. This is the attitude Jesus condemns. It presumes we are righteous through our own power, when it might be the case that we have not been thrown into a state of affairs that sorely tests the mettle of our virtue. It is one thing to be non-violent when the circumstances of life are relatively tranquil and quite another when one is immersed in brutal situations. Pregnancy means one thing to a woman who wants to bring a child into a stable and loving relationship and another to a frightened unmarried teenager. The observance of cultural mores, as important as they may be, do not justify a person. Only the goodness of God does.

When the circumstances of life support our efforts to be observant, we can easily assume a superior attitude toward those whose weaknesses are only too apparent. They may show failings in areas where we are resolute, but our disdain for them is a clear sign of both our ignorance of our own human frailty and our lack of human compassion for the frailty of others. Unfortunately, this attitude of arrogance can be brought to prayer by the pharisee in all of us.

Be Merciful to Me, a Sinner

Jesus extols the humility of the one who admits being a sinner and can accept the implications of that admission. The tax collector neither denied his culpability nor tried to excuse it. He straightforwardly acknowledged his sin and stood humbly and openly before the holy God to whom he was accountable. There is an unpretentious honesty in his manner. He knows who and what he is, and he knows who and what God is. He asks for mercy, knowing he does not deserve it but also knowing there is every reason to believe the compassionate God will grant his request. His prayer demonstrates contrition, humility, and confidence. Unlike the Pharisee, who looks only to himself, the tax collector, though he does not even raise his eyes to heaven, looks only to God. This is the attitude Jesus commends.

This is the kind of prayer described in both the reading from Sirach and the psalm response. It is those who can admit they are needy who turn to God in that need. It is those who trust that God will be their strength in the face of their weaknesses who are strengthened. The lowly, the poor, the oppressed, and the brokenhearted are not closer to God because they are lowly, poor, oppressed, or brokenhearted but because in their dire straits they turn to God rather than to themselves. God is merciful, and they experience this mercy when they pray for it; God is the source of their strength, and they are strong when they turn to God for strength.

An Example to Follow

Paul's own prayer demonstrates the attitudes that should be ours as we pray. Like the Pharisee, he acknowledges his success. He has competed well; he has finished the course; he has kept the faith. Unlike the Pharisee, he acknowledges that God is the source of any good he has been able to accomplish. The Lord stood by him and gave him strength. If there is any glory, it belongs to God. Paul's confident prayer springs from a humble heart.

Thirty-First Sunday in Ordinary Time
Wisdom 11:22–12:2

The universal love and providence of the Creator is celebrated in this most unusual reading. Unlike earlier traditions that envisioned creation as a kind of reordering of cosmic debris after the primordial battle, this passage depicts a Creator who is personally involved with every dimension of the natural world. We find here the same cosmic power, but it is coupled with love and mercy.

The first theme addressed by the author, who is known as Pseudo-Solomon, is the immensity of God. Compared to God, the universe is no more than the smallest component of it. Should a single grain of wheat fall from the scale, it would hardly be noticed. The same is true of one drop of morning dew. So is the entire expanse of the cosmos; it is as nothing when likened to God. Although the ancient understanding of the universe cannot begin to compare with the modern one, within the context of its worldview this comparison is no less remarkable than it would be today.

The author makes a daring statement. He says that God loves whatever God has made (11:24). While on the one hand we might wonder how anyone would think otherwise, on the other we must admit there is more than one place in the Scriptures where it appears that God is at odds with elements of the natural world. A closer look at those passages should show that they probably reflect Israel's struggle with nature religions or fertility practices. In these cases the magnificent forces found within creation had been somehow personified and were being venerated as divine beings. It was such worship, not creation itself, that was in conflict with God, and the denunciation found within the tradition is condemnation of the idolatrous practices that stood in opposition to God's sovereign reign.

Just as the power of the Creator is matched by the love of the Creator, so is this love manifested through mercy. The text says that God is merciful precisely because God is powerful. This too might sound like a curious statement, for in a world that glorified strength, mercy could appear to be a weak virtue. However, this passage dispels that false perception. Only one with power can move beyond the strict rules of retribution, and if divine power is boundless, then it is possible that divine mercy has no limits.

Perhaps an even more daring statement is found in a later verse (12:1). There the author claims that the imperishable (*áphtartos*) spirit of God is in all things.

What could sound like pantheism (God is identified with creation) might be better understood as panentheism (God is in all things but also transcends them). The implications of such an incarnational concept are noteworthy. First, it provides a clue to the reason God so loves creation. Second, it throws light on the intrinsic value of the natural world, both human and non-human (there is no mention here of angels or other supernatural beings). This passage originated too early for us to entertain the possibility that it contains trinitarian thinking. However, in the Jewish tradition the dynamic power of God, active in the lives of women and men, was often referred to as the spirit of the LORD (cf. Judg 6:34; 1 Sam 16:13; Isa 61:1; etc.). Only later would this idea develop in a new way.

Finally, Pseudo-Solomon is not naive when it comes to human weakness. He knows that people sin, and he also knows there is suffering because of it. This in no way nullifies his claims about the mercy of God. Instead, that mercy explains the way God deals with sinners. They are rebuked more as a corrective than as a punishment, and this is done in order to bring them to greater insight, to deeper commitment, and to trust in God.

Psalm 145:1-2, 8-9, 10-11, 13, 14

The responsorial psalm for today is both a hymn of praise of the greatness of God and a hortatory instruction. It opens with a declaration of praise, followed by the reasons for praising God. In the third and fourth sections the psalmist speaks directly to God again, praying that all God's works will give thanks and proclaiming the LORD's universal and everlasting reign.

The passage opens with an acclamation closely associated with the revelation of God and the acknowledgment of God's name, revealed at the time of the reestablishment of the covenant (cf. Exod 34:6). In these two verses covenant language abounds. God is described as gracious *(ḥannûn)* and compassionate *(raḥûm)* and filled with lovingkindness *(ḥesed)*. It should be noted that this divine goodness is not reserved for Israel alone but is extended to all God's works. This includes all people and nations but also all of natural creation. The covenant has been expanded to a universal embrace.

The works of the LORD include everything God has made as well as everything God has done, everything God has fashioned as well as everything God has accomplished. There is a comprehensiveness to this call for praise (vv. 10-11). The psalmist cries out to all the wonders of the created world, whose very existence testifies to the magnificence of the Creator. More than this, the God before whom the psalmist stands in awe is also a savior who has performed marvelous deeds on behalf of the people. God has delivered them from bondage, has provided for them in their need, has established them as a people, and has promised them a secure and prosperous future. As they unfold in the sight of all, these acts of graciousness themselves celebrate the LORD.

The faithful of the LORD are those who are holy *(hāsîd)*, those who are bound to God in covenant loyalty. Whether their holiness is the result of God's faithfulness to them or their faithfulness to God is not clear. It does not seem to matter to the psalmist, who is preoccupied with the praise of God and not with extolling others. These faithful are summoned to bless the LORD, to praise or honor God in reverence and awe. God is characterized here as a monarch who rules over a kingdom. The word for "glory" *(kābôd)* means "heavy" or "weighty." Used here, it implies that God's kingdom is substantial, distinguished because of its magnitude, comprehensive in its splendor. The character and extent of God's rule demonstrate the essence and scope of God's power.

The final section of the psalm extols God's reign and God's care for those who are burdened. The idea that gods ruled as kings was common in the ancient world, and so to characterize the God of Israel in this way was not unusual. What are unique are the exclusive claims made about the reign of Israel's God. It is resplendent, as one would expect. But it is also universal, including all, and it is eternal. In this light, the covenanted faithful ones are called not only to praise God for the wonders God has accomplished in and for them but also to announce the glory of God's rule to the entire human race, to all the children of Adam. It is not enough that they enjoy the privilege of belonging to God's kingdom. Through them, God invites the entire universe to participate as well.

2 Thessalonians 1:11–2:2

In this short reading Paul addresses two important issues: the fruition of the Christians' calling by God (1:11-12), and the correct teaching about the final coming of Christ (2:1-2). He addresses the Christians with familial titles, indicating both his relationship with them as together constituting children of God and members of the Church, and his personal commitment to them.

In a very moving manner this minister of the gospel tells his people that he prays for them, and he does so constantly. He is not merely intent on their accepting his teaching; he is committed to their spiritual well-being. Though he has been the minister of the word, it is God who has called them. It is Paul's prayer that they be worthy of that calling. Paul reminds them of this as an incentive for righteous living. However, he does not fail to insist it is God and not their own good works that makes them worthy of their call. Behind this assertion is the heart of Paul's teaching. That is, we are obliged to live ethical lives, but it is the prior grace of God and not our subsequent ethical behavior that saves us. For Paul faith is the acceptance of the call of God and the openness to the message of the gospel. God calls; Paul preaches; and God brings to fulfillment the fruits of the preaching.

The goal of Christian maturity is the glorification of the name of Jesus. In Greek, to glorify someone means to enhance that person's reputation. This might sound strange to us today unless we remember that Christian living is based not on performance of good works but on faith in Jesus. It is commitment to him that prompts Christians to live ethical lives. It is commitment to him that overflows into unselfish love of others. It is commitment to him that gives his followers the courage they need to endure in the face of difficulty. It is commitment to him that motivates their every action. Therefore, whatever they do gives witness to their faith, a faith that claims they have died with him and have risen through his power to a new life. In this way Christians do indeed glorify the name of Jesus. They in turn are glorified in him, for it is only through his grace that their transformation has been accomplished. It is all divine favor. It is to this transformation that they have been called by God.

There seems to have been some difficulty in the Thessalonians' understanding of the coming of the Lord, so Paul sets out to correct it. He first assures them that when Christ comes they will all be gathered together with him (cf. 1 Thess 4:14-17). The issue here seems to be the nature and time of Christ's coming, not whether the dead will be joined with the living. Paul taught that in faith and through baptism Christians have died with Christ and have risen with him and now live resurrected lives. This means that the day of fulfillment has already dawned. However, he also taught that fulfillment has not been brought to its ultimate completion. Paul teaches an already-but-not-yet eschatology. Here is the tension. To cling to one teaching and not the other results in denial of one aspect of faith. To maintain everything has already been fulfilled could lead some to believe they are free of all ethical restrictions (cf. 1 Cor 6:12); to hold that fulfillment is only in the future is to deny the resurrection itself.

This is the essence of Paul's teaching, and he insists the Thessalonians should accept nothing more and nothing less, whether it comes to them through some kind of prophecy or tongues, through teaching or logical reasoning, or even a letter purported to have been written by him. Though the eschatological day of the Lord is imminent, it is not yet present. Believers must continue to live their lives in patient anticipation of his coming, realizing they do so in the presence of his already having come.

Luke 19:1-10

The story of Zacchaeus demonstrates once again the mission of Jesus to seek and to save what is lost. It also reveals the animosity the Jews of his day had toward those who were in any way in collusion with the occupying Romans, as were the tax collectors. We must remember that the Jews prided themselves in being the people whom God saved from bondage. Therefore, any kind of servitude was repugnant to them. Not only did Zacchaeus belong to the hated class of tax collectors, he was chief among them. This means that he probably benefited both from the taxes paid and from the fees the tax collectors themselves exacted of the people. He conducted his business in Jericho, a prominent city on the east-west trade route. The city was probably a customs checkpoint, so tax collection must have been a thriving business there, from which Zacchaeus profited greatly.

Despite his obvious disrepute, Zacchaeus is described as possessing several very honorable qualities. His interest in seeing Jesus overrode any shame he may have experienced in having to climb the tree. This behavior has led some to consider him a comic figure. This is unfortunate because the character of his openness to grace might thereby be minimized. He responded immediately as Jesus had instructed, and he extended to Jesus the fullness of customary hospitality. The sincerity of his transformation is seen in the extent of his restitution. The law prescribed the return of the money extorted along with twenty percent of that amount (Lev 6:5). Zacchaeus is extravagant in his compensation, repaying fourfold whatever he might owe, and he does this is in addition to giving half his possessions to the poor. Such prodigality is his response to having been called by the Lord and honored with his presence.

The narrative draws bold lines of contrast between Jesus' attitude toward this man and that of the people who witnessed the encounter. Jesus first singled him out from the crowd and then graciously accepted the man's hospitality. The others, despising Zacchaeus, murmured against Jesus and condemned him for eating with sinners. They believed that only sinners keep company with other sinners. They also held that sharing a meal signified a very close relationship. Both these convictions led them to conclude that Jesus himself must be a sinner.

Jesus' intent in Zacchaeus' regard can be seen in the words he uses. "I must!" (v. 5). There is something obligatory here. Jesus does not ask permission to come to his house, nor does Zacchaeus extend an invitation. It is almost as if the plan of salvation requires that Jesus enter the man's house and his life. There is also urgency in the word "today" (vv. 5, 9). Jesus must come to Zacchaeus today so that today salvation will come his house. He was only passing through Jericho, and if they did not seize the moment, the opportunity could be lost. The urgency of the moment demanded that religious and social customs be set aside. Zacchaeus may well have been a sinner. His decision for restitution implies that he knew he was. So does Jesus' response to those who criticized him for socializing with a sinner. He never challenged their criticism. Instead he insisted that only those who are lost can be found; only those who are perishing can be saved. Those who revere themselves as righteous seldom understand this and as a result miss opportunities for their own salvation.

Themes of the Day

From today until the end of the Liturgical Year there is a definite shift in the perspective of the readings. They move from a focus on discipleship to concentration on the action of God. Today God holds out to us the splendor of the universe, the celebration of community, and the blessings of salvation. The psalm expresses our gratitude in praise and thanksgiving.

The Splendor of the Universe

The change of seasons is always an opportune time to marvel at the magnificence of the natural world of which we are a part. Its colors, its textures, its smells, all reflect the limitless imagination of the Creator. Perhaps the most marvelous feature of the world is the interconnectedness of all the elements of which it consists. Nothing is too small to make a difference; everything is dependent on everything else. Nothing is unimportant or loathsome; everything is worthy of God's care and mercy. Somehow the spirit of the Creator is manifested through each and every aspect of this universe. And we are part of it all. We are dependent upon the forces of life within this awe-inspiring world, and it is dependent upon us to carry life and consciousness and creativity forward into each new generation and to further it into new manifestations. The universe may be as a grain in the balance or a drop of morning dew, but each grain and each drop contains within it the possibilities of the future.

It is this world that supplies us with the nourishment we need for creativity. Its sounds and colors and tastes and textures feed our imaginations. Our works of art are re-creations of the artistic work of God. As we learn the laws that govern the natural world, we are able to duplicate them in our own industry. Part of the tragedy of ecological devastation is the disintegration of the very elements that feed our creative spirits.

The Intimacy of Hospitality

Offering hospitality is a profound social act. We reveal ourselves when we invite others into our homes. There our tastes and our choices are on display. When we offer hospitality, we invite another into our world, into our lives. We shift our attention from our own cares and concerns to the needs and comfort of the other. By the act of hospitality we transform strangers into friends and intimates.

Jesus not only accepts the hospitality of Zacchaeus, he boldly invites himself to the man's home. In a sense, he becomes the host, inviting Zacchaeus into his life, into the intimacy of his friendship. By this act he displays the unrestricted nature of his love. He establishes a bond of love with a man of questionable character, and he thereby transforms him into a man who repents and radically reforms his life. Although the home belongs to Zacchaeus, the real home into which Jesus invites him is the reign of God, and there Jesus is the host.

The hospitality Jesus offers dissolves all constraints. Relationships disregard the biased measures of propriety, forging bonds of reconciliation and issuing everyone an invitation to intimacy. The hospitality Jesus offers re-creates the world from one of insider versus outsider to one of universal inclusivity. Sinners become friends; the lost are found; all are restored to their rightful place as children not merely of Abraham but of God. The creativity of the Creator is matched by the compassion of the re-Creator.

The Blessings of Salvation

The compassion of God is manifested in the fact that God promises us a future. In that future all the blessings of salvation will be brought to fulfillment. Like Zacchaeus, we have been called, we have been invited to open ourselves to the Lord who is coming so he can extend to us the riches of his own hospitality. We have a future; our past will not hold us back. We have a future; divisions will be dissolved. We have a future; this is reason to cry out in praise and thanksgiving: "I will praise your name forever; let all your works give you thanks."

Thirty-Second Sunday in Ordinary Time
2 Maccabees 7:1-2, 9-14

The deaths of these brothers is described in grisly detail. The reason given for their murders leaves no doubt they are martyrs, faithful Israelites who died for their faith. The introductory verses of the reading tell us there were seven brothers who faced this fate, along with their mother. Although here we have a report of the death of only three of them, it is safe to conclude that the deaths of the others were no less brutal.

Israel had strict dietary restrictions, which they traced back to the promulgation of the law given to Moses. For reasons of which we are not certain today, they were forbidden to eat meat of animals that did not have cloven hoofs or did not chew their cud (cf. Lev 11:7). Since pigs did not fit into this category, they were considered unclean animals and were forbidden as food. Fidelity to these laws, along with circumcision and the observance of the Sabbath, became an identifying characteristic of the Jews. A rejection of them was considered apostasy. This is the issue treated in the reading for today. The king is demanding renunciation of their allegiance to God. Through one of the brothers who acts as spokesperson, the family refuses. The few words these brothers speak constitute acts of faith. That is why they are put to death.

As gruesome as the details of the martyrdom may be, the real point of this narrative is the faith in resurrection these brothers profess. Early Israel believed that justice would be accomplished in this life, either during the days of those directly involved or in the days of their descendants. The idea of individual reward or punishment became a major issue only after the experience of the Exile (cf. Ezek 18:1-32). Even then the people believed such justice would be served in this lifetime. This reading reflects the shift that took place in Israel's thinking around the time of the Maccabean revolt (ca. 167 B.C.E.). It was precisely because of the martyrdom of the righteous that the theodicy, the justice *(díkē)* of God *(theōs)*, became an issue. How could a righteous God allow the faithful to suffer such injustice? Although the Hebrew worldview and language did not provide the possibility to develop a concept of an afterlife, Hellenism did. The answer to the dilemma was sought in the idea of a life after this life. In this passage we find the beginnings of such faith.

The words of the three brothers reflect various aspects or stages in the development of this concept. The first brother asserts that God, who is really the ruler of this world regardless of what circumstances might suggest, will raise the faithful up to live again. The second is willing to be stripped of his tongue and his hands because he believes that his body will share in his resurrection. The third insists that only the righteous will be raised to life. These declarations reveal only a hint of the resurrection faith we have come to know. Its development will come in the future. However, it does provide an answer to the question of theodicy and a form of encouragement for those who must face the ordeal.

Psalm 17:1, 5-6, 8, 15

Although this responsorial psalm can be classified as a psalm of lament, there are hints within it of a temple ritual. In ancient Israel worshipers would bring their needs to the Temple and present them to the priest. In certain circumstances their complaint would take the form of a lawsuit. They would state their cause, name the defendant against whom they were bringing the complaint, give evidence of their own innocence, and pray that through the agency of the priest God would see fit to judge in their favor. This psalm reflects several of these characteristics. The petition itself suggests some kind of juridical situation. Although no defendant is named, the innocence of the plaintiff is first stated and then described. There is a declaration of confidence that God will look favorably on the psalmist. There is a hint in the final verse that the psalmist has experienced a theophany (a manifestation of God) and has spent the night at the sanctuary and in the morning will be assured of God's good pleasure.

The psalm opens with the same call to attention found in Israel's foremost prayer, "Hear, O Israel, the LORD is God" (Deut 6:4). However, in this prayer the one called is God. The summons probably originated in an oral culture, which explains its forcefulness. "To hear" means "to listen to in order to respond positively." That is precisely the gist of this call. It is because of the righteous nature of the psalmist's personal disposition that such a summons can be made in the first place.

Innocence is described in three ways. "Lips without deceit" is a phrase that refers to the reliable way the psalmist's situation has been reported. The Wisdom tradition contrasts two opposing ways of living: the way of the wise, or righteous; and the way of the fool, or wicked. The second and third allusions to the psalmist's innocence borrow from this tradition. They state that the psalmist has kept unwaveringly to the right path, has neither deviated from it nor stumbled while on it. Whether it is the certainty of personal innocence or the assurance of the justice of God that inspires the psalmist, the prayer is filled with confidence that God will hear the cry of the innocent who have been prevailed upon by others.

The prayer for help employs two graphic images. The apple of one's eye refers to what is most precious to the individual. The origin of the image is unknown, but its meaning is recognized in most cultures. The compassionate and caring God is frequently depicted as a protective bird under whose wings a fledgling is assured of finding safety and tenderness. The psalmist is taking a bold step in requesting such solicitude. Again, it is evidence of the psalmist's own innocence and of trust in God's provident justice.

To behold the face of God or to stand in God's presence is to have had some kind of religious experience. Within the context of the ritual described here, it could be an actual supernatural visitation or a formal word from the priest, who represents God's presence to the people. Since the psalmist speaks of waking, it could very well have been a visitation through a dream while the petitioner was keeping a night vigil. Whatever the method of divine response, the psalmist appears to be content. This in itself is an answer to the prayer. It implies that the petitioner is indeed in right relationship with God and has been assured of God's approval and subsequent presence.

2 Thessalonians 2:16–3:5

The epistle reading for this Sunday is a composite. It includes a wish-prayer of encouragement for the Thessalonians (2:16-17), a request of the Thessalonians for prayer on behalf of Paul himself (3:1-2), a prayer for encouragement (vv. 3-4), and a final benediction (v. 5).

Paul's prayer for the Thessalonians is twofold. He prays for encouragement and for strength. The first is an interior attitude; the second is the power needed for the external manifestation of that inner disposition. It is clear he believes that all the good things for which he pleads come from God. He says as much. It is God who has loved them and who, as a fruit of that love, grants them both this encouragement and hope.

The title Paul uses to identify Jesus contains three christological elements within it. He is called "Lord," the same title given to God in the Septuagint (Greek) version of the First Testament. This shows that he applies to Jesus all the characteristics and power the Israelites attributed to its God. He is called "Jesus," from the Hebrew name "Jehoshua," which means "the LORD [*Jah*] is salvation [*yᵉshûʿâ*]." Finally, "Christ" is an adjective that means "anointed one." It is a reference to the Jewish Messiah. In addition to these titles another christological theme is expressed. The grace Jesus won through his death and resurrection is the source of the love and encouragement the Thessalonians receive from God.

Having prayed for them, Paul now asks that they pray for him. However, the content of the prayer he requests is significantly different. He is not concerned with his own needs but with the progress of the gospel he preaches. He uses a dynamic image to describe this progress, that of a runner. It is not that the runner brings the gospel. Rather, Paul envisions the gospel itself as moving swiftly throughout the world and bringing glory (honor). In other words, Paul prays that the gospel be heard and respected, that it move unimpeded wherever it goes. He appeals to the experience of the Thessalonians themselves. As he compliments them, thus strengthening them in their faith, he suggests that they are an example of the way the word of God can take root in the minds and hearts of people and transform their lives. This kind of compliment can go a long way in encouraging them.

The second concern for which Paul would have them pray is his own deliverance from opposition. Here he is less concerned with the consequences of the persecution in his own life than with how this may set up obstacles for the progress of the gospel. The faithless to whom he alludes are not identified. This is probably a very general reference to those who know about the good news but who have closed their minds and hearts, who have even tried to undermine it.

Paul does not doubt the goodwill of these Christians, but he knows from personal experience the weaknesses of human nature. For this reason he places his trust in the faithfulness of the Lord. It is Christ who will strengthen the believers; it is Christ who will be their protection against the forces of evil; it is Christ who will keep them on the path of righteousness, which they presently travel. To this end he pronounces a blessing. It is the love of God that will ground them in their faith; it is the example of the endurance of Christ that will enable them to persevere in their commitment. This is the essence of the prayer for which Christ prays.

Luke 20:27-38

The gospel reading depicts Jesus in a theological contest with the Saduccees. They were a religio-political party that claimed to be descendants of Zadok, high priest at the time of David (cf. 2 Sam 8:17). Although originally they may have all been priests, such was probably not the case by the time of Jesus. They seem to have been a conservative, aristocratic group who cooperated with the Romans and enjoyed a certain amount of privilege as a result. Theologically, they accepted as authentic only what was actually written in the Bible. They were not like the Pharisees, who also revered the collection of oral traditions that grew up out of interpretation of the written tradition. Thus they would not have believed in the resurrection or in the existence of angels or demons, concepts treated in this gospel.

In their attempt to disprove the possibility of resurrection, they resorted to ridicule, thereby demonstrating what they considered to be the foolishness of such belief. (This reading contains elements similar to those found in the reading from 2 Maccabees assigned for this Sunday. Since both passages speak of seven brothers and both treat the question of the resurrection, the pairing of the two seems natural. However, these should not be considered as the same brothers).

If a man died without leaving an heir, the ancient law made provisions for the continuation of his name and the inheritance of his property. His brother was to take the widow to wife in order that an heir be born to the dead man (cf. Deut 25:5-10). This is the custom referred to by the Saducees. From their point of view their question points out the folly of resurrection faith.

In response, Jesus first draws a line of distinction between this age and the age to come. The age to come will not be like this age. Now, procreation is the way that life continues from one generation to another. In the next age, the conditions will be radically different and so will be the existence within it. There will be no death; all will be spiritual beings, like the angels. As children of God, they will have a share in the very nature of God.

Jesus then employs a traditional Jewish method of argument. Reading something within the text literally, he draws conclusions from it that were probably never in the mind of the original author. He refers to the narrative of Moses' encounter with God at the burning bush (cf. Exod 3:1-6). There God claims to be the God of the chief male ancestors of the Jewish nation. The text has God say "I am," not "I was." The implication is that God is still the God of these ancestors. However, the God of the Israelites is a God of the living, not of the dead. This means that somehow the ancestors are still alive. The very last phrase offers an explanation of how this might be the case. They were all joined to God through the covenant. Jesus' interpretation claims that death does not sever the union the covenant forges. Unless they choose to terminate their covenant relationship, they continue to be united to God, even after death. Such a manner of biblical interpretation may appear strange to us today, but this seems to be the argument Jesus employs to counter the challenge of the Saducees.

Themes of the Day

The last three Sundays of the year invite us into the future. Though we are accustomed to think of the close of the Liturgical Year as the end, it is really an opening into the end-time, into the future. Each of the remaining Sundays flashes a spotlight on some aspect of what God is doing in preparation for this future. Today we look briefly at the question of resurrection and the character of the life we are to live in anticipation of or in fidelity to it.

The Covenant Bond Is Not Severed

Both the reading from Maccabees and the passage from the gospel speak of resurrection. The first is a testimony of faith, the second demonstrates a measure of scorn that accompanies unbelief. Belief in resurrection is not the same as conviction of the immortality of the soul. The latter is based on the makeup of the human person; the former rests on the fidelity of God. The doctrine of resurrection is grounded in the concept of covenant, which claims that God has established a relationship with human beings. At issue is whether this relationship is severed by death. Is death powerful enough to break the ties that bind us in covenant, or is it God's desire that the covenant endure? The later traditions of the Bible, the place where this issue is addressed, clearly state that God's desire to be united with us is stronger than death.

Once we believe in the endurance of this covenant bond, we are pressed to thematize our conviction with metaphors that attempt to explain the implications of what we believe. Since God is a God of the living, we believe our continued union with God must unfold in some kind of life. Since the only kind of life we know is the life of the here and the now, the metaphors we fashion, like those that we find in the Bible itself, resemble certain aspects of our present experience of life. We must remember, however, that these are only metaphors that stand for and point to a mysterious reality, not precise descriptions of the future. We do not really know what it will be like.

Something Radically Different

The Sadducees insisted on understanding the next life as if it were merely a continuation of the present one. This was their error, the error Jesus corrected without reverting to the sarcasm they had employed. He does not say what this future life will be like. He simply states that it will be different. The social systems, the gender relationships, and the method of assuring the continuation of humankind will be radically transformed. Whether it is accurate to say that life itself will continue is not clear. What is clear is the assurance that our relationship with God will endure.

Living Proleptically

If this is the future that awaits us, how are we to live until it dawns? Actually, it has already dawned. This is the eschatological hope in which we live by the grace given us from God through our Lord Jesus Christ. Our future is already present; therefore, we are called to live lives that have been radically transformed. However, the future has not yet completely dawned, and so we find ourselves living both in this age and in the age to come. Thus we live proleptically; we live future lives, but we live them in the present. As difficult as this may be, we have the eternal encouragement of Christ. We have the promise that the Lord will strengthen us and guard us. We have the instruction of our religious tradition that directs our minds and hearts. When we live lives of the future, we truly enable that future to dawn in the present.

Thirty-Third Sunday in Ordinary Time
Malachi 3:19-20a

This reading is remarkable in its brevity; yet it is filled with vivid images, and it contains a powerful message. The setting is the Day of the LORD, the time of fulfillment of all of God's promises and the realization of the destiny of the world. It is the time when justice will be realized, when the scales of righteousness will be balanced, when the good will be rewarded and the evil punished. Initially Israel believed that this day would be for it a time of vindication and rejoicing. However, the prophets set them straight on this matter, insisting that Israel itself would have to face the righteous anger of God. This is the scene depicted in the first reading for this Sunday. Israel too would have to pay for its sinfulness; there would have to be just recompense.

The prophet employs the metaphor of a blazing fire to depict this. The image is of a conflagration that burns the stubble left over after the grain has been harvested. It has been dried by the heat of the sun, and it is useless except as fire starter. The day itself is so hot that, like a form of spontaneous combustion, it ignites the chaff. The ungodly are identified as the stubble that is consumed by the flames. Nothing is left of them, neither branch, which produces the fruit of the growth, nor the root, which promises new life. Every aspect is consumed by the fire.

On the other hand, the Day of the LORD will rise majestically for the upright, like the sun in the eastern sky that shines forth in righteousness. The healing of this experience of God is the total reversal of the flaming destruction in store for the wicked.

Psalm 98:5-6, 7-8, 9

The psalm response is an example of a hymn that celebrates the enthronement of God as king over all. The celebration originated as a popular Mesopotamian agricultural celebration commemorating the victory of life over the forces of death. The enthronement above creation of the victorious god signified the continuation of the fertility of the land and of everything that lived upon it. The feast was probably celebrated in the fall of the year after the harvest, when it appeared that death had a stronghold over life. The feast was a moment of encouragement and recommitment to the power of life.

Gradually the celebration took on cosmic significance. The god of life and fertility was thought to be the creator of heaven and earth. The enemy forces were no longer mere death but had expanded to include all of the forces of cosmic evil. Enthronement celebrations were generally celebrated at the turn of the year, when commitment to newness was appropriate. There is significant question among scholars as to whether Israel ever celebrated such a feast. However, there is no doubt about the presence of enthronement elements in Israel's prayer. This psalm is a perfect example of such prayer.

In the response for today, imperative after imperative summons all creation to praise God, who rules as king over all. The first verses elaborate on the musical element of the praise. The instrumental directions are quite specific. They could have originated out of an actual enthronement ceremony. Two instruments are explicitly mentioned, the harp and the trumpet. The first was frequently used as accompaniment for singing; the second might really be a reference to the ram's horn, which, like a clarion, announced days and seasons of ritual celebration. Here, as at the foot of Mount Sinai, it announces the coming of the LORD in glory (Exod 19:16).

The cosmic scope of God's rule includes both the seas and the entire world. While these words denote natural boundaries, the first has strong mythological flavor. *Yam*, the Hebrew word for "sea," is the name of an ancient god of watery chaos defeated during the primordial battle. What might have been a mythological threat in an earlier way of thinking is here merely a subdued body of water under God's control, called to praise God's rule. "World" (*tēbēl*) includes not only the land but all that lives upon it. Thus the entire universe is summoned to praise its ruler. "River" was the name of yet another mythic deity. It too is now but a participant in the celebration of God's sovereignty, along with the mountains, which were thought to be the place where God dwells. In this psalm all of these elements are part of the throng that sings praise to God.

The final verse is eschatological in character. The LORD is coming and is coming to judge *(shāpat)*. This does not appear to be a specific judgment, and so the presumption is that the reference is to the final judgment. The idea of judgment frequently engenders a sense of dread, since it implies the notion of passing judgment. Within the cosmic setting that lies behind this psalm, judgment means setting things in order so life can prosper. There may need to be some reordering for this to happen, but the idea is generally positive.

2 Thessalonians 3:7-12

The instruction Paul gives to the Thessalonians is meant to ensure both harmony within the community and a positive reputation, recognizable to those who do not belong to the community. Paul offers his own conduct as an example for them to follow. This should not be seen as an act of arrogance or self-serving pride. Rather, he is trading on the conviction that the values of Christian commitment are not taught only by word of mouth. They are also manifested through the witness of the lives of those who believe. Paul is saying that he himself has been faithful to the message he has been teaching and that the Thessalonians can learn from what he does as well as from what he says. There are implications to this for their lives as well. Just as he can serve as an example to them, they should be able to serve as examples to others. This is a very important way for the gospel to be taught to the world. It is also a measure of the authenticity of the word of the preacher.

There are three lessons that Paul seeks to teach. Two point to behavior he has avoided, the third to a way of living he has embraced. First, he has not acted in a disorderly fashion. This is a strange thing to say unless there were those who had come to the Thessalonians and had indeed acted in this way. Whatever the case may have been, Paul's behavior has been beyond reproach. Second, he has not presumed upon the hospitality of others. This is an important point, because it was common for travelers to rely on the hospitality of those through whose villages and cities their passed. However, there were certain well-established customs that governed how a guest should be treated and how long a guest should stay. Paul is probably referring to something quite different. His point becomes clear in what follows.

Paul's third lesson is found in his manner of living among the Thessalonians. He reminds his hearers that he worked long and hard so he would not be a financial burden to them. This suggests that besides the time and energy expended in preaching the gospel, he had other employment that enabled him to cover his own expenses while in their midst. He further reminds them that he really had a right to be supported by them during the time he was ministering to them. However, he had waived this right for the sake of the reputation of the gospel itself. He did not want to give anyone the impression that ministers of the gospel are a burden to the community.

This leads him to comment on a situation he has been told exists within the Thessalonian community. Playing on words, he condemns those within the community who have acted as busybodies rather than being actually busy. The reason for their idleness is not given, but Paul's condemnation indicates it was deliberate on their part, not a circumstance beyond their control. Paul counsels harsh treatment of such people. If they are unwilling to discipline themselves, then it is the responsibility of the community to discipline them. The community is told to withhold food from them. Proverbs similar to the one included here are found in both Jewish and Christian writings of the time. The community should no longer allow them to live off its generosity, because that generosity is then misplaced. Paul insists that if people want to eat, they must work like everyone else. Paul has offered himself as an example of this.

Luke 21:5-19

The admiration for the Temple expressed by some bystanders prompted Jesus to predict the destruction of that magnificent edifice. This was the second Temple of Jerusalem, constructed after the Jews had returned from Babylonian Exile. Though initially it could not compare with the splendor of the Temple built by Solomon, the renovations commissioned by King Herod gave it a resplendence that surpassed even Solomon's building. This Temple was certainly something in which the Jewish people could take great pride. Jesus may have exaggerated when he said that one stone would not remain upon another, but it was a way of characterizing the extent of the devastation that was to come to pass.

This reading does not address the destruction of the Temple itself but, rather, the events that will precede it, signs that should alert the people to the impending doom. We must remember that a sign, whatever it is, points to a deeper reality, a reality that may not always be easily recognized or understood. For this reason it is often necessary to have an interpreter of the signs. Before Jesus identifies the signs themselves, he warns his listeners against those who might appear claiming they have come in Jesus' own name to interpret the meaning of the events that are transpiring. They might even proclaim, "I am [*egō eimi*] he!" Or "The time *(kairós)* has come!" Jesus exhorts those around him not to follow these people.

The signs themselves are demonstrations of upheaval. They include political unrest and violence as well as disturbances in the natural world, all experiences people of the time believed would precede the end of the age. Once again Jesus warns his hearers. The end is not yet here. Something even more personal will transpire first. These long-expected signs portend the persecutions the followers of Jesus will have to endure at the hands of the government, their friends and acquaintances, even the members of their own families. The point is not that they will suffer—under such calamity all people will suffer. The point is that they will suffer because of the name of Jesus. In fact, the persecution—even death—they will be called upon to endure will itself be a witness to that name. It will be a testimony that fidelity to one's commitment to Jesus is a greater good than life itself. Faithful to the end, even if they are put to death they will be saved.

While Jesus may be talking about the events that will precede the actual destruction of the glorious Temple and the beloved city within which it stood, there are elements in his discourse that suggest an eschatological dimension of his teaching. First, signs are often understood as pointing beyond this world to the next. *Kairós* refers to a decisive moment, not to chronological time that unfolds gradually and predicably. It marks the time of fulfillment, and it connotes eschatological reality. We must remember that Jesus is describing these horrors at a time when the Temple stood in all its glory. Only he knew what would transpire in the future, and he is here preparing his followers for that future.

Themes of the Day

This Sunday we continue our reflection on the theme introduced last Sunday, the theme of the end-time. We see in the readings for today what we also saw last Sunday, that is, the complex eschatological meaning of end-time. It has already dawned through the death and resurrection of Jesus, but it has not yet unfolded completely. There is an already-but-not-yet dimension of the end-time. We believe we are living in the end-time, but are we at the beginning of it? In the middle? Or at its end? Some millenarians insist we are at the end, and the manner of life they preach reflects this belief. The Scriptures are not clear about this matter, so understanding it is left up to the way we interpret the biblical texts. All we have are hints about the character of the Day of the LORD, the role God will play at this time, and our manner of living as we await the unfolding of the end-time.

The Day of the LORD

The Day of the LORD was believed to be the time when God would come in majesty and power to set all things right. The good would then be rewarded and the evil would be punished. In order to set things right, the distorted order of sin and unrighteousness that held sway would have to be overturned. This explains the disruption and turmoil that is always described as preceding the day of final fulfillment. Malachi describes it as a blazing fire that will consume whatever opposes the will of God. Jesus describes this disruption in greater detail. As he envisions it, both human society and the world of nature will first have to endure the upheaval so that they can then be transformed in the age to come.

We must remember that these descriptions are metaphoric or symbolic in nature. As with all metaphors or symbols, we miss something of their profound meaning if we merely understand them literally. It is not helpful to relate elements of the description with particular aspects of the contemporary world. Doing this, we might tend to identify with those who are saved and relegate those who disagree with us to the ranks of those who must suffer the fury of God's justice. Instead, at times when it looks like evil will triumph, the concept of the Day of the LORD should instill in us trust that good will ultimately be victorious. Belief in the Day of the LORD is a way of testifying to our faith in the righteousness of God.

The Righteousness of God

Although the narrative readings for today concentrate on the disruptions that will accompany the coming of God, they also contain hints of the salvation that will finally arrive. Malachi speaks of the sun of justice that comes with healing rays; Luke promises that the faithful disciples will escape without a hair of their heads being destroyed. Just as the descriptions of the upheavals should not be understood literally, neither should these descriptions. It may be that the faithful followers of Jesus will suffer terrible agonies. The point here is that even in the midst of their pain, they will be protected. Just as the reason for the disruption is the offended righteousness of God, so the ground of their hope of protection is the same righteousness of God.

The healing rays of justice and the rescue of the lives of the upright are references to salvation. God does not come at the end to condemn but to save. Furthermore, the suffering that precedes the end is intended for purification and refinement, not punishment.

Upright Living

Christians are exhorted to live in this end-time with patient endurance of difficulties. They are instructed to carry their fair share of the work of the community lest they become a burden to others within the community or to the community as a whole. They must work diligently and conscientiously, awaiting the final coming of Christ without ever knowing precisely when that will be.

Since both human society and the natural world will pass through the crucible of refinement, both human society and the natural world will be transformed. As the readings of last Sunday pointed out, Christians can enable this time of transformation to dawn by living transformed lives even now. The suffering they will endure as a result of this way of living will act as the purifying fire that precedes fulfillment. If they persevere in this, they will secure their lives.

Thirty-Fourth Sunday in Ordinary Time
2 Samuel 5:1-3

The account recorded in the first reading for this Sunday depicts the anointing of David as king of the northern tribes of Israel (cf. 2 Sam 2:1-4). It takes place in Hebron, a city with a long history as a sacred shrine. It was the place where Abram had built an altar to the LORD (cf. Gen 13:18). It was also the place where Sarah was buried (cf. Gen 23:19). Traditionally it was the center of Judah's power. It is only appropriate that the new king should be anointed at this hallowed shrine.

The people acknowledge the intimate bond they share with this new king. They are his bone and his flesh, his very kin. Presumably this intimacy will strengthen the ties of loyalty that join them. For their part they recognize him as a worthy leader. In the past, when Saul was king, David had been able to gather around himself bands of people who would follow him wherever he would lead them. At that time such loyalty became a threat to King Saul's sovereignty. Now it would be an asset to David's power.

Although it was the people who anointed David as their king, they believed it was really God who had chosen him. In fact, the passage states that God informed David of his fate, describing it in terms of two metaphors frequently associated with kings in the ancient Near Eastern world. Because they were responsible for the well-being of the people, kings were often characterized as shepherds. The familiarity and personal concern associated with this metaphor suggests the nature of monarchy that was held up as an ideal. The second image is that of a commander or captain *(nāgîd),* one who leads by going before the people. Both images represent the king as a leader for the people, not one who is removed from them, expecting only to be served by them.

The elders were probably the leaders of the individual tribes who came together at certain significant times to make decisions that would affect all the people of their respective groups. In a very real sense they are the ones who governed the northern kingdom. These are the people who came to David. They are the ones with whom, in the name of the people they represented, David entered into covenant. They are the ones who then anointed him king.

This was not only a significant tribal act, but it carried personal repercussions as well, for by this act they were relinquishing some of their own authority and power and bestowing it on one individual.

Psalm 122:1-2, 3-4, 4-5

The responsorial psalm is an individual hymn of joy and praise of one who had the opportunity to go to the Temple in Jerusalem. Although the passage itself is short, the images it contains are vibrant and the sentiments it expresses are profound. Glorious temples were not only evidence of the wealth and importance of the rulers responsible for their having been built. They were more importantly concerned with the dwelling place of God on earth. For this reason an opportunity to go to Jerusalem and to enter the courts of the Temple was considered a great honor and a religious experience.

The city of Jerusalem was itself something to behold. It was built on Mount Zion, a hill that towered above much of the neighboring terrain. This not only gave it a vantage point from which to survey the surrounding territory, an important asset in case of possible attack, but its height enabled it to be seen from a distance, thus creating the impression of watchfulness and protection. Jerusalem was a city with walls and gates, suggesting both significant size and military fortifications. It was the seat of royal political power, and it became the religious center of the tribal confederacy that was bound together by common allegiance to God. In this capacity it also became the center of the administration of justice. The monarchy may have exercised significant influence in this area, but it was still accountable to the religious principles and values embedded in the religious tradition.

The strong fortifications of the city and its reputation as the site of the Temple and the place where God dwelt gave Jerusalem the reputation of being invincible. When one went to Jerusalem, one was visiting the center of every facet of Jewish life. This was truly the chosen city. It is no wonder it soon became a symbol of the reign of God.

Colossians 1:12-20

The reading is made up of a hymn of thanksgiving and an exaltation of the greatness of Christ. In the opening hymn the Colossians are invited to thank God for three blessings: a share in the inheritance of the saints, deliverance from darkness, and transference into the kingdom of God's Son. Paul claims that it was through the blood of this Son that redemption was won and sins were forgiven. This is certainly reason to be grateful.

As the reading continues we see that the effects of Christ's sacrifice in the lives of others is not the primary focus. Rather, it celebrates the excellence of

Christ, whose kingdom it is and through whom believers can gain access to it. The christology in the hymn praising Christ is referred to as "high christology." It extols the divine character and activity of Christ rather than his human nature and the physical life he lived on earth. In it, Paul uses several striking terms to characterize Christ: image of God, firstborn, the beginning, head of the Church. Each one adds a significant dimension to our understanding of Christ.

An image can either represent something or it can be a visible expression or manifestation of it. It is precisely because images function in these ways that the ancient Hebrews forbade fashioning images of God. Once God was so represented, God could always be represented in such a limited way. It is clear from the passage that Christ is here considered more than a symbol. Rather, he is a visible manifestation of the invisible God. To say that Christ is the image of God is not meant to limit our understanding of God. Rather, it extols the person of Christ. Firstborn can also be understood in two ways. It can refer to priority in time or to primacy in importance. Since this hymn is extolling the divine nature of Christ, the reference is probably not to Christ as the first created being but to the sovereignty of the power he exercises.

Christ occupies the place of preeminence over all the rest of creation, a preeminence that makes creation dependent upon him. He is the agent through whom all was created, and he is also the goal of all creation. This characterization is reminiscent of the feminine figure of Wisdom, who, though still a creation of God, was present at and somehow participated in primordial creation (cf. Prov 8:22-31). Christ's rule extends over the angelic realm as well (dominions, principalities, powers). He is said to be before all things. While this can suggest preexistence, it also means priority of distinction. The latter idea is certainly present in what follows; Christ holds all things together.

Paul ties creation together with redemption. Using the metaphor of body, he depicts both the union that exists between Christ and the Church and the preeminence that is Christ's as head of that body. However, the theme of church is not developed here, since this section follows one that addresses cosmic reality. Thus this reference may reflect the Greek idea of creation as a cosmic body with Wisdom or the Logos as its head. Redemption is accomplished through Christ's resurrection. Priority of time and preeminence are both present in the reference of firstborn from the dead, for Christ is both the first one raised and the one through whom all others will be raised.

Finally, as image or manifestation of the invisible God, the fullness of God dwells within Christ. In this capacity Christ is the agent of reconciliation. This reconciliation has a universal scope. It includes all created things in heaven and on earth, things visible and invisible. Though we are accustomed to think of reconciliation purely in human or social terms, the text is quite clear. All things are reconciled. (We are only beginning to explore the ecological implications of this.) The means of this reconciliation that Christ brings is the blood of the cross. Thus the sacrificial death of the human Jesus becomes the means through which the cosmic Christ reconciles all of creation with God.

Luke 23:35-43

The scene of the crucifixion is one of both contempt and faith. In the paradoxical fashion that has become so much a part of the gospel reality, Jesus is ridiculed for being who he really is. It is only at the end of the narrative, when speaking to the one person in the scene who does not jeer him but who professes faith in his innocence, that Jesus speaks with the royal authority that is his.

Jesus is reviled by the rulers of the Jewish people, by the Roman soldiers, and by one of the criminals being executed at his side. The inscription above the cross could also be construed as ridicule on the part of Pilate. These people who jeer him take the claims of Jesus in order to turn those claims against him. He has claimed to be the chosen one, the Christ of God, the King of the Jews—all messianic titles. If he were anything he has claimed to be, surely he would not be in these straits. It is clear from what those who jeer say they believe that if these claims were true either God or Jesus himself would intervene to prevent the events unfolding before their very eyes. What they do not realize is that he is indeed the Messiah; the error is in their messianic understandings and expectations.

The inscription on the cross plays a cryptic role. It was a Roman custom to display the crime of the condemned person so the passersby could both jeer the criminal and be sobered by the punishment inflicted. The inscription on the cross of Jesus reads "King of the Jews." While this is certainly the reason he was crucified, it is also a statement of fact. He was indeed King of the Jews, even though his manner of ruling did not conform to the standard of the day. True to the paradox of the gospel, what was intended as derision actually became a proclamation of faith.

There is already evidence of this faith in one of the criminals. He first recognized the innocence of Jesus and then his kingly character. It may not have been difficult to believe that Jesus was no threat to Roman rule. Many people probably believed in his innocence in this matter. However, this dying man professed a degree of eschatological hope. He seems to have believed that somehow Jesus would reign as king even after his death. What he asked was to be remembered by Jesus when he came into his own power. The only claim he has to make this request is the fact that he did not ridicule Jesus and he accepted his own imminent death as just payment for his crimes. In the eyes of Jesus, this appears to be enough, for he promises the man immediate entrance into paradise.

In Jewish eschatological tradition, the time of fulfillment was envisioned as a return to the pristine innocence and peace of primeval time. Descriptions of the end resemble descriptions of the beginning. Therefore, it is not unusual to think of the eschatological reign of Jesus as a garden of perfect paradise. Using this image, Jesus here assures the dying criminal that he will be granted entrance into Jesus' kingdom. Even from the cross Jesus rules with authority. Actually, it is precisely *from* the cross that Jesus rules with authority, because it was *through* the cross that he too entered into his kingdom.

Themes of the Day

The readings for this last Sunday of the Liturgical Year were not chosen in the same way as were the readings for the other Sundays of Ordinary Time. They do not follow a sequence of continuous reading. Rather, they were chosen to demonstrate the meaning of the feast we are celebrating today, the feast of Christ the King. This feast celebrates the power and authority of Christ by creating a collage of images that capture one or more characteristics of the Christ's kingship. Each image in some way significantly reinterprets the concept of king, investing it with new meaning. Gathered together they create a kind of litany that extols the kingship of Christ.

Shepherd and commander call to mind the care and protection Christ lavishes on those who place themselves under his care, who recognize his voice and follow him wherever he goes. According to this metaphor, the kingly rule of Christ is characterized by tenderness, not by the exercise of power.

King of Israel is, in the reading from 2 Samuel, a sign of universal rule. David was of the tribe of Judah and had been called to rule over the southern tribes. Now he is asked to extend his rule over people who were not his own. So it is with the reign of Christ. It extends to all, even to those who are not his original people.

Image of the invisible God acclaims the divine origin of Christ and, by extension, of the rule he exercises over all. The dominion of Christ includes everything over which God reigns.

Firstborn of all creation places Christ over the entire created world. The image of the caring shepherd reinterprets what could here be misunderstood as unfeeling dominion. Just as Christ tenderly cares for his sheep, in like manner he attentively tends the garden of the world over which he rules.

Source of all created things acknowledges both the sovereignty of Christ and his importance as the model after which all things were fashioned. In other words, creation mirrors the image of Christ the King. This is but another reason to cherish it.

Head of the body, the Church, underscores the intimacy and interrelationship that exist between Christ and all those who are joined to him through faith and baptism. This image challenges any idea of a distant and disinterested ruler. Just as a body needs a head, so a head needs a body.

Firstborn of the dead not only acclaims Christ's resurrection, it also guarantees the resurrection of those who will follow him into death. Christ is the kind of king who shares all of his privileges with others.

Crucified King is clearly the image that reinterprets all other images. It strips from the notion of king all honor and glory that flow merely from pride of office rather than from the exercise of dedicated leadership. For the sake of his sheep Jesus willingly endured humiliation and death. Nailed to the cross, his outstretched arms embraced women and men from every corner of the world. In his own body the created world was beaten down, only to rise again in glory. As head of the Church he became a victim so those who constitute his body could be spared many of the horrors he willingly endured. Finally, having conquered death by dying himself, he entrusts to all people the power over death he has won for them. He first exercised this authority as he hung dying on the cross, which forevermore will be seen as his glorious throne.

In the last words of the gospel, words with which the entire Liturgical Year is brought to completion, he opens the gates of his kingdom to a repentant sinner: "Today you will be with me in Paradise." These are the words we all long to hear, words that are empty when coming from one who has no authority but charged with power when spoken by the one who is King over us all.

Solemnities

Solemnities of the Lord

The Solemnity of the Most Holy Trinity Sunday
Proverbs 8:22-31

The mysterious figure of Woman Wisdom has intrigued interpreters since the day she first appeared alongside God at the time of the creation of the universe. Several characteristics about her have always been puzzling and never really adequately explained. First, it is clear she is not human, but is she divine? Only a deity would have been present before creation began, and yet the Hebrew verb *(qānâ)* can be translated "made" as well as "possessed." Further in the poem she is said to have been poured out (v. 23) and brought forth as if by birth (vv. 24, 25). She is called the first of God's ways, the one before all of God's other deeds. If she comes from God, might she be the personification of some quality of the Creator? Whatever her origin, she is present and active during God's wondrous acts of creation. She is there as *'āmôn* (v. 30). The meaning of this word is uncertain, but the context leads most commentators to translate it "craftsperson" or "architect." However, as active as she may have been in these primordial events, it is God who really creates.

The gender of this fascinating figure is also a point of interest. Why would a patriarchal society that normally advanced a male image as the norm represent in female form one of the most cherished characteristics of God, or of human beings, for that matter? Some believe she originated as an ancient goddess of wisdom who was later demythologized by the Hebrew monotheists. This may not explain why the representation is female, but it does account for the ambiguity in this passage regarding some of the semi-divine features included in her description. To suggest that she is the feminine side of God, as some do today, is to read contemporary interests back into early Israel. The ancients would most likely have revered a separate deity rather than one who possessed a two-gendered personality. The question of her gender remains open for interpretation even today. This is another reason why Woman Wisdom continues to be intriguing.

The created world itself is beautifully portrayed in this passage. There is no cosmic battle here, as is found in some of the other ancient creation myths. There is only one God, and that God effortlessly establishes the entire universe in tranquility and order. What in other myths were enemies to be conquered, such as the heavens and the sea, here are docile creatures that have been set in place by the Creator and have been given limits beyond which they cannot advance. This is a solid world, securely founded and wonderful to behold. If Woman Wisdom acted as craftsperson or architect for this magnificent project, then the principles of wisdom are woven into the very fabric of creation. This would explain the order that can be discerned within its workings.

There is rejoicing in this created world. God delights in Woman Wisdom; Woman Wisdom rejoices before God. Mention of playing should not make us think that Wisdom is a carefree child. This is the kind of rejoicing that springs from the very heart of the universe. It is delight in the glory of creation and in creation's God. Creatures would cry out in praise; God and Woman Wisdom sing out in delight.

The last verse brings all of this home to us. Wisdom takes delight in the inhabited part of the earth, in the human race. This brief statement locates humankind squarely within the created world. No other species is singled out in this way. The verse leaves us at an open threshold gazing at the universe that unfolds before us, aware that this mysterious primordial figure has a special interest in us.

Psalm 8:4-5, 6-7, 8-9

The responsorial psalm is a hymn that praises God for some of the wonders of the universe. The psalmist is depicted as gazing at the night sky, spellbound by its magnificence, marveling first at the wonders of the universe and then at the extraordinary role humankind plays within it. It is the splendor of the moon and the stars, once thought to be celestial deities but now considered creatures of God, that brings the psalmist to stand in wonder of God's plan for women and men on earth.

The psalmist's musings begin with a comparison of the scope of the heavens and the infinitesimal reality of humankind. Human frailty is depicted by means of poetic parallel construction (v. 5). A close look at the original male-gendered language reveals two characterizations that underscore this frailty. "Man" is *ʾĕnôsh,* a word that emphasizes human weakness, particularly human mortality. In parallel construction with this designation is a *ben-ʾādām,* a second characterization of human weakness. The psalmist insists there is no comparison between the magnificent and radiant bodies in the night sky and puny and short-lived human beings, yet God is mindful of them and cares for them. This provident attention would be enough to glorify the goodness of God, but there is much more that causes the psalmist to stand in wonder.

What is often translated "angels" is really the Hebrew plural for "gods" (ʾĕlōhîm). The psalmist here claims that human beings have been created just a little less than supernatural beings, and in that capacity they are given authority to rule over creation (cf. Gen 1:26-28). Although they are said to rule over all the works of God's hands, only the creatures of the earth are explicitly named. Perhaps the heavenly bodies still retain some of the privilege that was theirs when they were thought to be divine. Though under God's command, they are independent of human control. The language used paints a picture of royalty. Human beings are crowned, as royalty is crowned. They are endowed with honor and glory, two characteristics closely associated with ancient Near Eastern monarchy. The other creatures are put under their feet, an image that might imply conquest but also suggests the fealty subjects owe their rulers. The depiction in this psalm is most likely one of royal rule, not military victory.

As comprehensive as the control of ancient Israel's monarchy might have been, it was all delegated rule. Furthermore, the monarch was answerable to God for the exercise of that rule. Israel was God's people, and the land was God's land. The kings and queens were merely vice-regents, agents of God's will exercising dominion in God's stead, according to God's plan as set forth in the law. This is the pattern of royal rule that existed in Israel, and this is the image of royal rule presumed in this passage. The weak and fragile human beings, who were given control over the sheep and the oxen and the beast of the field, over the birds and the fish and whatever swims in the seas, do not rule autonomously. The realm that was put in their charge is not theirs; it is God's. While their choice by God is an incalculable honor, it is also a tremendous responsibility.

Romans 5:1-5

The overarching theme in this reading from the letter to the Romans is justification by faith. Every blessing mentioned in the passage rests on the believers having been justified by faith in Jesus Christ. There is also a trinitarian theme present, appropriate for the feast we are celebrating today.

According to Paul, the justification of the Roman Christians is an accomplished fact. They have already been reconciled with God; their guilt has already been forgiven. They are now in right relationship with God, and though God is really the author of their justification, it has been accomplished through their faith in Jesus Christ. In the thinking of ancient Israel, peace was both a sign of and the fruit flowing from a covenantal union between God and the people. This is probably the way Paul is using the word. Its presence indicates there is no longer enmity; instead, there is union.

Again and again Paul emphasizes the role Christ plays in this transformation. He is the one who, through his death and resurrection, has reconciled all people with God; he is the mediator of the new covenant of peace. The idea of gaining access suggests being admitted into the presence of someone of very high estate. Such access is only granted if one has earned the privilege to approach, which is certainly not the case here, or if someone who already has access is willing to usher one in. This seems to be the image Paul wishes to create. He is saying that it is through Christ we have been granted the grace to stand in the presence of God.

There is a touch of Paul's already-but-not-yet eschatological thinking here. Those who have been justified by faith already have peace with God, already have access to grace. However, they still wait in hope for the ultimate glory of God. Christian hope is not merely the expectation of future good fortune; it is not based on possibility. Instead, it is the guarantee of future blessing; it is based on the promises made by God. It is much firmer than mere desire; it is assurance. However, this assurance is not blind to the sufferings believers must endure. There is no indication that Paul is here speaking about persecutions. The reference is probably to the ordinary struggles of life that face every person. The word for "afflictions" *(thlípsis)* has theological significance. It refers to the necessary suffering that precedes the appearance of the reign of God. Paul probably has such suffering in mind.

Most likely Paul is here instructing his hearers to use the difficulties of life to their best advantage. There is no guarantee that suffering will make people better, mellow their emotions, or soften the edges of their personalities. It can also embitter, harden, and isolate them. Paul recognizes in suffering the potential for growth and transformation. This is the process he sketches for the people of Rome. He ends his recital of virtues with hope, and he explains that Christian hope does not disappoint us because it is grounded in the love God has for us. The image he creates here is of a love bounteously given, lavishly poured out.

The trinitarian nature of Paul's faith and teaching is clear. It is faith in Christ that justifies us with God; it is faith in Christ that gives us peace with God; it is faith in Christ that grants us access to the grace of God. Because of the reconciliation won for us by Christ, the love of God is poured out into our hearts through the Holy Spirit. In other words, Christ brings us to God, and the Spirit comes to us from that same God. God, Christ, and the Spirit are all involved in our ultimate union with God.

John 16:12-15

In this reading the gospel writer attempts to show the relationship between the Father, Jesus, and the Spirit by somehow relating all three to the teaching of Jesus. This is a very difficult and complex undertaking, and the resulting explanation is somewhat obscure. We will have to look to other passages or to Christian literature for a clear exposition of the doctrine of the Trinity. What we find here are seeds of theological thought that will come to fruition at another time. This passage, as brief and oblique as it is, gives us but a glimpse into the author's incipient trinitarian thinking.

In this passage it is Jesus' concern for the instruction of his disciples that prompts his discourse. He states that he has much more to tell them, but they cannot bear it *now*. By implication, they will be able to bear it at another time. The reason they will be able to understand in the future is that they will then have been instructed in truth by the spirit of truth. Thus the teaching of Jesus is referred to as the truth. The relationship of truth, the Spirit, and Jesus' teaching is not clearly delineated. Is the Spirit called truth because of the quality of the teaching of Jesus, to which the Spirit guides the disciples? Or is the teaching called truth because of the Spirit that guides the disciples to it? We don't know.

The Spirit is somehow to fill the void caused by the absence of Jesus and to fill it not so much with a presence as with a form of teaching. Jesus insists that the Spirit will not bring new teaching but teaching the Spirit has heard from another. Though not explicitly stated, the reference is to the teaching of Jesus, perhaps the very teaching the disciples were unable to bear while he was with them. However, the Spirit of truth is more than a messenger who merely repeats the words of another. Jesus says that this Spirit will also announce things that are to come. This could refer to an unfolding of the mysteries Jesus himself announced or alluded to when he was with them, mysteries that had not yet been brought to completion. Or it could allude to some of the ancient expectations that had not yet been brought to fulfillment. In this way the Spirit would teach and reveal what had already been taught yet was nonetheless new. It will be through this unfolding of the depths of the mysteries Jesus proclaimed that the Spirit will glorify Jesus and reveal him to be the chosen one of God.

The mission of the Spirit seems to be the guidance of the disciples into the deep meaning and radical implications of the teachings of Jesus. The truth the Spirit reveals is grounded in the teachings of Jesus, but it goes far beyond it. In this way there is continuity but not repetition. In a statement that seems to be an abrupt shift in thought, Jesus clearly asserts that what belongs to the Father belongs to him. This could mean that it was from the Father that the Spirit heard the teachings of Jesus, and it was also from the Father that the Spirit was sent to bring these teachings to fruition. The Spirit glorifies Jesus by bringing to light the deeper truth of his teaching, teaching that also belongs to God.

Themes of the Day

The relationship between the lectionary readings and the theological themes of this day is the reverse of what it is throughout most of the Liturgical Year. At other times the themes found in the readings constitute the theological meaning of the day. It is just the reverse with this feast. The readings are chosen because something in them either exemplifies or elucidates the doctrinal theology of the feast. This means that the readings will be interpreted through the lens of the feast and not the other way around.

God the Creator

Both the first reading and the psalm response celebrate the marvels of creation and, by inference, the marvelous Creator who brought them into being. They invite us to join the psalmist, standing back in awe of the creative power and imagination of God. We have only scratched the surface in our understanding of the myriad of species that are on our planet alone. One thing we have discovered about these creatures is that each is unique. No two persons are exactly the same, no stars, no snowflakes. What creativity! What imagination!

The passage from Proverbs states that God created all these things through Wisdom. While later theology will identify this remarkable Wisdom with both the Word of God, the Second Person of the Trinity, and the Holy Spirit, the Third Person, the reading itself does not suggest this. It might be best simply to extol the glories of the Creator and leave the differentiation of divine Persons to a later theological focus.

God the Redeemer

It is with Paul that we find the beginnings of trinitarian theology. In the epistle reading for today he very clearly credits God with our justification through faith and our possession of divine love. There is no doubt in Paul's mind about the source and mediator of our salvation. Justification, or salvation, is accomplished by God through our Lord Jesus Christ. The love of God is poured into our hearts through the Holy Spirit. Paul does not clearly state that the love of God we receive through the Holy Spirit sanctifies us, but one could certainly understand it in this way.

God the Source of Truth

The trinitarian theology we find in the reading from the Gospel of John resembles very closely that of Paul. In it Jesus reveals the intimate connection between himself and the Father as well as himself and the Spirit. The Spirit continues the mission of Jesus, neither adding anything to his teaching nor omitting anything from it. The Spirit's task is to lead us ever deeper into the truth that Jesus brought, truth that is really found in God. Here again one might be tempted to say that John is describing the sanctifying work of the

Spirit. However, the passage is not clear, and it might be anachronistic to assign such a role to the Spirit at this time.

One point is clear from these readings. While this is a feast that glorifies the central mystery of our faith, a mystery based on the way the three divine Persons relate to one another *(ad intra)*, the readings all address the ways God relates to us *(ad extra)*. This feast, which follows our celebration of the completion of the paschal mystery, is not intended for our clear articulation of doctrine; it is meant to give us an opportunity to commit ourselves to this God who, though beyond our comprehension, is present and active at the very core of our being. If we concentrate merely on the doctrine, we might be awed by an intellectual concept. But if we concentrate, as the texts for today suggest we do, on all the ways our triune God has blessed us, we may be more inclined to cry out with the psalmist, "O LORD, our God, how wonderful your name in all the earth!"

The Solemnity of the Most Holy Body and Blood of Christ (Corpus Christi)

Genesis 14:18-20

The few verses that constitute the first reading for today's feast make up a complete unit in itself, but the meaning is not completely clear. It is a description of a cultic event that includes a priest, possibly a sacrifice, a blessing, and a religious practice. It is a story about Abram, the premier ancestor of the Israelite people. One would think that because it was probably part of the folklore that grew up about him, he himself would be the principal actor in the drama that unfolds. However, this is not the case. Instead, all the significant action is performed by someone named Melchizedek. The only important action Abram initiates is the tithing, and that appears to be a response to what has transpired.

Names play an important role in this account. Their meanings reveal something of the significance of the actions performed. Melchizedek is a compound of two Hebrew words: *malᵉkî* (my king) and *ṣedek* (righteous). It describes the character of the man's governance. Some believe the priest-kings in Jerusalem, before its capture by David, often carried some form of *ṣedek* in their names (cf. Josh 10:1). Although there was a valley named Salem (cf. Jdt 4:4), the reference here is probably a shortened form of the name Jerusalem, the Jebusite city that was ultimately captured by David and made the capital of his kingdom (cf. 2 Sam 5:6-8). There are several allusions in this report to the cult in Jerusalem that could confirm this interpretation. The deity in whose name (God Most High) Melchizedek blesses Abram is closely associated with the cult that was practiced in Jerusalem (cf. Pss 46:4; 87:5). This was not a savior-

God, as was the God of Israel; this God was the Creator of heaven and earth, and Melchizedek, who was not an Israelite, was a priest of this God and conducted worship in the name of his God.

The rite celebrated here is some kind of a thanksgiving offering, probably for Abram's victory over his foes. The text does not tell us why it is this mysterious king-priest who presides and not Abram, or why Abram is blessed in the name of a god not his own. It may have been because of the status of Melchizedek. It may have been because this god was no mere patron-god, as was the God of Abram. Or it may have been that Abram participated in this worship because he was in the land of this god. Nor does the text tells us exactly what is done with the bread and wine. Was it part of the thank-offering? Was it a form of covenant meal to be shared with Abram? No explanation is given.

The words pronounced by Melchizedek are both a blessing for Abram and an exclamation of praise of God Most High. A blessing by the Creator would include a share in the goods of creation, the benefits of fertility of the land, crops, animals, and particularly of one's own procreative potential. It is at the conclusion of this blessing that Abram offers a tenth of his goods to the king-priest. In the ancient world tithes were offered both at sanctuaries and to rulers. Here the tithing is probably a tenth of the war spoils, offered as part of the thank-offering. We are not told of what it consists. The episode concludes as abruptly as it began. All we are sure of is the victory of Abram and his acculturation into the customs of the land into which he has migrated. However, it does introduce us to the importance of the city of Jerusalem with its king and its cultic life.

Psalm 110:1, 2, 3, 4

The responsorial psalm is a royal song extolling the Davidic king. This short passage contains two divine oracles, most likely spoken by a court prophet but intended for the king. The first (v. 1) is a directive; the second (v. 4) is a promise.

The confusion in the English translation, "The LORD said to my Lord," is cleared up if we realize that the first LORD is a rendering of the divine name (YHWH), while the second is a translation of the Hebrew for "master" (*ʾădōnî*). It is God who directs the human king to sit at God's own right hand, the place of honor. The scene reveals that God is the real king; the kingship of the human being is only delegated. Furthermore, it is God who enthrones the human king, subjugating his enemies as a footstool under his feet. Subjugation of enemies in this way is a common theme in ancient Near Eastern art. Although the text does not explicitly state that God actually vanquished the enemies, it is God who in this passage grants the king every other honor, so one can assume the defeat of the enemies was at God's hand as well.

The king is endowed with a scepter. This symbol of royal rule was probably originally a mace, a military weapon wielded in defense or attack. Now it is stretched forth as a sign of dominion. Again, it is the LORD who uses it to designate the scope of the human king's rule. The divine words that accompany the action indicate the king's authority and power even in the midst of enemies. The place from which this rule proceeds is Zion, the mountain upon which the city of Jerusalem was built. The mountain and the city represent the essence of Davidic rule.

The day of the birth of the king is not his natal day but the day of his enthronement. That is when he enters into a unique and intimate relationship with God. In some ancient cultures the king was adopted as the son of the god on the day of enthronement (for example, "You are my son, today I have begotten you" [Ps 2:7]). Daystar and dew symbolize the freshness of this new royal birth. Israel retained the idea of a special relationship with God but insisted that the king was still a human being, bound by the law as was every other Israelite (cf. 2 Sam 7:14). Still, the enthronement of a new king was always a time of great hope. People trusted in the relationship that bound the king to God, and they willingly submitted themselves to the king's governance. Image after image assures us that the choice of king is God's, that the ceremony of enthronement is officiated over by God, and that the dominion exercised by the king was assigned to him by God. This is a human king with divine responsibilities.

Finally, by divine oath the Davidic king is granted the priestly status that belonged to Melchizedek, the priest-king of Salem. It is believed that when David conquered the ancient Jebusite city of Jerusalem, he appropriated for his own God much of the religious tradition and many of the customs associated with that shrine. At his enthronement, each successor of David assumed the privileges, and perhaps some of the practices, that belonged to the office of that priest-king. Promised by God, these privileges would be the right of any legitimate descendant of David.

1 Corinthians 11:23-26

This account of the institution of the Lord's Supper draws on the Jesus tradition. The language used is technical and formulaic; what Paul received he now hands down (cf. 1 Cor 15:3). This does not mean that he received this tradition in direct revelation from the Lord but that he received it by word of mouth, the usual way a religious heritage is transmitted. This manner of expression establishes the ecclesial authority of the teaching. It also demonstrates Paul's own conviction that the risen Christ transmits the tradition through the agency of the members of the body of Christ, the Church. Since such transmission was a custom in both the Greek schools and the Jewish synagogue, the audience would understand what Paul was doing regardless of their ethnic or religious background.

how do you know?

That the account comes specifically from the Jesus tradition and not from the more general early Christian tradition is evident in the recital of the words of Jesus. They actually give instruction for the continual celebration of the liturgical reenactment. The fact that they are the words of Jesus gives divine legitimation to the *anámnēsis* (ritual of remembering) that is enjoined upon the community of believers. The words themselves are found within a succinct account of Jesus' Last Supper, wherein he draws lines of continuity between the old and the new covenants and also makes clear their differences.

Jesus' attention is on the bread and the wine. Faithful to Jewish table etiquette, as either the head of the household or the host he gives thanks and breaks the bread (v. 24). He identifies the bread as his body about to be given vicariously on behalf of those present. The fact that Jesus was actually with them when he said this makes the meaning of his words enigmatic. Was this really his body, or did it represent his body? Believers have interpreted this in various ways down through the centuries. One point is clear; they were charged to repeat among themselves what he had just done.

When the supper was over, Jesus took the cup and pronounced words over it as well (v. 25). This cup is identified with the new covenant (cf. Jer 31:31-34) and with the blood of the Lord, which, like sacrificial blood, ratifies the covenant. This statement shows how the Jesus tradition has taken the new covenant theme from Jeremiah and the blood ratification from the Jewish sacrificial system, incorporated them, and reinterpreted them. This verse ends as did the previous verse, with a charge to repeat the memorial.

NB

Jesus' sharing of the blessed bread and cup was a prophetic symbolic action that anticipated his death. The ritual reenactment of this supper would be a participation in his death and a sharing in the benefits that would accrue from it. In it the risen exalted Lord continually gives what the dying Jesus gave once for all. In the memorial celebration the past, the present, and the future are brought together: the past is the commemoration of his death; the present is the ritual of remembrance itself; the future is his *parousía*, his coming again. The reason for repeating Jesus' actions and words is that they reenact and signify his salvific death. Believers live an essentially eschatological existence, anticipating the future as they reenact the past.

Luke 9:11b-17

The gospel account opens with a summary statement about the ministry of Jesus: He preached about the reign of God and he healed the people of their illnesses. If his preaching had not attracted crowds, his healing certainly would have. At any rate, people from all walks of life thronged around him so that, as we see in this narrative, they had to be dismissed. It is the end of the day, the time when the major meal is customarily eaten. The scene is an out-of-the-way place, deserted but close enough to populated areas that the Twelve could suggest that food and lodging might be procured there. They could not have imagined what Jesus had in mind.

Five loaves and two fish would not have been much of a meal for Jesus and the Twelve, much less for the crowd said to have gathered on this occasion. Yet that was the fare the disciples were told to distribute. The crowd must have included women and children, but their number did not seem to interest the Lukan storyteller. He only mentioned the number of men. Jesus' actions over the food are brief but significant. He blessed it, he broke it, and he gave it as food. The eucharistic overtones are obvious. The prayer said over the food was probably more a thanksgiving than a blessing. If it was the typical Jewish blessing of the time, it might have resembled the following: "Blessed are you, O LORD our God, Ruler of the universe, who brings forth bread from the earth" (*Ber* 6:1).

It is difficult to know whether the historical Jesus actually spoke these words and, if so, whether it was done with a proleptic eye to his Last Supper, which was itself a foreshadowing of the final messianic banquet. However, we can be certain the gospel writer wanted these connections to be made. The episode recalls other feeding traditions that must have been called to mind on this occasion. The most obvious is the miraculous feeding in the wilderness with manna (cf. Exod 16:15). There is also a story in the Elisha cycle in which the prophet feeds a smaller crowd with loaves of bread, some of which were also left over (cf. 2 Kgs 4:42-44). The miracle in the wilderness described in today's gospel seems to have gathered together traditions of the past as well as expectations of the future, all of which point to the ultimate eschatological banquet.

A sometimes overlooked detail in this feeding account might allude to that final meal. There is a tradition in Jewish apocalyptic lore that the primordial beasts of chaos, having been decisively conquered, will be served at the eschatological banquet. (Such a final elimination of enemies is quite common in mythological literature.) These beasts were the sea monsters Behemoth (cf. Job 40:15) and Leviathan (cf. Job 41:1; Ps 104:26). Is it merely coincidence that this gospel narrative with its eschatological nuance adds fish to the menu?

The role played by the apostles cannot be overlooked. They are actually the ones through whom the crowds experience the munificence of Jesus. They distributed the food and, most likely, collected what was left over into twelve baskets. The author of the gospel shows by this that Jesus provides for his people through the agency of the Church.

Over the years there have been attempts to explain what really happened in this event. Was food really multiplied? Or did people bring out their own provisions and share them with others? Any attempt to explain away the miracle completely misses the point of the narrative. Its many-leveled meaning rests on the miraculous abundance God provides through Jesus.

Themes of the Day

This feast, which combines two previously separate feasts (Corpus Christi and the Precious Blood), is similar to Trinity Sunday in that the readings have been chosen to highlight aspects of the theology of the feast. The feast itself celebrates the living presence of Christ, which we know in the gift of his body and blood in the Eucharist. The readings themselves offer us portals through which we can enter this mystery. There is the portal of Melchizedek, the portal of sacrifice, the portal of banquet, the portal of the death of Jesus. No one theme exhausts the possibilities of entrance into the mystery.

The Sacrifice of Jesus

The feast itself identifies the essence of the mystery. The body and blood of Christ are offered as a sacrifice for us, and every time we reenact this sacrifice, we renew his sacrifice for us. The bread that is broken is the bread of a thanksgiving sacrifice, and the blood that is consumed is the blood that ratifies the covenant between God and us. However, the broken bread is really his broken body, offered for us, and the ratifying wine is really his blood, poured out in atonement for our sins. The body and blood of Jesus is the interim meal for the Christian community. They are to feed on it until the Lord returns. We see again the already-but-not-yet character of Christian eschatology, for the Lord has already returned. This means that the eucharistic meal is a reenactment of Christ's death, an anticipatory celebration of his coming, and a thanksgiving banquet with him present. The symbolism here is rich and many-layered.

The sacrifice Melchizedek offered was neither more nor less than a thanksgiving offering to the Most High God. Read on this feast day, the passage opens the door for us to step into the realm of thanksgiving. Although what we commemorate today is intimately linked with the death of Jesus, the sentiments this reading opens us to are sentiments of thanksgiving and awe before the high God of heaven.

The psalmist moves away from the content of the sacrifice and concentrates on the priest who offers it. He is not only a priest but a king as well. This feast would have us stop in our tracks and contemplate the royal as well as the priestly character of Jesus, who offers his body and blood as sacred food and drink.

The Banquet of the Lord

The multiplication of the loaves and fish is another portal that opens into the richness of this feast. It prefigures the eschatological banquet of fulfillment. Its miraculous bounty assures us of the abundance of that future banquet. The themes of these readings weave themselves in and out of one another, manifesting one aspect of the mystery only to recede into the harmony of the whole and there wait its turn to reappear like a simple yet complex fugue.

Its miracle of multiplication prefigures the miracle of Jesus as he changed the bread and wine into his own body and blood. Jesus handed himself over as food and drink on the very night he was handed over by others to become a victim of sacrifice. The banquet he prepared was a celebration of the new covenant; it was a banquet of thanksgiving; it was eschatological.

This feast invites us to enter through any portal, for each one will lead us to the mystery we celebrate: the mystery of the sacrifice of Christ; the mystery of the sacred bread and wine of the future; the mystery of the eschatological banquet of the present.

Index of Scripture Readings